A Borrowed Voice

Taiwan Human Rights through International Networks, 1960-1980

我的聲音借妳

台灣人權訴求與國際連絡網1960-1980

Written/edited by
Linda Gail Arrigo and Lynn Miles

A Borrowed Voice:
Taiwan Human Rights through
International Networks, 1960-1980

ISBN 978-986-84338-0-9
© Copyright 2008 All rights reserved

Edited by
Linda Gail Arrigo and Lynn Miles

Editorial Committee :
Lynn Miles, Linda Gail Arrigo,
Chiu Wan-sheng, Liao Tzu-fei, Chiu Hsueh-yi

Artwork by
Chiu Wan-sheng and Chiu Hsueh-yi

Illustrations provided by
Linda Gail Arrigo, Chiu Wan-sheng, Ken Kilimnik,
Taiwan Foundation for Democracy, Central News Agency,
Wu San-lien Taiwan Historical Materials Center

"Reminisences of Taiwan: Investigating Capital and Labor in a Subjugated
Economy," copyright Ken Kilimnik, 2008
"The Quiet Constancy of Miyake Kiyoko," copyright Winston Luo 駱文森, 2008

Printed by
Hanyao Color Printing Co., Ltd.

Printed in Taiwan

Printed May 2008

For further information contact Linda Gail Arrigo:
Taipei (886-2)-2662-3677, (mobile) 886-928-899-931
linda.arrigo@msa.hinet.net, linda2007@tmu.edu.tw

NT$600 US$20

Published by the Social Empowerment Alliance
No. 20 WeiShui Road, Taipei 104 Taiwan
Tel: 02-8772-1168
Fax: 02-8772-1167

陳菊　序

　　1979年6月，我被警備總部逮捕，一共拘禁了13天。但事實上本來會更久的，甚至不曉得會不會有出來的那一天。就我所知道，是在美國政府關切之下，國民黨才把我放了出來，雖然不久之後又因為美麗島事件再度入獄，坐了六年多的牢。

　　美國政府之所以會介入，就是因為當時被台灣政府驅逐出境、人在大阪的 Lynn(梅心怡)，不眠不休，馬上趕到東京，把台灣政治犯的資料，交給衛報等國際媒體，才讓世界各國的朋友都看見台灣，關心台灣人權，而協助台灣人民，渡過黎明之前的漫長黑夜。

　　至於 Linda(艾琳達)，更是多年以來，就一直在台灣，陪伴我們為反獨裁爭民主而打拼，當時包括雷震回憶錄在內的黨外人士訊息，就是靠著 Linda，向當時所有熟識的外籍人士，一一拜訪，一一懇求，一點一滴向他們訴說起台灣歷史的沉重，用她的真誠去打動對方提供協助。美麗島事件當時，Linda 甚至還與我們一同被捕。

　　他們二位，基於對普世性公義的嚮往，離開遙遠的故鄉，來到台灣，為人權奮戰，解嚴前如此，解嚴後亦然，甚至在政黨輪替以後，他們仍然為台灣的環保、勞工與弱勢等社會運動積極打拼，對民進黨政府亦不假辭色，用更高的標準嚴格監督，保持真正人道主義者的本色。在你需要援手的時候，他們不顧自己的安危相挺；在你需要勸告的時候，他們用最真誠的心對你說實話，這，就是真正的朋友。

　　他們用兩雙手，為台灣的政治犯，搭起一條連往自由世界的橋樑，留下一條救命的繩索。就憑著這座橋樑、這條繩索，維繫住了台灣民主的生存，而在多年以後，得以雲破日出，開花結果。

　　救回一個名叫陳菊的政治犯，不算什麼；Lynn 和 Linda，以及其他眾多的國際友人，還挽救了更多更多，更加重要的民主新苗，保存台灣的民主血脈。這一本書，記錄了1960到1980年間，在國民黨獨裁政權底下，國際救援組織，為台灣民主所做出的重大貢獻。期待所有台灣人民，都能記得這一段歷史，不僅對我們來自他方的好友永存一份感激，更能夠珍惜我們得來不易的民主。

Long-time activists for human rights in Taiwan met for dinner in Taipei in 1999 to reminisce about their many years of work together. Left to right, Linda Gail Arrigo 艾琳達, Miyake Kiyoko 三宅清子, Chen Chu 陳菊, and Lynn Miles 梅心怡.

The above preface to our book was written by Chen Chu, now mayor of Kaohsiung City.

CONTENTS

Chapter Four
True Christian Service to the Taiwanese People Compels Us 171

Chapter Five
We Are Willing to be Jailed for the Future of Taiwan 273

Chapter Six
The Rioters Are On Trial, Not the Government 375

Introduction

A Borrowed Voice
Taiwan Human Rights through International Networks, 1960-1980

Now that Taiwan has gone through the democratic transition of 2000 and another peaceful change of ruling party in 2008, it would seem that the principles enshrined in the Universal Declaration of Human Rights should be safe here. However, the future cannot be so secure, and every generation must take responsibility for its own decisions. It cannot be taken for granted that the advances of the recent past will continue.

This book is a raw history of a number of the foreign participants involved in exposing human rights abuses in Taiwan in the period 1960-1980, written by the people who lived it. It may be seen as oral history or biography, with the addition that the authors/editors have refreshed their memories through documents and archives, trying to reliably place events and people. It may serve as a primary source for historians, but the personal accounts recreate the period more vividly than any formal political history. While Taiwanese bore the brunt of White Terror retribution for resistance to the massive state machines that saw democratic rights as a threat to their power and profitable monopolies, foreigners often took considerable risks to try to ameliorate their suffering.

Here are the subjective experiences of the varied participants: students learning Asian languages as budding scholars or journalists; missionaries intent on spreading the love of Jesus; and US military personnel chagrined by the human cost of American policies. In this sense it contains also a history of the ideological ferment of the 1970s and reaction to US misadventures in Asia. There is much in this book about the struggle for democracy in Taiwan and the particular cases of repression that were the object of human rights appeals; and it concludes with analysis of declassified internal documents of the security agencies and their response to this unwelcome foreign attention to domestic human rights.

◎ Chapter One quickly lays out the background of US support for Asian dictatorships following World War II, and how the peoples of both China and Taiwan were ravaged by the White Terror of Chiang Kai-shek and his Nationalist government, a savagery in which the United States tacitly acquiesced.

◎ Chapter Two recalls the major cases of political repression of 1960-1970. It relates how the first reliable list of political prisoners was compiled by current and former political prisoners themselves, and smuggled out for publication abroad. They paid heavily for their actions.

◎ Chapter Three describes the growing organization and interconnectedness of human rights networks, 1971-1975, both those in Japan secretly collecting first-hand information through correspondents and visitors within Taiwan, and the increasing authority of Amnesty International with its Nobel Peace prizes. Jimmy Carter's human rights foreign policy from 1976 further put the Taiwan authorities on the defensive.

◎ Chapter Four focuses on the role of the foreign missionaries assigned in the 1960s to the Presbyterian Church in Taiwan, with its century-old roots in native Taiwan culture and society, and of the Catholic Columbans and Maryknollers who in the late 1970s took up social issues and chafed against the Catholic Church hierarchy's support for the Chiang regime.

◎ Chapter Five is the perspective from within Taiwan, 1977-79, as a democratic movement witnessed by human rights correspondents broke into the open. When Carter moved towards recognition of the PRC, the movement demanded that the future of Taiwan be determined by the people of Taiwan. The overseas Taiwanese and international links figured in helping the movement grow explosively and mount a formidable challenge to the regime leading up to the late-1979 showdown.

◎ Chapter Six details the 1980 overseas campaign for the arrested opposition leaders and Presbyterian ministers put on trial in March through May. The human rights campaign seems to have been crucial in opening the trials to international and domestic scrutiny. The chapter lastly analyzes the documents of the security agencies that have recently been declassified, showing their obsession with overseas Taiwanese activities and English reporting on the trials.

Why is the period of this book cut off at 1980? After the open democratic movement of 1979, even in spite of its suppression, and after election to national office of several of the wives of those arrested in December 1980, human rights information collection within Taiwan was successfully taken over by local people, facilitated by increasingly open communications channels with overseas Taiwanese. Travel became much more frequent and international telephone calls became affordable. The crucial function of information smuggling and of historical materials preservation overseas was, happily, largely displaced.

How This Book Came About

The authors/editors of this book participated in the events and organizations described herein. It was April 1977 when Linda Gail Arrigo, on her way to sociological fieldwork in Taiwan, joined Lynn Miles' Osaka-based network, the International Committee for the Defense of Human Rights in Taiwan. She and several other foreigners in Taiwan served in collecting information, translating it, and sending it on its way with couriers. Following the Kaohsiung Incident, overseas Lynn and Linda cooperated closely on the campaigns for the defendants, especially during the trials of March through May 1980.

Both were now persona non grata. Linda was allowed to return to Taiwan in 1990; Lynn was allowed to return briefly in 1992 and then after 1996. In 2005 they were both finally allowed permanent residence.

In December 2003, the Taiwan Foundation for Democracy sponsored a conference entitled "A Journey of Remembrance and Appreciation: International Friends and Taiwan's Democracy and Human Rights." The TDF invited more than 30 individuals from abroad who had made past contributions to the island's democratization, most of whom had been deported many years before, to give their accounts of what they had witnessed in the days of Nationalist authoritarianism. In addition to their written accounts submitted for the conference, Linda arranged for videotaped interviews of the participants as part of a planned film documentary. This was the first large-scale effort to openly acknowledge the role played by international citizens in the struggle for democracy and human rights in Taiwan.

In December 2007, another group of international participants was invited to join in the dedication of the Jingmei Human Rights Memorial Park (formerly the Chingmei prison for political offenders, Taiwan Garrison Command). In December 2007, the Council for Cultural Affairs provided Linda and Lynn with a small grant to produce the present book, provided that it was completed by the end of April 2008, a very challenging deadline. The book came out to be twice as long as originally expected. We hope the reader will be forgiving of the errors and omissions.

Reflections and Reservations

The history of international engagement with Taiwan's democratic opening is a story of borders challenged, crossed and erased. The boundaries to be broken were not limited to those defining the nation-state, but included the divisions of race, language, culture, and ideology. The struggle for democracy and human rights demanded a bridging, at least temporarily, of these differences.

The fact that human rights information smuggling was a secretive and often ad hoc enterprise means that this historical account cannot be complete. We regret that the efforts of a number of very active participants in the liberating struggles of the 1960s, 1970s, and 1980s remain unrecorded here. Some of this absence is intentional, as some then-participants are currently engaged as scholars, businesspeople and journalists whose dealings with China require anonymity regarding their previous political activities in Taiwan. Some have refused participation out of modesty. Case in point is our long-term collaborator Miyake Kiyoko, whose work was crucial in the early 1970s and who continues to remain active from Japan in current environmental and aboriginal peoples' issues, but who modestly declined to give voice to her own recollections as part of this project. Kiyoko's self-effacing stance is but one more aspect of the challenges we faced in encouraging memories from the many Japanese who go unrepresented in this work.

Putting this book together in a narrative of history called for long exposition by the authors/editors, and allowed some drama of autobiography. We hope that no one feels slighted because of this; the experiences were common to many. Just the ICDHRT alone had scores of people involved in some capacity over the space of a decade. Most of them go unnamed, and in fact some have gone unrecorded. We wish as well that we could have more fully recaptured the feverish activity and uplifting hopefulness of the seventies. It was a freedom movement on many different fronts, crossing borders everywhere, and still lives today.

Why "A Borrowed Voice"?

As we foreigners were sucked into the vortex of urgent concerns and campaigns for people in Taiwan we knew personally or knew about, persons in danger or even at that moment believed to be under interrogation and torture, we still faced in our minds and hearts nagging questions about the nature of our role and right to take action. As foreigners, even more so with white faces, we had less chance of being physically and immediately harmed ourselves. Deportation could be a high cost, but not fatal. This was one rationale for participation, that we might be able to help those local citizens who risked freedom and physical safety if caught by the authorities carrying letters and photographs documenting human rights abuses.

On the other hand, we faced a persistent uneasiness. Did our relative safety mean we were actually dilettantes dabbling in matters that would further endanger our friends with our amateurish methods – those both politically-motivated, and those innocent of political intentions? Did we have the right to "interfere" in the affairs of another country? The authorities repeatedly told us we did not. Were we launching appeals that would harden the authorities' determination to exert force, due to public embarrassment? Were we engaging in self-promoting displays, or presenting often lurid and unsubstantiated allegations as grist for "bleed and read" reports? The mainstream news often painted us as such.

We also worried for our own personal, family, career and economic viability. Could those with whom we held deep personal relationships – wives or husbands, children, friends, employers – be told about these risks posed to them through our political activities? Could those we loved possibly understand and accept our deepening experience of involvement and commitment? Decades later, many still cannot understand the reasons for our commitment, and many have not forgiven.

The time and money devoted to these seemingly gratuitous human rights activities often made it difficult to hold a full-time job, to advance in business or academic careers, or to maintain a household. If we were living in Taiwan, the security agencies would have taken the opportunity to scuttle any chance at stable employment and housing. But even in our home countries the stigma of engaging in dangerous and illegitimate activities cast a shadow, including career opportunities blocked by inability to travel to Taiwan or China. This was especially damaging for those whose careers were built upon their linguistic skills in Chinese developed through years of study and training. Employment in any kind of government post was immediately out of the question. Perhaps fortunately, most of us became involved in the struggle for human rights long before we ever realized the price that would have to be paid.

Regardless of the doubts and insecurities, we still welcomed the unknown visitor, smuggled out the forbidden letter, translated the news brief, or distributed the human rights abuse report. We were driven by the sense that it was our responsibility to stand up for those whose right to speak had been snatched away, those whose urgent voices were silenced by torture or imprisonment. And so we lent our own voices. Lending this voice brought to us a sense of peace and relief, an awareness that we had done what could be done against injustice, that we had not been complacent and (for Americans) complicit in our own government's callous support for an oppressive regime. Our actions were closely tied to a transcendent love for those whom we witnessed staking their lives on a statement of justice and truth. They depended on us to carry their voices to where they could be heard.

This sense of a "borrowed voice" is more explicit in the translation of our book title, which in Chinese comes out as: "I Will Lend You My Voice." The "you" in this translation uses the feminine form, suggesting that borrowed voice was typically that of the wife of a political prisoner, most often a woman stretched to and past the limit of her emotional and physical capacities. With the family breadwinner in jail or in the grave, she shouldered a huge burden. She might be threatened with loss of her home: confiscation of property was commonly part of the sentence for political offenders. But often the confiscation was left dangling, apparently a way for police agents to keep the family under duress.

All too often political prisoners and their relatives were intimidated to the point of fearing even the quietest of whispers. While they would sometimes talk to a foreign visitor whom they thought was less likely to be government spy (especially the case for Kiyoko Miyake, a small and unobtrusive woman whose visit to the home might not be noted by the watchers), they would not overtly condone any action that would embarrass their authoritarian overseers. In these circumstances it was an impossible task to reconcile their desire to withhold explicit authorization with what we saw as the imperative of human rights reporting arising from our conviction that reporting helped allay further arrests. Only relatively recently have we learned that most prisoners experienced improved conditions following international inquiries.

The intensity and emotional trauma of the experience itself often made it difficult for victims and relatives to provide a coherent account of what had happened to them. In many instances they would be reluctant to explain what had triggered their punishment by the authorities, even if their "crime" was consistent with the principles of human rights and seditious only in the eyes of the martial law regime. These circumstances, in tandem with linguistic challenges, usually meant that any report we brought into public scrutiny had to be painfully pieced together and might not be fully accurate in the details.

It is not surprising that such a mission could be full of doubts and recriminations, uncertainty and emotional turmoil. When passing through the airport gates, you smiled to mask the stiff expression of tension. If searched, you damned yourself for neglecting to carefully hide or code the incriminating information. If you coded it and got through, you puzzled over how to decode it, and sometimes scrambled the information. If you got through intact, you might plan the next task with a sense of satisfaction and a devilish grin. If caught by a searcher, you began to think of ways of feigning nonchalance or casually blaming somebody else for asking you to carry the material. If identified by the security agencies, you might try to invent ways to stave off deportation or begin to bid farewell to your friends. You might throw yourself deeper into human rights work, haunted by the fates of the Taiwanese prisoners you knew. If arrested, as was Watarida Masahira of the Taiwan Political Prisoners Rescue Committee (Japan) in December 1979, nearly thirty years later you might "thank the Kuomintang for making me a stronger person."

Despite the many travails, we lent our ease of passage and our voices to those who had neither. We provided "a borrowed voice" that we could only hope would speak out against the tortured silence.

Acknowledgements

The printing and some production costs of this book have been funded by the Council for Cultural Affairs of the Executive Yuan of Taiwan 行政院文化建設委員會, specifically the 2007 Subsidy Plan for the Green Island Cultural Park 綠島文化園區補助計畫.

We wish to next thank the Taiwan Foundation for Democracy 台灣民主基金會, which has been largely funded by the Ministry of Foreign Affairs, for sponsoring the conference of December 6-12, 2003, inviting back to Taiwan over thirty of the foreign nationals who made contributions to Taiwan's human rights and democracy. In the opening evening of the conference, the Foundation designed a moving ceremony in which the foreigners were individually introduced on stage and personally presented with an award by former political victims for whom they had been concerned. Most of the pictures of the participants in this book were taken at this conference.

Thirdly, the Wu San-lien Taiwan Historical Materials Foundation 吳三連台灣史料基金會 has in many ways served as a silent partner in the production of this book. Seven years ago they arranged for Lynn to bring back 102 boxes of carefully-preserved materials from the Osaka years of work of the International Committee for the Defense of Human Rights in Taiwan. The Foundation provided him with an 18-month stipend to further work on its organizing and cataloguing. In addition, the Foundation has devoted one year of work by Shen Liang 沈亮 to scanning and cataloguing this large body of material. Shen Liang has recently completed his master's thesis based on Lynn's archives. In preparation for this book, the Foundation has provided Linda and Lynn full access to the archives, and has scanned a number of documents for reproduction in the book.

Linda Gail Arrigo received post-doctoral awards from the Institute of Sociology, Academia Sinica, for the two years July 2002 through June 2004, which allowed her to organize her own archives from the human rights campaign of 1980, read the relevant publications that have since appeared, carry out interviews, and obtain documents from the National Archives Administration. Her reports and materials sent to Lynn prior to the Kaohsiung Incident are held at the Wu San-lien Taiwan Historical Materials Foundation. The photographs and historical objects she took out of Taiwan in 1980 and brought back in 1990 are held by the New Taiwan Foundation of Shih Ming-teh.

Lynn was also previously provided funds towards his writings on Taiwan by the Taiwan Publishing Co., Ltd. 望春風文化事業, of Lin Heng-tze 林衡哲. He owes a great debt of gratitude to Frank Cheng 鄭炳全 and the greater Los Angeles Taiwanese community. He also cannot find the words to express the full measure of gratitude for the occasional financial rescue his family has received at the hands of the Taiwanese-American community, most recently epitomized by the organizing efforts of Patrick and Sharon Huang 黃再天, 楊淑卿 of New York City.

For both Lynn and Linda, these years of human rights dedication have sacrificed our family relationships, and although it is not possible to make up for the past, at least we can say clearly that we realize in so many ways we have failed our families, and we plead for understanding and forgiveness, hoping that they may see that the good of one being the good of all, they too may be able to reap the larger harvest.

A great many friends were recruited for tasks in preparation of the conference and this book. For the December 2003 conference, Yoshihisa Amae, Rosanne Cerello, Li-ren Chen, Steven Ching-chiang Chung, Robin Dale, Elise DeVido, Stefan Fleischauer, Ben Ryan, Misato Sato, and Joshua Tin helped conduct filmed oral history interviews with the participants, and also accompanied them on some of the activities. Yoshihisa Amae, Ben Ryan, and Timothy Fox later worked in translating and transcribing the interviews, and Kelly Miles helped with some fast keyboard input.

Aside from Yoshihisa Amae providing an essay extracted from his Ph.D. thesis on the Presbyterian Church in Taiwan (PCT) and its role in Taiwan's democratization, Yoshi also assisted in interviews with Watarida Masahiro and Nishikura Kazuyoshi in December 2007. Yoshi further obtained photographs of the 1965 Centennial that grace Chapter Four, and the 1977 document is provided courtesy of the PCT Faith and Order Committee 台灣基督長老教會(信仰教制委員會), 永望文化.

Both Rosemary Haddon and Ken Kilimnik were able to find and scan pictures from their years in Taiwan between 1977 and 1980, which helped us recreate the feel of old Taiwan and remember friendships between local and foreign activists. Ronald Tsao (Tsao Chin-rong 曹欽榮) provided pictures of the December 2007 Chingmei Prison activities.

We owe the physical production of this book to Chiu Wan-hsing 邱萬興. He guided us in applying to the Council for Cultural Affairs, advised us in the layout and production process, provided many photographs from his own book (with Chang Fu-chung 張富忠) Green Era 綠色年代 and his extensive archives, and cheerfully pushed us towards completion. As we came down to the hectic deadline for this book, David Toman, Jerome Keating, and Tim Fox were drafted on short notice for editing and proofreading the galleys.

The cover of *A Borrowed Voice* has been created from two perhaps incongruously bright-colored 2007 paintings by Deh Tzu-tsai 鄭自才, which depict a birds'-eye view of the Green Oasis prison on Green Island, and the front gate of the prison visitation center, facing out towards the jutting coral rocks along the shore that are the mark of the site. The faint emblems of human rights reports and organizations, including Amnesty International's candle encircled with barbed wire, hover in the clear blue sky above. The artist sees bright colors despite years in prison and in exile; our authors present the stories of those whose efforts have in Taiwan borne fruit and hope for human rights.

Chapter One

He's Our Son of a Bitch

Asia's remoteness meant the hypocrisy could be easily ignored. The July 1943 signing of the Sino-American Cooperative Agreement by US Naval intelligence chief Milton Miles and Chinese spymaster Dai Li signaled the beginning of overt American willingness to overlook a political prisoner camp right under their noses. The pattern continued after the Chiang regime lost to the communists; fleeing to Taiwan in 1949, the Republic of China served US interests in isolating the new Peoples Republic of China. But as the White Terror continued into the 1960s, a few solitary voices, ironically emerging from the US military, rang forth with chilling stories of a 1947 massacre and a still-ongoing reign of terror. A few books planted the seeds of public questioning of American support for yet another Asian dictator, affecting those who would later form the international component of the movement for human rights in Taiwan.

第一章 1950年代： 美軍默許蔣介世進行白色恐怖

亞洲實在太遠了，以致於美國的偽善很容易掩飾。1943年7月由美國海軍情報首長 Milton Miles 和中國間諜頭子戴笠所共同簽訂的中美合作協議，也是美國公然默許國民政府以集中營處置政治犯的開始。蔣氏政權在中國與共產黨的戰爭中潰敗後，於1949年逃至台灣，然而國民黨與美國合作的模式仍持續著。在台灣，國民政府服膺美國利益，孤立中華人民共和國。然而，白色恐怖持續至1960年代，很諷刺的，總算有一些零星的聲音從美國軍隊裡傳出，如警世鐘般悽切的控訴著1947年大屠殺的故事，以及蔣氏政權所持續進行的恐怖統治。少數幾本書開始對美國所支持的幾個亞洲專制政權提出公開質疑，這些萌發的種子，促使台灣的人權運動有國際人士的關注及參與。

1950s Gulag : Quiet on the Eastern Front

by Lynn Miles

For Captain Milton Miles, then the head of the US Navy's China intelligence branch in the Pentagon, the December 1941 attack on Pearl Harbor was serendipity itself, bearing welcome impetus to the Navy's plan to put together a strategy that would put paid to General Douglas MacArthur's island-hopping project, which subordinated the Navy to an Army command leading a drive northward from the South Pacific. The Navy's rival plan was to plough straight west from Hawaii, ultimately closing the waters between Formosa and China to enemy traffic, spelling doom for Japan's war machine once its foreign supply of oil ran out. So Miles concocted a mission for himself, one that would land him back in his beloved Orient: get as close to Formosa as possible, and reconnoiter sites for an Allied landing.

In a trip lasting weeks and crossing four continents, he arrived at China through the "back door" (via the perilous crossing over the Himalayas), where he took up with infamous spymaster Dai Li, the same Dai Li that the Western media was referring to as the "Chinese Himmler" and "Chiang Kai-shek's dreaded henchman." When Dai Li learned of the importance that Miles attached to Formosa, he was happy to have his far-flung spy network secret the American intelligence man from place to place beneath the noses of the Japanese. A small island off Xiamen's coast was as close as Miles was ever to get to the island fortress that Japan had been operating as its model colony since 1895.

Twenty-four years later, Miles' 629-page memoir would make much of Dai Li's generosity, wisdom and charity, awarding him kudos for supporting an orphanage at Happy Valley, the guerilla training camp that Dai Li was running with American help. Miles left unmentioned that Happy Valley also hosted a concentration camp, where thousands of political prisoners were eking out the rest of their days unseen by foreign eyes. Once Chungking fell to the Communists and Chiang Kai-shek had to beat a hasty retreat to Taiwan in 1949, virtually all of them were summarily executed in their cells.

China Incubus

This American ignorance (not to say indifference) concerning the true circumstances of political imprisonment under the Kuomintang persisted well into the second decade of US-ROC control of Taiwan, where the Happy Valley concentration camp was resurrected as the New Life Correction Center on a small island far from public view. To gain access to the New Life facility, where many prisoners were serving life sentences under harsh conditions, it would take Amnesty International staff years of trying before they could gain so much as a peremptory first-hand look at the Green Island camp. That came in mid-January 1980, when the harsh Kuomintang crackdown on virtually the whole of the democratic opposition forced the world to take a hard look at the means by which Taiwan's rulers were stifling dissent.

4 July 1943 signing of the Sino-American Cooperative Agreement. Representing the US was Commander Milton "Mary" Miles, head of Naval Intelligence in China, while the "dreaded" intelligence chief, Dai Li, signed for the ROC. Within the same Happy Valley complex that saw happy cooperation between the Americans and Chinese, was a holding pen for political prisoners. When the Communists drove the KMT forces from the area in 1949, they discovered that the prisoners had been executed in their cells.

American military pay a visit to the New Life Correction Center on Green Island, circa 1958. For this period the KMT's prison-building program was a budget line item in their pitch for American funding. The photo was taken by one of the political prisoners charged with keeping a photographic record of the prison camp for propaganda purposes. (Courtesy of Chen Ming-ho 陳孟和)

Such an opening could not have come without a huge effort on the part of thousands of foreigners added to that of the millions of Taiwanese who were forfeiting their own comfort, safety, careers and family lives to remove the veil of secrecy in the intervening years. Nor could it have come without a growing awareness among civil society worldwide that, as years turned into decades, still going unmet were the war campaign promises made in 1942 by the five big powers constituting the United Nations — United States, United Kingdom, Union of Soviet Socialist Republics, France, and the Republic of China. These promises were the lofty principles laid out in the Atlantic Charter, on which Roosevelt and Churchill's signatures were not yet a year dry.

Let them fade a dozen more years, and we come to the US-ROC part in their overturning of Atlantic Charter purposes, fought for at the cost of 60 to 100 million human lives: the 1954 treaty and defense pact. For Formosans (as they were still being called by their new occupiers), to the burden of what was becoming a permanent ROC encampment now had to be added the sudden deluge of thousands upon thousands of High Noses. In 1954 US troop levels jumped from 811 to 4,174 personnel, peaking in 1958 at 19,000.

As the White Terror continued unabated well into the 1960s, several chinks began to appear in the Cold War armor. At first these were minor irritations to the Chiang cabal, little shaking its faith in official American willingness to turn a blind eye to willful and egregious violations of the fundamental tenets of the 1948 Universal Declaration of Human Rights that the ROC had joined the international community in designating as the supreme standard for proper relations between a government and its people. Individually at first, Americans started breaking ranks and scratching the surface, eventually going public with the regime's dirty secrets.

Among the first was Vern Sneider, who presented a credible account that moved many readers, especially those who had spent some time in Taiwan and had bothered to test *A Pail of Oysters'* basic premises against underlying realities on the ground, such as the fear that seemed to pervade all relationships. Speaking to a UC-Berkeley crowd of his first awakening when he came to the US in 1970, Taiwanese scholar Keelung Hong said that Sneider's work "describes not just the foibles of confused Americans out of their depths across the Pacific, but accounts of KMT terror, including the shooting of the character based on the interpreter Ed Paine recommended to Vern Sneider. The book opens with a KMT patrol seizing oysters gathered by Taiwanese coast dwellers. Sneider makes very vivid the terror in which Taiwanese lived in the late 1940s, the oppression of KMT bandit-troops, the massacre of 2-28, and also makes clear the common Taiwanese views that what land reform was really about was breaking up any Taiwanese power bases."

Following on the runaway success of *The Ugly American*, the 1958 novel that he co-authored with Eugene Burdick, former Navy captain William J. Lederer came out with *A Nation of Sheep*. The "sheep" in question were Americans who followed meekly whatever the media and their government told them about putative bulwarks of democracy and freedom on the Pacific Rim. One chapter, devoted exclusively to

The *Ugly American* had a huge impact on public feeling in the US concerning failed foreign policy. The who-lost-China debate of the 1950s gave way to popular indignation at the US leadership's poor record at "backing the right side." The book went through many printings, and within a few years Hollywood had produced a blockbuster of the same title.

When *Nation of Sheep* appeared in 1961, *Time's* reviewer pooh-poohed it as a hack job, and dismissed Lederer as a "heat generator rather than a light spreader," bemoaning the fact that "some 100,000 plain, puzzled Americans have made a 36-week bestseller out of this loosely written handful of horror stories about US policy in the Pacific." Taiwan Garrison Command and Government Information Office censors ensured that plain, puzzled locals would not get a chance to make it a commercial success in Taiwan, too.

Year after year after year, the *China Yearbook* managed to treat the February 28 Incident as but a small street skirmish. Discussion of the violent bloodbath that followed was strictly taboo. The point was not to hide from ROC citizens what had actually happened, but rather to keep the secret within Taiwan. By the time of the 1971-72 edition, the cat was already out of the bag, so such exercises in international obfuscation amounted to what the Chinese refer to as a "thief covering his ears while stealing the bell."

"what we aren't told about Formosa," detailed a long litany of crimes against the people by the Chiang regime.

Sneider and Lederer's works were banned in Taiwan, which virtually guaranteed them a ready audience among US military personnel, who got around the ROC censors by having copies mailed to them through the APO mail system.

By the time missionaries began pouring into Taiwan in the late 1950s and graduate students started arriving in numbers to take up Chinese language study or advanced research at Taiwan Normal, National Taiwan, and Cheng Chih universities, the informational dike was starting to show serious cracks.

Meanwhile, reports on most political arrests, rarely making it into the local media, fared even worse abroad, leaving the newspaper reader in London and New York quite benighted. The Lei Chen *Free China* Case of 1960, and the Su Tung-chi Case of 1961 might register a small rebuke in the form of a three-paragraph, inside-page story in the *New York Times*, but otherwise all was quiet. Likewise the arrest of Peng Ming-min et al after their 1964 statement supporting self-determination caused barely a ripple in the overseas press. But in the meantime the *China Quarterly* had run a series of critical studies citing the *Free China* banning; the quarterly's editor, Mark Mancall, put these articles, including several by Taiwanese scholars exiled in Tokyo, under one cover in 1964: *Formosa Today*.

The 1965 banning of *Wenhsing* and subsequent silencing of Lee Ao likewise barely stirred the *New York Times* from its slumber, warranted nary a word from *Time*, and garnered but cursory mention in more erudite journals like *The Nation*. All in all, human rights issues in Taiwan were off the radar as far as the American public was concerned.

Why so much attention paid to how the facts of the White Terror were getting so little traction abroad? First, because all revolutions begin with questions of manufactured consent and the fiat of dictators to deny historical fact wider dissemination. The struggle for people's loyalties began with the media. If Chiang and his minions were beholden not to the local citizenry but to Uncle Sam, and if the presumed masters of the US government were the people who elected it, then much depended on how the regime was perceived by the US public. More than anyone else, the Chiang regime itself was most aware of this, as proven later by minutes of high-level meetings that subsequently came to light.

Before an international network focusing on Taiwan human rights issues could emerge in the late 1960s, awareness of the crimes therefore had to be given a trial in the court of international opinion. These writings of the 1950s and early-to-mid 1960s were essential steps in that direction.

Chapter Two

The Republic of China Has No Political Prisoners

The decade 1960-70 began with the banning of Free China and the jailing of its chief editor, Lei Chen, who had attempted to form an opposition party; there was little international reaction. It ended with Peng Ming-min's escape to freedom abroad in 1970. In 1969 Amnesty International general secretary Martin Ennals made his first trip to Taiwan, prompting compilation of a list smuggled out by political prisoners themselves. By decade's end, undercover alliances had been forged between Taiwanese freedom fighters and their foreign counterparts. Overseas, as objections to the Vietnam War became daily headline fare, voices of opposition to US-supported dictatorships such as those from the Committee of Concerned Asian Scholars joined a growing chorus. The campaign to rescue University of Hawaii student Chen Yu-hsi provided a solid blueprint for effective international action. For the first time in its experience, the KMT faced an array of critics transcending national borders.

第二章 1960-1970： 台灣政治犯名單終有見天

1960年代，也就是1960年至1970年的十年，始於企圖成立反對黨的自由中國主編雷震於1960年被逮捕入獄，結束於1970年彭明敏逃至自由的國度。1969年，國際特赦組織 Amnesty International 的總秘書長 Martin Ennals 首度來台，並取得由台灣政治犯所提供的黑名單。在這十年的末期，台灣島內的自由鬥士與國外的接應者之間已暗中形成聯盟。在海外，反對越南戰爭的聲浪開始成為美國本土與世界的頭條新聞，反對美國支持獨裁政權的聲浪也急速增長，許多從事亞洲研究的美國學者也加入組織進行聲援。在1968-69年，國際動員成功救援就學於夏威夷大學的台灣大學生陳玉璽免於死刑的案例，成為後來有效國際救援行動的藍圖。這是國民黨首度面臨到結盟的跨國人權工作者的監督。

Formosa Found – 1960s Student Days

by Lynn Miles

When I started my voyage to Taiwan in August 1962, I knew very little of Formosa (as it was then all but universally called), outside of what my college classmate of the previous year, Ben Cheng, had told me. Although we had had our share of clashes, without hesitation I would have said that Ben was one of my best friends, even though my fellows at Central Methodist College (Fayette, Missouri) were agreed that he was quite the charmer, with much of what he said to be taken with a grain of salt.

For one, he told me that the accident that permanently altered his gait was because he had been speeding down a mountain road in his father's jeep, when he lost control and careened into a ravine. His sisters were later to laugh at that one, saying that in fact he was hit while riding a bicycle. He was on the level in telling me that his father was a big general, and that he had his own personal jeep, but it would be many years before I discovered just how important was his dad, who had passed away two years before I first met Ben, in 1959. But all that is neither here nor there, for I owe Ben a great debt for having interested me in going to "Free China" when I was a strapping 19 years old.

So it was that, having completed my freshman year of college, I felt a compelling wanderlust that I hoped to satiate with a couple of years of foreign travel. Little suspecting that this would turn into several decades in the "Orient," here I was, in August 1962, looking up from the Long Beach wharf at the towering hulk of the *SS Hai Tee*, and thinking it so big that no ocean wave would daunt it. It was a Liberty Ship, of the same vintage as the small fleet of Liberty Ships that had been mothballed at the end of World War II, and anchored in the inland graveyard of the Hudson River where it widened just above Stony Point. As a boy I had an occasional look at them because they were only a 30-minute drive from my boyhood home in the mid-sized town of Pearl River, NY. Now, in 1962, the Liberty Ship looked every bit as big and impressive to the 19-year-old standing on the San Diego docks as it did to the 8-year-old standing on the Stony Point shore.

We hadn't even left the harbor when it began to dawn on me just how small it really was, for on our way out we passed many ships that towered over us. Once at sea, we were also dwarfed by the rolling waves. This was all the more the case as we neared the end of our one-month journey, as we had to slow our 11-knot crawl and take up a slow circling maneuver several score miles northeast of Taiwan to wait out a passing typhoon. It was long minutes from the crest of one wave to the next, and for the first time I felt fear that the bow might plow under and never come up again. Swells nearly a hundred meters from crest to crest would coax creaks and groans from deep within the ship, prompting fears that it might break apart. But Second Mate Yao, who had

Flood control levee work

Typhoon Gloria killed hundreds throughout the island in September 1963. These shots were taken outside Huwei in April 1964. (Courtesy of Wu San-lien Taiwan Historical Materials Center)

befriended me early in the voyage, put these fears to rest. (It was just as well that he didn't tell me that Liberty Ships, thanks to a fundamental design flaw, had the worrisome habit of snapping in two in rough water.)

Another thing that Second Mate (as we called him) put to rest was the Chinese name that Ben had given me. When I boarded the ship, it was with a piece of paper that Ben had written out, listing the names and ages of all his siblings. There were eight of them. Hsin-yuan 心元 was the eldest, then a sister whose name I've forgotten; both of them had taken up permanent residence in the US, quite the rarity in those days for all but the scions of the very privileged. Ben 心本 came next, I believe, followed by three sisters and a brother, Alexander 心雄, who was later to rise to prominence as a high-ranking KMT patrician cultivated by Chiang Ching-kuo. Ben had told me before I left that his family would take me in when I arrived, and that his mother would be my "godmother." But when Second Mate Yao told me that the Chinese name that Ben had given me was a crude foreign concoction all lacking in elegance, I gladly accepted his offer to come up with a better one; I showed him the list that Ben had given me, and asked that whatever the name, it should have the heart心 character in it, which would make me a bona fide member of the family. So the Lin Mai-er 林邁爾 that left Long Beach arrived at Keelung in early September 1962 as Mei Hsin-yi 梅心怡. As time went on, I would learn that this was a fateful change of persona.

My first visual impression of Taiwan may well have been much like that of the ancient Portuguese mariners who gave it the name "Beautiful Island." This was largely thanks to the typhoon in whose wake we arrived, because it delayed us enough that we had to circle around in the waters north of Yonaguni late the day before arriving, and so had a chance to see cumuli stacked to the stratosphere, lording it over majestic mountains rising stark and clear in the typhoon-scoured skies.

From Little Devil to Foreign Devil

Arriving in Keelung Harbor the next morning, it was to the sight of water-born hustle and bustle, with sampans bearing peddlers clad in nothing more than underwear, sandals and conical bamboo hats, hawking their iced drinks, betel nut, and boxed lunches. There was not much time to linger at the deck rail as the *Hai Tee* docked, however, because a launch had brought out a "special person" to board the ship as she was being piloted at a snail's pace through the narrow harbor mouth. It was Alexander, Ben's brother, whose high station was immediately made apparent by the contrast between his carefree abandon and the nervous, eager-to-please demeanor of everyone on the ship, customs and immigration people included. The requisite entry stamp was quickly entered in my passport, customs dispensed with by the cursory wave of a hand, and in no time at all I was on solid ground and being ushered into a black Ford complete with chauffeur, leaving behind seven fellow passengers, all Americans, to fan away the stifling heat in their cabins while having their papers processed. Welcome to the life of privilege....

First impressions linger still of the muggy heat, even in the morning. And the drive along the main road leading into Taipei, with the chauffer, obviously very familiar

Lynn Miles

Leisure life and beasts of burden

Wiith the Shihmen Dam just having come on line the previous year, in early 1964 the stage was now set for Taiwan's economic take-off. Soon the ox would go the way of the endangered species. (Courtesy of Wu San-lien Taiwan Historical Materials Center)

with the dimensions of his car, managing to come within an inch or two of any number of pedestrians, cyclists and oxen pulling carts, moving along unperturbed, without so much as a glance at the near-death scrape with privileged authority that they had just experienced. And to the humidity, heat, and perilous traffic must be added the smells, becoming all the more noxious once we arrived at the Cheng family home on Antung Street, which was then still in what could be called the outskirts of Taipei. Back in those days, before the city planners got serious with such road-straightening projects as JianGuo South Road and FuXing South Road, Antung Street was the first semblance of a road that one got to when walking east from Hsinsheng South Road along Hsinyi Road. It meandered all over the place, following an old canal that has since been covered over; in fact, little is left of Antung Street itself, as JianGuo Road has since shot straight through as if it never existed. (In romanizing the street names, I am staying with the spellings then in use.)

The Antung Street canal was the filthiest, ugliest, most stinking open sewer I had ever seen, though within days I was to come across a few worthy contenders, among them the canal that ran down the middle of Hsinsheng South Road. As if the Antung Street canal were not deterrent enough to would-be trespassers, separating the Cheng residence from the canal and then the street was a high concrete wall, also ugly, capped with the barbed wire, spikes, bottle shards and *cheval de fries* embedded in concrete that could be seen atop the walls of any home wishing to advertise its inaccessible provenance. Once inside, the Cheng home itself was comfortable enough, with everything but the alcove covered with hardwood flooring, meaning that one removed one's shoes when entering. This was something I found difficult to get used to, as slipper-makers in Taiwan had yet to rise to the challenge of the foreign foot.

I stayed at the Cheng home through the end of the year as I settled into my new routine as language student at the Mandarin Center at Normal University. Quickly getting the most rudimentary phrases of everyday discourse under my belt, I loved to venture out to put them to the test. The grammar of spoken Chinese is simple in the extreme, so getting the hang of everything from haggling prices to asking bus directions was a matter of only weeks and soon enough I was clipping along; in any Western language it would have taken months to get up to first gear.

At home and school alike, just as aboard the *Hai Tee*, I was called "Little Devil," but it took me some time to accept that this was truly a term of endearment, rather than meaning that I was simply too young to be taken seriously.

All went peaceably and uneventfully enough in what, for that time and place, passed for the lap of luxury, a setting undisturbed by the press of circumstance afflicting average households. Well maybe not: there *was* this one incident which stands out. Preceding my arrival there had been letters from Ben, who remained behind in New York, announcing my arrival. When I first introduced myself to Ben's mother and siblings as Mei Hsin-yi, all pandemonium broke out. Mother began screaming and wailing, pounding the arm of her chair, and blustering away incoherently in her thick Szechwan accent.

Amnesty Spirit: No Pot Calling the Kettle Black

by James Seymour 司馬晉

I first went to Taiwan in 1960, just after earning my Masters degree at Columbia University. I had received an unexpected "gift of time" by virtue of the fact that the United States military had rejected me for minor (some might say dubious) health reasons. Having been given back at least two years of my life, I decided that I should do something that I really wanted to do. So I went to Los Angeles and boarded the Taiwan-bound freighter *Hai Ming*. [1] Aside from myself, the ship carried scrap metal from the United States, and one other passenger, my life long friend Hu Fu (Hu Fo) 胡佛，now professor at National Taiwan University.

After four weeks at sea, on Christmas Eve we pulled into the sleepy port of Keelung. The Foreign Ministry, under the questionable impression that I might be somebody important or at least worth cultivating, sent an official to meet me pier-side: Col. Konsin Shah夏功權, who would later enjoy a distinguished diplomatic career. I suppose the reason why I was taken that seriously (aside from the Republic of China's general desperate need for friends) was that I happened to have been related to some prominent people who were involved in US foreign relations.[2] Thus, for example the Foreign Ministry watched out for me, arranging trips to Quemoy and the Pescadores (Penghu), though not to Matsu as I wished. Happily, however, they left me pretty much alone.

I first lived with the family of Hu Fu at Ming-te Hsin-tsun 明德新村, near Ta Ping Lin, between Chingmei and Hsintien. In those days this was a rural area. There were few automobiles, and I usually bicycled to Taipei. I loved living out there, but eventually (when Hu Fu married and the house became crowded) I moved to National Taiwan University and lived with the Pao family in a detached room of theirs. The rent was the equivalent of US$10 a month, which doesn't sound like much (and, at black-market exchange rates, it wasn't much), but it was quite a stack of paper bills! (Out of fears that issuing higher denominations of currency would remind people of the inflation that had occurred on the mainland, for a long time the government refused to issue money in reasonable denominations.)

During these months I studied at National Taiwan Normal University's Mandarin Center. One incident there indicates the flavor of the times. Before Student Day (May 4?) we foreign and (mostly) overseas Chinese students were asked to write an essay to be posted. I asked what the essay should be about, and was simply told: Whatever your field of study is, write something about that. Well, my "field of study" happened to be political science. I decided to write an essay comparing chinese and American ideas of constitutionalism. I pointed out that in the United States, the constitution was taken very seriously (which it was, in those pre-Rehnquist years); its provisions were not casually cast aside. In Taiwan, on the other hand, whereas the constitution limited the president to two terms, that provision was rather casually cast aside when Chiang Kai-shek wanted to enjoy a third term. After I wrote my essay along these lines, I asked Hu Fu to clean up some of the worst linguistic *faux pas*. However, he opined that there was an even more serious issue; he was concerned that in terms of content what I had written would cause a

Not quite the reaction I had been smugly anticipating. In the years since, the typical reaction from people on first hearing my name is invariably, "Oh, but that's a girl's name!" But not this time. It turned out that the elegant moniker to which, thanks to Second Mate, I now laid claim was the very same name that my new godmother had given to a son who had died in infancy on the mainland at about the time I was born.

Had it not been for everyone's reaction, I would probably have regarded this as a miraculous turn of fortune. Right down to Mao-mei (Hairy Sister, the youngest), all were positive beyond a shadow of a doubt that this went far beyond possible coincidence; it just *had* to be another of Ben's childish pranks. My adopted family spoke as one in roundly condemning him, my explanations in barely-understood English falling on deaf ears. I retreated to my room to wonder whether the ironic whims of Eastern gods gave a whole new meaning to "inscrutability." When Ben got a strong dose of their ire by post, he deflected much of it in my direction, as if I had somehow known that he once upon a time had a brother with a girl's name, and the same name as Second Mate Yao had given me at that! For it all to blow over took a couple of weeks (the trans-Pacific exchange by mail taking that long), and soon enough I was reinstated as Little Devil.

Outside the house it was another story. Likely as not, on the street I was Foreign Devil. Stray a few hundred meters from where all palefaces were concentrated by the thousands on Chungshan North Road, and it was the same story wherever you went, even in Taipei. Venture even further afield, say into the countryside, and the whole village would likely as not turn out to check out the curiosity. Like the time I was relieving myself next to Taipei Station, not far from where the lists of those executed in the middle of the night on the river bank had been posted every morning in the early days of the White Terror. The wall along which the men's urinals were arranged in what was otherwise a unisex lavatory reached not much higher than one's elbows, so, as seen from the other side, there was no mistake as to what one was about. Not quite full exposure, but more exposure than one wanted, that's for sure. One could only adopt the attitude of the thief in the Chinese phrase, where covering one's ears while stealing the bell meant that no one else could hear: just strike the most nonchalant pose possible while vacating the bladder in record time. People in a hurry to catch their train barely noticed, but in one instance I was the object of attention of a gaggle of taunting barefoot youngsters. *Waiguoren! Waiguoren! Adoga!*

Martial Law, Political Slogans and Japan-bashing

Also leaving a lasting impression were the myriad ox carts. They were pulled not only by oxen but, where feeding the plodding beasts was beyond the means of the oxcart owner, then by coolies clad in nothing but shorts and sandals, and sometimes not even sandals. Often their loads amounted to tons, as they strained to move their loads through the teeming streets, leaning far forward against the taut strap, their arms dangling nearly to the ground. Brakes were unknown to these lumbering behemoths, and woe betide the unwary pedestrian who should chance to step in front of them.

Initial surface impressions of Taipei would not be complete without mentioning the

lot of trouble. So we produced a watered-down version. I was somewhat annoyed, fearing that the revised version was so bland that no one would get the point. Anyway, I took it and proudly presented it to my teacher, whom I addressed as Li Hsien-sheng (Teacher Li). Alas, when poor Li Hsien-sheng saw it, her jaw dropped, and she ran to the office of the director of the program. He came bounding in and declared that such essays must contain nothing political. (I declined to write a new one.)

This sort of thing, of course, was only the tip of the iceberg. I was gradually becoming aware of what lay beneath the surface. I knew that the enlightened mainlander Lei Chen 雷震 was serving a ten-year prison sentence. He had published a liberal journal called *Free China*.[3] Also, the American playwright Vern Schneider had written a novel called *A Pail of Oysters*, which depicted the plight of ordinary Taiwanese in the 1950s. This book was banned on Taiwan, a fact that made me absolutely determined to read it. At the CIA compound I knew a secretary, and she agreed to sneak a copy out of their little library for me. It was an eye-opener.[4]

Still, I had no interest in being a hero, nor did my local friends. But Hu Fu did realize his dream of forming a liberal academic group. They published the journal *Ssu yü yen* 思與 言, for which I guess my only contribution was providing it with the English name *Thought and Word*. This high-quality, if low-keyed, publication appeared for several decades, and managed to make occasional liberal points without getting its participants into trouble.

I spent most of my eight months in Taipei, but did take a couple of great mid-island hiking trips, both times with foreigners. (Local people seemed uninterested in such activities, or even found them bizarre). In early July Klaus Mäding, from Germany, and I climbed Yüshan 玉山, reaching the summit before sunrise on July 4. When the sun came up over the ranges to the east, it was fabulously beautiful. However, we were wearing clothes suitable for the summer tropics, and my main memory is how cold one was up there! On another occasion, with a group of American students, I made the three-day hike from Wushe to Hualien, via a trail through the mountainous forest. That gave me a glimpse of some aborigines.

I left Taiwan in August, and returned home – this time flying.[5] On the way, I spent a week or so in Japan. My purpose in going to Taiwan had been to try to learn Mandarin, so I had deliberately made friends mostly among Mainlanders. That meant that I hardly got to know well any Taiwanese folks. But in

In December 2003 James Seymour met with Mr. and Mrs. Lin Yi-hsiung at their foundation office in Yilan.

ubiquitous evidence of the trappings of the garrison state: trucks carting troops to and fro; jeeps by the thousands, many of them bearing four MPs with white helmets, their backs as ramrod straight as the carbines that they held at their sides, glinting in the sun; pillboxes, most of them unattended, but still there, prominently placed on major intersections as silent reminder of an ongoing civil war; anti-aircraft batteries alongside the bridges leading into Taipei; armed patrols on the beaches; stenciled slogans on the buses, warning you that the person sitting next to you could well be an eavesdropping bandit spy; mottos on every elementary school wall extolling us to greater efforts in the great mission of mainland recovery; and most exciting of all, middle-of-the-night shaking of buildings as phalanxes of tanks made their way out of the city along Roosevelt Road.

As for my political awakening, it came belatedly. When I arrived, I was very much a babe in the woods concerning the rightness of the "Free China" title, and was still in the woods when I left Taiwan a year and a half later. For the first year all of my associations were with mainlanders who were in Taiwan because they had thrown their lot in with the Kuomintang. Diehards to the last. Of course, there had been that conversation in the officers' dining room on the *Hai Tee*, where passenger Charlie's comment that the KMT's loss of the mainland was well deserved, thanks to its venality, corruption, ineptitude and cruelty, was met by the third mate's heated yet *sotto-voce* response, "You won't last long in Taiwan if you keep talking like that." In my book, that response alone should have won the debate for my fellow passenger, who never tired of pointing out that citizens of the ROC lacked the freedom to criticize the government. But, like the officers, I was prejudiced against Charlie for his know-it-all manner, and remember thinking something like, "How could Charlie, who has never been to China, presume to know more than the people running the ship, who spent years in Shanghai and later in Taiwan? He is insulting their patriotism!" For I still put a lot of stock in patriotism.

As for the KMT's corruption, I drew few conclusions from the fact that it was the Cheng family, KMT loyalists all, who drove me downtown to Hengyang Road, where they steered me into the back rooms of the jewelry shops to have my greenbacks exchanged at two and three times the official rate. This was at the very time that the *China Post* was chastising the government for not doing more to crack down on the black market. If black market currency exchange was the exposed face of corruption, as far as I could tell it was all-pervasive; the lack of security at the door leading into the back room hardly suggested a fear of raids by government treasury police; and the speed and flourish with which the young ladies dispensed with a stack of bills bespoke a wealth of experience in high-volume trade. The same could be said for the requests that kept coming in from all quarters for me to swing a connection with some GI, so that I could get Winstons or Johnny Walker at the PX, and in bulk so that a business could be established. Corruption reared its head on a daily basis, and it was difficult to tell from my vantage point whether the KMT was leading it, or was just another happy participant.

The *China Post* also fell into step with one of the periodic Japan-bashing juggernauts,

Japan my friend Ken Matsumoto introduced me to the exiled Huang Chao-tang 黃昭堂 /Ng Yuzin 黃友仁. Talking to Ng awakened me to the fact of how much about Taiwan I had failed to observe. He made me realize the extent of the repression and deprivation of the Taiwanese, first by the Japanese, then by the Kuomintang. Ng was an advocate of Taiwan independence, and although this was not an issue with which I have ever wanted to become closely identified, he made the case quite effectively.

Between 1961 and 1975 I concentrated on launching my academic career (getting my doctoral degree from Columbia, then teaching at New York University), and did not give a whole lot of thought to (much less revisit) Taiwan. Toward the end of that period, however, I did begin to develop an interest in the general issue of international human rights. In 1971 the American section of the British-based human rights organization Amnesty International was founded, and I became rather active in it.[6]

Then, in 1975, President Chiang Kai-shek died. The ROC government announced that a hundred days after his death there would be a commutation 減刑 of prisoners' sentences. The International Secretariat of Amnesty, in London, was eager that some political prisoners be included in the commutation. So they asked me to go to Taiwan on a mission, and appeal to the government accordingly. I traveled by way of London (where I was briefed for my mission), Moscow (where I spent two days at the airport due to a missed connection), and Bangkok. Finally I arrived in Taipei on May 15, remaining until the 21st. I don't remember too much of what happened in Taipei, but in the event, some political prisoners (I believe including Huang Hua 黃華) were included in the commutation. Amnesty was very pleased with the outcome, and believed, perhaps erroneously, that my mission had something to do with it.

That autumn, when I was back in New York, word was received that eight people were about to be placed on trial again. If memory serves, these included Li Ao, Wei Ting-chao, Hsieh Tsung-min, and five lesser lights. I was approached by the International Secretariat of Amnesty about the possibility of my going back to observe the trial. I still had a valid visa, and now in preparation bought a flight ticket. As a courtesy, I went to see Konsin Shah, who was the ROC's representative in New York at the time. He was, to say the least, unenthusiastic about my going; it was clear that I was now viewed as an interloper. Then, the International Secretariat began to have second thoughts. For one thing, there would not be time for me to go by way of London and be briefed. Finally, they phoned me with the word that the plan was off. But at this point Lynn Miles, in Japan, phoned London and urged that I be sent after all. He agreed to brief me when I passed through Tokyo. So around 5:00 a.m. New York time I received a call from London asking me to go immediately. Three hours later, I was on the plane.

Miles and I had never met. I had told him that I would be wearing a red necktie at a certain railroad station. He found me. He had prepared detailed written instructions. Soon I was on to Taiwan. I arrived in Taipei at Sung Shan airport on September 15, 1975, and took a taxi directly to the Garrison Command center in Chingmei, where (and at about that hour) the trial was to begin. Alas, when I arrived, I was not allowed inside.

I then went to the home of William Armbruster, who was a stringer for the Far *Eastern Economic Review*. Bill put me in touch with the elder statesman Kuo Yü-hsin and his young assistant Chen Chü. Through them I met many young dissidents, I believe including

eventually editorializing triumphant over the fact that the official embargo on Japanese medicines was finally getting results. That the facts otherwise could be seen on the shelves of the neighborhood pharmacy. Somebody was paying off somebody, went the conventional wisdom, spoken in ho-hum tones. When it came to business, greasing the palm of a policeman or politician seemed to be the natural order (what went in the West by the sobriquet "greasing the skids"), and what was politics if not the handmaiden of business? There were few complaints about it to be heard within my hearing, but that is probably because I was surrounded primarily by its beneficiaries and practitioners.

But later on, I was to hear it voiced as a complaint, and from the Cheng family. Prompting their pique was Kao Yu-shu 高玉樹, that uppity Taiwanese who so brazenly and successfully took on the KMT in the 1964 race for the Taipei mayor's seat, and won. His crime, in their book, was to steer contracts and land speculation in the direction of his business friends, which I suppose meant that they had their own friends who were now losing out. That Kao himself was raking it in was something I was able to verify for myself near the end of my stay, when an American friend of his son took me up to Yangminshan for an overnight at his palatial estate. So, on top of windfall profits being steered in a contrary direction, an even larger thorn in the Cheng family's side may have been the fact that a Taiwanese native son was doing so well for himself.

I say this because I was repeatedly the reluctant witness to remarks which, had they been spoken directly to a Taiwanese, could only have been taken as arrogant insults. Nearly all of my friends being mainlanders, I was forever hearing that, far from being genuine Chinese, the Taiwanese, addled by fifty years of Japanese brainwashing, were left with no real culture; they lacked the finer arts, and they had no history to speak of. While it would not be fair to say that this applied to all mainlanders, still the condescension was pervasive enough that their cultural superiority was a favored conversation topic among the foreigners that I was meeting. This was very much the case during my 1962-to-1964 stay, soon yielding to more subtle, codified forms.

Second Visit, 1965: Political Awakening

After a year's absence, I returned to Taiwan in November 1965 and stayed for two years.

A number of influences converged in 1965-66 to suck me into political curiosity and an activist tendency that, while quiescent from time to time, has never quit me since. It began in the States in early 1965, during my sophomore year at Central Methodist College, where a piece that I had written for the student newspaper had fired up the student body, which had in turn riled the administration to the point where by the end of the semester it had conspired, connived, manipulated and strong-armed several of the student government leaders to oust the editors of the paper. It would not be too much to say that we were railroaded out through repressive measures that would have done the KMT proud. By the end of the semester the paper was under full control of the administration, the same administration which had only months before

Chang Chun-hung 張俊宏, Chou Ching-yü 周清玉, Huang Hua 黃華, Lin Yi-hsiung 林義雄, Yao Chia-wen 姚嘉文 (and doubtless others, though my memory is not too clear as to exactly when I first met whom). I learned a lot from these not-yet-famous people, and gained great respect for them. (In five years, most of them would be in prison.) So although the trip was a failure in terms of achieving its goal of observing the trial, it was beneficial in terms of how much I was able to learn, and of establishing a network of relationships (*guanxi wang*) that would later be mutually beneficial.[7]

I made no more trips on behalf of Amnesty International, but during the next five years I did make two personal trips to Taiwan. The first was in early August 1978, and the second was mid-May 1980. During one of these trips I went to Tainan, where I saw quite a bit of the folks at the Tainan Theological Seminary, a hotbed of dissent, and also visited George Kuo at the agricultural research station at Sanhua. The second trip was in the wake of the big crackdown of the winter of 1979-80. I visited the relatives of the Meilitao Incident political prisoners. On the other hand, Han Lih-wu 杭立武 (the pro-government moderate human rights activist) invited me to lunch with Ma Ying-jeou 馬英九, then an official of the Kuomintang. He explained to me that the arrest of those involved in the December 1979 Kaohsiung demonstration had been justified. Just as in Boston, where he had studied, one needed a police permit to hold a parade or demonstration, so one needed a permit in Kaohsiung. The demonstrators hadn't had one and so were law-breakers.

At about this time I was occasionally attacked in the media, which was sometimes quoting officials like James Soong 宋楚瑜 (who referred to me as "Professor Chin" — Chin being my given name). Also, there was a notorious series of articles by Meng Hsuan in the *United Daily News*. Meng claimed to have interviewed me. (Actually, we had merely sat opposite each other at a large round table full of diners, and he picked up on a few of my remarks.) The articles were replete with innuendo (I was a "social misfit"), and misstatements. For example, he said that I had claimed to be the nephew of John Foster Dulles; he had checked into the matter and found that it was not true.[8] But Mr. Meng did pick up on one unfortunate but more-or-less real incident.

At various times I was invited to testify before Congressional committees about the human rights situation on Taiwan (transcripts available on request). On one such occasion (May 19, 1981), the sub-committee was chaired by Steven Solarz. The other sessions went well, as they were conducted by well informed and sympathetic chairmen. On this occasion, arrangements had been made by Solarz's aide, Edward Friedman, an old friend of mine and a solid liberal. All-in-all, I was expecting an easy time of it. To my surprise, Solarz's testimony was somewhat hostile. He kept pressing me to compare the human rights situation on Taiwan with that in the People's Republic of China. I was reluctant to make such a comparison. For one thing, I was thought of as an Amnesty International person, and even though I was not representing AI on this occasion, I did not want to stray far from the organization's policies, one of which was that one should avoid comparing the human rights situations in different places. Also, this was a time when China seemed to be making some strides, at least from having an atrocious human rights record to one that was merely bad, and I felt that it was not appropriate to make gratuitous invidious comparisons. And frankly, I did not want to make remarks that would let the Kuomintang off the hook so easily at a time when they had just been engaging in shameless repression. But Solarz (who would soon be out of office, tainted slightly with

been proudly trumpeting its willingness to leave the editorial content of the paper to the student editorial board. As if that wasn't enough, they also stooped to calling the editors communist, in public no less, with not a shred of evidence; once challenged to prove it, instead of retracting the statement, they just denied that they had ever said it in the first place.

There were many lessons that I drew from that experience, but the main ones concerned (1) the lengths to which corrupt, money-loving power structures will go to maintain that power; (2) the practical difficulties of speaking truth to power, even when the truth is being bandied in private; (3) the highs to be had from working closely with loyal friends fighting on the battleground of ideas and ideals.

So when I arrived in Kaohsiung aboard yet another China Merchants Liberty Ship on 21 November 1965, I was rum-running some contraband experience and attitudes: going up against authority, and questioning the official line as a matter of duty. Had I been an ROC national, I could easily have been disappeared in the night and put on the rack.

This experience at CMC in itself might never have amounted to anything so great as to be called a life-changing experience, had it not been what lay in store for me while a student at Normal University and later National Taiwan University in 1966-67. First, I met Frank Miller, also a student at NTU. He hailed from Mississippi, and was the only American I have ever met before or since who has managed to impose a true southern drawl on Mandarin. And, although I have met others since, he was the first American scholar that I had met who was reading contemporary Taiwanese literature seriously, rather than classical Chinese. It was he who put me on to *Wen Hsing* magazine and Lee Ao. It took only a few pages of Lee Ao's stuff to get me hooked, and pretty soon I was joining tens of thousands of students around the island in hungrily reading anything I could get my hands on put out by Wen Hsing Bookstore, publisher of both the magazine and a wide selection of paperbacks, many of them dealing with politically sensitive topics. Lee Ao was absolutely hot, and already by that time hands-down the regime's most formidable challenger, Yin Hai-kuang included.

I will return to Lee Ao, but before I finish with Frank Miller, I must also credit him with putting a copy of George Kerr's *Formosa Betrayed* in my hands. As for William J. Lederer's *A Nation of Sheep*, I believe this was also a copy borrowed from Miller (we all called him Miller, not Frank), which, like Kerr, was a damning indictment of US support for the Chiang dictatorship, but went further by treating each of the US-supported tyrannies in Asia, devoting a chapter to each. Both of them were chock-full of historical material fully indicting the US for its complicity in propping up leaders who were lording it over captive populations; both fell short of calling the US an imperial power or analyzing the systemic, capitalist dynamics of that power. So I still came away with the idea that, if only the US public knew the true facts of what was going down in Taiwan, all could be made right again through the application of fine democratic principles. For my underlying patriotism still got in the way of a readiness to concede that Taiwan was not a democracy in part because *America* was not a democracy. That would come later.

scandal) kept pressing the question, and took my reluctance to deal with the issue on his terms as raising doubts as to my credibility. Finally, I answered that Taiwan and the PRC were "in the same ball park." Although two things can be in the same ball park but still a long distance from each other, in a newspaper account Meng Hsuan rendered the phrase *"cha bu duo,"* meaning "not much difference." One of Meng's headlines was "Solarz Says Seymour Lies for the Chinese Communists." Congressman Solarz later sent me a letter that was a clear rebuke to Kuomintang propagandists such as Meng.

Actually, in those days human rights abuses in the PRC was a major concern of mine, and I devoted at least as much time and effort to the mainland as to Taiwan. Whereas I never did write and publish a whole lot about Taiwan, in 1980, after Beijing's brief "spring," I had edited a book of writings taken from "Democracy Wall" (1978-79).[9] (Later, I would turn my attention to the PRC prison system.[10])

Also, in March 1977 I had set up an organization called the Society for the Protection of East Asians' Human Rights (SPEAR), which between 1979 and 1984 put out a quarterly called *SPEAHRhead*. Each issue typically dealt with human rights issues in the PRC, Mongolia, and the two Koreas. Sometimes even Japan was covered. But of course so was Taiwan. After the Meilidao Incident I got hold of the complete transcript of the proceedings in Kaohsiung that evening (December 10, 1979). With the assistance of Linda Arrigo (who had been there in Kaohsiung and was able to help me supply needed explanations and commentary), an English translation was published *SPEAHRhead*. [11]

Unsurprisingly, after 1980 I was blacklisted and not allowed into Taiwan. But if the hope was that this would make me compliant, I'm afraid that the authorities must have been disappointed. For example, I published a translation of the embarrassing minutes of a secret meeting of Kuomintang military and civilian officials. On October 17, 1984, a group of top generals met with various civilian leaders, including chief censors (the current and former heads of the Government Information Office) Chang King-yuh 張京育 and James Soong. Until now, the latter two were perceived, at least internationally, as relatively clean-faced officials (even though, in those years, acts of government censorship were running at between 30 and 180 annually). Before long, the records of the meeting leaked out, though few Taiwanese were able to see them. Reading these minutes gave me a sense that all of these men were cowering in fear. They were determined to wage warfare on what they perceived to be a "formless enemy" comprised more than anything of heterodox ideas. I sent the document to the British magazine *Index on Censorship,* and they were eager to publish it with my commentary. It appeared as the cover story in their March 1985 issue.

Perhaps concluding that denying me a visa might have been counterproductive, in 1988 the government finally granted me a visa. The plan on the part of a group of us at Columbia University [12] was to undertake an academic election-observing study trip. I arrived with my colleagues in the wee hours of March 6, 1989, all of us exhausted after the flight from New York. However, at first the immigration officials would not let me pass, and the whole group waited while the officials tried to straighten things out. It being a Sunday morning, it was not easy for them to contact their superiors, but after a couple hours we were allowed to enter.

To my consternation, our government minders kept our observation group in the Taipei

Another important attitude-changing encounter came in early 1966, through an American professor of architecture teaching at Tunghai University. I met him through another Tunghai teacher, David Joy Chadd, aka David Witwer. Dave had been the editor-in-chief of *The Collegian*, the aforesaid student-run newspaper at CMC, and the only one of the four main editors to finish the spring 1965 semester not on probation. It was I who persuaded him that a year teaching English literature in Taiwan would be a year well spent.

Dave was thoroughly enjoying his new job. His students' English ability impressed him, and he was certain that soon he could begin teaching his first love, literature. Being a church school, there were mandatory weekly chapel services, but the resemblance to CMC ended there: the students were serious about their lessons, as were the teachers.

One of those teachers was Felix Tardio, who was bringing his teaching stint at Tunghai to a close so that he could devote full time to the writing of a book on Taiwan's architecture, which he found fascinating, delightful, ridiculous and dreadful. By early spring 1966 Tardio had moved to Taipei, where he burned the midnight oil, putting the last touch to his writings, soon to become the book-length companion to a volume of drawings that had been accepted for publication by some Taipei printing house which probably had no idea what it was getting into. Both of them were to be a critique — serious in the prose but riotous in the Art — of Taiwan's Architecture (both A-words capitalized throughout).

Architecture as Politics: Felix Tardio's Parting Shot

Sometimes, just to get out of our cramped fourth-floor flat opposite NTU, Jack Cooper and I would bike downtown to see Tardio. Jack was another veteran of the administration-student battle that I induced to come in late 1965. Felix was holed up in a funky Japanese-era hotel, the Fukuo, at 13 Hsinyang Street, just off Kuanchien Road, in the old Japanese-built section of Taipei between New Park and the railway station. I still have a vivid mental picture of the morning sun glancing off the huge waxy leaves of some tropical tree just outside his window. Tardio had his windows thrown wide open to catch the early spring air, but leftover winter chill still called for multiple layers of clothing. Big of build, he wore a turtleneck sweater under a corduroy jacket, elbows sporting patches, pocket full of pens. His trademark was a full, handlebar mustache and dark curly hair, reminding some of the Mexican revolutionary Pancho Villa, and others of the American comedian and popular talk-show host, Groucho Marx.

But when it came to humor, he was squarely in the Groucho Marx camp. He kept Jack in stitches with his tales of ongoing battles with Government Information Office censors over the deletion or "correction" of every last word. He showed us some of the passages which the GIO deemed impermissible. Naturally, all of them were criticisms of the ruling powers — these "misunderstandings" of his that in their eyes needed "correcting" before the book could go to press. Lee Ao was to explain to me later that the law prevented the government from banning a book outright until after

area. At one point I decided to leave town on my own and visit Ilan, where Lin Yi-hsiung and others were slated to speak. I slipped away into a stormy night, went to the railway station and took a train to Ilan. I was invited to sit on the platform, and may have spoken a few words to the rain-soaked audience. Soon word came that the police were about to descend on the place. I was swept away into a car (I think with Lin Yi-hsiung and Ho Kangmei) and the driver took a circuitous route to Taipei via Keelung.

In the early 1990s various brave exiles began trickling back to Taiwan, even though they knew that they would probably be arrested. Among them was George Chang 張燦鍙, chairman of World United Formosans for Independence (WUFI), who was the husband of my good friend and fellow human rights activist Tina Chang 張丁蘭, a founder of the Formosan Association for Human Rights. Another such person was my friend Lu Wang (Kang-Lu Wang) 王康陸, also a member of WUFI. George was arrested December 7, 1991 when he arrived at the airport under an alias, and held for eleven months. I'm not sure when Lu Wang was arrested and released. Anyway, roughly two weeks after George's arrest, I went to the prison where both were being held, and visited them (separately, through glass panes). They both seemed in good spirits. Sadly, after Lu Wang's release, he was killed in a suspicious automobile mishap next to the National Security Bureau. This

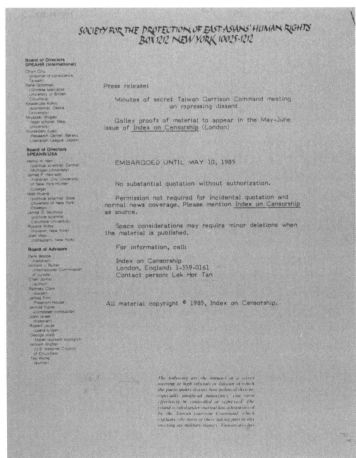

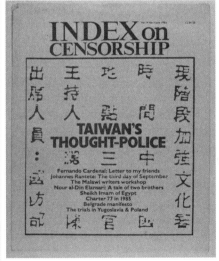

Seymour spearheads drive to expose thought police

Seymour's carefully timed release of internal documents showed that the ROC government was struggling to overcome bad press, both domestically and abroad. The revelations got big play in the Chinese language press in the US, and appeared in the August 1985 issue of *Index on Censorship*. See p. 25 for details. (Courtesy of Wu San-lien Taiwan Historical Materials Center)

its publication. Tardio seemed unaware of that, however.

But the extent to which Tardio was able to haggle his way past the censors speaks for his patient determination. Can't accuse the Taiwan government by name? Then use the general term, since everybody will know who you are talking about anyway:

> One great mistake made by many dictatorial countries is their failure to realize that the American, when traveling abroad, carries with him and continues to exercise those basic [four freedoms]. This is especially true of certain Asian countries where any mention of slightest criticism of the government is, in the minds of the government and police, taboo.

In this case, he was able to persuade the guardians of orthodoxy that if it be charged that "certain Asian countries" applied to the ROC, well, that was the fault of the reader, not the writer. So he was learning that it was possible, if you fought tooth and nail, item by item, to keep certain passages intact so long as he resorted to vague generalities and allusive ambiguity.

But even very direct criticism could be slipped by them in some cases. In the following passage perhaps their training in English had not prepared them for catching the true meaning of the words which I have italicized in the following:

> In Taiwan there are hundreds of men sitting in the central government's congress who still represent the provinces on the mainland. These men have been away from their homes for almost twenty years and still *go through the motions of* representing the best interests of their people on the mainland. As used here-in, "Chinese" shall mean all those living in Taiwan. In some eyes there is a difference between the Chinese Nationalists, who came from the mainland, and the native Taiwanese people. In this book there will be no such distinction....

If this is what was allowed to pass, then imagine what the deletions contained! Even with all the excisions, the book amounted to a collection of gentle prose trending toward suggestion, irony, and oblique phrasing when necessary, but all-in-all, for the discerning reader a few-holds-barred diatribe against government greed, detachment from public reality, and ineptitude.

Many were the hoops that Tardio was made to jump through in order to get his work of art to press. But, as he noted in a little message to the reader on a separately printed slip of paper inserted into each book before distribution, the sketches themselves were unaffected. And on that separate sheet of paper, which he never put before the GIO censors, he listed the page numbers and the passages which had been removed or replaced with something parroting the official view. If reading these today, you were to say to me, "All pretty tame stuff," I would come back with: "Monday morning quarterbacking!" Anything and everything in that era was couched in the most circumspect ways, and it was expected that the reader could get the drift with a healthy dose of reading between the lines.

Also enlightening was a conversation I had with my first close Taiwan-born friend, Lin Po-chao 林博照. For several months we shared a flat above the Good Friend Photo Studio, with a balcony overlooking the main entrance to NTU, where he was

INDEX ON CENSORSHIP 5 85

Taiwan

James D. Seymour

Spring wind blows no good

Classified government document reveals how Taiwan's Garrison Command plans to stifle dissent

Earlier this year we came into possession of two classified Taiwan government documents. One was the minutes of a secret October 1984 meeting of military and civilian leaders in which they discussed the repression of dissent. A translation of this document appeared in Index on Censorship 3/1985. The second document was a table detailing these men's plans.

The table, set out on pages 32 and 33, is less self-explanatory than the minutes were. In fact, when our June issue was being prepared, this document appeared to be moot. As we then indicated in our introduction, the minutes seemed mainly of value for the insights provided into the minds of the censors. Though opposition magazines continued to be banned, the actual implementation of the great plan (moving from 'passive' to 'active' repression) was not immediately carried out. We speculated that the reason for this had to do with the murder of Henry Liu, the American critic of President Chiang Chiang-kuo. At least one high government official was involved in that crime, a fact which caused serious international repercussions.

In April, some people were convicted in Taiwan for the murder. It may be that with the Henry Liu matter out of the way, the authorities have felt safe in moving ahead with their 'active' repression. The table has suddenly become relevant.

Taiwan was a Japanese colony until the end of the Second World War. During this period the Taiwanese enjoyed considerable political and legal modernisation, which their postwar Chinese rulers had not. Thus, the Taiwanese had mixed feelings about being 'liberated' by the corrupt Chinese Nationalist regime, which treated the islanders brutally. Since 1949 conditions have improved, but the Nationalists still rule the island under Martial Law. The organ which administers the Martial Law is the Garrison Command. There are also other government and police organs which carry on this work. The whole apparatus is structured in a Byzantine fashion, with the various security agencies often at odds with each other.

On 3 July, four people were arrested in connection with the leaks of official secrets. Two are Taiwanese: magazine publisher and former legislator Huang Tien-fu, and political activist Ch'iu Yi-jen. Mr Ch'iu had been chairman of an organisation called the

'Writers and Editors Association', a militant (but non-Marxist) group opposed to both the political establishment and the more moderate oppositionists. He holds a master's degree in philosophy from the University of Chicago.

Interestingly, the other two arrested people are 'mainlanders' — Taiwan-born young adults whose parents came from China proper. This background suggests that they had been trusted by the authorities, and indeed were typical of the people to whom the Nationalists intend to bequeath political power. Accused of originally leaking the document is Ch'en Pai-ling, an employee of the Government Information Office — one of the agencies in charge of censorship. Ms Shih Chia-yin, a political science student at Taiwan University, had been involved with a non-party magazine.

Three of these people have been released on bail, but as of this writing Ch'en is still a prisoner. Presumably, the group will be placed on trial. Acquittals in political cases are unheard of. The authors of the table tend to use euphemistic language. Thus, 'control of culture' primarily refers to repressing the opposition magazines. The word 'information' often means censorship, such as that carried out by the Government Information Office. Planned campaigns of repression go under such benign names as 'Spring Wind'.

Although last October's 'Spring Wind No 6' fizzled out, in late April 1985 a 'Zhongxing' campaign was launched; it had many of the earmarks of the plot which had been outlined in this table. (The term *Zhongxing*, meaning 'midway revival', is taken from ancient Chinese history. In 25 AD, the 200-year-old Han dynasty appeared to have died, but it was restored for another two centuries. The Chinese Nationalists hope for a similar revival.)

Apparently the groundwork for *Zhongxing* was better laid than had been the case with 'Spring Wind No 6'. Many secret meetings were held in addition to that described in our June issue. For example, under Project 4 of this table there is a reference to a 'Conference on Correct Opinion'. Nothing is known of this conference, but it apparently pronounced death sentences on many publications.

Zhongxing got under way when at least 1000 police (some estimates run much higher) were assigned to crack down on news-stands and shops, as called for in

Projects 5 and 6. And, in an unprecedented step, they invaded not only the magazine publishing houses themselves, but even the offices of various elected government officials. Often, the invaders wore plain clothes, lacked search warrants, and refused to show any identification. If anyone tried to deny them entry, the agents simply forced their way in.

The pre-April 'passive' repression had been mainly harassment. Although many opposition magazines were censored or banned, the authorities often failed to confiscate a complete press run. Thus, censorship did not have the desired effect of preventing the dissemination of unsanctioned ideas and information, which still found their way into the hands of a public otherwise largely dependent on government-controlled newspapers and broadcasts. The magazines might be distributed secretly and sold under the counter, or simply circulate underground in the manner of Soviet samizdat.

The switch to 'active' repression may mark a change in this situation, though it is too early to conclude that it will be completely successful. The Taiwanese people have shown a remarkable capacity to circumvent the information controls imposed on them. (In the minutes, one military leader complains of the intense reaction to the government's efforts. 'Publishers keep coming up with new tactics to flout our control.') The government has not demonstrated the capacity — and many of its members lack the will — to act as a totalitarian regime. Still, the accompanying table stands as a serious self-indictment of what could, in a democratic country, be deemed a criminal conspiracy on the part of the officials involved. ∎

On 9 August Ch'en Pai-ling was sentenced to 10 months in prison; the other three were acquitted.

The fluctuating fortunes of the independent and opposition press in Taiwan in the 1970s and 1980s are described by Gerrit van der Wees on page 34 ('Taiwan censorship statistics').

majoring in agricultural engineering and was about to graduate. Of a poor family from southern Taiwan, he was the eldest son and on track towards an advanced degree, when all of his best-laid plans for graduate study suddenly came crashing down thanks to my over-zealous curiosity and our ignorance concerning our immediate surroundings.

Beneath the Surface: Resentment, Anger and Fear

Having read *Formosa Betrayed*, I asked Mr. Lin what he knew of the February 28 Incident. What about Taiwanese-mainlander relations? We were in our room, it was mid-afternoon, and we could see that the neighboring student was gone from his room, there being no light bouncing off the ceiling between our rooms (the partition separating our rooms fell a foot short of the ceiling). Even without the threat of eavesdropping, however, Lin spoke very cautiously, in hushed tones, as if the ceiling itself might have ears. But by the end of an hour-long discourse, he had poured out his guts about disappeared uncles and publicly executed school boys. He had little good to say about mainlanders; the KMT power was a colonial regime (although he may not have used those words) —

> When upon our door there came a rapping,
>
> Lin now freeze-frame, quick surcease.
>
> Unknown to us, neighbor'd been napping,
>
> Our shadow-cloaked overseas Chinese.
>
> Afternoon interloper, hallway spy?
>
> Frantic guesses — what were the chances?
>
> No word from Lin, silent was I.
>
> We exchanged fearful glances....

Lin's face turned red, then ashen. The eavesdropper started out gently enough, "I overheard you. Sorry, but I have a slightly different view..." Then a litany, recited like a veteran of many a Three Peoples' Principles lecture. Lin's face switched from ashen to white. It was all he could do to stammer abjectly to every correction offered by our good-patriot neighbor. "Yes, yes, yes..." Weeks away from graduating from Taiwan's elite university, with his family's entire fortune put to that purpose, all now hinged on what the eavesdropper would do with the information. And with that, his twenty-minute lecture complete, our neighbor left as abruptly as he came, leaving Lin a quaking, stammering semblance of his former self.

Weeks passed, while we waited in suspense, to see if the guy might be an informer, whether there would come a message from the university department's disciplinarian, the party man, asking him to come in for a talk. Lin lucked out. The call never came.

But it was a severe lesson, and, as may be imagined, Lin clammed up for good. As for me, that should have been enough to put a tight lid on my reckless inquisitiveness — never again would I put my friends at such risk.

was a great loss to the democracy movement. (As for George Chang, he was several years later elected DPP mayor of Tainan. The head of the city council, non-DPP, was involved in some controversial land deals, for which George was prosecuted. At the time of this writing, Chang faces a 7-year prison term.)

During all these years I had the benefit and pleasure of associating with, and being enlightened by many people, some mentioned above. There is one person in particular whom I would like to recall. From the mid-1980s through the early 1990s I spent quite a bit of time in Hong Kong. There I befriended the Roman Catholic priest Edward Kelly. Though I was not Catholic (nor even particularly religious), Ed and I were kindred spirits who took an immediate liking to each other. Ed provided me with office space, first at the harbor-side American compound in Wanchai, and then in the offices of the You Dao Centre on Queens Road East.

Father Kelly's official position was Hong Kong chaplain to Catholic American military service people. But as there was little demand for his services, he carved out various niches where he could make a contribution to humanity. One of these was Taiwan. From his Hong Kong vantage point (rarely was he allowed into the island) he followed the day-to-day events on Taiwan, and published an irregular newsletter on the subject, with the English title of *Yuan*.

One of Father Kelly's projects, in which I'm particularly proud to have played a minor role, had to do with Taiwan's Dangwai magazines. Beginning in the late 1970s it was often possible in Taiwan for the opposition to begin publishing a magazine. However, typically, after a half dozen issues the operation would be closed down by the authorities. Ed obtained copies, and then collected missing issues from others like myself. Eventually, he was able to get the whole collection published in microform. Thus, this valuable record is available for researchers. (See page 239.)

Alas, in the early 1990's Father Kelly began to have health problems. He was unfailingly cheerful, and for a long time did not let on that in fact he had leukemia. Eventually he returned to his native Ireland, where he died in 1994.

All of these endeavors have been very satisfying, in part because of the opportunity they have given me to associate with great people like Edward Kelly and Lu Wang; I am only sad that these two cannot be here to enjoy this day. But of course the major satisfaction lies in seeing Taiwan as it now is: a prosperous, democratic land. I do not claim that foreigners played all that much of a role in this transition. It was the Taiwanese who made the great sacrifices and deserve virtually all the credit. But at least we interlopers were on the right side of history.

References in Chinese:

"American Congressional Hearing on Human Rights: Seymour Covers up for the Chinese Communists, is Refuted

Sorry to disappoint. Some time later, I was driving through the mountains with a Taiwanese businessman and his dog. We were on our way to several days of duck hunting in Chiaohsi, Ilan. As we crossed the Taipei-Ilan divide, and thinking that here, surely, there was no chance of third-party ears being anywhere near, I started to share with my host-driver-guide what I had read about 2-28.

"Oh no, we don't talk about that! No politics!"

"But it's not politics, it's people's lives. All I want to know is the facts. What actually happened? What's the big secret about it all, if terrible things in fact happened?"

"No, no, sorry. I don't want to get into all that with you. Things happened, but I don't want to talk about them."

"Why, what are you afraid of ? Here we are, only mountains and trees for miles around. Nobody can hear us." Throwing a thumb in the direction of the dog sitting behind in the back seat, I mocked, "Or maybe you think *he* is a spy!"

"Too dangerous. Never talk politics! It can only bring trouble!"

If I were to present these stepping stones toward political awareness in chronological order, then this last incident would have to come after I first met Lee Ao, the epiphany opening me to a whole new dimension. I have presented this last together with the others because they show that it was possible to come to some conclusions about the political realities then prevailing without necessarily making contact with anyone on the front lines of political dissent. These were everyday experiences, revelations available at any time to anyone curious enough to ask some simple questions. By this time, with *Nation of Sheep* and *Formosa Betrayed* to be easily procured through a plethora of channels, any foreign student who had spent more than a year in Taiwan and still didn't know that the KMT garrison had perpetrated an island-wide massacre in 1947, or that it had orchestrated the sacking of the American embassy and the USIS and the stoning of the ambassador's car in 1957, was spending too much time with the *Book of Changes* (both events, after all, had been covered by *Time*, the staunchest of Chiang Kai-shek supporters).

Culture as Politics: Meeting Taiwan's "Culture Punk"

What these everyday experiences also held in common was the fact that, had I been reported for any one of them, my visa would probably not have hung in the balance. A rebuke, mild or strong, would probably have been the extent of it, and without a doubt it would have gone worse for Miller, or Lin, or "TS" (whose identity shall remain a secret out of respect for the fact that the last time I saw him a few years ago, he was still in a cautious frame of mind bordering on paranoia).

Falling in with Lee Ao and his *Wen Hsing* associates was a whole different level of involvement. Why? Precisely what was the threat of this small group of intellectuals?

When taking up the despotic challenge presented by the power-holders, the position of the liberals was that, while conceding the point that the communists were an abominable tyranny demanding unwavering opposition, they were unwilling to lock

by Solarz," by Shih Ko-min, United Daily News, May 21, 1981.

"What's so Holy about James Seymour? He Meddles in Human Rights, Distorting the Truth! Visiting Taiwan Several Times, on Return to the U.S. He claims First-hand Material. He Peddles a Tempest, Openly Promoting Taiwan Independence," by Meng Hsuan, United Daily News, May 22, 1981.

Notes:

1. The ship belonging to the China Merchants Steam Navigation Company, which had been founded by Li Hong-chang. The captain was a great guy who taught me how to play wei-chi. We ate with the crew, and the food was reasonably good except for once a week, when a Western meal was presented.

2. I was the nephew of the recently-deceased U.S. Secretary of State, John Foster Dulles, and also of Allen Dulles (then still head of the Central Intelligence Agency). The latter connection gave me a certain entré into the large local CIA community.

3. A few years ago I came into possession of an almost complete run of this magazine. The issues are now in the Starr East Asian Library at Columbia.

4. After I returned to New York I was able to track down and purchase a used copy. Recently, I donated all of my Taiwan-related materials, including this book, to the Taiwan Culture Foundation (Tina Chang, Executive Secretary), 375 Yu Nung Rd, 7F, Tainan, Taiwan.

5. It was my first experience in jet planes, which still could not cross the Pacific without making two refueling stops (Wake Island, and Hawaii).

6. I founded a local AI chapter, Group 9, in the NYU/Greenwich Village area of New York City. One of the prisoners on whose behalf the chapter worked was Huang Hua. Group 9 is still going strong today, though I am no longer active in it.

7. After both AI missions, I wrote detailed reports for the International Secretariat. These were internal documents, and were never published. I hope some day these will become available. The second report was gathered with the assistance of Linda Arrigo.

8. There are two falsehoods here. First, in those days I was somewhat embarrassed to be the nephew of the unpopular (in America) Dulles brothers. I never mentioned my connection, and few of my friends knew. But, of course, it was true.

9. *The Fifth Modernization: China's Human Rights Movement, 1978-1979* (Earl Coleman, 1980). The introduction to this book was co-authored by my friend Mab Huang (Huang Mo 黃默).

10. *New Ghosts, Old Ghosts: Prisons Camps and the Laogai System in Contemporary China* (with Richard Anderson), M. E. Sharpe, 1998. Chinese version, Mirror Books (Hong Kong), 1999.

11. Issue no. 9, Spring 1981. (At this point the publication was prepared manually, but later it was *Taiwan Communiqué's* Gerrit van der Wees that got me going on Radio Shack machines.)

12. In 1980 I had left New York University for Columbia. (Details of my academic career are available on line at *http://www.columbia.edu/~seymour/jds_cv.htm.*)

step with everyone else in bowing to KMT authority. If they did not outright call the regime a one-party dictatorship, they instead made none-too-opaque allusions to a more circumscribed object of contempt — a poorly drafted education bill, for example. Or else they just kept their tongues, withholding the obligatory homage, letting their silence do all the talking.

The long *Wenhsing* piece by liberal pillar Yin Hai-kuang entitled "The Ethical Foundation of Freedom" may serve as example. In a magazine where longer articles typically ran to eight or ten pages, this one ran to seventeen. Under the heading "Freedom and Nation," he intoned: "Some nations absolutely protect freedom, like Switzerland, England, West Germany and Japan." That the Republic of China does not rate mention in the list speaks volumes, fairly inviting the reader to ask why the omission — and to supply the answer. Doubting the ROC's stature in the democracy sweepstakes thereby becomes an act of treasonous collusion between writer and reader.

This is but one example from among many, where the author pulls back from the precipice, relegating the "ROC" to some kind of undefined exile. He disdains to call a spade a spade, favoring omission, abstraction and circumlocution over commission, concrete and direct. Nowhere in Yin Hai-kuang's thirty-thousand-word exegesis do we expect him to say flatly, "The Republic of China has far, far to go before it can be considered to be a defender of freedom." But, for all his abstractions, we know — and so does the regime know — where he stands. (And so it was that, not too long after, while nobody was surprised at all to learn that Yin had lost his Taida teaching job, they went on as before signaling their respect by calling him "Professor Yin.")

If no less an internationally recognized intellectual giant than Yin Hai-kuang was forced to to cloak his accusations in the arcana of "logic," to suggest the obvious without ever stating it directly, then we begin to perceive the full dimensions of the *regime of fear* then confronting any intellectual who thought to challenge the official shibboleths maintained by brute force.

As for Lee Ao, although far exceeding the cautious self-imposed limits of Yin Hai-kuang, he still hewed to certain bounds. Especially in his first few years at the editorial helm, he was all but unknown outside of a small circle of liberals that began with Hu Shih in the days of *Free China* and then extending several years later to those *Wenhsing* editors who decided to print his first broadside. So for Lee Ao to have lashed out at the dread demons of political repression would have been to court sudden disappearance. Instead of tilting at officially sanctioned talismans straight on, he first cultivated his persona as "cultural delinquent," reserving his slings for the educational and cultural establishment. This assured him a popular following among the young while at the same time sparing him the ultimate fate awaiting the true iconoclast straining against the restrictions imposed by a garrison state. But even so, in a pattern that we were to see repeated time and again with a score of *Dangwai* publications in the seventies, *Wenhsing* moved step by calculated step into the abyss of all-out, undisguised political dissent.

14

COMMENTARY

The Asian Wall Street Journal Weekly August 5, 1985

Taiwan Pays the Price of Repression

By JAMES SEYMOUR

Taiwan's continued survival as a de facto independent entity depends primarily on the U.S. Regardless of the Taipei government's emphasis on weapons purchases, what is most important really is its international public relations.

For decades the Nationalists mastered the art of public relations, but there are signs that they are losing their touch.

Mid-October seems to have been the turning point. First, on Oct. 15 came the murder in California of Henry Liu, an outspoken critic of Chiang Ching-kuo. This gaffe, for which at least one high Taiwan government official is responsible, is a departure from the past practice of committing all such dirty deeds at home. This time, Americans were incensed.

Equally outrageous was a secret meeting of various high officials that took place two days later. To the participants' great embarrassment, the minutes of this meeting leaked out. Though the government banned every domestic magazine that tried to publish it, a translation has been provided in the June issue of Index on Censorship, a London bimonthly.

'Thought Pollution'

At the secret meeting the authorities discussed the problem of "thought pollution." (One can only recall the 1983 Communist campaign against "spiritual pollution" on the mainland.) They laid a detailed plot to move from "passive" to "active" repression of the opposition, especially its magazines. Although these plans weren't carried out immediately (probably because of the furor over the Liu affair), they have been implemented in recent months. The repression has been a devastating blow to the island's chances for democratization, and thus for American sympathy.

The participants in the Oct. 17 meeting, mostly military men, see politics as a form of warfare. But they find political battles more difficult to fight than those that are

is invisible. A more-tangible foe would be easier to ferret out. Most of the stated tactics for doing so are the obvious blunt tools like the banning and confiscating of dissident journals. Already this year more than 70% of Taiwan's independent political magazines have been seized. Some methods sound more benign than this, but on closer inspection are just as sinister.

As one of the newer tactics, certain Taiwan officials came up with the idea of having dissidents sued in court for defamation. Libel law in Taiwan isn't simply a

Jonathan Loew

matter of a slanderer having to pay his victim financial compensation. The punishment also involves a prison sentence, typically of one year. Furthermore, in this one-party dictatorship (originally designed by Leninists), political trials are conducted by a partisan judiciary, and acquittals are unknown.

Taiwan is a place where pseudo-intellectuals have brilliant careers as long as they toe the party line. This gives rise to much resentment, and in their writings the more genuine intellectuals try to attack such people. But the government always has the last word, as its numerous critics have found out.

The Nationalists (or at least their Tai-

was actually launched against a New York anti-Nationalist Chinese-language newspaper. For venue, the state of Virginia was picked because of its conservative judges and tough libel laws. But when the case went to trial, the statements that had been published were found to have been true.

In Taiwan, truth is the first casualty of libel suits.

The authorities actually deny that they are promoting libel suits. In February, Government Information Office head Chang King-yuh said the government "isn't involved at all," and that the suits are "between individual citizens." This is the same Mr. Chang who had been the most active participant at the October meeting where plans were laid to promote these actions:

"I propose that an office of legal advisers be established in government organs at every level, so that whenever an organ or any of its officials is the subject of a libelous attack, they can apply to their legal advisers to act on their behalf in making inquiries and bringing charges," Mr. Chang said, adding that "a revision of the civilian and criminal code, providing heavier penalties . . . would make the people who are responsible for producing extremist publications afraid to arbitrarily attack and libel leaders and government organs."

He also called for tax and commerce officials to harass "illegal" publishers. "By increasing their difficulties, we can gradually prevent them from printing and selling," he said.

Vanishing Credibility

The credibility of Mr. Chang's February disclaimers vanishes in the face of these earlier secret utterances. Credibility is an essential commodity if the Taipei government is to have American support and thus survive.

The drama of the leaked minutes isn't over. On July 3, four people were arrested in connection with the leaks. Two are Tai-

chairman of an organization called the Writers and Editors Association, a militant (but non-Marxist) group opposed to both the political establishment and to the more moderate oppositionists. The two men have been released on bail.

The other two arrested were "mainlanders"—people who the authorities normally trust most. Chen Pai-ling worked in the Government Information Office under Mr. Chang. Mr. Chen, who is said to have originally divulged the document to a young woman named Shih Chia-yin, remains in prison awaiting trial. (Ms. Shih has been released.)

The Role of Laws

It must be understood what traditionally minded Chinese mean by the term "law." At the October meeting, the party's culture czar, James Soong, spoke of "relying on laws" to control the opposition magazines. In modern countries laws are precise rules, uniformly applied; from reading them people can learn what they may and may not do. But in imperial China laws tended to be vague, and were sometimes even secret. Instead of protecting the citizenry, laws served as tools to enhance the power of the elite. The Nationalists boast of being the guardians of traditional Chinese culture, and in many ways they are. They have a long way to go to achieve a modern legal order.

The officials of this stridently anti-communist government who participated in the October meeting appear to be running scared, but it doesn't seem to be the Chinese Communists (with whom they have so much in common) that really frighten them. Rather, they are terrified of homegrown liberal ideas, which are seen as part of a conspiracy to overthrow the government. Indeed, while there is virtually no pro-communist sentiment on the island, the calls for majority rule become more insistent every year. They can no longer be ignored.

James Seymour is an associate re-

Op-ed pieces hit where it hurts

Seymour's fastidiously crafted essays won him a wide audience throughout the 1970s and 80s. This August 1985 op-ed piece didn't help him any with his blacklist problems. (Courtesy of Wu San-lien Taiwan Historical Materials Center)

Seymour and Miles first met when Seymour passed through Japan on his way to Taiwan in 1975 on a fact-finding mission for Amnesty International.

If the steps were calculated, not so the consequences one was courting, for they were outside the known parameters of any publicly rendered calculus. One could only contemplate and speculate. In fact, the regime of fear was founded on nothing so much as it was on the unknown. If torture and/or prolonged detention ending in swift execution (one's family being given posthumous notice if at all) had been the sure and inevitable result of a particular line of action, then, with the element of fear of the unknown eliminated as a weapon of repression, history would surely have taken a different course, with a different breed of activist likely stepping up to the plate. But fear of the unknown? This was the most potent fear of all, bound to produce in the person contemplating even the most modest level of opposition a guaranteed modicum of neurosis. That much is fairly well understood, and back in my college days was presented as gospel in Psychology 101; who has not learned how rats needed little time to be conditioned to neurotic helplessness after being presented with a stimulus that sometimes brought on food, other times electric shock? In private conversations with me months later, Lee Ao was himself to discourse at length on how the lack of any sort of defining guidelines added up to a loose and arbitrary construct consciously designed to keep the opposition in fear of the unknown reprisal.

In this regime of fear, the most hideous and unimaginable of crimes now became imaginable possibilities. The umbrella of fear had many spokes, extending to the classroom and workplace, worship service and family meal, newspaper column and casual conversation, sober riposte and idle jest. Fear was able to reach out, extending into avenues of human endeavor far removed from politics. One could not ride the public bus without being exhorted by stenciled advisories to be ever on the alert for spies. But it was in the political realm that people would, as Aung San Suu Kyi did when accepting the 1990 Sakharov Prize for Freedom of Thought, call fear by its name, just as a year later in her acceptance speech for the Nobel Peace Prize, she pointed out that it had its international dimension: "the lonely struggle taking place today is part of the much larger struggle worldwide, for the emancipation of the human spirit from political tyranny and psychological subjection." By far the most lethal arrow in the quiver of psychological subjugation is fear.

If I have dwelt overlong on issues as they concerned the beleaguered intellectuals of Taiwan 1960-65, it is because I doubt whether my personal witness — to roommate under duress retracting his "confession," to businessman friend telling me to put a lid on the political direction of my questions — suffices to explain how, within a short time, I was to be moved to action. The missing catalyst was supplied by the *Wenhsing* liberals, who were able to show me not that "freedom" of that time was an empty slogan, but that someone could stand up and say so. In this, Lee Ao stood head and shoulders above everyone else for the sheer audacity with which he brought a trenchant pen to bear in the face of fearsome risks.

Crossing the Line: A Midnight Drive

Consorting with Lee Ao, then, was the big leap, if not directly into action, at least into the line of fire between the regime and its opponents. I first met Lee Ao in early

The following is the complete text of the 1981 letter from Congressman Steven Solarz:

Dear Jim:

    I want to thank you for your testimony on the human rights situation on Taiwan before the Subcommittee on Asian and Pacific Affairs on May 19, 1981.

    It has been brought to my attention that some newspapers on Taiwan have used the frank exchange of views that we had in order to discredit people who try to improve the human rights of the people on Taiwan.

    In fact, I favor all constructive efforts to correct human rights abuses on the PRC or on Taiwan by you, Amnesty International, the Society for the Protection of East Asians' Human Rights, or any other responsible people.

    When I was on Taiwan in January with Congressman Pritchard, we addressed our concern for political and religious freedom to the authorities on Taiwan. I have sent appeals for clemency for Reverend Kao [Chun-ming, leader of the Taiwan Presbyterian Church], and others by letter to General Wang Ching-hsu.

    Anyone who thinks I do not put the highest value on such efforts to improve human rights is badly mistaken.

    Sincerely,

    Steve

1966, a couple of months after the banning of *Wenhsing* the previous December. By that time I had probably read all of his three or four paperbacks that Wen Hsing had published (there would be six or eight more in quick succession after the closing of the magazine). I met him through no one's introduction. He simply appeared at my door one day, after receiving a fan letter from me addressing him as the "Mark Twain of China" (a far-fetched analogy, but I had been reading *Letters from Earth*, not *Huckleberry Finn*). I knew who it was the moment I opened the door, somehow, and we instantly hit it off.

Thereafter I was a frequent visitor to his place, a fourth floor flat with a front balcony that had a unobstructed view to the south, mainly comprising a large plot of paddy, and Hsinyi Road Section 4 beyond. And here began my real education. On several evenings we stayed up talking until daylight, and by the end of it there was a high stack of books on the table, most of them taken from his library stacks (his library itself being a collection of libraries, occupying another whole flat adjacent to his). The core topic was the historical legacy of the KMT, its corruption, mendacity, and disregard for fundamental liberties.

Although there were no directly observable indications, probably few of my visits to his place got off without a report added to my file. But I had no sense that associating with him would get me in hot water, and during this, my second stay in Taiwan (lasting until late 1967), never once do I remember living in fear of the unannounced visit from the agents of authority.

This was even the case when I finally crossed the line into action of the sort that would rank as abetting what was beyond any doubt a crime in the ROC's book: helping Lee Ao escape Taiwan. It was to be done by the after-midnight dash into the Tienmu residential compound of one of the US embassy's political officers. Lee Ao called me up late one night, identified himself as "Mr Lee," and said that he had something to discuss that could not wait until morning. He came by and picked me up (outside of government officials, military brass and high party cadre, he was only one of two people I knew of who owned a car). Once we were on the road, he explained that the next morning some of his political enemies would be making public a letter that he had written some years ago to Hu Shih. Nearly up until the arrest of *Free China* chief editor Lei Chen in 1960, Hu Shih had been the patient moderate who had for several years stood between the magazine and the regime. As former ambassador to the US and currently, at the time of *Free China's* closing, the head of Academic Sinica, it was thought that his international stature would be enough to force the regime to think twice about overt, ham-fisted repression. And whether or not the KMT indeed did think twice, ultimately Chiang Kai-shek gave the order to shut it down and lock Lei up "for at least ten years." According to Lee Ao's letter to Hu a year or two later, Hu's courage was again failing him in his last years, just as it had failed him when he should have stood up to the KMT on the mainland.

Now Lee Ao's enemies in Academia Sinica, led by Hsu Kao-juan, those who resented Lee Ao's claim to being the foremost authority on Hu's writings and thoughts, those whose dander was up over Lee Ao's portrayal of the early Hu as something of a

The iconoclast at home

In February 1967 Lee Ao still found much to poke fun at, seemingly unperturbed by the banning of his magazine. This was before his house arrest beginning in January 1970, and his March 1971 arrest and imprisonment. Miles first met him in early 1966, and was a frequent visitor to his spacious, book-filled apartment for the year and a half until he left for Vietnam. (Courtesy of Wu San-lien Taiwan Historical Materials Center)

liberal (in several volumes, all of them by this time banned), but especially those who had come under direct attack by the "cultural punk" — all of them were now poised to give Lee Ao a "red hat" (paint him a communist). This was in late 1966, after Lee Ao had already been effectively silenced, not only through closing of *Wen Hsing,* but also banning of most of the dozen books that he had rushed to print in the ten or so months following the magazine's demise.

He had been tipped off, and now we were in a car bound for the home of someone in the embassy who had once given him his name card with his residential address on it. I was to play the driver, but more importantly it would fall to me to deal with the guard at the entrance to the compound, speaking entirely in English and Lee Ao being "drunk and asleep" in the back seat. But as it turned out, when we arrived the place was utterly dark, not a light on in the whole house. Either no one was there or the family had gone to bed. The gate was closed and the guard was off duty. Lee Ao decided against ringing the doorbell outside the gate, so we gave up and went home. Never again was I to hear from Lee Ao so much as the slightest hint that he was contemplating a repeat of his bid for political asylum abroad. I read this as a sign that either the fear factor was wearing thin or he had resigned himself to the price to be paid for his stunning performance as the *enfant terrible* of the Taiwan literary, intellectual and political world.

Lee Ao's fear that the letter was to be made public was borne out, with his enemies organizing a press conference where they clamored for the authorities to deal with Lee Ao harshly, as a traitor. (In his letter he had confessed as to sentiments that he had shared with his high school teacher, that things were better on the mainland under the Reds than they were under the KMT in Taiwan.) Lee Ao was later to mock them with a "letter of thanks," for publishing his letter here, there and everywhere, whereas if he had published it himself it would have been banned.

For me, being pressed into middle-of-the-night service as American driver hardly qualifies as a feat of derring-do, I admit. But it does pass the litmus test of risking one's personal comfort and safety in the face of tyranny. Do I get a few points for that? If not, how about the time I ventured, again late at night, into the heart of darkness (Wanhua) to meet Peng Ming-min and Michael Thornberry at the home of Leo van den Berg, a Dutch priest with the Belgian order, the Congregation of the Immaculate Heart of Mary (CICM, Congregatio Immaculati Cordis Mariae).Van den Berg had prior experience in China, so his Chinese was good, as was Thornberry's, so the conversation was probably conducted in Chinese. On the other hand, Peng had an impressive command of English, so I can't be sure. What I do remember out of all that was said that night, was that it was their consensus that the US adventure in Vietnam was both immoral and fated to fail, for the same reason that it had "lost" China. Not even Lee Ao, at least within my hearing, had so roundly condemned the US on moral grounds.

Aside from this, during my 1965-67 stay, there is nothing that I can point to that would have, if discovered, gotten me into deep political doo-doo with the despots. But this still left the cultural ka-ka. Enter the Barbarian.

Lynn Miles

Metzke, Miles & Morrow

Designed by Lynn Miles and Peter Metzke, the Barbarian opened in Sept. 1967 in the heart of Hsimenting, Taipei. It was here that habitué Michael Morrow prepared for his fateful trip to Vietnam.

Michael Morrow : Missing in Cambodia

Excerpted from *Time* Magazine, International Edition, 25 May 1970.

Few correspondents know their way around as well as Richard Beebe Dudman. Resourceful without being reckless, in 20 years on the *St. Louis Post-Dispatch* he has learned to operate with equal ease in Cuba or Washington, the Middle East or London, Viet Nam or Paris. But no newsman can be at ease on assignment in Cambodia.

One day this month, on his sixth visit to Indochina, Dudman left Saigon in a turquoise scout car for a firsthand look at developments across the Cambodian border in Svay Rieng province and perhaps Phnom-Penh. Driving the car was Michael Morrow, 24, a founder and correspondent of Dispatch News Service, the tiny agency that distributed Seymour Hersh's Pulitzer-prizewinning story on My Lai. Between the two men sat Elizabeth Ann Pond, 33, on leave from her job as Viet Nam correspondent for the *Christian Science Monitor*.

Noncombative. The trip was supposed to take less than two days. Beth Pond, in fact, was due the next night at a small dinner party being given by South Vietnamese President Nguyen Van Thieu. But the group ran into difficulty at a Cambodian army roadblock on the outskirts of Svay Rieng town. Ronald Ross, correspondent for the *Minneapolis Star and Tribune*, was in another vehicle ahead of them. "I looked back and saw Dick and Beth arguing with the Cambodians about getting through," he says. Ross continued on his way. Dudman, Morrow and Pond have not been heard from since.

Back in Saigon, fellow correspondents concluded that the Viet Cong had captured the Dudman group after it finally got past the roadblock. Morrow, whose wife was born in Hanoi, speaks Vietnamese, so there was hopeful speculation that he could explain their noncombative role as journalists. In fact, each of the three has criticized U.S. military involvement in Indochina. In 1963 Dudman was even refused a visa by South Viet Nam after he wrote articles unfavorable to the Diem regime.

> *Interesting that* Time *should single out Dudman as the one who best "knew his way around," when it was Morrow who had the language capabilities.* Time *was willing to use the "politically loaded" term of "regime" for the Diem cabal, something that it was unwilling to do when Diem was in power.*

5000 Years and American Coffee Get Their Come-uppance

Sometime in the spring of 1967 I met Klaus-Peter Metzke, a German art student on some sort of work fellowship with the Goethe Institute in Taipei. He was spending most of his working hours out at the National Palace Museum, and much of the rest of it venting before all and sundry his views on the "infantile incompetence" which attended the museum's archiving methods, descriptions of pieces, lighting of the exhibits, classification, preservation methods, choice of selections for showing and those for leaving unseen in the vaults within the mountain, etc., etc., ad nauseum.

He was especially passionate on the subject of "five thousand years." If he had a hard time communicating an order to a waiter, he would chalk the communication gap up to "five thousand years." Did contemporary notions of hygiene allow for spitting on the floor of the restaurant? "Five thousand years!" If he flagged down a taxi that had suddenly veered across two lanes of traffic, putting everyone in the vicinity in frozen peril, that too came within the scope of "five thousand years." A teahouse waitress who took ten minutes to deliver a luke-warm cup of coffee invited a scornful "Ha! Can you believe it! It took her only five thousand years to learn how to do that!"

In the sweepstakes to see which country could catch the bigger share of his sarcasm, America came in a close second. Coffee, food, materialism, wine, journalism and letters, cars and motorcycles, mass consumerism, the educational system, beer, art, lack of public transport, fashion, health care, tobacco, prudish notions concerning sex — all were rich veins to be mined, grist for his mill. For a time, I believe that I was about the only thing American that he appreciated. Just why he took to me was beyond my divining, but for certain we were an improbable pair. We became close friends nonetheless, and within a couple of months we were living together, the better for me to play foil to his uncommon take on the world, to be ridiculed and made the butt of his unrelenting jabs, gibes and jests.

In late spring 1967, when Peter was in full stride, four sheets to the wind in his unrelenting diatribe concerning both "American coffee" and anything that went by that name in Taipei, he located a good source of freshly roasted coffee beans, and started talking up the idea of creating a coffee shop, a bistro for artists and intellectuals. It would offer a combination of premium coffee and avant-garde ambiance unmatched anywhere this side of Tokyo, and presume to lay claim to Taipei's nearest brush with a bohemian ambiance. The more he talked about it, the more his enthusiasm worked its magic on me, and soon I was sold.

I introduced him to TS, the young businessman to whom I had been teaching English, the one with whom I had had that conversation on the duck-hunting expedition. TS became interested in the project, agreeing to finance the start-up. He would also pay us something for our contribution. Peter and I had our hearts on converting one of the old tea warehouses along the Tamsui River just northwest of the Yuanhuan Circle, but our third partner wanted a location better calculated to attract the night crowd. We settled on a basement on Omei Street in Hsimenting, the downtown nightlife district. Peter and I set to designing the tables, chairs and lamps.

Just to Win One Battle

by Richard C. Kagan.

Richard became deeply involved in the anti-martial law and anti-KMT movements from 1965-1981. In 1981, he was blacklisted for being a pro-independence activist. During the 1980s, he testified before the U.S. Congress and spoke before others against martial law and the formidable pressures of the KMT in abusing their Taiwanese critics. In 1994, he returned to Taiwan. Although finally being granted a visa, he was accused by a pro-KMT resident in St. Paul, MN of being a terrorist. On this basis, she actively argued against his return to Taiwan as an educator. Kagan is now Professor Emeritus at Hamline University.

I had attended the University of California at Berkeley in 1957-1960, and 1961-63. My undergraduate major changed from being pre-med to history and political science. In 1963 I received an M.A. in East Asian studies. I transferred to the University of Pennsylvania and passed my Ph.D. general examinations in 1965. After that I received a National Defense Education Act Fellowship to study Chinese at the Stanford Center in Taipei, where I studied for eighteen months from 1965 to 1967. At that time the directors of the Center were Harriet Mills and James Dew. For the summer of 1967 I studied in Japan and then spent four years in Cambridge, Massachusetts, where I finished my Ph.D. and held part time jobs. Finally, in 1971-72, I was a researcher at the East Asian Center at the University of Michigan. I spent one year at Grinnell College and then obtained a teaching job at Hamline University in St. Paul Minnesota where I remained for 34 years. I retired as a professor emeritus in 2004.

Intellectual and Political Background

At Berkeley, I was a member of the radical political movement called Slate. We were engaged in reforming pedagogy, in civil rights, and in criticizing America's domestic and foreign policies with regard to economic injustice and support of foreign dictators. I picketed against racial discrimination, and was one of the organizers of the demonstration against the House Un-American Activities Committee in San Francisco in 1960.

When I graduated from Berkeley, I had decided to work in the barrio in East Harlem, New York City. I also decided to become a Jewish conscientious objector. I had a diploma from the School of Judaism in Los Angeles and so was very familiar with the religious arguments. I supplemented these with an anarchistic view that the state could not order me to kill somebody without my consent. I was told that I had little chance of winning my petition. With the anticipation of going to prison, I decided to prepare for an 18-month sentence. It was the general procedure to go to the federal prison in the district where you were arrested and convicted. So I decided to go to Yale for the summer and learn Chinese. I believed that a prison cell and the prison routine would be a good environment for studying Chinese characters. And the prison in Danbury, Connecticut was a highly regarded prison. I did go on trial (really a hearing before a federal prosecutor) in Bridgeport. He judged that I should be a medic in the military. I refused on the same

We painted and decorated the interior ourselves. As for the name, at first we were in favor of "The Rebel," but our partner, with fears of the midnight tax audit the stuff of nightmares, would have none of it: "Too political." But having had one proposal shot down, we were now one up on him, which, as they put it in contract bridge, meant that he was now "vulnerable." We seized the advantage and pressed the attack, this time sallying forth with "the Barbarian 野人." We won him over "against his better judgment," and soon all three of us were absolutely euphoric over the fine statement that we were to be making with the name.

In pitching the name to TS, we undoubtedly soft-pedaled the fact that this creative flight was really a part of Peter's "five thousand years" crusade. As to what arguments we used, memory fails. Perhaps we pointed out that the original meaning of "barbarian" was simply one who spoke a different language. Certainly we argued that, whereas "rebel" might invite unwelcome political interpretations, "barbarian" carried no such baggage, for what we were looking to build was a *cultural* oasis, a refuge for folksingers and poets.

Unless you occupy a prime location where the out-for-an-evening drop-in crowd is more or less guaranteed, ambiance makes all the difference to the vendor of casual coffee. The quality of the java also rates as a third factor, but, except in isolated instances, still ranks well behind location and atmosphere as most reliable indicator of your approaching bottom-line fate. The Barbarian was fortunate to have all three factors in its favor. Our prime Hsimenting position meant we could expect a certain, guaranteed "cold call" crowd from among those whom we labeled (not without affection) "the cinemaniacs." They would settle down for coffee until showtime, none too particular about either the coffee or the surroundings, just content to escape the crowd of hawkers, "yellow oxen" (ticket scalpers), vendors and other cinemaniacs out on the street.

Literati and Punks: Barbarian Nights

The Barbarian also had as neighbor the newly reborn Wenhsing establishment, (野人) recently moved from its premier bookstore location alongside New Park to a place just down the street from us. It was now a "gallery of the arts," its publishing house having offended the powers that be by one Lee Ao too many. The Barbarian typically had a sudden surge in business before the gallery's cultural forums or movie showings, some of which were very well attended.

For whatever reasons, the Barbarian's business boomed, so that, within a month or two of its September 1967 startup, it had to turn away customers in the evenings. The cinemaniacs gave us adequate turnover, but of the remainder (basically our "regulars") many would ensconce themselves with a book and a *café noir* at one of the Barbarian's nine tables, sometimes for hours on end. Our steady clientele tended to be younger and more rebellious in their outlook. Some of them, like artist Shiy De-jinn 席德進, had traveled abroad, and added to our collection of overseas record labels that had yet to win the piratical attentions of the Taipei knock-off trade.

Richard Kagan goes native, 1978.

anarchistic view that I would not let anyone decide whom I should give medical services to — that is, I would not necessarily prioritize Americans, allies, and the hostile wounded.

Now, I had finished up with Yale and had not applied for graduate school. However, Berkeley gave me a slot and I studied East Asian history. The appeals board in California reversed the federal prosecutor's decision and gave me conscientious objector status. My local board in North Hollywood, California, however, overrode this order and decided that I was morally unfit to be in the military and downgraded me to a 4-F status.

During the two years of my Master's education I worked in a maximum security prison for adolescents in Kentucky. This prison was segregated. My job was to help with the

Place of prominence in our musical offering went to Derek and the Dominoes, the Doors, and Dylan. Target of the sort of rebelliousness stirring within the breast of your typical Barbarian habitué was mass culture, more or less to the exclusion of politics. The taboo on so-much-as-whispered political discourse still stringently in force, it was generally assumed that at any given time at least one government informer would be seated among our clientele. Many of those who came "just to hang out" were people that Peter and I very much wanted to see there — people operating on tight budgets but contributing to the overall cultural fund. So, even had the fear of repression been absent, I doubt whether we would have tried to take the Barbarian in a very political direction, since a lot of cultural people, then as now, were turned off by politics. Some found it simply boring, others beside the point, still others intimidating.

Neither Peter, TS, nor I had anticipated that such a little place would need so much day-to-day attention. When the Hsimenting *taibao* (punks) began taking a keen interest in the place, our "cultural punk" customers began to look to other watering holes. The following spring, by which time Peter and I had already left Taiwan, TS was close to giving up. The manager would have to call him nearly every night to oust the last of the punks, who had been there for five hours on one cup of coffee, burning holes in the lampshades with their cigarettes. Sometimes it required a call to the police before the place could be closed up for the night, so obstinate were the petty potentates in assertion of their squatters' rights. But calls for police action brought on a different set of problems, for they would then have had their hand out for even more "protection money." We all suspected that it was a racket, the punks and cops working hand in glove.

This was too much for TS, and he up and abandoned the café business, much the wiser when it came to heeding the advice of a couple of culture-starved foreigners. It was only in 2001 that I learned from him that there was no basis to the rumor, heard repeatedly over the years and even appearing in print, that the authorities ordered the Barbarian closed on the grounds that it was a breeding ground for degeneracy and dangerous thoughts among the young. Rather, it was the constant bother of having to run over to the Barbarian at closing time every night just to tough-talk the punks into leaving. (As for TS's admonition against political talk of any kind, it endured well into this century, so there can be no doubt that if there had been political currents running through our venture, he would have bowed out the moment he became aware of it.)

Of the four decades since the Barbarian's short-lived skirmish with cultural authority, I spent 25 years exiled abroad, but the thousands of miles separating me from Taiwan did not prevent me from encountering scores of people who would tell me that they had once been regular customers. Some of them ended up figuring prominently, others peripherally, in the *dangwai* movement of the seventies. There were those who were to claim that however "apolitical" the funky ambience of that cramped cellar dive, it was to play a formative part in their political development. Since Peter and I had been there on a daily basis, and since I cannot recall any incident of a political nature, I can only conclude that this points up the continuity between politics

integration of the inmates (so-called "residents"). During this time I became deeply involved in the civil rights movement, and faced arrest and pre-emptive brutality several times. (Earlier, I had also worked with migrant workers in Goshen, California.) I left Berkeley for the University of Pennsylvania because, in part, I objected to their requirement of signing a loyalty oath before being allowed to work there.

At the University of Pennsylvania, I became active with a small group of scholars of Asia who opposed American foreign policy in East Asia, and especially objected to the support of the regimes in Saigon, Seoul, and Taipei.

Arrival in Taiwan

I flew to Taiwan in early September of 1965. We landed at night at Sungshan Airport. It was a dark and silent experience that seemed to suggest the oppression on the island. Fortunately, my wife (Leigh Kagan) and I were able to stay in the beautiful Japanese home of Mark and Kyoko Selden at #20, Section 3, Chinan Road in Taipei. They moved out after about a week, and we took over their house, and slept in their former bedroom. Our daughter was born a week later, on September 25. Our living environment could not have been better.

However, my intellectual baggage was soon unpacked. I became interested immediately in the civil rights activists, and the critics of the KMT and American foreign policy. I went to parties with Chinese and asked them who were the dissident leaders with radical beliefs. I ended up with a list that included iconoclast Lee Ao 李敖, professor of philosophy Yin Hai-kuang 殷海光, writers Wang Tuo 王拓 and Yang Ching-chu 楊青矗, Peng Ming-min 彭明敏, Kang Ning-hsiang 康寧祥, and many, many students including Parris Chang 張旭成, Huang San 黃三, and Chen Yu-hsi 陳玉璽. I read their writings and interviewed them. I had many, many hours of discussions about Taiwan's history and current politics.

My interest in the radicals brought me some excessive and negative attention. At the Stanford center, Harriet Mills and James Dew made it clear that we were not to be engaged in any local politics, or activities that were proscribed by the Nationalist government — such as reading or sharing "communist" materials. During the end of my studies in Taiwan, I was allowed to work in the Ministry of Justice Investigation Bureau's library. One day, I found and purloined a copy of classified instructions to the special agents by Wang Sheng 王昇. I showed it to some friends. I had wanted to have it copied through the embassy but was told that I would be arrested at best and harmed at worst. After I returned it, I was charged with stealing and was not permitted to return. However, later through some pressure from friends, I got back in to continue my studies. But this lasted a short time because I was soon off to Japan.

My mail was opened. Sometimes, I just received the letter and not the envelope.

My most significant political activity was the planning and organization of Peng Ming-min's escape from the island. I happened to live across the street from Milo and Judy Thornberry. Initially, we became friends because our children were born at about the same time. We shared the experience of having an infant, and the purchases of diapers and other infant items. He was a Methodist missionary who regretted his church's orientation to the Chiang Kai-shek family and KMT regime. Gradually, he learned about the sufferings of the Taiwanese. He secretly invited Peng to his home where they discussed

and culture. The two are not easily separated. Lee Ao, after all, was in his heyday labeled a *"cultural punk"* 文化太保. In like fashion, then, the Barbarian, which began innocuously enough with our having a little fun with Peter's war on the 5,000-year cultural orthodoxy, had tread into political territory in ways that neither Peter, TS nor I had anticipated.

With the US venture in Vietnam requiring an ever-increasing need for replenishing Uncle Sam's cannon-fodder requirements, the draft board back home had been on my back since the time of my first Taiwan sojourn in 1962. They were more than mildly miffed that I had not bothered to contact them and ask for permission to leave the country. The same pattern was repeated in late 1965 with my second Taiwan stay, again with a deferment, just expired, granted on the basis of my second year of college enrollment in the United States. Again I received a form to be filled out, forwarded by my parents in New Jersey, and again I sent the form back with proof of enrollment at Shihta. Again came the letter of reprimand, this time stronger, and again, all bark and no bite: the rebuke could be taken with a grain of salt so long as one was left the option of filing, once more, for student exemption status.

A sigh of relief that my life had been spared for another year might have been the appropriate response, but I was beginning to feel that, so long as I remained outside the country, the draft board could not touch me: they were a paper tiger. When the 1966-67 school year came around, and I was no longer enrolled in school, yet once more came the forwarded draft board letter and form.

I was in a jam, the same predicament faced by thousands of young men my age back in the States who were beginning to see popular opposition to the war register on the TV news, leaving a gut feeling that the US mission in Southeast Asia diverged from the pious vows of selfless commitment to the great cause of anti-communism.

What to do? There being little else that I *could* do, I ignored them. As another letter came, and another, each of them more insistent than the last, I began to wonder what recourse they had. Could I go on ignoring them indefinitely, or would some sort of extradition request come into effect? Although I had not investigated the matter, I had little doubt that if the ROC were to receive such a request, they would act on it (though one might hope that, as in all matters bureaucratic, they would take their good time before so much as lifting a finger, in which case I might have time to abscond or otherwise devise an appropriate survival response).

Meanwhile, edging its way into my consciousness was the fact of mounting resistance to both the Vietnam War and the draft. Forced inductions into the US Army had gone from 82,000 in 1962 to 382,000 in 1966, by which time incidents of draft resistance were much in the news. 1967 was the year of the Spring Mobilization, which saw thousands of people young and old parade up the streets of New York, some of them chanting, "Hey, hey, LBJ, how many kids did you kill today?" Emboldened by the addition to their ranks of Dr. Benjamin Spock, who had made his reputation as upstanding, respectable "everybody's baby doctor," organizers took the fight to Washington, which saw one hundred thousand people come out for a "Stop the

politics, religion, and eventually planned for Peng's escape.

During the period I was a student in Taiwan, besides the many visits at the Thornberrys, I had three significant meetings regarding Peng's presence:

1. One time I had to deliver a message to Peng that was very secret and confidential. It seemed to be about some political issues on the island that regarded his freedom. At that time, he was living in a Japanese-style house near Taiwan University. He was under a rather liberal imposition of house arrest. I put on a raincoat and helmet, mounted my Honda 75cc motorcycle, and drove right into his house. There I delivered the letter and then drove out. I was chased by a security jeep but managed to squeeze into an alley that had only room for bicycles and small carts. The next day, in my casual clothes, I walked by the house to find that the guards were equipped with large police motorcycles.

2. Another day, I had a friendly visit from Jim Newcomer, the secretary of the American ambassador. Jim had been a graduate student at Columbia University. He had secretly been a mole for the CIA at a Communist Youth Festival in Europe. Then he learned Chinese and joined the State Department. He was posted in Taipei. But after a while, the right-wing press in America "discovered" that he attended the festival and assumed he was a communist. The State Department would not fire him, but was forced to restrict him from meeting KMT officials. He was very sympathetic to the Taiwanese but was not allowed to meet with them either. His ambassador, Walter McConaughy, was a do-nothing official who did not care very much for his posting. In any case, while Jim was at my home, Peng turned up. Jim made a hasty retreat out the back door, telling me that it would harm him terribly if it was known that he had a meeting with Peng.

3. I had a secret meeting in 1967 with pro-Peng leaders. It was so secret that I gave the Thornberrys my daughter's passport and told them that if I disappeared, they should get in touch with my parents and send her back to California.

After I returned to the States, I helped the Thornberrys organize Peng's escape. We gave him a code name — the refrigerator. We said that we needed a new door — meaning arm; and new evidence for the type of refrigerator — meaning passport. I also raised money from the missionary community in America to help with the airplane ticket and other accommodations.

Finally, I made an appointment to meet with Secretary of State Henry Kissinger on the day of Peng's departure. He knew Peng. The idea was that if Peng was caught, Kissinger would be asked immediately to intervene. I never met with Kissinger because Peng made it safely out of Taiwan.

The true story of this escape was not made known until December 2003 when the Thornberrys finally met with Peng in Taipei. Until then, the government claimed that either the CIA had engineered the escape, or that fishermen in Taipei had helped him escape to Japan.

Besides the political intrigue, the most important relationship for me was with Yin Hai-kuang, the very popular and liberal professor of philosophy at National Taiwan University. Originally a KMT member, Yin slowly became dissatisfied with the regime. He promoted

Draft" March in October.

In Taiwan, where US imperial follies in Vietnam hardly registered as a public issue, the Barbarian was also a natural gathering-place for young Americans, most of whom had developed strong feelings about the war. Among them was Mike Morrow, who would meet his Hanoi *huachiao* girlfriend in the Barbarian several afternoons a week for instruction in the rudiments of Vietnamese. Soon bound for Vietnam, where he would be working for International Voluntary Services, Mike and I talked a lot about the Vietnam War, and its parallels with the Chinese civil war. We agreed that the US was undoubtedly backing the "wrong side," just as it had backed the KMT. In Vietnam, as in China two decades before, the target of the US-supported repression was no longer confined — if indeed it ever had been — to the communist insurgent threat, in the meantime burgeoning like Topsy to include the students, intellectuals, and a number of social-minded Buddhist organizations. The insurgency had now become a national war of liberation in which "our" side, again and alas, was willy-nilly forced into the role of villain. As with the KMT, "we" had become the prop without which the regime could not possibly survive, having long since forfeited the support of the captive populace.

Mike and I discovered that we shared more than a sense of frustration at the ugly pattern of US colonial support for Asian dictators: he and I were in the same predicament with our draft boards, making all erstwhile discussions about the putative rightness of the American cause quite beside the point. He regarded the question of whether or not the draft board had the power to initiate extradition proceedings as irrelevant: "All they need to do is get a court order, and, if you ignore that, then it could easily go to the State Department. Then it's no passport, just like that. What are you going to do, stay in exile on a foreign passport all your life?" Mike's solution was to meet the tiger in its lair. Once in Vietnam, he would get a deferment — "alternative service in a war zone."

It sounded a whole lot better than getting drafted and shipped off to die in somebody else's country, helping them fight for a "democracy" that they themselves did not seem to want badly enough to struggle for it themselves. The allure of "Mike's Move" was that it could satisfy all of my requirements perfectly, for I could stay *outside* of the war while at the same time having an *inside* look at it. I decided then and there: Vietnam just had to be my next destination. (I must note in passing that those who worked long, hard and at considerable risk to resist the draft have been right in making the distinction between draft *resister* and draft *evader*. By evading the draft I may have saved myself, but at the expense of having someone else being called up in my place. Running away from the draft barely slowed the military machine, if indeed it slowed it at all, in its appropriation of new cannon fodder.)

Bye-bye Civilizing Barbarian, Off to Barbarizing Civilization

There were other factors that led me to leave just when the Barbarian was in its heyday, just when the cultural descent that I've described began to set in. I certainly did not lack for reasons. One was that fellow Barbarian Peter was grumping and

Richard Kagan and James Seymour, both of whom presented telling human rights testimony to US congressional hearings in the 1970s and 80s, find something to agree about, 2003.

the anti-authoritarian government ideas of the economist Friedrich Hayek. Yin was thoroughly iconoclastic and fearless. He broke down the hierarchical codes of teaching by sitting with his students on the lawn for class at the university. I visited him many times and later corresponded — though under a pseudonym at his request. (Later, together with others, I helped raise money for Yin's daughter to attend the University of Washington.) My favorite trip was to his home, which was in a cul de sac and was under the surveillance of the security police. My Ph.D. was on Chen Tu-hsiu, who had been the Dean of Beijing University, a founder of the Communist Party, and a Trotskyite. I had a German Shepherd whom I called "To-lo-sz-ji," or "Trotsky." I would bring him to Yin's house where he would play with Yin's dog. We would let them go out in the alley and then call them back. His dog's name was "Jie-shi" which was the first name of President and Generalissimo Chiang Kai-shek. We no doubt disturbed the surveillance agents when we called the dogs back to the house.

I helped many students financially, as well as a couple who intrigued a complicated departure from the island.

With regard to the American community, with several peers such as Len and Nina Adams, Ted Farmer, Gordon Bennett, and others, we organized the Committee of Concerned Asian Scholars (CCAS). This group was dedicated to criticizing American imperialism in

grousing all the time, saying that now, with our underground haunt set in a daily routine, there was nothing creative left for us to do. "We are in a mind-numbing, enervating rut, a dead end. We must rescue our creativity!" Several times he had talked about going off to Angkor Wat to do some stone rubbings.

Something else to think about was the fact that JAL stewardess Fujiko, then my sweetheart and later to become my wife, would be making only two or three overnight stops a year in Taipei but monthly overnights in Bangkok. Saigon and Bangkok were only minutes apart by air, so if all my arrangements lined up properly, I could soon be sharing furlough with her on a frequent basis in the luxury of a classy Bangkok hotel. So it was that I began checking the China Merchants freighter departure listings in the *China Post*. "Peter," I exclaimed, "we're Bangkok bound!" But getting Peter out of the Republic of China was no easy matter, and the whole exit rigmarole provided ample grist for the mill of his misanthropic musings.

"Idiots! I go to the foreign affairs police to get an exit permit, and they tell me I have to get a form stating that I've paid my taxes. I tell them, 'But I did not have any income, I was not working, so why should I pay any taxes?' So in the end, what do you think they want from me? A statement from 'some authority' saying that I was not working. They want 'proof' that I was not working! How can one 'prove' one was not working!? Idiots! Five thousand years, and what have we got? Mindless paper-pushers!"

After a stopover in Bangkok lasting several weeks, I took the short hop to Saigon, and was soon pounding the pavement looking for a job that would put me in harm's way as a way of keeping me out of harm's way: a six-month contract that would allow me a one-year deferment from forced induction into the army, which in turn would likely have meant a two-year tour of duty in Vietnam. Acting on the tip that Mike Morrow had given me at the Barbarian months before in Taipei, I immediately looked up International Voluntary Services, only to be told that they were not hiring in country. What to do? Already living on borrowed funds, my options had run out.

It so happened that the German "tourist" with whom I had been sharing a hotel room had just landed a job with Alaska Barge. He handed me a list of defense contractors and wished me luck. I began making the rounds of their head offices at Tan Sun Nhut, the mammoth US air base just outside Saigon. Within a week I was on a military flight bound for Qui Nhon, halfway up the coast of what was then South Vietnam. There I began working as a Dynalectron technician, a civilian attached to a military unit, the Unserviceable Aircraft Parts Section of a medical evacuation ("medevac") helicopter maintenance and supply company. It was like being in the army, but without the salutes, senseless work details and boot polish. I got paid well enough, especially considering that my only expenses were rent for a small bedroom and cheap meals at the on-base cafeteria. Another plus was that I got to see the beauty of Vietnam from the open doors of a Huey a thousand feet up whenever I took it into my head to invent a reason for going somewhere on "business." Even better still, I got to learn first-hand the crazy thought patterns that passed for "military judgment," repeating the cockamamie misadventures of *Catch-22's* Yossarian in trying to cope with the

Asia. It also had the purpose of promoting Taiwan's struggle against the U.S.-supported government in Taipei. Although very sympathetic to Mao Tse-tung and Ho Chi Minh, the Committee never supported the Mainland's claim to Taiwan, or a Marxist revolution in Taiwan. The early issues of this publication, the *Bulletin of Concerned Asian Scholars*, attacked Taiwan's martial law, and supported human rights and the labor and woman's movements in Taiwan. In 1968, the committee was re-organized and expanded, and became one of the major academic critics of the Vietnam War. Its journal continues to be successful and prestigious. The journal has been renamed *Critical Asian Studies* and is now published by Routledge.

During my departure from Taiwan, I was considered a "problem" to the government. I managed to sneak several proscribed Chinese books out in my luggage, including the works of Henry Liu 江南. In order to protect me, my friends escorted me to the airport with a comical dragon dance, and a U.S. embassy official walked me through customs to the plane.

Political Action

During the period 1967-71, I lived in Cambridge, Massachusetts, with my wife, Leigh, who was a graduate student at Harvard. I spent most of my time finishing my dissertation (1969), and teaching at Boston State College (1969-71). This college was primarily a working-class college with a focus on urban affairs. There was a large contingent of Boston policemen who were getting specialized degrees or training. This formative experience of working with ghetto kids and the officers of the state increased my commitment to social change, economic reforms, and racial equality.

I became CCAS chairman and a member of the editorial board. Besides our major goal of opposing the Vietnam War, we wanted to encourage contacts with the People's Republic of China. This eventually led to two CCAS trips to China, in 1971 and 1972. The preparations for these trips revealed the deep splits in our organization and in the politics of fighting American imperialism. In 1968, we had arranged a meeting with Beijing's representatives in Warsaw. As a leader in CCAS, I had some rights to go. However, members of our delegation wanted me to tell them about my connections with the Taiwan independence movement. I refused and was not able to be on the team.

In 1972, Leigh was the delegation's leader to China. Peng Ming-min contacted us and asked her to give a message to Chou En-lai. He was seeking Chou's support against the KMT. However, during her reception with Chou, Leigh was not able to give him the request.

In 1971, I received a scholarship to the East Asian Center at the University of Michigan to prepare my thesis as a book. At the same time that I did work on the manuscript and was turned down by one press, I edited Ross Y. Koen's book, *The China Lobby in American Politics*. Macmillan Press had published this book but the first printing was withdrawn and destroyed when the CIA objected to Koen's linkage of the KMT with the opium trade from Burma and Thailand. I felt strongly that this book should be re-published, and wrote an introduction describing the political context of its suppression and the U.S. government's support of the KMT. I was told directly that if I published this book, I would never get a job as a college professor. After Random House published it, I was blacklisted from teaching. Two colleagues told me this. It was in part due to my anti-war activities,

madness of war. All these experiences confirmed for me the futility of the war effort, as I watched morale slip to ever lower depths with each passing week.

The parallels between America's misadventure in Indochina and its forlorn who-lost-China debacle two decades before were not lost on me, so it was not too long after my December 1968 arrival that I began harping aloud to the effect that the Vietnamese, whatever their weaknesses in firepower terms, still had the upper hand and would emerge victorious, for reasons long since committed to paper by everyone from Sun Zi to Mao Zedong. My ranting fell on deaf ears until all hell broke loose in what has later come to be known as "the Big Tet." That was the only time I saw combat close up, with ear-less corpses stretched out before me, puffing up in the midday sun. In the short space of my six-month tour, I could see more and more Americans, military and civilian alike, coming to agree with me that the American effort was doomed to fail. It would be going too far to say that I was a minority of one at the start of my tour, but "dissenters" like myself were few enough in number as to invite accusations of treasonous leanings for musings that were still generally unpopular; whereas, by the end of my tour, so overwhelming had become the mounting evidence, that I believe that the poison of my defeatist conclusions had infected pretty well the whole company. Long gone was all talk of the high purpose of "our mission," and by the time of my June 1968 return to the States, it was a matter of "look out for number one, and devil take the hindmost," as my comrades took turns in boasting of how few days they still had left in "Nam."

One of the perks that came with my Dynalectron contract in Vietnam was a furlough in country of choice, called "R&R," interpreted to mean, either "Rest and Recuperation" or "Rest and Relaxation" or "Rest and Revitalization" or "Rest and Recreation." Compliments of the Military Air Command, in spring 1968 I was airlifted from the Vietnam killing fields to the comfort of my "baby's arms" in Tokyo, with stops each way in Taipei. Going north, I saw Lee Ao, who, knowing that he would see me again soon on a Taipei stopover on the southward leg, had a letter ready for me to take out, addressed to Sun Kuan-han in Pittsburgh. Kuo I-tung 郭依洞, popularly known by his pen name of Po Yang 柏楊, had been arrested several weeks before, ostensibly for his part in the translation of a Popeye cartoon, and Sun had been writing letters to Chiang Ching-kuo asking for leniency. Lee Ao's advice to Sun was not to waste time writing polite letters of entreaty to the authorities, but instead go as public as he could overseas. Only then would the regime take notice. That this advice made a deep impression on me would become clear in the way I reacted to Lee Ao's own arrest three years later.

Goatskin Salesman Meets Provisional Government Emigré

Moving to Japan in late 1968, I was soon working for a Pakistani trading firm in Kobe. While my name card read "Assistant Manager" I was in fact spending most of my time treading the pavement, repping cheap leather tanned in Chittagong around the Buraku ghettos of Kobe and Osaka. By the end of 1969, I had made two Taiwanese friends.

but even more so due to my attack on the KMT. A professor at Stanford University also warned me that if I criticized the KMT I would not be able to return to Taiwan to do my research. At this time, there was a great deal of pressure in the China field to be very careful about criticizing Taiwan's government because it would hurt one professionally.

During this same period, there was a campaign to attack my character. At a meeting of the Association for Asian Studies (AAS) in 1969, I had introduced Ross Koen and had him speak on my panel, called "The Effect of McCarthyism on the Field of Chinese Studies." The panel included Owen Lattimore, O. Edmund Clubb and others who had been harmed by the McCarthyite anti-communist campaign. During the discussion period, I was openly accused by a person in the audience of pushing a wheelchair victim off of a cliff. The next year, a professor from Yale asked the AAS to obtain a restraining order to keep me from attending the convention in San Francisco. I was allegedly a terrorist planning to harm the book exhibit.

1972-78 was a period of relative quiescence. I had obtained a teaching position at Hamline University and spent a great deal of time preparing classes and taking care of my daughter, son, and wife. In January of 1975, I took a dozen students on a study tour of China. My experience was chilling — not just because of the cold temperatures in Yenan and Beijing but because of the political climate and the attitudes toward Taiwan. The guides and government authorities were tremendously hostile toward Taiwan. For instance, after I was asked what countries I had visited and replied that they included Taiwan I got a strong group criticism. None of these people knew anything about Taiwan except that it was official policy to liberate the former province of China. When I returned to the United States to give lectures on my trip, many listeners criticized me for being anti-China and anti-Mao.

1978, Return to Taiwan

In the summer of 1978, I took a group of students from Hamline University to Taiwan for a research-study course. I began to contact my old friends and contacts from my student period. I re-visited the Tainan Seminary of the Taiwan Presbyterian Church. While there I made an evening phone call to Professor John King Fairbank with regard to an article I was writing on the Chinese labor movement of the 1920s. Early the next morning, I was called into the office of the president of the seminary, Dr. Hsiao Ching-fen 蕭清芬. (He is the father of Bi-khim Hsiao 蕭美琴, later translator for President Chen Shui-bian in 2000 and then a Democratic Progressive Party national legislator; she was just a small child at the time). He wanted to know what I was doing with Fairbank. The KMT had long believed that Fairbank was pro-China. The secret police that were listening in on seminary phone calls reported that I had been talking about a job with Fairbank. They accused Hsiao of harboring a spy, and a pro-communist foreigner.

That summer I also was at Tunghai University in Taichung where I talked to a biology professor, Edgar Lin 林俊義, who had written for the ***Bulletin of Concerned Asian Scholars*** on the environmental problems in Taiwan. We could only talk while walking on the campus of Tunghai University. When I returned to Minnesota I wrote an article on martial law that appeared in the *Bulletin*. I also wrote a manuscript on Taiwan's history, martial law, land reform, and the problems of Taiwan's environment. This manuscript was later published in part by the Food First Institute, which was run by Frances Lappe.

The first was a young man named Kuo. Fluent in Mandarin, Taiwanese and Japanese, he was the son of the owner of a fairly large textile plant in Taoyuan. Having grown up in Kobe, with summers spent in Taiwan, he had now taken a Japanese wife and was being groomed for the future directorship of the family firm, meanwhile looking after their interests in Japan. Visiting his family in Taipei a few days in December, I discovered them to be quite rich by the standard of that time (private cars were only then starting to come into use, and what traffic jams as Taiwan could boast for that era had been made up of three parts oxcart, seven parts taxicab).

Kuo had heard of Lee Ao, but not read him, and showed only mild interest in the fact that Lee Ao and I were friends. He made clear from the start that he did not care in the slightest to engage in idle political conversation.

Quite the opposite was the case with Huang Liang-teh 黃兩德, who discussed nothing else. I first met him when a Swiss business friend took me for lunch to a small Chinese restaurant, Kappa Tenkoku, on one of the dark alleyways off the main Motomachi Shopping Arcade. We went up to the second floor, where the walls were covered with flags, posters and newspapers declaring the proprietor's fervid interest in Taiwan independence.

Huang's *nom de guerre* was Huang Chieh-yi 黃介一. Drafted into the Japanese Imperial Army during the war, he was shipped off to Shanghai to perform bayonet drills on live Korean captives and patriotic political prisoners, thereby making a passing grade in this ultimate of loyalty tests, and to otherwise serve the Japanese godhead. Having no formal schooling in Mandarin, he nevertheless spoke it fluently and with only the slightest trace of an accent, and managed Shanghai dialect with greater ease than he did Japanese. The bayonets that he drove into these hapless prisoners pierced his own heart also, leaving him scarred, and sentenced to a long life of political penance.

Repatriated to Taiwan at the end of the war, Huang had taken up residence in his hometown of Keelung, where he early became the object of the attentions of some agents working for the KMT's Gestapo chief, Tai Li 戴笠. When the darkness of 2-28 fell over the land, Huang went calling on the home of a Keelung doctor friend who was involved in efforts to reform the city government. His friend had been "picked up for questioning" several days before and had never returned. Even so, the place apparently was still under surveillance, for, just as Huang was leaving, he was stopped by several plainclothesmen. His Mandarin being much better than theirs, he was able to pass himself off as an undercover mainlander in the employ of a rival intelligence agency and presumably enjoying Chiang Kai-shek's express patronage. He gave them a good tongue-lashing, and they left. It had been a close call, and, as others of his friends went missing, Huang knew that his own days were numbered if he did not flee the country. He arranged for secret passage to Japan, where he took up asylum.

My friendship with Huang was to span over a decade. Once prominent in the Provisional Government exiled in Tokyo, his star had declined within a movement which, once Thomas Liao 廖文毅 had been enticed back to Taiwan, had itself waned

During the summer, I made a trip to the Penghu Islands off the west coast of Taiwan in the middle of the Taiwan Strait, where I discovered two significant secrets.

First, the KMT had been helping Saigon in the Vietnam War. They sent food (subsidized by America) and advisors. President Thieu's brother was ambassador to Taiwan from the Saigon regime. After the war, there were many Chinese-Vietnamese who fled from the communist regime. Hanoi had actually caused the exodus of many of these Chinese families into China and into boats where they became part of the tragic refugee traffic of the "boat people." The KMT allowed the loyalist Saigon Chinese to enter Taiwan. But most were kept on an outlying part of the Penghu Islands. Taipei was suspicious of these refugees, thinking some may have had anti-Saigon feelings or could even be spies. For the most part they were families who had drifted in the South China seas and found a port in the Penghus. I visited them, interviewed some, and took pictures. The U.S. ignored these people. It was no surprise that the regime in Taiwan would receive America's support over the human rights of the refugees.

Second, while on the boat to the Penghu Islands I learned about the *fan-gung i-shih* 反共義士, or anti-communist heroes. There was a man on board who had an anti-communist tattoo on his arm. When I asked about it, he explained only in part. Later, after interviewing another man who would not let me see his face or take his picture, I learned more about this group. Basically, during the Korean War, the American government did not want Chinese Nationalist troops to fight with the Allies against the Chinese communists and the North Koreans. But they were put in charge of the P.O.W camps. There the Nationalists carried on propaganda and torture. They tattooed captured soldiers. Everyone knew that if these soldiers returned to China they would be harmed. For their own safety they were urged to come to Taiwan. Once there, they were placed in a military unit where they were watched carefully. For years, they were not allowed to venture out of sight of their handlers. The younger ones were drawn into the ranks of the secret police in Taiwan. Here they participated in violence against Taiwanese dissenters. Their function and existence were kept secret. During the Kaohsiung Incident in 1979, it was this cohort of people who beat up both the protestors and police. They often became agents provocateur and saboteurs. I later testified at the Human Rights Subcommittee of the House of Representatives about the history, organization, and activities of this group.

I returned to the States to write up my articles. During the Christmas break, I returned to Taiwan. It was at this time that President Carter normalized relations with Beijing. Deputy Secretary of State Warren Christopher was dispatched to Taipei at the end of December 1978 to explain the new relations between Taipei and Washington D.C. Demonstrators attacked his entourage from the airport. These were well organized by the government. There were even portable toilets along the road.

Wanting to cover the event, I went to the American Officers Club in north Taipei. I observed from a cab. I took pictures of the demonstrators. They were all about the same age, in their early twenties with short haircuts and the same blue uniforms. Clearly they were a select group from some military or secret service. When they saw me, some rushed the cab. The driver streaked down the alley but was stopped. The guards demanded to see my camera and ordered me to give them the film. I had changed the film quickly during the drive. So I gave them the wrong film.

into borderline irrelevance. It was difficult to understand his feelings about Liao, who he sometimes described as a traitor, sometimes as a great patriot who had paid a high price and had gone back only out of compassion for his family, members of which were being jailed and threatened with torture and death.

When Huang parted company with the Provisional Government crowd in Tokyo and went his own way, he started what he called the Three-in-One Movement 三角一運動, the triangular symbol of which was plastered all over the upstairs of his restaurant. It advocated a campaign of defiant non-cooperation through a three-pronged attack on the KMT's legitimacy: don't vote, don't serve in the military, and don't pay taxes.

At that time I regarded as preposterous, pie-eyed optimism any strategy aimed at moving the mass of people in Taiwan to action — or should I say "inaction," as his program called for classic passive resistance. It was hard enough for someone like Lee Ao to reach the public with his writing, so how could expat dissidents like Huang have a ghost of a chance of getting up a crowd? But even had there been the freedom to agitate openly in Taiwan, it is questionable as to whether his campaign would have caught on enough to constitute a serious threat to the government..

Huang was well aware that he was but a whisper in the raging storm of international politics. I admired him greatly for the courage to carry on in the face of such monumental odds, even more for his resolve to never return to Taiwan until the hated KMT dictatorship was removed — a vow that he kept well into the post-martial law years.

As I prepared to make my next trip to Taiwan in late 1969, I asked Huang if there was anything I could do while there. He gave me some fliers to pass on to friends or to "just leave on the seat of a bus." He asked me to bring back Keelung and Taipei phone books, and gave me the phone number and a message of greetings to a friend, Kao Yu-shu 高玉樹, in whom he showed repeated interest over the years, seemingly confirming the portrayal of Kao by KMT supporters as a crypto Taiwan Independence traitor.

Fateful Honeymoon: Small Part in a Big Plot

I saved my money, and by the end of 1969 my job seemed secure enough that my fiancé Fujiko and I felt that the way was now clear for us to take up joint residence before tying the knot. Fujiko wanted to use up her accumulated vacation time and free mileage from her airlines job. Use it by the end of the year, or lose it. So we decided to take our honeymoon before the New Year chimed in, then deal with the marriage later. Fujiko's choice of destination would have been Europe or Polynesia, but we ended up with the pauper's budget alternative. The silver lining, I reminded Fujiko cheerily, was that in Taiwan "we" could see old friends.

"Don't peek, you'll get in trouble! It's against the regulations, and the authorities are very strict about it here." December 1969. From the air, first glimpse of Taiwan's majestic mountains had passengers reaching for their cameras, but Fujiko had long practice at restraining them. Should I have been surprised that she, the daughter of

February 1980: Kagan Testifies

The following is excerpted from Human Rights in Asia: Noncommunist Countries, *a record of hearings held by the Subcommittees on Asian and Pacific Affairs and on International Organizations of the Committee on Foreign Affairs of the US House of Representatives. Kagan appeared on the first day of the 3-day hearings, 4 February 1980.*

The instrument which has maintained Taiwan in a culture of fear is martial law. This last year has been a year of refurbishing martial law.... Indeed, the most flagrant abuse of human rights in Taiwan is the institution of martial law. Its existence accounts for the abuses against the integrity of the individual – torture and inhuman incarceration on Green Island – against the political rights of political representation, self-determination, freedom of belief, and against the social and economic rights of "the enjoyment of just and favorable conditions of work," and the "right to strike."

The maintenance of martial law justifies a large military force and necessitates the creation of a surveillance industry which produces manpower and equipment to open mail, tap phones, spy upon, threaten and otherwise harass the public. For example, special post office employees check all airmail letters and packages against three lists of suspicious addresses and spot check others. The lack of a return address on a letter is cause for inspection. These measures have created a deep and pervasive sense of fear in the population.

The largest demonstration for human rights occurred on December 10, 1979, the 26th anniversary of the new United Nations Universal Declaration of Human Rights. A riot resulted; the Chinese Government claimed there were 400 demonstrators injured, 183 police with iron bars and incendiary devices. However, US Government authorities now confirm that the December 10, 1979 incident in Taiwan was actually instigated by the Chinese Government itself. Nevertheless, the Chinese authorities have successfully rounded up the opposition human rights leadership, destroyed their publications, and produced a tremendous fear among the population.

Reports of torture and threats of long jail sentences have circulated widely. My own contacts with officials in Taipei and with expatriates in America reveal a complex situation. I have been told that the President of the Republic of China felt pressured by the military and the police to arrest the opposition leadership. The President was faced, it seems, with outright revolt from the security appartatus.

a police captain from the most conservative part of rural Kyushu, would, even on vacation, take to enforcing the KMT regulations? Add to that her strait-laced, by-the-rules way of life even after moving to the "big city," and there was little to suggest that she would have taken up with an outlaw like me. Harbinger of heavy scenes to come....

"Give it a rest, Fujiko. You're not working now, we're on vacation. Just look at those mountains! On the east coast they can be seen from fifty miles away. Centuries ago sailors from Portugal had to sail to the far end of the globe before they could find an island which might do justice to the word 'Formosa.'" How I hoped that my enthusiasm for the jade island would infect her too!

This is the way Fujiko and I began life together, by clashing over the appropriate response to wantonly abused authority. But more than that, as with my second marriage, how we felt about Taiwan became one of the main defining features of a chasm that spread between us. She had already told me that all of the JAL crews rated Taipei as one of the least — or was it *the* least? — glamorous stops on the international route. The people were rude. The airport stank with an odor that you thought could not be matched anywhere, until you landed in downtown Taipei streets, a sullen pall hanging over the city, the sun not to be seen again until the flight back home. It was even said that the experienced airline stewardess boarding a plane in Tokyo could immediately tell by the smell whether it had picked up passengers in Taipei or not. Attribute these derogatory observations to the product of a racist mind, if you like, but thereafter I noticed that the international airport's move from Sungshan to Chiang Kai-shek did nothing to diminish the violence on the international traveler's olfactory senses at moment of first arrival.

Even when Fujiko later confided to me that, on our first meeting, she was surprised that I "smelled just like them," I still imagined that with time surface impressions would fall away and soon enough she would find lots to love in the country that had become my second home.

Most of our ten-day honeymoon was to be spent touring the mountains in a car borrowed from the rich businessman father of the young Kuo whom we had befriended in Kobe. Before leaving for the hot springs of Lushan, however, I just had to phone Lee Ao. He invited us out for dinner. Waiting at the restaurant entrance, Lee Ao escorted us to the table, where Peng Ming-min was waiting to surprise us. Peng carried on with Fujiko in elegant Japanese, which allowed Fujiko later to pronounce him very professorial.

Peng finally turned to business. He wanted to know whether we would be willing to carry a letter out of the country, for mailing in Japan. We agreed to get together with Peng upon our return from the mountains, and with the details of a clandestine rendezvous hammered down, made off for Lushan. Back in Taipei within the week, we called on Peng's house a couple of days before returning to Japan. On the day of our scheduled departure, Lee Ao was to have seen us off at the airport, but was sick, and his brother Lee Fang 李放 went in his place. In those days, upon exiting

After this event, I went to Tainan and visited with faculty and students at the Tainan Seminary. One particular person gave me documents to carry to a meeting of the opposition set for Christmas day at the Ambassador Hotel, secretly planned by Shih Ming-teh, aka Nori, Linda Arrigo's husband. (I had met Linda earlier. In fact, after a celebration of her marriage in late 1978, she came to my apartment followed by many secret police. I burned some of my documents that night for fear of being caught and my materials confiscated.) In any case, I checked into the Ambassador Hotel on the eve of December 24, 1978. I had the documents strapped to my stomach. Early in the morning — maybe 6 a.m. — my bedroom door was opened and three men looking like military in plainclothes entered. I reacted instinctively. I had been trained in combat judo. (One of the initial reasons that I had been refused a status as a conscientious objector was that I had been in fights. But later when I finally received my CIA materials on my life through the Freedom of Information Act, I learned that they pointed out that I had self-defense knowledge but was not a terrorist.) I knew that if they shut the door, I would have no chance of surviving their attack on me. So I ran through their legs, knocking them off balance, ran down the hall, and went down the fire escape. I ran around to the entrance of the hotel. Either then or later, I noticed the Chinese newspaper headline pointing out that a professor had been murdered. I was in a state of shock. Had this been fore-planned about me and then printed? I learned later that the day before Malcolm Caldwell, who was a fellow member of the CCAS, had been murdered in his Phnom Penh hotel by assassins who were working for Cambodia's Pol Pot.

At some point my contact, a short Taiwanese man, approached me and asked for the documents and my other materials. He would return them to me later. I was frightened and naïve. I gave him the materials and my film. I never saw them again.

I then took a taxi to get away from the hotel. As we traveled down the main road and crossed the tracks that led to the train station, the taxi driver said that there were two motorcycles following us. He believed they were driven by the secret police. He crossed the tracks and told me to jump out and run into a building, go upstairs and then come out at the opposite side. The police would not know what to do. He picked me up and took me to a safe house. It was an art store. The proprietor gave me a scroll of a tiger and wrote on it that it was a gift for my son.

By now, I knew I was in trouble. I kept a low posture and left the country in the beginning of January. I did gather many documents and interviewed many radicals. From this I wrote my monograph on Taiwan, and published an article on Taiwan's politics in *Dissent* magazine.

1979-80

I arrived soon after the Kaohsiung Incident of December 10, 1979. As soon as I could, I went to Kaohsiung to interview people. What I found out was that the "anti-communist heroes" and other secret groups of ruffians had been primarily responsible for the violence and injuries of the police. The witch-hunt that stirred afterwards was carefully organized to round up the *Formosa* magazine dissidents and neutralize them. This strategy was a reprise of the White Terror, but much more focused. It was at this time that I began to bring information from abroad to the Dangwai (non-party) leaders and intellectuals.

During my trips to Japan, I was introduced to Lynn Miles. Through him, I became engaged

the terminal, one had to cross a stretch of tarmac parking apron and then mount steps atop a truck next to the plane, which sat parked some fifty meters from the terminal. As we reached the top of the stairs, we turned and waved to Lee Fang, our signal that we had gotten through exit formalities without detection of our precious consignment.

A small favor for an old friend. That would have been the end of it, had not Peng given his Ministry of Justice Investigation Bureau minders the slip — clean off the island. Several weeks after we had last seen him in Taipei, we were reading in *Newsweek* that Peng had taken up refuge in Sweden. The GIO meanwhile was issuing firm denials to the press, saying that the putative Peng in Stockholm must obviously have been an impostor, since they held in their very hands proof positive of Peng's Taipei presence.

And what was that proof ? Daily reports of Peng's comings and goings in Taiwan. The GIO (as Lee Ao was to tell me gleefully a year later) had been misled by the Investigation Bureau, who, in turn, had been hoodwinked by their own agents in the field, still filing false reports of daily excursions around the island in close pursuit of their quarry — a fairly routine practice among field agents at the time, making it possible for them to supplement their meager income by filing for travel expenses incurred by these phantom journeys. It did not go well for them when they were confronted with international wire service reports that equally insistently claimed that Peng was in Sweden. When the sham was exposed, according to Peng (in his memoirs), the axe fell on the necks of people all the way up to the deputy director of the MJIB: "The department chief who had so viciously threatened me as we sat around the Christmas tree at the Investigation Bureau clubhouse was the highest-ranking man to be sent to prison. He was the scapegoat at the higher levels, charged now with having pressed me too hard."

Reading Peng's memoir of the escapade, *A Taste of Freedom*, I feel a tinge of sympathy for these MJIB people, even after having spent decades in exile myself, with the carrying of this letter purportedly being my most glaring offense against the established order.

Lee Ao's Confession: A Telling Indictment

Some years later, when I was to bump into Peng in Tokyo or Seattle or New York, he would always ask about Lee Ao. Had I had any word from him? He repeatedly said that had that letter been intercepted, it would have foiled his escape plan, but never revealed its exact importance or to whom it was sent. Nor did he reveal to anyone my part in his escape.

That I should later be charged with "helping Peng Ming-min escape" as reasons for the authorities' blacklisting me had to do with Lee Ao's prison confession and not the breaching of a confidence by Peng. This only became clear after Lee Ao was arrested fourteen months later, and was forced into revealing his role in the letter affair. Copies of Lee Ao's military court indictment had been leaked, with parts of it appearing two years later in a Hong Kong magazine, which published the livelier passages from the

in obtaining mules for taking in documents. There were several ruses: to memorize names and phone numbers; to hide documents in or under "porno" journals such as *Playboy*, and to hide documents behind framed pictures. These trips were always stressful. Later, after I was made *persona non grata* or blacklisted, I had my students who lived in Japan meet up with Lynn and then deliver materials into the island. One such student was Mark S., who was also blacklisted. Another student became involved in demonstrations at Tunghai University. In all, I remember organizing at least three students for this activity. This network increased the ability of Lynn to serve as the major operative in getting information to Taiwanese radicals. (I spent many enjoyable hours talking and eating with Lynn and his friends. I later wrote an unpublished novella about Lynn and his life in Japan.)

My knowledge of Taiwan's struggle for human rights and democracy soon got me national attention. In February 1980, I was invited to co-lead with Professor Sydney L. Greenblatt a delegation to Taiwan, together with Ramsey Clark who was coming to Taiwan to attend the trials of the Kaohsiung Eight. Our group consisted of a couple of scholars, a photographer, and some Amnesty International human rights people. We were the first civilian human rights group to visit Green Island. In looking at the prisoners and their biographies that were posted on the walls, I became aware that many of them were mainlanders. Although I knew that Chiang Kai-shek's government had eliminated many mainlanders who opposed it, I was stunned at the number of ex-KMT members and mainlanders who were in the prison. This corroborated my own experiences in the 1960s when mainlander friends of mine were harassed and put under surveillance, even arrested and imprisoned. These included Huang San, Yin Hai-kuang, and supporters of Lei Chen.

Because of the KMT's repression of the population in general and the terror against the family of Lin Yi-hsiung 林義雄 and others in particular, the trial was delayed and thus we could not attend the trial. Ramsey did write an article about his trip that was published in *The Nation*.

We stayed in a hotel in the old part of Taipei city. One night a woman appeared at my door and tried to force her way in. I had the feeling that I was being set-up. Since I kept her out, I was not able to confirm this. We were clearly watched wherever we went.

My major contributions to the democracy movement in Taiwan occurred in the early 1980s. On February 6, 1980, I appeared before the U.S. House Foreign Affairs Committee to testify on martial law, the Kaohsiung Incident, and Taiwan's struggle for human rights. My testimony was received then and later with some strongly expressed negative criticism. Two members of the State Department wanted to know how I got my information on the KMT secret police and the provocateurs at the Kaohsiung Incident. Representative Henry Hyde and one conservative scholar of China minimized my argument about martial law. They responded by saying that Taiwan's martial law was "soft." They pointed out that Israel and Canada both had martial law. Richard Bush, a former State Department official now with Brookings Institute in D.C., singled me out in his book on U.S.-Taiwan relations as a person who was bested by Hyde and others. Bush never interviewed me about my ideas. In his book, I am the only person he is thoroughly critical about. The State Department and the U.S. government in general downplayed and minimized the physical and psychological effects of 2-28, the White Terror, and the post-Kaohsiung Incident period.

indictment text interspersed with "insider" commentary.

The commentator, whose identity was masked by a pen name, speculated as to the authenticity of both the "confession" and the indictment itself. This made a lot of sense, because at that time the military authorities rarely allowed defendants, lawyers or family members to take indictments from the courtroom, if indeed courtroom there was. So the purpose of the whole article was to tantalize the reader with the question as to whether the indictment and confession were fact, or perhaps some government black information campaign.

But, at least as far as the part concerning Fujiko and me was concerned, the "confession" rang true, since, as far as I knew, only Peng, Lee Ao, and his brother had known about the letter and how it was carried out.

Yet there was one glaring error in the report. In his "confession," Lee Ao credited not his brother, but himself, with having seen us off at the airport. Prior to his 1971 arrest, Lee Ao had told me quite emphatically (in loud tones, so that those at the other end of the wiretap could hear) that it was not his intention to get tortured as a way of forcing from him some putative secret information. "I have no secret information. Everything I do is absolutely legal. I may let them work to get their information, but torture? Not necessary! 'Tell me what you want to know, and I will tell you. If you don't like the truth, then tell me what it is you want to hear, and I will tell you." Of course, as was almost always the case even in times of tension, these words were said with his signature mock equanimity, as if he were talking about bargaining about the price of a new coat and not whether to let them proceed with the screaming ordeal. But now, some years later, I was faced with a curiosity: what to make of the fingering of himself, and not his brother, as the one who facilitated the safe exit of Peng's letter?

Later, in 1992, my confusion was cleared up when I was able to meet Lee Ao for the first time in over twenty years, the Hong Kong article being the only account of his "confession" that I had seen in the intervening decades. I reminded him of his having forcefully told me prior to arrest of his "cowardice" (no holding out under torture) in 1971, then asked him to reconcile his divulge-all-when-pressed policy with his covering for his brother, as revealed in the indictment that came to public light. Why had he gone to the trouble of covering for his brother by saying that it was he himself who had seen me off at the airport?

"No, no, that was not the case. It was just a typo." Simple as that. He laughed that I should think him capable of putting the safety of his brother before himself: "What do you think I am, a hero?"

When the HK report came out, more important than the puzzle presented by seeing Lee Ao's name where Lee Fang's should have been was finding myself identified as the courier of the Peng letter. With Lee Ao having been sentenced and now serving time for the crime of having helped Peng escape, and with there no longer being any doubt as to what the authorities knew about me in that connection, I could no longer nurse the hope, already on its last legs, that I could somehow escape the sentence of long years of blacklisted exile.

By 1981, I was made *persona non grata*. But I still worked on behalf of the interests of the Taiwanese opposition. There were many cases in which I gave financial support to Taiwanese, or helped them leave Taiwan. Much of my interest, of course, was in dealing with students. I contacted the University of Minnesota to inform the administration about KMT and government spies among the students.

Through the invitation of Ramsey Clark I was involved in a slander trial. The Chinese-language publication of the Taiwanese-American community in New York City, *Taiwan Tribune* 台灣公論報, had criticized a medical doctor in Washington, DC for being a KMT operative and a person of low character. This man was a mainlander of some prominence. He sued for about a million dollars, claiming that the charges against his character harmed his medical practice, and that he was not affiliated with the KMT. I testified that the profane Taiwanese language that was used was really not that derogatory, and that he actually was a representative of the KMT. I had found his membership in an overseas KMT committee. Thus, as a public servant of sorts, the charge of slander could not be rigidly applied. Ramsey won the case.

Another issue revolved around the nuclear power plants being built in northern Taiwan. There was a joint venture with an American company to supply the containment walls around the reactor. Due to corruption, only half of the cement that was charged for was used — thus making the wall thinner than it should be. The rest went into the pockets of the Chinese. The American president of the company was nonetheless detained and put in a sloppy condition of house arrest. He went on trial. It was all a set-up. I had been given the documents regarding this case and I wrote and spoke about them. It was one of the few case studies of corruption in the nuclear power plant industry.

The two cases above seemed to be hemorrhages from the old China Lobby. They revealed that the KMT's dirty tricks were still at play.

After 1980

The real test of American involvement in Taiwan occurred later in the early 1980s. President Chiang Ching-kuo's health was deteriorating, and several widely publicized murders had occurred, including those of Lin Yi-hsiung's mother and twin daughters in February 1980 in Taiwan, Professor Chen Wen-cheng 陳文成 of Carnegie-Mellon University in July 1981 in Taiwan, and the Chinese-American writer Henry Liu in October 1984 in California. Next to Chiang Ching-kuo, the most powerful man in Taiwan was General Wang Sheng, who ran the political college for the military and had a following of thousands of military officers. In addition he had been put in charge of a special unit that sought out and arrested or assassinated political figures. He seemed to be the heir-apparent to Ching-kuo.

Ray Kline, the CIA's major operative in Taiwan, was very close to Wang Sheng and later wrote a hagiographic biography of Wang. There was a touch of narcissism in this book. There were many photographs of Kline as well as Wang. The book supported Wang's claim that Taiwan was a backwater, and implied the only future for the Chinese in Taiwan was to suppress the Taiwanese and/or return to the mainland. The propaganda book by Wang that I had liberated during my student years bore out Wang's intentions and attitudes. What Kline left out was Wang's deep anger at Western values and imperialism. (Part of the above analysis of Wang derives from his secretary, Lee Tsai-fang, who was

To return to December 1969, Fujiko and I got on the plane, breathed a sigh of relief, and were airborne. Once in Japan, we mailed Peng's letter, and were soon reading about Peng's miraculous dash for freedom in the international media.

I spent the whole of 1970 in Japan, living in the upscale bedroom town of Ashiya and working in Kobe and Osaka. The end of that year I got into hot water with the Japanese immigration authorities for violating my visa status, and was ordered to leave the country and apply for a new visa. That I was married to a Japanese national won for me what the immigration authorities in Japan assured me was preferential treatment — "normally we would just deport you and prevent your re-entry for ten years." I had violated my visa status by working as language instructor at big trading companies for an Osaka-based company called English Companion, while the immigration authorities' files still had me down in their files as running around touting the quality of Pakistani sheepskin in the Burakumin neighborhoods. My crime lay in my failing to notify them of my change of employ, and especially the change in "type of employment," which, when done by the book, would have required a change in visa status. I could be thankful for their leniency in a country which put Taiwan to shame when it comes to blindly following whatever is on paper.

Just get myself to a Japanese consulate abroad, apply for the new status, duly noting my marriage to a Japanese national, and "within two weeks" I would be rejoined with my wife. These assurances proved wide of the mark by many orders of magnitude — it would not be until June that I finally got the visa.

For most foreigners in my predicament in Japan, the favored destination was Seoul or Pusan, as one could purchase round-trip passage on the over-night ferry for under US$100. There were any number of small hostels in both cities catering to the expat crowd, just in from Japan on an overnight visa run. But I decided on Taiwan, again thinking that I could mooch free lodgings while catching up on current events that had been eluding me, not least of them being Lee Ao's personal predicament following Peng's escape.

Ping-pong Diplomacy as Practiced by a Hermit

On 4 January 1971, I arrived at Lee Ao's doorstep penniless and quite at his mercy. Either put me up, or introduce a friend who would lodge me in exchange for English lessons. Lee Ao chose to put me up, first warning me that I could be bringing trouble on myself. Before climbing the four flights of stairs to his apartment, I had passed in front of his place, suitcase in hand, as if I were lost and could not make out the correct address. Across the alley and down a few doors sat a taxi cab, in which I could barely make out two shadow-figures, obviously spies. I thought that by appearing to be "lost" perhaps I could somehow fool them into thinking that I was there to visit someone else in the vicinity. If that failed (as was most likely), at least I might hope to convince them that I was not a frequent flyer among Lee Ao's adoring flock — perhaps visiting for the first time, on the basis of a printed address that someone had given me.

But now that Lee Ao made the offer, I was forced to decide quickly. After all, they

head of the World Anti-Communist League, and who accompanied Wang to D.C.)

The CIA called a classified meeting in Alexandria, Virginia to discuss the possible heirs to Chiang Ching-kuo. There were three scholars invited, myself among them, and also two former ambassadors present. I was the only one to support Taiwanese independence and to warn that if Wang Sheng became the president, there was a real possibility that civil war would occur. (A potentially steaming civil war seemed to be looming if Wang Sheng inherited the mantle; alleged Taiwan Independence advocates had blown up his son's house in Los Angeles in 1980 after the Kaohsiung Incident arrests, killing a relative.) One of the most important off-the-record remarks made during this meeting was that if internal struggle did break out, the United States would move in to prevent the Taiwanese from taking over. The fear was that a successful coup by the Taiwanese would initiate an attack from China. To prevent this, Washington would have to intervene. I do not know how widespread this view was, but it was clear that relations with China trumped democracy in Taiwan.

Return to Taiwan

When I returned to Taiwan to teach a two-week course at Tamkiang University, I found a totally different society. The progress from my student days was remarkable. It was as if a century had gone by — not just thirty years.

I look back now at a wonderful period in my life of hope, idealism, friendships, and even enchantment. The struggle for human rights and democracy is really a struggle of self as well as social liberation. Embedded in the many days and nights of debate, travel, and planning, I never believed that there would be such a glorious future. I was not aware how many other people were engaged in the same movement, and how we would all come together in a refreshing wave of freedom and satisfaction. I wish I had worked harder, met more people, been more curious, and more capable. I felt good about my work because I learned so much from my friends (as well as my enemies). I came to respect a whole civilization of people who were struggling for the same things I was.

I can apply to my life the wonderful song from Passover — the celebration of the freedom of the Jews from their punishing life in Egypt. The exultant song lifts up our awareness with the idea that if we had won just one battle it would have been enough *dyainu*.

What more can we ask for than to "wish we find our love, our own true love." That is what Taiwan has been for me.

Kagan speaking about his past experiences at the December 2003 conference on human rights in Taipei.

had seen my suitcase. There was also Lee Ao's own safety to consider. Would my presence, I wanted to know, bring him more trouble than he already had? On the contrary, he assured me, my staying with him might deter them from any hasty action that they preferred to keep out of the international spotlight. (Even after I was long gone, Lee Ao's adversaries would have it repeatedly impressed on them that he enjoyed an international following.) As Lee Ao was always reminding me, the KMT feared loss in prestige internationally above everything else.

This may have been typical Lee Ao generosity, to suddenly turn my position as supplicant upside down, making me the one conferring favor. But Lee Ao was not one for giving his own role as loyal and self-sacrificing friend short shrift, so I tend to think that he was telling the truth. In any case, without other options, I was happy not only to have a place to live, but to have the opportunity to talk with him for many hours over what the Japanese authorities had assured me would be a couple of weeks, if that.

Several days after that, Lee Ao was visited by officers of moderate station in one of the intelligence agencies, with questions about my background, purpose, etc. Lee Ao refused to tell them, saying that they would have to do things by the law, and must have the foreign affairs police check me out. They complied, sending over someone whose credentials were carefully screened by Lee Ao before he could proceed. Lee Ao sat fast beside me, now and then throwing in comments, playing advising attorney for all it was worth.

I told them my story as to how I had been "forced out of Japan," arriving here more or less against my will, penniless, and at Lee Ao's mercies. I, who had just a few days before been trying to pass myself off as "stranger" to Lee Ao's neighborhood was now recast as longtime friend — so close in fact, that I could think of no one else who might want to put me up.

The officer was going through the motions of examining my passport — what did he expect to see, a notation that I worked for the CIA? — he came upon the words "*Shitsudoo*-113" scrawled in pen below my "CANCELLED" Japanese visa. He asked to "borrow" the passport for a day.

Lee Ao, heedless of the possibility that his living room was still being bugged (he had already removed one bug and sent it off to the UN), said excitedly, "They probably think you are a very heavy-duty spy now, since even the Japanese wanted you out." Certain that the story I had given them would not wash, and that they would exhaust all means at their disposal to try to figure out what business and what agencies brought me to his door, Lee Ao speculated as to what interpretations they might come up with for this cryptic code from the Japanese authorities. Great fun it was for him, to play with the different scenarios they would concoct for his shadowy houseguest.

Although he was able to read English, his command of spoken English was quite limited, and certainly not such that he could carry on a conversation. But he had committed to memory some witty gems, one of which he was forever repeating: "with enemies like these who needs friends?" This was to make the point that he had

Taipei Police Guard Against 'Incidents'

By LEONARD PRATT

TAIPEI (AP) — Nationalist Chinese police have carried out a series of arrests and interrogations in the last week, apparently in connection with fears of anti-government or anti-American incidents in Taiwan in the near future.

Security in the capital of Taipei has been tightened to guard against such incidents, which some officials fear could come as early as this weekend.

While well-informed sources said as many as 20 persons had been arrested or detained, only five could be definitely identified.

Two are former students of Peng Ming-min, a Taiwan dissident who escaped from the island 13 months ago. Both served time with him in prison for advocating the overthrow of the Nationalist government.

The two — Wei Ting-chao and Hsieh Tsung-min — were arrested early Tuesday and their homes searched. Wei's girl friend, whose family name is Chen, was arrested Wednesday.

Detained for interrogation were Chen Yi-sung, a lawyer and former politician, and Li Ao, a historian and writer. They were released, but have refused to see reporters.

Government spokesmen had no immediate comment on the arrests, which seemed to follow no clear pattern other than that most involved have at one time spoken or written in opposition to the Nationalist government.

But it was learned the arrests were linked to authorities' feelings that they have reason to anticipate incidents of some kind this weekend.

Two explosions have occurred in Taiwan in the last four months — at a U.S. Information Service library and at the Bank of America — and neither has been solved.

Sources pointed out this Sunday is Feb. 28, the 24th anniversary of the start of anti-government uprisings in Taiwan in which some 10,000 Taiwanese were killed by Nationalist troops.

They also referred to "possible incidents" in the United States over the weekend that could trigger incidents in Taiwan on Sunday.

Police patrols in Taipei have noticeably increased within the last week, particularly at night.

Pacific Stars & Stripes 7
Sunday, Feb. 28, 1971

Taiwan to Expel U.S. Missionary Couple

TAIPEI (AP) — An American missionary couple with close contacts among persons opposed to the Nationalist regime were ordered to leave the island by Thursday, police spokesmen said Wednesday.

The expulsion appeared linked to current government concern over potentially dissident elements.

Police said the two are the Rev. Milo L. Thornberry Jr., 37, and his wife, Judith, 38.

Their address in the United States was given as that of Mrs. Thornberry's parents, 10930 Cactus, Dallas, Tex.

A Methodist minister, the Rev. Mr. Thornberry had been working in a seminary north of Taipei run by the Presbyterian Church of Taiwan.

Informed sources said foreign affairs police took the couple into custody Tuesday and told them they had 48 hours to leave the island. They had been under house arrest since with police refusing to let newsmen speak to them. Telephone calls to the house are not put through.

Huang Kai-tung, public information director of the Taipei police headquarters, said in a statement that the Thornberrys had "violated the foreigners residence regulations of the Republic of China." He would not elaborate.

A spokesman refused to say whether the U.S. government will protest the deportation order, but he added: "The governments have been in touch about the order."

During their six years on Taiwan, the Thornberrys became friends with many persons now out of favor with the Nationalist government. Some of them were among persons arrested last week in a crackdown on anti-government circles.

Pacific Stars & Stripes 7
Friday, March 5, 1971

Taipei jitters leading to arrests gets foreign coverage

Mention of the February 28 Incident of 1947 in foreign press reports was quite exceptional in the early 1970s. Leonard "Bud" Pratt, the AP correspondent, was one of the few foreign reporters willing to report on cases of political repression. While AP enjoyed worldwide distribution, the February 28 and March 5 reports by Pratt (above) did not make it into the *China Post* and *China News* – nor any of the Chinese language papers of the day. The only readers with access to the *Stars & Stripes*, published by the US military and printed in Okinawa, would have had to have access to the military distribution outlets in Taipei.

Richard Kagan

"never had it so good" until the goons took up residence in a taxi across the alley from his domicile.

Never had it so good? Thanks to the Garrison Command surveillance detail, "robberies in the neighborhood are down to zero per cent. The neighbors now sleep soundly at night. And so do I. This puts me one up, and so they 'owe me one.' An 'accident' might otherwise befall me, but not with my bodyguards on the job. I live in the middle of perhaps Taipei's only oasis of safety. I couldn't have done better if I had elected to live upstairs from a police station."

Lee Ao also claimed to be gratified by the sudden decline in frequency of visits from fans, followers and friends, for whom a courtesy call on Taiwan's number-one "culture-punk" might have invited unwanted attention from overzealous control freaks. Only the most loyal of friends dared pay so much as perfunctory calls. Meng Hsiang-ko 孟祥柯, aka Promethius Moon, was a regular, plus a handful of others, either themselves already under suspicion or already involved with Lee Ao beyond the faintest hope of hiding.

Where others might bemoan their loneliness, Lee Ao seemed to feed on it. Paramount among his reasons was that he could now devote himself to his writing with all the more concentration. To Lee Ao this was not the cloud's silver lining, but the whole silver cloud offering golden opportunity.

Or so went the pose. Wasn't this show of you-can't-hurt-me defiance just part of Lee Ao's game? I couldn't be sure. It was hard for me to accept without question that Lee Ao inwardly really welcomed the cloud that all this attention cast on all his daily affairs. After all, keeping visits to a minimum should have been no more difficult than the policy that he openly adopted later when he was no longer "protected" — declining to answer the doorbell. And there was also the matter of the little counter-conferences that Lee Ao was conducting periodically in his living room.

These went under the name of "Ping-Pong Diplomacy," on a ping-pong table that was hastily set up in the living room for the occasion. Lee Ao and Wei Ting-chao were the champions, and I never stood a chance against either one of them, just as Chiang Kai-shek never stood a chance in the "Ping-Pong Diplomacy" of the newspapers, in which Henry Kissinger and Chou Enlai won every round. Was it that I got tired of playing on the Chiang Kai-shek team, or was it that I wearied of the humiliation of having my butt beaten time and again with such apparent ease? Lee Ao, on the other hand, was always eager to play, challenging all comers to some "Ping-Pong Diplomacy."

Other than Wei and Meng Hsiang-ko, Hsieh Tsung-min was the only regular visitor to that police-protected fourth-floor flat that I can remember, if we don't count the plainclothes callers from various branches, the men whose job it was to keep their dossiers on Lee Ao up to date, the men whose heads would surely roll if Lee Ao pulled a Peng-like disappearing act on them.

Political Prisoner Lists and Propaganda of the Deed

On one of his visits Hsieh gave me a copy of a list of 214 political prisoners that he

Huang Hsin-chieh, left, and Peng Ming-min, right, in the United States in 1989. Professor Peng Ming-min issued the Declaration of Self-Salvation in 1964 together with Wei Ting-chao and Hsieh Tsung-min. Huang was sentenced to fourteen years in 1980 following the democratic movement of 1979, and served almost seven years.

Wei Ting-chao was released from his second imprisonment in 1977. Wei and his wife happened to run into Linda in 1978 on a festival day in Chungli. (Picture by Linda Gail Arrigo.)

Linda interviewed Roger Hsieh (Hsieh Tsung-min) several times in 2004, concerning his transmission of the political prison lists abroad in 1969 and 1970, and his subsequent torture. (Picture by Linda Gail Arrigo.)

said had been put together by people that he knew, still in prison. He said that a copy of it had already been forwarded to Amnesty International secretary-general Martin Ennals on his previous visit to Taiwan several months before. Even so and leaving nothing to chance, we decided that it would not hurt to have duplicate copies taken out, and Fujiko, who had by now arrived in Taiwan to share my narrow balcony bed at Lee Ao's, spent three or four days transcribing the list in her own hand.

From the way Hsieh talked, I got the impression that, like Lee Ao, he was well-connected with foreigners. Both of them had met with Ennals. But Hsieh, fairly fluent in both Japanese and English, had also cultivated a few American military acquaintances. From what I was to learn later, it would not be going too far to say that Hsieh had infiltrated US intelligence, but for now let it suffice to say that such connections made it possible for him to communicate with the world outside via the US military post office. This afforded him a slightly greater margin of safety in getting information to and from contacts overseas: inspected or not, at least the missives arrived; and, if inspected, there was still a chance that the intelligence gleaned was not shared with ROC intelligence. But more than that it also meant that, if his "secret channels" were to end up being discovered by the ROC intelligence people, they would have to take serious note of the apparent closeness of Hsieh and his "secret angels" working from inside American intelligence.

In late January 1971, the Taipei office of the Bank of America was bombed, following on the 12 October 1970 bombing of the US Information Service office in Tainan, in which there were serious injuries. No one I talked to, Lee Ao, Hsieh and Wei included, professed to know anything about who lay behind these acts of "propaganda of the deed," even going so far as to speculate that they could have been the work of one or another intelligence branch simply as a way of boosting their own budgets (no terrorist threat, no work) or more generally as a way of heightening political tensions.

By the middle of February, the political grapevine was alive with rumors that Taipei would see some kind of "commemoration" of the 24th anniversary of 2-28. Notwithstanding his having been "cut off" from the world, this grapevine was well within Lee Ao's reach, as he kept in close communication with his minders. All he was able to find out was that, at least as far as these individuals were concerned, the bombings were the work of real adversaries, not rival branches posing as terrorists. They were still hard at work trying to nail the culprits. Another rumor: there had been some tinkering with the high command, and a new general had been put in command of the newly-reinforced northern garrison responsible for security in the Taipei Basin.

On the countdown to 2-28, the level of tension ratcheted a notch higher with each passing day. A week before the big day on which all attention was now focused, the Gestapo made its move. Hsieh and Wei were arrested on February 23rd. As for Li Cheng-yi 李政一 and the others in the case, I am not sure exactly when their numbers came up. They may have been arrested the same day (it would be months before I first heard the names of the others).

Lee Ao found out about Wei and Hsieh's arrest in the morning, when Wei's sister

Touring the central Taiwan countryside, from the hills of Taichung to the sea, in early 1967. Except for the upper right one, all photos were taken by Lynn Miles. (Courtesy of Wu San-lien Taiwan Historical Materials Center)

appeared all out of breath at his door (by cutting through some paddy fields you could get from Wei's to Lee's in under five minutes). Once she had left, Lee Ao hunkered down, expecting that his turn was next. He slouched over his desk, lost in thought. It was a rare moment, seeing Lee Ao at a moment of crisis, when his humor failed him.

But not for long. Soon he was back at it again. "Well, good! At last I have a chance to test out that toothbrush." The said toothbrush, rakish avatar in his much advertised more recent writings, served as a taunt thrown in the face of his tormentors, declaring his readiness for the arrest that could come without notice, perhaps in the middle of the night. By placing his toilet kit under his bed, he was saying, "I'm ready, bring it on!"

But by afternoon Lee Ao's equanimity *did* fail him altogether. That was when Wei's sister came rushing over to convey still more alarming news. Wei's girlfriend had also been taken in. Her captors were not the security people, but ordinary uniformed police. She was now being held at the local police station.

Lee Ao was fired by fierce indignation, this time real passion, not feigned. "This they cannot do! She is completely innocent, totally uninvolved in any kind of activity! They are just going to use her to break Wei. Last time they could not break him, so this time they are going to stoop to this level."

It struck me as curious, then and since, that he should think that there were certain rules of the game that they must follow, like them or not (another instance, already mentioned, was the time that he forced the plainclothesman to go back and send a proper immigration officer). After publishing exhaustive screeds cataloging instances of the KMT going above the law, how could he now profess shock that the KMT was disregarding the rules at will? What I got from this was that, as far as Lee Ao was concerned, the arrests of Wei or Hsieh or Lee Ao himself, while illegal, were still allowable by the rules of the game because they were dissidents, but not the arrest of Wei's girlfriend, an innocent.

With a look of grim determination, Lee Ao put on his overcoat and went out in search of Wei's girlfriend, where he planned to confront her captors, to catch them in the act of breaking the rules of the game.

Before he left the house, Lee Ao handed me a list of foreign correspondents and asked me to get in touch with them while he was out. I was able to reach Leonard Pratt of AP and Don Shapiro, who I believe was working then as stringer for the *New York Times*. I got on the phone and passed on Lee Ao's request that they join him at the police station.

A few minutes later there came a call from Lee Ao, saying that Wei's girlfriend was about to be removed from the police station and delivered downtown. They were waiting for a Gestapo vehicle to pick them up, and would soon depart. Lee Ao wanted to give chase. He asked me to go down to where his "bodyguards" were sitting in a taxi on the street below, and tell them to get over to the police station

Lynn Miles

9

Traveller's Tales

- PRIME Minister William McMahon would appear to have enough domestic troubles to be going on with in an election year without the added complication of trying to come to terms with the puzzle of working out a China policy (and the much more difficult task of knowing what Nixon will do next). The tale of Sino-Australian relations over the past couple of years would be completely farcical if it did not have such tragic undertones.

Basically Australia was happiest with its head in the sand, its embassy in Taipei, its troops in Vietnam and its wheat in ships sailing for China. That was a case of having one's cake and eating it. Why rock those boats going to China by doing anything as stupid as rationalising one's policy? Sir Robert Menzies once summed up the apparent contradictions in Australia's foreign policy by saying: "Nelson at the battle of Copenhagen discovered that by closing one eye he could often do a wise thing. We Australians have discovered that by closing both eyes you can often do a wiser." Bob Menzies had the clarity of mind to know what he was getting away with (and it is good news indeed that he is apparently fast recovering from his recent stroke; Australia still has need of him – or of his like).

- THE ostrich days are over, but Canberra still appears to have sand in its eyes. The last year has been remarkable for the number of contradictory statements, by members of the Government, on China policy and on the nature of contacts claimed to have been established. Hopeful initiatives have been torpedoed by clumsy ministerial speeches. No one – least of all the Chinese – could know what Canberra's true policy was as it floundered confusedly in President Nixon's wake.

Some of the contacts were made in Hongkong, the go-between being an Australian businessman, James Kibel, who together with his father and brother has been trading with and visiting China for several years. An invitation was delicately extended to an Australian politician, Andrew Peacock, to visit China with his wife. This fell through, ruined by Deputy Prime Minister Douglas Anthony who has since improbably announced he would like to go to China himself. Now poor Jim Kibel is carrying the can for such official nonsenses. McMahon has indicated his dissatisfaction with Kibel's efforts as an honest broker, which even inspired an appalling piece of anti-Semitism from a senator, who claimed that Australia's foreign policy was being run by Manchester Jews.

- REPORTS that Australia's trade commission in Hongkong was to be raised to formal diplomatic status to facilitate contacts were denied by Trade Commissioner Roy Barcham. A few days later the change was made. At the same time a "ministerial source" was quoted in Canberra as prophesying China's release of Francis James, a somewhat eccentric Australian journalist, about whose sensational travelogues of journeys inside China this Traveller mused cynically in the issue of June 26, 1969. Journalists and Australian officials waited at the border, while the Review's columnist Richard Hughes commented (Mar. 11) that he hoped the ministerial source would not prove to be another embarrassing Canberra leak which would lessen James' chances of swift freedom. The journalists waited in vain; James has yet to appear.

- AMAZINGLY, it was speculated that his release might have been postponed because the outspoken writer might say something which would "place further strain on Peking-Canberra relations." I would have thought that the Australian Government itself had done so much to impair relations that anything James said could only improve matters.

- AN Indian visitor to Europe, I read in the *Hindustan Times*, was surprised to hear the "rulers of Bangladesh" described as "Hindu" in a news bulletin broadcast by the American Forces Network on February 14. To make sure he had not misheard, he sent a query and received a reply from David Mynatt, AFM News Director in the Department of the Army. The reply quoted the news item in full. It concerned over 10,000 people who had been rounded up by the authorities in the "infant republic of Bangladesh," who were suspected of collaborating with Pakistani troops last year. The item went on: "The suspects are all Muslims ... the new rulers of Bangladesh are Hindu ... and there is no love lost between the two." Mynatt gave the source for the item as Associated Press. But the AP representative in New Delhi said the last two sentences had been added by the Armed Forces Radio and had not formed part of the AP report.

- IN the spring of 1970, Review contributor Arnold Abrams interviewed Hsieh Tsung-min in Taipei, a few months after the then 35-year-old native Taiwanese was released from political prison. Hsieh was vocal in attacking the Kuomintang government for its undemocratic practices and suppression of Taiwanese, and described in serio-comic detail how he was constantly followed by secret policemen. He was willing to have his remarks quoted and even his picture published.

"I have nothing to lose," he told Abrams. "My freedom? The way I must live – is that freedom? I have no freedom to lose, nothing to lose, not as long as I stay in Taiwan and Taiwan remains in the hands of this government."

- A YEAR ago Hsieh was rearrested along with his friend Wei Ting-chao, who had been involved with him in the "Professor Peng case" of 1964. In that year the two men and Peng Ming-min, their former professor at National Taiwan University, were convicted of sedition for preparing an anti-government tract called "A Declaration of Formosans." Peng was amnestied and later escaped from Taiwan; he is now a researcher at the University of Michigan and a leader of the Taiwan Independence Movement in the United States. Hsieh and Wei completed their full prison terms of five and four years respectively.

The government has said nothing about why the two men were arrested again, despite numerous inquiries. Now word comes from reliable sources that Hsieh and Wei and several others have already been tried in secret by a military court on charges of treason and that the prosecutor asked for sentences of death. So far as is known, no verdict or sentence has yet been rendered. No details of the specific charges against the men have become known.

Parenthetically, Arnold Abrams was refused a visa (no explanation has been forthcoming) by the Chinese Nationalist government last month when he attempted to make another second trip to Taiwan for the Review.

FAR EASTERN ECONOMIC REVIEW

APRIL 1, 1972

Death sentence for Hsieh, end of a visa for Abrams

As this 1972 column appearing in the *Far Eastern Economic Review* proves, talking to reporters posed dangers not only for the talker but for the reporter. Hsieh Tsung-min may have had "nothing to lose," but what about reporter Arnold Abrams?

posthaste (he was being careful to keep them abreast of his every move, lest they get it into their heads that he was really trying to give them the slip). Then I was to call Pratt and Shapiro, and tell them that he would get in touch later when he learned where exactly she was being taken.

I called Pratt and Shapiro back, but no answer. They were probably already en route to the police station, I decided, so I went over there myself out of fear that they would arrive there to find Lee Ao gone. When I got there *everybody* was gone — even the police. I had to go all through the police building and compound before I could find anyone at all, and that someone pretended ignorance as to Lee Ao's visit, the whereabouts of Wei's girlfriend, or any of it.

A little while later Pratt and Shapiro arrived, and we all stood around wondering what to do. Just when we decided that perhaps the best course of action would be for all of us to head together over to Lee Ao's in hopes that he would soon be back, he showed up. He was unable to suppress his delight at a comic Keystone Cops episode in which he had played an involuntary role. "They tried to arrest two of my bodyguards! When the police took off with Wei's girlfriend, I asked my bodyguards if I should hail my own cab or take theirs. They said 'Hop in!' So we gave the coppers hot pursuit. But we were intercepted by another police car at an intersection. They cut us off, preventing us from following the first car any further. They then tried to arrest my bodyguards. You should have seen it, right there on the street! Did those police ever lose face when they discovered who they were dealing with!"

New Domicile: Moving Out of the Line of Fire

His mock indignation and rollicking good fun were soon cut short. With a tap on his home telephone line, the authorities knew that I had solicited the attention of the foreign reporters, under Lee Ao's adroit field command. My commanding officer was, in their opinion, out of line (they, too, had their "rules of the game"), and was taken for a ride downtown. He returned late that evening, as somber as I'd ever seen him. He said that they had confided in a grave tone that he was at the top of their short list. If he persisted in challenging them, they would have no choice but to arrest — and hang the consequences.

"Things are taut as can be right now. The security people are all upset, with zilch to show in the way of progress toward nailing the culprits behind the bombing cases. They genuinely seem to be expecting something to happen within the next week. After that, perhaps things will settle down a bit." Lee Ao explained that the Garrison Command was demanding that he rid himself of his foreign tenants – now numbering two. They were insisting that we had to decamp that very day. But, he said, "until things blew over," we were still free to come visit from time to time, and thereupon with a silent nod toward the ceiling (where we all believed the listening devices were hidden), he silently passed us a key to the front door, then said aloud, "You are always welcome here any time." The key was to be used in the event that we might be calling in the morning, as Lee Ao often worked through the night and slept until well after lunch.

Prisoner of Conscience Chen Yu-hsi

by Kawata Yasuyo 川田泰代

The following excerpts are taken from *Prisoner of Conscience, Chen Yu-hsi*, by the journalist and Amnesty International Japan Section co-founder Kawata Yasuyo 川田泰代 (Mrs. Kawata died in May 2002.) It was first published in Tokyo in 1972, and translated and updated by Chen supporters in Honolulu in 1975, not long before they received word that Chen was about to be granted the right to leave Taiwan for further studies in the U.S. Their persistent lobbying, petitioning, letter-writing, lobbying, marching, and ROC flag-lowering, student and citizen organizing, and chasing after the media resulted in more public indignation than Chen's captors had bargained for.

For well over a decade, the Chen Yu-hsi trial would remain the anomalous example of how that which had been programmed as a slam-dunk, closed, star-chamber proceeding run by the military according to a script written at high levels (complete down to sentencing), could be pried open and exposed to international scrutiny. So overwhelming was the pressure that visitors, family and overseas observers were allowed into the court, there to witness Chen's vehement objection to the court's allowing his forced confession and his angry demand that the court supply proof. After sentencing and while still in the Taiwan Garrison Command custody in Hsintien, he was allowed to be interviewed by a reporter working for the mainstream press, something not seen before, and not to be seen again for over a decade.

Some of the main items, below, are taken from the chronology in the back of the book. They provide the context for Kawata's story of both Chen's predicament and the effort of herself and friends in Tokyo working with people in Hawaii to rescue him. Running to 38 pages, the very detailed blow-by-blow chronology was done by John Reinecke of the support group in Honolulu, and is based on the one appearing in Kawata's *Ryoshin no Shujin* (*Prisoner of Conscience*), published in 1972.)

Life Events of Chen Yu-hsi

1939.1	Chen Yu-hsi is born in Changhua, the eldest son to a poor farm family.
1964.9	After graduating from NTU in 1961, he begins MA program at University of Hawaii (UH), specializing in mathematics and economics.
1965.6	Begins summer term at Harvard as UH East-West Center (EWC) grantee, joins in anti-Vietnam War activities, which he continues upon returning to UH EWC in September.
1966.9	Begins teaching assistantship at UH Dept. of Economics.
1967.3	Awarded teaching fellowship at Brown University, to work on Ph.D.
1967.6	ROC Cultural Affairs Office notifies EWC that he is being denied approval to continue studies. Chen is later told that he must return home, and confides to friends that he's afraid of doing so.

Fujiko and I packed our bags and went down to the street. I walked out to Hsinyi Road to get a taxi. Once we were all packed and ready to go, Lee Ao stepped in front of the goons' taxi so that they could not pull out and shadow us in hopes of learning our destination. Despite that afternoon's warnings that he would be severely dealt with if he continued to monkey with them, he was still testing the limits.

We went first to the International House, figuring that if we were followed, instead of going through all sorts of zany maneuvers to shake our tails, we would simply stay the night there. Once it was clear that we had not been followed, we took another cab from the I-House over to the second-floor apartment of American grad student Bob Hegel. Everyone, even his wife Charlie, called him "Hegel." Hegel and Charlie lived not far from Taita. We had met them at some USIS function in late January, and had visited their place frequently in the three or four weeks since. They were always eager for news of Lee Ao, and were continually trying to link us up with other foreign students who might be interested in keeping abreast of contemporary political developments but without running any risks.

Hegel and Charlie also put us in touch with several Stanford students who had been quietly involved in behind-the-scenes efforts to get an open trial for Chen Yu-hsi 陳玉璽 and then, upon his August 1969 conviction and sentencing to seven years' imprisonment for "repeatedly spreading propaganda in favor of the Chinese Communists," his release. Chen's original "crime" was to have read Mao Zedong in the University of Hawaii library, which had a lot to do with the vigor with which his defenders abroad were able to raise a big fuss about KMT interference with student life on American soil. But even with the scandalous human rights issues that the Chen case brought into the public limelight, it was no easy matter to get students to stick their necks out, if even only to meet another foreign student. I salute Hegel and Charlie, for both generosity and courage at a time when only their apartment saved Fujiko and me from a spell of homelessness. Nobody knew exactly what the risks were (as I pointed out earlier, it was the unknown that was the real fear factor), but they took them nonetheless, when nobody else in the expat academic crowd would be moved to concern themselves on our account.

The only other exception was Jeff Barlow, another American graduate student, who had arrived in Taiwan the year before, already with some political experience under his belt. I believe that he had been one of the founders of the Committee of Concerned Asian Scholars (CCAS), which had set up recently as an ideological counter to the established academic organization in the Asian studies field, the Committee of Asian Scholars. Jeff was very good at making the connections between what was happening in Vietnam and elsewhere in Asia and the world, on the one hand, and US support for the repression in Taiwan, on the other. It was from Jeff that I learned that back in the US top-ranked sinologist John Fairbank, the same Harvard professor that Lee Ao's enemies had pegged as a communist, was coming under withering fire from radical scholars outraged at his endorsement of "Johnson's war" in Vietnam. Jeff's wife Janelle, not a scholar, had come Taiwan-ward as Jeff's spouse, and not in connection with studies or work assignment.

1967.8.15	Chen leaves Honolulu on a ticket to Taipei. However, he stops in Japan (Aug. 17) on a sixty-day tourist visa obtained in Honolulu.
1968.1.8	To extend his stay, Chen files application with the Tokyo Immigration Office for special permission to remain in Japan as a student. His guarantor is Attorney Miyazaki Ryusuke 宮崎龍介. Prof. Matsuoka Iwaki, chairman, Dept. of Business Administration, Hosei University, submits a letter of recommendation. [Chen was making arrangements to study at Hosei instead of returning to Taiwan.]
1968.1.23	On orders from the Immigration Bureau, Chen deposits 100,000 yen (about $280) as guarantee money for good conduct during his extended stay in Japan. "Temporary release from visa requirements" is granted to Chen while his application for a "special permission visa" is being processed.
1968.2.7	The Nationalist Embassy in Tokyo secretly gives the Immigration Bureau a memorandum promising humane treatment of political dissidents by the Nationalist government [this is part of an agreement to accept "repatriation" of mainland Chinese criminals being held in Japanese prisons in exchange for Tokyo's forcibly sending Taiwan dissidents back to Taiwan].
1968.2.8	On instructions from the Immigration Bureau authorities, Chen reports at 1:00 p.m. at the Tokyo Immigration Office near Shinagawa Station. His attorney is unable to accompany him. He is accompanied by a young and inexperienced Chinese who is not allowed to enter the room where he is being questioned. Chen is forcibly detained and put in a cell overnight. He is allowed to telephone an officer of the Overseas Chinese Association, which had undertaken to assist him, but this man does nothing even after being called a second time. About 2:30 p.m. Attorney Miyazaki is informed by the office of Chen's detention; he calls Mrs. Kawata, who in turn telephones a person she hopes can help.
1968.2.9	At 9:30 a.m., Chen, handcuffed, is deported from Haneda Airport aboard China Airlines. A special agent of the Nationalist government guards him aboard the aircraft. Upon arrival at Taipei he is arrested by the Taiwan Garrison Command and is immediately jailed incommunicado. An acquaintance at the Tokyo Immigration Office is told that Taiwan is recalling students from all over the world, that their lives, property and jobs are assured, and that Chen has left of his own volition and at his own expense [assurances which Kawata demonstrates in the main text to be lies].

On 18 June 1968 Chen is indicted, and three days later UPI reports that the death sentence might have been demanded. But by the end of June, thanks to the efforts of Kawata et al in Tokyo and Reinecke and friends in Honolulu, the following accounts had already reached the public:

April 25	*Contact* (newsletter of the EWC Grantees Association, Honolulu): article and editorial

On the several occasions where I crossed paths with visiting scholars and American grad students, without exception everyone was very interested in hearing the latest on Lee Ao. But no one could be induced to go pay him a visit. I would plead that if we could get maybe a dozen people or so to visit him over the next couple of weeks, the danger of exposure which might bring on added surveillance of the visitor would merit future brownie points at the pearly gates, and in any case were nothing beside the magnitude of the risk that Lee Ao was now taking. We should take to heart Lee Ao's observation that it was its image in the United States that the KMT really cared about, so we would be treated with kid gloves. The old strength-in-unity argument.

Only Hegel, Charlie and Jeff were willing to try. They assured me that I could count them as the first three toward my stated target, one dozen. I hugged and kissed them each, sure that lining up another nine people like them would be a cinch. But *not one* grad student would take up the challenge. I was met by a solid wall of indifference, passivity, fear, paranoia — the demurrals came in all colors.

Less Leg Left for Grabbing: Last Days with Lee Ao

Meanwhile I was doing what I could, visiting Lee Ao every few days, letting his guard detail see that at least one American was paying attention — and then giving them the slip downtown, as they tried to discover my current domicile (why didn't they come right out and ask me?). I think that my visits also helped give Lee Ao a bit of a lift, as he seemed to enjoy hearing about the various tricks of evasion that Fujiko and I tried, some successful, some not.

It was also on one of these visits that, while taking time out to go out on the balcony and gaze upon his "bodyguards" whiling away the hours in a taxi four floors below, we got into a discussion concerning whether or not Hsieh, Wei and others like them had tapped into the true feelings of their fellow Taiwanese concerning the question of Taiwan Independence. I asked him what scenarios could be imagined, should conditions become open enough in the future to allow a plebiscite on the question of Taiwan's future. Lee Ao said that there could be little doubt as to what the outcome might be. The blame for this, he said, rested entirely with the Kuomintang, so thoroughly had they alienated the people of their "model province." After all, he said, if you rephrased the question only slightly, instead asking whether the people wanted to be free of the Kuomintang, then it was clear that the people on the mainland had already voted, with independence from KMT rule the result.

Immersing myself in these moments of Lee Ao's greatest loneliness (but there would be greater), his manifest helplessness had a profound effect on me. If you had then said to me that one day Taiwan would be as free as the US (not saying much, but for the moment we'll let the comparison pass), with Lee Ao, probably the most prolific Chinese writer in history, selling book after book to huge audiences, there is no way I would have believed you. Had I believed you, I am sure I would have drawn great strength from it. As it was, without such faith to sustain me then, I now think that the only thing that managed to keep me going was the pleasure to be had in helping someone in so lonely a position.

April 28	Tokyo *Observor*, article by Nakajima Teruo
May 2	*Contact*, material on Chen case and letter by EWC Chinese Students Association
May 3	*Honolulu Star Bulletin*, article
May 23	*Contact*, report on EWC Grantees Association's Investigation Committee on the Chen Case
May 26	*Asahi Journal*, article and editorial
May 30	*Honolulu Star Bulletin*, letter from Bertrand Russell asking "as many people as possible to bombard the Chiang Kai-shek dictatorship... with demands for the release of Mr. Chen"
June 27	*Tokyo Shimbun*, half-page article

KAWATA'S ACCOUNT

We now turn to excerpts taken from Kawata's account of how she managed to rouse public opinion in Japan, which worked well together with the huge ruckus being made by Chen's former classmates at UH, making this a transnational campaign of the first order.

Most Japanese people, preoccupied with the immediate concerns of everyday life, tend to play down the importance of saddening news, or rather, they push such news from their consciousness without a second thought. There are, however, a number of important, unresolved problems we Japanese should face. One is Japan's aggression against China before and during World War II, including the Nanking Massacre. Another is the repression suffered by people elsewhere in Asia and the Pacific under Japanese colonial rule. My pursuit of justice for this young man stems both from a personal interest in his future and from my urge to right past national wrongs against the Chinese people as a whole. ….

I think it was about noon on February 7, 1968, that I received a phone call from Chen Yu-hsi, who sounded rather apprehensive about something.

"I'm on my way to Mr. Miyazaki's house now and will ask him to accompany me to the immigration office."

"Really? Well, I hope everything works out okay."

I never dreamed that would be my last conversation with Chen.

On New Year's Day that year I had not put up any special decorations because I was living alone and felt lazy. I locked up the house and left to visit friends. When I returned I found that someone had been by and had left a small package in my mail box. It was a present of moon cakes, accompanied by a white New Year's greeting card on which five pine leaves had been drawn. On the card was written with a fine pen, "The roots of the pine of Sino-Japanese friendship will never die. Chen Yu-hsi."

I could see that the heightened repression, together with the threat of even more repression to follow, was taking a toll on Lee Ao's spirit. Banished were the jokes, gone the spunky bravura. The people with whom he was "trading information" had made clear that they were "deadly serious this time" and would countenance no more dashing heroics from him. He took quite seriously their threats to somehow tie him to the bombings, and, as he had already said, once you were at their torturing mercies there was no question but that they could carry out any threat they liked.

Beyond buttonholing members of the foreign press, and trying to drum up interest and support among the foreign students, I also paid several visits to the USIS and the political desk at the US embassy, in hopes that my comings and goings would be recorded by the Garrison Command. I figured that a notation in that security dossier of theirs with my name on it, to the effect that I seemed to carry some cachet with the US diplomatic and/or intelligence crowd should help them think twice before expelling me from the country out of hand. They would have to proceed carefully with this young American of suspect background. This is what Lee Ao, had he known about it, might have dubbed the "foreigner grabs the foreigner's legs" 洋鬼抱洋腿 gambit. The fact of the matter was that there was little leg to grab on to; my generosity with information was met with stinginess in the way of assurances that the information would move anyone in official circles to do anything other than "pass it up and see what happens" — I often wondered if it accomplished even that. More likely collecting my information was just another feather in the cap of some security bureaucrat wanting to spice up his résumé.

And so things went, with Lee Ao's situation neither worsening nor improving, until I called him on the evening of March 4th to tell him that "I will be coming early in the morning," so "that won't be needed" 不要那個.

To anyone listening in on the phone line, "that won't be needed" sounded suspiciously like code meant to put one over on the wiretappers. It was very stupid of me, I admit it, and I have spent year upon year since then wondering as to whether this little slip-up provoked what followed, or merely became a serendipitous pretext for it.

As for Lee Ao, he was quite aware of what I meant by the "that" in "that won't be needed." And, even if he disagreed with my trying to play cat-and-mouse code games, he probably decided that there was no point in trying to set me right on the policy within hearing of our larger audience. Instead, he simply said, "OK."

So what did I mean by "that won't be necessary?" Lee Ao had given me a key, so that Fujiko and I could come and go as we liked. When we were forced to move out, Lee Ao told us to keep the key, as we were still free to visit. "Just be sure that you come no earlier than eleven in the morning, or you'll find the door bolted. If you want to come earlier, give me a ring first, so I can leave the door unbolted when I go to bed." Lee Ao generally went to bed when the sun was coming up, and slept through the morning. Even had I known how to say "don't bolt the door" in Chinese, I would still probably have chosen to leave it vague like that, so that those bugging the line would not know

It caused me to wonder when and where he learned such beautiful Japanese. I guess he wanted to demonstrate the results of his efforts to improve his knowledge of our language during the four and a half months he had been in Japan. After staying in my home for approximately a month and a half, Chen moved into the *Zenrin Gakusei Kaikan* (Good Neighbors Students' Residence), dormitory for Chinese students some three miles from my home. He came to visit me from time to time, but would return to his dormitory as soon as he had finished his business, without having anything to eat. He would say that his friends at the dormitory were waiting for him. Most of his business concerned procedural problems in applying for special permission to stay in Japan for an extended period.

Many years have passed since I returned home and found that New Year's card from Yu-hsi in my mailbox. During this time I have expended an unbelievable amount of energy in trying to become like the "immortal roots of the pine of Sino-Japanese friendship." In leaving behind his deepest wishes summed up in this one short phrase, he dropped onto my shoulders the heaviest burden I have ever known. ....

I asked Kikuko Akimoto, a colleague on the *Fujin Bungei* (*Women's Literary Review*), who is also employed by All Nippon Airways, to investigate the matter. A few days later she reported back: "A man named Chen Yu-hsi was on board a 9:30 a.m. China Airlines flight to Taipei on February 9. The manifest clearly indicated repatriation. Do you think this is the right person?"

China airlines is the flag carrier of the "Republic of China." It was obvious that Chen had been deported.

"How can I ever explain this to Chen's classmates and friends in Hawaii who gave him contributions so he could stay in Japan instead of going straight to Taiwan?" I was troubled with such questions and suffered day and night wondering how to fulfill my responsibility for Chen Yu-hsi, whose formal address in Japan was still listed as my home even on the date of his deportation.

In any case, I needed legal advice. So I put the letter from Chen's father into my purse and in the midst of a severe snow storm went to the home of Attorney Ryusuke Miyazaki, Chen's legal guarantor.

With his white beard and simple clothes, Mr. Miyazaki reminded me of Premier Ho Chi Minh. He lived in a residence built like a Zen temple, a little oasis in the middle of Tokyo. Mr. Miyazaki, with his youthful intellectual capability, listened carefully and then gave me immediate and very appropriate answers.

"Kawata-san, why don't you write to his father? Please tell him to have his son write to you if he is back home. Suggest in a slightly exaggerated manner that Ryusuke is worried."

"Should I consult some of my Chinese friends to help me write the letter?"

"No, I think you should write it yourself and do it as soon as possible. There is something particularly strange about this affair because even in the most extreme cases, the Immigration Bureau usually detains people for at least three days before deporting them."

"I hear censorship of the mails is very strict on Taiwan; do you think it's likely that my letter will be opened?"

that I had a key. No matter how you looked at it, I was a victim of my own cleverness.

When I arrived the next morning at the landing in front of his door on the fourth floor, I saw a pair of shoes, all polished and gleaming, carefully placed in front of his door, toes pointed outward. When friends visited, they were allowed to park their shoes inside the door; but all emissaries of authority were immediately reminded of their low station with the request that they park their shoes outside. Just another chance for Lee Ao to put them in their place, show them who's who.

One sight of those shoes, and I was immediately alerted to the fact that someone was inside, and by the shine on those shoes knew that it had to be someone of no mean station. That being the case, it would be foolish to use the key, since Lee Ao would also be up, hence no need to let myself in — just ring the doorbell. I say "foolish to use the key" even more because I did not want to reveal to third parties — especially these particular third parties — that Lee Ao had loaned out his key.

I rang. Nobody answered. I peered into the fisheye lens in the door, and could see that the light was on in the living room. For sure, Lee Ao had to be up. I rang again. This time the door opened with a whoosh, and Lee Ao demanded loudly and with dramatic flourish: "Why didn't you use your key?!" He thereupon had me come in and explain, without his coaching, what I had meant by "that won't be needed." Since my story gibed perfectly with the one that Lee Ao had already given his visitor, this particular spook seemed satisfied that it was all an "unfortunate misunderstanding." Never was there any apology for listening in on Lee Ao's phone.

Misunderstandings like this could precipitate calamitous responses, and Lee Ao was persuaded that at a time like this he did not need any more visits from his foreign friends. Thus ended Fujiko's and my visiting rights. That was the last I was to see of Lee Ao for nearly 22 years. A few weeks later, with no pesky foreigners to witness and disseminate the fact, Lee Ao was taken in and tortured, in an effort to implicate him in not only the bombings, but in helping Peng to escape, and in passing the list of political prisoners on to Amnesty International.

Improbable Confederates: Nakano Fujiko and Robert Ricketts

Among Lee Ao's allies we must count the reluctant freedom-fighter from Japan, Nakano Fujiko, my much-suffering wife of the time. She had been dragged into all of this, a fight neither of her making or understanding. All she could do was sit by and watch me try to help Lee Ao while not advancing my/our own prospects one bit.

She had endured enough. On top of all the daily political tension that she was subjected to, and partly because of it, her hair fell out. The main sticking point was my having given such high priority to Lee Ao's cause, so little to my efforts to return to Japan with the visa that would enable me to live and work there. What about our lives, our future together? Didn't that matter too?

The reasons for Fujiko's discontent were all valid, and all I can do is express much-belated remorse: I had no right to force this fight on her, it's true, but at the same time I could not turn my back on Lee Ao so long as I was there, even if my own contribution

"Yes, you should write on the assumption that your letter will be read by censors."

This wise old man's advice encouraged me to act boldly. ....

During the course of Representative Inomata's investigation into the Chen affair, the Immigration Bureau of the Ministry of Justice was forced to disclose the existence of the above memorandum and to supply a copy to the Judiciary Committee. Attention should be paid to the fact that this memorandum was issued just one day before Chen Yu-hsi was detained for immediate deportation. The young Taiwanese intellectuals who did not support the Chiang regime were marked as political criminals and deported by the Japanese government on the basis of a piece of paper handed to Immigration Bureau Director Susumu Nakagawa by the Taiwan Ambassador.

It was further revealed that sixty drug smugglers were returned from Japan to Taiwan as part of the deal for returning Chen Yu-hsi and Liu Wen-ching 劉文卿. The framework for this trade was set up by the Director of the Immigration Bureau without so much as obtaining the consent of the Minister of Foreign Affairs. The manner in which this deal was carried out demonstrates the contempt held by the Japanese Immigration authorities for other Asian peoples. One political dissenter equals thirty drug smugglers! Japan, where is your dignity?

None of the provisions of the Japanese Immigration Law of 1952 prescribes immediate deportation for persons like Chen Yu-hsi and Liu Wen-ch'ing. This action was taken simply as a matter of convenience for the two governments.

Tsutomu Ikegami, a public prosecutor with the Tokyo Superior Public Prosecutor's Office and author of a book, ***200 Questions Concerning the Legal Status of Aliens***, drafted a new immigration bill which was introduced in the Diet in March 1969. In response to the question, "What kind of treatment do you give to those persons who could not and who did not get permanent visas on the basis of the Japan-Korea agreement?" Mr. Ikegami wrote, "From the point of view of international law, you may do with them what you like."

When I came to realize that the same interpretation could easily apply to Chinese residents in Japan, especially those critical of the oppressive policies of the "Republic of China," I was appalled at the power held by such outdated officials as Prosecutor Ikegami. What does Mr. Ikegami think of the United Nations Charter, and of the Universal Declaration of Human Rights — subscribed to by Japan — which is proclaimed as "a common standard of achievement for all peoples and all nations," regardless of their political status. ....

The reaction to the *Asahi* coverage was immediate. Soon I received a letter from one of the young

Kawata Yasuyo's *Ryoshin no Shujin (Prisoner of Conscience)* first appeared in Japan in 1972. (Courtesy of Wu San-lien Taiwan Historical Materials Foundation)

Kawata Yasuyo

was reduced to that of frustrated foreign witness. Now wearing a wig on her head and a scar on her heart, Fujiko returned home to Japan. I still had to stay behind, not to help Lee Ao, who now that he was in jail might be better helped outside Taiwan than in, but to look after my visa application, and to track its progress as it inched toward the top of an Immigration Bureau "IN" basket in Tokyo.

My Taiwan visa was good for one month. I renewed it without incident in early February, but, with all that had transpired between February 20 and March 5, I entertained no hope whatever of getting it renewed again. With still no encouraging word coming on my Japan visa, I could not return to Japan, as the new visa, if and when it came, had to be received in Taipei (or else I would have to go elsewhere and apply all over again, with yet another wait of who-knew-how-many weeks). So I really had no choice. Even had I shared Fujiko's disgust for this land of gloom and doom, I had no choice but to sit tight in Taipei.

"The paranoiac is the exact image of the ruler. The only difference is their position in the world." (Elias Canetti, *Crowds and Power*, 1960) Of Robert Ricketts, there were several things about him, in those deep-chill Cold War days of early 1971, that have left a lasting image: his constantly-fidgeting hands and his cautious, secretive manner. Actually, the word "cautious" does not come close to describing what I took at the time for an overly excited streak of paranoia.

The terms of our meetings were at his insistence, right down to the location. The venue for our conspiratorial murmurings never varied. It was probably owing to our aversion to using the phone — tapped? — that we kept to the one place for our clandestine meetings: the cafeteria in the west compound at the MAAG complex just across the river from the Grand Hotel. Palefaces here one and all, with the occasional Afro-American — all presumably friends.

Well, not quite. For Ricketts and I shared the belief that, every bit as much as the government of Chiang Kai-shek was the enemy of freedom in Taiwan, "our" government was equally at fault in the deprivation of rights there as in many other parts of the world. Indeed, it was more at fault because the apex of world power was situated in Washington, not Taipei, and the way towards ridding ourselves of this killer state on Taiwan ultimately hinged on decisions made thousands of miles away as much as they did on executive fiat wielded from just five miles from where we sat.

So Ricketts and I, at odds with both governments, were improbable allies in what was then a very lonely cause. In fact, for a while it was as if we two were the only ones who seemed to think the situation sufficiently dire to warrant some personal risks to alert the world to the fact that the ROC government was lying when it said that it was doing a fine job of advancing human rights and freedom in China. In the coming years I would meet many, many foreigners, mostly Americans and Japanese, but also a plethora of other nationalities, who, out of deep-felt sympathy and compassion coupled with a simple desire for dignity and justice, willingly gave of their time, energy, money, comfort and safety, but in 1971 things were lonely indeed.

Previous to our first meeting, my only purpose in venturing so far north of town was

women who had written to the editor of the *Asahi Journal*. It read, "Summer vacation begins in June, and students will be going to different places. We want to hold a students' meeting before them in order to bring Chen Yu-hsi's case to the attention of the whole student body. Please send us relevant source materials." I was quite impressed with this young woman's sensitivity for justice.

When I had asked for help from the male officers of Sino-Japanese friendship organizations, the responses of the men in charge were diametrically opposite to those of the women students I have described. When I sent them a number of copies of the *Tokyo Observer* with the Chen article, they never raised any questions about it. In addition they stopped notifying me of their meetings. These men involved in trade with China were completely uninterested in problems which did not relate directly to their business interests.

As the Chen case unfolded it was noticeable that those who responded first, both in Japan and abroad, were often women. In fact, the person who decided that Chen's case had to be placed on the agenda of the House Judiciary Committee was Michiko Watanabe, Director of the Education Propaganda Department of the Socialist Party of Japan. Mrs. Watanabe, the mother of four grown-up children, studied under the late Inejiro Asanuma, who used to say that American and Japanese reactionaries were the common enemy of the Japanese and Chinese peoples. For these words he was stabbed to death by a right wing fanatic. Mrs. Watanabe seems to have inherited much of Mr. Asanuma's political abilities. [….]

On August 1, the prosecutor had demanded the death sentence for Chen. It was now August 11. With the trial finally over, and the decision imminent, I decided I no longer needed to rely on other people to speak up for Chen and that I would take off my mask. I had begun to think that nobody else was seriously concerned about Chen receiving the death sentence. I am very grateful, even now, to the executive members of Beheiren for asking me to participate in this conference although I was not a Beheiren member. They invited me on the basis of reading news articles on the Chen case. I spoke on the final day of the conference. My speech was included in a book entitled *Anti-War, Pro-Reform*, which was a record of the conference. Since most of the audience knew little about Chen, I had to present much material with which readers of this book are already familiar and which I am omitting here.

> Just about a year ago, on August 17, 1967 he came to see me with an introduction from a friend of mine in Hawaii. For some reason, he seemed afraid. I asked him what was the matter and he told me that if he returned to Taiwan he would be thrown into prison for about ten years.
>
> So, I asked him what he had done. He related how he had participated in a demonstration in Hawaii in opposition to the bombing of North Vietnam. A TV camera man took some footage of him when he was waving his hand during the demonstration; the film was shown on the television in Taipei, the commentator suggesting that Chen was agitating his fellow students. Friends in Taipei wrote him warning, "Stop doing such things or you're going to be in serious trouble."
>
> When in 1967, Chen was accepted for the Ph.D. program at Brown University the Taiwan government ordered him home immediately. This is when he started to

to sample the American cooking at the MAAG cafeteria. But once Ricketts entered the picture, hamburgers, fries and even ice cream were only incidental considerations. Now there was real business to be done. Ricketts, who chose the location of our meeting, could have walked me through the gate, but he wanted instead to meet in a corner of the cafeteria, where our association would less likely draw attention because the clientele was off-duty and therefore dressed in civilian attire. We always did it his way; our comings and goings were always performed singly, and with an eye out for lurking spies.

Even then, as far across the room from the service counter and cash register as we could get, Ricketts was constantly casting his glance over my shoulder to see who else was about, and speaking at a barely audible level as is if invisible spies were seated at the empty table next to us, taking notes on our every word.

Underground Publishing: Hatching a Plan

Ricketts was introduced by Janelle, wife of Jeff Barlow, who was close friends with Hegel and Charlie, with whom I had been living since my late-February expulsion from Lee Ao's place. Of the foursome, only Janelle was in Taiwan for reasons other than to pursue advanced research related to China or Taiwan. Up until I met Ricketts, she was the only American I knew connected in any way with the US military. Her office was over at the MAAG compound off of Hsinyi Road (now home to DaAn Park), where the CIA and the various military intelligence agencies were headquartered. Her duties were strictly secretarial; although she was not inclined to break the oath of silence that she had signed when taking the job, she was not above passing on what little gossip she picked up around the coffee maker.

Ricketts and Janelle worked for different agencies, but their offices were within the same building in the same compound. Somehow the two of them became friends, and she learned of his secret meetings with Hsieh Tsung-min, which, had they been discovered by either ROC intelligence or the US military, would have spelled the end of Ricketts' Taiwan tour. When she told Ricketts about me, he expressed interest in getting together. I don't recall now whether our first meeting was before or after Hsieh's arrest, but within weeks of our first cloak-and-lager conference, we were already decided on a plan of action whose agenda included the dissemination of an English-language news-sheet that would be printed outside Taiwan, secreted into Taiwan through the US military mail system, and disseminated to foreigners, in hopes of enlightening the expat crowd (primarily US military) about the real facts of KMT repression. One could, whether a student from Stanford University here to research the status of Ming-era upper-class women, or an intensively-trained military language specialist from Monterey here to daily don ear phones and eavesdrop on mainland military conversations from atop the mountain at Linkou, or just a clerk shuffling papers — one could spend two years in Taiwan and never once catch wind of anything other than the official US view, which pumped up the Chiang regime in the most glowing terms imaginable.

Our plan was hatched sometime in March 1971, probably not long after the arrest of

suspect he would be arrested if he returned to Taiwan. His friends in Hawaii told him to go to Japan and stay there until things cooled off. They also told him that if he had trouble staying in Japan he could go to the People's Republic of China — that because he believed in the reunification of China, he would be welcomed there. So thinking, he came to Japan.

The reason I agreed to participate in this conference was to enlist your support in stopping Chen's death sentence. However, there have been frequent changes in the case and according to this morning's newspapers he received a sentence of seven years imprisonment. Needless to say, I am experiencing a slight sense of relief, and I have had to change the format of my talk to you....

I would like to have you look at this case as an internal problem of Japan. Because I fear there will be many other cases in the future like Chen Yu-hsi's I would like you to give serious thought to how we should handle the problem of the deportation of political offenders by the Immigration Bureau.

Please consider the reasons he was indicted and imagine that you are a Taiwanese and found yourself in his shoes. The Taiwan authorities claim that Chen Yu-hsi was always reading the *China Pictorial Review*, and the *People's Daily* and the poems of Mao Tse-tung while he was studying in America. They also say that he visited Wu Pu-wen, vice president of the Tokyo Overseas Merchants Association and asked for Wu's assistance in going to the mainland. Through Wu's introduction he worked for the Chinese newspaper *Great Earth News* in Tokyo. In addition, between December 2 last year and January 17 this year, he supposedly wrote two articles for *Great Earth*. Simply for having committed these "crimes," Chen could have been punished with two death sentences and one sentence of life imprisonment. Seven eminent persons, most of whom were personally acquainted with Chen, agreed to lead a movement to save this young scholar and hold a press conference on June 24....

I would like to relate to you the background behind Chen's deportation in the fall of 1967, shortly after Prime Minister Sato returned from an official visit from Taiwan, the then minister of justice, Isaji Tanaka, and Immigration Bureau Director Susumu Nakagawa went to Taiwan to conclude a secret agreement with that government's national security bureau. The Japanese officials wanted Taiwan's cooperation in receiving 200 Chinese drug smugglers being detained at the Omura Detention Center in Yokohama. Former prime ministers Kishi and Ikeda had tried to get Taiwan to take the drug smugglers back, but Taiwan kept refusing.

陳玉璽

PRISONER OF CONSCIENCE CHEN YU-HSI

by YASUYO KAWATA

Kawata Yasuyo's *Ryoshin no Shujin (Prisoner of Conscience)* was translated by Nishikawa Toshiyuki 西川俊幸 and ,Lonny Wiig and was published in Honolulu in 1975. (Courtesy of Wu San-lien Taiwan Historical Materials Foundation)

Kawata Yasuyo

Lee Ao. Here is how it was supposed to have worked. Ricketts and I would bang out articles on a second-hand typewriter that we would buy exclusively for this purpose, paste them up into newsletter format, get them printed in Okinawa (where Ricketts had already lined up a printer), and have them shipped into Taiwan compliments of the US military. We had not yet worked out how they would be gotten into the hands of our target audience without their original distribution source being traced.

Ricketts worked for 7th Psyops, short for "7th Psychological Operations Group," an Army unit whose main task was the creation and dissemination of black information and appeals to the China population to rise up and overthrow their communist masters. Headquartered in Okinawa and supporting US military operations in Japan, Korea, Okinawa, Taiwan, the Chinese mainland, the Philippines and Vietnam, the unit listened in on enemy communications, surveyed public opinion, produced bogus poll results, and prepared radio broadcasts, fliers, magazines, counterfeit money and postage stamps, and engaged in other tricks of the black propaganda trade. Many of their publications were dropped over enemy territory from high-flying planes. The hope of this huge effort was to "exploit troop weaknesses and vulnerabilities." Their covert budget for just Vietnam was US $3.7 million in 1967 alone. Between 1965 and 1972 over fifty billion leaflets — 1,500 per person — were distributed in Vietnam and Laos. Yet there was little evidence that the material was sophisticated or culturally sensitive enough to have much of an effect. No matter, they went on producing fliers by the billions on the fastest printing presses in Asia.

So, in a sense, the 7th Psyops, with "Credibility through Communication" as its motto, had already provided the model that we intended to follow (although on a modest scale appropriate to two people working on a budget of several hundred dollars): surreptitiously work up propaganda and circulate it under the noses of the oppressors. While the paper progeny of Ricketts' nine-to-five efforts were crossing the Taiwan Straits, the product of his off-duty pursuit of a different truth was, if all went right, to make the 50-minute hop from Kadena Air Force base in Okinawa to an air base in Taiwan.

A different truth…. It must be admitted that at the time both Ricketts and I were firm in the conviction that it had to be seen as *the* truth, in stark contrast to what could only be regarded as glaring lies coming from our government. Thinking in terms of absolutes, we began to adapt as if on the terrain of all-out warfare. We fell to using many of the enemy's methods — avoidance of the phone when on special business, cryptic messages, code words, counter-surveillance, propaganda bearing a political agenda, black-and-white portrayal, being careful sometimes to the point of paranoia as to what we would say in a particular crowd either about the "Free China" that we were living in or about our activities — this was all cloak and dagger but without the dagger.

Adopting the adversary's methods is one thing, hijacking his printing presses is another. It sure would be great if one day we could hear from Ricketts and learn in detail how he planned to do this. The US military had at its disposal a colossal printing plant with a full complement of professionals to run it, not to mention all

Finally the Sato Cabinet concluded a deal with the Nationalists which was exposed during the Judiciary hearings on the Chen case. In this secret arrangement the Taiwan government agreed to accept 30 drug smugglers for each political prisoner the Japanese government agreed to deport. The first victim was Chen Yu-hsi....

In summary I would like to make the following points:

—Beheiren should expose the contradiction that Chen Yu-hsi from Japan is a "political criminal," although Japanese law doesn't include the concept of "political criminal."

—We should think deeply about the problem of political refugees in Japan so that in the future there will be no more Chen cases.

—We should make certain that Chen has permission to return to Japan any time he is able to leave Taiwan.

—Because I have seen how a death sentence can be reduced to seven years imprisonment, and how, by making a big fuss the Taiwan independence movement prevented Liu Wen-ch'ing from being arrested once he was back in Taiwan, I now believe the following generality about political prisoners: "The more noise you make the less punishment they get."

sorts of ways of distributing the product. It was Ricketts' plan to let 7th Psyops' do our printing and MAC to do our airlifting to Taiwan. That was the plan.

Ricketts had already met with Hsieh, who had provided him with a copy of the political prisoner list that Lee Ao and Hsieh have since written about as the one secreted out of the country at the request of Martin Ennals, Secretary General of Amnesty International. Now that Lee Ao, Hsieh, Wei Ting-chao and others had been arrested, the premier issue of Ricketts' *Taipei Tattler* would make use of this list of 214 prisoners as companion piece to the main feature, which would focus on Peng's escape, the bombings of the USIS and Bank of America, and of course the arrest of prominent dissidents in a bogus conspiracy to tie the regime's most vocal opponents to acts of covert terror.

Before the first issue ever so much as went to press, however, I was forced to leave Taiwan, with Ricketts soon to follow. Some months later I had forwarded to me in Japan a clipping from the *Stars and Stripes*, the newspaper serving the US military throughout Asia (also edited and printed in Okinawa). Short on details, it reported that Ricketts and two others had been removed from Taiwan to Guam, where they would stand trial in a military court.

Many years later in Japan, I bumped into Ricketts at a demonstration against the Sanrizuka land takeover to make room for the new Narita Airport. He had taken a very long and circuitous route in getting from Guam to Japan. There had been stops in a number of countries, including Sweden, where he had won asylum as a political refugee, staying long enough to develop a command of Swedish.

While I had first viewed Ricketts' paranoia as being fanciful in the extreme, it was not long before I discovered that his fears were very much reality-based. Hsieh had introduced him to a relative of Peng Ming-min. Having absconded abroad in early 1970, Peng had left his relatives to the watchful care of the various intelligence branches. Just how Ricketts managed to rendezvous with them without arousing suspicion of the Gestapo is something that must await a fuller accounting by Ricketts himself. Somehow the meeting came off without incident, at least for a time.

It was the US intelligence people who had first learned about it – from Ricketts of all people. Just how much Ricketts had told Peng's nephew (or was it cousin?) about his own work and military connections, I cannot recall. But we may be certain that it was enough to encourage Peng's relative to think that perhaps Ricketts might be able to put him in touch with the CIA.

It may have been in the nature of wondering out loud, or it may have taken the form of an emphatic request. At any rate, Ricketts went back to the office with this notion of Peng-CIA liaison, and passed it on to his superior, who in turn passed it on up the chain of command. It went to the CIA headquarters in Langley and came back down by a parallel route to the local CIA station, located in the same building in the same compound on Hsinyi Road where Ricketts worked. The reply traced the same route back again, via Langley and the Pentagon, then back down to the 7th Psyops in Taiwan. Within a couple of weeks Ricketts was called on the carpet by his boss. In the

Letter from Hawaii

REINECKES' 1968 APPEAL LETTER FOR CHEN YU-HSI

Chapter 6 of Kawata's book, entitled "The Movement in Hawaii Goes Forward," quotes from a number of letters at length. She introduces the one below as follows: "I also received a copy of the letter which John and Aiko Reinecke, the couple who took a keen interest in Chen, sent out to several hundred persons on September 27.... Although the Reineckes devoted their energies to helping Chen not primarily for political reasons but because they loved him as a friend, they empathized with him because of their own experiences. After many years as school teachers they were fired from their jobs in 1947, even before the McCarthy period began; and later Dr. Reinecke was sentenced to five years in prison for 'conspiracy,' though his sentence was set aside upon appeal to a higher court."

Dear friends,

Here in Honolulu a group called the Student Faculty Union intervened very actively in the Chen case. The East-West Center Grantees Association which should have taken the initiative in the matter, did not do so; for many of the grantees had scattered at the end of the spring term and few of the remaining ones were deeply concerned. A member of the SFU knew a former grantee named Timothy Wong, an American of Chinese ancestry who had been a Peace Corps worker in Thailand and a graduate student in Taiwan, who speaks Mandarin Chinese and is familiar with Chinese outlook and customs. We were lucky that he agreed to go as observer to the trial. Very sensibly, he would not go until he was sponsored also by the Associated Students of the University of Hawaii and the Grantees Association but it was your contributions (over $600) which in great part made his trip possible.

Wong arrived most opportunely in Taiwan on July 26, for Chen's court-martial was held on August 1 and Wong just had time to make arrangements with the Foreign Office to attend it. He sent back a careful, objective report which covers four single-spaced thirteen-inch pages. Also attending the trial were members of Chen's family and UPI and AP correspondents — but no one from the Taiwan press. We understand that over 200 persons are arrested every year in Taiwan for sedition, but only half a dozen have come to open trial. Such is the power of world public opinion to which your letters and telegrams contributed....Ten days after the trial the court found Chen guilty of sedition and gave him the minimum sentence of seven years. His father, so the Foreign Office has informed the SFU, has applied for a re-trial. Wong came back from Taiwan hopeful that the re-trial will be granted and that it will have a favorable outcome. We do not know if a date has been set for it; one guess is that it will be in October or early November.

The Chen family are small businessmen and until recently Yu-hsi's father farmed a one-acre plot. The family has had to bear a crushing load of legal and other expenses. The lawyer who was engaged to represent Yu-hsi charged $750 U.S. We understand that for the re-trial the family is engaging a still more prestigious lawyer who may charge in the neighborhood of $2,500 U.S. We have been able to send a little money to help toward paying the legal expenses, and we hope to get a big drive started on the University campus. ...

sternest terms he was told that thereafter he was to have no contact whatever with anyone related to Peng or any other dissident. On pain of expulsion from Taiwan and possible court martial, Ricketts was from that time on under direct military orders to stick to business and not interest himself in local politics.

In March and April of 1971 when Ricketts was telling me these things, his very meeting with me was in violation of his superiors' orders, while it went without saying that if he were caught in a conspiracy to educate other US military personnel concerning the "Free China" that they were defending, court martial would probably be the result. Since it was generally understood that a dishonorable discharge from the military would remain as a lifelong impediment in the way of getting good jobs in post-military life, the risk that Ricketts was willing to take was infinitely greater than anything I would ever have to confront.

When I met Ricketts in Japan some ten years later, he told me that it was Hsieh's capture and interrogation that ultimately did him in. Ricketts was arrested by the MPs and underwent prolonged questioning. They knew about his connections with Hsieh, which, he believed, they learned about by torturing the information out of Hsieh. But by the time that Hsieh's ordeal had begun (it was to last into the summer), I had in all probability contributed to Ricketts' undoing through an unforgivable blunder.

One day, after an overnight session of newspaper clipping and filing at Ricketts' apartment, Ricketts had to go to work. I took him up on his invitation, quite out of step with his usual habit of putting security first, to share his taxi as far as the MAAG compound, a thirty-minute walk from where I lived. After dropping Ricketts off at the MAAG gate, I took the taxi to the corner of Hsinsheng South Road, from where I walked home, making sure that I was not followed. Upon getting home, I discovered that I was missing my black vinyl zip-up binder, which contained my journal and interview notes — not to mention my passport. I had left them in the taxi!

That was on April 16. I immediately reported the loss of the passport to the Foreign Affairs Police, which brought daily calls from them, as they were anxious to see me out of the country. Since they had already made it clear that I would not be allowed any further visa renewals, I could imagine that they were certain that my loss of the passport was far from accidental, but just a way to delay my departure for however long it might take me to procure another passport.

Recovered Passport, Telltale Journal, Hasty Leave-taking

On April 21 I received a call from the Foreign Affairs Police saying that my passport had been found, and that I could come and pick it up. Within an hour of that call I was visited at home by the Foreign Affairs Police officer assigned to my case, and told that I had to leave Taiwan the next day, that I should go downtown immediately to pick up my passport, and immediately make arrangements to fly out on the earliest available flight back to Japan. He dropped hints that if I was not cooperative, then force would be applied. Spare myself a lot of trouble, he said, and, more importantly, make sure that I would still be welcome to visit Taiwan in the future by leaving with

Appendix B to Kawata's book

TIMOTHY WONG'S REPORT ON CHEN YU-HSI'S TRIAL

August 2, 1968

Taipei, Taiwan

TO: East-West Center Grantees Association

Associated Students of the University of Hawaii

Faculty Senate Committee on Academic Freedom

Student-Faculty Union

FROM: Tim Wong

SUBJECT: The trial of Chen Yu-hsi on August 1, 1968, at Taiwan

PRELIMINARY NOTES

1) Up until at least two days before the trial, most sources — including Chen's lawyer-- reported that the trial would be closed. I did not know of its actual date until late in the evening of July 30, 1968. On the morning of July 31 I met with Mr. C. C. Lai of the Ministry of Foreign Affairs and he gracious agreed to seek permission from the Garrison command for me to attend the trial. This request was quickly granted and I arrived at Ching Mei, the trial site, the next morning in the company of Mr. C. Y. Chang, also the Chinese Foreign Ministry. There I discovered that the trial was to be an open affair after all. UPI and AP represented the foreign press among the observers, which included students from National Cheng Chih University. To my knowledge, no local Chinese news reporters were present. No news of the trial was mentioned in *Chung Yang Jih Pao*, Taiwan's leading newspaper, today.

2) Chinese law is based in form on the Continental System and has many important differences from Anglo-American law. At Chen's trial, I noted the following:

a) Other than the defendant who acted as his own witness and was free to speak, no witnesses were called to testify.

b) There was no cross-examination of the defendant from his own lawyer.

c) The judge played a very active role, questioning the defendant and gathering and presenting incriminating evidence much as a prosecutor would do in the United States and England.

d) The accused, rather than his counsel, prepared and presented his own defense in court.

e) In no time during the entire proceedings, did Chen's lawyer voice objections on points of law in the matter of defense counsels in England and the United States.

a clean record. Through all of this he was my "friend" of course, only thinking of my good.

When I went downtown to pick up my passport, they told me that the driver had turned it in, notebook, binder and all, to the ROC MP at the gate to the MAAG compound. The MP in turn brought it back to his headquarters upon return from duty station. Ricketts and I spent a few idle hours on my last nights in Taiwan, speculating on what sort of agencies had attempted to get in on the information bonanza as my notebook made its way from the MP to Foreign Affairs Police headquarters. With the passport and incriminating journal now back in my hands, Ricketts and I went through nearly a hundred pages of journal entries to see just who might have been injured by any of the revelations to be found within. We decided that none of our dissident friends would likely be hurt. If anything, Lee Ao and Hsieh actually might have been helped by my having taken down their speculations as to who could possibly have been behind the USIS and Bank of America bombings. That Hsieh had been talking to foreigners might hurt him, but, on the other hand (more speculation) perhaps it would help him for them to know that he had foreign friends. But as far as my notes themselves went, they did not really incriminate anyone, especially not Lee Ao, whose signature style was nothing if not in-your-face. So in our estimation, the only person likely to have been damaged by my notes was Ricketts. This meant more fuel for the fires of his paranoid musings.

Fortunately, I had not put to paper a description of Ricketts' publishing scheme. Praise God for the lacuna. But from the loquacious entries in my log could be gleaned enough useful "intelligence" to make it more than clear that Ricketts and I were in frequent association, if not up to our necks in some nefarious conspiracy. On top of that, there was the fact that both of us were friends with Hsieh, and Hsieh was now in the hands of the Gestapo. If my notes reached Hsieh's interrogators, they would be surely asking him more about Ricketts and Miles. What Hsieh might have to say to his jailers about either of us was entirely a matter of guesswork.

With the "lost" passport back in my possession, the stage was now set for me to act on the orders of the Foreign Affairs Police to drop my application for a work visa at the Japanese consulate, and instead apply for a tourist visa so that I could leave before my ROC stay had expired. I was to be out of there within days.

All the speculation and conjecture concerning what the security people knew about our publishing plan went on in the chaotic setting of my hasty preparations for departure. Again Ricketts and I were up all night, this time to sort through papers that I would be leaving behind, from ones that I wanted to ship back to Japan. Since Ricketts would be doing the shipping through the military APO system (using a San Francisco mailing address), anything that I left with him for forwarding would reach me without the risk of ROC constabulary interception.

The next day I checked my bags at the airline counter. All went smoothly. Since bombing of civilian airliners had yet to intrude upon international travel as a way of scoring political points, so too the x-ray and other security devices now seen at all

f) A confession was submitted and used as the major incriminating evidence even though the defendant repeatedly repudiated it, claiming to have written it under undue duress. The judge countered by counting out in the course of the trial that Chen had been transferred from the Security Office to the Martial Law Office. At the latter place Chen had taken part in two different inquiries but had made no change in his confession at either time.

THE SETTING

1) The trial was held at Ching mei, a suburb of Taipei, at a temporary court room of the Garrison Command. It was a fairly small room with bare cement floors, benches, a few chairs, ceiling fans, fluorescent lights illuminating a picture of Generalissimo Chiang and a flag of the Republic of China.

2) Aside from Chen's family, I counted sixteen observers, including myself and Mr. Chiang. Chen's father, uncles, and brother all of whom came in just before the opening, swelled the number to about twenty.

3) Three judges sat in front along with a recorder and a prosecutor. Chen's counsel Fu Po-p'ing, sat below this panel behind his own table to the audience's right. A sergeant-at-arms stood beside the table at which the prisoner was expected to stand during the entire trial.

4) Chen appeared at 9:02 a.m., looking physically healthy but tense. He wore a white sports shirt of synthetic material, slim, dark trousers that were just a little too long, badly torn socks, and high-cut, laceless shoes that resembled galoshes. At 9:03 the Military Tribunal began the trial in earnest.

international terminals were a thing of the future. The bags preceded me onto the plane, while I worked my way through exit formalities. But, when my name came up on their security list, I was shunted to a side room. After long, long minutes, my bags were retrieved from the plane, and a team of inspectors went through them meticulously, opening every book and scanning every piece of paper for telltale traces of my presumed espionage trade. When they lit on my copies of *The John King Fairbank Clique Conspiracy in Taiwan* 費正清集團在台灣大陰謀, their eyes lit up expectantly, only to dim in disappointment at the realization that the two-volume set had a Taipei publisher and carried a GIO registration number. The search yielded them nothing, while all the passengers on the plane were made to wait. We were 45 minutes late taking off as a result.

So on 22 April 1971, I said goodbye to Taiwan, wondering if I should ever be allowed to return. The daily calls from the Foreign Affairs Police and the rigorous search I was given upon leaving did not bode well for the future at all.

But neither did my prospects for getting a visa that would allow me to stay in Japan with Fujiko, who by now was at rope's end. Arriving in the Fukuoka Airport, it was my luck to get an immigration officer who went through my passport carefully. Coming upon the stamp and notation alongside it of my previous exit in January, he escorted me to a side room. I was made to sit for several hours, which suggested that perhaps they were awaiting orders from Tokyo. The problem was that I was supposed to be arriving on a work visa, but instead I held only a tourist visa applied for and received the previous day in Taipei, with the ROC Foreign Affairs Police breathing down my neck. Japanese immigration made me sign a declaration that I would not attempt to work while in Japan on this visa, that my sole purpose in being here was to rejoin my wife for awhile and prepare the papers that were holding up my teaching visa. So it is that I made it back into Japan by the skin of my teeth, with an unmistakably stern warning that if there were any visa irregularities, this would be my last visit for a long time to come. I knew that these warnings were not to be shrugged off.

Married barely over a year and railroaded out of one country, the challenge now before me was to see how I could avoid the same fate in another.

Chapter Three

Foreign Interference in Domestic Affairs

By the mid 1970s, "human rights" had become the watchword of the day, so much so that in 1976 US. presidential candidate Jimmy Carter set as his campaign plank "adherence to human rights principles as a fundamental foreign policy consideration" -- and won. He was perhaps not so much leading a movement as deflecting criticism of the US. But Amnesty International had already won one Nobel Peace Prize and was about to win another. Starting with concern for Hsieh Tsung-min, tortured after sending lists of political prisoners out of Taiwan in 1970, a clandestine network operated by Lynn Miles from Osaka grew up nearly overnight, and within a few years joined with others to loosely link thousands, Taiwanese and foreigner, within Taiwan and without. ICDHRT, FAHR, SPEAHR, OSDMT, and many more small volunteer-based organizations focused on Taiwan boasted increasingly global reach.

第三章 1970-1975：國際人權組織串連

七十年的中期「人權」成了當時的流行口號，甚至連美國總統候選人吉米卡特都在1976年承諾美國外交政策將首重在人權原則的基礎上，這是卡特競選的重要主軸，爾後，他也如願當選美國總統。他當權的時候，國際特赦組織也已贏得了諾貝爾和平獎，不久之後又再度獲獎。對台灣的關注是始於1971年救援謝聰敏一案。謝聰敏因爲將台灣政治犯名單送至國外，而被捕並遭虐刑求。梅心怡在日本大阪展開的國際秘密救援網絡隨即開始串連，在一夕之間就聯繫了數以千計的台灣人和外國人。關注台灣人權的組織還包含了「捍衛台灣人權國際委員會」、「台灣人權協會」、「保護東亞人權協會」、等小規模以志工爲主的人權團體，使台灣人權的實況得以持續讓外界知曉。

Into the Big Wide Open

by Lynn Miles

In the decades since the 1974 startup of the International Committee for the Defense of Human Rights in Taiwan (ICDHRT), I have been asked many times just who made up the organization. The questions have come from all quarters: journalists, human rights allies, friends who wanted to help out, and even a few people who, pretending friendship, were really working to bring us down. Old habits dying slowly, in the ensuing decades I have preferred to keep our inner workings hidden from all but a select few, even long after we long ceased to exist as an organization, figuring that if the principal actors wanted their stories to be told, then they could do the telling.

With the ever-irrepressible "Borgia" (code name back in ICDHRT days for Linda Arrigo) after me for full disclosure, it is time to lift the veil. Certain people deserve credit, for better or worse, where for too long I had been getting more than my fair share. So this is to be their story as much as mine.

Dispatch News Service and David Boggett

Returning to Japan from Taiwan in May 1971, I was in a funk. My friends were in prison, not likely to get out for a long time to come. Although outward indications were still lacking, there could be little doubt that I was already blacklisted from returning to Taiwan for at least as long as Lee Ao, Hsieh and Wei stayed on ice, perhaps longer. My visa status in Japan was anything but certain, and my marriage was nearly on the rocks thanks to my having taken an excessive interest in Taiwan human rights issues when I should have been putting all my time and energy into rescuing my own situation from the inaction of the Japanese Immigration bureaucrats.

So, first priority had to go to getting that visa so I could work in Japan. Having had to abandon my visa application in Taipei, and sworn to abstinence from income-generating work until being granted a valid visa, I was back to square one; actually, the situation was quite a bit worse than when I had left Japan for Taiwan at the beginning of the year.

Finally I was notified by the authorities in Tokyo that my papers were in order, and that I could proceed to a foreign country to file my application for new status. Again I was told that it would take a week to ten days. This time I did not take a chance on being allowed into Taiwan. So I took the quick flight to Pusan, and, as was customary with all the other ex-patriots in Japan doing the South Korea visa run, filed my application at the Japanese consulate, then immediately turned around and flew back to Japan, to do my waiting there. (This was also intended to prove to wife Fujiko that I had put all Taiwan human rights work behind me)

Just when I thought Lady Luck had finally begun to smile on me, there was another

Foreground and Background: An ICDHRT Gallery

Without trustworthy information sources there would have been no International Committee (as we called it). So our 1970s-era tale begins with the undercover operatives. Against daunting odds they managed to stay beneath the GIO and Garrison Command radar while meeting with dissidents, contacting prisoners' friends, families, and former fellow inmates, and finding creative ways to sneak information abroad. Next came those who translated and organized it for dissemination (Karen Smith, Sugihara Toru 衫原達, Nicki Croghan and others). Finally, we needed someone willing to forfeit future chances of entry into Taiwan by going before the public.

Dennis Engbarth and Miyake Kiyoko 三宅青子

Miyake Kiyoko goes at the top of the list, for she was our solitary source beginnng in 1972 (the ICDHRT was formally established in 1975). She shuttled back and forth between Taiwan and Japan until, in late 1975, she was uncovered and came under threat. She left for Japan in early 1976, but continued to find ways to get information out. Dennis sprang into action late in 1976, frequently coming to Japan or Hong Kong to meet up. His long, detailed reports needed but the most minimal of rewrites to become the ICDHRT's exhaustive information releases of 1976-79.

Kuo Yu-hsin 郭雨新

The ICDHRT having no formal membership, we should better call Kuo Yu-hsin a fellow traveler. After his late-1975 defeat in a hotly contested election, he left for the US to settle with family in Washington, DC. On several visits to Tokyo and Osaka in 1977 and 1978, he was a key player in getting materials into English and having them disseminated widely.

Kawakubo Kimio 川久保公夫

We called him "Godfather." Dean of the Osaka City University Economics Faculty, Kawakubo Kimio (flanked by Hsu Hsin-liang, left, and Wei Ting-chao, right) was our face before the Japanese public. His was the experienced counsel that steered our decisions, his was the wealth of contacts that won us entrée, and his was the voluble writing that won a wide readership in Japan. On the board of Amnesty International's Japan Section, he visited Taiwan in December 1975.

Lynn Miles

setback. Upon arriving in Fukuoka for the second time in as many months, this time from Korea, I had the profound misfortune to meet up with the same immigration officer who had welcomed me on my arrival from Taipei. Remembering me well, he was not at all pleased to learn that I again was attempting to enter Japan bearing a tourist visa. No amount of assurances on my part would sway him from the suspicion that my real reason for returning to Japan was to take up work again. "If you can work in neither Japan nor Korea, at least you can live more cheaply in Korea than in Japan."

Without much time spent in consultation with Tokyo, the Fukuoka immigration authorities put me back on the same plane that I had arrived on, a Pusan-Fukuoka shuttle. No sooner had the airline rolled to a stop on the receiving apron at the Pusan terminal, than Korean immigration rushed on board and escorted me off. Red-carpet treatment all the way. I became the responsibility of Mr. Heh, who had cleared me for takeoff from Pusan that morning, on the basis of the valid Japanese tourist visa freshly stamped in my passport. Again I was taken to a side room for intense questioning. Soon many of Mr. Heh's colleagues dropped in to hear my tale of woe. I saw no reason why, with the ROC and ROK being the "closest" of allies in what for Taipei was a diminishing circle of friends, I should want to drag my Taipei past into all of this, so the blame for my predicament fell entirely on the Japanese. Casting their former colonial masters as villain in this story of heartless injustice played well to anti-Nippon prejudices. How callous of the Japanese, these Korean immigration officials agreed to a man, that they should prevent this young American from rejoining his new bride in Japan. They all took great pity on me, and declared their contempt for the cold and unfeeling monsters.

Mr. Heh called some reporters, and a press conference of sorts was hastily thrown together. I was encouraged to repeat my sob story for the media, and was displayed as state's evidence in this shocking example of Japanese inhumanity. Thus did I provide grist for the mill of the Koreans' long-standing hatred for the Japanese, something that I would have plenty of opportunities to learn about in the following decade.

That done, Mr. Heh and I settled down to the practical problem of where I was going to stay until my visa came through. Since I had only prepared for an overnight stay in Pusan and had no money, I was clearly a charity case. At a loss to find a place where I could stay gratis for however long it might take for my Japanese visa to come through, Mr. Heh invited me to stay as a guest in his home! Never before or since have I met an immigration official so unwilling to turn a deaf ear to his subject's plight. During my one-month stay in Korea, I spent all but a week of it in Pusan as his house guest, eating meals with him, playing with his son on the heated linoleum floor of his living room, and going out with him in the evenings for dinner and drinks. He even gave me some pocket money so that, while he was away at work, I could take a bus downtown to while away the hours in a coffee shop, studying my Hangul and reading up on Korean history.

One week of my waiting time was spent in Seoul, where I doubled up with David Boggett, himself guest of a professor whose name he had been given by Amnesty International in London. As for how I met Boggett, it all started with Mike Morrow.

James Seymour

We first met in 1975, on his way through Japan on an Amnesty International mission. From then on we were in frequent touch by phone, telex and mail, sharing information closely until (and after) I left Japan in 1984. Widely published on Asian human rights generally, he appeared in US Congressional hearings on Taiwan in 1977 and later. Very careful with his facts, he was the torch-bearer of the Amnesty International spirit, making it possible for him to stand aloof from the battle between independence and unificationist partisans of the 1970s and 80s.

Linda Gail Arrigo and Chen Chu 陳菊

Do they really need introducing? Linda and I first met on her way into Taiwan in 1977, when she declined to work undercover for the ICDHRT. But in 1978 she took up with Chen Chu and Nori (Shih Ming-teh), and the rest is history. Did she consider herself a part of the ICDHRT? The answer came in August 1979 when on her own she placed an ICDHRT ad in the first issue of *Meilidao* magazine. From 1977 to 1979, Chen Chu (right) deluged Miyake (center) and me with urgent, information-packed reports, sometimes carried out as undeveloped film.

Denis Wong

Introduced by Dennis Engbarth, Denis performed multitudinous duties from his lonely outpost in Hong Kong, where he settled in after leaving Taiwan in 1977. His trips to Taiwan were sure to reap rich informational harvests. A generous host, he put up ICDHRT activists whenever they joined up in Hong Kong. When Chen Chu managed to get Lei Chen's *Memoirs* out to us in early 1978, he negotiated their publication with the Hong Kong publisher of *The Seventies* 七十年代.

Lynn Miles

Mike, whom I had first befriended in 1967 when he was a regular patron of the
Barbarian coffee shop in Taipei, had suddenly leaped into the international spotlight
when he and three other American journalists were captured by communist guerrillas
during the 1970 US invasion of Cambodia. When he returned from captivity, the
behind-the-enemy-lines story of the four Americans was bandied about in the press,
which even carried mention of his credentials as reporter for Dispatch News Service.
Had it been just Mike who was captured, it probably would not have rated a story, but
he was in the company of very established journalists from the St. Louis *Post-Dispatch*
and *Christian Science Monitor*.

Reading in *Time* and *Newsweek* that Morrow was still alive, I had written to him
asking if Dispatch might be able to use any material on Taiwan. He replied with an
introduction to Dispatch's Kobe representative, Emer Manawis, who in turn put me in
touch with Boggett, then living in Sakai, near Osaka. Boggett said that he was about
to leave for Korea, but that we should get in touch upon his return, and we could
work together. Boggett wanted to expose the human rights situation in South Korea,
just as I was casting about for ways to do the same regarding Taiwan, so we thought
we had a good basis for pooling efforts. So now, in June 1971, getting plenty bored
whiling away the hours in Pusan coffee shops, I decided to venture up to Seoul to
see Boggett, and hopefully firm up the schemes whose preliminary outline we had
loosely sketched on the phone several weeks before in Japan. We decided that the two
of us had enough information to begin work as a poor man's news service.

The visa allowing me to work in Japan finally came through, and I returned to
Ashiya. By the end of the summer, Boggett was back in Japan, too, and we got
together. He said that the several stories that he had submitted for distribution in the
US by Dispatch News Service had been rejected as being too in-depth for a general
newspaper audience. Mike Morrow and David Obst (another former Barbarian
habitué) had started Dispatch precisely in response to frustrating rejection letters
just like the ones that Boggett was now receiving. Morrow was among the very few
American journalists who could speak Vietnamese, so he had access to Vietnamese
from all walks of life, including dissident figures, students and people involved in the
push for political reform. But stories about these people did not interest the editors
back home, so Morrow and Obst decided to start up their own news service to fill the
need for more in-depth reporting. Obst thereupon headed back to the United States to
set up Dispatch's Washington office.

In Mike's telling, once inside the Washington beltway, Obst started angling for bigger
fish. He linked up with Seymour Hersh, who immediately shot to fame with the My
Lai story, which Dispatch (Obst) released. This report of a massacre of an entire village
by US troops in early 1968 only became known through a leak in the Pentagon, and
once Dispatch sold the story (to 36 newspapers), the Pentagon now had a PR problem.
The mainstream media picked up on it, and within weeks the affair had blown up
into a full-fledged scandal that occupied the front pages of the newspapers and got
top billing on prime-time TV news shows, especially after *Life* magazine published
photos of the executed elderly, and the lifeless mothers clutching their dead babies in

The Quiet Constancy of Miyake Kiyoko

by Winston Luo 駱文森

From 1970 to 2000 Winston Luo worked as an advisor for the Asahi Shimbun, *setting up interviews whenever reporters came from Japan. He served as a reporter for Kang Ning-hsiang's* Capitol Morning News *from 1989 to 1990, and for the* Liberty Times *from 1991 to 2002.*

Miyake Kiyoko is a Japanese human rights fighter. Born in Kyoto, she turns 70 this year. Diminutive and slight of build, she has a genial personality, and is a bit on the introspective side, while at the same time being determined and passionate. She is an upholder of democracy and defender of human rights.

Her father hailed from ten generations of medical doctors. He himself majored in medicine, and later, while teaching at Kyoto University, served as personal physician to the Japanese royal family. Upon the establishment of Manchukuo as a Japanese colony, he ventured to Manchuria to work as the curator of a museum. It was when he returned to Kyoto that Kiyoko was born. In October 1944, with the reconquest of the Philippines by General Douglas MacArthur imminent, he had the opportunity to return to Japan, but gave up his passage to a younger subordinate, and so it was that he was killed in the Philippines.

Miyake's mother also died, leaving her and her younger brother orphaned at an early age (another younger brother had already died). She and her brother were then put in the care of relatives, Miyake herself being sent to live with a maternal uncle in Osaka.

While in university, she took an interest in helping people with physical and mental disabilities, working for a time on farm at which they were employed. She also had a passion for mountain climbing. Her first visit to Taiwan, in 1961, was in order to climb

Taiwan's highest mountain, Yu Shan. The year before, while a member of the Japan Mountain Climbing Association, she got to know some climbers from Taiwan that the JMCA was hosting. This all came about because she was friends with someone who was operating a mountain lodge in Japan.

And thus began an association with Taiwan lasting over four decades. That first 1963 trip brought her together with some intellectuals in Taiwan, themselves belonging

Miyake in the mid-1960s. The picture was taken at the Good Friends Photo Studio opposite National Taiwan University. (Courtesy of Chen Chin-tsai 陳進財)

a ditch outside the village. Dispatch's marketing of the Hersh scoop also marked it for the second time as a player in the majors when it came to the mass marketing of Vietnam War-related material.

More than that, sale of the story brought Dispatch a huge and quite unforeseen boost in income. This was the undoing of Morrow and Obst's partnership, not to mention their friendship. Morrow wanted to hold Obst to their original agreement concerning the splitting of the proceeds. But Obst would have none of that, contract or no, since it was thanks to Obst's work, and not Morrow's, that Dispatch was able to land the story; he thought he deserved the share that would ordinarily go to Morrow. The situation became very confused, and for a time there were two services operating concurrently under the name of "Dispatch.

In any case, it was to Obst's Washington office that Boggett had submitted his stories, and it was Obst who had penned the rejection letters in terms that made it clear that Dispatch could no longer be regarded as an "alternative" news service that hoped to deliver the Asian reality that the mainstream media was ignoring. Obst was riding high on the My Lai wave, and could not be bothered with stories about tortured dissidents in countries with which the US was allied.

Marcel Valance and Hsieh Tsung-min's Prison Letter

By late 1971 Boggett, having pursued countless media outlets to no avail, finally decided to start up a magazine. He set up office in a modest Kobe apartment overlooking the harbor, and went to work. First issues were banged out on an IBM Selectric, which had fonts with raised letters on interchangeable balls that whirled and bobbed as you typed. You had to type each line twice, the first time to determine how many spaces needed to be inserted in order to justify the right margin, the second time to produce the final. If an article came out three lines too long, you had to retype an entire paragraph to accommodate a deletion to make it fit. For a job that might take 15 minutes in these click-of-a-mouse days, then it would take an hour or more to come out with a nicely justified column of type. Headlines for the stories were done by transferring the letters one by one from a plastic sheet. It called for a good eye and careful hand. One head took 30 to 40 minutes to execute, and often if you botched a letter you had to start all over again. And then there was the cutting and pasting, using rubber cement so that things could be picked up and moved around.

While these methods seem downright antediluvian by today's computerized standards, I am not suggesting that more advanced methods were not at the disposal of our contemporaries. The problem was that Boggett was not about to wait another half-year or more while he put together an organization and somehow raised the huge start-up funds necessary to keep a publishing venture going for several years. The result looked every bit the DYI effort that it was.

To this enterprise Boggett gave the name "Ronin." This was years before Hollywood gave the term widespread currency in the West. In the Japan of that time, the term applied to a student who, having failed to gain acceptance into the university of her/his choice, was taking a year off, dubbed the "*ronin* years," to cram for the next

浪人 ⦂RONIN VOL.1 NO.3

In his letter, the full text of which appeared in our last issue, Hsieh Ts'ung-min wrote from his Taiwan Garrison Command prison cell that he "had to take a lenient attitude toward their insane torture by promising... to admit Mr. Lee Ao, a very brilliant scholar and the most popular writer in Taiwan, was a commissioner of Formosan Independence Movement." An introduction to the life, thought and work of Lee Ao, whose photograph appears below, is to be found on pages seven and eight of this issue of RONIN.

The Taipei grapevine, oracle of so much popular wisdom, offers the following one-liner: "In Taiwan there are two madames, one of them moral." In the essay below, here appearing in translation for the first time, Lee Ao discusses the vagaries and double-standards of Taiwan's prostitution-control laws, as arbitrarily applied to the case of Taiwan's foremost procuress — and, it is said, along with Madame Chiang Kai-shek, one of the two foremost 'madames'. Originally entitled "The Unveiling of Ho Hsiu-tzu", it was included in a book of Lee Ao essays, Rambling Talk (Taipei: Wen Hsing, 1965.)

pacifying a procuress :

the other madame

Under the defeated circumstances of the "Taiwan Prostitution Control Law," the situation before us can be summed up by only eight characters: "Open Prostitution Lies Outside, and Illicit Prostitution Falls Within." The universal, wild lawlessness of illicit prostitution has already reached the point where our very bones tremble. And the flame of illicit prostitution is not at all being shown in the darkness; rather they are making a public show of themselves all around. In November 1960, twenty brothels on Kuang Fu Road in Taichung up and presented a collective petition to the city assembly, announcing that their illicit prostitution business already had a history of over forty years, and they demanded that their "prosperity" be assured "so as to benefit the people!" And who can't play this kind of game? In May of this year, a brothel in Hou Tsai Yuan of Feng Yuan village also presented a petition to the head of the police department, saying that their history went back more than ten years, that their roots went deep, their stem stood firm. And the police sent some troopers to occupy the place but could only manage for a while, as to put a stop to it for all time was out of the question. I'd say that's not quite as good as setting them up on a new road!

But something rather special within the corner of this tapestry stands out, that being the illicit prostitution enterprise under Ho Hsiu-tzu's hand.

That Ho Hsiu-tzu has set up Chiao-min Salon, a beauty parlor, and other lustrous sundries, so as to transact a fat business of illicit brotheling, is an internationally known fact. The restricting of illicit prostitution is a move of which we approve, Ho Hsiu-tzu being no exception. Furthermore, to apply the blade first to the flagrant example of this old procuress is a legitimate control.

But if we go into a little greater detail, we find that there are places where Ho Hsiu-tzu surpasses others. To speak plainly, in the fundamentally immoral profession of prostitution, the illicit brothels of Ho Hsiu-tzu still evidence a comparative morality. Ho Hsiu-tzu's first-term husband was Chen Ping-kuei, chief of Taihsing County in Kiangsu during the period of Japanese control. After Chen died she hitched up with Chou I-pei, county assemblyman of Hsinchu County. She herself graduated from Taipei's First Girls' School, the top girls' school in Taiwan during the Japanese occupation, so her knowledge and knack obviously differs from that of the other

When Miyake came to me with Taiwan political prisoner information in 1973, I was interested in helping, but was quite caught up with *Ronin* editorial duties, which also involved me in lots of different social issues in Japan, South Korea, the Philippines, and elsewhere in Asia. So initially the only encouragement I could give her was to say that I would translate materials she sent me and pass them on to Amnesty International. Miyake had to bide her time. In late 1971, *Ronin* No. 2 carried Hsieh Tsung-min's "Letter from Prison," followed by the No. 3 issue (above) with an introduction to Lee Ao and a translation of his piece on Ho Hsiu-tzu, Taipei's leading brothel operator.   -LM (Courtesy of Wu San-lien Taiwan Historical Materials Center)

to a mountain-climbing club, and that is how she first learned about the real human rights situation in Taiwan. In order to come to Taiwan in the first place, the climbing group she was with needed a guarantor in Taiwan to sign off on the expedition. Chen Chin-tsai 陳進財, on the staff of National Taiwan University's Electrical Engineering Department, was then a member of a climbing group made up of NTU students and teachers, as well as of the China Youth Mountaineering Club (under the China Youth Corps). Chen helped the Japanese group manage the paperwork, going so far as to apply his father's chop to the application forms.

After her second trip to Taiwan in 1964, they decided to get married, and on her third trip in April 1966 she moved to Taiwan to stay for good, as his wife. Her only long-term residence in Taiwan ran until early 1976, when Chen was working for Wing On Travel Agency, and was assigned the directorship of their Tokyo office. From early 1964 to early

year's unified exam. In feudal times, *ronin* 浪人 were laid-off samurai, some of whom became so driven by circumstance as to take to gangsterism as a way of life, but there were also the stories of the occasional *ronin* hero who took up his sword on behalf of the oppressed or to redress an injustice.

In short time, our chief editor was to rue the choice, as he told me with a baleful shake of the head: once the first issue of *Ronin* came out and was smuggled to his underground confederates in South Korea, he discovered that what "*ronin*" conjured up in the Korean mind was the grim reminder of Japanese imperial soldiers who in 1945, having been left behind on Korean sacred soil at the end of the War, were without means of quick return to Japan. They were forced to shift for themselves, much after the underpaid and forcibly conscripted soldiers doing the bidding of Chiang Kai-shek's henchmen Chen Yi 陳儀 and Peng Meng-ji 彭孟緝 and in 1946-49. This led to a lot of stealing, raping, and mayhem little calculated to ameliorate the low esteem in which they were already held, owing to a long ledger of wartime atrocities. (Formosans of yore might well imagine it!)

But for the magazine it was too late for that, full steam ahead, and Kim Chi Ha take the hindmost. And so it was that we fell victim to quirky god-tricksters, the puckish pranksters that fool around with names. Today with even Hollywood wise to the practicality to be had from serving up exotic persona, we were on the cutting edge, out there with Graham Greene. For we really *did* want to be rebels! We were very much against the established order, and saw many big wrongs that needed immediate righting. We were burning with impatience, our complaints with injustices only increased with each new activist we met, and by the end of the year we were off and running as publishers of what could be, in the beginning anyway, rightfully and in all honesty called a "periodical."

The prevailing view in the Japan of the time seemed to be that, for good or ill, in any case a *ronin* was without a fixed place, and as such was to be feared, pitied, or both. Whatever, more than romantically flaunting the rootlessness of his own existence, Boggett's choice of the name represented a way of romantically striking the pose of challenger of abused and abusive authority: our *ronin* was to be the *ronin* that stood on the side of the oppressed.

And we did grow to the name. We warmed to the idea that this cultural chasm spanning the waters was something that *ronin* might be perfectly positioned (culturally speaking) to bridge. Naturally it would be done using the favored language of the imperialist masters. Our strange mix of caring and defiance, of militancy and anti-militarism, probably had more than a tad of the stereotypical *ronin* to it. One did not have to wear shades to see pink.

So it was no small achievement, I thought, that Boggett was able to raise any money at all, for young hot-bloods on the left took it as a given that rich people were rich precisely because they refused to stand with the oppressed. I was rather hard on the upper class in those days, taking the Marxist-materialist view that one's economic station trumped everything else. (Today that same view might be called Christ-

1976 would have meant a stay of twelve years, but it was broken by a stay of three years in Hong Kong by Chen, beginning in February 1973. Miyake joined him there for part of that time.

Having returned to Taiwan in 1974, the birthplace of their only child (a daughter), the couple then moved to Tokyo in 1976. The move to Japan was also prompted by anxiety brought on by frequent visits from the security agencies; an undercover agent named Ma, pretending to be a friend of a number of political prisoners and sharing some information about them with an American student working for Lynn Miles' Osaka-based International Committee for the Defense of Human Rights in Taiwan, got Miyake's name from the student. This meant that, with her "cover" as assistant in a travel agency having grown perilously thin, she would be working thereafter under the shadow of suspicion. On top of that, over several years, Chen had been taken in twice for questioning by the authorities, largely having to do with his associations with various intellectuals like Hsieh Tsung-min 謝聰敏, Wei Ting-chao 魏廷朝 and Pao Yi-min 包奕明. So Miyake and Chen moved to Tokyo in 1976 with their nine-year-old daughter.

(Chen's third detention came in the summer of 1979, when he returned to Taiwan with a group of seven or eight Japanese. I served as the leader of the group, which included a photographer from *Mainichi Shimbun*. On leaving Taiwan on August 6, the group was thoroughly searched at the airport, and some photos that Wei Ting-chao had handed Chen were discovered. He was arrested and taken to the Security Section, the dreaded interrogation and torture center behind the Presidential Building. He was questioned for three days and three nights, then released and allowed to return to Japan.)

Not long after her arrival in Tokyo, she was put on the blacklist by the Taiwan Garrison Command, and was prevented from returning to Taiwan until 1990, at which time the authorities announced that the blacklist was a thing of the past. But there was still plenty that she could do, however much the blacklisting might put a dent in her travel plans. She continued to carry on her Taiwan political prisoner information gathering and relief work, albeit from afar, and soon she became an important center of activity in the international rescue network. It was also shortly after she settled down in Tokyo in 1976 that she became very busy with working behind the scenes to get the Taiwan Political Prisoner Rescue Association going.

Chen's work for the travel agency allowed Miyake to make contact with lots of people going to and coming from Taiwan, so although she was blacklisted from actually going

Despite her aversion to reporters and cameras, Miyake has managed to get herself into the news. The above two newspaper items span 37 years. The 19 April 1966 *United Daily News* tells how Miyake and her husband first met on a climbing expedition. Written by Wu Chin-fa, currently the Deputy Chairman of the Council on Cultural Affairs, the foreground opinion piece appearing in the *China Times* on 6 December 2003 is a tribute to her unceasing work over the decades. (Courtesy of Chen Chin-tsai 陳進財)

spiritualist: "Give away everything you own….")

Ronin's main benefactor was an affluent physician from Sakai. Having spent several years in Korea, Manchuria and China during the war, Dr. Furukawa (I've forgotten his given name) spoke fair Chinese and a smattering of Korean. He often traveled to South Korea, where he had many friends, quite a few of whom had risen to positions of postwar prominence. One of them was a South Korean parliamentarian who had been arrested by the South Korean CIA on charges of conspiring with several students to go to North Korea to be trained as spies. One of the students had spent some time at Cambridge University, where Boggett had graduated not long before coming to Korea and Japan. Representing the Cambridge student body, he had come to Seoul on a fact-finding mission. He concluded that while there may have been some contact between North and South Koreans in Europe, it certainly did not prove a conspiracy, and in any case did not warrant a death sentence.

It was while investigating the case in Korea that he was introduced to the name of Furukawa. When I first contacted Boggett in June, he was living in Furukawa's house, preparing to go again to Korea. Now returned from Korea and living in Kobe, he was still dependent on Furukawa not only for his own living expenses but also for the publishing project.

The magazine's first, October 1971 issue focused on human rights in South Korea. My contribution extended no further than to helping with the typing, paste-up and mailing, but I became increasingly involved with each successive issue. My name was kept off the masthead, but as my actual role in the editing and production grew, Boggett insisted that I list myself as assistant editor. No way! He said that then he would be forced to give me a name and put it in himself, as it would be presumptuous for him to claim all the credit. So for "Marcel Valance" as perfect *nom de guerre*, let David Boggett have all the credit. Whatever he gave me as his reason for that particular choice made no lasting impression on me.

Our second issue front-paged a "Letter from Taipei," written by Hsieh Tsung-min from prison after he had "received the gist of charges in this morning (August 28th, 1971)." The opening review of Hsieh's résumé moves to the reasons behind the long wait before deciding to print the letter:

> In February 1971, after a rash of bombings (US consulate in Kaohsiung, USIS in Taichung, Bank of America in Taipei), a new wave of arrests followed. Hsieh's letter takes up there…. It has been known to some outside Taiwan for some months, but only now is being made public in response to the news that Hsieh has been sentenced to death in a military trial conducted in secret in Taipei on March 1st of this year. No news has come out of Taiwan about Wei, but as he faced the same charges at the same trial, it is probable that he received the same penalty.

There were a number of questions that the letter raised. One passage in particular had me wondering.

> The KMT lives by the theory of conspiracy, and at the same time, they constantly

With Miyake passing into "exile" in her home country, her work eventually became public knowledge. Two articles from two different newspapers report on her winning of a human rights award in New York. (Courtesy of Chen Chin-tsai 陳進財)

to Taiwan herself, she was able to stay on top of breaking developments. Of course, information from abroad was also reaching people inside Taiwan thanks to her efforts.

She is also known for having succeeded in getting a list of Taiwan political prisoners into the hands of overseas human rights activists in 1971, while she was still in Taiwan. It was at the height of the authoritarian control of the Kuomintang that, starting in 1971, she worked with another human rights activist, the American Lynn Miles, to rescue Taiwan's prisoners of conscience, often with no regard for their own safety. Miles has later written that during the period 1971-76 she was one of his primary information sources, if not <the> primary one. She would run around calling on the families of those in prison and showing her care for them, all the while collecting information and materials concerning the true facts behind their loved ones' imprisonment. Once her materials reached Amnesty International, the facts would then capture the understanding and concern of people around the world. In that way it became known that, under the long oppressive rule of martial law, there were people who were being tortured and suffering the inhumane practices of state terror, finally living out their days under tragic circumstances in prison.

She was also moved to compassion by the poverty she saw on a trip to the Penghu Islands, and decided that she wanted to do something to alleviate their plight. That in turn led to her decision to try to do more for the families of people who had been thrown into jail for political reasons, so she started taking practical steps to collect information about them for Amnesty International. She was instrumental in delivering to these families not only material relief items, but also the psychological solace that comes from knowing that people overseas cared about them. She became an important intermediary between these families and people involved in rescue work outside Taiwan, so it is no wonder that her contribution is still remembered today by so many former political prisoners and their families.

In a later interview with the media, Miyake pointed out that at that time detailed information about the prisons was very hard to come by. How many prisons were there?

suspect the conspiracy of others. During these months, they asked me over and over in this way: Did American Ambassador tell you how to destroy this government? Did he tell you why the US aid is reduced? How Japan tries to take over this government? Dear Friends, I never met any member of American Embassy.

It was hard to fathom how they were accusing him of working to destroy the ROC government on orders of the US government, only to end up accusing him of having a hand in the Bank of America bombing.

The letter contained no mention of Ricketts, no mention of me. (Was I to feel neglected or relieved?) But through its agents on the street outside Lee Ao's, the KMT was aware that Hsieh and I had met on at least two occasions. How much did they know about his rendezvous with Ricketts? What did they know of my connection with Ricketts? What was I doing visiting the MAAG compound where the intelligence agencies are headquartered, that day when I left my passport behind in the taxicab? And what about my visits to the embassy and the USIS? The regime hardly needed to be paranoid to smell a conspiracy here. Ricketts and I must have played interesting roles in the scenarios that suggested themselves to Hsieh's captors.

Patrician Leftist, Professor Patron: Kawakubo Kimio

With Ricketts not only kicked out of Taiwan but altogether out of the picture, who was feeding me information from Taiwan? At first, no one was. I was completely cut off, quite in the dark.

But all that changed thanks to Dr. Furukawa, whose circle of influence spread far and wide. It included people active in the Taiwan Independence Movement, a number of whom were with the group of young professors and activists putting out the Japanese-language monthly, *Taiwan Chenglian* 台灣青年, in Tokyo. Furukawa invited several of them to come down to Osaka. His friend Prof. Kawakubo Kimio 川久保公夫 of Osaka City University, whom he knew to be interested in Taiwan human rights issues, was also invited. Kawakubo invited me. That was when I first met Kyo Sekai 許世楷 and Oh Ikutoku 王育德. Koh Yujin 黃有仁 (aka Ng Yuzin, Huang Chao-tang 黃昭堂) may also have been with them. The three were among the most active in *Taiwan Chenglian*, one of the two main TIM factions in Tokyo (the other one, the Provisional Government group, had fallen on hard times upon the return to Taiwan of its guiding light, Thomas Liao 廖文毅).

At that Osaka lunch I also met Oh Giroo 王義郎, a *Taiwan Chenglian* board member from Kobe, for the first time. International business law professor at Kinki University, Oh was to become a close friend during my fifteen-year stay in Japan. His knowledge was encyclopedic, his interests far-ranging. He was extremely well-read in all kinds of things Chinese, ranging from medicine to literature, science to history, alchemy to chemistry, cuisine to equestrian warfare. He was at home in Japanese culture as well, with an equally broad range of reading habits and interests. His modest apartment was wall-to-wall library, with room barely left over for a TV set. I often went to him for help with translations that I was doing. Oh would always cook up a tremendous meal before we sat down to work.

And where were they? Even the families were in the dark. But with persistent effort she was finally able to make headway and get a fuller picture, and soon she was sending information abroad.

Although Miyake and Chen have a daughter, now 41, they dissolved their marriage some time ago.

Her involvement in the rescue work for political prisoners in Taiwan has spanned over four decades. On 10 December 1988, she was presented with the Taiwan Human Rights Award in New York, conferred by the Formosa Association for Human Rights, so that her work finally has gotten the recognition that it deserves.

Over the years, Peng Ming-min, Hsieh Tsung-min, Kuo Yu-hsin, Chen Chu and many Taiwanese living abroad in the Japan and the U.S. have kept up contact with Miyake. In August 2007, she was visited in Hachioji City, not far from central Tokyo, by Kaohsiung mayor Chen Chu, on the concluding of a sister city agreement between Chen's city and her own. On meeting for the first time in some years, the two of them tearfully embraced each other for the longest time, so it can be readily seen just how appreciated Miyake's work for human rights has been for many people.

One of many of Prof. Kawakubo Kimio's writings on Taiwan human rights, this one appeared in the April 1977 issue of *Sekai Seikei* (*World Political Economy*). For Kawakubo and others in Japan, information having to do with political cases in Taiwan came primarily through Miyake until 1976. (Courtesy of Wu San-lien Taiwan Historical Materials Center)

Although Furukawa soon faded from view once *Ronin*'s leftist leanings became more than he could ignore, Prof. Kawakubo remained a staunch friend of Taiwanese of many different political persuasions for the fifteen years that I was in Japan. I first knew him as constant friend and patron of *Ronin*, but learned quickly enough that his concern extended to many people struggling for the basic human rights guaranteed by the Universal Declaration of Human Rights (UDHR) throughout Asia. Search the Japanese left in those days for intellectuals, journalists and educators who took an interest in Taiwan, and you might come up with several score who knew a little about the political or economic side of the picture, but even among these "experts" you would find that what they knew concerning human rights in Taiwan rarely exceeded the most superficial levels. This was because, except for the Trots, or those who held that "Pravda" still meant "Truth," or the anarchist fringe (those who held that no one, not even themselves, had a corner on the truth), rare was the left-leaner, in Japan as elsewhere, who did not accept that the PRC had full right to decide Taiwan's future. In other regions of the world, too, the left might hold high the flag of self-determination, but if the talk turned to the people of Taiwan's claim to UDHR-sanctioned rights, you would be dismissed out-of-hand as either a leftist-adventurist, or a CIA agent.

Except for this motley collection of marginalized Trotskyites and anarchists, the left had yet to turn a critical eye on the Beijing regime. This same went for respected mainstream journals and pundits too: adherence to the Beijing line bordered on blind fealty. For the leftists especially, that the Taiwan Independence Movement (TIM) was a running dog of American and Japanese imperialism barely rated mention, and the perversities of the Chiang regime were but arrows in their quiver of hatred directed not at the KMT but at the KMT's American backers.

Still unanswered is the question as to how information came to me from Taiwan, now that Ricketts had been removed as my only hope of linking up with the human rights information-trafficking underground. The first information to reach me from anyone in Taiwan was the above-cited Hsieh letter. In August Hsieh discovered that the cell next to his was occupied by a Japanese tourist who had been arrested for activities carried out under the direction of TIM cohorts in Tokyo. Hsieh passed the letter to him, and upon release he brought it back to Japan, handing it over to the *Taiwan Chenglian* people, who in turn gave me a copy.

For the next several years, however, little in the way of hard information came from the independence people in Tokyo. From early 1972 to mid-1975, the single most important source for nearly everything coming out of Taiwan, as far as we in Osaka were concerned, issued from Miyake Kiyoko 三宅清子, still in Taipei at the time. Married to a Taiwanese, Chen Chin-tsai 陳進財, she had given birth to a daughter, who was five or six by the time Miyake and I first met on one of her trips to Osaka. In spite of the ever-present danger to herself and her family, she was meeting with a number of dissidents, including Hsieh's sister Hsieh Hsiu-mei 謝秀美, Su Hung Yueh-chiao 蘇洪月嬌 (intrepid and outspoken wife of Su Tung-chi 蘇東啓), Chen Ku-ying 陳鼓應, Tien Ma-ma 田媽媽, and later Chen Chu 陳菊, Chang Chun-hung 張俊宏 and

LETTER FROM PAEK   July 31, 1975   TAIPEI

In Taipei, day after day the crazy heat, 36°C or higher, continues.

Since J will be leaving for Japan soon, I will entrust this letter to him. What with his being so busy, I really appreciate his taking the trouble to help us out. Well, the political prisoners who were released from prison as a result of the most recent "reduction of sentences" number exactly one hundred from Green Island, and a total of only thirty from Pan Ch'aio, Ching Mei and other places. Recently I have met two of them, but now that they have come out, for them to immediately disclose conditions on the inside and for these reports to gain wide circulation would not go well for them, for it would obviously mean that they were the ones responsible for the leaking of the information. So just now they don't want to talk. Furthermore, as many of them are suffering from severe nervous exhaustion and some of them are close to nervouse breakdowns, I would just as soon leave them alone for awhile. So I'll just pass along the names of those released that are knonw to us now:

Ch'en Yung-shan ⎫
     Ying-ho ⎭ brothers   ° Lin Ch'in-t'ien
* Huang Hua   ° Liu Chia-ch'in
* Lin Chung-li   ° Huang Shu-lin (crazy)
° Lai Shuei-ho
° Hsü Tseng-teh

Almost all of those who have come out (and especially from Green Island) are suffering from physical complications. (*) signifies very serious illness, and (°) indicates relatively light sicknesses which, if not given medical attention, could become serious.

Here is a summary of what they have told me (about the situation on Green Island).

1. There are 10 to 12 people to a 6-mat room [one mat equals approximately 1.3 m^2]. The windows in the cell are very high, so that when one stands up s/he still faces only wall. In the summer there is no air-circulation, turning the room into a hot steam kettle.

2. Prisoners are allowed a bath once a week, twice (cold water) in the summer. In the sweltering heat of the summer, a majority of the prisoners bathe by splashing water on themselves from the water running through the toilet under the floor. To go without a bath is more insufferable than the filth and stench. Washing of clothes is also done in the toilet bowl. At Ching Mei baths are allowed only once a year.

3. Aside from the exercise time of one 30-minute period per day (Green Island) and three 10 to 15-minute periods per week (Ching Mei), they are locked up in their cells the wholse time with nothing to do.

4. The most insufferable thing of all is the occupying of the same cells by the crazies and the sane ones.

5. No matter how serious their sickness is, so long as they are able to walk they are not bothered with. The doctor (military personnel) only asks from beyond the screen door and steel bars, "How are you doing?" They don't inspect the person's body at all, and if one should complain about

"Paek" was one of two code names for Miyake used by the ICDHRT and others working with her. "Okada" was the other. The translation of this letter was most likely done by myself, although by this time Karen Smith had returned to Japan from Taiwan, so it may have been her work. Miyake's reports were typically just the bare-bone facts. -LM (Courtesy of Wu San-lien Taiwan Historical Materials Center).

many others. Speaking Chinese well and lacking the telltale physical features that would have prevented her from passing as a Taiwanese when walking the streets, she could visit the homes of dissidents and their families without drawing attention of the surveillance people, thereby both sparing the families the terror of a follow-up visit from an intelligence agent and herself interrogation leading to deportation.

Self-effacing Lady with a Big Will: Miyake Kiyoko

When Miyake and I first met in Osaka, I was just getting involved in Amnesty International, both in organizational work in Japan (the Japan Section in Tokyo, Group Five in Osaka) and in direct communications with Asian Research in London. Upon Miyake's return to Taiwan, we kept in close touch, and whatever information she sent me, I forwarded to AI-London. Miyake eventually became the main source for Taiwan human rights information and contacts not only for AI, but also the Osaka-based ICDHRT, and the TPPRA, headquartered in Tokyo with a nation-wide membership. Throughout the seventies, materials from Miyake, all of them translated into English, found their way into the hands of a broad spectrum of individuals and groups abroad, from journalists and diplomats, to scholars and church people.

Unknown to all but a few dozen people in Taiwan, and another few dozen outside, Miyake was the channel, our undercover source, the one whose identity we went to great pains to hide (letter drops, code names for individuals, espionage-style rendezvous). Hundreds getting her information had no idea as to her role. Once received, we put everything into English, and assigned our source this time one alias, that time another, sometimes Chinese, sometimes Korean. Since my own cover was already blown, I could not communicate with her directly. When she wrote from Taiwan, her letters always bore a bogus return address. Instead of writing directly to me, she would address her correspondence to "Quince O'Toole" at OLS, an Osaka advertising and translation agency where I was working a few hours a week. Anything addressed to "Quince" was passed on to me, so I was sure to get it. This method served us well for years.

In her post-martial law writings, Chen Chu dubbed Miyake the "mother of Taiwan human rights." Having been in the thick of the overseas mobilization for support of the human rights struggle in Taiwan throughout the seventies, I might readily concur. Certainly, if any foreigner rightfully deserved the title of "mother," it would have been Miyake, a rock of constancy and compassion throughout the seventies and well into the eighties and nineties (she remains active today). Whether in Taipei, Hong Kong, Tokyo or Osaka, Miyake was a reliable informant.

The establishment of the ICDHRT, in 1974 in Osaka, and the TPPRA, in 1976 in Tokyo, was as much to her credit as to anyone else. In the mid seventies, returning to Japan for one of her periodic visits with her Osaka family, she would come bearing magazines that had been banned, or books, or election fliers. Whenever she came back we would organize a small meeting. At first it was just Kawakubo and I, but with the months and years the circle grew to include Sugihara Toru 杉原達, Karen Smith, Teddy Rothman, Oh Giro, Lin Po-yao 林伯耀, Enatsu Ken'ichi 江夏健一, Nicki

Case Study : Liberating Su Tung-chi

by Lynn Miles

In the early 1960s, second only to the case of Lei Chen case for international notoriety was the Su Tung-chi Case of 1961. One of Lei Chen's "crimes" of the previous year was to link up with local native-born politicians in an attempt to form an opposition party. The venture was stopped in its tracks by the arrest of Lei and the closure of his magazine, *Free China* 自由中國. Among the Taiwanese politicians, Su Tung-chi 蘇東起 had been the most prominent of Lei's confederates.

As a popular county councilor in Yunlin County, Su pressed ahead, bringing a motion to demand Lei's release. Notwithstanding the Kuomintang majority in the county council, the motion passed, winning for Su the everlasting enmity of the authorities. He and his wife were both arrested in September 1961, and the following May he was sentenced to death, later reduced.

In late 1974 Miyake sent out word that prisoner Su was gravely ill. Not content to leave Amnesty International to mount a postcard campaign, Kawakubo and I decided that something public had to be done in Japan. So an organization was hastily cobbled together. we rushed together some translations and dashed up to Tokyo for a press conference, which was very poorly attended, and, as far as we knew, resulted in not one news story. But this began for me a long and ultimately successful effort to establish rapport with reporters in Tokyo, so ranks as an important ICDHRT milestone.

Included in this International Committee launch were Vickie Lo 毛清芬 and Kuo Sue-eh 郭雪娥 (wives of independence leaders 羅福全 and 郭榮桔).

Councilor Su Tung-chi

Sentenced to Death

July 1962 saw the first number of the very well-written and nicely edited English quarterly by Ong Joktik (Wang Yu-teh) 王育得 and colleagues of the group that was ultimately to become the World United Formosans for Independence. The quarterly lasted not a year, but its Japanese counterpart, *Taiwan Chenglian* 台灣青年 continued for over three decades. (Materials on this and following page courtesy of Wu San-lien Taiwan Historical Materials Foundation)

Croghan, and a host of others, always at a coffee shop or restaurant in Namba or Dotombori, where we would be treated to a very thorough briefing on the latest Taipei happenings.

As the circle grew, so did our range of international contacts, so that by the mid-seventies there was a functional network in place making possible the distribution of Miyake's information to far-flung places in what was then record time. By no means was she the exclusive source, and by no means was I the only person outside Taiwan working connections with people inside. Nor does honesty allow me to leave the impression that it all began with the two of us. In my opinion, what we did begin was a consistent channel operating over the span of a decade, for getting information in and out of Taiwan. As our relationship developed, we learned to trust each other: I to trust the correctness of her information as well as the significance she sometimes attached to it, and she to trust that I would put something together quickly in English, and send it out to an ever-expanding mailing list. When the situation warranted, I would send a telex off to AI-London, or to Jim Seymour in New York, or dash up to Tokyo with a satchel full of reports for distributing to the international press hanging out at the Foreign Correspondents' Club.

By 1975 the information network touched by this first, informal coterie spanned the globe. We were mailing scores of people directly, and perhaps reaching thousands indirectly, from new-left activists with strong sympathies for Beijing to US Congressional aides, from Taiwan Independence advocates to Chinese freedom fighters, from graduate students in Hawaii to research assistants in Stockholm, from the Asia Research Department at the London head office of Amnesty International to local AI groups assigned by London to work on the case of a Lin Shuei-chuan 林水泉 here or a Tsai Tsai-yuan 蔡財源 there, from the CBS bureau chief in Hong Kong to the *Newsweek* head office in New York, from dozens of foreign correspondents stationed in Tokyo to the head office of the International Press Institute, from a group called Tapol (meaning "political prisoner" in Indonesian) in London to NACLA (North American Congress on Latin America) in Washington, from a Buddhist social action group in Los Angeles to the offices of the World Board of Missions of the United Methodist Church in New York, from the Center for Society and Religion in Sri Lanka to the Canadian Churches for Global Economic Justice, from the Convent of the Good Samaritan in Nara to the Asian Development Foundation in Melbourne, from small anarchist periodicals produced entirely by volunteer efforts of passionate partisans in Hong Kong to mainstream publishers in Paris. The quest for recent information on political developments affecting human rights in Taiwan was ever-burgeoning.

Although we never had a board of directors or even a publicly named staff, the ICDHRT's reputation spread as we became an authoritative information source. Certainly this was the case with a number of political arrests and incidents between 1976 and 1978 — so much so that our destruction became a priority of the ROC authorities. But by that time, Miyake and family had already been hounded out of Taiwan, and her preeminent role as field reporter was taken over by others, mainly the Americans Dennis Engbarth and Linda Arrigo, who had entered Taiwan in 1976

Lynn Miles

4   Amnesty International Newsletter   June 1973

consultative status with the Organisation of American States. All Groups working for Latin American prisoners should mention this fact when writing to officials.

CHANGES OF ADDRESS: The Austrian Section is now located at A-1170 Wien, Braungasse 45 A, telephone (Section Office) 0222/46 64 715 and (Private - Dr Irmgard Hutter) 0222/46 57 423; Anne-Marie Rodeyns of the Belgian Section is now at 104 Avenue de l'Université, 1050 Brussels, telephone 02/4893 76.

POSTCARDS FOR PRISONERS

FROM PAST CAMPAIGNS

News of four South Vietnamese

Huynh Tan MAM, who was on the *Postcards for Prisoners Campaign* in May 1972, has been included on the list of prisoners to be released to the National Liberation Front. This means that the Saigon Government is classifying him as a communist prisoner, whereas AI considers him to be a non-communist political prisoner.

Thieu Thi TAN and Thieu Thi TAO, the two sisters who were jointly on the Campaign in November 1972, remain in prison. But their mother, arrested last spring for protesting their detention, has been released.

Tran Huu KHUE (February 1973) has been sent from the notorious prison camp on Con Son Island back to the National Prison in Saigon. His deportation from the latter last summer brought an AI letter of protest from Secretary General MARTIN ENNALS to President NGUYEN VAN THIEU because of Mr Khue's frail state of health.

THIS MONTH'S CAMPAIGN

Jiri MULLER, *Czechoslovakia*

Jiri Muller, aged about 30, is a prominent left-winger but not a member of the Communist Party. He was arrested in November 1971 in Brno and tried in Prague in July 1972, charged with subversion of the Republic. He was sentenced to 5½ years' imprisonment. He suffers from a chronic gall bladder complaint, acute nervous disorder and failing eyesight.

Jiri Muller was an official in the Union of Czechoslovak Youth (University students section) and a pioneer of reforms in the student movement as early as 1965. In reprisal he was expelled from the youth union and the Technical University in Prague in 1966. In 1967 he was interned for seventeen

vakia; *and to:* Dr Jan Nemec, Minister of Justice, Praha-Nove Mesto, Vysehradska 16, Czechoslovakia.

The cards should refer to Article IXd of the amnesty of February 25 1973, under which the President was to reconsider cases of seriously ill prisoners.

SU Tung-chi, *Taiwan*

Su Tung-chi's arrest was one of a large number made in Taiwan in 1961 as a result of the Lei Chen affair. Lei Chen is a well-known mainland Chinese living in Taiwan who, seeking to reform and liberalise the political atmosphere there, tried to form a new opposition in Taiwan. In March 1961, elections were held in Taiwan and, as predicted, the Nationalist Party won an overwhelming victory.

As a result, Lei and his followers founded a "Society for the Discussion of Better Elections" which publicly criticised the government. After a brief lull, Lei and three of his colleagues were arrested. Lei was sentenced to 10 years' imprisonment and the others to lesser terms. Soon afterwards a number of public figures, who were probably seen by the government as potential opposition leaders, were detained. One of these was a young Taiwanese named Su Tung-chi who had come forward to sign a petition seeking clemency for Lei.

Su was from a well-known family in the Yun-lin district of Taiwan, a graduate of Meiji University in Japan and a very popular leader in his home area. He had held several appointive posts and had been elected repeatedly to local government office despite apparent Nationalist opposition.

In September 1961 Su's home was raided by security officers and both he and his wife were arrested, although she was eventually released. Su was found guilty by a military court of having twice plotted rebellion and was sentenced to death. This was commuted subsequently to life imprisonment. There is, however, no evidence to suggest that these charges have any foundation, and it is believed that Su was sentenced merely for his criticism of Lei's imprisonment.

Please send courteously-worded cards appealing for his release to: Generalissimo Chiang Kai-shek, President of the Republic of China, President's Office, Taipei, Taiwan; *and to:* Chiang Ching-kuo, Prime Minister of the Republic of China, Executive Yuan, Taipei, Taiwan.

Charlton NGCEBETSHA, *Rhodesia*

Charlton Ngcebetsha is a leading member of the non-violent African National Council, founded to oppose the proposed Anglo-Rhodesian settlement terms. He is one of six ANC leaders arrested earlier this year to curb the movement's influence. On his arrest he was taken to Que Que Prison where he is still believed held. He is an elderly man with a long-standing heart condition and Que Que is reportedly one of the worst prisons in Rhodesia. Recently his health has been causing concern. *Please send courteously-worded cards appealing for his release or transfer on humanitarian grounds to:* The Minister of Law and Order, The Hon. D. Lardner-Burke, Private Bag 704, Causeway, Salisbury, Rhodesia.

Published in London by the International Secretariat, the 4-page *Amnesty International Newsletter* featured a "Postcards for Prisoners" campaign each month. The three prisoners selected for special attention were always one each from communist, capitalist and unaligned countries. The July 1973 campaign was based on information supplied by Miyake. Su Tung-chi was released in 1976. (Courtesy of Wu San-lien Taiwan Historical Materials Center)

and 1977, respectively.

There were others who stepped in to fill the breach, like Helen Chauncey and Kathleen Kearny in Taiwan, Jim Seymour in New York, and Denis Wong in Hong Kong, who kept in close touch with me in the Osaka office. Step by step we became better connected to an ever-widening circle of friends in Taiwan who were showing an interest in sharing our agenda. A piece of breaking information might come to us on one occasion from a foreign student passing through Osaka on his or her way home from having spent a couple of years of study in Taipei, and another from a reporter just back from a quick visit there.

Among the boxes of Taiwan human rights files that gathered decades of post-seventies dust, first in my Osaka apartment, then on a farm in New Jersey, then in a Connecticut garage, then in a San Gabriel, California garage, there is one which I labeled "The Team." It contains the files, each of them with a red flap, with the name of the "agent in the field" who was supplying the information. Red-tagging of the file of our informants began in 1974 or 1975, when there were only a few of them, and was designed so that we could locate and pull them quickly in the event of an emergency requiring quick evacuation from the Ashiya apartment (we were thinking more along the lines of a fire than of a police raid). Protecting sources was the sine qua non of a successful human rights campaign that relied on trusted contacts. Everyone involved was quite aware that sources were precious, so we took elaborate security measures, covering where possible all traces of the means by which we kept informed. Were we to surrender our cloak of secrecy, with it would go our sources, after the precedents of Thornberry, Abe, Ricketts and myself.

This collection of informants and activists accumulated through a decade of intensive international human rights work; it often approached the level of elaborate protocol that you might expect from a large, well-established bureaucracy long engaged in espionage. Perhaps the fitting metaphor for the ICDHRT was that of laundromat, much like the way in which money goes in and comes out without leaving a trace as to its origins. Or even better, the backstage dressing room, where reports came in the back door in the middle of the night, had telltale references excised, certain identities masked and otherwise dressed up for the stage. As a result, many anonymous tips went out into the world with the "International Committee for the Defense of Human Rights in Taiwan" on the letterhead. Attribution in most cases impossible, the ICDHRT became the authority of last resort, where actually it was at first Miyake and later a few others within Taiwan, all of whom needed to keep their association with ICDHRT secret, who deserve the real credit. They were the unsung heroes.

Ronin Consumes Me, Miyake Steps in

In the few years between 1972, when I first met her, and 1975, when Taiwan work came to take nearly all of my non-remunerative, non-family time, there was just Miyake-san, making her once- or twice-annual trips back to Tokyo and Osaka, meeting me at a restaurant or coffeeshop, and filling me in on the latest scuttlebutt. I got the impression, correct or not, that I was one among many of the people she was

Lynn 076.01-031

LIST OF TAIWAN POLITICAL PRISONERS (

Legend to the list appears at bottom of list. Where asterisk appears in any entry, please consult that n

	NAME	PROV-INCE	AGE	OCCUPATION	DATE AND AGENCY OF ARREST		CHARGE		details
1.	Yang Tzu-chieh	D	42	Retired military personnel	—	—	2/3		
2.	Juan Kuei-yao	F	43		—	—	5		
3.	Ch'iao Heng-wei	D	54	Menial, Legislative Yüan	—	—	5		
4.	Li Ta-en	B	56	Chief, Tainan tax office	—	—	5		
5.	Wang Yü-an	F	38	Publisher, Cheng Yen Publishing Co.	CFC	69.6.30	7		
6.	Shen Ch'iu-ho	F	48	Proprietor, Pai Ch'eng Book Store	—	—	5		
7.	Ch'iu Yen-liang	E	28	Student, NTU* Dept of Archeology	SS	1968.6	2/3		
8.	Wang Chia-fah	E	40		—	1954	7		
9.	Chang Yüan-lung	D	46	Restaurant proprietor	FBI	62.7.16	2/1		
10.	Fan Ken-ts'ai	C	46	Taiwan bank	—	—	5		
11.	Hua Ch'un-lin	D	—	Retired military personnel	FBI	68.5.7	7		
12.	Ch'en Ch'i-mao	B	—	Trading house	—	—	5 (2/1)		
13.	Wang Che-hsiung	H	—	Colonel, regimental vice-commander	FBI	1961	2/3		
14.	Chang P'ei-hung	A	—		—	—	7		
15.	Sun Yü-p'u	D	—	Police officer	PD	1965	5		
16.	Chou Hsia	I	—	Retired captain	FBI	1960	2/3		
17.	Chou Li-chün	—	—	Sec'y, Materials Sect, KMT Cent. Com.	—	—	5		
18.	Lin Hsin-chao	A	—		—	—	2/3		
19.	Ching Kuo-shu	M	—	Reporter	—	—	5		
20.	Ho P'	L	—	Special Commissioner, Chin Ting	—	—	2/1		
21.	Tang Hsi-ling	A	54		FBI	1969.4	7		
22.	Cheng T'ien-yü	B	54	Sec'y, Keelung Municipal Assembly	FBI	1968.9	2/1		
23.	Ch'i Jung-pao	A	—	Student	—	—	7		
24.	Hung Ch'ing-po	B	—	Farmer from the mainland	—	—	2/3		
25.	Su Yung-nien	E	51	Retired captain & education officer	FBI	1961	2/1		
26.	Hsu Mo-kuang	B	—	Deckhand from Hong Kong	—	—	2/1		
27.	Chang Wei-kuang	C	—	Police officer	—	—	2/1		
28.	Lin Feng		—	Teacher (Chin Ting)	—	—	7		12yr
29.	Ch'i Sheng-kang	H	20	Student (Huwei High School)	—	—	7	Listened to [mainland] broadcasts	12yr
30.	Lo Chen-hsiang	E	—	Craftsman of rattan ware	FBI	—	2/1	Took part Red labor union	12yr
31.	Ch'en K'un-shan	A	32	Accountant	PD	—	2/3	Plotted Taiwan Independence	12yr
32.	Liu Chin-shih	A	37	Tanner	PD	—	2/3	Participated in WUFI*	10yr
33.	Yu Ch'ien-ch'ang	A	—	Student, Yüan Lin H.S.	—	—	7		4yr
34.	Huang Chien-jung	A	34	Naval officer	—	—	2/3	Plotted Taiwan Independence	10yr
35.	Ch'en Hsien-teh	A	38	Primary school teacher	—	—	2/3	Plotted Taiwan Independence	5yr
36.	Huang Tong-fang	A	22	Reserve military prison guard	TGC	1969.6	—	Passed letters for jailed F.I. elements	5yr
37.	Cheng Ming-kao	A	—	Primary school teacher	—	—	7	Discontented with status quo	5yr
38.	Chang-yang Ch'ing-li	A	—	Pork seller	—	—	7	Crime 25 years ago	5yr
39.	Tai Jung-teh	A	—	Hydroelectrical engineer	FBI	1968.4	7	Discontented with status quo	7yr
40.	Lin Yung-sheng	A	—	Student, Tamkang College of Arts	SS	—	2/3	Taiwan Independence plot (*Pi Chien Hui*)	5yr
41.	Lo Tzu-huan	A	23	Student, Shih Chieh Tech.	SS	1969.6	2/3	Taiwan Independence plot (*Pi Chien Hui*)	5yr
42.	Li Yi-yi	A	33	Merchant	—	—	2/3	Plotted Taiwan Independence	5yr
43.	Wu Yi-nan	A	—	Naval reserve officer	—	—	2/3	Plotted Taiwan Independence	5yr
44.	Liao Teng-chu	A	32	Electrical engineer	SS	—	2/3	Plotted Taiwan Independence	10yr
45.	Hsieh Jung-chou	A	21	Lumber yard business	PD	—	7	Criticized the Kuomintang	4myr
46.	Chang Tzu-yü	A	40	Worker, textile factory	—	—	7	Discontented with status quo	5yr
47.	Lin T'ien-che	A	—	Tailor	—	—	2/1	Took part Red organization	5yr
48.	Wu Yao-chung	A	34	Ass't prof, Professional College of Arts	SS	—	2/3	Ch'en Yung-shan Case [Taiwan Independence]	10yr
49.	Lo Wen-sung	A	34	Advertising	FBI	—	7	Criticized the Kuomintang	7yr
50.	Chan Hsing-wang	A	45	Village elder (*li chang*)	—	1967	5	Disrupted elections	6yr
51.	Fang Jung-huei	A	28	Teacher	—	—	7	Discontented with status quo	4yr
52.	Ch'en Yu-hsi	A	32	Student abroad (America)	SS	1968.9	7 (2/1)	Issued leftist treatise in Japan	7yr
53.	Kao Po-tso	A	42	Doctor, mountain highlands	—	1969	5	Mtn Highland Youth Corps (anti-KMT group)	12yr
54.	Kao A-ming	A	40	Primary school teacher	—	1969	5	Mtn Highland Youth Corps (anti-KMT group)	12yr
55.	Ku Shih-chi	C	43	Accountant	FBI	60.10.5	2/1	Implicated in Feb. 28 [1947] Incident	12yr
56.	Yeh Chiang-shuei	A	50	Worker, Kaohsiung Steel Works	—	1960.12	5	Implicated in Feb. 28 Incident	10yr
57.	Yeh Ch'eng-hsiang	A	54	Worker, Kaohsiung Steel Works	—	1960.12	5	Implicated in Feb. 28 Incident	10yr
58.	Yü Chi-ten	A	44	Census taker, ward office	—	1960.12	5	Implicated in Feb. 28 Incident	10yr
59.	Sun Jung-ts'an	A	44	Laborer	—	1960.12	5	Implicated in Feb. 28 Incident	10yr
60.	Ou-yang Mi	C	56	—	FBI	1965.12	5	Escaped from communist-held territory	5yr

Reprinted from RONIN

Detailed Prisoner Information Reaches the Outside

The list compiled in prison by Tsai Tsai-yuan 蔡財源 was passed to Hsieh Tsung-min 謝聰敏, who in turn got it to AI shortly before his February 1971 arrest. It was published in *Ronin* No. 8 in late 1972. (Photo of Tsai by Tsao Chin-jung 曹欽榮. Chinese list courtesy of Dr. Chen Wen-cheng Memorial Foundation. *Ronin* courtesy of Wu San-lien Historical Materials Foundation.)

Lynn Miles

contacting in hopes that we could broadcast her information far and wide. She and I agreed that human rights violations in Taiwan would need a big boost in international attention before there could be any hope of things changing for the better. The fight for truth and justice in Taiwan was doomed to a futile battle unless the international conscience could be roused in support.

Our working relationship developed by fits and starts. At first I was little more than Miyake's frontier way-station and translating service. Beyond that, there was little else that I could do (or would do, so immersed was I in the *Ronin* editorial and distribution work). With the first four issues that were produced in *Ronin*'s first year, the vast bulk of the work being done involved just David Boggett, Nonaka Noriko and me. Noriko was a young Japanese volunteer who was surviving somehow on the income from occasional translation work. She seemingly had limitless time, energy and passion to devote to the *Ronin* project. She stayed until Boggett, who tolerated her amorous advances up to a point (patiently, I thought), finally decided that his love for *Ronin* would have to take precedence over hers for him. She left after a tearful, acrimonious episode, but within a year was on friendly terms with him again.

There went our main typist, a big loss, since Boggett, who typed with two fingers, and not near so accurately or quickly as Noriko, had only me to rely on now, while a good part of my time was taken up teaching and being a poor partner for Fujiko. For most of *Ronin*'s life, Boggett (we all called him "Boggett," not "Dave" or "David") and I were the entire magazine staff. I played a far subordinate role, which I was still straining mightily to keep anonymous, not only in hopes that I could return to Taiwan some day soon but also in hopes of hiding my involvement from the Japanese authorities. Boggett was out and around, spending his time chain-smoking cigarettes and drinking too much coffee and too much beer as he hobnobbed with stellar lefties and academic heavies. It was he who collared the contributing writers, ranging from American reporters and illustrators to Korean poets and Japan-born Korean columnists.

He was a hot item. Although he and I had arrived in Japan at about the same time, within a year he was well ahead of me in spoken Japanese, forging ahead and damn the consequences (which were occasionally funny, sometimes frustrating) while I hung back, afraid. He was boldly going ahead, while I was forever seeing problems seemingly insurmountable. If he saw a problem, he would step right up to meet it head-on and without hesitation, while I had barely begun to mull it over in my brain. I was the stay-at-home intellectual, he the activist par excellence, constantly on the move, tirelessly enlisting new comrades.

That he should be so frolicking and fancy-free, so able to jump up and take off for Tokyo or Seoul or Hong Kong at a moment's notice, was for me a matter of no small envy. His language ability, or more precisely his ability to command attention in spite of his language ability, was another, as was the quickness with which he could penetrate the workings of Japanese society. It also stunned me that he could operate so openly, and without a care for what the authorities might want to do. In Japan he touted his concern over repression in Korea in the most public way, all the while

The New Missionaries

by Jack Hasegawa

> *We called the ICDHRT-organized trips to Taiwan "missions," and the people who performed them "missionaries." Think "Mission Impossible" and you get the picture – strictly undercover. Have spy pen, will travel. Contacts were limited to former prisoners, prisoners' friends and loved ones, in-country foreigners with connections like Miyake Kiyoko and Dennis Engbarth, reporters long resident in Taiwan like Dirk Bennett and Bud Pratt, and those few natives brave enough to consort with foreigners, like Dr. Tien Chao-ming 田朝明 and Chen Ku-ying 陳鼓應. Then there were the in-the-open missions performed by AI. In September 1973, we had word from Miyake that Hsieh's case was going to be retried, and the IS agreed to forego the usual London briefing and allow Jack Hasegawa to go directly from Japan (see pp. 164-170).*

I remember arriving in Taipei with a small suitcase, a large briefcase, and a great deal of anxiety. I thought that my American passport would protect me from arrest or imprisonment. Deportation was the only thing I really feared. Early deportation or denial of entry into Taiwan would have meant that I would not be allowed to try to find Mr. Hsieh, or learn anything about his whereabouts or condition....

Potential contacts were telephoned on my behalf by people whom I might plausibly meet in my role as a college professor and former missionary....

While I remember very little about the individuals I met, or what we talked about, I remember vividly the oppressive weight of fear. I was, and remain, a naïve and trusting person. I had little experience of secret meetings, identifying or evading government "tails," or copying down whispered addresses or telephone numbers while pretending to do something else. In fact, my experience in the civil rights movement and community organizing was exactly the opposite.... Everything in Taipei was on the most micro level possible: one quick meeting, yielding the name of one other person; one person giving one telephone number or one piece of information. Every meeting was fraught with real danger, more than I fully appreciated while I was there, even after the many briefings I had received in Japan. It is not fully possible to understand how frightening life in a police state can be if you have never actually lived in one. Even at its height, in the US the racist violence by Southern law enforcement officers was relatively open. As frightening as it was, it remained within the framework of American law and operated within the arena of American public opinion.... In Taiwan, the fear was more paralyzing, perhaps because much of the violence was hidden.....

I tried to be at the door of whatever office I had chosen for the day when it opened. I went first to the Ministry of Justice. That visit established the pattern that I encountered day after day, office after office. There was a long wait, while someone was located who could speak English. That person, almost always a well-dressed young man, gave me tea and crackers, and asked how he could help. Once I explained my desire to see

brushing aside considerations that his behavior would likely get him black-listed in Korea. As for Japan, he thought that his high visibility would force the immigration authorities to tread lightly, for fear that his ouster might stir up a fuss. He practically dared them to take him on, thinking that his friends would rally to his corner if he were ever so rudely treated by the Japanese authorities.

Boggett was also the consummate showman, to which was added a small measure of the con man. He enjoyed pumping things up, dramatizing them. And he could hustle contributions, without which we could not even dream of continuing as a magazine. The contributions poured in, as articles and artwork, and as money. He really knew how to put the collar on a potential contributor. All these things and more I envied in him. At times I resented them, too, since they only reminded me of how tied down I was by teaching and earning the wherewithal to sustain a family.

By October 1972, *Ronin*, originally intended as a monthly, had come out with seven issues in its first year. By the third issue, Boggett had had enough of the time-consuming method of our own typed input and paste-up, and had raised money enough to cover professional typesetting. We still had the paste-up to do, but now our *modus operandi* was more by the book. Freed of the chore of typing and retyping each line that took up so much production time, we could devote more energy to the other facets of running a radical rag on a shoestring.

A number of political developments rocked East Asia in 1972, not least among them the shocking suicide as political statement by Mishima Yukio 三島由紀夫, and the declaration of martial law in the Philippines and South Korea. With the geographical compass of *Ronin* 's concerns so blatantly declared in graphic terms right on our masthead (a small map bounded by latitudes 20 and 50 degrees north, and longitudes 93 and 143 degrees east), Boggett felt that we could not ignore these dark developments, and busily went about soliciting articles from activists in each of those countries. By October we had articles from Japan, Okinawa, Korea, Taiwan and the Philippines, from such contributors as Oda Makoto 小田實, the reform-minded Filipino legislator Bonifacio Gillego, and Korean truth-to-power poet Kim Chi Ha 金芝河, each of them having achieved fame and popular following in their homelands for having championed justice for the oppressed, each of them virtually ignored by the mainstream media outside their own countries.

Of *Ronin* 's first seven issues, the second and third were the only ones carrying anything about Taiwan, with pieces on and by Hsieh Tsung-min and Lee Ao respectively. The vast majority of the material in all seven issues was from and about Korea, a good part of it supplied by a young aspiring journalist named Norman Thorpe, whom Boggett had befriended in Seoul and who had gone in with him on the *Ronin* project from the beginning. By late 1972 I was feeling glad to be a part of a bona fide albeit ragtag magazine with a growing reputation in academic, intellectual and activist circles. At the same time I had long since begun chafing at the humble station of my anonymous role. My status had degenerated to that of mere office manager. Our peripatetic editor was not really to blame for this; rather it was the fact that I was tied down by family and job. My time being so limited, it bothered me

Hseih Tsung-min, and to receive permission to observe his trial, I was asked to wait, while my new friend went to see what could be done to help me. On the first day, and in every subsequent visit, my "friend" returned crestfallen to say that Mr. Hsieh was not in custody by this agency, and that he had not been able to find any information about him. Perhaps I should try the city prosecutor's office, since that would be the place where records would be kept if Mr. Hsieh had been arrested on a criminal charge. Sometimes the person helping me would even offer to go with me to the next place, and act as my interpreter.... [T]he result was always the same. Nobody knew anything about Mr. Hsieh's current location or about any upcoming trial. I don't think anyone, over the several days of this search, denied knowing who Mr. Hsieh was, but, for all his fame, no one was able to help me find him.... Finally, one of the hapless men assigned to deal with me said that he would give me a note to someone at a higher level, back at another ministry, the one that would be surely able to help. He told me to take a cab, and that the cab driver would know where to go.

When I got in the cab, the cabbie took the piece of paper, and drove off. When I didn't respond to his query in Chinese, he looked in the rearview mirror and switched to Japanese, which he spoke quite fluently. My Japanese was not as good as his, and he sometimes had trouble understanding me. He asked whom I was going to see at this next building. I said that I was to see the person mentioned in the note. He said that there was no name, just the name of the ministry, and its address. He asked why I was going there, since foreigners did not often go to this place. When I told him why I was in Taipei, and what I wanted to do, he pulled over to the curb.... This anonymous taxi cab driver explained that the civilian government would have no involvement in a case of political protest, like the case of Hsieh Tsung-min, who was quite famous. He said I should go to the military headquarters if I really wanted to find out anything....

When I was finally deposited outside of the appropriate building, I went in to find a front desk that looked much like a police headquarters. There was a long counter across the room with benches near the doors and uniformed men working at desks behind the counter. I presented my passport and asked the uniformed man who stepped up to see what I wanted if he could speak English. He said, in English, "Wait there," and pointed to the benches. I sat down, but was very shortly joined by a tough-looking major. He spoke English very fluently with a slight southern accent....

When I asked if he knew where Mr. Hsieh was being held, he replied without hesitation that "Mr. Hsieh is in our custody." While I don't remember the details of what he said, he made it clear that Mr. Hsieh was under investigation as a threat to national security, and that the investigation would continue for as long as necessary. There was no tea, and no smiles. In fact, I don't think we ever left the benches by the doors, to go into an inner office. The major was polite but blunt. He said there was no trial scheduled, and that there was therefore no reason to ask for observer status. When I asked to see Mr. Hsieh, the answer was a simple "No." When I asked if there was anyone else who might give permission, I got the same impassive "No." After some further discussion, the major said that I could write a note to Mr. Hsieh, and ask any questions that I wished, and that he would deliver it.... When I finished my note, and he had read it, he stood up and said "Come back tomorrow," and left. I don't think I saw him again. When I came back the next day, I was handed a letter at the desk. I think it was in Chinese, and I think it was in some kind of official envelope, but these details are really lost to me now.

Jack Hasegawa

that the thousand editing chores left me no time for researching Taiwan and working materials into publishable shape. If Korea was Boggett's beat, Taiwan was mine, but I was getting very little information into print, mainly owing to the sporadic and fragmentary nature of what little hard news I was able to get. I was beginning to see the gains for the Taiwan authorities in sending international critics into lasting exile.

In the meantime, Boggett's commendable success in catapulting not only *Ronin* but himself into the public spotlight reaped the predictable reward. Once he left Japan, he discovered that not only was he *persona non grata* in South Korea, but he had worn out his welcome in Japan as well. He therefore set his sights on Hong Kong, where he determined to set up a legal presence on the cheap through a barrister friend who had volunteered his services. By registering *Ronin* in Hong Kong, he would keep it safe from the censors in Tokyo and Seoul.

While all this was going on, Miyake was making her repeated homecomings. With each return to Osaka, where she had grown up, she would call me up, and we would get together for coffee, while she updated me on Taiwan human rights developments. Her main contact was Hsieh Tsung-min's sister, Hsiu-mei, who was defiant and daring in the face of authority and could speak fluent Japanese. Since nothing concerning Taiwan issues had appeared in *Ronin* for over half a year, Miyake's gentle but ceaseless prodding was enough to put me into a lasting funk over my failure to help propagate the tidings of repression in the country we both loved and ached to see liberated from the Chiang despots.

At long last, I woke up. I could see that to Miyake I was probably beginning to sound like some of the rejection letters that I had once received when trying to get material about Taiwan published elsewhere. As I have explained, *Ronin* had come about precisely because this kind of information was not reaching the public. The dictatorships in Seoul, Taipei, Manila, Djakarta, Singapore, Kuala Lumpur and Saigon all depended on Washington for sustenance. The fact that they were threatening, beating, disappearing, executing, imprisoning, torturing, assassinating, raping and otherwise abusing their own people was kept from the American public. *Ronin* had been founded on the notion that this informational void had to be filled.

Ronin's State-of-Siege Report and Prisoner List

With the seventh issue behind us and Boggett's imminent return looking not very likely, I finally gave notice that I would be unable to keep up the pace until I got some Taiwan materials together. Boggett was sympathetic, for there was no getting around the fact that I was a part-time volunteer, nothing more. So he gave the eighth issue to me. It was my baby, cover to cover.

Entitled, "State of Siege in Taiwan, the 23rd Year," the issue's main feature was the list of 214 political prisoners that Tsai Tsai-yuan 蔡財源 had compiled for Hsieh Tsung-min, who had forwarded Amnesty International's request for information into political prisoners being held at the Chingmei Detention Center run by the Taiwan Garrison Command. Giving name, province, age, occupation, date and agency of arrest, charge, actual offense, and sentence and date of sentencing, it was, according

I made notes each day on what I remembered for the report I was to submit to Amnesty International on my return. I also tried to find places to put sensitive information. I knew that others had carried letters in their shoes or stuffed into the linings of their suitcases, so I tried to find places that had not been tried so often. I left a few days later with all of my notes written on the inside of my necktie, which I had opened up and then re-stitched with the little sewing kit provided by the hotel! Mr. Hsieh's letter and the other information I had managed to gather was given, along with my report to the Amnesty International chapter. I later heard that they had been able to obtain medical attention for Mr. Hsieh, and to get medicine to him.

Ennals had sent letters not only to Chiang Ching-kuo, but also to the ministers of justice and defense, perhaps in anticipation of an orgy of buck-passing. It did not matter. To the last, everyone professed ignorance of any such communication. Finally the trail led to the Garrison Command, where Colonel Tseng Chuan-you told Jack to write a formal letter.

Jack Hasegawa

to *Ronin*'s companion piece, "not unlike a number of other lists that have successfully made it out of Taiwan at great risk to their bearers," but was "the first list having such telling detail and comprehensiveness to find its way into publication."

The accompanying "Suppressing the Rebellion" was basically a column-by-column analysis of the list's contents. For example:

> Age. Of the 174 victims whose age is given, the average age is 39.1 years. A breakdown by province and age yields interesting results: the average age of those hailing from Fukien and Kiangsu (51.3 and 51.2 years) is ten years higher than the average for all provinces, while the average Taiwanese is ten years younger (33.6). Of the 45 people listed in their twenties, no less than 42 are Taiwanese; of the 33 listed in their thirties, 30 are Taiwanese.

The section looking at "law under which charged" offered supporting material, mostly mined and translated from various sections of the ROC law books. "36% of the 214 cases" were tried under Article Two Paragraph One of the Statute for Punishment of the Rebellion, one of "the most stringent and commonly used laws presently on the books; this law makes the death sentence mandatory." My high school English teacher would have red-marked the passage for syntactic failings, but hopefully would have left unscathed the introduction that the "editorial we" gave to the Taiwan Garrison Command,

> an organization staffed primarily by military officers personally selected from the upper echelons of the ROC's military apparatus by Chiang Ching-kuo during his tenure as Defense Minister. Although originally conceived as a branch of the Ministry of Defense and subject to the conventional checks of civilian control, it is generally known that in the last decade or so it has come to enjoy an autonomous status all its own and is said to now answer to no one but Premier Chiang Ching-kuo. Through a series of purges, personnel transfers, forced retirements, and even executions (some of which appear in the list), Chiang has forged Taiwan's version of the KGB into an apparatus extremely loyal to him. Indeed...the Taiwan Garrison Command became, with Chiang's ascension to the Minister of Defense slot, his main power base, from which he began to build and consolidate his position while terrorizing his political rivals and eliminating their power through intimidation and coercion. One can imagine the immensity of the TGC's power when it is remembered that all political trials are conducted in secret by a military tribunal under the TGC, where one may be accused and convicted of crimes committed decades ago on the mainland or on Taiwan before the Nationalist takeover.

Today this summary impresses me as being not especially illuminating about the modus operandi of the TGC. To the extent that it glosses over other Chiang Ching-kuo relations that developed on his path to the apex of ROC power, it is misleading as well. And willfully so, I think, considering that at the time the lines were written I was already aware of the story, well-circulated in Taiwan when I was last there in 1971, that Chiang had been seen walking around with *The Intellectual* in his pocket as signal of quiet endorsement. That the Prince had ultimate recourse to means of brutal and terrifying force, and that on occasion he made use of such means, cannot be denied, but gentle suasion was not unknown to him. Such subtle complexities did not exist

Report from the Other Side

by Karen Smith

At any given time, the ICDHRT had an activist core, largely made up of young people, who did the nuts-and-bolts work. They were mostly Americans and Japanese, but beyond that one could not say much about them, because their identities had to remain secret in order for them to be able to travel to and from Taiwan. One such was Karen Smith, who, taking a year off from Yale University, landed for the first time in Taiwan in September 1972 for a year of advanced language study. She revisited in 1975, after passing through Japan and meeting me, at which time she indicated an interest in using some of the contacts that I gave her, and agreeing to act as a go-between. In 1975 she took up residence in Kyoto, and thereafter put in many hours interviewing, writing, editing, typesetting, and any number of other chores that constituted the daily work of a small organization working on a shoestring and with no paid staff.

*Both editions of **A Tortured Silence** contained her translations, and both were typeset between the two of us.*

In late 1976 she ventured to Taiwan again, this time with definite ICDHRT items on her agenda. She met with Chen Ku-ying, Dr. Tien, Hsieh Hsiu-mei, and a number of released political prisoners, and queried them extensively about people still inside, people trying to get out, people suffering serious disabilities, and other information pertaining to the prisoners. Her reports immediately became some of the most detailed available anywhere in any language for that time. Until her departure from Japan two years later, she continued to be one of ICDHRT's more active activists.

Reports like the one below, excerpted from a typed draft based on notes that Karen was able to safely bring out in January 1967, were the raw material of Amnesty International case documents. As with with much of the reporting done by Miyake Kiyoko from 1972 to 1976, some of Karen's earlier work went into the AI Country Report on Taiwan in October 1976 - LM

During the 1947-50 period the KMT had no power to pacify the island. They were plagued by conflicting factions and guerillas on the inside and the ever-continuing threat of a mainland invasion from the outside. But once the US entered the Korean War, finally ensuring support of the KMT regime with the Seventh Fleet and CIA training, the KMT could forget its fear of external threats and concentrate on wiping out all internal dissension. Thus US policy to make Taiwan an instrument against Red China gave the KMT a free hand within Taiwan.

So many were killed around 1950 that it's impossible to count. Many people, once arrested, were never heard from again. 1950 equals if not exceeds the slaughter of 2/28, with at least another 10,000 killed. However, in one way 1950 was much more

in a *Ronin* world populated by heroes and villains, and precious few (if any) complex characters in between. This was propaganda war, with *Ronin* siding with "the people" in their struggle against the dictators and their imperial masters.

If this style of journalism did not rise above the level of hyperbolic editorializing, at least *Ronin* was true to the list as originally constructed, and readers so inclined could draw their own conclusions from it. This is more than could be said of the list's presentation by the monthly *Taiwan Chenglian* editors, who divided it into two sections, one made up of native-born Taiwanese, the other mainlanders. Was it that they could brook no placing of the word "Taiwan" in a column titled "province?" Or was it that they wanted to make the point that native Taiwanese victims of the repression outnumbered their China-born prison mates? With the *Ronin* presentation, the reader would have seen beyond the opposition to the Chiang family came from all quarters, while the accompanying analytical piece made the TI point that Taiwanese predominated among the political prisoner population.

Filling the rest of the eighth issue's sixteen pages, the human-interest story of Po Yang demonstrated that the definition of "thought crime" according to these draconian laws knew no bounds. After carrying out the letter to him from Lee Ao in 1968, I had been in occasional contact with Dr. Sun Kuan-han, Po Yang's public defender abroad. A Westinghouse engineer living in Pittsburgh, he offered a wealth of material, including a long letter from Po Yang, written on the eve of his 4 March 1968 arrest.

In addition to the usual thousand copies of the magazine, we had our printer run off another thousand copies of poster-sized sheets of just the list, mailing bulk copies to AI and other NGOs, a batch to the Foreign Correspondents Club in Tokyo, a bunch to foreign reporters in Hong Kong, as well as to religious and human rights organizations in the States. And some of them we smuggled back into Taiwan.

And now the stage was set for me, *Ronin*'s printed contraband in hand, to try my luck as cub courier. When I had last left Taiwan in 1971, I was given "special treatment" during the "exit informalities," but my visa had been left in my passport, unmolested by "canceled" stamps. The visa soon expired of its own, however, so when I was biding my time in Seoul waiting for my Japanese visa, I used the opportunity to apply for a new ROC tourist visa. Good for multiple visits and valid for four years, that it was granted without a hitch I took as a hopeful sign: still off the blacklist, I was as yet free to come and go to Taiwan.

But I could not be sure. Just having the visa did not ensure entry. Deciding to put the visa to the test in December 1972, just days after *Ronin* number 8 came out, I postponed distribution of the issue until after I had returned to Japan. I could only hope that the KMT spies in Japan had not picked up on my editorial progeny.

Fears that I might have been found out were given added impetus by Boggett's and my occasional coffeehouse conversations with one Michael Chang 張景齡. Michael's official status in Japan was "student," as he was enrolled in a bona fide Osaka institution of higher learning — Kansai University, I believe it was. He contacted Boggett after reading about *Ronin* in the *Sankei Shimbun*, the fifth largest newspaper

ruthless, for 1950 marked the KMT's intent to completely wipe out all threats to its power, Communist or otherwise. According to the head of a detention center at that time, up to 8000 people were kept in that one detention center at any one time; with 16 to 20 people in a small room there wasn't room for everyone to sit down, and prisoners divided themselves into three rotating shifts of standing, sitting and leaning. Every night, under an infamous bridge in Yungho south of Taipei, truckloads of people were taken out and shot. Residents could hear the gun-shots through the night. At that time, if you were given "only" a life sentence, you were congratulated.

This might have been case aside as history long past, except that people arrested in the furor of that time are still in prison, wasting away, serving life sentences. Many of these men were imprisoned in their early twenties, and have now spent half their lives in prison, forgotten by the world.

For example, in the 1950 Matou Cast, named after the Tainan village of that name, 33 people were taken and convicted of being Communist and plotting with Communists. Some actually were Communists — but some were not. Convictions were based on reading Communist literature or simply knowing those who did — guilt by association. Most were farmers working at a local sugar factory. Three were executed: Hsieh Chang Jen 謝常仁, Tsai Kuo-li 蔡國禮, and Chang Mu 張木. Of those given life sentences, Li Kuo-min 李國民 was beaten insane; Chen Shui-chuan 陳水權 is suffering from a serious heart ailment; Lin Shu-yang 林書揚 has anemia and hemorrhoids, 50-year-old Lin Chin-mu 林金木 has gastric ulcers; 49-year-old Yang Chin-hui 王金輝 is in satisfactory health; the situations of the remaining four are unknown and they could well have already died in prison: Huang A-hua 黃阿華, Chung Yi 鐘益, Tsai Jung-shou 菜榮守 and Sun Ching-kao 孫清誥.

In a similar 1950 case, in Taichung, in central Taiwan, 63 people were convicted, of whom seven sere executed: Chang Po-che 張伯哲, Chen Fu-tien 陳福添, Teng Hsi-cheng 鄧錫章, Li Ping-kun 李炳崑, Chen Meng-teh 陳孟德, Li Chi-jen 李繼仁 and Chien

A tortured silence

The silence is being broken by a few brave souls so that others may discover Taiwan's under side—the one not shown in travel posters, the one of pain and torture and endless years spent in prison.

To the outside world, the Taiwan government trys to present the "Ihla Formosa" of the travel posters: serenity, peace and quiet, mist-shrouded mountain-sides, farmers patiently plowing their fields with water buffalo, children playing in streams, the crystal clarity of the alpine sky, the zen eternity of temple sutras, the mid-afternoon break when everyone takes off for a doze... And to the potential multinational investor it peddles another portrait: "Asia's number-one success story," a modern infrastructure, a labor force that is as cheap as it is intelligent and industrious, cheap and plentiful hyrdoelectric power, free export zones, new deep water ports...

But there is another side to Taiwan that the government does everything in its power to conceal, cover up or play down: the political imprisonment of hundreds, perhaps thousands, of political prisoners, the sudden closing of free-thinking magazines, the executions of diehard opponents in factional struggles, the confiscation and banning of thousands of domestic books and the banning or "editing" of foreign ones (if you are ever in Taiwan you might want to check out the "new" Web-ster's definition of "China"), the state-of-siege vigilance and spying on one's neighbor in the schools, churches and other social organizations.

Since 1949, the "Republic of China" has had a constitution that is the equal of any anywhere. And it has ratified the Universal Declaration of Human Rights. But these textbook facts mean nothing to the people like Pai Ya-ts'an who, at the very moment you are reading this, are being tortured in the underground cells of the Taiwan Garrison Command's downtown Taipei headquarters, only a stone's throw from Chiang Ching-kuo's office in the Presidential Building. Nor to those being "interrogated" months on end at the TGC's Special Cases Section at Liu Chang Li, a few miles away. Or to the old man in "the box" in the prison camp on Green Island—a man whose name nobody knows, (cont. on back page)

From planning, translating, typesetting and layout, *A Tortured Silence* was the work of Karen and myself. The premier issue of what the International Committee for the Defense of Human Rights was promising would be a quarterly appeared in December 1975. We printed 1000 copies, and somehow distributed them in short order. Karen was able to take copies with her when she visited Taiwan late that month. -LM (Courtesy of Wu San-lien Taiwan Historical Materials Center)

Karen Smith

in Japan and generally conceded to be well to the right of center. The "big four" — *Nippon Keizai*, *Asahi*, *Mainichi* and *Yomiuri* — had by that time recalled their Taipei correspondents so as to meet conditions imposed by Beijing, as had Kyodo News Service, leaving the Taiwan beat to *Sankei* and Jiji News Service. Although the *Sankei* story did not fail to mention that *Ronin* was concerned about East Asian human rights, and hoped to be the English voice for those oppressed by their governments, nonetheless the treatment of a publication at the opposite end of the political spectrum was friendly.

Cub Courier: Running the Blockade

Boggett initially accepted Michael's name card at face value, which is to say he was a student (never mind that he looked to be in his thirties). He gave him copies of the *Ronin* issues with the Hsieh Tsung-min and Lee Ao articles, and asked for any materials that might shed light on the true state of human rights affairs in Taiwan. Michael told him that as far as he knew, everyone in jail in Taiwan was a communist, but he would be glad to see what he could find out.

Michael, for his part, also wanted help. He asked Boggett for information on the magazine's "Taiwan desk." David, knowing of the pains to which I was going to keep quiet in hopes of again going to Taiwan, told him that our "Taiwan desk" was currently in Taiwan, but would be visiting Japan in a few months, at which time he would set up a meeting.

When Boggett told me all this, I decided that I wanted to meet Michael, even if he was filing reports for the ROC. At *Ronin* we were by degrees being weaned off the idea that one could not talk with one's adversaries — on the contrary, more talking was what was needed.

So Michael and I met, in a coffeeshop around the corner from the Hanshin Hotel in Umeda, just a couple of blocks from the Osaka headquarters of *Sankei Shimbun*. I presented myself as a friend of both Boggett and "Valance." In fact, I said, it was "Valance," whom I had first met in Taipei, who introduced me to Boggett. As for *Ronin*'s publication of the letter that Hsieh secreted out of prison, or the translation of a Lee Ao piece on Madame Ho Hsiu-tze 何秀子, or the introductory pieces accompanying both of them, I vaguely recall an effort at deceiving him there, too. Suffice to say, my main objective at the start of our friendship was to put Michael's suspicions to rest concerning the extent of my involvement.

The deception was not entirely one-sided. I remember that on our first meeting Michael told me that Lee Ao and Hsieh were Taiwan Independence elements doing Beiping's bidding, in an effort to split Taiwan from China. Although this line of argument had already passed muster when foisted on an audience with no direct experience of the cockamamie logic of those state-of-siege times, today it may seem laughable that someone could, without the slightest hint of irony, maintain that behind the "splittest tendencies" of the "seditionists" in Taiwan lay the black hand of their imperial masters in "Beiping," as Beijing was called then in Taiwan. But to anyone not under the spell of *China Post* jeremiads galled at the gullibility of the West,

Made in Taiwan

by Karen Smith

State Secret:
Taiwan's Political Prisoners

AMNESTY INTERNATIONAL JAPANESE SECTION GROUP2

Things haven't changed much in Taiwan over the last thirty years.
With writers and editors still being popped off to prison for the slightest diversion
from the official Kuomintang (KMT) line,
with "politicians of the people" frustrated at the polls and in every attempt at organizing,
the author writes that "most people on the island feel helpless to decide their own fate."
What are the people thinking about their own fate and that of their home?
Karen Smith visited Taiwan in December 1976 and was subsequently blackballed by
the ROC government for this article, which appeared in WIN Magazine in March.

Like repression anywhere else, the repression in Taiwan is both physical and psychological; spies among one's colleagues, a plethora of "security" agencies, censors, unknown reports, detention centers

Or a mis-step can land a person in prison. Hwang Hwa, a political prisoner released in the July, 1975 mass commutation, received another 10 year sentence last year for "seditious" writings in the *Taiwan*

(Courtesy of Wu San-lien Taiwan Historical Materials Center)

Ching-yun 簡慶雲. Of the twelve given life sentences, Wang Wei-ching 王爲清, 47, has a heart ailment, Li Chen-shan 李振山, 58, is mentally ill, Wu Yue-ming 吳約明, 58, is going blind, Liu Chen-sung 劉眞松, 48, [...illegible...] Wang Ju-shan 王如山, 64, has a bad stomach, while Hsieh Chiu-lin 謝秋臨, 53, Wang Yung-fu 王永富, 51, and Chen Lieh-chen 陳列珍, 58, are reported to be in satisfactory health. Unknown to be alive or dead are Hsieh Kui-fang 謝桂芳, Wang Teh-sheng 王德勝, Chang Tsai-yun 張彩雲 and Chiang Han-tsu.

The conditions under which these people must survive have been deteriorating over the years. Back in 1950, when there were over 2000 people on Green Island, prisoners were not locked up but could walk freely around the barren island, miles from Taiwan's eastern coast. They could go swimming, plant vegetables, and get all the exercise they needed. Food was good, at least by prison standards, and two good square meals were served a day.

In 1954 women prisoners were moved to Panchiao. In 1964 a new prison was built in Taitung and the government moved most of the political prisoners to Taiyuan. For the few scores of people left on Green Island, life was still better, since they now had more room and facilities to themselves. In Taiyuan, however, people were locked up all day except

it was laughable then too, and a laugh was about all Michael got from me. I told him a good deal more about the extent of my association with Lee Ao — "there is no way you can hope to convince me that either Lee Ao or Hsieh were fronting for the communists."

Michael did not seem all that interested in coaxing intelligence out of me anyway. On the contrary, he soon took a different tack, coming out of the closet as GIO hatchet-man and trying on a new cloak of urbane gentility. Mindful of my eager desire to return to Taiwan, he kept offering enticements, letting me know that through his humble services I could gain entrance. His attitude toward my attitude was summed up in his most-used phrase, "don't scratch their faces." As we say in English, I was "in their face." Diplomacy was the proper antidote for government repression. Instead of public attack, I should try behind-the-scenes suasion — quite the opposite of the advice that I had gotten from Lee Ao.

The conditions were always the sticking point. In return for his clearing the way for me by putting in a word with his GIO superiors, he wanted me to promise that I would not hold a press conference while in Taipei. It was to be strictly a private visit so that I could "look up old friends." I cannot now remember whether I pointed out that it would have been the height of conceit to presume that were I to try to pitch a story to assembled journalists in Taipei, anyone would bother to come. What I told him for certain was that to curtail my own freedom of speech in this way would be to betray my friends, who were in prison precisely on freedom-of-speech issues. I could not cooperate with the government where they had refused.

Michael never gave up with this approach, and I always figured that if I ever decided that selling out my friends was an acceptable course of action, I would let him get the credit for converting me to the great cause of the ROC and its righteous anti-communist crusade. In the meantime, however, I think that I did not really help him very much with the kind of information that would win him points with the folks back at GIO headquarters. That Michael never asked about "Marcel Valance" again after our first few meetings suggested to me that he had seen through the ruse, and knew that Valance and I were one and the same.

I arrived in Taipei on 23 December 1972. They weren't using computers yet, but little difference did that make; all my worries about having to put up with a thorough search of my baggage and possible seizure of printed materials went for naught, as I did not even make it past immigration. Or, more exactly, I was allowed in and then immediately called back: having stamped me in, they presumably had better thoughts or more likely came upon my name on a check of second and third lists. They put a "VOID" stamp on top of the entry stamp in my passport, and escorted me to the same flight I came in on, there being no other flights that night back to Japan. They put pressure on the airline company to get me to pay for the round-trip flight to Hong Kong, but I told them to bill Chiang Ching-kuo. (In future adventures like this, I resolved to myself, I would use China Airlines, said to be the private fiefdom of the Chiang/Song families.)

Lynn Miles

for a one-hour exercise period — only those with life sentences or who had some special connection with the guards were allowed outside prison gates to work in the gardens. In 1969, six prisoners swiped a gun from a guard and killed him. Five of them were executed and one is now serving a life sentence on Green Island. This violence influenced conditions on Green Island. A new prison was built there in 1970, and by 1972 all political prisoners had been transferred back to Green Island. Taiyuan has been turned into a prison for military people only. This can be misleading, however, as every able-bodied male in Taiyuan must serve in the military, and if during this period he talks too freely or shows some signs of "questionable thinking," he could be sentenced to a term in Taiyuan. Were he not in the military, he could be a political prisoner at Chingmei, Hsintien, or Green Island.

The sun on Green Island is scorching — the aborigines who live in the area have been turned almost black by it. Sweet potatoes are about the only food that can grow on its coral soil and food must be shipped in. Many prisoners suffer from poor nutrition. But then, as one ex-political prisoner put it: What does it matter if the food is good or not if you have one hour of exercise when you're locked up in one small cell with nothing to do for the other 23? Lifers who have been in prison for the last 25 years feel that present conditions are the worst ever. More and more people become sick with various "prison diseases" — high blood pressure, hemorrhoids, TB, heart and stomach ailments — and insanity. In one special section are rows of cages too small to lie down or stand up in. The case of one prisoner, who received his PhD in Germany, went insane after eight months in one cage. When he was let out, he was almost blind, but when his vision got a little better he was put back in. No one knows how many prisoners die within Green Island's walls. It's known that two of those convicted with Su Tung-chi 蘇東起 — Chen Liang 陳良 and Chan Tien-tseng 詹天增 — opposed the KMT even while in prison and were shot, although they had been given life sentences. There are an estimated 200 political prisoners left on Green Island now.

One ex-prisoner gave an account of his arrest and trial: "I was taken in a private taxi — so as not to arouse public notice — to a temple in Hsimenting. I was taken to one building housing many rooms. They interrogated me, but because I presented no real 'problems'or resistance, I was transferred to Chingmei 20 days later. Those who don't cooperate stay at the temple until they do — usually people are transferred within four months but there have been some cases where people were kept there for two or three years. My basic crime was that I had read a lot of books and felt many aspects of society were irrational, and had gotten into debates, saying things I shouldn't have. Chingmei is complete unto itself — the pre-trial detention center, the court, and the prison are all within its walls, although the sign on the gate just says it's a detention center. The trial itself is a farce — I well knew that as soon as I entered the temple they had already decided my sentence. My lawyer looked at my file before the trial even began and told me I would get ten years. That was because I had been cooperative — ten years was considered a favor. At that time just listening to a Mainland radio broadcast could get you five years. During the trial, there's really nothing a lawyer can do — he just reads the government's file and asks for the court's leniency because the 'defendant sincerely regrets his deeds.' But usually the court just rubber-stamps the preliminary sentence handed up [by the Garrison Command]."

Arriving in Hong Kong, I was still to run another gauntlet. On my entry form I had left blank place of intended residence. This was immediately seized upon by the immigration officer, who demanded to know where I planned to reside during my Hong Kong stay. I replied that it had never been my intention to land on their doorstep in the first place, that I had been sent there against my will. Should we be surprised that this set off all kinds of alarms? Soon I was swarmed by officials of various ranks and descriptions, who methodically gave me the third degree at a first-gear pace. They had all the time in the world, and anyway, with me holding only my return Taipei-Osaka ticket, and no flights headed to either of the only two possible dumping-places for me (Japan and the US), there was no rush. They decided against letting me in, and had the airline prepare to ship me back to Japan first thing the next day. I spent that night sleeping on a bench in a behind-the-scenes waiting room, guest of the immigration authorities at Kai Tak Airport. It was an opportunity for me to learn first-hand about others who were stuck in that same room, night after night, sleeping in their clothes, with the "next day" always offering promise of a return ticket home. Stranded and entirely without rights, they were unknown to anyone outside the small circle of immigration officials charged with finding a country that would take them.

Once back in Japan and sobered by what was belatedly verging on certainty that it would be some years before I would ever be able to visit Taiwan again, I looked up Michael and apologized for being "out of touch" for so long. I had intentionally steered clear of him for several months, and had pleaded overwork when turning down his phone requests for a coffeehouse conference. The truth was that once I had decided to go, I did not want to go through the ordeal of sorting out how much to tell him, how much to keep secret. I had been at a loss as to the better course of action. Tell him that I was going, but fudge about the details and purposes? Or, not let on at all? If the latter, how would I explain my silence once I got back to Japan?

When I told him how rudely I had been treated at the airport, he was all sympathy. Well, if I had only told him beforehand, it could have been the red carpet. Crocodile tears? Perhaps, but I began to feel closer to him, all the while quite aware that he was defending the government that I was calling to accounts.

The final nail in the coffin burying my dreams of return to Taiwan came several days later, when Professor Kawakubo agreed to accompany me on a visit to the ROC consulate, known as the East Asia Relations Association (亞東關係協會, Ato Kankei Kyokai), in Osaka, to inquire as to why the visa issued on December 22nd in Osaka was not honored in Taipei on December 23rd. One of the higher officers came out to the main counter, looked over my passport, said something like, "That's strange, let me look into it," turned on his heels and went into a back room with my passport. When he came back a half hour later, he said "I'm sorry about the mistake." He returned the passport to me — with the visa canceled. Never again would I be re-admitted, at least not until Lee Ao and Hsieh had regained their freedom.

My trip may have been just so much wasted airfare, but it was not a complete wash, since it brought me to an important decision: attempts at secrecy would thereafter

Political Trials on Trial: AI Catches Fire in Taiwan

by Lynn Miles

Released to Amnesty International's national sections in Germany, Japan, the Netherlands, Sweden, Switzerland and the USA, as well as to all AI coordination groups working on Taiwan, the October 1976 Country Briefing on Taiwan was a huge boost to everyone working in the field. When it arrived in Japan, everyone was eager to see AI's take on the number of prisoners, inasmuch as released prisoners who had talked to Miyake, Hasegawa, Smith and others had been saying that they still numbered close to 1000.

"There is no official figure for the number of political prisoners held in Taiwan. Government officials refuse to recognize the term 'political prisoners' and only admit to the existence of imprisoned 'rebels.' ... In 1975 sources close to the government admitted that there were about 400 persons detained for political reasons. But Taiwanese abroad estimated that 8,000 persons are in prison for their expression of dissent." (p. 3)

AI "has on file the names of more than 200 political prisoners," as if to say that AI, the stickler for hard information, was content to leave the reader with parameters of 200-400 and 8,000. Our hearts sank. What use was a report like this? But further on, by adding up the inmate populations of the political holding pens at Chingmei ("slightly less than 300"), Hsintien (no number given), Panchiao ("400"), and Green Island ("over one hundred") the reader could easily do the math and realize that in AI's opinion the number was more like 800 – somewhat lower than estimates given by Miyake and Smith's informants, but a whole lot more political prisoners than the government was admitting to publicly (zero). We ran off hundreds of copies, sending them to the international press in Tokyo and Hong Kong, and smuggling them in to friends in Taiwan.

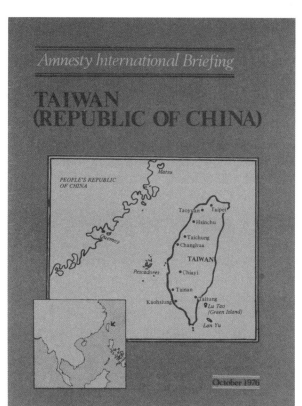

As it turned out, the report was a powerful weapon, and the ROC was now on the defensive, not only as to the matter of numbers, but also as to the way it was conducting its political trials behind closed doors. The AI Country Briefing got wide circulation not only wherever AI had national sections, but also in Taiwan itself.

be reserved solely to protect the identity of information sources, not to hide my own. Everything was now to be out in the open.

I was quite aware that, when compared to what was being suffered by many in Taiwan who wanted to leave but could not, my case hardly constituted grounds for complaint. The fate of overseas Taiwanese wanting to raise human rights issues concerning their home country, too, was often much worse. The memory was still fresh of Taiwanese victims of collusion between the Japanese immigration and ROC authorities, forcibly put on planes and sent back to Taiwan to face the worst. Many of them were the victims of a pervasive spy system blanketing the US and Japan, at a time when "KMT spies on campus" had yet to make a splash in the headlines.

Before finishing with Michael Chang, I should mention that I was never certain that the term "spy" really conveyed what he was all about. He made no secret of his GIO connections. Far from it, he fairly advertised them. His political stance was open and above-board, and it was obvious even on our initial meeting that he was a true-blue KMT loyalist. So while on the one hand I felt like I was "talking with the enemy," on the other I could not really regard him as enemy at all, but as friend. If one truly believed in nonviolent revolution, then the virtues of talking as opposed to fighting had to be practiced in the real world. Michael was for talking. And, after dozens of meetings with him over several years, I actually began to feel that his respect for my position was real, not feigned.

The bridge now crossed, there was no turning back. From that time on, I threw myself into human rights work as a crusade, to the point of neglecting Fujiko and soon what was to become a family of three. Having already miscarried, Fujiko had begun to worry, but in December 1973, daughter Natania Miwako was born. The name Miwako, made up of the characters 美 (beautiful) and 和 (harmony), was conferred by Enatsu Kenkichi 江夏健一, who explained that the first character stood for America, the second for Japan. Professor Enatsu was himself of mixed blood (Chinese father, Japanese mother), and, as with many like him, he had dropped his Chinese name in return for the gift of being received as a naturalized Japanese citizen. More than once he looked up friends in Taipei for me when he went there for a conference on multinational corporations. He is now vice chancellor at Waseda University.

Family Respite, ICDHRT Roll-out

Through the end of 1973 I was putting in eighteen- and twenty-hour days, seven days a week, editing *Ronin* and getting it printed and distributed. With Natania's birth at the end of the year, Fujiko, who had herself been involved in rescue and movement work from time to time, had to give it all up. Now, to the pain of the delivery had to be added the pain of seeing me so totally consumed by work that had nothing to do with our daily livelihood. So much of my concern and passion was now being squandered on an ever-broadening landscape of the oppressed and unfortunate, with so little to spare for her.

It was not just Taiwan and South Korean human rights work that was taxing her patience with me. She couldn't understand, for example, how I still found time to take

ASIAN WALL STREET JOURNAL, 27 DECEMBER 1976.

Taiwan Admits to 254 Political Prisoners, But Premier Says Rights Aren't Denied.

By DIANE YING
Special to THE ASIAN WALL STREET JOURNAL

TAIPEI — Premier Chiang Ching-kuo disclosed that 254 persons are serving jail terms in Taiwan for seditious activities, but he denied his government has ever violated human rights in handling these cases.

The disclosure was apparently spurred by increasing U.S. expressions of concern over human rights issues and charges from abroad of political repression in Taiwan.

U.S. President-elect Jimmy Carter's strong position on the lack of political freedom in South Korea also has obviously caught the attention of Taiwanese officials. And recently, U.S. Congressmen, including House Foreign Affairs Committee Chairman Thomas Morgan, have inquired about the condition of Taiwan's political prisoners.

"Fair Trials"

Premier Chiang's statement, deliver Constitutional that jailed for subversive or sedition have had

announced that eight persons had been sentenced separately to three to 15 years in prison by a military tribunal in Taipei for undertaking subversive activities on behalf of the Chinese communists.

The agency also released pictures showing the defendants in court and con evidence of pro-Communist pu tape recordings of Chinese com casts. The trial was closed to th the agency didn't acknow whereabouts of several others I newspaper ad.

Several Recent Incidents

The committee that sponsored believed to be backed by Taiwanes dissidents abroad linked either to the Independence Movement or the sources said. Activities by the two gr outlawed in Taiwan.

N.Y.Times 76.12.26

Taiwan's Premier Says 254 Are Held As Foes of Regime

Special to The New York Times

TAIPEI, Taiwan, Dec. 25—Prime Minister Chiang Ching-kuo said today that 254 persons were serving jail terms on Taiwan for ... activities. He invited ... ations to investigate. ... ent disclosure on po-apparently spurred an concern on the and by recent pub-Mr. Chiang's Chi-... nment with politi-

... l in his statement cases had been ... rocess, and he

...litary tribunal for undertaking sub-sive activities for mainland China. The ncy also released pictures showing the

Amnesty Int'l Pledges Aid for Fan's Family

WASHINGTON— (CNA) — Amnesty International, a human rights organization that won last year's Nobel Peace Prize, today promised whatever help is necessary to Chinese Communist defector Fan Yuan-yen to bring his wife and two daughters out of the Communist-controlled mainland of China.

Martin Ennals, secretary-general of Amnesty International, said Fan's wife and daughters "certainly are prisoners of conscience," to whom the London-based organization's help should be extended.

Fan, a former Chinese Communist pilot, fled to freedom aboard his MIG jet fighter last July 7. From Taipei he wrote to U.S. Secretary of State Cyrus Vance asking for assistance in getting his wife and daughters out of the mainland.

"We will do whatever we can to help him (Col. Fan)," Ennals

*China News
78.1.20*

said in reply to a CNA question at a press conference in Washington this morning.

Fan has not appealed to Amnesty International for help, Ennals said, "If a request is made," he added, "we certainly will do what we can to help them out."

Ennals came to Washington from London to kick off a campaign to bring pressure to bear on South Africa to end political repression.

Asked why Amnesty International has so far refrained from criticizing the Chinese Communists for their gross human rights violations on the Chinese mainland, Ennals said there are many ways to help end repression in totalitarian countries. "Speaking out against them is just one of them," he added.

Starting last year, Ennals said, Amnesty International, began working on individual cases of political repression on the Communist-held Chinese mainland.

Asked whether Amnesty International representatives will be allowed to visit the Chinese mainland, Ennals said he simply did not know.

Amnesty International wants to send representatives to the Chinese mainland, Ennals said. "But I do not know whether they will be allowed to visit," he pointed out.

Top: Within two months of the public release of Amnesty's *Briefing* on Taiwan, the government was compelled to answer its main charges directly, both as to number of political prisoners, and also as to the fairness of its trials, which would be open to "any international organization that is based on goodwill toward us." Did that rule out AI? We wondered.

Center: The February 1977 issue of the *Li* 笠 poetry review did a special issue introducing AI.

Right: In 1978 Dangwai candidates Chen Ku-ying and Chen Wan-chen published a full translation of the report as part of their campaign literature.

Right: The best the government could come up with was an if-you-can't-beat-'em-join-'em strategy, singling out for coverage AI's reports on the PRC.

a couple of weekend trips to the industrial complex whose smokestacks were pouring poisons into the air and water of the surrounding neighborhoods of Yokkaichi, just south of Nagoya. So bad was the pollution that hundreds of people, especially the very young and the very old, were getting extremely sick. Several had died after spending months of indescribable agony as their lungs gave out and they became increasingly reliant on the last-ditch technofix of life support. Others were barely hanging on, living testament to indescribable agony. And there were those who had chosen suicide as the alternative to a few more lingering years of ceaseless pain.

In the meantime, Miyake had come to stay with her uncle in Osaka.

Except for our family tour of the US by Greyhound bus in March, stopping off in various cities for me to give lectures to small groups in Taiwanese homes, I was kept occupied changing diapers for most of 1974. But as usual Miyake was not about to let me off the hook. She regularly got in touch with me on her return visits, and we'd get together in some downtown Osaka café. I generally kept abreast of the situation through her, but now the question became one of what I was to do with the information once I had I received it. Miyake, for one, was very dissatisfied with the slowness with which *Ronin* was managing to get her information into print, and even more with the fact that, after information was forwarded to the Asia Research Department at AI's London office, nothing at all would be heard back from them as to what action they were taking. So it went, case after case, with each set of information originating with Miyake and ending up in London, seemingly a dead end. With this information-bearing underground railroad apparently traveling London-ward, never to return, Miyake was fed up with what she saw as inaction.

Having returned to Taiwan, in early 1975 she wrote that Su Tung-chi's medical condition was growing critical, requiring release from prison for medical attention. I dutifully passed the information on to London, but Kawakubo and I decided that we could not leave it at that. Something more had to be done, because AI could not be expected to react for some time. Once the Research Department had compiled sufficient information (they would need other sources to back up our reports), they might pass on recommendations that an Urgent Action alert be issued to all of the AI national sections. Even so, precious days and even weeks would pass before any form of public action was taken. (Started up in March 1973, an "Urgent Action" was AI's answer to precisely the same sort of complaint, probably originating at the grass roots level from all over the world. Until that time an AI group was forbidden to take up any other cases than their three adopted political prisoners, assigned to it by the International Secretariat.)

Kawakubo was for going to Tokyo and doing a press conference. But in whose name? He wanted to use the name of Amnesty, since it was well known to foreign and domestic press alike. But, well aware that AI had clearly-stated strictures against taking the AI name and using it for just such publicity without prior clearance from London (rarely if ever granted), I was dead against it. In the first place, I had just returned from ten days in London, where I had spent a good part of it virtually camped (a couple of times overnight) in the Asia Research Department, so I had

Political Trials on Trial – 2

The Chen Ming-chung Case : Amnesty Methods Tested

In the annals of post-war ROC political trials there was nothing to compare with the international controversy stirred up by the Chen Ming-chung case of late 1976. And never before had Chairman Nishimura Kanichi 西村關一 of the Japan Section seen such a long and perturbed letter from Martin Ennals, Secretary General of the AI International Secretariat, concerning a cable that I had sent London on November 15, and one received in Honolulu a few days later. My cable: "Absolutely reliable report from immediate family says... Chen Ming-chong sentenced to death on ca 10 November." The one to Hawaii gave "report from London" as the source and "Amnesty International Osaska" as the sender. Otherwise they were identical.

On the basis of the cable to Hawaii a feverish petition campaign for stay of execution got underway in the US. Soon big-name signers were on board, including Nobel Laureate George Wald of Harvard University. Naturally the GIO got wind of it. One can only imagine what went on in the high councils back in Taipei when they heard of the fund-raising campaign for an ad to be placed in the *New York Times*.

Whereas Chen's wife had been told by his lawyer that he had been indicted on November 2nd and tried and sentenced on November 9th, she was later to see on the TV evening news on November 27th that he had been tried and sentenced to 15 years that morning. No little coincidence, this was the very day that the ad appeared in New York.

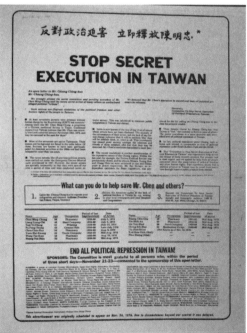

Top: A November 22 *Honolulu Advertiser* story reports on an upcoming demonstration at the ROC consulate by the Coalition to Free Political Prisoners. They embellish the story by saying that AI reported that Chen was tortured.

Bottom: The *New York Times* ad organized by the Chicago-based Committee to Stop Secret Execution of Political Prisoners in Taiwan, and signed by Marc Mancall, James Seymour, George Wald, and some fifty others. Further embellishment: "Confirmed reports from Taiwan indicate that Mr. Chen ... may be executed in the next few days."

a good idea what kind of reaction such a Tokyo press conference might elicit. Our excellent relations with London would have vaporized in one fell blow; already it was clear from AI's correspondence with me that I rated as an important informant, and on occasion was even allowed to advise, so I did not want to jeopardize this hard-won cachet.

In the second place, I personally had no quarrel whatever with AI concerning the policy, which had every reason in the world to protect its hard-earned reputation. At the same time that I was dealing directly with the AI office in London, I was also in close touch with Kurata Masahiko 藏田雅彥 and Ogita Yutaka荻田裕, the two young full-time staffers in the Tokyo office of AI's Japan Section, and I had had some dealings with Reverend Mun 文牧師, who was heading AI's troubled chapter in Korea. What AI was guarding against in preventing loose use of its name was the possibility that individuals or groups, interested in rescuing a particular prisoner of conscience or in singling out a rogue regime for rebuke, would pursue their own agenda at AI's expense. That both Kawakubo and I were active in AI (we were both instrumental in establishing Group Five in Osaka, and at one time we both served on the board of directors of the Japan Section) did not matter. In this instance, were we to stage a press conference in AI's name it might create the impression among the press that AI was more intent on hammering on the ROC than the on PRC.

This being an emergency, Kawakubo was still for stretching the rules, but for once I had to put my foot down. Both for practical reasons and issues of principle I did not want to do it, no matter how pressing the need to rescue Su in his life-and-death crisis, hidden away from public view.

So that is how the ICDHRT was born. With no mission statement, no bylaws, no board of directors, not even a named staff person or a proper letterhead, the ICDHRT was quickly concocted as the name for a shadow group in which I came to be recognized as the main actor, but which also included scores of others at various times.

We scheduled a side room at the Foreign Correspondents' Club in Tokyo, and held our press conference. Had the announcement gone out in the name of AI, attendance would undoubtedly have been much better. As it was, we were blessed with the company of only a handful, nearly all of them our own people.

To this day I do not know whether a story about Su Tung-chi's health condition resulted from that press conference. But, since one of the reporters was from CNA (Central News Agency, the news-dispensing arm of the ROC government), at least the government knew that someone was running around the press club trying to make noise about it. Doubtless the CNA reporter passed along word that our press conference was poorly attended, but that would have been of small comfort to a government that had to worry about where else we might be taking concerns for Su's health. That alone should have worked in Su's favor. And even without our feckless attempts, soon the ROC would be hearing from others, too, thanks to the AI Urgent Action alert going out to its national sections and local chapters.

While I was disappointed that so few reporters should trouble to take a half-hour out

The GIO approach to damage control was to maintain that, the cable to Honolulu being a "forgery," the November 9th trial had never taken place. AI-London also had its damage control problems, hence the long Ennals letter asking for an explanation. I was caught in the middle, for while I believed the original information to be correct, at the same time I felt betrayed by the ICDHRT colleague who had made use of an internal AI communication behind my back. The silver lining was that his action and the response it elicited may well have saved Chen's life.

To us in Osaka the case proved two things: that (1) sentencing in political trials was not according to a fixed procedure, but decided entirely based on political considerations, so therefore (2) as Kawata had put it in her book, "the more noise you make the better." The closed martial law system was now in the hot seat.

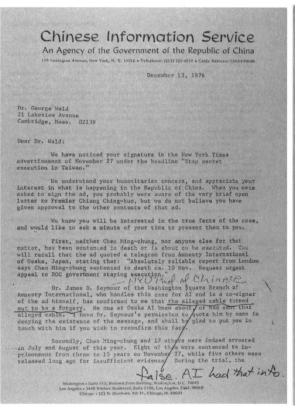

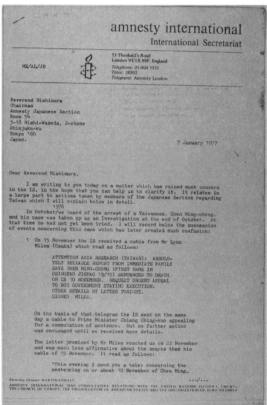

Left: On December 13 the Chinese Information Service in New York wrote to George Wald: "During the trial, families of the accused were present and they were defended by counsel" – lies – and that he was convicted of "infiltrating armed forces units, smuggling in arms through other Southeast Asian countries to prepare for a Chinese Communist invasion." Consider that in the past, death sentences had been meted out for lesser crimes. (Courtesy of Wu San-lien Taiwan Historical Materials Foundation)

Bottom: The five-page letter from Martin Ennals to Nishimura Kanichi. "I am confident that you will understand the absolute importance for the movement as a whole, that only reliable and authorized statements are made in the name of Amnesty International. In future and until I hear from you, we will only act on letters and cables sent by you personally to the International Secretariat as representative of the Japanese Section." (Courtesy of Wu San-lien Taiwan Historical Materials Foundation)

on their way back to the office from lunch at the FCCJ, and dejected over the thought that even with our follow-up effort at buttonholing journalists in the dining room, nothing was likely to appear in the international media, we began to reap the harvest of those efforts in other ways. With time I learned that foreign reporters stationed in Tokyo, be they from New York or Paris or Cairo, simply would not file a story coming out of Taiwan based solely on our information. However, come the day when they made their trip to Taiwan, they would pull out the file containing all the materials that we had mailed them, and give us a call. Several of these journalists, too, eventually joined the small legion of ICDHRT crypto-couriers.

In those days, foreign news organizations normally had their East Asian correspondents stationed in either Tokyo or Hong Kong. The larger institutions able to afford two offices had people in both places (a few were just setting up their Beijing bureaus). The ICDHRT's mailing list eventually extended to nearly a hundred correspondents whose areas of coverage included Taiwan and who were therefore expected to be making trips to Taiwan in the future. With many of them we would get a call shortly before their departure asking for an update and some introductions, in which case I would hastily assemble whatever I wanted to have carried to friends in Taiwan and boogie on up to Tokyo.

Coddling the Press, Pampering the Pillars

Although I knew that any one of them could be working for the CIA (by that time it was coming to public light that the CIA had infiltrated news organizations), I hoped for the best and trusted them with sensitive information, like the names and phone numbers of people I was in touch with in Taiwan. Had any one of them been spies, I think our activity would have come to a quick end with the expulsion of Miyake and, later, several others, so I am inclined to believe that none of them were working for the other side.

Some of them *were* more than mere reporters, however. When I discovered that, in return for our briefings and introductions, it was possible to ask favors of them in exchange, they sometimes became surreptitious agents working on our behalf. Some might consent to acting as couriers, while others might share with me their notes or whatever documents they carried back. We even bagged a couple of scribes who took on the AI crusade as their own, and intentionally joined GIO-organized junkets so that they could sneak out of their Taipei hotels at night to meet with people and gather information that were more for AI's purposes than their own editors'.

The London *Guardian* correspondent, Robert Whymant, deserves special mention as a sympathetic spirit who could be easily enlisted at the drop of a hat. He was the only Tokyo-based foreign correspondent for whom our reports, on occasion, might serve as the basis for a short story, filed from Tokyo, without waiting for a trip to Taiwan or some other second source to corroborate the information. Whymant knew that the same information we were getting also went to Amnesty International. When he went to AI for the confirming quote, for example, he may not have expected that they could add to his information, but having that second source, and one with the

Bookstore owner Li on trial: A case for propaganda

TAIWAN

Proving the Threat

While frequently citing the danger of communist subversion, the Taiwan government has, in recent years, found its main internal security problem in native Taiwanese demanding a larger share of power, or in the activities of disgruntled liberals. But last week, in what they took great pains to point out as proof of the communist threat, the authorities announced that seven men had been arrested and convicted of being agents for Peking. It was apparently the first operating spy ring that had been cracked for more than a decade.

For six of the accused it was the second time around. Sentenced as communist troublemakers in the early 1950s, they had served their jail sentences and had been released. But, in the words of the government indictment, they had "failed to repent and continued to work secretly for the communists." Two were named as the ringleaders — businessmen Chen Ming-chung and Chen Chin-huo — who were said to have worked under instructions from the Chinese Embassy in Tokyo. Their assignment was described as "instigating, indoctrinating and organising ex-convicts" so as to have trained cadres ready to respond to a communist invasion of Taiwan. According to the Nationalists, they had also smuggled in arms from Thailand, the Philippines and Indonesia.

The two ringleaders were given the longest sentences, fifteen years, which would have been longer, said officials, if they hadn't fully admitted their crimes and shown remorse during their military trials. The only member of the group who had not previously

fallen foul of the Nationalists was Li Pei-ling, owner of the San Sheng Bookstore in downtown Taipei. Described as a long-time communist sympathiser made "even more perverted and radical" by failures in business, Li was accused of having smuggled in hundreds of volumes of communist books to be used by the ring for the indoctrination of members. Some 400 books, mostly writings by Mao Tse-tung, as well as numerous tape recordings of broadcasts from the mainland, were confiscated by security police.

In addition to the seven convicted men, six others had been arrested and questioned, but then released because of insufficient evidence. But a three-year reformatory sentence was handed down on 23-year-old Nina Huang, who was said to have been recruited by the communists last year in Japan and taken to Peking for a visit. The reason for the light sentence, said officials, was her youth, naivete, and cooperation with her interrogators. However, insiders say it may have also been linked to her father, Huang Hsun-hsing, who is an independent legislator and regarded by the government as a constructive critic rather than a radical.

And the government went out of its way to use the trials for propaganda purposes, releasing photographs taken inside the court to the press. Such photographs had never been made available in security cases before. The accompanying Government Information Office news release drove the point home. "This is a typical case of Chinese communist machination which has now been detected and exposed. All the people in the republic should, from now on, heighten their vigilance in order to maintain their own well-being and social tranquillity."

The December 17 *AsiaWeek* presents a GIO-issued photo of the "open trial." Chen Ming-chung is nowhere in evidence, nor are the three lawyers. *AsiaWeek* cites government sources as saying that the ringleaders "failed to repent" and "had also smuggled in arms from Thailand, the Philippines and Indonesia." "And the government went out of its way to use the trials for propaganda purposes, releasing photographs taken inside the court to the press. Such photographs had never been made available in security cases before."

Issuing of photos to the press might have been taken as a step in the right direction had we been willing to believe that they were not simply enactments before the government's own cameras.

Most curious of all about this case was that Chen Ming-chung's wife had been detained by the Garrison Command on the very day that her husband's lawyer subsequently told her that he had been tried (Nov. 9). She had been threatened not to discuss the case with anyone (meaning her sister in Washington).

authority of Amnesty International at that, made his story credible with both editor and reader. Had Whymant's inclination to rely so heavily on either the ICDHRT or AI been known to his colleagues at the FCCJ, it would have been looked upon with contempt ("entirely unprofessional!") but as I grew more experienced in both talking to reporters and reading their news stories critically, I realized that many correspondents, even those with the most "professional" of standards, were not above basing an entire story on government sources. One even came upon reports whose main foundation was an unnamed "defense analyst" (CIA?) or "high-ranking Pentagon official," with a few choice second-party quotes to give the appearance of balance — just the usual tricks of the journalist's trade.

This was among one of many handicaps that came with trying to win public attention for information emanating from a largely clandestine human rights organization operating on a shoestring. Another was that the reporters whom we were badgering would tell us that even if they wrote about the concern of the moment, the story would never make it past their editors back home. I heard this one often, and each time I was left to wonder how much of this was a valid reason, or how much a cover for laziness or disinclination to get involved in another story when they already had several half-completed stories on their desk contending for completion.

For the reporter there was also the added consideration, never spoken, that to do a story on human rights in Taiwan might jeopardize the reporter's standing with the ROC government hacks working at the FCCJ, either openly as GIO point men or under cover for the CNA or *United Daily News*. To reporters willing to string along for an "inside" look at the troops on the front lines in Quemoy while ignoring the troops on the front lines in the Garrison Command's torture chambers, these agents were capable of dispensing infinite largess, from free airline tickets to lodging in the Grand Hotel. For correspondents reporting for smaller organizations, without ROC-paid junkets there could have been no thought of a visit to Taiwan at all, as it was beyond the means of their meager salary, and the home office could not afford it. For reporters representing the larger organizations like *Time*, *Newsweek*, the *Washington Post* or the London *Times*, staying on the good side of these agents wasn't necessary, not only because their organizations were able to cover travel and other expenses, but also because the GIO was falling all over itself (sometimes in the most fawning manner imaginable) to accommodate top-flight correspondents whose stories might be read by a US senator.

Information packets started going out to more and more reporters, and the ICDHRT slowly insinuated itself into the consciousness of enterprising reporters as important information source on the human rights situation in Taiwan. By late 1975 our media-for-the-media send-outs had covered the July reduction of prison sentences on the death of Chian Kai-shek, the October arrest and November sentencing of legislative candidate Pai Ya-tsan 白雅燦, and the December banning of the *Taiwan Political Review* 台灣政論.

Over the years, the ICDHRT could take credit, to greater or lesser degrees, for stories appearing in such pillars of establishment thinking as the *Washington Post*, *Christian*

Political Trials on Trial – 3

Peoples Liberation Front Case: Shutting out Melinda Liu

If the Chen Yu-hsi Case of 1968 and the Chen Ming-chung Case of 1976 proved anything, it was that inundating the ROC with an international show of concern could, if not save the political victim from imprisonment, at least force a lessening of the sentence. As time went on, more and more pressure was coming to bear on the martial law authorities to put on their trials out in the open.

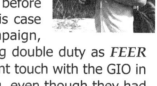

Coming a year after the Chen Ming-chung Case, the People's Liberation Front was announced by the GIO on November 5, just 12 days before the upcoming elections for seats in the provincial assembly. This case also saw international mobilizing, again with a signature campaign, this time for the *Washington Post*. Since Melinda Liu was doing double duty as *FEER* correspondent and *Washington Post* stringer, she kept in frequent touch with the GIO in hopes of learning the trial date. They were not at all forthcoming, even though they had announced in advance that it would be an "open and fair trial."

It was not until the elections were well over that the military got around to trying the case. As if following the Chen Ming-chung Case script to the letter, it was held the same day as the signed ad appeared in the *Washington Post*. ICDHRT called Melinda Liu from Osaka, and she was not at all afraid to talk, giving us ample material for our next information packet.

Left: of our write-ups by now were based on the timely, fact-filled reports sent us through various channels by Dennis Engbarth(above), easily the most prolific of our correspondents. He had entered Taiwan in late 1976, and started filing early the next year. Little editorial work was needed to dress up his reports for a wider public.

Above : Again a closed trial posing as an open one. On the phone to me in Osaka, Melinda Liu said that all the newspaper accounts read as if taken verbatim from a government press release – not surprising, she said, since the only reporters extended "invitations" were ROC nationals.

Science Monitor, Le Monde, London *Times, Suddeutsche Zeitung, Wall Street Journal* and *Frankfurter Allgemeine Zeitung*. By the time the Meilitao Incident broke, five years after our founding, the ICDHRT came to enjoy the confidence of correspondents in the major Western radio and TV media, such as the BBC in the UK, and National Public Radio, ABC, NBC and CBS in the United States.

I have chosen for mention as the "pillars" the ones which, according to criteria that are well worth examining but which we must here leave unchallenged, are listed in standard college texts like *The Media Elite* In point of fact, with the exception of the *Guardian Times* and *Christian Science Monitor* correspondents, it was only after several years of effort that we began to make any perceivable headway with the "major media." Before that, it was always a Bo Gunnarson, representing some little-known Swedish paper; or some German radio network that I had never heard of; or someone passing through while stringing for the *Toronto Mail* or the Pacifica Network (listener-sponsored radio with a potential listening audience of one-third of America); or a Thai television crew in town for three weeks and then it was off to Taiwan; or someone stringing for the International Labor Organization organ; or a Kobe housewife from Vancouver freelancing successfully for large North American magazines like *McLean's*; or an unpaid reporter for a trendy-lefty magazine like *Liberacion* in Paris; or the correspondent for *La Prensa* of Havana. There were many of them, with these being but a few that I am able to call to mind.

All I remember is that I spent a good part of my time going up to the FCCJ, probably averaging five or six trips a year over the years 1975-1980. From my door to the FCCJ door was a ten-hour round trip. This was preceded by a day or two of frenetic activity. Sometimes I had to go without sleep altogether in order to fulfill my professional commitments (teaching, translating, copywriting), taking a day or more off from work to prepare printed materials for presentation once in Tokyo.

Sometimes, where English classes or translation/copywriting gigs could not be rescheduled, I had to hand the work to someone else or cancel it outright. Mostly, however, my employers gladly made the adjustments, not least because the person responsible knew what I was up to in a general sort of way, and approved of it.

Sometimes this meant loss of pay, but rarely did it mean conflict with Fujiko, because I was still bringing in enough to pay the bills on a professional schedule that only occupied twenty-five or thirty hours a week. If you don't count such perks as residential allowance, paid commuter pass, paid vacation leave, annual bonus and accumulating retirement pension, my income was on a par with the Japanese *sarariman* (salary man) many years my senior, and we were living quite comfortably in a suburban town that enjoyed a national reputation as home to the rich and famous. So, at least as far as my family was concerned, we could not complain.

Not so the family of Wei Ting-chao 魏廷朝:

> I was kept there [at the security section on Hsi'ning South Road] for three months, of which ten-odd days were spent at Liuchangli.... But I wasn't beaten, the first time I wasn't beaten. But one time while I was caught sleeping, I was

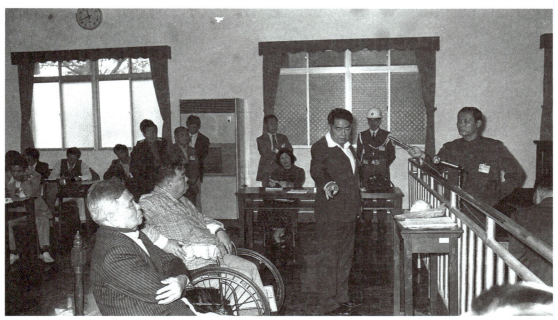

Political Trials on Trial – 4

The Wu Tai-an Case: Star Chamber Star Performance

Once the Kuomintang capitulated to the rising demand for open trials, then their fallback position became one of controlling the lead witness. Dangwai leader Yu Teng-fa was the target, and once the Garrison Command could depend on Wu Tai-an to perform reliably in front of the kliegs, all was ready, and they proceeded with the trial in March 1979. Having dutifully performed his role as accuser, his turn as defendant came a month later, where again he put on a sterling performance – abject contrition and begging the court's forgiveness. His histrionic function now exhausted, he was found guilty and put to death (see p. 349).

beaten and lost a tooth. They didn't let you sleep, exhausting you so that you were left with no spirit to resist. For several weeks they didn't let you sleep, wouldn't let you rest. That was their simplest method. (ICDHRT interview, July 1977)

Acceptable Pain and AI's Information Scraps

Forced wakefulness as torture? I came to a quick appreciation of why AI had always listed sleep deprivation among the favored tools for breaking a prisoner. Getting by on less shut-eye than most people, I was on occasion forced to go without for two, three or four days running, but it was still very much an ordeal. More than once I had to perform a marathon of preparatory work before getting on a Tokyo-bound Bullet or Hong Kong-bound plane. Once aboard, I could fall right to sleep with no risk of over-shooting my destination. Even so, napping was a mixed benefit. It mattered little that I had showered and changed into new clothes before departing, because by the time I arrived they were smelly and rumpled. I myself looked no better, and stank worse — this in a country where nationalities are identified by smell, in a country where the Korean minority was snottily summed up with the observation that they all reeked of garlic.

On top of the adrenaline working its odious miracle, there was also the dreaded cottonmouth syndrome. I would guzzle juice and water just to be able to talk. Tea tasted terrible and coffee even worse; beer took on the flavor of rancid milk. Many foods lost their taste, or assumed new, obnoxious odors, making some of them downright unpalatable. Vision was terribly impaired. Worse still was the disorientation in time and space. Day three often saw the onset of dizzy spells. Worst of all were the toothaches (which had final say, ultimately putting a stop to the practice, for fear that I would soon run out of teeth).

As you can imagine, my logical processes and verbal acuity, nothing to boast about even in the best of times, were not well prepared for the task of explaining in clear and concise fashion what it was that brought me to Tokyo. Blunders and miscalculations there were aplenty. One time, with Chen Chu's first arrest (which, I admit, is to present the extreme case), I arrived in Tokyo fresh from a three-hour nap on the Shinkansen, my first sleep in over 72 hours. Making straight for the FCCJ by way of the loop line and with my destination only ten minutes away, I could not resist the temptation to nod off for even two minutes' blessed sleep between stations. I did quite well at waking up to the squeal of brakes at the approach to each station, there to read the platform sign. But, upon getting off at the correct stop, I discovered that I had left my briefcase, full of all the materials that I was going to hand out at the FCCJ, on the train overhead rack. My everyday, beaten-up shoulder bag, stuffed with address book, date book, and a collection of materials was to still with me, nothing vital had been lost, no security breached. But even so, without the briefcase I could just as well have turned around and gone back home.

On advice of the station master, I waited for the train to make the full one-hour loop around to the same station. Finding the trove of materials where I had left it, untouched, allowed me to join the legion foreigners who are always happy to attest to

State of FEER

by William Armbruster

My first visit to Taiwan came in the summer of 1972 when I began five months of language study at National Taiwan Normal University.... I arrived back in Taiwan in August 1974 and immediately began teaching English and studying Chinese. I failed, however, in my initial efforts to break into journalism. I made contacts with the GIO and leading dissidents and sent some articles to different news organizations, but I was unable to get anything published.

My big break came the following year when I visited Hong Kong and met Loren Fessler, a former *Time* magazine correspondent who had begun his journalism career as a freelance writer in Taiwan for *Time* and the *New York Times* back in the 1950s. Loren encouraged me, and a couple months later he came to Taiwan. His visit coincided with several developments that seemed to indicate a more flexible approach by the government... including the recent start-up of a new magazine called *Taiwan Political Review* (*TPR*) and the reduction in prison sentences for several prominent dissidents, including Lee Ao, a former editor of *Wenhsing*, as well as the government's decision to permit Chen Yu-hsi, a former political prisoner, to return to graduate school in Hawaii. Loren urged me to write an article about these events. He took my story back to Hong Kong and presented it to various journalist friends of his, including Derek Davies, then editor of the *Far Eastern Economic Review* (*FEER*). and Daniel Southerland, then Hong Kong correspondent for the *Christian Science Monitor*.

As a result, I became the Taiwan correspondent for both publications. My first *FEER* article appeared in October 1979 under the headline "A Gust of Liberalism." "Gust" was probably too strong a word (reporters don't write the headlines); "breeze" would

At the December 2003 Taiwan Foundation for Democracy conference, Armbruster and Jack Hasegawa enjoy a few light moments between sessions. Behind them is Lu Chao-lin 盧兆麟, who was arrested in November 1950 and given a life term, which he served at Green Island. His sentence was reduced to 25 years in the commutations of July 1975. He passed away this last February 28.

Japanese honesty as a national character trait.

If you say that this was an absurd path to productivity, I suppose that on looking back there is no denying it. I was crazy, demented, bent to a mission at the expense of a lot of things that many people take for granted as worthy of prior consideration — sleep, money, meals, convenience, pursuit of hobbies, sports and idle pleasures, time with wife, time with children. The mission sometimes subsumed all else, the missionary consumed by a passion surpassing all conventional understanding.

While I may have been an extreme case when it came to burning the midnight oil, I was in good company. People visiting from Taiwan, couriers returning from Taiwan, colleagues getting briefings and preparing materials prior to entering Taiwan, activists passing through Japan — many were they for whom a stop-off in Ashiya meant working through the night in our living room, then bedding down for a short nap in the morning among the bags, travel paraphernalia and papers. We were all working hard because we knew the horrors to which the tortured were being submitted with each passing day. Every day therefore counted to the utmost, and if you could advance the agenda of public condemnation by even a day, you had spared someone a great deal of pain — pain far greater than what we suffered. We felt that we had miles to go, not before we could sleep, but before any of our locked-down friends could sleep. so we pushed ourselves to the very limit of our endurance.

We were on the frontier, the twilight zone, between those who were living outside, in relative security and comfort, and those inside, in the prisons. What the two sides had in common was a concern for others. The difference between them was that one side was being made to pay for that concern. Take the case of Tsai Tsai-yuan 蔡財源, whose crime was to have passed the list of prisoners to Hsieh, the list that we had printed.

> It is an extraordinary sensation for us, having been trying in vain since early 1971 to get any scrap of information about Tsai Tsai-yuan, suddenly to be presented with such a horrifying picture of his condition.... At this stage, what we need most urgently is advice about parcels. Do you really think that a parcel of toilet things, addressed to Tsai at Chingmei Prison, would reach him safely? And would pills, such as aspirins or vitamin tablets, be allowed through the customs? We are very anxious to give what practical help we can. Needless to say, there has been nothing to show whether the letters have reached him or not. (Letter dated 1 October 1975 from J. M. Child, Tamaki Group, Amnesty International New Zealand Section)

Amnesty International grew by leaps and bounds in the 1970s, beginning the decade with a world membership of under 20,000 and finishing it with 200,000. Primarily Europe-based in its inception, by 1973, when I joined the Japan Section (the section was just two years old) AI was working mightily to become a global movement with national sections on every continent. At the same time, it took great pains to maintain some kind of balance, to stay aloof from the ideological battle, mainly (but not exclusively) left versus right. This was partly to make it more difficult for the governments, offended by foreign interlopers presuming to pass judgment on their human rights performance, to call into question AI's impartiality, but more

have been more appropriate. In any event, I thought the publication of the TPR was particularly important because of its willingness to criticize martial law....

One of the saddest stories I reported was the life sentence imposed on Pai Ya-tsan, who planned to be a candidate in those elections. He was arrested, however, in October, even before the campaign began, for posting manifestos calling on Chiang Ching-kuo to disclose his personal wealth. He also called on the government to establish diplomatic relations with the Soviet Union and to begin negotiations with China. In February 1976 the government announced that Pai had been convicted of sedition in an open trial. When I read that report in the *China Post*, I immediately called the GIO, asking why there had never been any advance announcement of the trial if indeed it had been an "open trial." Not surprisingly, I didn't get a straight answer to that question. Later that day, Pai's sister, whom I had never met, showed up at my home, asking if I knew anything about her brother's trial. She told me that her family had been surprised when they read the newspapers that morning that her brother had been convicted in what was supposed an "open trial."

The *TPR* only lasted five months before the government ran out of patience with its criticism and shut the magazine down in early 1976. I dutifully reported that development, just as I had reported on the charges of fraud in the December 1975 elections and the arrests of dissidents such as Pai and Yen Ming-shen, another unsuccessful candidate for the Legislative Yuan.

Such reports from Taiwan were relatively rare in those years; the previous correspondent for the *Far Eastern Economic Review*, for example, was an American who worked for

> Incidentally, inasmuch as I could not get a room at the Hotel China, I spent the first two nights at Bill Armbruster's. It was useful to have a good chance to talk to him, and I was careful not to be obvious. I doubt that the govt knew that I was staying there. We took precautions against the place being bugged. Oddly, he was one of the "reporters" at the Gen. Li briefing. I trust just a coincidence! Anyway, he is very careful (almost paranoid), and I don't think anything was compromised.

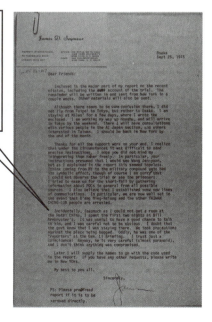

Upon completion of his Sept. 1975 Amnesty International mission, James Seymour's first stop after leaving Taiwan was Japan. Here, in a 25 September 1975 letter presenting his preliminary mission report to AI in London, Seymour reports that he has "established some new lines of communication" (Armbruster?), and gives his impression of the cub reporter: "almost paranoid." "We took precautions against [Armbruster's] place being bugged."

No matter how enterprising and no matter how interested in covering the human rights story, to any reporter without big-organization backing, paranoia came naturally. After all, hadn't the AFP reporter Albert Yuan languished in jail for years?

(Courtesy of Wu San-lien Taiwan Historical Materials Foundation)

William Armbruster

importantly it stemmed from the fundamental AI philosophy that freedom of expression of thought, so long as it was non-violent, had to be defended, no matter how contrary to *anyone's* beliefs.

To the liberal, this was a basic article of faith, but to the KMT such foreign ideas were anathema. Official ROC agencies like the CNA and GIO jumped into action, attacking AI as all lacking in objectivity and bent on scoring points for the communists. But when this caught the attention of dissidents who reasoned that any organization meeting with such strenuous objection from the KMT had to have been a friend of theirs (Chen Chu told me this in 1997), the government line switched to one of publicizing reports on the mainland while censoring or altogether ignoring those on the ROC and its allies.

Liberals who subscribed to the AI philosophy came naturally to the organization, which was nothing if not a redoubt of liberal ideology. Then there were the anti-communists and people on the right, whose main bogeymen were the USSR and PRC and their satellites. The remainder comprised those who had taken on the anti-communist regimes like the ROC and ROK — what in those days we joined with the PRC in calling the "puppet regimes of US imperialism." These, "the lefties," probably held about as much weight in the Japan Section as the liberals at the time that I got caught up in section politics. I made no effort to disguise the fact that I was more or less within the "left bloc" of the Japan section, but our politics hardly qualified as "left" among the Japanese intellectuals of the time.

According to the AI program, a national section was forbidden to take up individual prisoners in particular countries. Rather, besides the administrative and publicity functions for the country within which it operated (for example, for the Japan Section it meant translating materials about AI's Campaign for the Abolition of Torture into Japanese), it had to work to keep the aforesaid war between ideologies from breaking into open feuding, in the name of satisfying AI's condition of balance. In Japan this was a tall order, especially in that time, when lynchings and executions among different fanatic, fascist-"left" factions were regularly in the news.

In order to keep up this ideological cold-war balancing act, which was challenged anew by each inchoate member burning to bare a particular regime's dirty laundry, AI devised an organizational structure and operational agenda to which each national section was required to adhere. A national section might consist solely of individual members, in which case the annual dues it paid the International Secretariat was less, but so was its voice in the decision-making counsels. The one sure way to increasing your influence globally was to increase your membership. But you were also required to develop local chapters, known as groups. Once a group had more than the required dozen members, then a new group could come about through cell division.

The Kansai Group became Group Five in the Japan Section, the other four, organized several years before, all being in Tokyo. Right off the bat we had several-score paying members, with the amount of dues (calculated on the basis of membership) going to Tokyo (and some of that onward to London) having a bearing on how much influence

the GIO. He obviously wasn't going to report anything that might jeopardize his position there. In early 1976, the government was very sensitive about any criticism, fearing that reports of political repression might harm its relationship with the United States, especially since Jimmy Carter, the apparent Democratic presidential nominee that year, was making human rights a major focus of his campaign.

Several times government officials suggested that I stay away from politics and focus on business and the economy. There were, however, no threats against me. Nonetheless, I operated on the assumption that my mail was opened and that my telephone was tapped. Thus, in my calls to and from dissidents, I never used their names, nor did they identify themselves, although if they were calling from their home or office phones, I'm sure those were bugged.

I was also concerned that government agents might try to use me as a way to collect evidence against dissident students. I was afraid, for example, that if I was talking with two students and one of them became very critical of the government, he might be saying those things just to get me and the other student to say things that could be used against us. I wasn't really concerned for myself; the worst thing likely to happen to me was deportation, but a student or other dissident could end up with a jail sentence.

One of the most disappointing events in my years in Taiwan came when I learned that a mainlander friend, during a visit to my home, had been rifling through my desk drawers, apparently looking for my mail. This man, who had previously helped me in many ways, was always asking about my contacts with the dissidents, so I had been cautious in what I told him, but I thought that he was just curious. After my American roommate saw him opening my desk drawers and told me about it, I concluded that this man was probably a government agent, so I severed my relationship with him.

Despite incidents like this, I loved living in Taiwan. I prided myself as an objective journalist, but I felt strong admiration and friendship for many of the dissidents, including Lu Hsiu-lien, who was then the leader of the feminist movement in Taiwan, and Chen Ku-ying, a left-leaning professor of philosophy at National Taiwan University. I also liked many

we carried in Tokyo, never mind the distance.

By the early seventies, AI individual membership worldwide had mushroomed into the thousands, while the roster of groups numbered in the hundreds. By early 1974 there were over eighty groups in the United States alone, and by early 1975 over 180 in Sweden. In 1974 its co-founder and chairman, Sean MacBride, won the Nobel Peace Prize, and three years later the prize went to the organization itself.

From the 11 December 1977 acceptance speech by Mümtaz Soysal, of AI's International Executive Committee: "We are gratified that the Nobel Committee should see fit to award the 1977 Peace Prize to the 168,000 individuals in 107 countries who comprise the active members and supporters of Amnesty International. I am here in their name." Everyone in the Japan Section took great heart from these words, which more than made up for the fact that Sean MacBride's 1974 Peace Prize had been shared with former prime minister Sato Eisaku, quite the villain among civil libertarians. For weeks on end we were toasting each other's fame and fortune, at each of us being able to claim a 1/168,000th share of the prize.

AI's POC Adoption System and Prisoner Profiles

Meanwhile and much behind the scenes, AI-London was assigning each of its groups around the world three individual prisoners for focused action: one each from the communist/socialist, the capitalist, and the developing blocs. Before the case of a prisoner was forwarded to a local group for adoption, the International Secretariat research department responsible for that part of the world would investigate to see whether the case met AI's basic criteria defining a POC: "We have set up an office in London to collect information about the names, numbers and conditions of what we have decided to call Prisoners of Conscience, and we define them thus: 'Any person who is physically restrained (by imprisonment or otherwise) from expressing (in any form of words or symbols) an opinion which he honestly holds and which does not advocate or condone personal violence." (This statemen is from the 1961 appeal that launched AI, by one of its founders, the British labor lawyer Peter Benenson)

In Taiwan and South Korea, the two countries where I was active, cases would start out as "investigation cases" handled by the Asia Research Department, which was, for most of the time that I worked closely with the head office (1972 to 1979), headed by the French sinologist Arlette Laduguie. Where a government might claim that the offender had committed or conspired to commit an act of violence (often the case with "subversion" cases), if the prisoner failed to pass the POC test, he or she might still be forwarded to a local group, not for adoption, but to be taken up as an investigation case, in hopes that the group could learn more than the Research Department about the truth of the allegations.

This meant that Pai Ya-tsan, for example, was quickly accorded adoption status, since in his public questions to Chiang Ching-kuo he had never so much as suggested violence. So his defenders were entitled to preface his name with the "POC" title, which was already gaining some currency among the wider public outside AI. Hsieh Tsung-min, on the other hand, had his case go out "for investigation," all because the

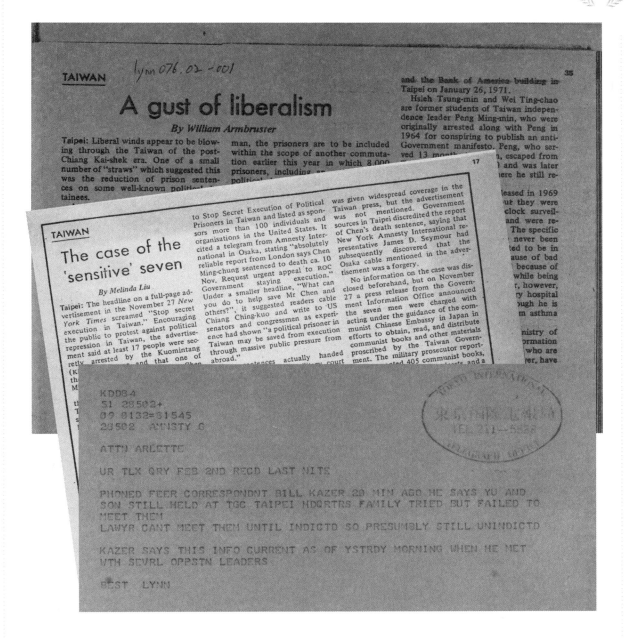

Armbruster was succeeded by Melinda Liu (1976-78), who took human rights reporting a step further. (o n one trip to Hong Kong she passed on copies of the banned *Long Live the Elections* to the ICDHRT for publishing abroad), and she in turn by Bill Kazer in 1978, and then Phil Kurata in 1980. Liu was by far the most daring of the four reporters of that period.

Top: Armbruster's opening *Far Eastern Economic Review* salvo of October 1975 perhaps shows the influence of the Seymour visit. Center: Melinda Liu's long and illustrious career began as lowly FEER correspondent in Taipei. Bottom: As this early 1979 telex to Al-London shows, Bill Kazer was unafraid to take calls from overseas discussing human rights cases. (Courtesy of Wu San-lien Taiwan Historical Materials Foundation)

government was trying to pin the Bank of America bombing on him (as made clear in his "Letter from Prison"). I remember arguing strenuously with Arlette about this (diplomatically of course, by mail), for how could the burden of proof fall on Hsieh, when he was locked away, and especially since just days before his arrest I had heard him speculate as to who might have been responsible?

Because Kawakubo and I, both working on Taiwan, were among the Kansai Group founders, for starters we asked that KG be assigned a prisoner from Taiwan as one of our three adoption cases. But by that time AI, growing like Topsy, had picked up so many groups that it had taken the next logical step, which was to set up a coordinator for all groups adopting, say, Taiwan prisoners in, say, Sweden. And so it was that the KG became a Taiwan Coordinating Group. For that reason, the group did not have regular meetings at which they would sit down and draft polite letters of entreaty or inquiry to the authorities, and letters of encouragement to the prisoners, all of them going to one prisoner each in three countries.

With perhaps as many as five hundred groups worldwide, and with each group adopting or investigating one prisoner held in an anti-communist country, the number of Taiwan prisoners whose cases were taken up at one time or another by AI probably exceeded one hundred. Whether the prisoner was actually adopted as a POC, or, failing to meet the two criteria, was assigned as an adoption case made little difference, because in either case the government in Taiwan was going to be hearing from concerned individuals in numbers. If the prisoner was an investigation case, the group was instructed to emphasize that fact when communicating with the Taiwan government.

The prisoner information that AI Secretary General Martin Ennals had requested of Hsieh Tsung-min and Lee Ao in 1970, and which cost Hsieh and Tsai Tsai-yuan so much torture and suffering in 1971-72, was already beginning to pay off in 1973-74. In those years the offices of the ROC president, and the heads of the Executive and Judicial Yuans were all getting insistent inquiries from people all over the world, especially in Europe and North America, concerning people with whom they had no personal acquaintance.

For the KMT, this show of concern was a social and political phenomenon entirely new in their long years of authoritarian, answer-to-nobody experience. At first all they could do was put up a wall of silence.

> "Subversion" in Taiwan is a catch-all charge directed against any and all political dissidents in Taiwan. So it may be that he was simply involved in discussions or meetings of a group of dissident intellectuals in his university. (AI Asia Research Department, Chin Him San adoption/investigation profile sheet, 26 February 1974)

This is the advice of researcher Peter Harris, who prepared the prisoner adoption sheet on Chin Him San 陳欽生, a Malaysian national attending Chengkung University and arrested in March 1971. All that AI knew about Chin was that his brother had contacted AI in London, proclaimed his brother's innocence, alleging that he had been tried without legal representation. Sentenced to 12 years for "subversion," Chin, again

Yonaguni Rendezvous

By Kobayashi Ryujiro 小林隆二郎

Another leg of my long journey toward freedom. In 1975 I was running around Osaka preparing for a folk concert in support of the Korean poet Kim Chi Ha, jailed by the Park Chung Hee regime in its campaign of repression against free expression. Prof. Kawakubo had offered use of the AI office, where I first met Lynn Miles, who gave me a detailed run-down on the human rights situation in Taiwan.

In May 1977 he contacted me urgently. I rushed over to his apartment. "Kobayashi-san, you have been to Okinawa lots of times. Since you know it so well, I need you to go there with me, to fetch a man who is on the run for having criticized the government." He wasn't joking and it was urgent, so I agreed on the spot.

The two of us set off for Yonaguni sometime in late May. We planned to fly to Naha, from there to Ishigaki, and finally to Yonaguni, all in one day. We made it to Ishigaki, where an early summer breeze was blowing. Then it was announced that the Yonaguni flight had been canceled due to bad weather. The next morning, taking a 19-seat, two-engine prop plane, we arrived at Yonaguni. 124 km southwest of Ishigaki and 111 km east of Suao on Taiwan, it is the southernmost of Japanese territory. 27.5 km around, it has only three villages: Sonai, Hikawa and Kubura.

Our man was holed up in Kubura, where we announced our arrival by walking down the main street, Miles singing Chinese and English songs at the top of his lungs. 40 minutes later, a man appeared. Miles began speaking with him tentatively, in Chinese. "He's our man," he whispered to me. Soon we were joined by Chang Chin-tse 張金策 – and then another, Wu Ming-hui 吳明輝.

We had time to kill until the afternoon flight, so the four of us walked up to the spot where they had been delivered off the south coast, and forced to swim the last 100 meters. They had a few cuts and bruises to show for it. Miles insisted that we climb to the highest point on the island so as to catch sight of Taiwan, but it was too hazy.

We took our time walking to the airport. We bought their tickets, and we talked our way through the scenario carefully. At no time were the two of them to speak, either to each other or to us. Miles handled the tickets, and we got on the flight. The same routine was repeated on the Ishigaki-Naha flight. We stayed the night in Naha, and by noon the next day we had arrived safely in Osaka. Later I heard from Miles that within ten days the two were in Washington appearing before a Congressional committee, giving their testimony about repression of human rights in Taiwan.

according to the brother, was now on Green Island.

Each prisoner profile was prepared by a London staff researcher, giving date and place of arrest, legislation under which held, date and place of trial, charge, sentence, place of detention, lawyer's name and address, date and place of birth, occupation, health, family, address of family, need for relief, language for correspondence, and reason for adoption/investigation. All cases assigned to a group came with such a profile. Most, like Chin's, also came with a suggested course of action. In his case, AI-USA Group 82 was instructed to first contact the brother in Malaysia and, if he "suggests you contact people inside Taiwan — either the prisoner himself, or friends of the prisoner — you should not attempt to do so yourselves but should refer his suggestions for discussion to a special Amnesty group in Japan that deals with internal Taiwan contacts: Lynn Miles, Amnesty International Kansai Group."

From AI groups in Sweden, Belgium, the Netherlands, Germany, France, the United States, Canada, India, New Zealand, Australia and other places, in 1973-74 letters asking for more information on their prisoner started pouring into the downtown Osaka Ad Building, home to the offices of *Ronin*, AI Japan Kansai Group, a startup Japanese photo publication called *Asian Eye*, and later *Libero*, an Japanese-English quarterly that some anarchist friends had launched.

That Asia Research should be passing my name out as primary conduit to people inside Taiwan was little help, for what could I do beyond forwarding the letter to Miyake in hopes that she could find a way to establish contact with the families? I rarely responded to such letters directly, even if I had some helpful information, since I already had my hands full as it was. Any information that Miyake sent me would be translated within a day or two and dutifully passed on to London, so the groups concerned would eventually be getting what little information there was anyway. I constantly regretted that I did not have more time, for silence from me would only be added to the silence from all other quarters, the end result being that the groups concerned might give up hope and quit writing.

POC Families, the Tenuous Link

But at least hope could be helped along in the other direction, so I made copies of these letters in readiness for the departure of the next courier, who would hand them over to Miyake, or Chen Ku-ying, or Dirk Bennett, or whoever the courier of the day was meeting, hoping that word might get to the family that in fact there were people outside pressuring the government concerning their loved one.

> The most important problem is the shortage of information concerning the prisoners.... The groups get very demoralised because they write letters to the authorities and/or families of their prisoners, but never get an answer. As this is almost the only thing they can do they soon stop writing and sit and wait until they get new advice from me, which I am not able to provide them with.

Letters like this one, from the Dutch Section Southeast Asia Coordinator, came to us at the rate of several a month. Now and then snippets of information came as attachments to attachments to letters, showing that the circle of concern about POCs

Formation of Amnesty International's Taiwan Coordination Group

by Klaus Walter

It was all pure coincidence...

During my recent visit to Taiwan on the occasion of the opening of the Chingmei Human Rights Park, December 10, 2007, Linda Arrigo asked me to write down how I became involved in the defense of Prisoners of Conscience (the AI term for non-violent political prisoners) in Taiwan. Well, here is the written version of what I told to a group of students on the evening of Human Rights Day 2007:

In the mid-70's, being a law student myself, I had become active in German party politics (the Social Democrats (SPD) youth wing) on a communal and regional level. After having changed university and city, I did not feel at home any more and was more and more disappointed by the (obviously common) atmosphere of a low-level corruption and cooperation between party politics, public administration and the economy, especially building contractors. So I was rather looking for alternatives where to invest my "political energies" and I happened to come across Amnesty International. I liked the idea of "sitting between all chairs" (a German proverb meaning not being inclined towards either right- or left-wing politics). At that time a normal Amnesty group was working for the release of three political prisoners, usually one from a Western-oriented country, one from an Eastern block country, and one from a "Third World" country.

In 1976 I joined AI-group 1400 in Bonn, as they had adopted prisoners from Argentina, the then-Soviet Union, and Mali. I knew Spanish (my grandmother was born in Argentina) and so I thought my knowledge could help there. When I attended the first group meeting, I noticed the cases from Argentina and the Soviet Union were being handled by very experienced AI-members, whereas for the Mali case they were looking for somebody willing to take care of it. And I also knew some French, so I began to do some "research" about the case's background (apart from doing the normal routine work every AI-group does, i.e. writing letters to the authorities and asking for the release of the very person).

After some months I had build up a connection to a left-wing African trade union's delegate in Paris, France, whom I visited, and I finally found out that there had been a slight confusion with the name of the prisoner we were working on (in Malil many people have the family name Traoré - like Chen in Taiwan or Müller in Germany), so it turned out that the person had already been liberated some weeks before.

Case solved, case closed, I applied for a new case -- and a few weeks later we received a new case dossier, this time from Taiwan: Tai Hua-kuang, a young man from mainland who had engaged with a few others (among them Lai Ming-lieh and Liu Kuo-chi) in a group called the "Taiwan Revolutionary Movement", which had sent "threatening letters" to US companies in Taiwan. His sentence was life imprisonment. Of course his confession had been extracted under torture, and therefore AI was seeking a retrial. Full of enthusiasm, me and my group began letter-writing campaigns in addition to trying to find out the

in Taiwan had spread far and wide, and that these AI groups were more determined than the letter from the Dutch section let on. Over time I saw enough of these letters to gain confidence in their determination. Clearly, they were not at all content to sit back and do nothing if silence was the response to their politely-worded requests for information from the Garrison Command or the Premier's office:

> I am writing to you as a member of Amnesty International Swedish Section, Group No. 192. Since three years we are working for a Taiwanese doctor, Mr. Chen Chung-tung 陳中統... doing research work on cancer at the University of Okayama, Japan. He returned to Taiwan in February 1969 to get married. He was then arrested, accused of having joined the Formosan Independence Movement in Japan, of having brought subversive literature into Taiwan, and of having enlisted three friends for the movement. He confessed after having been denied food and also and having been threatened.... Dr. Chen was sentenced to fifteen years in prison, which seems unduly harsh, even for the Chiang Government.... Five groups in Sweden, USA, Germany, Australia and Ceylon are now working to get him released.... The only way to influence the Taiwanese Government is to give the case international publicity and create opinion against his long term of imprisonment. The biggest part of our work has been a great campaign among the most outstanding of Dr. Chen's colleagues all over the world, about 40 of them Nobel Prize winners. The original letters of appeal were sent to the Premier of Taiwan, and the copies were handed over to the Embassy of Taiwan in Washington by one of the cancer specialists, Dr. Lloyd Law of the National Institute of Health in Bethesda. We have also written to a large number of organizations and persons with a connection to or knowledge about Taiwan, but unfortunately without any visible result.

The result of all this letter writing and public pressure would not start to become visible for another couple of years, but it was most assuredly being felt in high circles at the time. Read Lee Ao's *Memoirs* for those years and you get the impression that Lee Ao was the KMT regime's only headache. Far from it.

This is not to say that we, too, did not have our headaches, the main one being a reliable channel of communication. I am not speaking of the logistical difficulties of keeping the line open between Miyake and myself — difficulties, to be sure, but sooner or later a messenger was always found, the Rubicon of fear and intimidation put in our way by the regime safely crossed. Rather, the problem was with the families.

In an interview published in the *Bulletin of Concerned Asian Scholars* in 1985, Kang Ning-hsiang 康寧祥 spoke of "families of the prisoners of the Formosa period," who

> ... emerged as a more cohesive group than the legislators and councilors. In the past the KMT jailed a lot of people. When the men were imprisoned the women would not have dared to protest openly. No one was expecting that when the men were jailed after the Kaohsiung Incident, their wives would come out and run for office.

For him the threshold was crossed with the Kaohsiung Incident. But if anything he understates the case: move back in time but a few years, and so isolated were the families that few dared speak *privately*, and forget about taking their case into the

background. After about half a year, with not a single answer from the government in the "Republic of China" and having no AI-Taiwan coordination group in Germany which could have given advice on how to proceed further, my group suggested the case to be given to an AI-group in the USA, because Tai Hua-kuang had been there as a student and we thought that AI groups in the US could perhaps find out more and create more efficient pressure for this case. When I went to the AI office in Bonn to give the case back, the case allocation officer in the office, where I had been helping as a volunteer on several occasions, told me that instead of giving up we should try to form a coordination group for Taiwan. The section needed a group like that to take care of some 25 to 30 Taiwan cases, since there were no specialists to coordinate the work. He put me into contact with a Taiwanese minister, Roger Chao, in Wuppertal (some 70 kms from Bonn) and his wife Ursula, an AI-member. Okay, I thought, why not, let's try!

Soon I found some members from my Bonn group to work on this, some members from Wuppertal joined in, and we began collecting information from the groups already working on Taiwan prisoners, from public sources and from the Taiwanese exile community in Europe. We attended meetings of the "Taiwan-Heimatverein", the "Formosan Christians for Self-Determination," etc., organized country seminars for the AI-groups working on Taiwan cases, outlined letter-writing campaigns for the different categories of prisoners, and shared all possible information with the other AI groups.

One group of prisoners was of special interest for us: there was a rather large group of Green Island inmates who had been there for a really long time, since the early 50s or so. We called them "Long-Term-Prisoners" (mostly people imprisoned in the aftermath of 2-28 and with little of no information on the real reasons for their arrest and sentence). Many of them had no family in Taiwan and little or no contacts to the outside world -- and practically nobody cared about them.

One special highlight I remember was a public event organized by us to inform the German public of this in 1978. We had invited Prof. Peng Ming-min to speak about the political situation in Taiwan in Wuppertal's Von-der-Heydt-Museum. Ironically the site was occupied by sympathizers of the German Baader-Meinhof group of prisoners trying to press us for help to get the so-called terrorist prisoners released.

All this was in the years 1977 to 1979. At that time, the Taiwan coordination group in Germany was dealing with some 30 Taiwan cases in Germany, Austria and Switzerland (as these AI-sections did not have own Taiwan

Klaus Walter returned to Taipei after a long absence, for the December 2007 opening of the Jingmei Human Rights Memorial Park.

Klaus Walter

streets. The numbers of POC relatives intimidated by visits from plainclothesmen and sometimes uniformed military personnel undoubtedly ran in the tens of thousands for the years 1947-1975. With the government controlling links not only between the POCs themselves but them and their friends and families, a way had to be found to break through the wall of silence and somehow locate those brave enough to speak with outsiders.

We forwarded to Miyake and others copies of these letters coming to us, asking for more information. If writing to the families was also met with silence, perhaps that meant that the families were not getting the mail in the first place. Miyake over the months managed to connect with a few families (at first I believe that this was done with the help of Hsieh Tsung-min's sister Hsiu-mei), and through them was able to collect the indictments or judgments against various POCs. These documents were almost invariably copies done on some kind of wet-process copying machine. Upon receiving them from Miyake we made copies and distributed them to AI-London ("AI-London" being our term for the International Secretariat's Asia Research Department), Jim Seymour, *Taiwan Chenglian*, the Formosa Association for Human Rights (FAHR) and other groups abroad, some Hong Kong journalists and activists, and the handful of foreign correspondents in Tokyo who could handle Chinese. In selected cases, instead of simply copying the documents, we summarized them in English. Full translations were rare.

It was the job of Miyake and our mysterious other messengers to convey to the families the hope (not to say conviction) that adoption of their loved ones by far-flung AI groups could make a difference. If the families ignored the warnings that they were getting, whether at the prison from the mouth of the very person that they had gone to see or from uninvited visitors from the local police station or the Garrison Command, they first needed to understand that those very words of warning, threat and intimidation bespoke a fear, indeed a phobia, that the truth might fall into foreign hands. But even so, as the case of the 1980 murder of prisoner Lin Yi-hsiung's family was to prove so chillingly, the threats could not be taken lightly.

So there was fear on both sides. For the prisoners and their loved ones, the threat of losing property, jobs, education, freedom of exit, even human lives, were all too real. And the KMT? They feared losing ill-gained wealth, privilege and control.

> We have recent reports that the Appeal Court hearing of Mr. Hsieh Tsung-min, sentenced last year to 15 years' imprisonment under the Statute for the Punishment of Rebellion, is to take place on October 1st and thereafter in Taipei. (Amnesty International Secretary-General Martin Ennals, letter to Chiang Ching-kuo, 20 September 1973)

What were the sordid little secrets that the KMT government tried at all costs to stop at the border? That there had been over a year of detention before the case even came to trial. That there had been no lawyer, or that the lawyer was really a government lacky, working for the other side. That coercion had been used to get the confession, with methods ranging from sleep-, food- and water-deprivation, to pins under the fingernails, to electric shock to the genitals, to suspension of the suspect from the

coordinators, we agreed on giving advice to their groups as well). Hsieh Tsung-min was one of them, but we also followed the political situation, like the Chungli incident, etc.

An on Human Rights Day 1979, the Kaohsiung incident happened. Immediately afterwards we had the news, we had to deal with the lists of prisoners, trying to figure out the transcription of names and comparing the info received from various sources (there is a basic rule of AI: all information must come from two different and reliable sources). We received news from Linda Arrigo, Lynn Miles, Jim Seymour, Gerrit van der Wees, and the Presbyterian Church -- and we had to find out about the real situation. Soon the number of groups working for Taiwan prisoners increased when all the Kaohsiung prisoners were taken up as Prisoners of Conscience. Lu Hsiu-lien, Chen Chu, Yao Chia-wen, Lin Yi-hsiung, Shih Ming-teh, and Rev. Kao Chun-ming were among those our groups began to work for.

We joined forces with the Taiwan coordination groups in other sections like France, the Netherlands, Sweden, US, and Britain, and we managed to initiate a major AI campaign for Taiwan prisoners which took place in 1981, focusing mainly on the "long term prisoners" and the Kaohsiung incident prisoners (including those from the Presbyterian Church).

In many cases we could establish a regular contact. Later Chen Chu and Lu Hsiu-lien, but also Lin Yi-hsiung and others, came to Germany to visit us and have talks with politicians (usually from the Bundestag, the parliament, as the government did not want to have contact due to the lack of diplomatic relations).

In 1984, after having finished my studies, I became a staff member of the German AI section, and slowly handed over the responsibilities of the coordination group to my successor, Dr. Renate Müller-Wollermann, who officially took over in 1987, and has been doing this ever since.

I myself did not stop being involved in Taiwan matters, though. In 1989 I was part of the first "development" mission at the international level in AI. We helped to form the first three Amnesty International groups in Taiwan, with Bo Yang and Ruth Kao being in the front line of the new groups. In 1996 I came again to Taiwan and held a lot of talks, among them one televised talk with the then Minister of Justice, Ma Ying-jeou, on the death penalty in general and the Hsichih Trio in particular. I also visited the three defendants in Kueishan prison at that time. And finally in December 2007, it's a real pity that this case still is not solved at the time of the writing these lines.

Maybe this story is similar to the story of politics in Taiwan itself: It is not so spectacular, but it is full of progress and successes, and really good developments: all the former prisoners have been released, torture is not practiced anymore, the use of the death penalty has been reduced -- but everybody takes it as normal. You still should take note of it and appreciate the facts.

wrists (those wrists having first been tied behind the back), to being strapped onto a block of ice for hours at a time... as time went on the horrifying list became still more horrifying.

For me, on hearing these things, horror gave rise to something bordering on despair. Compassion came easily. What came difficult was the ability to contain the anger, and to concentrate on practical tasks in a systematic way so as to be most effective in bringing pressure to bear. I began to feel an overwhelming flood of impotence, as it seemed to me then that a few hundred, maybe even a few thousand, letters from abroad would not make up enough to force the gates. The snail's pace and paucity of information coming out of Taiwan also brought much frustration.

Barely Detectable Waft of Liberalism

But the times were changing, and by mid-1975 one could feel that we were now seeing some movement in the right direction. In an October article for the *Far Eastern Economic Review*, Bill Armbruster gave three 1975 developments that "point to a political liberalization that may be a hallmark of the post-Chiang Kai-shek era." The three: "the reduction of the prison sentences [of "8,000 prisoners, including an estimated 200 political detainees"]; the decision to allow Chen Yu-hsi 陳玉璽 to return to America; and the appearance of the *Taiwan Political Review*."

Within a week of the appearance of Armbruster's upbeat assessment, Pai Ya-tsan 白雅燦 was arrested. On the first day of the Legislative Yuan election campaign Chang Chun-hung 張俊宏 was taken in, and Kang Ning-hsiang 康寧祥 was threatened (all eyes looked to Kang in those days, as the Dangwai figure least likely to be arrested). By the end of the year Armbruster's bellwether, the *Taiwan Political Review* was banned, and the next year Huang Hua 黃華 and Chang Chin-tse 張金策 became the repression's targets of the hour. Within a few months Armbruster's reports began sounding a much more somber note. And while it took me a long time to get over his putting the number of political prisoners at a mere 200, after all these years, I think that Armbruster's original tribute to a general easing of the situation was essentially correct in the broadest terms.

Beyond saying that "outside forces and events may have more impact on Taiwan's future than any domestic issue," Armbruster made no attempt to explain exactly what lay behind this unforeseen "gust of liberalism." Perhaps he did not want to get into that can of worms for reasons having to do with his own personal security. He had put up Jim Seymour, who was in Taipei on Amnesty International business for the second time that year, and was afraid that their association might be found out (in a letter to me, Jim wrote "almost paranoid"). Taking extra precautions to hide the fact of his link with Jim in his writings, he would not have wanted to share what he knew about AI campaigns over the previous couple of years; so just possibly AI efforts figured among the "outside forces and events" having a braking affect on the regime's repressive tendencies.

In addition to the quiet, polite letter-writing campaign that went on from week to week and year to year, these efforts also included several high-level missions to the

The Taiwanese Christian Self-Determination Movement in Germany

by Chao You-yuan 超有源

Representing Taiwan at the German Protestant Church Congress

The German Protestant (Lutheran) Church holds its nationwide "German Protestant Church Congress" (Deutscher Evangelischer Kirchentag, DEKT) once every two years, with approximately 100,000 participants. Many activities take place during the three days of the Church Congress. The liveliest of these activities is the "Market of Possibilities" (Markt der Möglichkeiten) which offers all kinds of groups the opportunity to set up stalls or exhibitions. This in turn gives the visitors the opportunity to show their concern for society and to get to know the world from different angles and issues. Our "Taiwanese Christian Self-Determination Movement" has been participating in the "Market of Possibilities" with a stall of our own beginning 1975.

The first time we took part in a Church Congress was in 1975 in Frankfurt. The theme of our stall was "Taiwan belongs to the Taiwanese, it does not belong to Chiang [Kai-shek], and it does not belong to Mao [Tse-tung]," in this way we strove for an independent stand for the Taiwanese.

In the course of the Formosa [Meilitao] Incident many Taiwanese democrats were arrested and imprisoned. In order to come to the help of these political prisoners, we organized a petition during the 1981 Church Congress with the aim to send postcards to the political prisoners. The caption on the postcards reads: "We deeply care for you and call upon the Taiwan authorities to release you soon." When thousands of visitors to the Church Congress learned of the fate of these political prisoners, they wrote and signed these postcards and paid for the stamps out of their own pocket. These postcards were then sent to Taiwan. Although many years later we learned that none of the political prisoners ever received a single postcard, we do believe that at least to some extent these messages exerted pressure on the Taiwan authorities.

On one occasion Mr Hsieh Tsung-min 謝聰敏 came to Germany to pay a visit to the Amnesty International group in Bremen that had been campaigning for him in the past. A young girl who had sent a postcard to Mr. Hsieh that had been returned to the sender handed this postcard over to him personally. At the time when she had signed and sent the postcard this girl was only 8 years old. By the time she handed it over to Mr Hsieh, she was already 18, but nonetheless Mr. Hsieh was deeply moved.

Komitee für Menschenrechte in Taiwan (KMRT)/

Committee for Human Rights in Taiwan

Everyone in our group of Taiwanese was a member of Amnesty International. However, we later learned that members of Amnesty International were not supposed to work for their compatriots in their own country. For this reason we established the "Committee for Human Rights in Taiwan" 台灣人權協會. The Committee for Human Rights in Taiwan was

ROC. First there were the visits by AI Secretary General Martin Ennals, in 1969 and
1970. I know nothing about that mission other than what Lee Ao and Hsieh Tsung-
min have written about it (that Ennals wanted details on POCs), on the one hand,
and what Ennals himself has written about it (that it was to evaluate the Yuyitung
brothers' trial), on the other. There was also an attempted visit by the influential New
York sinologist and AI-USA member, Ivan Morris, in 1971. That was before I was
involved in AI work, or at least before I was in close communication with people in
London, so I know nothing about what the Morris mission hoped to achieve.

My first involvement in setting up an AI mission was in 1973, when we learned
that Hsieh was facing re-trial. This came quick on the heels of other alarming news,
saying that his health was in serious jeopardy. Always in situations like this, the more
distant the link, the more difficult it was to take claims of atrocities, cruelty, barbarity
and neglect at face value. In the first place, it was human nature to want to deny
the unpleasant, shut out the horrifying. In the second place, just plain everyday life
experience told you that some people might exaggerate or distort the truth to gain
some kind of advantage otherwise not forthcoming. It was natural for the families
to want to see their loved ones released. Would they embellish on the truth, or
exaggerate the threat to health or life in order to get that much more purchase on the
reader/listener/receiver's sympathy and concern?

And there was one more consideration, both for AI itself and for those who hoped
to gain AI's trust: once, just once, should you be caught publishing a false report
or making unfounded claims against an offending government, and you could
take for granted that that government's Ministry of Truth would do its utmost to
see to it that the whole world heard about your "lapse in judgment," your "bias,"
or, most damning of all, your "secret agenda." It mattered little whether you were
talking about someone's health condition, whether the trial had been open or not,
or whether there had been a lawyer present. One false statement and you were
nailed. They would shoot down your reputation —forever if they could. If they
had absolute sanction over the domestic media, they would do this mercilessly and
quite effectively, meaning a setback of perhaps years. Internationally, they would
be listened to as well, in certain quarters at least. Naturally for the IS Asia Research
Department, this called for extreme caution when treating reports, many of which
came to them third, fourth and fifth hand.

With the Hsieh situation of October 1973, it came third-hand: from Hsieh's sister to
Miyake to me to Arlette Laduguie in London. Over the preceding year, news from
Hsieh Hsiu-mei had been reaching AI that her brother was gravely ill, partly because
of injuries sustained during interrogation, partly because of prison treatment later.
Now came more ominous news: Hsieh was to be tried again, perhaps as retribution
for the letter that he had secreted out of prison the year before.

Ennals reminded Chiang Ching-kuo of the "courteous treatment" he had received on
his previous visit to Taiwan. He asked that an AI delegate be allowed to attend the
Hsieh trial. "I need hardly add that such a trial observer would have no intention of
trying to interfere with the course of Chinese justice." Rather, AI's sole interest was

established in 1978 with seven members. As it was a clandestine organ¬ization the list of members was kept secret. The main purpose of this committee was to show care and to let the political prisoners and their families know that there were people abroad who knew of their fate and who cared about them. We wanted to let them know that they weren't alone – because in the atmosphere prevailing in Taiwan at the time "political prisoner" amounted to a synonym for today's "terrorist". When there was a political prisoner in a family, other relatives, neighbors and friends wouldn't dare to entertain any further contact with them. Our foremost task was therefore to provide them with moral support and to express our concern in all kinds of ways.

Our second task was financial support. We frequently had money or parcels taken to Taiwan by church members who handed them over to the persons we wanted to support.

In order to rally public support, the Committee for Human Rights collected material on Taiwan's political prisoners and made them available to the international media; in addition to this we frequently carried out petitioning activities demanding the release of Taiwan's political prisoners. Through these activities Taiwanese all over regularly connected with each other, including Taiwanese from Sweden, Austria, France, the USA, Canada, Brazil and Japan, e.g. in 1979 overseas Taiwanese expressed their solidarity with Yü Teng-fa by writing letters to Chiang Ching-kuo.

The "Occupation" of the Press Division of the KMT's Office in Bonn

By 1981*, after the Formosa Incident, the number of political prisoners in Taiwan had risen sharply. In order to demonstrate how the Taiwan authorities were suppressing the democracy movement and ignoring human rights, my ex-wife Ursula and another German student who had studied in Japan painted their faces white and "occupied" the KMT's Press Division in Bad Godesberg near Bonn. They declared that they wanted to make a phone call to the Taiwan authorities to demand them to immediately release the democrats Annette Lu (Lü Hsiu-lien) and Chen Chü, otherwise they wouldn't leave. As they had notified the German media in advance, all kinds of media, newspapers and TV stations sent journalists to report on this event, which lasted for three hours. The next day they all published detailed reports on the background of this incident. From that moment Germans began to feel

Chao You-yuan

in "satisfying the considerable international interest that there has been in the Hsieh case by making as detailed an appraisal of it as possible." He ended by assuring Chiang that AI "is continuing its research into Prisoners of Conscience on the Chinese mainland," hopefully heading off charges that AI had a pro-communist bias.

This was the Amnesty approach. Polite and diplomatic, it was above all cautious to the extreme. "We have reports that" was the standard opener, meaning that AI was always ready to stand corrected by the government, and would be only too glad to broadcast the glad tidings of so-and-so's release, or humane treatment, or fair trial.

But the AI approach also consisted of persistence. Stonewalling against the AI was no use, and the silent treatment ultimately doomed to failure. And, if the accused regime closed the country to official AI emissaries, it would go none the better for them, as that fact would be used by AI to argue for greater international scrutiny, not less.

So this fourth visit in as many years by an organization rapidly assuming an international reputation must have struck terror in the hearts of the GIO and other agencies whose job it was to fend off these international liberal do-gooders. In 1971, the ROC in its great magnanimity had permitted a University of Hawaii representative to attend the Chen Yu-hsi trial. That was supposed to have been an exception, a special case, as was the "courteous treatment" accorded AI in the Yuyitung trial. But now these noisome foreigners were making a regular thing of it, traipsing all over our sovereign republic, turning over stones, presuming to judge us on *our* human rights record. *Us! Free China!* One example:

> I am writing to you as an official representative of Amnesty International's London-based International Secretariat. Mr. Martin Ennals, Secretary General of Amnesty International, wrote concerning our interest in the appeals court hearings of the case of Mr. Hsieh Ts'ung-min, which we believe was scheduled to be heard from today.... We have no intentions of interfering in the processes of Chinese law. We merely wish to observe the procedures under which Mr. Hsieh is tried and sentenced. We know that the government of the Republic of China shares our concern for humanitarian treatment and the preservation of basic human rights for prisoners of conscience all over the world. (Jack Hasegawa, Taipei, letter to ROC Minister of Justice, 1 October 1973)

Despite his Japanese-sounding name and the fact that his facial features never led him to be taunted as a *gaijin* 外人 in the land of his distant ancestors, Jack was about as Japanese as I was. He was a member the Society of Friends, from a country whose Quaker roots go back to pre-revolutionary times in the Americas. Within a generation of emigrating from England, the Quakers were both numerous and politically strong in the box-shaped state where William Penn, himself a Quaker, established his British crown-sanctioned regime.

Two hundred years later, growing up in New Jersey in the fifties, I would often hear about the Friends, some of them relatives of mine who had refused military service based on their religious pacifism. In 1968 the Quakers' pacifist image took a dive in my estimation when the country put into the White House one Richard Nixon, a conniving crook, proven liar, dark knight of lawyerly deviousness, and quite likely

concerned with the fate of so-called "Free China" in Taiwan. To their surprise there were in fact so many political prisoners who were imprisoned for fighting for human rights and democracy!

[*Editor's note: Linda believes this happened in early 1980 soon after the Kaohsiung Incident, because Ursula told her about it when Linda visited Germany in mid April 1980.]

"Homeland News" in Europe: Taiwan's Political Prisoners

We reproduce below an article provided by Reverend Chao You-yuan 超有源 that appeared in "Homeland News", the newsletter of the World Taiwanese Associations, European Branch, October 1976. The article is transcribed from a speech given by Ursula Chao, then wife of pastor Chao, at the 6th Annual Conference of the Taiwan Associations of Europe and Germany from October 1-3, 1975. The following is a summary of this article:

The editors present a brief overview of the statistics on Taiwan's political prisoners, which according to official KMT figures only amount to 254 individuals for the total period from 1949 to 1976. But according to figures compiled by Taiwanese living overseas on the basis of their contacts with Taiwan, in 1968 alone 1,500 individuals were arrested on political grounds and 200 of them were sentenced to death.

In 1975, when the speech was given, there were 500 political prisoners on Green Island, 20% of which had been sentenced to life imprisonment. Ursula Chao continues by describing the appalling medical conditions there and the kinds of torture the prisoners were subjected to. She describes a few cases, among which the most prominent are Hsieh Tsung-min and Shih Ming-teh.

Ursula Chao points out some examples of how overseas Taiwanese, especially in the US and in Japan, tried to gain international attention for the plight of these prisoners. For instance, in 1973 Taiwanese women in the US founded an association that wrote with their own blood the word "humanity" in Chinese, and they sent it with their signatures to the authorities in Taiwan. Ursula Chao mentions the work of Amnesty International, the abbreviation of which is "ai," which is exactly the romanization of the Taiwanese word for "love". She concludes by appealing to the audience to help, to donate money and to work with Amnesty International for the support of Taiwan's political prisoners.

Reverend Roger Chao and his wife with Chen Chu, now mayor of Kaohsiung, at the Jingmei Prison Human Rights Park, December 9, 2007. (Courtesy of Ronald Tsao.)

Chao You-yuan

co-conspirator in the murder of John Kennedy, and yet, somehow, a "pacifist" of
Quaker persuasion.

The Big Stick: Speaking Softly

Jack Hasegawa did a lot to revive my esteem for Quakerism. At the time that he took
on the October 1973 AI mission to Taiwan he was working as director of Friends
World College's year-abroad program in Kyoto. That he would be going directly to
Taiwan without stopping over in London for the normally requisite briefing by the IS
pointed up the fact that the mission was organized hastily, but just as easily it could
have been taken as proof, if any were needed, that the organization was still, in its
pre-Nobel Prize days, financially strapped: cutting corners was the order of the day.

Some among the ROC constabulary might have made the mistake of thinking that
just because Jack was a warm, genial, modest and soft-spoken kind of guy, he would
be a pushover for the likes of the GIO. They were soon to be set right. When Jack
deplaned on October 1, he hit the ground running, and never let up the whole time
he was there, even though at one point he was fighting an incapacitating intestinal
disturbance and fever.

His first stop was the Taipei offices of the Presbyterian Church of Taiwan, where
he met with Reverend Jamie Sutherland, a Canadian missionary. Fearing that the
office phones were tapped, Sutherland took Jack out to a public phone, where they
attempted to reach Wei Ting-chao's brother, Wei Ting-yu 魏廷昱. None of the numbers
that I had given Jack (which had been passed to me by Miyake) got him anywhere. He
quickly exhausted our short list of family contacts.

Not knowing any Chinese, since Jack easily passed for Japanese in Japan, he would
presumably just as easily have passed for Taiwanese in Taiwan, so long as he didn't
have to speak. He would therefore have posed less threat to the families if he had
gone directly to their door rather than trying to set up an appointment by phone. But
he was under advice from the AI head office about security agency threats against
families talking to foreigners, and was instructed to make his first contact by phone so
as to ascertain whether the families in fact would welcome the chance to meet with an
AI representative despite the threats — the standard AI approach.

It was not only because Jack could not speak Chinese that he first looked up
Sutherland. If AI was so nervous about making initial contact with the family, that
still left the question as to what exactly one was to say at the outset, once you got
through on the phone. "Hello, would you like to meet with a representative of AI who
is now visiting in Taipei?" If the family member were to answer "yes" and the phone
were tapped, then when the security agent came calling they would have no way to
explain themselves.

To London, I raised the strongest objections to this approach. Much better if Jack were
to go directly to their door, unexpected and uninvited. In the first place he would
probably be able to tell at a glance whether the place was being watched, and act
accordingly. Secondly and more importantly, it would offer the family an opportunity
to concoct a story for the spooks. In any case, they could always maintain afterwards

Apologies to the Kuomintang

by Lynn Miles

In the pitched battles of the sixties and seventies described in the preceding pages, there were times when some of us so passionately believed in the rightness of our cause that we often lost sight of the humanness of our adversary. We were no Gandhi, meeting them with a smile and gentleness that belied the force of our conviction. We wantonly painted things black and white – for weren't there lives at stake?

What we were forgetting was that, as Dennis Engbarth was fond of saying, "The Kuomintang is not monolithic, you have to look for nuances." Many of those nuances are unfortunately not much in evidence in this book. It's all heroes and villains.

While people should be held accountable for their actions, at the same time we must realize that while all this high drama was going on, there was an underlying consciousness that was growing apace. Initially the gap was not so much a matter of language differences as it was of humanist concepts. But we were learning from each other. Each of us, in our time and according to our own lights, was learning exactly what the Universal Declaration of Human Rights was all about, how much of that wartime promise still remained unfulfilled, and indeed how the UDHR itself still needed developing.

So, not presuming to speak for anyone else, I should just like to apologize for myself, for having so easily dismissed the words of my GIO friend in Osaka, Mr. Chang Ching-ling, who said, "Don't scratch their faces," meaning, give diplomacy a chance.

Now it is time to look beyond nationality. The "international" in the International Committee should stay with us into the future, as should the "universal" in the Universal Declaration. With the resilience, resourcefulness, and tolerance of the Taiwan people behind it, today the Kuomintang is well placed, if it so chooses, to lead in taking the human rights agenda beyond Taiwan's shores. And one good way to build on the positive image that Taiwan enjoys in the world today is to promote the lessons we have learned about the applicability of nonviolence as the only really viable means of bringing peace with justice. When we speak of "the Taiwan experience," we should not be talking about rights as they are, but rather rights as they have been achieved. And for that, we have history, an uplifting history, a history in which we all, adversaries though we were, learned to work out our common future.

Until we have put our all into the effort, no one can say for sure that the dream of John Lennon, a world without borders, a world without nations, is a dream beyond realizing. We have so much to gain, so let's give it a try. And should we succeed, then there will be no more foreigners. But that does not mean that we should cease looking out for each other: there will always be room for the borrowed voice.

that, whatever information passed between them and Jack, they had not sought him out, but he them.

Since AI wanted to take the cautious, telephoned approach, when Jack met Kawakubo and others of the ICDHRT in Osaka just prior to his leaving, we decided that the best tactic would be for Jack to first meet with Sutherland, who might figure out a way to sneak something past the eavesdroppers on the phone. Perhaps he might consent to inviting the families out for a coffee somewhere on some other pretext, and then introduce Jack unannounced when they got there.

In any case, Jack's first attempts at meeting with family members failed. Since cables and letters about the Hsieh case had been sent directly to the government and had presumably already been received, Jack proceeded to the Executive Yuan, where

> I was moved from desk to desk, and finally delegated to a young man named Herbert Fu, who turned out to be from the Government Information Office. He knew nothing, could find out nothing, and while eager, he said, to be my friend, was afraid that his agency could not help me. He then took me on a rapid tour of what I think was the Foreign Ministry. I asked them repeatedly what building we were in, but he always replied with the Chinese name, saying that he didn't know the English translation. We went into one office labeled "Foreign Affairs Section," where there was a fifteen-minute shouting match (Herbert, being the younger by about 20 years, was shouting very respectfully), the object obviously being that the GIO wanted to pass me on to this unidentified "Foreign Affairs Section," though I kept assuring them that the Hsieh case was not a foreign affair, but a domestic one. It turns out that since I was clearly foreign, it should be handled by some foreign affairs section. Herbert lost, and we were ushered across the hall to an office marked "Immigration." A scene similar to the one before occurred, before we were turned out with little ceremony. Back in the GIO office, after a number of phone calls, I was informed that I would be received at the Central Police Headquarters, and was given a note. (Later translated, it simply said, Taipei Central Police Headquarters, Foreign Affairs Section.)

These words are from Jack's report to London. Had I shown them to any reporters having dealings with the GIO, especially reporters expressing an interest in doing stories with a human rights focus or asking for an introduction to the political opposition, they would all have recognized the pattern (see, for example, David Tharp's treatment of their treatment, page 143). This was as true when I was in Taipei twenty years later, as it was in 1973. Long years of experience had kept the GIO up to speed at pouring on the unction while giving reporters the run-around. Nonetheless, Jack's mission was judged a success by AI and everyone involved, for he put the government on notice that they would have to tread carefully. And he was able to bring out information after successfully meeting with the relatives of Lee Ao, Wei and Hsieh.

Chapter Four

True Christian Service to the Taiwanese Compels Us

As soon as they stepped into the world of the majority Hoklo-speaking population, foreign missionaries with the Presbyterian Church in Taiwan in the 1960s discovered a local reality very different from government propaganda. Others were enlightened by George Kerr's recently-published Formosa Betrayed. They felt morally obligated to help alleviate the suffering, and one small group of missionaries engineered Peng Ming-min's 1970 escape from Taiwan. In contrast, the Catholic Church in Taiwan was "fed, wed, and bedded" with the KMT hierarchy, to quote Sister Nadine Tierney in 1978. Still, Colombans and Maryknollers, whose policy was to speak the language of the people they served, felt for the native Taiwanese. They ascribed to a theology of liberation; many founded workers' social centers. Both Presbyterians and Catholics were punished in 1979/80 for their friendships with democracy activists, but that did not break the spirit of the PCT.

第四章 1965-80： 基於我們的信仰及聯合國人權宣言

1960年代被派往台灣基督長老教會的外國傳教士，一開始在國民黨政府的宣傳樣板中難以接觸真實的台灣，很快地，在逐步深入河洛話族群的民眾後，他們終於有機會接觸到台灣本土的真相。有些人則受到 George Kerr 當時的作品「被出賣的台灣 Formosa Betrayed」所揭發的事實所感召，他們深覺基於道德或信仰都有義務要做些什麼，以減輕受害者的痛苦，於是，一小群外國人的精心安排讓彭明敏得於1970年逃離台灣。相反的，在台的天主教，如 Nadine Tierney 田修女於1978所言，則是保守地順從國民黨的統治不管世事。然而，屬天主教的 Colombans 和 Maryknoller 的政策卻是說著他們服務對象的語言，與在地人同感同理。他們同屬於解放神學，且堅持入世工作。無論是長老教會或天主教，都於1979/1980因支援從事民主活動的朋友而受到懲罰，但是長老教會所堅持的信念並未中斷。

Pioneers in Taiwan's Human Rights and Democracy: The Role of the Foreign Missionaries of the Presbyterian Church in Taiwan

by Yoshihisa Amae 天江喜久

Introduction

While Taiwan's democratization was mainly an outcome of the interaction between the rulers and the ruled, foreigners, both inside and outside the island, played a significant role in stimulating the political transformation, especially in the early stage, i.e. 1960s and 1970s. My essay here examines the role of the foreign missionaries and other church-related agents; it is based largely on my Ph.D. thesis completed at the University of Hawaii, [1] and it draws upon the personal accounts written for a conference sponsored by the Taiwan Foundation for Democracy, which on December 8-9, 2003, brought together three dozen foreigners who made contributions to the democratic struggle from the 1960s through the early 1990s, many suffering immediate forced deportation or banning from future entry to the country that may have been their home for decades. The conference was entitled "International Friends and Taiwan's Democracy and Human Rights: A Journey of Remembrance and Appreciation."

Many of these were missionaries who belonged to the Presbyterian and Reformed Churches and were directly or indirectly involved in events such as the escape of Taiwan independence activist Peng Ming-min in 1970, and the drafting, issuing, and distributing of the three public statements issued by the Presbyterian Church in Taiwan in 1971, 1975, and 1977. Another large number that tended to come into conflict with the authorities were Catholics of the Columban and Maryknoll orders, which in the 1970s in particular articulated programs such as the Peace and Justice mission, following Christ's directive to care for the downtrodden and disadvantaged, an emphasis often known as "liberation theology", particularly through labor activism. In both cases their involvement was not without risk and penalty. Many of them were expelled or locked out of Taiwan as *persona non grata* and were not permitted to return to the island until the blacklist was abolished in the early 1990s. My own research centers on the missionaries of the Presbyterian Church in Taiwan.

The Presbyterian Church in Taiwan: A Church with a Local Spirit

The loss of the KMT in the Chinese civil war and its subsequent flight to Taiwan in 1949 brought many foreign missionaries to the island, some from missions in China from which they had been expelled by the Chinese communists. By 1955, over 300 missionaries had settled in Taiwan, and by 1960, their numbers reached 600 Protestants (Baptists, Methodists, and other denominations) and an equal number of Catholics. [2] Most of them were either pro-KMT or apolitical, and were either

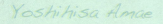

Reverend Kao Chun-ming, General Secretary of the Presbyterian Church of Taiwan (PCT), and others were put on trial on May 16, 1980 for harboring the fugitive opposition figure Shih Ming-teh. Rev. Kao was sentenced to seven years imprisonment. It seems the security agencies were long seeking a pretext to punish Rev. Kao for his leadership in the three public statements of the PCT on human rights and national self-determination.

On June 16, 1965 the PCT celebrated its centennial, dating from its founding in Tainan in 1865 by the Reverend James Laidlaw Maxwell

unaware of the political plight of the native Taiwanese or simply averted their eyes from such a reality. Language was another factor. The vast majority of missionaries used the official national language, Mandarin Chinese, which was considered the language of the oppressor by the native Taiwanese. Thus, they ethnically identified with the Chinese mainlanders and their mission works were focused among them.

A brief historical context is needed to understand the situation as well as to appreciate the involvement of these missionaries. Since the loss of the Chinese civil war to the Chinese communists, and under the ideological warfare of the Cold War, in which atheistic communists were deemed demonic in general by the Christian community, especially by the Catholics and the evangelicals, the Republic of China almost automatically received support, sometimes enthusiastically, from the West. The KMT regime, led by a "great Christian leader" Generalissimo Chiang Kai-shek and his wife Soong Mei-ling, known as Madame Chiang Kai-shek, was often portrayed as "Free China" and the "bastion of democracy." Regardless of the massacre of the native Taiwanese after the 2-28 Incident in 1947 and the political purges since 1949, known as the "White Terror," Taiwan was constantly showered with praise from the West. The religious community was not an exception to this. Fundamental preachers, due to their anti-communist ideology, were unconditionally and uncritically pro-KMT, and for this reason blind to the plight of the native Taiwanese.

In contrast, the Presbyterian Church was already long established in Taiwan, and had weathered the Japanese occupation. The PCT, the major Christian religious denomination in Taiwan, was founded when English Presbyterian missionaries arrived in southern Taiwan in 1865, followed by Canadian Presbyterian missionaries in the north in 1872. These missionaries brought modern medicine and education, and thus their converts, although only a few percent of the population, tended to become the leading medical and commercial elite as Taiwan modernized under Japanese colonialism. By the mid-1970s, the PCT encompassed over 150,000 adherents and nearly 1,000 congregations, organized island-wide through internal democracy up to the highest post of General Secretary.

Missionaries affiliated with the PCT, as well as the Fathers and Brothers of the Maryknoll Mission, whose policy globally was to indigenize, learned the local Holo (Hoklo) language (commonly known as *Taiyu* or "Taiwanese") upon their arrival to Taiwan. This gave them access to the native Taiwanese, many of whom had suffered political persecution under the KMT regime. More importantly, being affiliated with a church with a strong local spirit, PCT missionaries were informed about the tragedies of the 2-28 Incident of 1947 and the White Terror under martial law since that time. Theology was another factor, and probably was the most important one, in explaining why these missionaries got involved in caring for the human rights of the Taiwanese people.

Some of the missionaries learned about the tragedy of 2-28 and other incidents through George Kerr's, *Formosa Betrayed*, but many were not exposed to this reality until their arrival to the island. It was against such a political myth that the missionaries had to stand up. In this process, they came into communication with

I Objected to Government Pressure on the Presbyterian Church to Withdraw from the World Council of Churches

by Donald J. Wilson

I arrived on Taiwan in December of 1959 to serve with the Presbyterian Church of Formosa, as it was then named. While I and my family were U.S. citizens, we were serving in Taiwan under the auspices of the Presbyterian Church in Canada.

Soon after arriving in Taipei, we were told by the Canadian Mission Committee that we should study the national language, Mandarin Chinese, then referred to as *guo-yu*, since the mainland Chinese and the Kuomintang were in command of the government. Martial law was still in effect (and remained in force throughout my entire time of service in Taiwan) even though it had been declared as an "emergency" measure in 1949, when the mainland fell to the People's Republic of China and about two million mainland Chinese escaped to Taiwan to establish a continuing national entity there.

I began to learn quickly that all was not well between the native Taiwanese population and their "brothers" from the Mainland. In addition to the strict enforcement of martial law, and the imposition of *guo-yu* as a national language, there was an obvious distrust between the two million newcomers and the approximately thirteen million native Taiwanese. Our mission office worker, who was Taiwan-born, told me that when he heard someone speak *guo-yu* his initial reaction was to take two steps backward. I did not fully realize why this was so until eight months after our arrival, the Presbyterian Church of Formosa's Personnel Committee told me they wanted me to shift my study of language from *guo-yu* to Taiwanese, the Amoy dialect of Chinese, and the mother tongue of the vast majority of the population and of the Presbyterian Church.

As soon as my new studies began in Tainan people began to tell me privately about the history of "ji-ji-bat" (2-28), or February 28, 1947, when upwards of 20-30,000 Taiwanese, many of them community leaders, were taken and killed or "disappeared" because of their fierce resistance to the oppression imposed by the mainlanders who had come to rule following the departure of the colonial Japanese government in 1946. This period of learning Taiwanese and orientation to what had happened in the recent past made me aware that Taiwanese were very fearful and cautious about publicly criticizing the government, and helped me realize that there was a huge human rights problem in Taiwan.

My service in Taiwan was primarily in Taipei, the seat of the KMT government. There I taught in the Taiwan Theological College and later served as associate general secretary for the Presbyterian Church in Formosa. Personally I made the acquaintance of Dr. Peng Ming-min, a prominent professor at National Taiwan University who was accused of "sedition" in 1964 because he circulated literature calling for the end of martial law. When he was imprisoned, I paid pastoral visits to his wife at their residence in Taipei, because Taiwanese friends were fearful of doing this. Later when Dr. Peng was released to house

opposition figures.

The Great Escape of Professor Peng Ming-min, 1970

The first collective effort by the PCT-affiliated missionaries in Taiwan's human rights was rescuing Professor Peng Ming-min 彭明敏, a renowned scholar of international aviation law. In September 1964, Peng and his two former students, Hsieh Tsung-min 謝聰明 and Wei Ting-chao 魏廷朝, were arrested on charges of sedition after attempting to publish a manifesto for self-salvation in which they asserted the right of the people of Taiwan to determine their own future, i.e. Taiwan independence. Peng, thanks to his fame which elicited an international outcry, was soon released from prison and was instead put under house arrest. He had many international friends, among them the missionaries, and the reality of the past as well as the ongoing political oppression was propagated overseas through their efforts.

Donald Wilson, a missionary to the PCT from the Presbyterian Church in Canada, arrived to Taiwan in 1959. Wilson taught in the Taiwan Theological College in Taipei and then later served as Associate General Secretary for the PCT. He had learned about Peng's case, and when Peng was imprisoned he paid pastoral visits to his wife at their residence in Taipei. The visits continued after Peng was released from prison and was put under house arrest. Wilson recalls a military jeep posted at the end of the street. According to Wilson, other Taiwanese friends were fearful of visiting Peng. After returning to the United States and Canada with his family in 1967, Wilson was refused a visa. [3]

Milo Thornberry and Judith Thomas became acquainted with Peng through Donald Wilson. The Thornberrys arrived in Taipei in December 1965. Sent by the United Methodist Church, Milo came to Taiwan to serve as a chaplain at Soochow University, but, at his request as well as that of the seminary, he was instead loaned to the PCT and was appointed as associate professor of church history at Taiwan Theological College, where Judith taught English. According to the Thornberrys, their acquaintance with Peng and other political activists such as Hsieh Tsung-min, Wei Ting-chao, and Li Ao 李敖 brought them to realize how oppressive KMT policies were. The couple felt strongly compelled to do something to oppose the social injustice committed by the government. [4] Their human rights activities comprised three areas. First, they arranged meetings for foreign visitors in which Peng and other Taiwanese friends would inform them of the political repression on the island. These meetings, which were held at the Thornberrys' residence, were clandestine in order to protect the Taiwanese informants from being arrested. Visitors included church and government dignitaries and journalists, as well as academics. Second, in order to provide more information, the Thornberrys obtained a mimeograph machine, and used it to print and circulate original as well as reprinted articles which focused on various aspects of Taiwanese society. Several hundred copies of the collection were handed to visitors in Taiwan as well as to interested parties in the U.S. [5] The foreword to the collection read:

We are a group of men and woman of local and foreign nationalities

arrest, I continued to visit in their home, even though a military jeep was posted at the end of his street.

As associate general secretary in the Presbyterian Church I participated in major confidential discussions held in Tainan in 1966-67 concerning the pressure the Nationalist government was placing on the Presbyterian Church to withdraw its membership from the World Council of Churches. The government resented the fact that the WCC had called for the inclusion of the People's Republic of China in the United Nations. The government had sent its representatives to the sessions of the General Assembly to pressure for its withdrawal from the WCC. This I saw as an infringement on religious liberty and I urged that the Presbyterian Church maintain its relations with the WCC as a matter of religious commitment and fidelity to being a part of the worldwide body of Christianity.

After my family returned to the United States and Canada on furlough in 1967, I was unable to obtain a visa and my denomination was quietly informed that I was *persona non grata*. I continued to be unable to visit Taiwan until 1980, when again I was refused a visa to participate in a human rights conference sponsored by a well known American religious study group known as CRIA, the Council on Religion and International Affairs. Only after much pressure upon the KMT was I granted a visa. However, at every meeting of the Human Rights Conference, a government spokesperson always personally and publicly addressed me and instructed me to inform the officials of the Presbyterian Church of Taiwan that they were wrong in making statements about the denial of human rights in Taiwan and in calling for a national democratic government.

My last visit to Taiwan was in 1985 when I was invited to address the General Assembly of the Presbyterian Church of Taiwan on the occasion of its 40th anniversary celebration. I am proud of the prominent role of the Presbyterian Church in Taiwan in struggling for the independence of Taiwan, supporting a nationally elected democratic government, and advocating human rights.

Donald Wilson came to Taiwan in December 1959 under the auspices of the Presbyterian Church in Canada. He maintained contact with the family of Professor Peng Ming-min, then imprisoned.

Donald J. Wilson

residing in Formosa (Taiwan), whose professions comprise the fields of religion, education, and public affairs. Our primary purpose in compiling this paper is to point out some issues that should provoke thoughtful discussion of the realities in this country. While we are aware of the disadvantages of remaining anonymous, we choose to do so both for the sake of our own safety and for that of our families and friends. That such secrecy is necessary is, in itself, indicative of the nature of the regime by which this island is governed.

We know that a vast amount of public funds and great official efforts are being expended abroad by the Chinese Nationalist Government to maintain an image of this country as a worthy member of the "free and democratic" world. We know also that abundant official publications boasting of the Kuomintang's (Nationalist Party) achievement in Formosa are being distributed to foreign visitors here. Thus we feel acutely a need to present a more balanced picture to those who are concerned with what the real situation in Formosa might be. With these things in mind, we have compiled several articles — some previously published — which are at considerable variance with the governmental propaganda and which we feel, as a result of our own observations and personal experiences, reflect more truthfully the actual situation in Formosa under Chinese Nationalist rule. Emphasis is given to the political situation because we are convinced that this political situation affects the whole of life here— partly by making impossible any changes in the present structures that might contribute to the realization of social justice — and that any discussion of the problems in Formosa is superficial unless this basic political problem is recognized. [6]

The Thornberrys secured a mailbox in Hong Kong for their Taiwanese friends to correspond with friends overseas without fear that their mail would be read by the authorities. The letters were brought to them by foreign friends who moved back and forth between Taiwan and Hong Kong on a regular basis.

The third involvement concerned the political prisoners and their families. Many families of the political prisoners lived in severe poverty and isolation, thanks to security agents harassing relatives who dared to offer them any help. The Thornberrys were able to identify these families and provide them with financial assistance. They were able to distribute thousands of dollars to persons in great need through generous donations from the American Friends Service Committee (Quakers) and other personal sources. [7]

Meanwhile, the Thornberrys maintained regular contact with Peng Ming-min, and by late 1968, they felt that his life was in danger. They reached a consensus that Peng needed to leave the island. On one occasion, the Thornberrys invited Mark Thelin, faculty at the Tainan Theological College and Seminary, and his wife Virginia to brainstorm on an escape plan. The Thelins recall how the five of them met at the

Helping Peng Ming-min Escape: We Must Oppose the Oppression Our Country Is Supporting, Else We Are Complicit

by Milo Thornberry 唐培禮牧師 and Judith Thomas

Preface: The human rights work we did in Taiwan was carried out as a team. We discussed and agreed on every activity and we each fully participated in all of them. In that same spirit of teamwork, we are writing this joint account of those activities. While we are no longer married to each other, we continue to share and delight in our three adult children: Elizabeth Thornberry Maher, Richard Thornberry, and Katherine Thornberry, and our two grandchildren, Sean and Cassidy Maher. We are both very happy and honored to have this opportunity to return to Taiwan with our children after more than thirty years and to see at first hand your amazing progress toward democratization

We arrived in Taipei on December 30, 1965, just in time to celebrate the solar New Year in our adopted country.

We were sent by the United Methodist Church, which had a long history of missions on the China mainland and a more recent history of association with then-President Chiang Kai-shek and his wife Soong Mei-ling. Indeed, the Methodist presence in Taiwan was established after the Nationalist government moved to Taiwan, and most of the church's missionary work was associated with the people who came to Taiwan from China after World War II. For this reason, we were expected to learn Mandarin Chinese rather than Taiwanese, and we began language study immediately after the New Year.

Milo's first eighteen months were spent studying Mandarin at the Taipei Language Institute. The assumption of our church was that he would become chaplain at Soochow University. Instead, at his request and the request of the seminary, he was loaned to the Presbyterian Church of Formosa and was appointed as associate professor of church history at Taiwan Theological College in Taipei. Later, he also served as a visiting professor at Tainan Theological Seminary and as a member of the regional faculty of the East Asia Theological School.

Three months after our arrival, Judith's language study was interrupted by the birth of our first child, Elizabeth. When she was three months old, Judith resumed study part-time and was able to continue beyond the initial 18 months normally allowed. She managed to do a little formal study of Taiwanese as well. (Alas her Taiwanese teacher told her that she spoke Taiwanese with a "mainlander" accent!) In the summer of 1968, we moved to the campus of Taiwan Theological College, halfway up Yangmingshan, where Milo taught church history and Judith taught English.

During the year before our arrival in Taiwan, we both read whatever literature we could find written in English about the island. We also had the opportunity to meet Rev. George Todd, who had spent time in Taiwan with the Presbyterian Church. He had a strong influence on us as he talked about the ways he had found to move below the surface

Thornberrys to discuss a possible exit plan through the wee hours in the morning.
[8] After six months of preparation, the Thornberrys had formulated a plan in which
Peng would disguise himself and leave the country on a scheduled flight from
Taipei's Sungshan Airport, which then served as Taiwan's international airport. The
disguise was particularly difficult because Peng had lost his left arm in Japan under
the American bombing of Nagasaki during WWII, and so was easily identified.
According to Judith Thomas, such an audacious plan was conceived after reading
an article in a weekly news magazine about eastern European dissidents escaping as
tourists. [9]

Peng obtained a Japanese passport via his friend who came to Taiwan as a tourist.
He replaced the original photo with his own, and by December 1969, he was ready to
leave. Lynn Miles carried a letter to Japan for Peng just about Christmas 1969. Peng
spent the 24 hours prior to his departure at the Thornberrys' residence, from whence
he left for the airport. Under the watch of the Thornberrys' friends, Peng passed
through immigration with his forged Japanese passport. [10] Some ten days later, in
mid January 1970, he surfaced in Sweden, where he had obtained political asylum
with the assistance of Amnesty International members.

The Thornberrys were put under house arrest on March 2, 1971 on the accusation of
having imported a bomb by courier from Japan. [11] The couple was then deported
from Taiwan in 48 hours. According to the *New York Times* article, reporting the arrest,
plainclothes officers were stationed throughout the day at the Thornberrys' residence
on the campus of Taiwan Theological College; the telephone had been disconnected,
and visitors were intercepted by a policeman and were asked to leave. [12] Rowland
Van Es, an American professor of Tainan Theological Seminary, who trailed the
Thornberrys to the airport, recalls military guards being posted every 10-20 yards
along the entire route to the airport. [13]

Public Statements by the Presbyterian Church in Taiwan in the 1970s

In those days, missionaries with the PCT felt that the Taiwanese church needed to
speak on behalf of the "voiceless" native Taiwanese who have been deprived of their
political rights and basic freedom. Such thought was expressed through the work
of Dr. Wolfgang L. Grichting, a German sociologist who visited the island in 1970
for his project on religion and society in Taiwan. During this visit, the scholar met
up with Milo Thornberry, Wendell Karsen, and other missionaries. The outcome of
the meeting appeared in his book titled, *The Value System in Taiwan*, 1970. Grichting,
commenting on the PCT, wrote:

> The PCT needs to prophetically and courageously attack the roots of the
> present social problems in Taiwan from the perspective of the Gospel
> with the spirit of speaking the truth in love, letting the chips fall where
> they may, and being willing to bear passively and patiently whatever
> consequences this may elicit. [14]

The recommendation soon became a reality. In December 1971, on the backdrop of
the ROC's expulsion from the United Nations and the impending visit of the US

of Taiwan life and understand the often unheard perspectives among the people. Most important, George encouraged us to get to know Rev. Don Wilson of the Presbyterian Church in Taiwan. "He will introduce you to people who can help you gain a fuller understanding." As soon as we could, we met Don, and it was subsequently through him that we met Peng Ming-min, his wife, and his extended family. We quickly become good friends, and spent many good hours in discussion and learning.

Meeting Dr. Peng was the most important event in our journey to a greater understanding of the political situation in Taiwan. Gradually, through his own story, through personal contacts provided by him and others, and through our own continued study, we came to realize just how oppressive the government's policies were. Our decision to take personal responsibility for acting against these policies was not casually made. We had many discussions about whether we, as foreigners, had any right to get involved in political activities of another country. The deciding factor for us was the fact that our own country, the United States, was already deeply involved in Taiwan's politics. Indeed, we took the actions we did on this basis: if we do not oppose the oppression our country is supporting, then we will be complicit in that oppression. We must, therefore, act in opposition.

In those early days, we talked about what kinds of actions we were willing to participate in. We were open to a wide range of activities, but we were also clear that we would not do anything that involved violence. We saw ourselves as engaging in activities that would, in a free and democratic country, fall well within the bounds of the law. At the same time, we knew that these actions would, under the martial law in effect at that time, be seen as illegal. In order to be effective, we therefore needed to carry out our actions as unobtrusively as possible.

As American citizens, whose government's support was essential to the Nationalist government, we knew that our actions carried much less risk for us than similar actions would for any Taiwanese national. That knowledge led to another principle that we adopted: in our human rights activities, we would not be involved with any Taiwan citizen who was not an adult with full understanding and acceptance of the risks. This decision meant that we were never involved with any of our students in these activities, nor did we discuss such activities or the general political situation with any of them.

Our human rights activities fell into two broad areas of concern. The first related to ensuring that foreign visitors to Taiwan as well as persons outside Taiwan heard a perspective different from the official one proffered by the Government Information Office. While in language school we were also expected to help provide hospitality to Methodist visitors from the United States. We found that few had any idea of realities on the island. Since we had met Dr. Peng within a year of arriving in Taiwan, we were eager to arrange meetings in which he and other Taiwanese could give their perspectives to these guests. Many of these meetings were, of necessity, clandestine because our Taiwanese friends risked imprisonment if their actions became public. In order to provide a confidential setting for these meetings, we opened our home to visiting journalists, academics, and other foreigners, as well as our Taiwanese informants.

In order to provide more information to these visitors, we worked with some foreign friends to create a packet containing both original and reprinted materials discussing various aspects of the Taiwan situation. We secured a mimeograph machine and printed

President Richard Nixon to Beijing, the PCT published a statement on "Our National Fate." This statement was originally an ecumenical work. Daniel Beeby, a British missionary who was then serving as vice president of the TTCS, made a proposal to announce a statement at a meeting of the Republic of China Ecumenical Cooperative Committee. [15] According to Rev. Huang Wu-tong 黃武東, who attended the meeting, Beeby made a motion at the end of the meeting, saying: "As you know, in a time as such when Taiwan faces great challenges, we, the church, shall not remain silent but speak out based on our Christian faith!" Beeby's proposal was supported unanimously, and afterward those present approved the statement in the name of the Committee. [16] However, when information about the committee's action was obtained by the government, the church leaders were harassed and pressured by the authorities. As a result, all churches except the PCT withdrew from being signatories of the statement. The PCT then modified the statement and announced it as its own. [17]

In the statement, the PCT called on the government to "hold elections of all representatives to the highest government bodies to succeed the present representatives, who were elected twenty-five years ago on the mainland." [18] Further, the PCT declared that the future of Taiwan should be determined by the fifteen million people in Taiwan: "We oppose any powerful nation disregarding the rights and wishes of fifteen million people and making unilateral decisions to their own advantage, because God ordained, and the United Nations Charter has affirmed, that every people has the right to determine its own destiny." [19] This document is regarded as the first public announcement on the self-determination of Taiwan published on the island. [20]

Foreign missionaries were involved in the making of the statement in at least two major ways: its drafting and dissemination. The draft of the statement was prepared in Chinese and English. The original draft prepared by Beeby was modified by John Tin and Rowland Van Es, his colleague. Wendell Karsen, missionary with the Reformed Church of America, however, was the one who was responsible for the final wording of the English draft. Working at the PCT General Assembly in Taipei at the time, Karsen was asked to come to the office at 11 pm to join the PCT Executive Committee members who were working on the statement. Discussing the text line by line, he recalls how he had paid special attention to the English translation, in order to retain the "double meaning" of the text, designed to evade government accusations while delivering the real message to those who are familiar with the political situation. [21] This involvement eventually cost the young missionary his position in Taiwan. Karsen, who left for the United States on a furlough in July 1973, was put on the KMT blacklist and not allowed to return to Taiwan until 1992. Upon Karsen's denial of re-entry to Taiwan, the Reformed Church of America issued a statement in May 1974, expressing solidarity with the people in Taiwan. The statement reads, in part: "We have become aware of the hopes and frustrations of the 15 million people living in Taiwan, being denied their right to self-determination through the foreign policies of many nations, including our own." The church also called on its members "to acquaint themselves with the Taiwanese quest for human dignity, and to write to

several hundred copies of nine articles, two of which were written for the collection by knowledgeable friends. We did not circulate these articles among Taiwanese because it was never our intention to try to persuade Taiwanese of realities in their own country. The packet was intended for foreign visitors who wanted to know more about the Taiwanese situation. To that end, we distributed the articles to many visitors in Taiwan as well as to interested parties in the U.S. The source of the collection was, of course, kept secret.

A second area of involvement concerned political prisoners and their families. Working with Taiwanese friends who had been in prison, we obtained lists of other prisoners' names and forwarded them on to Amnesty International for public recognition and personal contact.

We also learned of the dire predicament of many families with a family member in prison for political activity (which often meant as little as voicing a criticism of the government). Possibly as a remnant of the traditional *bao jia* system, these families were systematically cut off from financial help — e.g., relatives who acted to help them were visited by special police and warned not to help. The result was that many of these families were living in severe poverty. With the help of our friends, we were able to identify these families and provide help for them through funds brought in from outside the country. The American Friends Service Committee (Quakers) was a major help in this endeavor, along with other persons of good will who worked hard to raise money and get it to us in unconventional ways.

Together with our foreign donors who provided the funds and our Taiwanese friends who bravely traveled about Taiwan distributing them to families, we were able to distribute thousands of dollars to persons in great need. This work ended only after our deportation and the arrest of some of the distributors.

There remains one activity that we remember with great satisfaction. During 1969, as we continued to meet regularly with Peng Ming-min, it became increasingly clear that his life was being threatened. He was called in for "consultations" with the internal affairs police, who talked of how easily they could attack him in the guise of an accident such as an out-of-control car hitting him as he walked along a street. We were very concerned about not only his safety but also his emotional health in living with such continual trauma of threats and restrictions (he was under surveillance both at home and when he went out).

After much discussion with Dr. Peng and a few other foreign friends, we reached a consensus that he needed to leave Taiwan until conditions were less dangerous for him. There was no hope that the government would allow him to leave legally; the only recourse was some kind of clandestine departure. None of us had any experience with such an undertaking. We had many discussions together and were ultimately able to come up with a plan to help him leave Taiwan safely. We had assistance from many friends outside the country, including the family in Sweden he initially stayed with, who were connected with Amnesty International.

The activities described above comprise the majority of the work we did in Taiwan that was specifically focused on human rights. We want to add that there were some things we were unofficially accused of doing that we did not do. Upon our arrest, some press reports in Hong Kong and in the People's Republic suggested that we had links with the CIA or

their representatives and senators, asking them to support self-determination for the people of Taiwan." [22]

The dissemination of the documents was not at all easy in those days. Under martial law, freedom of speech and press were not enjoyed by the people of the island. The media was controlled by the government and discourse alternative to the government propaganda was quickly suppressed. The PCT first attempted to publish the statement in the local newspapers as a paid advertisement, but such a plan was aborted after the government security agencies found out and intervened. According to Karsen, the head of the Garrison Command called Kao Chun-ming 高俊明, General Secretary of the PCT, and demanded that the statement not to be issued. Kao resisted the pressure and the PCT general assembly called all pastors to read the statement from the pulpit on January 2, 1972. The secret police scheduled "tea times" with all PCT pastors, using carrot and stick, to stop them from carrying out the order. While some caved in, most of them read the statement as scheduled. [23] The statement was also published in the *Taiwan Church News,* the PCT weekly newspaper. However, the publications mysteriously disappeared in the mail and failed to reach the subscribers. [24]

Meanwhile, Karsen had arranged trusted colleagues who were going off the island to smuggle the document out to Hong Kong. From there, it was sent to worldwide churches, the Vatican, Christian organizations such as the World Council of Churches (WCC) and the World Alliance of Reformed Churches (WARC), the U.S. State Department, and overseas news services. In an accompanying letter, the PCT requested the overseas churches to circulate the statement as widely as possible in their respective countries. Major news agencies carried the story, while many church publications, particularly in the US, featured it, with some calling upon their government to take action to protect the rights of the people of Taiwan. The statement was forwarded to their senators and congressmen as well.

The response to the statement was positive. The overseas churches all expressed their support for the PCT. [25] For example, the Vatican replied: "the Holy See, in the future, as in the past, will do everything in its power to cooperate in guaranteeing the peace, liberty and human rights of the people of Formosa." The director of Republic of China Affairs at the US State Department, in his reply, assured the PCT that, "… while we intend to normalize our relations with the People's Republic of China, we will remain firm in our commitments to our friends and allies … I hope that the above may help to alleviate some of the concerns that you and your Church may feel about the President's trip to Peking." [26]

Such positive response was not unrelated to the years of the PCT's commitment to ecumenicalism. The significance of the statement should not be underestimated. It was, after all, the first public challenge to the legitimacy of the KMT regime from the largest and most organized civil institution in the island. The word spread well beyond the walls of the church, encouraging countless supporters and activists of democracy and human rights in Taiwan and abroad.

some other U.S. secret agency. In truth, neither of us was ever associated with the CIA or any other governmental agency.

We were told that an unofficial report from the Nationalist government to the U.S. ambassador accused us of attempting to import explosives for the Taiwan Independence movement. That accusation was also untrue. We were never asked to assist in any violent actions and we never did.

Finally, we want to emphasize and acknowledge that there were many, many persons — both foreign and Taiwanese -- who helped in these projects. Some of them cannot be publicly recognized because of positions they still hold. We are still in awe of the numbers of people who quietly made sacrifices, took risks, met serious consequences, and remained committed to their principles.

We know that we risked much less than many of the people we worked with during that time, especially the people of Taiwan. At the end of the day, we were sent back to our homeland. Many of them were imprisoned or exiled. They are the heroes who deserve to

Milo Thornberry and daughter on train to Ilan with Taiwan Foundation for Democracy, December 2003. Milo and Judith and their children were put under house arrest at the Taiwan Theological Seminary in Yangmingshan and deported in March 1971.

Judith Thomas receiving recognition from Peng Ming-min; Judith hatched the plan for Peng's escape from Taiwan and carried it out together with Milo at the end of 1969.

The PCT issued two other statements in this decade: "Our Appeal" (1975) and the "Declaration on Human Rights" (1977). In the latter statement, addressed in an open letter to the US President Jimmy Carter, the PCT advocated self-determination for the people in Taiwan and boldly urged the government "to take effective measures whereby Taiwan may become new and independent." Both statements, unlike the first one, were initiated and drafted on their own, with little help from foreign missionaries. Yet, again, the missionaries played the role of courier in disseminating the document. The statement was smuggled out to Hong Kong with the help of foreign missionaries and their friends, and then subsequently announced to the international community. [27] Elizabeth Brown, the English secretary to General Secretary C.M. Kao, also entrusted a copy to Linda Gail Arrigo, a member of Lynn Miles' network in Osaka, to spirit out of the country to human rights organizations.

The Expulsion of Daniel Beeby

The involvement of the missionaries in events which were deemed by the authorities "seditious" was not without severe penalties. Soon after the 1971 Statement was issued, Daniel Beeby's request for a visa extension was denied on the grounds that the applicant was now *persona non grata*. After having served at the seminary for more than twenty years, Beeby was notified by the government that he must leave the island within 10 days. On March 5, 1972, a farewell service was held at the Taipingching Church 太平境教會 in Tainan. Arranged by Rowland Van Es, the solemn service was recorded by a CBS television crew whose members were in Taiwan on their way back to the US from Vietnam. Rev. Kao Chun-ming gave a sermon entitled "Who is the True Patriot?" and read Matthew 5:10: "Blessed are those who are persecuted because of righteousness, for theirs is the kingdom of heaven." Beeby, in his fluent Holo Taiwanese, spoke to the emotionally-charged congregation:

> There is one thing which I do not quite understand to this day. That is there are many people — [native] Taiwanese and Mainlanders alike — who do not want to stay but leave Taiwan. The government forces them to stay and would not allow them to leave the island. On the contrary, there are many like myself who love Taiwan and wish to stay. Yet the government won't let us stay but instead forces us to leave. Therefore, I must bid my farewell to all of you. Thank you very much for holding such a solemn "funeral" for me. Tomorrow, I will leave the island. Please do not trouble yourself to see me off at the train station. [28]

Despite Beeby's request, the following day about seventy students and faculty members of the TTCS accompanied Dr. and Mrs. Beeby from their campus residence to the Tainan train station. Together they sang "We Shall Overcome" as they marched to the station. [29] The emotional farewell brought tears to many in the crowd. According to Kao Chun-ming, at each train stop on the way to Taipei, members of the PCT came to the station platform to bid farewell to the Beebys. [30]

We Were Glad to Play a Small Role in Professor Peng Ming-min's Escape

by Virginia and Mark Thelin

First of all, we want to emphasize that our contributions have been extremely minimal. The major work in building democracy has rightly been carried out by local people. We were lurking on the fringes of a couple of the milestones on Taiwan's road to democracy, but that was about all. Mark's sociology teaching over the years may have broadened some student minds and inspired some new and different views of society -- an influence impossible to measure. To illustrate: A graduating senior sociology major in the 1960s said this of his lectures and assigned readings in a sociological theory course Mark was teaching, "Before I took this course, I thought Karl Marx was The Devil. Now I know he was just a man, but one passionately interested in improving the lives of workers everywhere." (This kind of influence cannot be quantified.)

One concrete example we can cite of assistance to democratizing forces relates to Dr. Peng Ming-min. Mark first met him when directing a seminar entitled "Interns in Industry" during the summer of 1963. This was a project involving the supervision of twelve university students and seminarians who spent six weeks of their vacation working in offices and factories of the Taipei area. They were doing this in order to acquire an understanding of industrial relations "from the inside", as participant observers. The organizer of the project was Dr. George Todd, who introduced Mark to Dr. Peng at dinner one evening in the Peng home. This was shortly before the Todds returned to the United States, having completed a three-year term as visiting faculty at the Tainan Theological College and Seminary. Mark and Dr. Peng became better acquainted through subsequent meetings.

After Dr. Peng's arrest in September of 1964, Mark visited the Peng family each time he went to Taipei for a meeting or on a research project. He went on home leave in the United States for the academic year, 1965-66, during which he married Virginia (Ginny) and returned to Taiwan in September, 1966. By that time Dr. Peng had been released from prison, and the acquaintance with him was renewed. Early in 1969 we and our toddler son, Carl, visited Taipei, staying at the home of Rev. and Mrs. Milo and Judith Thornberry on the campus of the Taiwan Theological College. Milo and Judy had also made the acquaintance of Dr. Peng. They told us that he wanted to get together with the two of us couples to brainstorm and to come up with a way he might leave Taiwan unnoticed by the authorities. He could not get work, because of his prison record, and had been refused an ROC passport despite having received a job offer from an American university. He had to wait until after midnight to come to meet us in order to avoid being seen and followed by the "watchbird" stationed outside his home during the day.

At the Thornberry home we five discussed the situation through the wee hours of the morning and worked out a possible plan of action. After that we Thelins heard nothing further about the matter for almost a year. Then, on a trip to Taipei, Mark contacted the Thornberrys and was told that Dr. Peng had successfully left the Island, the government,

In Taipei, sympathizers secretly arranged a press conference at the President Hotel. Wendell Karsen contacted reporters of the foreign press in Taipei, including Reuters, UPI, AP, *The New York Times*, *The Washington Post*, and *Newsweek* magazine. [31] Before heading to the airport from the railway station, Beeby asked his KMT escort if he could make a quick stop at the hotel to bid his friends a farewell. Unaware of the arrangement for the press conference, the officer from the Garrison Command gave permission. Beeby walked into the room where the reporters gathered, held a press conference, and the story of his expulsion was widely reported overseas. [32] Beeby told the press that he saw "a new determination on the part of people in the Church to speak out on things wider than the saving of souls." [33] When the couple stopped in Hong Kong on their way to England, Beeby told the press that Taiwan should be "a viable and separate country." He also urged that the principle of self-determination be observed for the Taiwanese people. [34]

Beeby's expulsion shocked the students and the faculty at the Seminary, as well as the PCT members at large. Rev. Hsu Tien-hsien 許天賢, who at the time was studying

Expelled Foreign Missionaries Originally Assigned
to the Presbyterian Church in Taiwan

Name	Period of Stay in Taiwan	Position when Expelled	Date of Expulsion	Alleged Reason
Donald Wilson	1959-1967	Faculty, Taiwan Theological College (TTCS)	Left Taiwan on a furlough in 1967, not permitted to return	Acquaintance with Peng Ming-min, a political prisoner
Milo Thornberry	1965-71	Professor, Taiwan Theological College	March 1971	Involvement in the escape of Peng Ming-min
Daniel Beeby	1950-1972	Acting President of TTCS	March 6, 1972	Involvement in the 1971 Statement
Rowland Van Es	1967-73	Professor, TTCS	1973	Involvement in the 1971 Statement
Wendell Karsen	1969-1973	Missionary to the PCT	Left Taiwan on a furlough in July 1973, not permitted to return	Involvement in the 1971 Statement
David Gelzer	1975-84	Professor, TTCS	January 1984	Involvement in the election campaign of Ruth Kao 高李麗珍

apparently, not yet knowing it. (We leave it to Milo and Judy to explain how he left, as they were involved in carrying out the plan and we were not.) Shortly after that, *Newsweek* published an article stating that Taiwan's leading dissident had suddenly turned up in Sweden, and speculated that the CIA must have flown him out on a U.S. military plane or else sent him off in a fishing boat. How strange it was to read this, to know how it had been done and that it had nothing to do with the CIA -- and not to be able to tell anyone for many years!

We were also on the margins of the Kaohsiung Incident through knowing Dr. Linda Gail Arrigo, who had been pursuing her doctoral dissertation research at Stanford University. She had come to Taiwan in 1977 to study young women who were working in factories of what was developing as the export processing zones. She was interested in the possibility of a short-term faculty appointment at Tunghai and also needed a sociology student who could assist her in carrying out her research. She was able to get the research assistant but not the teaching appointment, as there was no opening at Tunghai for someone with her specialty, which was anthropology.

Ten days or so before the Kaohsiung Incident (and by then having married Mr. Shih Ming-teh), Linda appeared on our doorstep one evening. She wanted to find students to write articles for *Formosa* magazine. Mark told her this was likely a very dangerous thing for them to do, but she was sure everything had changed, Taiwan was opening up dramatically, and that there was no danger at all. In short, she believed Taiwan was entering a new era politically. She also told us of the planned rally (with permit denied) for Human Rights Day, December 10, 1979, in Kaohsiung. We warned her to be careful.

In the immediate aftermath of the Incident we heard many rumors that whatever violence had happened was the result of provocation by police action, that policemen and soldiers had been sent to various hospitals to increase the count of the injured, etc. Ginny began writing all this up as a report to be hand-carried out of Taiwan. (Mark had done the same in a five-page, single-spaced letter to Dr. George Todd following public disclosure of Dr. Peng's arrest; this was in November of 1964. Dr. Todd later referred to the letter as a kind of "sacred document", summarizing the events as reported in the newspapers and with the addition of an occasional interview. Because of postal censorship in those days such letters, documents or related materials had to be taken out, either by ourselves or others who chanced to pass through Taiwan and happened to have seen us along their way.)

In the meantime, Mr. Shih Ming-teh, leader of the rally, had gone into hiding to escape arrest. Since we knew his wife, we began to wonder if he might appear on our doorstep sometime seeking shelter and to consider what we would do if he did. Instead, a policeman appeared one day demanding that we tell him what we knew of Mr. Shih's whereabouts. Only Ginny was at home, and at that moment was typing up the report to be sent out. She was fearful the policeman would search the house and find what she was typing, so she was quite nervous. She frankly admitted that Linda had visited us shortly before the Incident, answered some other questions, and was surprised when the policeman rather abruptly left. That afternoon, however, at her office in the study-abroad center at the Taichung campus of Chung-hsing University, a student from her political issues class appeared and grilled her for two hours as to what she knew about Linda and her husband Mr. Shih, *Formosa* magazine, and the Kaohsiung Incident. She truthfully indicated throughout that she didn't know much, and must have passed the test, as we

at the Seminary, recalls how shocked and puzzled he was to learn about the Beebys' departure. He could not understand why a couple who dearly loved Taiwan was forced to leave the country. He soon came to conclude that the problem lay in the authoritarian political system. [35] Hsu later became actively involved in the opposition movement. He was arrested and imprisoned after the Kaohsiung Incident.

Wang Hsing-nan 王幸男, who attended the farewell service, remembers Beeby's expulsion as one of the incidents which inspired him to challenge the KMT regime. [36] In October 1976, Wang returned to Taipei from the United States, where he had been living since 1970, and mailed parcel bombs in the disguise of a dictionary to three high-ranking government officials. The bomb claimed the left hand and the sight in the left eye of Hsieh Tung-min 謝東閔, the Chairman (Governor) of Taiwan Province. Wang had returned to the United States, but later was kidnapped from Hong Kong in a ploy by the Taiwan security agencies. Under torture, he attempted to commit suicide by gulping boiling water; saved by an emergency opening to his windpipe, he survived to be sentenced to life in prison. [37]

Lobbying for Taiwan

The torch of Taiwanese self-determination lit by the PCT was carried on by the exiled church leaders. Through the initiative of Shoki Coe 黃彰輝, Hwang Wu-tong, Lin Chung-yi 林宗義, and C.S. Song 宋泉盛, a group called Formosan Christians for Self-Determination (FCSD) was launched in Washington D.C. in March 1973. They appealed the Taiwanese cause to the American public and international friends through publications, public speeches, mass rallies, and lobbying. The FCSD opened branches in fourteen U.S. cities, and the movement spread to Europe with the opening of its office in West Germany in February 1974.

In March 1976, Shoki Coe, C.S. Song, Y. Chao 趙有源, Daniel Beeby and Boris Anderson, former missionary to the PCT, were invited to testify about the situation in Taiwan before the British Parliament. When the PCT announced its Human Rights Declaration in August 1977, the FCSD conveyed it to churches and secular organizations in the United States, including the US Congress and the State Department. PCT Moderator Weng Hsiu-kung 翁修恭 visited Representative Jim Leach (R-Iowa) in Washington D.C. in April 1978 and shared the PCT's view on Taiwan's future. Leach brought the issue to the attention of his colleagues on the floor of the House and urged them to continue American support and friendship for the people in Taiwan. [38] After President Carter announced his decision to normalize the relationship between Washington and Beijing in December 1978, members of the FCSD lobbied Congress for passage of the Taiwan Relations Act.

U.S. Congressman Leach felt that the members of the House Foreign Affairs Committee needed to hear the "authentic voice of the Taiwanese people." [39] Thus, through the arrangement of the office of Jim Leach, Peng Ming-min, Ben Wei 魏瑞明, and two PCT pastors from Taiwan, Rev. Wang Tsai-hsing 王再興 and Rev. Andrew Hsieh 謝禧明, paid visits to the members of the House Foreign Affairs Committee. According to Ben Wei, many Congressmen were moved by the appeal of Rev.

had no further trouble at that time.

Throughout the years we spent in Taiwan under martial law, there were many minor incidents which clearly indicated that our speech and actions were being rather closely monitored. We tried to be as supportive as possible of democratic tendencies within the limits of great caution.

Professor Mark Thelin taught sociology at Tunghai University in Taichung for several decades. After retiring from Tunghai, he spent a few years teaching at the Tainan Theological Seminary before Mark and Ginny moved back to the United States in about 2002.

Mark Thelin, for decades a professor of sociology at Tunghai University, with his wife Ginny in front of Tainan Theological College and Seminary, December 2003.

Wang who, in tears, pleaded with them not to abandon the people of Taiwan. [40] Congressman Leach and Peng Ming-min were both invited to testify at the hearing held by the Subcommittee on Asian and Pacific Affairs of the House Foreign Affairs Committee on February 15, 1979.

The Taiwan Relations Act, a vital piece of legislation that stipulates the US commitment to Taiwan's security and the human rights of the people of Taiwan, was approved by the Senate on March 29 and signed by the President on April 10, 1979. According to a study by David Lee, the House Foreign Affairs Committee favored better terms for Taiwan than its Senate counterpart, the Foreign Relations Committee. [41] For example, compared to the Senate Bill, which relied on the rubric of the "people on Taiwan," the House bill directly referred to Taiwan by defining who and what it meant, including the authorities exercising control over Taiwan. The House bill also specified boycotts and embargos as acts which, if directed against Taiwan, would be of grave concern to the United States. [42]

Joint Service for the Thirtieth Anniversary of Universal Declaration of Human Rights

The church was able to tackle sensitive issues on human rights in the name of religious conscience. On December 10, 1978, the PCT and the Catholic Church sponsored a joint service in commemoration of the thirtieth anniversary of the Universal Declaration of Human Rights in Taichung and Tainan. Due to government pressure, the Catholic Church in Tainan officially withdrew from co-sponsoring the service. A few Catholics attended the service in a personal capacity. In Taichung, the Maryknoll Fathers and Brothers, a Catholic group based in Taichung, co-sponsored the service with the PCT despite the pressure. The services in both places were well-attended. Close to a thousand filled the sanctuary in Tainan. [43]

John Tin preached a message titled, "Bible and Human Dignity." Tin preached the importance of human rights; Jesus respected human rights; He who was by nature God humbled himself and became a servant to men; Jesus made friends with tax collectors and prostitutes, who were discriminated in the society; at the end, he was arrested and crucified as a political prisoner; however, God elevated this political prisoner to be a savior of the world so that through him we might recover the original image as God created us in the beginning, with freedom, life, and unalienable rights — human rights; for this reason, men should not be oppressed and be deprived of their rights by any groups or governments; Jesus came to the world to actualize the Kingdom of God; therefore, Christians must follow the footstep of Christ and protect human rights. Tin also preached that no governments have a right to ban Bibles in any language; Christians must not accept banning of the Bible, for it is a violation of human rights. After the sermon, pastors recited Bible verses in different languages and then the entire assembly sang "We Shall Overcome," "Our Homeland," and Hymn 430 in Holo Taiwanese. It brought tears to the eyes of the participants. [44]

The service in Taichung was also a full house. Rev. Kao Chun-ming preached on the same title: "Bible and Human Dignity." Kao, quoting from Isaiah 61, preached that

Repressed Memories: Soldiers Standing Every 10-20 Yards on the Route to the Airport

by Rowland and Judy Van Es

I have never set any of this down on paper before. I have repressed many memories of the 60's and 70's, all of which will tell you something of the civil rights or human rights condition in Taiwan in that time frame. I even feel very uneasy doing it now in 2003 in the month of November. The searing memory of a soldier bearing a loaded rifle posted every few yards along the path from airplane to terminal (and also at every street corner in Taipei as it turned out) still stays with me. I will just give a few reminiscences without trying to collate them or connect them well. Perhaps they will help set the atmosphere.

I was not aware of any human rights movement per se. At first there were a few individuals who confided some things to me. A pastor or two who helped me mature. They were, to me, shining lights. I found those among the church people, and they gave me some hope. The number of these people grew as the years went by.

I was fortunate to have read George Kerr's book *Formosa Betrayed* before I came. I trained at Missionary Orientation Training Center at Stony Point, NY, an interdenominational effort, for 1964-1969. I had precious little other preparation for what we found; I trained for one year at Taipei Language Institute. One language school teacher took us under his wing and helped us a little from the humanitarian-Christian point of concern. Then, because Mandarin was oppressive in Taipei, we went to Tainan Theological College campus for 1/2 year in Tainan before I began teaching. Much of what ensued and developed during our stay from 1967-1973 was from just trying to be involved in sanity measures in a rather insane situation.

My introduction as a teacher! I remember it quite vividly. A "professional student"(yes, we had those in the seminary as well) challenged my use of Taiwanese! Just as I was about to begin my first lecture in my teaching career, I was accosted by this man in the back of the room, who asked me if I was aware that the official language in Taiwan was Mandarin and if I thought I should break the law by using another language to teach. I was sweating subject matter as well as language. I had gone over my first lecture with my language teacher several times. And now this student was harassing me based on a passage of scripture, Romans 13:1 "Let every person be subject to the governing authorities; for there is no authority except from God, and those authorities that exist have been instituted by God." I quickly learned an exegesis of this passage that I had not learned in seminary. My journey toward standing for rights was advanced. Something needed to be done about that.

I was asked to help facilitate the verification of some case studies of families of political prisoners, who were in great need. I would take affidavits and so forth. At one point, I was told that the mother of one of the families had "unwisely" purchased a school uniform with money provided her. Her watchers thus were able to determine that she was receiving help. She should have known better. Her girl should have continued to stand at the back of the room without uniform to learn. The adjustment of families of political prisoners to

Christ came to "bind up the brokenhearted, to proclaim freedom for the captives," and "to proclaim the year of the Lord's favor." Contextualizing this verse, he said, "we do not want to just shout 'anti-communism, anti-communism' and not care for the brokenhearted people and human rights of the workers …The most effective anti-communist policy is to eliminate poverty and establish equalitarian society." Kao also referred to the suffering of the Jews. "The history of Israel is a history of sorrow … Their ancestors were enslaved in Egypt for 430 years and held captive and worked as slaves in Babylon. In Jesus' time, Israelites were treated as second-class citizens under the Roman Empire and their 'human rights' were deprived by the rulers. This was the time when Jesus preached the good news of liberation. His liberation was not that by military or force. Jesus' liberation depended on that by the truth … Today we boldly claim that every individual and every nation have their human dignity. Because God has ordained to us 'human rights' and the [ROC] Constitution guarantees them. To the international community and to our government, we need to assert the right to national self-determination. Those 17 million people in Taiwan, regardless of provincial origin, language, and class, are all 'one family'." [45] Participants from the Maryknolls included Father John Kennedy 高德輝, Father Ronald Boccieri 郭佳信, and Father Chin Hua-ming 秦化民 (English name to be researched). They impressed the audience by saying that only two things could stop them from attending the event: deportation or a car accident. [46]

The human rights prayer meetings by the PCT and the Catholics in Taichung may even have inspired the Dangwai leaders to hold a massive political rally in Kaohsiung in commemoration of International Human Rights Day. Shih Ming-teh 施明德, with his secretary Chang Mei-chen 張美貞, attended the meeting at Wuchi Presbyterian Church 梧棲長老教會 in Taichung on November 14, 1979. Impressed by the service, Shih asked the church leaders whether the Dangwai could co-sponsor the prayer meeting on December 10 for the anniversary of the Universal Declaration of Human Rights. They replied that while the Dangwai people are welcome, the capacity of the church is not large enough to accommodate everyone, thus suggested that the Dangwai hold their own human rights convention. Rev. Hung Chen-hui 洪振輝, vice moderator of Taichung Presbytery at the time, urged Shih that the Dangwai become more active in the promotion of human rights. [47]

The PCT Provides Sanctuary for a Dangwai Leader

Democratic activists sought foreign missionaries for help in case of impending arrest. The reasons are: 1) the authorities would think twice before raiding the place due to their international connection (mistreatment of the fugitives would trigger international criticism and a possible wavering of their support for the ROC) and; 2) they may escape the country through their help; if not, at least, the news of their arrests cannot be concealed.

In June 1978, Chen Chu 陳菊, an activist who was the nexus of Dangwai communications although she was only in her mid-twenties, sought refuge at the mission house of Ronald Boccieri, a missionary of Maryknoll Brothers and Fathers, in Lotsu, Changhua 彰化埔心羅厝天主堂, a remote village in central Taiwan. After

the life they must lead should be quick and certain.

If I found this story hard to believe, it was reinforced by one a student of mine who told me, with some weeping. I had been a little provocative with a "prophetic account," and he responded at night in my house. In middle school he had written an essay about "His Hero!" Secret police came to his father, a school principal, shortly thereafter. His son was terribly misinformed and it was his fault. His son had described the principal as his hero and told them why. His father was responsible for having him answer correctly that His Hero was none other than Chiang Kai-shek. His father was still in prison.

One contact investigating families of political prisoners was particularly dedicated, I thought. He had been incarcerated on Green Island over ten years. He was clever in making contact with the families, but he never feared being caught doing so. There were years when he had not seen the face of another human — his food being handed around the corner as he looked out of his cell facing the sea.

Another contact was a factory manager. I'm afraid our meetings covered only a short period. He seemed to be a bright man — about my age. I never got to know much about him. Since students and friends had told me of friends and relatives that disappeared from campuses or off the streets and were not heard from again, I was not to question his lack of contact.

Of course I was kept in line by stories from other friends and pastors that they knew "officials" were asking about me. There seemed to be an official surveillance of the school and other less official ones. The principal told me once that he was asked at length about where I might be going when I left the back gate of the seminary with a racket tied to my bike. That took hours! I debated whether I would attend the picture taking at the Foreign Languages Department of Cheng Kung University. Would the place just be filled with the "wrong kind" of people? I had some really old students in those classes. One year I was asked especially by some young students to eat together with them at a meal they would cook. I had a great time. One student in particular tried nicely to tell me some of the facts of life in a Taiwan university — to make it safer for me. My stories about Ullyses and other Greek heroes sometimes seemed to be very pointed.

Having been taught to be careful not to impose my Western ideas and ideals where they did not belong, I was surprised to have colleagues encourage me to subscribe to such periodicals as *Time*, and *Newsweek*. In fact I shared a subscription to *The Stars and Stripes*, a U.S. military newspaper I would never choose, because we could read "raw news" in there. We didn't have to accept their editorial stance or anything else. Taiwanese friends helped me learn how to read! (I opened a "How to Read the Newspaper" class in the Philippines in later years based on this experience.) I remember having to go far into many a night to "perfect" a letter to the editor of one of these periodicals. It would be in response to some article that provided a teaching platform for true Taiwanese values and/or perspectives. Some of these were even published! Unfortunately, not all the issues of these periodicals would get to our house. They would be intercepted by the censors. Many an article arrived blacked out with ink.

My reading lessons were enhanced by my work on the General Assembly Executive Committee project for drafting the 1971 "Statement On Our National Fate by the

several days, the security agents raided the place and on the evening of June 23, 1978, Chen was arrested and imprisoned for several months. [Editor's Note: She was released, however, due to international pressure, as will be described in a subsequent chapter in more detail.] Boccieri was subjected to public criticism within the Catholic Church on Taiwan for his involvement, and nearly 300 church figures signed a statement rebuking him and the other two foreign priests who drove her from Taipei, at a large prayer meeting held in the wake of Jimmy Carter's December 16, 1978, announcement that the United States would recognize the Peoples Republic of China as the legitimate government of China. [48] He was blacklisted by the government and forced to leave the island in November 1979. After having spent thirty years in Taiwan, which he considered to be his home, and having learned to speak Holo, Boccieri felt "heartbroken."

This case of political leaders protected by religious personages seems to have set a precedent for political dissidents. When following the Kaohsiung Incident the government began on December 13, 1979, to arrest all opposition activists, Shih Ming-teh sought help from the PCT. General Secretary Kao Chun-ming arranged a sanctuary for Shih and Shih was able to evade arrest for 27 days, but was finally apprehended on January 8, 1980. Two young Presbyterian ministers from the Tainan Theological Seminary, Shih's lieutenants in the *Formosa* magazine organization, Tsai Yu-chuan 蔡有全 and Lin Hung-hsuan 林弘宣, were arrested the day before, and others who had assisted Shih as a fugitive were arrested within the next few days, including Rev. Kao's secretary Shih Jui-yun 施瑞雲, and a senior woman minister of the PCT, Lin Wen-chen 林文珍. Finally, Rev. Kao himself was arrested on April 24, 1980, and all were consequently tried on May 16. Kao was sentenced to seven years in prison, which he accepted with equanimity and transformed into an opportunity to understand the spiritual needs of the convicts he met in prison. Yet, the involvement of the PCT in the Kaohsiung Incident induced larger attention from the international community. The news went out through church channels throughout the world. The international pressure compelled the government to open the court for public hearings. Moreover, it eventually compelled President Chiang Ching-kuo to offer clemency to imprisoned activists. [49]

A Show of International Concern for the Presbyterian Church in Taiwan

The announcement of the Human Rights Declaration in 1977, in which the PCT called Taiwan to become "new and independent," aggravated the church's relationship with the government. The PCT experienced various harassments ranging from denial of travel permits to police surveillance, and bashing in the state-controlled media. [50] This was a difficult time for the church as its contact with the international church community was getting cut off. Previously, the government had forced the PCT to withdraw from the World Council of Churches, which the government alleged to be "communist."

At the same time, the government began to draft a new law on religious organizations that would allow it direct mechanisms for draconian punitive action against the church congregations, such as confiscation of church property, if pastors engaged in

Presbyterian Church in Taiwan." The wording had to be just right. I learned much about English as well as about Taiwanese. It was refreshing to have to discuss Mr. Nixon's visit to China with the secret police, but I tried not to show it. Their lead — in question was "Do you have any thoughts about the visit of President Nixon to mainland China?"

I remember being actually scared on two occasions. One was leaving Tainan in March 1971 to go to Taipei to verify that Mike and Judy Thornberry were all right (in a manner of speaking). Word had come that they were under house arrest on Yangmingshan. Do you remember how difficult phone communication was in those days? I finally got to the campus and peered across the street, which was cordoned off, and shouted at Judy, whom I could see. She stood in the doorway behind the screen door momentarily and shouted that she was relatively okay, had even done some shopping, and had Liz in tow, but could not even go to the bathroom by herself. I could hear but could not see Mike, who was apparently holding Richard. I nervously stayed and trailed them to the airport as they were being deported to try to make sure they were not spirited away somewhere else. Military were posted every 10-20 yards all the way! I have never acknowledged this with them, my wife knew only pieces — I didn't want to worry her or give information she might have trouble with if questioned.

I reflected on things we had told each other and things we had done. And I was immensely sad. I remembered sharing about the times I preached at church and had to answer many questions the next day in my own house about things I had said in the sermon. How I had wished my own students were as attentive to what I said as was this man from the police questioning me. I remember keeping ignorant of certain facts, not nailing them down in detail, because I was fearful of yielding precious information if I myself were tortured. I did not want to be the source of information that would bring harm to others.

Another adrenalin rush came during the farewell for the Beebys' at Thai-peng-keng Maxwell Memorial Church 太平境馬雅各紀念教會. [Editor's note: This church, the earliest Presbyterian church in Taiwan, is the memorial church for the first evangelist Dr. James L. Maxwell, M.A.M.D., sent to Taiwan in May 1865 by the Presbyterian Church in England. Dr. Maxwell chose Tainan, then the capital of Taiwan, as his base for preaching the Lord's salvation through medical treatment.] I was making sure the CBS camera team, on their way back from Vietnam to the USA, would get footage of a "real story." Pastor Ko Chun-beng's (Kao Chun-ming 高俊明牧師, C.M. Kao) sermon of "Who Is the True Patriot?" was excellent. At one point the camera panned the congregation, and automatically the balcony group drew back, fearful of being identified on film, even for American television. But a seminary professor realized the occasion, and drew himself up with a clearing of his throat, and he leaned out even over the railing. The rest of us in the crowd suddenly lurched forward to be caught in the floodlights. For me, that was real drama and a proud moment. After the service a distinguished lady said to me as she stepped into her car, "You know, Pastor Bän, I hear that my son is well." I wondered what the woman I knew as Elder Phe [Editor's note: This seems to be the mother of Peng Ming-min] was fully implying. We lived on the edge in those days. I reflected on whether she knew my own part in her son's departure, of if she guessed, or if she might even be saying thank you. Communication among people was like that in 1972.

When the Beebys' ten days were up and they had to go to the Taipei airport, I rode two

Rowland and Judy Van Es

criticism of the government or the "national purpose" of recovery of the mainland. In mid-1978, this law was reviewed at an academic conference by the government-sponsored Chinese Association for Human Rights. Linda Gail Arrigo attended the conference, and found that although the academics at the conference were fairly critical of the law, the newspaper accounts stated that the proposed law had met with their approval — generally a propaganda prelude to passing a law. This was a grave threat to the PCT, which since its founding had been an internally-democratic and autonomous institution, based on the original Presbyterian model.

The PCT was able to make a breakthrough from this isolation through the help of foreign missionaries. Through the contact between Wendell Karsen, an expelled missionary now in Hong Kong— at the time serving as the Executive Secretary for Education for the Hong Kong Christian Council— and David Gelzer, professor at the TTCS, the PCT arranged an emergency theological consultation from December 4 to 6, 1978. Eighteen theologians and clergy from England, Germany, Canada, the United States, Japan, the Philippines, Indonesia, Switzerland, Malaysia and Singapore gathered in Taipei for a three-day conference to discuss the role of the Christian church in Asia and the PCT in particular. Twenty-eight members of the PCT, including most senior leaders, participated in the conference. The conference was arranged in secrecy to avoid sabotage by the authorities. Karsen and Gelzer used coded letters in their correspondence with one another. All participants arrived in Taiwan on tourist visas without formal invitations from the PCT. [51]

During the conference, participants shared their churches' experiences with authoritarian governments. Dr. Yap Kim Hao, the General Secretary of the Christian Conference of Asia, emphasized the need for the churches in Asia to search for their identity. Yap argued that the Asian churches had been passive and had become victims of their own culture and tradition. The challenge for the church, he continued, was how to "do theology" by wrestling with politico-social issues such as corruption, poverty, inequality, and crime from a philosophical, critical, and theological perspective. Yap stated that in face of all these problems the Christian church must nonetheless criticize the tyranny of power in order to defend human rights and justice. [52] Sr. Christina Tan of the Roman Catholic Church in the Philippines asserted the need for the church to move from "passive resignation and silent watching from the sidelines to active participation in helping the people to regain their land, their voice, and their freedom…the church must awaken the people, inspire them to bravery and courage." [53]

In his speech on the mission of the church in Taiwan, C. M. Kao, the General Secretary of the PCT, emphasized the importance of speaking the truth in love. He explained that the three statements were made based on their faith that Jesus was the Lord and that human rights were bestowed by this Lord on every person and every race. The PCT, for this reason, believed that only the people in Taiwan, 17 million of them, regardless of their place of origin or the language they spoke, had the right to decide the future of Taiwan. Kao explained that in each statement the church spoke in love, but was ignored by the public. He demanded to know if the government had any

cars behind them on the train. I wanted to make sure they were able to leave and leave decently. As always, I was shadowed. Since they were able to make all their appointments in Taipei before departure (particularly the news conference at the President Hotel on the way to the airport), I finally just went on inside the airport and said goodbye to them. What a large gathering of various kinds of people — all taking pictures of everybody else. I have many shots of cameras looking back into my lens, spies recording who was sending the Beebys' off.

We did try to keep some secrecy. Midnight visits by other professors were frequent. Often we had to pull our chairs to the middle of the room and put on some distracting noises in the background to help defend against listening devices. These kinds of meetings increased when the government threatened to close the Tainan Theological College through taxation policies. I was visited in this way by a Maryknoller whom I accosted with a not-too-friendly "Whom did you bring with you?" He assured me he had lost his trailer and had even climbed over the back wall to avoid being followed. But the following day I was still asked why I had been visited by "so and so." I know these accounts are commonplace to people who lived in Taiwan in the '60's and 70's, but when I returned to the USA I realized that's not how people who enjoy human rights live.

The American officials who supported the Chiang regime didn't seem to want to know about these things. At a dinner at the USIS of Tainan, I happened to be seated right next to the ambassador. I asked if he had read Kerr. He turned to the person on his left and made some inane remark about the weather.

In 1973 I was forced to leave Taiwan. It was suggested that I would not be able to return if I went to check on our youngest son in the USA. He had needed emergency surgery, so my wife had taken him in March. My oldest son and I packed up our house so that others might use it during our furlough. When we got to the Taipei airport things were not pleasant. The questioning became intense, as the inspectors went through our luggage. One person took out a romanized Bible and accosted our eleven year — old about this and other things. [Editor's note: The government had banned versions of the Bible translated into romanized Taiwanese and aborigine dialects, to enforce compulsory use of Mandarin Chinese.] Our son looked at me with some panic. I insisted on being with him at all times, and would not let them take him into another room for questioning. Finally, the airport manager accompanied me to our plane seats and bid me good-bye. There was a scene in the aisle shortly as the men came back "to take me for further questioning." I can still see the look on my young son's face! Fortunately, the plane was allowed to leave because "He had already been seated, and departure time had arrived." They were prevented from taking me off the flight, but it was a long trip to the USA.

My closure on Taiwan had to come in the form of remembering some files I had of *Far Eastern Economic Review* articles and some receipts that were the "wrong kind." I also had the seedbed of several articles on events in Taiwan that were indicative of the lack of human rights. When the final word came that I had no chance to get another visa to go back to Taiwan I had to think of a way to destroy those things before trying to send my household goods in Taiwan on to the Philippines. I selected a colleague and described the files as best I could and boldly asked him to burn them, that's right -- burn them -- without asking any questions. He did so. And then my goods were submitted for shipment to the Philippines.

plan to overcome the island's increasing international isolation. He also called for the people in Taiwan to abandon the colonial mentality of willingness to be ruled by others and take up the responsibility of being in charge of the nation's course. Kao also emphasized the role of the church in the salvation of all people, whether they be native Taiwanese or Mainlanders. He appealed to all Christians to fearlessly put down their roots in the land, lay down their lives, and strive together with fellow citizens to share the suffering of the people. [54]

On the second day of the conference, the PCT held a tea party for the participants to meet the KMT officials and other Christian church leaders in the island. In welcoming the honorable guests, PCT moderator Weng shared with them the observation that the consultation was held in Taiwan since "for a time of period, PCT pastors could not leave the country in the name of the General Assembly." Weng told the group that the church is one body, thus if one church suffers the whole body suffers together. [55] Chu Bo-chun 居伯均, Director of the Civil Affairs Bureau of the Internal Affairs Office, was invited to give a welcoming speech. He assured the foreign guests that the ROC is a "democratic country which enjoys perfect freedom of religion, and the people have the freedom to choose their own faith." Then, he wished everybody a successful conference. [56] However, his hypocrisy was revealed in the following session when the PCT and the German church signed a sisterhood church relationship. Hartmut Albruschat, a representative of the West Berlin Brandenburg Church, expressed his regret over Moderator Weng's failure to obtain a government permit to attend the sisterhood relationship signing ceremony which was originally planned in Berlin in November. To this, Director Chu suddenly stood up from his seat and left the room without witnessing the exchange of the signed documents, leaving the guests in a state of shock. [57] On the following day, the group was invited to a luncheon at the Taipei Grand Hotel, hosted by the Taipei City Mayor, Lee Teng-hui 李登輝. Several members of the KMT Central Headquarters also attended his gathering. Mayor Lee told the group that he is a Christian himself, and according to the report in the *Taiwan Church News*, his humble and sincere attitude won praises of the delegation. [58]

The meeting was an historic occasion, as the PCT was being isolated from the international Christian body by the government's restriction on freedom of travel by PCT leaders. Despite the short notice, the PCT succeeded in inviting a fine group of church leaders from all over Asia. The conference reassured the PCT of support from the international church body, boosting its confidence. The government officials who attended the meetings seemed to have been impressed by the support the PCT enjoyed in the international Christian community. [59] The draft law on religious organizations remained merely a proposal that had not yet passed approval by the national legislature, a rubber-stamp body.

Other Church-Related Foreign Visitors

The overseas churches occasionally arranged delegations and individuals to visit Taiwan to show their solidarity with the PCT. In March 1979, the Evangelical Church in Germany sent Eberhard Kuhrau, Director of the Overseas Department in Westdeutscher Rundfunk, the largest broadcasting agency in Germany, to visit

I was able to get my church, Reformed Church in America, to make statements of support for the Presbyterian Church in Taiwan and for their actions and statements. One of my happiest moments was to hear the PCT general secretary tell me in 1995 that the RCA is the one church that has stood with the PCT through thick and thin. We can testify that that does not happen accidentally.

Rowland and Judith Van Es lived in Taiwan 1967-73. They helped investigate the living conditions of the families of political prisoners.

Taiwan. During his two week-long stay, Kuhrau visited all places and institutions in Taiwan, among which many of them were the PCT-affiliated organizations such as the Tainan Theological College and Seminary, Chang Jung High School, Chang Jung Girls School, Taiwan Church Press, and Taiwan Theological Seminary. He filmed the liberal atmosphere in these church institutions and contrasted that with the oppressed, totalitarian lifestyle in the society under martial law. At the TTCS, the German journalist made a presentation to the faculty titled "The Contribution of the German Mass Media in Germany's Democratization Process in Postwar Germany" and held a discussion with the students on the topic of public response to the broadcasting of Holocaust images on televison. [60]

When the PCT General Secretary Kao Chun-ming was arrested on April 24, 1980, the overseas Christian churches sent delegations to visit and to show their solidarity with the PCT. In early May, WARC and the WCC together dispatched representatives to Taiwan. During their stay, WARC General Secretary Edmond Perret, with five other PCT leaders, attended the court hearings for Kao and nine others defendents arrested for harboring Shih Ming-teh. [61] Perret, with two other representatives, William Thomspon, General Secretary of the United Presbyterian Church (USA), and Uwe Hollm, Vice Bishop of the West Berlin Evangelical Church, held a press conference, in which they expressed their support for the PCT while expressing their regret for not being able to meet government officials to explain the purpose of their visit. [62] The case was tried on May 15, and the sentences announced June 6: seven years for Kao. From May 31 to June 5, delegates from the Scotland Church flew to Taiwan and visited Kao in Chingmei prison. Then in September and October, American and German churches sent their representatives to Taiwan and visited Kao in prison. Numbers of other visits were recorded until Kao was released from prison in August 1984. In addition, the Presidential Office was flooded by countless letters from overseas, appealing for the release of Kao and other Kaohsiung Incident convicts. A letter sent by U.S. Representative Jim Leach, addressed to President Chiang Ching-kuo on April 29, 1980, was of a very strong tone. The early release of the prisoners cannot be unrelated to these overseas efforts.

Conclusion

The role of foreign missionaries in Taiwan's democratization was not obvious, especially given the furtive nature of action within Taiwan under martial law. Yet the external communications channels maintained by the foreign missionaries almost certainly made Taiwan's security agencies hesitate to crack down. The efforts by each missionary at that crucial time in Taiwan's history later paved the way for the opposition movement to rise in the late 1970s, and again in the 1980s after the hiatus of the Kaohsiung Incident and trials. Their contributions were:

1. encouraging/inspiring the PCT to be prophetic on social injustice committed by the government;

2. playing a messenger role in disseminating the PCT statements as well as delineating the reality of the political oppression in the island, which was generally whitewashed by KMT propaganda; and

It was Wonderful, the PCT's General Secretary Reverend Kao Chun-ming, Re-elected, Even in Prison!

by David G. and Elizabeth Gelzer 郭大衛牧師夫婦

An invitation from the Presbyterian Church in Taiwan (PCT) brought me and my wife, Elisabeth, to Taiwan. I was asked to fill in as professor of theology at Tainan Theological College and Seminary (TTC&S) for the late, regretted friend and colleague, Rev. Ong Hian-ti (Wang Hsien-chih 王憲治牧師), thus enabling him to complete his doctoral studies. Having lived and taught in West Africa for 23 years, going to Taiwan became a new, exciting adventure, since I had little knowledge about the history of the PCT and the political situation in Taiwan. In the U.S., I had heard about the Republic of China, a "bastion of anti-communism," whose strong friend and ally was the late Senator Barry Goldwater and many in the Republican Party. There was also the feeling among many Christians in the States that President Chiang Kai-shek was friendly and kindly disposed towards Christians in Taiwan. But what was really going on in Taiwan, neither I nor most of the people in the U.S. knew.

Arriving in September, 1975, the afterglow of the televised funeral of Chiang Kai-shek lingered on, particularly among conservative Christian groups on the island. They thought that the country was on the verge of embracing Christianity. The regime's invitation to Billy Graham to hold another campaign added to the euphoria felt among these numerically small evangelical groups. The campaign was held in Taipei under cloudy, often rainy conditions. Curious but sadly true, the Graham group organized the week-long campaign solely with these small American-organized and American-controlled churches. The largest Protestant and autonomous church, the Presbyterian Church in Taiwan (PCT), was completely ignored. As an eleventh-hour concession, the organizers permitted students from the Presbyterian seminaries to serve as "helpers." They were to lead those who had "come forward" to one or the other church group represented. Some 45,000, in the course of the week, had made "a decision." And yet, the only church able to receive, nurture and integrate them, was the PCT. It had the leadership, pastors and lay; it had the educational infrastructure to help inquirers to grow in faith and knowledge, and it could and did all this in Japanese, Hakka, native Taiwanese or Mandarin.

At the end of the campaign, Billy Graham was received by President Chiang Ching-kuo who thanked him and presented him with a citation. Mr. Graham announced this to the closing meeting of the campaign, adding that when back in the States, he would go and see the president and show him how he had been honored!

It is necessary to begin here, because the uninformed reader may get the impression that all was calm and peaceful between church and regime in Taiwan. It seems clear, moreover, that Mr. Graham and his team were kept in ignorance about the conflict between the regime and the PCT. The conflict had erupted four years earlier, already when the church issued a "Statement on Our National Fate," on December 29, 1971. Therefore, whatever

3. international networking with overseas Christian and human rights organizations, which in turn put pressure on the KMT government.

Such contribution was possible, though not without risk and penalties, due to their status as religious workers, and was effective especially in the late 1960s and early 1970s when no other civic organizations enjoyed such resources and networks. For this reason, they can be called the pioneers among the foreigners in their involvement in Taiwan's democratization. Not all missionaries got involved, but many did out of their religious conviction.

Ronald Boccieri, a Maryknoll Brother who was expelled in November 1979, a year after sheltering opposition activist Chen Chu, was once admonished by the Papal Nuncio to stay away from trouble since the responsibility of the church is to "make sure to stay in Taiwan." Boccieri responded: "We disagree. Our first job is to preach the gospel." [63] Like Boccieri, to these missionaries who got involved in the human rights of the Taiwanese people, their actions were not a contradiction or a diversion, but an extension as well as an application of their faith. Thus, the primary reason for their involvement was theological. Their gospel did not divide the ecclesial and the secular. Instead, it encouraged and inspired the church to engage in the society so that God's justice may be revealed.

Second, an aspect which set them apart from others, was in fact their language skills. Unlike other foreign missionaries, those affiliated with the PCT and the Maryknoll Brothers and Fathers spoke Holo Taiwanese, the language of the oppressed and the native. This gave them access not just to the other side of Taiwanese society but it also seems to have unlocked the hearts and fears of the native Taiwanese in communications with them. The combination of the two explains why they were able to do the things they did in the crucial period of Taiwan's democracy, and it is well reflected in their acceptance of the adversities that they faced in the witness to their faith, as shown in their individual interviews at the December 8-9, 2003, conference in Taipei, "International Friends and Taiwan's Democracy and Human Rights," which brought together many of the missionaries who had been deported and banned so long ago.

Notes:

1. Yoshihisa Amae, "Taiwan's Exodus: The Presbyterian Church in Taiwanese Nationalism, 1945-1992" (Ph.D. dissertation, University of Hawaii, 2007).

2. Hollington Tong, *Christianity in Taiwan: A History* (Taipei: *China Post*, 1961), 84.

3. Donald Wilson, "Donald J. Wilson, 1959-1967," in *International Friends and Taiwan's Democracy and Human Rights* (hereafter referred to as *IFTDHR*), Vol. I, 114-115 (Taipei: Taiwan Foundation for Democracy, 2003).

4. Milo Thornberry and Judith Thomas, "Our Human Rights Activities in Taiwan," in IFTDHR I, 29.

5. Ibid., 31.

6. Ibid., 31-32.

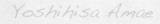
Yoshihisa Amae

these groups may or may not have said to the Graham team about the PCT, it is safe to assume that it was not good!

I soon learned what was at stake for the PCT. After World War II, the Synod of the North of Taiwan, the fruit of Presbyterians from Canada, and the Synod of the South of Taiwan, the fruit of Presbyterians from England, joined to form the Presbyterian Church in Taiwan. Its membership was around 200,000, spread the length and breadth of the island, its language not Mandarin but Taiwanese, its people centuries already of the soil of Formosa, not swept in as refugees from the China mainland. Once before, in 1895, the dream of freedom and independence was brutally crushed by Japan. And now, with the U.S., after nearly 29 years, finally recognizing the People's Republic of China as the legal government of China, the dream of a free and independent Formosa seemed a new possibility. Already the first and second Taiwanese principals of TTC&S since the founding of the PCT had been declared *personae non gratae*.

The de-recognition of the Chiang regime, the Republic of China (ROC), by the United Nations, in 1970, awakened the PCT to speak out:

> "... Based on our belief that Jesus Christ is the Lord of all men, the righteous judge and Savior of the world, we voice our concern and our request, and in doing so we are convinced that we speak not only for the Church but for all our compatriots ... because God has ordained and the United Nations Charter has affirmed that every people has the right to determine its own destiny."

Two months after the Billy Graham campaign, the PCT, on 18 November 1975, issued a second public declaration, "Our Appeal Concerning the Bible, the Church and the Nation." And less than two years later, 16 August 1977, at the moment when President Carter was proceeding towards normalizing relations with the PRC, still more forthrightly, the PCT issued "A Declaration on Human Rights by the Presbyterian Church in Taiwan."

These three declarations by the PCT are the foundation of Taiwan's slow but inexorable march toward its independence. For the PCT, this march brought suffering, oppression, imprisonment, spying, surveillance, etc. But with these declarations, the PCT gave voice back again to the people of Taiwan, intimidated and made voiceless by the regime's threats, punishment and imprisonment. For anyone to speak the word "freedom" was tantamount to treason.

This story, outlined in skeleton form, is essential to an understanding of how independence was achieved by the Taiwanese. It is important also because powerful organizations such as the American Chamber of Commerce in Taipei would attribute this achievement quite differently: to the miracle of the American "market economy" introduced to Taiwan and spread with significant American investment in the country. That such has taken place is undeniable. But it is not that which lies at the heart of Taiwan's road to independence.

For seven years, till Mrs. Gelzer and I were expelled from Taiwan, in addition to my work as professor of theology, I was asked to join and became an intimate member of an unofficial *ad hoc* group (unofficial, but labeled "AHG") made up of a local pastor, a Presbyterian layman and several TTC&S colleagues as well as a staff member of the General Assembly Office in Taipei. With each new public declaration issued by PCT, the

7.   Ibid., 33.

8.   Virginia and Mark Thelin, "Our Contributions Toward Democracy in Taiwan," in IFTDHR I, 24. Mark Thelin had known Peng since 1963 through an introduction by George Todd, a visiting faculty at the TTCS. When Peng was arrested in September 1964, Thelin wrote up a report on the incident and forwarded it to George Todd, who had then returned to the US after completing his three-year term at the TTCS. During Peng's imprisonment, Thelin visited his family in Taipei on a monthly basis. The Thelins' involvement in the escape plan was minimal. According to the Thelins, they did not hear about the matter of Peng's planned escape for almost a year after they attended the meeting at the Thornberrys. Thelin learned about the successful escape from the Thornberrys not so long after the fact. See Thelin, Ibid., 23-24.

9.   *Taipei Times*, December 13, 2003: 16.

10. Ibid.

11. Wendell Karsen, "Taiwan: The Struggle for Human Rights: Memoirs of a Foreign Participant, 1969-1984," in *IFTDHR* I, 70.

12. *New York Times*, March 31, 1971.

13. Rowland and Judy Van Es, "Rowland and Judy Van Es," *IFTDHR* I, 39.

14. Wolfgang L. Grichting, *The Value System in Taiwan* 1970: a preliminary report (Taipei: [s.n.], 1971), 197.

15. This is an ecumenical group, which consists of many Christian organizations, including the Presbyterian Church, Lutheran Church, Baptist Church, and Catholic Church.

16. Hwang Wu-tong, 黃武東回憶錄 *Memoirs of Hwang Wu-tong* (Irvine, CA: Taiwan Publishing, 1986), 303.

17. Kao Chun-ming, Kao Lee Li-chen, and Hu Hui-ling, 十字架之路：高俊明牧師回憶錄 *The Road of the Cross: Memoirs of Rev. Kao Chun-ming* (Taipei: Wang chun feng, 2001), 230.

18. *The General Assembly, Public Statements*, 4th ed. (Taipei: Presbyterian Church in Taiwan, 2002), 8.

19. Ibid., 7.

20. Huang Jiashu, 台灣能獨立嗎？透視台獨 *Can Taiwan Become Independent? A Perspective on Taiwan Independence* (Haikou, P.R.C.: Nanhai, 1994), 91.

21. Karsen, *IFTDHR* I, 73-74.

22. "Reformed Church in America Urges Self-Determination for Taiwan," *Reformed Press Service*, No. 117, May 1974, 2.

23. Karsen, *IFTDHR* I, 74-75.

24. Ibid., 75.

25. Taiwan Church News 1078, March 1972, 1-3.

26. Ibid.

27. Stephanie Wolfe, a summer missionary volunteer from the United States, was instructed by another missionary to bring the letter to the United States and deliver it to President Carter. She smuggled the letter out of Taiwan and mailed it special delivery to the White House immediately upon her return in late August. See Lauren C. Steele, "Summer missionary volunteer smuggles letter from Taiwan" *The Auburn Plainsman*, October 13, 1977, A-11. Reprinted in 望春風 *Mayflower* Vol. 99, November 1977: 17, 20.

tension between the KMT and the church mounted. The regime's aim was to isolate the PCT from the church without, to silence the church within, and to "imprison" its leaders by canceling passports and visas and monitoring and interfering with public services of worship and meetings. It also had informers planted in church sessions, staff meetings of colleges and seminaries who were required to report after regularly what had been said and decided by the respective bodies.

My presence in the AHG was behind the scenes, doing what the AHG asked me to do. The AHG could be called together at any time, day or evening or late in the night, in response to an emergency or a suddenly opened-up opportunity, demanding a decision or a response. The AHG also developed proposals for the Assembly's Executive Committee as a way of dealing with a new crisis that required immediate action. Time and space do not permit more than a brief listing of some of the areas in which I became involved. But whatever it was, I did it at the behest of and with the full support of the AHG, as part of the PCT and never on my own.

The immediate question was, how to speak to the world, with the KMT tightening the noose around the PCT ever firmer?

In the political arena of ROC-USA relations, both in the Senate and the House there were members who understood and sympathized with the PCT's public declarations. Messrs Kennedy, Glenn, Pell, Leach and Solomon, among them, during visits to Taiwan, in addition to their official visits with the regime, made contact with the PCT Assembly office in order to hear what was really going on in Taiwan. After the Kaohsiung Incident and with the imprisonment of the PCT's General Secretary, the Rev. C.M. Kao, the AHG would suddenly be called to come to Taipei and give an update on the situation. More often than not, the visitors would ask for a written report. The AHG would comply and the result, elaborated in Taiwanese — with summary translation for me — became my responsibility to put into English. It had to be done immediately, because the visitor would be leaving the next day. As a diplomat, he could take highly sensitive material with him, without being subjected to painstaking searches by the police. Once, while in Washington, in the office of Senator Claiborne Pell, I discovered one of the AHG's reports which he had used during his intervention on the floor of the Senate. It was written by me on my Hermes 2000!

Mail was censored, telephones were tapped. And yet, on several occasions when a message had to be sent out by telephone, the AHG asked me to transmit it. I could do it in French, German, or Swiss dialect, depending on the final addressee. My recipient overseas would then re-transmit it to the intended receiver. Even if the message had been "overheard," its coming in a non-English garb would probably have slowed the listener's deciphering, or the foreign pronunciation would put it beyond his/her comprehension.

As the tension between the KMT and the PCT intensified, the tone of the *Taiwan Church News (TCN)* became more outspoken, more courageous. Two members of the AHG shared editorial duties. The weekly was never shut down. But more often than not, there were delivery problems. To inquiries with the main post office in Tainan about it, the same reply always came: the paper had been duly shipped. If somewhere it appeared not to have arrived, that was not "our" problem. Or the post office would claim that during the shipping the copies must somehow have "gotler lost." The editors decided to start an

28.   Hwang,回憶錄 *memoirs* , 309.

29.   Rowland and Judy Van Es, interview by author, Tainan, July 27, 2004.

30.   Kao, 十字架之路, 239.

31.   Due to the sensitivity of the case, the letter of invitation was secretly hand-delivered to the reporters without a signatory. See Wendell Karsen, interview by author, Taipei, December 6, 2003.

32.   Ibid.

33.   *South China Morning Post*, 7 March 1972, 1.

34.   Ibid.

35.   Hsu Tien-hsien, interview by author, Tainan, April 29, 2004.

36.   Wang Hsing-nan, interview by author, Tainan, May 6, 2004.

37.   Wang was imprisoned in the Green Island prison until President Lee Teng-hui awarded him clemency in May 1990. He was elected a member of the Legislative Yuan from the Democratic Progressive Party in 1998 (re-elected in 2001, 2004, and 2008).

38.   Congress, House of Representatives, Congressman Jim Leach of Iowa, "Tribute to Taiwanese Religious Leader," E2121, *Congressional Record — Extension of Remarks* (25 April 1978): 45.

39.   Leach's concern for Taiwan was more or less affected by Cynthia Sprunger, his legislative staff, whose father worked as a medical missionary in the Mennonite Christian Hospital in Hualien, Taiwan.

40.   Ben Wei, interview by author, Taipei, December 14, 2004.

41.   David Tawei Lee, *The Making of the Taiwan Relations Act: Twenty Years in Retrospect* (Hong Kong: Oxford University Press, 2000).

42.   Ibid., 123-124.

43.   *Taiwan Church News* 1398, 1399, 1400, December 17, 24, 31, 1978, 2.

44.   Ibid.

45.   *Taiwan Church News* 1401, January 7, 1979, 8.

46.   *Taiwan Church News*, December 17, 24, 31, 1978, 2.

47.   Hung Chen-hui, "高雄事件始作俑者," in 台灣基督長老教會與美麗島事件 *The Presbyterian Church in Taiwan and the Meilidao Incident*, ed. Chang Li-fu, Hung Rwei-lang, and Cheng Yang-en (Taipei: Presbyterian Church in Taiwan, 1999), 64-65.

48.   Father Alan Doyle, Maryknoll Taiwan, e-mail to Linda Gail Arrigo, March 18, 2008: "Boccieri's figure for the letter should probably be 279, certainly not 500 people signing. As I remember the prayer meeting in Taichung took place some days before Carter was formally switching US recognition to China [January 1, 1979]. The generalized anger at the US by some for this move probably contributed to the circulation of the letter that the three priests [Ronald Boccieri, plus Father John Kennedy 高德輝神父 and Father Al Borsari 秦化民神父 who drove to Taipei to pick up Chen Chu, according to Chinese-language accounts] leave Taiwan. The priests were American and the coincidence of the timing did not help."

49.   Kao was released after serving 5 years and 3 months in jail, and Lin Yi-hsiung's term was reduced from 12 years to 6. According to the memoir by Lee Teng-hui, CCK ordered Lee to negotiate with the PCT

English, digest-version, of TCN. Second generation Taiwanese in the diaspora no longer were able to read chinese characters. The PCT's partner churches in the U.S.A., Canada, Great Britain and on the Continent also needed information, immediately accessible to them, especially regarding the church and Dr. Kao, imprisoned. I was asked to launch this project.

My Taiwanese "eyes" were students, staff and volunteers with whom I discussed the choice of articles from *TCN* to be translated. I chose its title, *Occasional Bulletin*. One of my students, an artist, designed for me an indigenous "burning bush," contemporizing the classic Reformed symbol then part of the PCT's masthead. I put my "eyes" reading into article form, typed the articles on stencils on my typewriter, and had them mimeographed at the Taiwan Church Press. The *Occasional Bulletin* helped to keep channels open with the churches around the world. *TCN's* editor, during my close association with the paper, became the object of much criticism, threats and warnings. But he remained strong, courageous, giving his editors freedom to write, inform and reassure their readers about their role during these stressful times.

The gift of the Evangelical (read, Lutheran) Church of Berlin-Brandenburg, via the Berlin Mission Society, a state-of-the-art printing press, was a godsend. It accelerated the speed with which the press was able to communicate with the church and the world and relieved me from "type-setting" the *Occasional Bulletin*. The single-story historical building in which type-setting was still done by hand became obsolete. It gave way to a three-story building, facing Youth Road, also erected on the campus of Tainan Theological College and Seminary, housing presses in the basement, a book store on the ground floor, offices on the second, and on the third the editorial offices.

When the People's Republic of China expelled all missionaries from the mainland, the Maryknoll Society along with Protestant mission agencies followed the defeated forces of the ROC to Taiwan. For all of them, the move was supposedly temporary, until the "recovery of the mainland" had been achieved. Soldiers, administrators, and missionaries came as Mandarin speakers to a land whose mother tongue was overwhelmingly Taiwanese. And now, no longer Japanese, but Mandarin, was the official language on the island. Those that came with Chiang Kai-shek used Mandarin, as did Presbyterians from the Presbyterian Church of the U.S.A. (South), and the mainland Maryknoll missioners.

But after World War II, when reinforcements arrived in Taiwan from the Maryknoll Society and from the Presbyterian Church of the U.S.A. (North), the PCT recommended to foreign missionaries — with the exception of those destined to work in schools and colleges — that they learn Taiwanese, the language current and liturgical of the people. It was obvious, inevitable, and, of course, the aim, to help identify the missionaries with the Taiwanese people.

After the Kaohsiung events and the imprisonment of key opposition members — whether guilty or innocent -- and that of Dr. Kao, speaking Taiwanese brought Presbyterians and Maryknoll Fathers and Sisters together in action and prayer. The locus was the Thai-Ping-keng Presbyterian Church in the heart of Tainan. Neither our Presbyterian colleagues (South) nor the Maryknoll Fathers (mainland) approved our stand (which they considered anti-Chiang Kai-shek, anti-government, anti-American, and One-China policy). The regime's action against the PCT-affiliated and the Maryknoll missioners was the same: both were declared *persona non grata*.

David G and Elizabeth Gelzer

on the early release of Kao. See Lee Teng-hui, 見證台灣 蔣經國總統與我 *Witnessing Taiwan: Chiang Ching-kuo and I* (Taipei: Yunchen wenhua, 2004), 51-53.

50. For more details, see Chen Nan-chou, 台灣基督長老教會的社會政治論理 從台灣基督長老教會三個聲明宣言之研究來建構台灣教會的社會政治論理 *The Social and Political Ethics of the Presbyterian Church in Taiwan* (Taipei: Yongwang wenhua, 1996).

51. Karsen Wendell, interview by author.

52. *Taiwan Church News* 1398, 1399, 1400, December 17, 24, 31, 1978, 6.

53. David G. Gelzer, "Report on a Consultation on the Mission of the Church in Asia Today," December 4-6, 1978, Taipei, 3, private collection.

54. Ibid., 7.

55. *Taiwan Church News* 1397, December 10, 1978, 2.

56. Ibid.

57. Ibid.

58. Ibid.

59. J. Martin Bailey, "Taiwan: The Church, the Government, and American Reality," *The Church Herald*, 26 January 1979, 7.

60. *Taiwan Church News*, March 25, 1979, 1.

61. *Taiwan Church News* 1472, May 18, 1980, 6. Perret had previously visited Taiwan from January 31 to February 6, 1980 to observe the situation in Taiwan after the Kaohsiung Incident.

62. *Taiwan Church News* 1472, May 18, 1980, 1. Their visit was portrayed and criticized by the media as intervention to domestic affairs.

63. Ron Boccieri, "Taiwan Memoirs," in *IFTDHR* II, 46.

Yoshihisa Amae 天江喜久, then writing his Ph.D. thesis at the University of Hawaii on Manoa, on the Presbyterian Church in Taiwan and its role in Taiwan's democratization, assisted at the December 2003 conference welcoming the missionaries who were deported for their human rights activities. In 2007 Dr. Amae was appointed professor at the Taiwan History Institute of Chang Jung University in Tainan, the university of the Presbyterian Church in Taiwan.

Yoshihisa Amae

The history of threats, intimidation, persecution and imprisonment perpetrated under the KMT regime against Taiwanese members of the PCT must also include the following brief accounts.

The Re-election of Reverend C.M. Kao as General Secretary of the PCT.

The infamous Kaohsiung Incident in December 1979 resulted in military court mock trials in March and May 1980 and imprisonments. Dr. C.M. Kao was given a seven year prison term! The loss of the church's general secretary was compounded by the sudden crisis in leadership. During Dr. Kao's imprisonment, a British missionary was asked to assume the interim administrative duties. She worked closely with the moderator, Ang Hsiu-kiong, a pastor in Taipei. The church had to face the critical and delicate question: Should, or would, the General Assembly re-elect Dr. Kao, now in prison, or choose another person? For the church his re-election became a litmus test of its solidarity with Dr. Kao, his innocence, and his prophetic leadership. At the same, his re-election, in the eyes of the KMT, would be the church's unmistakable signal to time the KMT to stop its growing interference in the affairs of the PCT.

Then, shortly before the General Assembly's meeting to be held on the campus of the Tainan Theological College & Seminary, we learned that the KMT bribed the 49 delegates from the tribal churches to vote against Dr. Kao's re-election. If they complied, the rest of the bribe of NT$50,000 would be paid to them. The night before the opening of the assembly, the 49 were lodged and entertained in a hotel near Tainan. When the agenda called for the election of the moderator, five KMT officials had the audacity to enter the assembly; they took seats in the front row so as to identify those who participated in the discussion. Not only had they entered uninvited but also, without requesting permission from the moderator to speak, they warned the delegates not to re-elect Dr. Kao, a prisoner: inevitable negative consequences would result from such action.

The moment of the election was here. The moderator gave directions on how the voting was to take place: Two urns had been placed in front of the auditorium on either side of the center aisle (in plain sight of the KMT officials). One urn was for positive votes, the other for negative votes. Every delegate had to come forward and personally drop his ballot into one of the urns, indicating "Yes" or "No." The delegates would be asked to rise to be counted. The total number of ballots would be tallied with the official number of delegates in the hall. The Moderator explained once more the one question before the house. He offered prayer and asked the delegates to stand and sing the hymn, "Kiù-chú Iâ-so, góa líp-chì (*Savior Jesus, I await*)."

Being a full member of the PCT, with my turn at hand, I, too, moved forward and cast my vote in the "Yes" urn. A hushed silence reigned in the hall as the ballots were counted and recounted to verify that the number of ballots cast agreed with the number of delegates. The result: 235 "Yes" and 49 "No." (The 49 votes with the KMT had held firm.) It was wonderful, the PCT's General Secretary, re-elected, in prison! Emboldened, the delegates also ratified, by the same count, the 1977 statement, "A Declaration on Human Rights by the Presbyterian Church in Taiwan," reaffirming it on the eve of President Jimmy Carter's landmark announcement of December 16, 1978 to recognize the PRC as the legitimate government of China (and by the same token to de-recognize the ROC's claim of sovereignty over the mainland).

On June 16, 1965 the PCT celebrated its
centennial, dating from its founding in
Tainan in 1865 by the Reverend James
Laidlaw Maxwell

Yoshihisa Amae

The International Consultation in Support of the PCT

During Dr. Kao's imprisonment and while Ang Hsiu-kiong was moderator of the General Assembly, a partnership was established between the PCT and the Evangelical Church of Berlin-Brandenburg (ELCBB), the go-between being the Berlin Missionary Society. The moderator was then invited to come to Berlin and sign the agreement. But the KMT, systematically curtailing the freedom of PCT pastors, refused the moderator's request to leave Taiwan. Hemmed in on all sides, the AHG came up with a ploy: organize a "consultation," bring representatives of the partner churches in as a visible sign of solidarity for Dr. Kao and the PCT. The consultation would be held in December, around Human Rights Day. But would busy executives in their respective churches be able to free themselves for such an event? And how could the PCT bring this off with mail and telephones under surveillance? The AHG presented the proposal to a clandestine meeting of a quorum of the Executive Committee. Doubtful whether such a meeting could be arranged at such notice, the Executive Committee nevertheless decided to go ahead.

An expatriate and the only one in the group with a passport, I said I would be pleased to go to Hong Kong. I was to get in touch with a Methodist and a Reformed Church missionary, both of whom had worked in Taiwan. The former showed little interest, as his denomination had adopted the "One China" policy. The other, Reverend Wendell Karsen, was in favor of giving the plan a try. He gave me his telephone card, facilitating greatly my telephoning freely, and arranged for my lodging in the guest house of Chung Chi College. Ensconced there for a week, I obtained the commitment from all of the PCT's partner churches in Great Britain, Germany, Switzerland, Canada and the U.S.A. To ensure secrecy, the "delegates" were asked to send the information about their arrival, etc., to Hong Kong. My colleague and I, in turn, worked out a code, so that I could receive the relevant information without it being detected, before transmitting it to the Assembly office. The delegates would come as tourists, in time connect with the PCT, and meet with the Taiwanese members at an undisclosed place.

The highpoint of the "consultation" was a tea party to which five KMT officials had been invited to witness the signing of a partnership agreement between the PCT and the ELCBB (it was supposed to have been signed in Britain.) Before the signing, the overseas guests introduced themselves, including a word about their church/ organization's numerical strength and the length and nature of their relationship with the PCT. The KMT visitors appeared to grow increasingly perplexed about the meaning of the swelling host of Christians, represented by delegates who had come from afar in solidarity with the members of the PCT in these trying times.

The *pièce de résistance* was the words of the Asia Secretary of the Berlin Mission. He came, he said, because when the members of the ELCBB learned that the moderator had been refused permission to come to Berlin for the signing of the partnership agreement, they were sad and disappointed. And now it was up to him, as delegate of the ELCBB, to redeem this unfortunate situation. All the while the five KMT guests grew increasingly restive. Then, just before the moderator and the Asia secretary were about to sign the document, the five arose, whispered something into the ear of the presiding chairperson of the tea party, and disappeared. Later, through the grapevine, it was reported that the security forces were completely baffled. It remained a mystery to them how these VIPs had been able to enter Taiwan unnoticed.

David G and Elizabeth Gelzer

台灣基督長老教會總會
台北市長春路89號之5
THE GENERAL ASSEMBLY
THE PRESBYTERIAN CHURCH IN TAIWAN
89-5, CHANG'CHUN ROAD, TAIPEI, TAIWAN 104
REPUBLIC OF CHINA
CABLE ADDRESS: "PRESTAIWAN" TAIPEI
TELEPHONE: (02) 541-6956   (02) 511-6534
(02) 581-6607   (02) 581-6690

GENERAL SECRETARY
C. M. KAO

真理・生命・和平・合一
FAITHFUL SERVANT

＋＋＋＋＋＋＋＋
＋　台灣基督長老教會人權宣言　＋
＋＋＋＋＋＋＋＋

　　致美國卡特總統，有關國家及全世界教會

　本教會根據告白耶穌基督爲全人類的主，且確信人權與鄉土是上帝所賜

鑑於現今台灣一千七百萬住民面臨的危機，發表本宣言。

卡特先生就任美國總統以來，一貫採取「人權」爲外交原則，實具外交

史上劃時代之意義。我們要求卡特總統繼續本著人權道義之精神，在與中共

關係正常化時，堅持「保全台灣人民的安全、獨立與自由」。

面臨中共企圖併吞台灣之際，基於我們的信仰及聯合國人權宣言，我們

堅決主張：「台灣的將來應由台灣一千七百萬住民決定。」我們向有關國家

特別向美國國民及政府，並全世界教會緊急呼籲，採取最有效的步驟，支持

我們的呼聲。

　爲達成台灣人民獨立及自由的願望，我們促請政府於此國際情勢危急之

際面對現實，採取有效措施，使台灣成爲一個新而獨立的國家。

我們懇求上帝，使台灣和全世界成爲「慈愛和誠實彼此相遇，公義和平

安彼此相親，誠實從地而生，公義從天而現」的地方。（聖經詩篇八五篇十

至十一節）

主後　一九

趙信恩（出國中）
翁修恭　代行
高俊明

十六
日

台灣基督長老教會總會
台北市長春路89號之5
THE GENERAL ASSEMBLY
THE PRESBYTERIAN CHURCH IN TAIWAN
89-5, CHANG CHUN ROAD, TAIPEI, TAIWAN 104
REPUBLIC OF CHINA
CABLE ADDRESS: "PRESTAIWAN" TAIPEI
TELEPHONE: 5416956. 5116834

GENERAL SECRETARY
C. M. KAO

FAITHFUL Declaration on Human Rights by the Presbyterian Church in Taiwan

To the President of the United States, to all countries concerned, and to
Christian Churches throughout the world:

Our church confesses that Jesus Christ is Lord of all mankind and believes that
human rights and a land in which each one of us has a stake are gifts bestowed
by God. Therefore we make this declaration, set in the context of the present
crisis threatening the 17 million people of Taiwan.

Ever since President Carter's inauguration as President of the United States
he has consistently adopted "Human Rights" as a principle of his diplomacy.
This is an epoch-making event in the history of foreign policy.

We therefore request President Carter to continue to uphold the principles of
human rights while pursuing the "normalization of relationships with Communist
China" and to insist on guaranteeing the security, independence and freedom of
the people of Taiwan.

As we face the possibility of an invasion by Communist China we hold firmly to
our faith and to the principles underlying the United Nations Declaration of
Human Rights. We insist that the future of Taiwan shall be determined by the
17 million people who live there. We appeal to the countries concerned -
especially to the people and the government of the United States of America -
and to Christian churches throughout the world to take effective steps to
support our cause.

In order to achieve our goal of independence and freedom for the people of
Taiwan in this critical international situation, we urge our government to face
reality and to take affective measures whereby Taiwan may become a new and
independent country.

We beseech God that Taiwan and all the rest of the world may become a place
where "Mercy and truth will meet together; righteousness and peace will embrace.
Truth shall spring out of the earth; and righteousness shall look down from
heaven." (Psalm 85 verses 10 and all) (Today's English Version and King James'
Version)

Signed   H. E. Chao
              Moderator of the General Assembly
              (at present out of the country)

              H. K. Weng   *H. K. Weng*
              Deputy Moderator of the General Assembly
              (Acting in the absence of the Moderator)

              C. M. Kao   *C. M. Kao*
              General Secretary

16th August 1977
(Translated from Chinese. The Chinese text governs.)

We Knew in Our Hearts That True Christian Service to the Taiwanese People Would Compel Us to Join Them in Their Struggle

By Wendell Karsen 嘉偉德牧師

Introduction: Discovering the Shocking Real History of "Free China"

My wife Joyce and I, along with our three children, Stephen, 8 years old, Philip, 5, and Rachel, 1, landed in Taipei at the Sungshan Airport on December 6, 1969. We had been sent there by the Reformed Church in America to work in partnership with the Presbyterian Church of Taiwan in a ministry to university students.

We had undergone five months of cross-cultural training in the USA in preparation for overseas service.We had a minimal introduction to Asia in general, but not much on Taiwan in particular. As a result, we arrived in Taiwan with the usual American stereotypes about the island and its Nationalist government that had been promulgated so effectively for many years by the American "China Lobby."

It was with considerable shock that within a short time after our arrival, we began to discover these stereotypes were all based on myths. We were shocked to hear about the February 28, 1947 tragedy in which some 20,000 innocent Taiwanese civilians were slaughtered by Nationalist troops. Almost every Taiwanese we met who dared to talk to us about this knew somebody who had been killed at that time. We were shocked to learn that the large number of military encampments spread throughout the cities and rural areas of Taiwan under the Garrison Command were used primarily to intimidate the Taiwanese people and only secondarily to defend the island against a communist attack. We were shocked to find that the regime paid thousands of people to spy on their neighbors and report any expression of dissent or disagreement to the secret police. We were particularly shocked to learn that great pressure was put on pastors and members of the Presbyterian Church of Taiwan to report on each other, and that because of the presence of some "Judases" within the church, nobody knew who they could fully trust. The list could go on.

As we learned the Taiwanese language, became acquainted with both Taiwanese and foreigners who knew the truth, read books like George Kerr's *Formosa Betrayed* and observed life around us, we knew in our hearts that true Christian service to the Taiwanese people would compel us to join them in their struggle to free themselves from the oppression and exploitation of the Nationalist regime.

I immediately began jotting all the information I was gathering down on paper and sending periodic reports out with trusted friends since we were warned that our mail was being read and our telephones were tapped. These were mailed to the Reformed Church in America's leaders, and other key people and organizations, asking for action on behalf of the Taiwanese people in general and the Presbyterian Church of

Ruth Kao's Bid for National Legislator : How to Lose an Election and Yet Win It

With Dr. Kao in prison, a grassroots movement arose in southern Taiwan to persuade his wife, Mrs. Ruth Kao, to run for a seat in the Legislative Yuan. She hesitated, saying she lacked experience in public affairs. She asked for reactions and advice. She received much encouragement to take the step into public life and exposure. She heard the plea of the people, "represent and speak for us." She accepted and one of the AHG became her campaign manager. Everywhere she went in the legislative district and spoke to and with the people she was well received and gladly heard. The results of the elections were being televised. By 9 pm the reports from all of Taiwan had been posted, all with the exception of the Tainan district. By 10 pm we were still waiting for news. What, we wondered, could possibly be the problem? Close to 10:30 pm, the Tainan district reported that Mrs. Kao had lost by 17 votes! Not much later we heard that Mrs. Kao, early on, had outvoted her KMT opponent by thousands of votes. The election committee, faced with an overwhelming defeat of the KMT candidate, rearranged the ballots to the KMT's satisfaction. Everyone knew immediately that fraud had been committed. And in the streets of Tainan the people celebrated Mrs. Kao's victory.

David G. and Elizabeth Gelzer were in Africa for 23 years before being invited to Taiwan in September 1975. Rev. Gelzer helped maintain international communications and moral support for the PCT while the KMT "tightened the noose" in 1977-80.

Wendell Karsen was sent to Taiwan in late 1969 by the Reformed Church in America, with the mission to cultivate social commitment for youth. He was not allowed to return to Taiwan after furlough in 1973. This however allowed him an important role in 1979-80 in helping external communications of the PCT through Hong Kong, coordinating with David Gelzer. With his wife Renske, December 2003. Maysing Yang is visible in the train seat behind.

Taiwan in particular. I also wrote letters to major newspapers and magazines under fictitious Chinese names exposing the human rights abuses of the Chiang regime and advocating self-determination for the people of Taiwan.

The Grichting Research and Quiet Contacts with the U.S. Embassy

Dr. Wolfgang Grichting, a German sociologist, came to Taiwan at the beginning of 1970 to do a study on religion and society (politics excepted) in Taiwan, and to publish a book detailing his findings. Professor Grichting circulated an extensive questionnaire throughout various levels of society through churches, universities and other institutions and organizations. After he had collated the results, he looked for people, and particularly PCT missionaries, living on Taiwan who had an informed understanding of Taiwan's society to help him interpret his data. Dr. Grichting was introduced to Milo and Judith Thornberry, American United Methodist missionaries, seconded to the Presbyterian Church of Taiwan, who had arrived in 1965. They lived on the campus of the PCT's Taiwan Presbyterian Seminary in the YangMinShan mountain area outside of Taipei where Milo taught church history. A series of confidential evening meetings was quietly arranged by the Thornberrys in their home to help Dr. Grichting in processing his findings. The book was subsequently published in 1971 under the title *The Value System in Taiwan, 1970*.

I was responsible for the section on the PCT's ministry to the aged and the young, and my analysis and suggestions for action were published on pages 195-199 pretty well as I wrote them. One of my "in-between-the-lines" recommendations read: "The PCT needs to prophetically and courageously attack the roots of the present social problems in Taiwan from the perspective of the Gospel with the spirit of speaking the truth in love, letting the chips fall where they may, and being willing to bear passively and patiently whatever consequences this may elicit." Little did I know then that this was exactly the course the PCT would take, beginning that very year! For a number of years, I did not think the Investigation Bureau or the Taiwan Garrison Command ever knew about these meetings or who had participated in them, but I was mistaken. The Thornberrys were expelled in 1971 for helping Professor Peng Ming-min escape from Taiwan; it was a severe blow to all of us.

Following President Franklin Roosevelt's mistaken prognosis of the post-WWII Asian world, the USA continued to pursue his policy of propping up the Chiang regime's Republic of China as the future hope of the region, even after Chiang's civil war defeat and his Taiwan retreat. The regime's American supporters, the powerful "China Lobby," continued to spin and promote the myth of Chiang's benevolent rule in "Free China." Fortunately, there were some who suspected otherwise, even among the US Embassy staff in Taipei, and who were trying to uncover the real truth and report it to the US State Department.

Sid Goldsmith and Burton Levin were two such staff members. Since the "Taiwanese question" was such a sensitive one, they had to be careful and quiet in the way they went about gathering information. They gleaned what information they could from intelligence sources and local opposition publications, discreetly dined with

December 22, 1979

REPORT ON SITUATION IN TAIWAN
BY LAURIE S. WISEBERG, EXECUTIVE DIRECTOR,
HUMAN RIGHTS INTERNET
1502 OGDEN ST. NW, WASHINGTON, DC. 21101

(This report is being written in my personal capacity, not as an officer of the Human Rights Internet.)

(Excerpts from 16-page report)

From November 15 to 20, 1979, I visited Taipei. The purpose of my trip was to make contact with individuals and organizations in Taiwan actively concerned with human rights. Today, most of the people I met with are either in jail on charges of sedition, under threat of arrest, in hiding, or (in the case of an American woman) deported.

During my five day visit, I talked with perhaps as many as sixty Taiwanese and with several Americans living in Taiwan. None of the people I talked to could be described as "revolutionary", even by the remotest stretching of the definition. Most, of course, wanted to see a change in the current regime. The Kuomintang has ruled Taiwan for over thirty years under martial law. All power remains centralized in the hands of the 2 million mainlanders while the 17 million Taiwanese remain unrepresented. ...

The major force for human rights outside the political opposition in Taiwan has been the Presbyterian Church

The major force for human rights outside the political opposition in Taiwan has been the Presbyterian Church. Organized into more than a thousand local congregations, the church has about 170,000 members, embracing primarily Taiwanese, but Taiwanese from all social classes in the country. The Presbyterian Church has had a particularly strong following among the mountain tribes who, like aboriginal peoples throughout the world, are the most neglected segment of national society. As early as 1971, the General Assembly (on the occasion of President Nixon's visit to mainland China) of the Presbyterian Church spoke out for self-determination for the Taiwanese and for electoral reform: "...every people has the right to determine its own destiny." In recent years, the Church has opposed martial law, defended the right of the church to preach in local dialects and to issue a Taiwanese bible, supported genuine free elections, and issued a Declaration

opposition politicians like Kang Ning-Hsiang, and the like. I was introduced to them at a public function in 1971. When they realized how much I knew about the Taiwanese scene and what kind of connections I had, they asked if I would be willing to quietly meet with one or both of them from time to time at the Embassy. They guaranteed that my name, the RCA or the PCT would never appear in any report they would give. I was hesitant because I felt that I could be linked with US intelligence. On the other hand, here was a rare opportunity to argue the Taiwanese case right at the highest echelons of the American Embassy and to feed them accurate information, so I accepted.

This precipitated one of what would subsequently become many discussions between my wife and myself as to whether or not we should engage in such an activity, risk discovery and possible expulsion from Taiwan, and thereby jeopardize our missionary work. Our consistent conclusion was that this was part of our missionary work! We had come to serve the people of Taiwan, and our conscience and the Christian faith we professed left us no choice but to take such a risk on behalf of an oppressed people, some of whom were risking their lives in the struggle for human (and God-given) rights. Sid, Burt and I worked out a way that I could unobtrusively enter a back door of the Embassy and go right to the meeting room without being seen by anyone other than an alerted security guard. I used a very circuitous route to the Embassy to make sure I was not being followed. I passed on any relevant information that I had on the regime's harassment of the PCT, their treatment of political prisoners, news about Taiwanese dissidents inside Taiwan and in the United States, material on Taiwanese concerns and aspirations, etc.

The PCT's December 1971 Statement on "The Fate of Our Nation"

The expulsion of the ROC regime from the United Nations in October 1971 and the impending visit of President Richard Nixon to the PRC in February 1972 produced considerable anxiety among the Taiwanese. They were afraid that a deal was going to be made between the USA and the PRC, with the connivance of the ROC regime, at the expense of, and without any consultation with, the Taiwanese people. PCT church leaders felt that somebody must speak up on behalf of the Taiwanese people in a "now or never" situation.

A statement was drafted by Dr. Dan Beeby, President of the Tainan Seminary, edited by Dr. John Tin and others, and sent to the PCT General Assembly Office in Taipei. PCT representatives then presented it to the Taiwan Ecumenical Cooperative Committee (ECC) (loosely akin to a national council of churches) as a draft with the request that it be adopted and issued as a joint statement by the Committee. However, agreement could not be reached. The PCT then decided to issue a statement on its own. The Executive Committee secretly met at the General Assembly Office on the evening of December 17, 1971, to discuss and refine the statement and to organize its distribution throughout the island and abroad.

That evening, a courier from the PCT General Assembly Office knocked on our door at 11:00 p.m. and got me out of bed. He said the PCT Executive Committee was

on Human Rights. Although the church has attempted to articulate matters of principles — not to support specific political policies — it has been perceived as a major threat by the KMT.

The Kuomintang, sensitive to international opinion, has been afraid of moving directly against the Presbyterian Church. It has, therefore, resorted to a whole myriad of subterfuges to undermine it. In 1970, it forced the Presbyterian Church to disaffiliate with the World Council of Churches on the grounds that the latter is a communist organization. It has forbidden high school and university students to take part in church activities and harassed those who defied this ruling by interrogations, threats, and flunking them out of school. It has used other denominations against the Presbyterians. It has used the media to attack the church. It has denied passports to Church members wanting to travel abroad. And it has used civil servants and party members to cause a great deal of trouble for the ministers at the local level. More recently, the KMT tried a more direct attack by introducing a new law entitled "Regulations for Shrines, Temples and Churches."

Allegedly establishing new regulations "in order to guarantee religious freedom," the law is a particularly pernicious redrafting of an old law introduced by the Japanese at the height of Japanese imperialism in Taiwan, and subsequently repealed. It was targeted particularly at the Presbyterian Church: the Catholic Church is not subject to the law because it does not apply to "churches having a hierarchy," while other denominations have been assured it would not apply to them. Under the name of freedom of religion, the law would require each congregation to set up its own juridical body of not less than five persons in which title to church property would be vested and which would have the authority to call ministers to order. Since half of the body is required to be "religious propagators" (i.e., ministers), this is theoretically impossible for local congregations which have only one minister. More pointedly, however, the law is aimed at undermining the right of the General Assembly of the Presbyterian Church to hold land on behalf of local congregations: with the new law, the KMT could whittle away at the base of the church by forcing local congregations to break away, with their land and property, from the general church body. Moreover, the law would require that "religious propagation must be done in public and in the Chinese language," while most Presbyterian ministers preach in Taiwanese or in the local language of their congregation; it would require that "religious doctrine, ceremonies and activities may not contravene the law, public order or good social customs" with the latter unspecified;

assembled at the office, was working on an important public statement, and would like me to come and help. I threw on my clothes and immediately went to the office, knowing that something big must be up.

When I arrived, the General Secretary, Dr. C. M. Kao, explained the circumstances surrounding the issuing of the public statement. We all then discussed the text line by line. There was also a concern that the English translation, which was to be sent to news and church agencies around the world, should *exactly* reflect the double meaning of the Chinese text. For those both inside and outside of Taiwan who knew the true situation, the text was worded in such a way that they could "read in-between-the-lines" and discern the real message — a call for a new constitution, for elections that reflected the true political situation on the island, and for self-determination for the people of Taiwan.

The next task was to decide how to disseminate the Statement throughout Taiwan and abroad, both in Chinese and in English. We drew up a list of churches, Christian organizations and news services abroad to which we wished the English version to go. I agreed to contact trusted colleagues who were going off island during the next few days. Meanwhile, the Statement would be issued on December 29 and published in Taiwan's newspapers as a paid advertisement. All PCT pastors would be asked to read the Statement from their pulpits the next Sunday, January 2. The meeting was finally adjourned, and we returned to our homes in the wee hours of the morning, tired but elated that such a momentous step had unanimously been taken, yet a bit apprehensive at the possible fallout.

The plan was implemented, but not surprisingly, ran into immediate difficulties. The newspapers at first agreed to run the paid ads. However, once the government censors saw the text and reported to their superiors, the security people ordered the newspapers to cancel them! The cat was now out of the bag. The head of the Taiwan Garrison Command called C.M. Kao and demanded that the Statement not be issued. Kao replied that since the Statement was an official act of the PCT Executive Committee, he was duty bound to carry it out. Meanwhile, ecclesiastical stool pigeons within the PCT alerted their security handlers who reported the plan to have the pastors read the Statement from their pulpits. The secret police immediately scheduled "tea times" with all PCT pastors and, using both carrot and stick, tried to bribe them or intimidate them into not reading the Statement on the following Sunday. Some caved in, but most of the pastors courageously read the Statement anyway.

Meanwhile, I had found people and means to get the English version of the Statement out to the world with immediate effect. The major news agencies carried the story, while many church publications, particularly in the USA, featured it, with some calling upon their government to take action to protect the rights of the people of Taiwan. My own denominational magazine, *The Church Herald*, in response to my urgings, along with those of other colleagues who were knowledgeable about and committed to the Taiwanese cause, published a particularly strong editorial calling for action.[6]

Wendell Karsen

and would provide authority to local governments to close down a church or dismiss its minister if the church is seen to be acting "against national policy" otherwise not defined. Thus, the law would be a threat to the integrity of the church and to religious freedom. It was on those general grounds of principle — that the law was unconstitutional because it violated freedom of religion guaranteed in the Constitution — that the Presbyterians have opposed it. Other religious groups have voiced concern about specific articles but have not taken a stand against the law, per se. Nevertheless, the strong criticism leveled against the proposed law by the Presbyterian Church has caused its shelving for the time being.

A final note of interest about this law and the Presbyterian Church concerns the attempt of the KMT to shift theological colleges, presently under the jurisdiction of the Ministry of Interior, to the jurisdiction of the Ministry of Education. If theological colleges came under the latter's control, it would make it possible for the Ministry of Education to send Political Guidance Counselors onto the campuses — as the Ministry does with all other high schools and universities it controls — to regiment the student body to party discipline. As punishment for the church's resistance, the KMT has made it impossible, as of June 1979, for graduates of theological colleges to take the TOEFL test of English proficiency (administered by the Educational Testing Center of Princeton University) which is a prerequisite for any Taiwanese student seeking admission to a U.S. University. We have, thus far, heard no protest from either Princeton or from the U.S. government.

The Catholic hierarchy has sought good relations with the government and has been prepared to be used by the government in order to avoid the uncertainty of turmoil

Catholics in Taiwan are about equal in strength to Protestants, comprising about 1 per cent of the population. By and large, however, the Catholic Church has been a conservative force — a conservatism recently expressed in their invitation to Senator Barry Goldwater to attend the anniversary celebration of Fujen Catholic University. The Catholic hierarchy has sought good relations with the government and has been prepared to be used by the government in order to avoid the uncertainty of turmoil: its objective, above all, has been security. One exception to this has been the Maryknoll Fathers who, unlike the mainstream of the Catholic Church, have used Taiwanese with their parishes and have been responsive to human rights concerns. With the normalization of relations between China and the U.S., Chinese Catholics were

Looking back, the issuing of the 1971 Statement by the PCT turned out to be a catalytic act that bolstered the long struggle for human rights in Taiwan that would culminate in victory with the election of the Democratic Progressive Party's candidates in the 2000 election. For the first time, the regime had been publicly challenged by the largest, best-educated and best-organized group of Taiwanese on the island — the 200,000 strong Presbyterian Church of Taiwan.

Working to "Set the Prisoners Free"

I had been on Taiwan only a few months when I began to hear gruesome tales of how political prisoners, who were arrested simply because they advocated justice and self-determination for the Taiwanese people, were treated. Most of them were sent to a notorious fortress prison on a place called Green Island off the east coast of Taiwan. "Confession" under torture was the norm. Political prisoners in this period were seldom executed, but without adequate blankets in winter, nutritious food, medical care and sanitary conditions, they slowly deteriorated physically, mentally and emotionally. I also learned that once a person had been imprisoned for political reasons, the secret police would visit the employers of every member of the person's extended family and order them to fire them, thus leaving the family destitute, since nobody else would dare to hire them. The prisoner's family was made an abject lesson to others.

As a Christian pastor, these reports aroused both anger and compassion within me. When an opportunity presented itself, I was more than ready to help them as best I could. I believe that it was in Hong Kong while on vacation that I met an Amnesty International representative who, when he heard what I had to say about Taiwan, asked if I would be willing to be a contact person for Amnesty there. Since the deportation of the Thornberrys, they had found it very difficult to obtain accurate information on political prisoners in Taiwan. I agreed. Later, trusted people at Tainan Seminary asked me if I would serve as a conduit to funnel funds provided by the Presbyterian Church USA to families of political prisoners.

I had learned most of what I knew about political prisoners and their families from one of my Taiwanese tutors at the Taipei Language Institute who seemed trustworthy at the time – Gui Ek-Bin. When asked if he would be willing to help his people by getting me specific information and by delivering funds, he agreed. He began to feed me detailed information on the names and conditions of political prisoners during my private Taiwanese lessons at the Institute, and I passed that on to Amnesty International through safe channels. He did not divulge the sources of his information to me, and I did not ask. Later, he also gave me specific information as to which families of political prisoners needed help, what kind of help they needed and how much it would cost. I then secretly delivered funds to him in the privacy of our classroom at the Institute, and he in turn delivered signed receipts to me from the families who received help that I then passed on to Presbyterian Church USA people through safe channels.

This went on for some time until shortly before our family was to leave Taiwan for a furlough in the USA in the summer of 1973. One day, the PCT's new Associate

called upon to demonstrate their patriotism which took the form of an attack on the Maryknolls and led, eventually, to some backlash within the religious community itself. The Maryknolls have been forced, therefore, to opt for a lower profile and to be less directly involved in human rights cases. From the other side, the Bishops' Conference in Taipei has recently set up a Bishops' Commission on Human Rights for China, but what precisely its role is to be is not clear. One may assume that it will focus almost exclusively on violations on the mainland rather than at home.

Very similar in character is the Chinese Association for Human Rights, created in February, 1979, and housed on the same premises as the Anti-Communist League. The Organization claims that the stimulus for its creation was the nascent movement for human rights on the mainland, the American de-recognition of the Republic of China with the anger this aroused in Taiwan over the threat to their security, and a general concern over human rights. Thus far, the Association has yet to evidence much concern about violations of human rights in Taiwan, with the exception of one forum it held on the next election that is anticipated. A test of the genuine concern of the group will be the extent to which it acts at all in the present crisis. During the Yu Teng-fa affair, it is alleged to have defended the right of the Kuomntang to prosecute and imprison the 78-year-old former magistrate of Kaohsiung County to 8 years in prison.

One of the problems posed by the establishment of the Chinese Association for Human Rights is the degree to which it legally pre-empts the human rights field in Taiwan. According to current Taiwanese law, there can be only one association per issue in the country: e.g., one for consumerism, one for women's issues, one for environmental issues, and one for human rights. To be legitimate an association must seek approval from the government and register. After an association is established around a given issue, a new association which may wish to set itself up can only do so if the registered association is prepared to accept the new group as its affiliate. Through this simple device, the government can control all associations....

"I am told that that afternoon has now taken on heightened significance. For almost all of the women present that day as listeners have become the very people they sought to help: the wives and families of political detainees."

I also spent several hours on another evening listening to the wives of former political prisoners talk about their experiences:

Coordinator for Student Work, with whom I worked, asked me to come with him to see C.S. Song's brother, who was a top executive at the state-run oil company. When we arrived, Song startled me by asking how involved I was with Gui Ek-Bin. I replied that he had been my language teacher, and that I continued to see him on occasion. He then made it clear that he suspected there was more to it than that. He said that Gui could not be trusted and advised me not to see him again.

I left unsure as to what to do. On the one hand, Song's information could be true and Gui could be suspect. On the other hand, as a top oil executive, Song could well have some kind of connection with the regime and was simply being used to sow seeds of suspicion to disrupt the relationship. Since I was about to leave Taiwan on furlough anyway, I decided not to see Gui again until after my return. Later, I heard that Gui had been arrested and that, as the result of a combination of threats and bribes, he had divulged our activities. To this day, I do not know if the report on Gui was true.

Conscientizing University Students

My assignment as an RCA missionary was to assist the PCT in its ministry to university students. This was a key ministry in terms of reaching out to those who would become Taiwan's future leaders. It was also a very sensitive ministry as far as the regime was concerned, particularly since I spoke the Taiwanese language. I was appointed as Associate Coordinator for University Student Ministries by the PCT and served in that capacity along with my able Taiwanese colleague, Reverend Chia Hi-Beng (Andrew Hsieh Hsi-ming 謝禧明牧師).

A key goal of this ministry was to help students become aware of the true situation of the society in which they lived and to motivate them to do something to address its problems and serve its people. Courses, programs and activities were offered by campus ministers and volunteers at a string of PCT student centers strategically located near key university campuses. Each center also had a student hostel where students could live together, build community and explore ideas that were not being addressed in their university courses.

We were also acutely aware of the KMT's brain washing program that all university students were constantly exposed to. This was particularly true during the summer months when students were encouraged (read "pressured") to join the "Kiu Keng Kok" (KKK as we called it, common name the Chinese Youth Corps 中國青年救國團, formal name until 2000 was the China Youth Anti-Communist National Salvation Corps), camps which were modeled after the Hitler Youth Corps camps designed by the Nazis. Students were enticed to these camps through sports and other types of enjoyable activities and fed a steady diet of KMT propaganda.

We were determined to give these students another choice by developing a number of summer programs that aimed at furthering the goals described above. We ran a summer music camp at Tunghai University in Taichung. We designed an around-the-island study tour for seminary students who rode a bus around Taiwan, talking to people and analyzing social, economic and political realities. They lodged overnight at PCT churches, discussed their findings and explored what those findings

the knock on the door at 7 a.m. and the police rushing; coming home from work to find a husband gone and learning from neighbours that he had been taken away by the police; the difficulties of supporting a family and taking care of young children while a husband was imprisoned. The stories are common enough in many dictatorial societies. Yet, the women who listened with me, largely upper middle class wives of professionals -- the wives of the Meilitao politicians — were being exposed to this for the first time. They had never before sat together in a room to hear other women tell of the imprisonment of their husbands. They were particularly moved by learning about the conditions of families of political prisoners who were peasants or workers, without any legal aid and in total penury. One of the issues discussed that afternoon was the possibility of forming a woman's organization that could provide some support to political prisoners and their families. I was asked to say a few words and spoke about human rights groups in other countries, of the central role that women have played in Bolivia, in Argentina, in South Africa, and of supportive international solidarity that is now emerging. I am told that that afternoon has now taken on heightened significance. For almost all of the women present that day as listeners have become the very people they sought to help: the wives and families of political detainees.

...

suggested for ministry and for the future of Taiwan. We offered English camps that featured spiritual exercises, physical activities and social service projects, along with English lessons conducted by native speaking American volunteers, in seven university towns. Students lived together in community for five weeks at PCT campus ministry centers and discussed current personal and social concerns.

We designed two social immersion experiences for seminary students. One group went to rural areas to live and work with farm families. They learned about life in Taiwan from a rural perspective, discussed their observations and explored ideas for addressing the concerns and meeting the needs of rural people from a Christian perspective. Another group went to Taipei and took up factory jobs. They lived together in a student center hostel and spent their evenings sharing their conversations with fellow workers and their observations of the conditions under which they worked. They too explored the spiritual, social, economic and political implications of their findings and formulated strategies for future ministry .

In all, some 300 students opted to participate in our demanding and challenging programs while resisting KMT pressure to join the KMT Youth Corps. But perpetual "students," recruited by the secret police to be their eyes and ears on university campuses around the island, were sent to infiltrate. They were easy to spot. In fact, we would always deliberately accept a few obvious ones so we would know whom we were dealing with. Only when they were not around would the "real" conversations take place.

However, when a program proved to go beyond the limits tolerated by the regime, more direct action was taken. A case in point was the summer industrial exposure program. Seminary students working and talking with factory workers about their problems, opinions and concerns made the secret police very nervous. In the end, they moved to shut the program down. One night they swooped down on the Taipei hostel where the students were living, arrested the lot and clapped them in jail! The charge was disturbance of the peace. People in the neighborhood surrounding the student hostel had supposedly complained that the students were gambling, drinking and raising a ruckus. The charges were, of course, completely false.

We learned what had happened in the wee hours of the morning. Rev. Hsieh bravely volunteered to go to the jail well after curfew (we were still under martial law) and demand their release. The police said they would release the students under one condition – the program had to be shut down and the students sent back to their homes. Rev. Hsieh and I decided that we had no choice but to comply, since not to do so would have unduly endangered the students, and the PCT's Tainan Seminary.

Experiences like this, although appearing as defeats at the time, had a great impact for good on the young people who went through them, along with their families, friends and classmates. They underlined the oppressive nature of the regime and exposed its hollow rhetoric for what it really was.

The Beeby Expulsion Incident

Dr. Rowland Van Es, a fellow RCA missionary and professor of Old Testament at the

In December 2003 the Taiwan Foundation for Democracy sponsored a conference entitled "International Friends and Taiwan's Democracy", which invited back to Taiwan about thirty foreigners who had made contributions to Taiwan's human rights, most of whom suffered deportation. Lin Yi-hsiung 林義雄 and his wife invited the group to his foundation in Ilan. Below, group picture on the first day of activities. Upper right, Albert Lin 林哲夫, Rowland Van Es, and Milo Thornberry and his daughter.

PCT's Tainan Theological Seminary, shared my concern for human rights in Taiwan, as did most of the faculty and student body at that institution. Rowland and I had worked out a code, based on Old Testament characters and events, that we could use to communicate with each other concerning sensitive subjects.

In late February 1972, I received an urgent coded post card from Rowland. Dr. Dan Beeby and his wife Joyce had received word from the police that they were to be expelled from Taiwan in ten days' time! Dan Beeby, an English Presbyterian missionary, had become an ardent supporter of human rights for the Taiwanese during his many years as president of the Seminary. He had managed to walk a tightrope. On the one hand, he had quietly encouraged the faculty and students to be discreetly involved in these issues, while on the other hand he had avoided precipitating the kind of overt action that would bring down the wrath of the secret police on the institution and its parent body, the PCT. The agents on campus, and the security apparatus behind them, had been unable to accuse him of fomenting any direct action against the government. However, over the years, police reports and security innuendoes had added up until the regime decided it could no longer tolerate him and that it would quietly expel him from the island.

Apart from a concern for the Beebys and the personal trauma of their being suddenly uprooted from a place, the regime's goal of isolating the PCT from its overseas partners and getting rid of and silencing any foreign missionaries who knew the real truth about Taiwan, would in time be accomplished. The only way this could be prevented was to make sure the Nationalist regime would pay a heavy price in terms of world opinion and think twice about taking such action against anybody else. But how could that be done?

Because this crisis was too sensitive, and the time was too short, I decided to act alone. By coded post card, I learned from Rowland the exact timing and method to be used by the authorities in expelling the Beebys. He reported that the Beebys had been told that the Kaohsiung Chief of Police, along with other officers, would quietly escort them from Tainan by a certain train on Monday, March 6. Once they arrived in Taipei, they would then be moved to the airport by car under police escort and immediately flown out to Hong Kong on a certain flight.

Several things were in our favor. President Richard Nixon was completing his earth-shaking visit to the People's Republic of China and had just signed the Shanghai Communiqué. Now, a number of reporters for the major newspapers and news services of the world were en route to Taipei to see how Taiwan would react to this shock.

I thought up a plan and relayed it to Rowland for his and Dan Beeby's approval. I would write an anonymous letter addressed to these reporters. It would explain the situation and invite them to a press conference with Dr. Beeby in the President Hotel's Philippine Room after his arrival in Taipei, at 2:40 pm. The room was reserved and paid for under a fictitious name. Upon arrival in Taipei, Dr. Beeby would ask his police chief "friend" if he would do him one last favor and let him say

What I Learned from Sister Nadine Tierney Was, "You Have to Love the Person Who Is Giving You a Hard Time"

by James Collignon, M.M.

I was born in St. Cloud, Minnesota on July 19, 1926. In 1953 I was ordained a priest and then went to the Catholic University in Washington, D.C. to gain a Master's degree in music. In 1957 I went to Taiwan for the first time. Several times I returned to the U.S. for work, but altogether I was in Taiwan for twenty-five years.

My first impression of Taiwan was how militarized the island was at the time. The military itself was present almost everywhere, middle and high school students wore military type uniforms, patriotic slogans were prominently displayed, and everyone had to fly the national flag.

My first inkling that much was going on under the surface of the relative calm around me began with several of my language schoolteachers who would speak quietly about the repression of native Taiwanese. Then in my first parish, in Chiong-hoa (Changhua) City, people would never speak directly about their concerns but you could feel it as you got to know the language and culture better.

A real breakthrough in my understanding came with the election of John F. Kennedy as U.S. President in 1960. I supported Kennedy and the KMT government had actively opposed Kennedy's election. I could tell that my Taiwanese friends were secretly happy about Kennedy's surprise victory.

As I came to understand the language and the culture under girding it, I vividly remember asking why Taiwanese called themselves "sweet potatoes – han-ji-a." After giving me the standard answer that Taiwan was shaped like a sweet potato, my Taiwanese friend then added, "Pigs like to eat sweet potatoes"(*Ti-a ai chiah han-ji*) – a very deft analysis of the plight of the Taiwanese under the KMT's corrupt, repressive regime.

After working in Taiwan for six years, I was assigned to the US to teach at Maryknoll's Major Seminary. This was the era of the Second Vatican Council and real ferment within the Roman Catholic Church. Pope John XXIII "opened the windows" of the Church to let in the Spirit. The breeze was both refreshing and challenging to all of us. When I returned to Taiwan in 1965, I was filled with enthusiasm for the dynamic changes Vatican II had unleashed and excited to bring this "good news" to the island.

Though I studied both Taiwanese and Mandarin, Taiwanese was the language I used most. That knowledge directed many of my sympathies. During this period of work in Taiwan one glimmer of hope was the incipient credit union movement. I was in a small parish in Chiong-hoa County, Sio Po Sim, the home to one of the initiators and key organizers of the credit union movement, Matthew Wang (Ong Bu-chhiong). Matthew had a vision that later proved to be quite correct: use the real need people had to pool their savings so they could borrow from each other at low interest rates as an opportunity

goodbye to a dear friend staying at the President Hotel on the way to the airport. I then hand-delivered the invitations by slipping the addressed envelopes under the various reporters' hotel room doors. Amazingly, all went according to plan. The train journey proceeded without incident, the police chief granted Beeby's request, and thirteen reporters showed up for the press conference, which lasted for half an hour! The police were flabbergasted, but realized that they could not intervene. Beeby proceeded to tell them about his service to the people of Taiwan and the circumstances surrounding his expulsion.

Dr. C.M. Kao and a few other PCT leaders bravely came to the airport to bid the Beebys farewell. By that time, Rowland and I, along with other Taipei friends and colleagues that we had notified, had also arrived. We all gathered around Dan and Joyce, had a moving prayer together and escorted them to the immigration gate. Meanwhile, Dan had given us the thumbs up and whispered to me: "Some day we will meet again in Taipei and drink a toast in celebration of a free Taiwan."

The word had already flashed around the world. When the Beebys arrived in Hong Kong, a group of reporters was there and they held another press conference! When they arrived in England, there was a further press conference. We were thankful. The Beebys had been expelled, but in the process, the Nationalist regime had received a black eye in terms of world opinion.

The Kuo Yu-Hsin Case

I had heard about Kuo Yu-Hsin from PCT leaders I trusted. He was a Presbyterian layman who was referred to as a "father figure" among the Taiwanese opposition. He was a long-term representative of the Ilan constituency in the relatively powerless Taiwan Provincial Legislature and eventually became its speaker. Kuo was one of a handful of Taiwanese politicians who continually tested the parameters of what criticism would be tolerated by the Nationalist regime. He was also an articulate voice for the aspirations of the Taiwanese people. The KMT did its utmost to defeat him with bribes, intimidation, slander, accusations, etc., but he was so popular with his constituents that they never succeeded. We met incidentally at church and at other general functions a few times. I was cautious since he was a well-known opposition figure.

One day, he sent a message to me by courier. He had received word from reliable sources that an attempt was to be made on his life. He was advised to escape from Taiwan and ask for political asylum in the USA while he still had a chance. Could I possibly figure out some way to get him out of Taiwan alive? And could we meet to discuss it?

Escaping from Taiwan was no small matter, especially for a well-known personality like Kuo. The island was a tightly controlled fortress, and people like Kuo were carefully kept track of by the secret police. I suggested getting him out by using a ruse similar to that which the Thornberrys had used just after I arrived in Taiwan to help the famous dissident, Peng Meng-Min, escape in January 1970.

Meanwhile, a missionary friend from Japan, Jim Anderson, was in Taiwan as a tour

to also build leadership, a sense of community and concern about each other's daily struggles. The credit union movement proved to be a key means of rebuilding leadership in the Taiwanese community, leadership so dramatically destroyed by the 2/28 massacre and the subsequent repression inflicted by the government.

The first stirrings of the credit union movement in central Taiwan almost failed. I am proud of my efforts to call a meeting of Chiong-hoa pastors and encourage them to press forward with the credit union movement. Real credit must be given to Mr. Wang and the other Taiwanese organizers of the time who were skirting the edges of the permissible and were under constant government scrutiny. In a small way those of us in the church community who supported the credit union effort gave these courageous men and women some protection – something to be proud of looking back over those difficult times.

[Editor's note: Matthew Wang (Wang Wu-chang 王武昌) in 1971 finished training at the Coady International Institute, a social justice education program affiliated with St. Francis Xavier University in Nova Scotia, Canada. According to its website, "Two high-placed mentors in Taiwan were able to create a kind of legal umbrella under which Matthew could develop his dream (of a cooperative and credit union movement). Cardinal Yu-Pin, the country's highest-ranking Catholic prelate, had maintained a good working relationship with the government. In addition, the bishop of Matthew's home diocese was a very supportive Maryknoll missionary from the United States. With their support Matthew founded the Popularum Progressio Institute (PPI) in 1972, named for Pope Paul VI's inspirational encyclical. ... Within just six years, more than 6000 had taken the program (in grassroots leadership). These enthusiastic volunteer leaders then returned to their communities and trained others." This successful program was sponsored by the government after 1984.]

I found not only very little enthusiasm for the Vatican II changes among my own Maryknoll group as well as the broader Taiwan Catholic community, but, in fact, real resistance and opposition. When I was assigned to a Taipei parish, I began to have more contact with local Presbyterian Church ministers and some Presbyterian Church functionaries. I often found a higher level of comfort within this community than the Roman Catholic world.

Eventually these Taipei contacts and my own teaching at the Tainan Cheng Kung University and the Teachers' College in Kaohsiung brought me to offer my services at the Tainan Theological College before and after the Kaohsiung Incident. In fact, the College already had a music teacher and really didn't need me. But I offered myself in an act of solidarity with the Presbyterian Church. It was well known that the sympathies of our Catholic Church were with the Nationalist Party and I wished to demonstrate that this was not universal. The faculty and students of the College very graciously received me. At that time the seminary came close to being closed by the government, or so we perceived things, and I felt an action such as mine was necessary.

I confess to feeling real fear at times when I was riding my bicycle from the College to our Maryknoll House in Tainan. I was concerned that I might be hit "by accident" by a vehicle operated under KMT agents' control. It was perhaps a precursor sense of the terrible political maiming of Wu Shu-chen that was to take place later.

We often laughed at danger, however. One standing joke was the shoe repairman on

leader for a group of Japanese students. I explained Kuo's situation to him. I asked him to inform my friend John Nakajima, the general secretary of the United Church of Christ in Japan, and ask if he would be willing to set it up on the Japanese end. The operation was referred to as "the student center construction project." A week later, I received a coded letter from Jim saying that Nakajima had agreed and that he would implement "the plan" as soon as they got the go ahead from me. Nakijima would find a Japanese who generally resembled Kuo in terms of height, weight, features, etc. The Japanese would wear a fake mustache, glasses and a distinctive suit, shirt and tie, have his passport photo taken and apply for a passport. He would then deliver his passport and his fake mustache, suit, shirt, tie and hat to me to pass to Kuo by courier, and Kuo would exit the country with them. This plan was being put into action when Kuo sent me an urgent message saying we should put the plan on hold!

In the end, Kuo was permitted to leave the island and immigrate to the USA to join his daughter. There he carried on his fight for self-determination for the people of Taiwan for a few years before his death. But apparently my contacts with Kuo had not escaped official detection. Kuo Yu-hsin corresponded with me from time to time through 1978. He was always grateful to me for having taken such a risk to help him when he needed it. When I was banned from Taiwan and put on the black list, his card to me of May 23, 1974 upon hearing the news read: "For whom doth the bell toll? It tolls for thee."

Paying the Price: Provincial Re-entry Permit Revoked!

As we increasingly became more involved in the human rights struggle in Taiwan, my wife and I knew that, despite our efforts to keep our activities as clandestine as possible, the risk of expulsion or of visa denial was increasing. We had therefore been very careful not to discuss any sensitive matters in our letters, and to warn people writing to us to refrain from doing the same. We had also been careful about what we said in public or on the phone, and to whom we said it, since the regime had routinely infiltrated "professional students" into our classes and student programs to report on what we said and did.

Now, however, it became clear that we were under more than routine surveillance. Our trusted Amah (home-helper), Lu A-Gim, courageously reported to us that she had been followed home by the secret police on several occasions. They were pressuring her to report on the comings and goings at our house, and on the conversations that were held there, and offering her money to cooperate. We solved her dilemma by encouraging her to cooperate with them, and by giving her safe "information" that she could report to them.

The time had now come to make arrangements for our up-coming furlough in the States. Close to our departure in July 1973, however, the warning bells grew louder. After our farewells to C.M. Kao and other PCT officials and friends at the airport, our family was singled out of the immigration line and asked to go to a private room. There, uniformed people from the Investigation Bureau and other security agencies proceeded to go through our luggage with a fine-tooth comb! On the previous

campus who would always show up to repair shoes outside our meetings with foreign dignitaries when they came to visit the Theological College. The solidarity these visitors offered clearly helped save us from being shut down, but the shoe repair spy kept diligently performing his listening duty as he tapped away outside our doors.

A real bright spot for me during these Theological College years was an opportunity to co-teach, with Reverend David Gelzer, a course on Vatican II, using the text "The Church in the Modern World." I served as translator into Taiwanese for David, as well as an "interpreter" of the Catholic underpinnings of this document.

I offered to teach a similar course at the Catholic Seminary in Tainan. But opposition to change was still quite strong in the official Catholic world, and the offer was turned down.

One person I remember quite well from my Tainan stay was Rita Yeh 葉島蕾. She had studied in Minnesota, gave up her studies to do something for her country and returned to Taiwan to work. Although her father was, I believe, a mainlander and she grew up on military bases, she became very pro-Taiwanese in Minnesota. She was accused of sedition and imprisoned. Quite an impressive person, she worked with a suicide hotline organization called Lifeline.

A final strong memory from this stay at the Tainan Theological College is how comforting the morning services were. We would read from the prophets Isaiah and Jeremiah during these services and the texts came vividly alive for us as the prophetic cries of anguish and hope from centuries past resonated in our own world. We took great solace in these statements of faith that there would be a bright future after the difficult days we were facing.

By 1981 the immediate danger to the Theological College had passed, so I returned to the States to work. When I tried to return to Taiwan in 1983, my application was turned down by Taiwan's authorities with no reason given. I was not able to return until 1996.

While I was in Minneapolis, Sister Nadine Tierney, a Maryknoller who had served in Taiwan, came through on a speaking tour that had been arranged by Clergy and Laity Concerned. Nadine was speaking on college campuses about martial law in Taiwan and the human rights violations that were happening there. She had just come from an engagement at the University of Wisconsin where she had received a very rough reception from students from Taiwan.

The tour had been a difficult one and Nadine felt she simply could not continue. She asked me to pick up some of the speaking engagements that were still lined up. This posed an interesting dilemma for me, as my visa was hostage to Taiwan's authorities and they were sure to hear of any such activities. I decided that continuing Nadine's education of the U.S. public about the human rights situation in Taiwan and what the U.S. should try to do about it was more important than returning to Taiwan, painful though the decision was.

So I found myself on tour. First stop was Vanderbilt University and it proved to be a tough start. I was heckled by students from Taiwan with one young man firing question after question at me. Behind him sat his "handler," a young woman who was clearly feeding him his lines. "You say there are spies in Taiwan, how many?" the young man asked. "100?" "200?" "1,000"? I remembered two things at that point: first a report I had read that said

afternoon, I had paid a farewell call on C.M. Kao at his General Assembly Office. During our talk, he had given me some confidential documents and asked me to deliver them to the Formosan Christians for Self-Determination leaders in New York. Figuring that the average agent could not speed-read in English, I had scattered the documents in between scores of other papers in files in my large carry-on briefcase. When I saw how extensively they were going through our things, even paging through every children's book page by page, I quietly shoved my briefcase behind the seat on which I was sitting and did not submit it for inspection. After they had delayed the entire flight for over half an hour and found nothing suspicious, they allowed us to board. I whispered to my wife and children to follow close behind me so as to conceal the briefcase that I now quickly slid out from behind my chair. It was only when we were almost to the end of the hallway leading to the door of the plane that I overheard someone exclaim, "We forgot to check his briefcase!" By this time, the other passengers, who were disgruntled at being delayed, and who were wondering what was going on, were all ears. I said in a voice that all could hear, "You have held up this plane long enough! My wife and children are now finally seated and I do not want to delay these people any longer. I have nothing to hide. You can search through anything else you want to search, but please do it here." They finally retreated in embarrassment without searching my briefcase (which I had shoved out of sight behind a seat), and the plane pulled away from the gate.

We spent several weeks visiting historic sites on our way back to the States. Upon our arrival at the Chicago airport, we were met by my family who drove us to the house where we were to live during our six-month furlough in Wheaton, Illinois. While we were celebrating our family reunion, my father handed me a letter that, he said, had just arrived from Taiwan. I went into the bedroom, opened the letter and received the shock of my life! It was from David Lai Chun-Ming, the Presbyterian pastor and colleague who had signed as our personal guarantor on our provincial re-entry permit form. It was a carefully worded letter that had obviously been written with somebody looking over his shoulder. He had received a visit from the police, he wrote, who had asked him to withdraw as our guarantor which, sadly, he felt that he must do.

Paying the Price: Multiple Re-entry Visa Denied!

After several months of negotiations, the PCT joyfully informed us in early January that their hopes of getting a visa for us had not been unfounded. The Foreign Ministry had finally informed them that four-year multiple re-entry visas had been granted to us and that a telegram had been sent to the ROC Consulate in Chicago instructing them to issue them! Overjoyed, but wondering if the news was too good to be true, I phoned the consulate to make an appointment to get the visas stamped in our passports. It turned out that the official I dealt with was a Taiwanese who was familiar with the PCT and with missionary activity. However, when he checked his cable file, the only back cable that he had not yet received was the one with the number that the PCT had given us! Nevertheless, since it was a missionary case, and since I had given him the correct number, he agreed to give us the visas nevertheless, figuring one out of every three people on Taiwan had to report in some way to the authorities on their neighbors' behavior and, far more importantly, advice Nadine had given me – you have to love the person who is giving you a hard time.

I made it through that talk and went on to give many more. I realized that most of the student objectors were under great pressure from the very spies in their midst who were indeed reporting on them. Not only were their own careers and, perhaps, lives in danger, so were those of their families back in Taiwan. Nadine's advice held me in good stead throughout.

A final adventure to report was the 1986 trip to accompany Hsu Hsin-liang as he attempted to return to Taiwan. We made it as far as Tokyo but were barred by the authorities from boarding our flight from there to Taiwan. Those who were not allowed to proceed went on to Hong Kong where we held a press conference. With people like former Attorney General Ramsey Clark and human rights activist Linda Arrigo in the delegation, we had quite a time.

Finally allowed back to Taiwan in 1996, I found myself in a Taipei parish surrounded by a truly different place. Taiwan had become a free country and I loved it!

As I reflect back over my long association with the wonderful people of Taiwan, I continue to marvel at their warmth, their friendship and their tenacity in the face of adversity. I always believed that being a missionary meant learning as much as teaching. I must say thanks to my Taiwanese friends for all they continue to teach me.

that it was simply a bureaucratic error! Feeling somewhat apprehensive, I went to the consulate on the next day, and our visas were promptly stamped into our passports! We were going back!

I immediately phoned the good news to RCA and PCT authorities, to our family and friends, and to our supporting churches. Having originally been scheduled to return to Taiwan in mid-January, we went into high gear – purchasing air tickets, holding a garage sale, buying last minute supplies, packing our suitcases and bidding our farewells. The Lombard Reformed Church, that had been our home church while in the States, hastily arranged a farewell dinner and gave us gifts.

Two days before we were to depart, in the middle of our garage sale, the phone rang. It was the Taiwanese official at the Chicago Consulate. He said, with some relief in his voice, "Oh. You haven't left yet! There is an urgent matter. Will you please come to the consulate as soon as possible." Only after I pressed him did he finally say that he was sorry, but that he had received an urgent cable from Taipei ordering him to cancel our visas! Upon hearing the news, my wife dissolved into tears, and I got a great lump in my throat. We were not, after all, going to be able to go back to a place and a people that we had grown to love.

Paying the Price: The Aftermath

The RCA General Program Council voted to send a stiff protest to the ROC Government. They were concerned about other RCA Taiwan missionaries' visas, and about the plight of the Taiwanese people in general and the PCT in particular. I wrote a letter explaining our circumstances and the situation in Taiwan and sent it to our 40+ supporting churches. I also wrote an article about the human rights situation in Taiwan (that was published in the RCA's Church Herald) and contributed to an RCA Taiwan information packet that was sent to all RCA pastors and their congregations, including suggestions for action. I drew up an extensive plan for a "Taiwan Teach-in" at one of our RCA campsites. I also spoke in scores of RCA churches, and to other groups, about the situation in Taiwan and asked our people to press their legislators to advocate self-determination for the Taiwanese people. In short, the RCA and I used the publicity generated by our visa denial as a launching pad for an educational campaign concerning Taiwanese human rights throughout our denomination and beyond.

Still wanting to serve the Chinese people, my wife and I responded to a call from the Church of Christ in China, Hong Kong Council, to go to Hong Kong to do youth and education work beginning in May 1974. Meanwhile, our entire household, including my extensive library, was still in our home in Taipei. RCA medical missionaries, Dr. and Mrs. Sam Noordhoff, kindly helped to pack up our things and ship them to Hong Kong. With saddened spirits, we were forced to leave Taiwan behind, but "Ilha Formosa" and the Taiwanese people would always have a big place in our hearts.

I did not know it then, but my wife Joyce, who died of cancer in 1989, would never be allowed to set foot on Taiwan again, and I would be on the regime's official blacklist for nineteen long years.

Wendell Karsen

Edward "Ned" Kelly, "The Source" in English for Taiwan Banned Publications

By James Seymour

Father Edward Kelly ("Ned" to his Irish friends) was born in 1936 and raised in Ireland. He earned a doctoral degree in Chinese studies from Columbia University. For several decades he was a leading supporter of the cause of social and political democracy in Taiwan.

From 1971 until 1994, Ed Kelly was intermittently based in the British colony of Hong Kong. He served with the Ireland-based missionary society Columban Fathers, his assignment being to keep abreast of developments in China and Burma. The work of the Columbans (not a religious order) involves solidarity with the poor and protection of the integrity of creation.

In 1974 he went to the United States to teach. In 1978 he transferred to Taiwan, joining the local chapter of the Columban Fathers. There he was intimately involved with democratic activists. He fell somewhat out of favor with the authorities, and in 1984 he moved back to Hong Kong, now to serve as regional chaplain to Catholic sailors in the United States Navy. There, with the assistance of lay people, he founded Association for International Teaching, Educational and Curriculum Exchange (AITECE), whose purpose it was to provide teachers for China and to promote friendship between China and the West.

But he continued to be closely involved in Taiwan issues, and remained in constant touch with the democratic movement on the island. In order to keep this work quiet and separate from his other activities, he established in Wanchai the Youdau Centre 優道中心, which would play a crucial role as a link between Taiwan and the outside world. His publication *Yuan* (源, "source") made opinion-makers around the world aware of the situation on the island. In the period 1982-1986, he also played a key role in collecting opposition magazines, which had generally been banned by the ruling Kuomintang. These were later published on microfiche by the Netherlands-based Inter Documentation Company in Leiden.

In the last decade of his truncated life, Father Kelly turned his attention from Taiwan, where the forces of justice and democracy were winning, to China, where they were not. Now traveling frequently to China's poorest regions, Kelly worked both to promote educational exchanges, and also to help the impoverished Chinese create enterprises which would provide them with a dignified livelihood. His preferred way to raise the standard of living in poor villages was to promote handicraft industry.

Edward Kelly was a man of rare wit and charm. He also had extraordinary talents. There are many others, of course, who have a grasp of people's spiritual needs, their economic requirements, and also political realities. What was unique about Ed Kelly was that, on the one hand, he realized how these are all connected, and on the other hand, he insisted that they are discrete. He bore all three aspects in mind, but he never let one get in the way of the other. He always insisted that the goal should not be to create "rice Christians," but to allow the Chinese to find their own way. If that led to Catholicism, fine; if it did not, the

Aiding the Cause from Hong Kong

Although we had been re-assigned to Hong Kong, we could not, of course, simply walk away from our PCT colleagues and friends and from the Taiwanese human rights issues. I continued to be in touch with Amnesty International people in Germany, Ronin Publications people (Lynn Miles) in Japan, Formosan Christians for Self-Determination people in the USA, church officials and publication editors in the USA, and representatives of other human rights organizations whenever I could contribute something relevant regarding the on-going human rights struggle in Taiwan. Since I was personally acquainted with some top people in the US Consulate in Hong Kong through the church, I had periodic meetings with them, and with important official guests who were passing through, and I was able to educate and advocate concerning the human rights situation in Taiwan.

I met with PCT officials whenever they came through Hong Kong and at other venues, like Singapore, when we attended common meetings together. These meeting gave me an opportunity to learn first-hand the latest PCT and human rights news. People like C.M. Kao, Hsieh Hi-Beng, and others could, in turn, learn from me how Taiwan's situation was "playing" in the outside world. I could also help them send sensitive communications to churches and organizations around the world when it was needed. Furthermore, since I had begun to make regular visits to the People's Republic of China in 1977, I could give them objective reports on the situation on the mainland, and on the re-emerging church there. These meetings were also very helpful to them emotionally, as a safe way to communicate with the outside world.

The PCT Conference on the Mission of the Church in Asia

During my early years in Hong Kong, the PCT issued several more courageous public statements that had strong political overtones. A statement issued on August 16, 1977 even called for the recognition of Taiwan as an independent nation! There was also great concern over the impending USA recognition of the PRC as the sole legitimate government of China (which would actually occur on December 16, 1978). The Taiwanese once again felt that they might be sold out by the KMT regime through some accommodation with the PRC at their expense. The PCT, with its on-going internal struggle with the regime, felt more isolated than ever. In light of these developments, in late October 1978, with also the crucial December 1978 elections approaching, PCT leaders decided to explore whether or not they could quickly organize a conference on the mission of the church in Asia. Such a conference would show the regime and the world that the PCT was not an isolated and forgotten Church, but a Church with partners around the world that would stand with it during this critical time. To have maximum impact, the conference would need to be convened as soon as possible, hopefully within the next five weeks!

Some people involved in these preliminary discussions felt the time was too short for the implementation of such a major conference. However, it was agreed that Dr. David Gelzer of Tainan Seminary, a UPUSA missionary, would be sent to Hong Kong to meet with a few leaders there, including me, to explore possibilities. (I was

missionary work was nonetheless important.

Father Kelly died on October 6, 1994 in Dublin's Mater Hospital after a long struggle with leukemia. He was buried in the Columban Cemetery of Dalgan Park in Navan, Ireland, alongside many of the distinguished early Columban missionaries to China.

Father Edward Kelly in Hong Kong. Picture courtesy of Association for International Teaching, Educational and Curriculum Exchange (AITECE), which he helped establish. After living in Taiwan 1978-84, but unable to return, he quietly translated Taiwan opposition materials and distributed them from Hong Kong under the title Yuan.

then serving as the Executive Secretary for Education for the Hong Kong Christian Council). David arrived in Hong Kong and met with a few people who were not very encouraging. The time was too short; the logistics were too difficult; the ROC/PRC struggle was too sensitive an issue in Hong Kong; and so on. He then came to see me. Having been personally involved in the Taiwan human rights struggle, and knowing that I was being asked to help very close friends and colleagues, I had quite a different view. In the end, I convinced David that not only did I think such a conference could be pulled off, but that the PCT should think in terms of a worldwide conference that would involve church leaders from PCT partner churches in Asia, Europe and North America. Only this kind of a conference would have the desired impact.

I offered to act as the conference coordinator from Hong Kong. Such organization would have to be done outside of Taiwan anyway since, should the regime get one whiff of what the church was up to, every effort would be made to keep such a gathering from ever taking place. David was very encouraged. We set up a code that we could use to publicly communicate.

David returned to Taiwan and conferred with PCT officials. A coded cable came back. Our "Secondary School Religious Education Project" was a "go"! I immediately made a series of phone calls to my contacts abroad: Yap Kim-Hau (Gen. Sec. of the Christian Conference of Asia) in Singapore, Newton Thurber and Marvin Hoff (officials of the UPCUSA and the RCA), in the USA, Dan Beeby (United Reformed Church professor at Selly Oaks Colleges) in the United Kingdom, John Nakajima (General Secretary of the United Church of Christ) in Japan, Kim Kwan Sung (General Secretary of the Korean National Council of Churches) in Korea, LaVerne Mercado (General Secretary of the NCC Philippines) in the Philippines, Rev. Earle Roberts (General Secretary, Canadian Presbyterian Church) in Canada, Hartmut Albruschat (Official of the German Evangelical Church [EKD]) in Germany, Richard Deutsch (Chairman of the Basil Mission) in Switzerland, Kwok Nai-Wang (General Secretary, Hong Kong Christian Council) in Hong Kong and others. All I had to share with them were the proposed dates and the general nature of the conference. The PCT would provide meals and lodging, but participants would need to cover their own airfare. People would need to clear their schedules, provide travel funds and trust my word in lieu of an official formal invitation from the PCT which, of course, could not be sent for security reasons. All understood that everything had to be kept secret. They all rose to the occasion.

Phone calls and telegrams flew back and forth between Hong Kong and key contacts. News was relayed to Taiwan, and detailed conference plans relayed back to Hong Kong, by coded letter and telegram. In the end, after four weeks of intense communication and planning, 18 church leaders from nine countries arrived in Taiwan as individual "tourists" and made their way to the conference venue where they met the 28 PCT participants. Only the South Koreans did not show up. They were denied exit permits by their own repressive regime! Once I knew that the delegates had arrived and that the conference was underway, I sent a one-line telegram in romanized Taiwanese, signed with my Chinese name, wishing them God's blessing. The telegram was read out to the meeting and entered into the record. They

"He Sent Me To Bring Good News To The Poor, To Set The Downtrodden Free"

by Neil Magill

This is a brief summary of my time in Taiwan. The newspapers and TV gave a lot of coverage to my deportation and return in 2000. Some people in Taiwan wrote a book in Mandarin about me entitled "The Father Ma Affair" after my deportation from Taiwan.

I was born in Derry, North Ireland. I studied at St. Columban's Seminary, University College, Dublin and Trinity College, Dublin. I received a B.A Degree in Politics and History and a M.Phil.

I arrived in Korea in 1973. It was a time of political unrest and daily there were street demonstrations against Pak Jung Hee, the President. I attended some of the Masses in Myungdong Cathedral and was inspired by Cardinal Kim's homilies, even though I only understood a little of what he said. It was a conversion experience for me to see the Cardinal, bishops, sisters, and priests join factory workers and students to demonstrate on the streets against the dictatorship of President Pak. This made the gospel alive for me and gave meaning to the words of Jesus: 'He sent me to bring good news to the poor, to set the downtrodden free'. After four years in Korea I felt at home and saw possibilities for a happy ministry there.

During vacation in Ireland the Superior General asked me if I would be willing to go with four other Columban priests to start a mission in Taiwan. Two of that original group have since died. That's a sobering thought!

I agreed to go to Taiwan and it was back to language school again in Taiwan studying Mandarin. After a few months in Taiwan some new Taiwanese friends kept asking me why I wasn't studying their language. At that time I went to the Maryknoll language school in Taichung to begin studying Taiwanese. I never regretted that decision. The reaction of people when I tried to speak Taiwanese was totally different from when I spoke Mandarin. Their faces lighted up and friendship was easy. Coming towards the end of my second year in school an old Maryknoll priest told me to go to one of the big industrial estates to see the teeming thousands of workers, women and men going into the factories on bicycles and motorcycles. He asked me "What is the church doing for them?" and "Is anyone interested in their plight?"

Coming from a working class background where my father worked on building sites I had an affinity for the plight of workers, and without hesitation I decided I was going to commit myself to the workers in Taiwan. The Columbans supported the idea and the bishop didn't object. The beginnings were difficult … moving to an area where I knew no one and searching for a small house to rent.

Each day at midday and in the evenings vendors would move into the large industrial estates and set up a stall, cook noodles and prepare basic meals. The workers, during their short breaks, would come out, get a bowl of noodles, sit on the pavement, and eat it. I joined them most days for meals by the side of the road in an attempt to get to know

all knew who it was from, of course, without mentioning my English name.

During the hectic days of planning and implementing the conference, little did we know that its timing would prove to be so providential. Only ten days after the closing of the conference, the USA recognized the PRC and President Chiang Ching-kuo abruptly canceled the island-wide elections! Tensions between the regime and the PCT continued to heighten, but the conference had reassured PCT leaders that they were not standing alone.

The Arrest of Reverend C.M. Kao, PCT Secretary General

As soon as word of the Kaohsiung "riot" on December 10, 1979, and its aftermath reached Hong Kong, I immediately notified my contacts around the world. The RCA's Marvin Hoff, the UPUSA's Nueton Thurber, Amnesty International, the Asia Forum for Human Rights and others quickly responded by telegraphing protests to the ROC government and asking for the release of the victims of these events, particularly the Presbyterians. However, in the end, the regime put nearly all the main figures of the opposition on trial and gave most of them long sentences. But they were not going to let things rest there.

Kao's involvement with hiding Shih Ming-teh, General Secretary of *Formosa* magazine, became known to the regime, and they seized on this opportunity to arrest a person whom they considered to be a chief nemesis, on April 24, 1980. PCT supporters abroad were shocked when we received this news. We were also galvanized into action. Again, even stronger protests were lodged with the ROC government. In Hong Kong, I was able to obtain 54 signatures of Hong Kong missionaries and other church members on a letter that I cabled to President Chiang Ching-kuo. Prayers were offered around the world on Kao's behalf and on behalf of the other seven defendants, many religious persons among them. However, on May 16, 1980, we received the sad news that he was sentenced to seven years in prison!

During that time, my colleagues and I made every effort to keep Dr. Kao's unjust imprisonment at the forefront of people's minds and prayers. His moving writings from prison were printed and circulated. Letters continued to be written to newspapers, and to the ROC government, calling for his release. In a series of radio broadcasts over Radio Television Hong Kong (the official government station) highlighting stories of Christians who had been imprisoned for their opposition to injustice, I dedicated an entire broadcast to Dr. Kao's story and included his poems and songs written from prison.

After four long years, we were overjoyed to receive and pass on the news that he had been released!. We were also proud of his PTC colleagues, who, despite tremendous pressure from the regime to do otherwise, had maintained Dr. Kao as their general secretary during the whole time of his imprisonment. It was obvious that his courageous example, his transparent humility, and his strong faith and hope in the face of suffering had galvanized the PCT, and all who were struggling for human rights in Taiwan, into an unstoppable force.

some of the workers. At first I was viewed with suspicion as they suspected any foreigner was the owner or had a high management position in some factory. The workers asked me these questions and I told them I was there to get to know them and to understand their working conditions. Eventually they asked me where I lived and soon some were coming to visit me in the evenings after work and shared with me their plight … long working hours in unsafe environments for a very low wage.

About that time Pope John Paul 2 had written an encyclical "On Human Work," which I had got translated into Chinese. It was a powerful document, and I had statements from it pasted on the walls of my room. The workers, who didn't know there was a Pope as they were not Christian, were very impressed with these statements. *"Workers are entitled to a just wage which will support their family." "Workers are entitled to a day off each week." "Workers have human dignity." "Workers are co-creators with God."* etc. "If only we were treated like that!" was their common response.

Soon we organized nightly sessions studying the labor law of Taiwan … it was like the social teaching of the church, a best-kept secret in Taiwan. Some people from the fledging Democratic Progressive Party helped us by giving seminars on the labor law, just wages and the role of Trade Unions. Young lawyers gave their services free of charge to workers with grievances. My little house got too small and this time the workers searched with me for a bigger room to rent. At that time my path luckily crossed with two very important and committed people, Su Yi-jang and Lyou Su-chi. We met at a demonstration at Taoyuan airport. [Editor's note: This must have been the November 1986 demonstration organized by the new DPP to "welcome" Hsu Hsin-liang's return to Taiwan to spearhead the opposition party. See further description in Michael Fonte's account.] They were committed to the struggle of the workers and to building a democratic society. They had a huge impact on me as they understood the local situation and taught me much about society, the economy and how to do things according to their culture. They also had a big impact on guiding the future direction of our New Life Workers' Centre. I will always be grateful to them and to this day we keep in contact and are good friends.

As more workers came to the classes on how to organize and form trade unions, others dropped out. It was only later that some of them told me that the police had gone to their homes and threatened them. Managers of factories threatened to dismiss and blacklist them if they continued to attend our newly formed Workers' Center.

We continued with the work and cooperated with other groups interested in working for better conditions for the workers. Then the big move came when the workers at the Center decided to take to the streets to highlight the unjust wages and conditions they were working under. The Center, my two co-workers and myself, came under the strict eye of the government and local church. The bishop warned me not to encourage the workers to demonstrate or go on strike. To demonstrate was the right and decision of the workers, not mine. The police paid regular visits to the Center and demanded that I remove the posters with the statements from the Pope's encyclical. 'These are Communists posters' they argued. Imagine the Pope a Communist! I thought he himself would enjoy that one. I refused and told them there was freedom of religion in Taiwan and this was part of our church's teaching.

On another occasion they stole documents from the Center and sent spies to our nightly

Long Years on the Blacklist

From 1976 on, I made several attempts to return to Taiwan, without success. In May 1992, the Christian Conference of Asia sponsored a consultation on the mission of the church in Asia. It was to be held in Hsinchu, Taiwan, and I was invited. When I inquired as to whether I might still have visa problems, my PCT colleagues assured me that things had now changed. Ninety per cent of the names on the blacklist had been removed. They were sure my name must have been among them. But they were wrong! At that time, I was serving the Hong Kong Christian Council as its secretary for education and communication. Our general secretary, Dr. Tso Man-King, was confident that he could prevail upon the ROC Foreign Ministry to change its mind since the then Foreign Minister, Dr. Frederick Chien, had been a member of his church in Washington, D.C when he was the ROC ambassador to the USA. He was also wrong! The PCT was bound and determined to change this. A PCT person who held a DPP seat in the Legislative Yuan attached a rider to some bill allowing me permission to enter Taiwan for a two-week period. It passed and I got my "good behavior" tourist visa! And just in the nick of time – the day on which we had hoped to leave for the consultation.

Meanwhile, it seemed that even nature itself was against us. Upon getting word that I would now be granted a visa, Hong Kong got hit by one of the biggest floods it had had in years. All transportation ground to a halt and many stores and offices closed. Determined to get my visa at last, I took off my socks, put on an old pair of shoes, rolled up my pant legs and waded through a half mile of swirling waters to the ROC's downtown office. They were open and I got my visa! With visa at last in hand, I waded to my office, called my wife and made preparations to leave for Taipei the next morning. There was no time to contact anybody. We would need to do that after our arrival in Taipei.

Upon our arrival at CKS Airport, I was still a bit apprehensive as to whether the immigration people would actually let me cross that magic line this time or not. I sent my wife Renske through first, figuring that with her on the inside, I stood a better chance of making an argument in case of difficulty. Sure enough, when I stepped up to the counter and had my name punched into the computer, all the bells and whistles went off again! The chief officer in the back jumped up and told me to stay where I was. He disappeared into the chief of immigration's office and I thought, "Here we go again!" However, upon emerging some five minutes later, he barked an "Okay!" to the officer and I was in! Home at last after nineteen years!

Although hastily arranged, it is hard to imagine the emotion of visiting old homes and haunts and meeting old friends and colleagues in Taipei, Hsinchu, Tainan and Kaohsiung again after so much time and such significant events had transpired.

Reverend Wendell Karsen, now retired, has recently written his memoirs of his stirring experiences in Taiwan, Hong Kong, and Indonesia, entitled Church Under the Cross. Over the years he assiduously maintained files and correspondence that allow historical accuracy in this account, and he has donated his files concerning Taiwan to the archivist of the Presbyterian Church of Taiwan.

Wendell Karsen

classes. Then I began to get threatening phone calls at 2 or 3 am in the mornings. The gist of these phone calls was "If you don't leave Taiwan you will be killed." Some months later a police car with four laughing cops knocked me down on the street. When I struggled to look around I saw laughing cops in the car. At that time there was no such thing as e-mails and I depended on letters from my family. My mother wrote to me each week as did other family members and friends but for months on end I received no mail. It was confiscated. I protested, but to no avail. This all gave me greater courage and determination. But it was a stressful time.

At our nightly activities in the New Life Workers' Center we had classes on the environment and other social problems. We planned and took part in demonstrations against the destruction of the environment and the exploitation of young women in prostitution.

My support at that time came from the Columban community in Taiwan, from our Columban General Assembly documents which clearly took a stand for the poor and oppressed, from liberation theology from South America, and most of all from the commitment and sacrifices of the local factory workers and those struggling for democracy.

I had spent eleven challenging and exciting years in Taiwan when in 1989 the KMT government forcefully deported me. They unknowingly picked St Patrick' Day! I left Taiwan dispirited, angry, broken-hearted and with no chance to say good-bye to my friends, the workers, or the Columbans. All I had were the clothes on my back. I had no chance to say goodbye to friends. The police van which took me to the airport had a few burly cops in it who held me down and removed my glasses. A police car with the siren blaring led the way. Looking through the van window I could see people in the streets stop at the sound of the siren and look at the police escort and van. What were they thinking, I thought to myself?

I felt like a criminal.

My bishop and other bishops, my Columban colleagues, along with Trade Unions, friends within the DPP, and various groups spoke out harshly against the government but it all fell on deaf ears.

Some years later in 2000 the newly elected President, Chen Shui-bian, invited me back. Ms Chen Chu, Head of the Labor Affairs, paid my ticket. President Chen met me at his office for an hour and apologized for what the previous government had done. This was a blessed moment for healing all the hurts I had carried because of the deportation.

Today as I look back over those years, I am very grateful to the Taiwanese people for having the opportunity to spend eleven years with them and for all that they taught me, the big nose foreigner "a-tok-a." My life has been enriched because of their welcome and hospitality, their culture, and their friendship. My world vision has been broadened. The Taiwanese taught me the need for solidarity to bring about social, economic, political and environmental change. Taiwan is my second home and it has a special place in my heart.

If I had to, I would willingly do it all again for the sake of the gospel and the exploited workers in Taiwan

A Borrowed Voice

In China, Maryknollers Worked with Ordinary Rural People in Local Dialects – So in Taiwan They Learned Taiwanese

by Richard Madsen

I grew up in a devout Catholic family in Alameda, California. My father was a worker in a steel foundry in Oakland and my mother was a secretary in the parochial school run by our local Catholic parish. Most of our social life was centered on the parish. I was educated in Catholic schools.

At the age of 13, I decided I had a vocation to the priesthood — not just to any kind of priesthood, but to the missionary priesthood. I was inspired by articles I read in the Maryknoll Magazine about missioners working in Africa. This seemed to beckon to a life of meaningful adventure far beyond the boundaries of Alameda. After graduating from elementary school at the age of 14, I entered the Maryknoll high school seminary in Mountain View, California. I went through the whole Maryknoll seminary system — four years of high school in Mountain View, four years in the college seminary in Glen Ellen, Illinois, one year in the novitiate in Bedford, Massachusetts, and four years in the Maryknoll Major Seminary in Ossening, New York. Most of my classmates had similar backgrounds — devout working class backgrounds. In high school and college, we received an excellent classical education in Latin and Greek and Thomistic philosophy. In the major seminary we studied modern theology and canon law — by that time influenced by the heady new ideas coming out of the Second Vatican Council. Even though we were part of a foreign missionary society, we were taught almost nothing about non-Western history and cultures.

Nonetheless, we had echoes of Chinese culture all around us. Founded in 1911, Maryknoll's first missions had been in China. The architecture of the major seminary was in a vaguely Chinese style — distinguished by sweeping curved roofs. My first teachers in the high school seminary were "old China hands," Maryknollers expelled from China after 1949. Our rector during my first two years in the major seminary was Al Fedders, one of the old China hands who had come to Taiwan in 1952, after he had been expelled from China and who had helped to set up the Maryknoll mission there. On the first floor of the major seminary was a room devoted to Maryknoll martyrs. It was dominated by a big picture of a Maryknoll priest being tortured by Chinese Communists.

I received my assignment to Taiwan in January, 1968, one of the most turbulent months in the history of Maryknoll. The rector of our seminary abruptly left the priesthood, to marry a Sister from the Maryknoll cloister. A number of other Maryknollers also left the priesthood around the same time, including several Maryknollers in Guatemala who had become involved with revolutionary activities. All of a sudden it seemed that the floodgates of change were opening. From then on,

Old housing along the river in Tainan, 1978. Photograph by Ken Kilimnik.

almost every month brought news of another Maryknoller leaving, another radical new idea being proposed, another breach in accepted norms carried out.

In this unsettling atmosphere, my class of deacons was abruptly called to an assembly by our superior general, John McCormack, who read out our mission assignments. When I heard that I was going to Taiwan, I was stunned. I had never had any interest in going to Asia. I was afraid that Chinese would be too difficult to learn, and I certainly didn't want to be tortured by communists. I knew almost nothing about Taiwan, except that the Maryknoll community there was mostly dominated by conservative old China hands (which turned out to be not exactly true). This was the way these assignments were made in those days. Very few people who were sent to Taiwan would have had much interest in and much prior knowledge of the place.

I knew a fair amount about Latin America and had assumed that I would be going there — or perhaps to study theology in Europe, because I had a special aptitude for academic work. I didn't know what to think or what to feel about my assignment. I repressed a deep feeling of disappointment, and obediently made my plans to go to Taiwan. The day after receiving our assignment was the Chinese New Year, the Year of the Cock. John Bourque who was also assigned to Taiwan and I went down to New York Chinatown, where amidst the din of firecrackers, I had one of my first authentic Chinese meals ever.

The ensuing four months before ordination brought more turbulence, within and without Maryknoll. The Tet offensive brought increasingly passionate controversy over the Vietnam War. Martin Luther King was assassinated, and riots broke out across American cities. A week before our ordination in June, Robert Kennedy was assassinated. It was in this atmosphere of collapsing certainties that John Bourque and I arrived in Taiwan, in the beginning of September 1968.

Mike Fonte and some other younger Maryknollers who had been ordained just a few years before us met us at the airport. One of the first things Fonte told us was that our assignment had been a big mistake. We were being assigned to work in the mountains with the aborigines. But Fonte and the others thought that there really wasn't any need for more priests to work in the aborigine missions and that the place for real creative work was with the local Taiwanese on the plains. The aborigine assignment was the unfortunate result of bad decisions made by the old China hands. Welcome to Taiwan.

Because we were assigned to work with the aborigines, we were getting a different language training from most of the younger generation of Maryknollers. Almost all of them had studied Taiwanese at the excellent language school at the Maryknoll Center house in Taichung. Maryknoll was one of the few religious societies that had most of its members learn Taiwanese. This had come from its traditions of working on the mainland, where most Maryknollers worked with ordinary rural people in their local dialects, rather than trying to interact with urban intellectual elites. A consequence of this in Taiwan was that the Maryknoll missionary community was somewhat isolated, a world unto itself. For the most part Maryknollers didn't have many

An Art Program to See the Beauty in Your Own Village

by Ronald Boccieri

My first impression of Taiwan was that everybody was anxious about saying "the wrong thing." "Don't mention this, don't say this, don't ask that question," were the operational phrases I kept hearing repeated. It was unnerving, but I buried myself in the study of Hoklo Taiwanese during those first years as I worked in Catholic parishes in Chuili and Poli.

Slowly, though, as my language ability grew, I became more aware of some of the things the catechists were saying about 2-28 and other incidents in Taiwan history. So I kept at my language study, working with Mr. Lim, my truly wonderful, patient teacher, from 8:00 to noon every day, hoping that I could gain the keys to understanding both the culture around me and the half-hidden history of these warm, patient people.

When I was assigned to work in Lam-tau (Nan-tou) around 1966, I was introduced by a person there to Sia Chong-bin (Hsieh Tsung-min). I was told to meet him in a certain place and the preparation for the meeting was like something out of a movie – wear a hat, have this magazine tucked under your arm, etc. Mr. Sia was quite a person and my conversation with him gave me a deepening understanding of a whole world of struggle and conflict below the surface of daily life. I have reason to believe that, under torture, Mr. Sia divulged my name and from that time on the authorities kept an eye on me. Sometimes the spying was quite obvious and almost laughable.

When I moved to Lo-chhu (Lo-tsu) 埔心羅厝天主堂, a small village in Chiong-hoa County (Changhua 彰化), I was hauled in by the police and taken to the secret police headquarters in Taipei. I asked my Regional Superior to accompany me. He conveniently "had a cold and couldn't talk." I told him, "I don't need you to talk, just to accompany me." Nothing doing. Like too many of the Catholic Church leaders of the day, he wanted to keep as clear of the secret police as possible. My friend Father Dick Downey agreed to go with me to the headquarters.

The interrogation was pretty intense. "Are you a communist?" I was asked. "You don't use the term communist bandit!" the police shouted. "That is not a Christian word," I answered. "You associate with bad people," came the next accusation. "That's part of my calling," I replied. "Jesus was accused of the same thing. I try my best to follow his example."

It became clear that the head of the parish council was being used as a spy and would send in reports on me. I noticed that he never had a drink at any of the weddings or other celebrations. Good Italian-American that I am, I never trusted anyone who didn't drink at social occasions, so I thought something was up. Much later, after I was kicked off the island and then returned years later, the parish council head and I were together at a festive occasion. He had a drink and then told me that he had, in fact, been forced to report on me.

After the secret police incident, I was also hauled into the Chiong-hoa city police

interactions with other religious orders, like the Jesuits. And they were somewhat insulated from the Church hierarchy in Taiwan, which was dominated by bishops and priests that had escaped from mainland China, led by Cardinal Yu Pin, born 1901 in northeastern China, who was extremely closely connected with the KMT and was a major religious spokesperson for global anti-Communist crusades.

John Bourque and I, on the other hand, were being sent to the Jesuit-run language school at Hsinchu, where Mandarin was taught. I didn't know the difference between Mandarin and Taiwanese,but. I did quickly learn the difference between the Jesuit Mandarin language school and the Maryknoll Taiwanese language school. The Jesuit school taught missionaries from many different religious orders. Most of them trained their priests, brothers, and sisters in Mandarin. Because of this, I developed wider connections than most Maryknollers had done with other foreign missionaries on Taiwan.

The choice of language school had an influence on how I initially came to understand Taiwan. All of our teachers, of course, were mainlanders, and many were retired KMT soldiers. We were taught about greater Chinese culture, not about Taiwanese culture. We learned to see the world from the point of view of mainlanders. But when we interacted with our fellow Maryknollers in Taichung, we got a very different perspective. Their teachers, of course, had been Taiwanese — and often Taiwanese who had a deep feeling of social responsibility for the island. And in the course of working with Taiwanese communities, most of the Maryknollers had developed a deep sympathy for them. From people like Mike Fonte, Ron Boccieri, and Jim Nieckarz I gradually got a feel for the situation of the Taiwanese.

It wasn't a politically sophisticated feel. None of us had a very deep understanding of Taiwanese politics. A Jesuit at the Hsinchu language school quietly lent me a copy of *Formosa Betrayed*, which gave me my first understanding of the situation. I hid it under my bed. But in casual conversations with fellow Maryknollers, I don't think the 2-28 massacres were ever mentioned, at least in terms that conveyed the scope of the atrocities. In general our attention as Maryknollers was focused on church things. The younger generation was in deep conflict with the generation of old China hands about the theological basis of our work and about the proper way to do missionary work. (All this was complicated by the fact that after a big spurt of conversions in the 1950s and early 1960s, not many new people were becoming Catholics.) The older generation was politically cautious. Don't do anything to get into trouble with the authorities. 'Don't rock the boat. We are guests in this culture. Concentrate on church work'. Some of us in the younger generation reacted against this and developed a generalized propensity for rocking the boat. Some of us were inspired by fellow Maryknollers in Latin America who had caused trouble and gotten into trouble.

In any case, some of us wanted to get closer to ordinary people in Taiwan, against the wishes of the older generation of Maryknollers who thought we should stay in our clerical enclaves. As part of this, Mike Fonte and I developed a plan to live in the house of one of the Taiwanese language teachers in Taiwan. During the summer (when I was on vacation from the language school in Hsinchu), we moved out of the

Richard Madsen

headquarters for an interrogation. During their questioning, which had the same ring to it as the previous one, they quoted me as saying a certain phrase. I knew that the only place I had used that phrase was at a meeting of my own American organization. Unfortunately, it seems that spying, which the Taiwanese couldn't avoid, was also being done by those who could have, and should have, resisted doing so.

In my Chiong-hoa County work, I began to meet more and more Protestants. I had hepatitis and later sciatica nerve problems that laid me up in the Presbyterian hospital in Chiong-hoa and there I met many fine Christians. Later I took a pastoral counseling course at the hospital and was asked to preach. I was honored by the request. These were much more active people, engaged in political meetings. I would go into the meetings furious at some recent nonsense by the police and the government and would come out laughing. My Protestant friends never lost their sense of humor even in the darkest of times and this was very, very good for my soul.

Tan Giok (Chen Chu 陳菊) brought Si Beng-tek (Shih Ming-teh 施明德) down to see me at one point and I really was so out of it that I didn't know who he was. I found out his long history of struggle against the repression around us and the terrible torture he had endured. He came back several times, and Yao Ka-bun (Yao Chia-wen 姚嘉文) also came to our little church to visit. Whenever they would come, the police would arrive as well, come into the church courtyard and start taking down license plate numbers.

One day in June 1978, another priest friend, Father Al Borsari 秦化民, called me and said that Tan Giok (Chen Chu) needed to get away. He asked if she could stay in our church complex. My answer was immediate, "Yes, of course." Tan Giok stayed with us for three days and each day the small village was infiltrated more and more by strangers who wanted to "sit around and play chess." Tan Giok stayed calm the whole time, mostly writing in the small back house we had on the parish compound.

On the third day, the niece of one of the special dedicated ladies we had in Lo-chhu came to talk to me. "My aunt says that all these strangers in the village are police. She says you should be careful."

As we sat down to supper that night, the "strangers" came over the compound wall and barged into our dining room. We hurried Tan Giok into a small room, locked the door and turned to wait for the police. The officer in charge started barking at me in Chinese. I replied as politely as I could that I didn't speak Chinese, I only spoke Hok-lo Taiwanese. I had purposely never learned Chinese because I felt it was being used at that time as a tool of suppression of the native Taiwanese.

The officer started speaking in English, which was actually quite good. I refused to speak in English and responded in Hok-lo. Finally, the officer said, "I'm going to break down that door and search your house." "No need to break down the door," I replied. "Here's the key. If you find anyone in there, please treat that person with kindness." The police took Tan Giok out to the courtyard and I followed. Outside I decided it was time to give the young Taiwanese cops a little sermon. Five thousand years of Chinese culture, I said, and this is how you treat a young woman? "I will take the part of your mother and father and hang my head in shame for you. Kian-siau, kian-siau."

The poor cops were doing their job and could only stare at the ground. Off they went.

Maryknoll Center House in Taichung and into the teacher's house. Our experiment lasted about two days before Al Fedders — our former rector in our first years at the major seminary and now the head of the Maryknoll Taiwanese language school — found out what we were doing and angrily told us to come back.

But it was this impulse to get out of the normal insulated clerical environment and to get closer to ordinary Taiwanese people (driven initially not by any deep knowledge of Taiwan but by a desire to differentiate themselves from an older generation of clerics) that later led some Maryknollers into their political involvements. For some of us, this path led fairly quickly out of the priesthood. Some, like Ray Kintzley and John Traugott, married local Taiwanese women. Others like Mike Fonte and myself left Taiwan after about three years to study Asian studies in American graduate schools and left the priesthood after that. Others, of a slightly older generation, like Boccieri and Nieckarz, and Jim Collignon stayed in Taiwan and got involved in incipient human rights and Taiwan independence movements — and got expelled from Taiwan because of this.

After two years of Mandarin language school, in 1970 I was allowed to go to National Taiwan University (Taida), where I lived in a dorm with ordinary students and studied sociology. My knowledge of Mandarin helped gain me access to Taiwan's young intellectuals. (Most Maryknollers who had studied Taiwanese never learned to read and write. I did gain a fairly good reading knowledge at the language school in Hsinchu and then learned a lot by reading magazines like *The Intellectual*, in which a younger generation of scholars were gingerly pushing the limits of acceptable discourse. At Taida, one of my roommates was a mainlander (but from Fujian, so he could speak the Taiwanese dialect) and the other was Japanese. I got to know a number of Taiwanese students and I was deeply impressed by the intensity of their commitment to finding a way forward for Taiwan. But they usually didn't directly express explicit political ideas that could get them into trouble. More often there were indirect political references. For example, once we were discussing eating dog meat, and I asked what kind of dog was best to eat. The answer was "Pekinese."

When I was at Taida, I became especially close friends with Sister Nadine Tierney. She too had studied Mandarin and worked as a kind of campus minister to university students. She was an extremely warm, open-minded and outgoing person. She was at that time not directly engaged with politics, but later in the 1970s, when she had moved to Kaohsiung to run a center for workers, her openness and her sympathies led her to become involved with people in the *Formosa* magazine movement.

All that was in the future, though. At the time, in 1970, I was mainly struggling with culture shock.

I was the only American in the dormitory of the Law Faculty at Taida. The crowding and lack of privacy were especially difficult to get used to. And in contrast to the clearly pronounced Mandarin and neatly written characters of the teachers in the language school, the speech and handwriting of professors and classmates were almost indecipherable. But I eventually adapted and developed a feel for the

Richard Madsen

But the Chinese priests in Taiwan went bananas. They should have known better and their lives weren't in jeopardy. But they were furious at me. "You don't love the Chinese people," was their complaint.

When I met with the Bishops, I was told, "We understand, but you can not do these things."

I saw the Papal Nuncio at a Thanksgiving feast. "Well, I understand there's been some trouble," he said. "Our responsibility is to make sure the Church stays here in Taiwan," he added. "We disagree," I responded. "Our first job is to preach the gospel."

I came to realize that an art program might well give Taiwanese a sense that they could be creative, they could see the beauty around them and express it instead of doing things by rote as the schools and government insisted. They didn't have to copy anybody else, they could be free to express themselves and look with fresh eyes at their own culture and landscape.

I wanted them to gain a sense of pride in being Taiwanese, being rooted in this land and its festivals, its architecture, its fields, its families. They were constantly being told that they were second-class citizens, country bumpkins who didn't have anything to offer. The response was heartwarming as creativity bloomed.

Ron Boccieri at his rural mission in Changhua. Picture taken about 1978 by Ken Kilimnik.

passions and aspirations of Taiwanese intellectuals. Near the end my stay at Taida, student protests broke out over threats to Taiwan's claim to the Diaoyutai Islands. I was impressed to see my student friends all of a sudden exhibit a harsh anti-Americanism. [Editor's note: The Diaoyutai ("fishing platform") Islands are a group of small uninhabited islands to the northeast of Taiwan that were administered under Taiwan during the Japanese period, but after World War II were considered attached to Okinawa. The issue in 1971 was that the U.S. was returning their sovereignty to Japan together with Okinawa – just when oil explorations seemed to indicate seabed reserves. This set off protest at first against America and Japan, but later against the impotence of the Republic of China.]

The rigors of life at Taida were alleviated by often raucous parties with fellow Maryknollers — plenty of good food and scotch, and most importantly, laughter.

I left Taiwan in June of 1971. My first stop was in Hong Kong, where we received the astounding news that Henry Kissinger had carried out secret meetings with Chou En-lai, which would eventually of course lead to an American rapprochement with the PRC and a shift in the political landscape of Asia. I entered graduate school at Harvard and several years later left Maryknoll to marry Judy Rosselli, whom I had first met when she was a Maryknoll Sister in Taiwan. I ended up writing a number of books on the moral dimensions of Chinese society, American society, and U.S.-China relations.

In the fall of 1999, Judy and I returned to Taiwan for our first extended stay in 30 years. I arrived the day before the 9-21 earthquake and, based at the Academia Sinica, I did research on the response to the earthquake by Taiwanese religious groups like Tzu Chi Buddhist Compassion Relief. In fact Judy and I helped Tzu Chi volunteers build houses for earthquake victims in Taichung County. It was an ecumenical effort that I believe shows that some of the seeds sown by Catholic missionaries in the 1960s fell on good soil and have borne good fruit, albeit of unexpected varieties. During our stay in Taiwan, we had some wonderful encounters with the Maryknoll Fathers and Sisters. I saw in the New Year among the Maryknollers at their Centerhouse in Taipei, sipping scotch with, among others, one of my dearest friends among the old China hands. I couldn't have imagined a more meaningful way to begin the new millenium.

Richard Madsen is now a professor in the Sociology Department of the University of California at San Diego.

The seed for this art program was planted one day when I was still serving in the Lam-tau (Nan-tou) parish. At the offering of the gifts, Mr. Ko, one of the nicest, kindest people you would ever want to meet, came up the church aisle bearing the offering. His big, floppy farmer's feet were bare, as was the reality for all the farmers in the area. One of the nuns of the parish was not happy that Mr. Ko had walked down the aisle, no matter how gently, in bare feet and she said so. Wait a minute, I thought, let's listen to our people, these wonderful farmers. What indeed did they have to offer? They were being ripped off by the Agricultural Association whenever they had to sell their rice or buy fertilizer. On the one hand they really had nothing to offer. On the other, they had themselves, their dignity, and the whole cloth of their lives of struggle, family and friendship.

The art program gave an opportunity to these people to walk with their heads held high, bare feet and all. But the police repression was closing in on me and my people. Wherever I went, someone called ahead to let the police know I was coming. That final year I was in Taiwan, the art program, which had had up to 90 kids in attendance at times, saw only five sign up. Not one kid from the parish signed. The police had told their parents not to let their children attend.

I realized I couldn't do this anymore. I had to be supremely careful about anything I said in public and felt it was time for me to take a rest. The government told my Society that they should let me go home for a year and then I could come back.

I returned to the States and was able to have a great year of study. But when I tried to return, our new regional superior found out that I was number 1 on the *persona non grata* list. I was heartbroken. But I'm glad to have lived to see the day when my Taiwanese friends walk proudly, have stood up and claimed their birthright, have build a strong democracy and have grabbed hold of their beautiful culture and shown it to the world.

Farmer Ko is walking around heaven in his bare feet smiling down on us.

Reminisences of Taiwan: Investigating Capital and Labor in a Subjugated Economy

By Ken Kilimnik

Mark Twain once quipped, *When I was younger, I could remember everything, whether it happened or not, but now when I am getting old, soon I shall remember only the latter.* With that warning, I begin my story.

I came to Taiwan on July 4, 1975 to teach English at a *bushiban* (private cram school) in Tainan. At the time, I believed Taiwan like South Korea to be politically and economically subjugated by Japan and the United States, based largely on what I had heard from Japanese and other Americans during a summer traveling seminar I had participated in Japan in 1974 that was sponsored by the World Friendship Center in Hiroshima. That experience had caused me to apply for a fellowship from the World Federalist Society's "Action for World Community" program, for which work I chose the theme, human rights in South Korea.

When I arrived by plane from Tokyo on July 4, 1975, the contrast with Taipei and the U.S. could not have been greater. Taipei seemed to be composed of only store facades — all the stores seemed to be on the sidewalk, and the traffic was mostly bicycles, motorbikes, old buses and taxis, with wild drivers weaving in and out through crowds of people. It was about a month after Chiang Kai-shek had died, his son Chiang Ching-kuo had just assumed power, and the streets of Taipei were full of military jeeps. Four Americans met me at the airport in Taipei, including a journalist, Bill Armbruster; another named Scott; Brad, who was married to a Hong Kong Chinese girl; and Karen Smith, for whom I brought messages from Lynn Miles and a gift from Tokyo. They all thought I was nuts for going to the south of the island and for a job paying nothing.

I was met by the *bushiban* director's son, Earl W., in Taipei the next day with a couple of his Chinese friends, and after having dinner we drove that evening to Tainan, arriving on July 6 at 3 a.m. Earl's dad, Ed, struck me as a stern schoolmaster and he warned me right away against mentioning the People's Republic of China in class or talking about communism. I had told myself that my reason for going to Taiwan was different from that of other Americans I had met there — it was to learn about Taiwan so I could gather useful information and make it available to people back home in America. I had no desire or intent to change the status quo in Taiwan.

My initial school soon proved to be rewarding in one sense and exhausting and maddening in another. It was rewarding because my students were so open and friendly, but exhausting and maddening because I was expected to teach 23 hours a week without being paid more than a pocket allowance of $25 a month.

One of my students, Raymond Chuang, invited me to his father's weaving factory on July 8, my second day of teaching. There were three huge vats of dye and some 300

Dirk Bennett and Ken Kilimnik at their Japanese-style house in Taipei, about 1978. Photo by Ken Kilimnik.

An ornate Japanese-period house in Tainan. Photo by Ken Kilimnik.

looms, all run by young girls. By July 9, I had already felt two earthquakes, listened with trepidation to the incessant roar of military jets and propeller planes to and from the west (across the Taiwan Strait) with trepidation, and had eaten at one lunch alone cow ears, along with liver, ham, chicken, egg, rice, soup, and Coke. My Chinese host family and my Chinese students in English classes were much amused by my efforts to speak Chinese. In my classes we once discussed television programs, one young man asserting that the programs on television were controlled by Japanese corporations who advertised on them; most of my class agreed. I found it was the older students, who had lived under Japanese occupation, who were more critical of the government in class, complaining that under the Japanese they used to have outside speakers come to class and speak, but never now. The younger students were more interested in talking about the movies or taking trips to the sea and the mountains.

By chance I met a salesman for Sea Land Services, an American shipping company, named Peter W. during my second week in Tainan. Peter said that he thought Chinese people were like Italians – both eat good food, are pretty dirty, and are extremely friendly to foreigners but never tell them the truth. He warned me to expect that from people in Taiwan. With Peter's help I was able to visit the export processing zones in Nantze and Kaoshiung. After persuading him I was not a CIA agent, he admonished me not to talk politics with him, and he kindly took me along on some of his sales visits and introduced me to other salesmen who in turn brought me along on their visits to plants. Through his efforts I was able to visit several American and Japanese factories there and to interview their managers, both American and Japanese, as well as interview workers on the plant floor with the aid of translating friends. Using materials from these visits I wrote several detailed articles for the IUE News, an American labor union newspaper, as well as articles for AMPO, a Japanese "left-wing" English language magazine in a special issue they published on export processing zones in English. Later I learned that working hours inside the zones were actually far less than many on the outside, such as in restaurants. One waitress in a downtown coffee shop in Kaohsiung told us she worked 30 days a month – without time off — but still managed to go to night school.

In the meantime, I was busily increasing my teaching and private tutoring to yield over US$125 a month. In evening we held class on the roof and watched magnificent sunsets, singing songs like "We Shall Overcome" and reading poetry. Afterwards we often went to a coffee shop where the favorite questions to me were whether I had girlfriends and believed in God. (I had Christians, Buddhists, Confucianists and non-believers in my class.) I found the omnipresent advertising to be annoyingly imitative of American culture — whether on television, at the movies (we saw "The Godfather" with English subtitles) or even my *bushiban*'s use of the name "Green Hill" with a fetching American girl in short pants on a poster and Green Hill's name and logo printed on mugs, shirts and stationary.

Despite the admonishment of the *bushiban* boss, I tread on thin ice in class by asking students whether there were any differences of opinion in Taiwan. The only one saying yes was the oldest, a Dr. Tso. He said it was a shame that the Government

The whole group of human rights activists and Taiwan Foundation for Democracy staff at the historical site of the old Dutch fort in Tainan, precisely on Human Rights Day 2003.

Ms. Chen Chu, early human rights worker, jailed 1979-1986, and now mayor of the major industrial city Kaohsiung. With Ron Boccieri, who gave her refuge in June 1978 at his church compound in Lotsu, Changhua, and was for this publicly castigated by the Catholic Church hierarchy in Taiwan and expelled, after thirty years in Taiwan and learning Taiwanese.

tolerated no difference of opinion. Another time he related the story of Wu Feng, a Chinese official who offered his head to the aborigines in 1769 in order to stop their practice of headhunting. When I asked if there were a moral in the story, he said we should give the story to some government officials to stop the rampant bribery. His was, however, the only critical voice in class. Most of my students wanted to go into business and the most ardent in class eagerly recycled the government slogans about retaking the Chinese mainland.

By now, almost two months into my stay in Tainan, I found it remarkable that every family I had visited (and I was frequently invited to people's homes, in contrast to Japan) had a color television, no matter how small or shoddy their home. My host family as well as most of the others I visited cherished plans for their children — male and female — to study in Japan and the U.S., although in my classes it seemed the college girls' highest aim — even among those who studied in college — was to work as a secretary. (My host family was an exception: with three sisters, one planned to be a chemist, the other a concert pianist, and the third was already working in her mother's export business.)

I confided my aims for visiting export processing zones to Peter W., who had apparently grown to trust me more. Two months after we had first met, he told me wistfully that he would like to read a critical book about Taiwan from the U.S. He had wanted to do so when he was serving in the army by borrowing books from the United States Information Services library in Tainan, but knew that if he had done so, he would have been questioned and even arrested. Later he confided in me that relatives of his were killed during the 2-28 rebellion in Taiwan in 1947. Peter said that at that time the Nationalists killed off the Taiwanese intelligentsia. So despite what Peter said to me at the outset about Chinese never telling the truth, with me as a foreigner, in private settings, it seemed that many felt they were able to open up and tell me things they wouldn't dare tell another person from Taiwan. When I asked my students once to write something about the history of Taiwan, the only hand-in I got was about an aborigine revolt against the Japanese.

I caused quite a stir by leaving my bushiban to teach English at the neighboring YMCA school. Although I didn't think so at the time, in retrospect it is clear to me that many people went out of their way to pamper me and in retrospect put themselves out far more than I realized at the time. My best friend was Chen Dou Lu, a 24-year-old just out of the army who drove me everywhere on his motorcycle. A conservative politically, he couldn't understand, he said, why the United States didn't invade North Vietnam, and insisted that Taiwan was free, although he did complain that there were only 20,000 college places each year for some 90,000 applicants. That Taiwanese had to learn four languages (Mandarin, Taiwanese, English and Japanese) was to him an indication of their subjugation to other people, but the most I heard him criticize the U.S. was to complain that the U.S. dominated the air waves in Taiwan (meaning music, not planes). Knowing of my visits to Kaohsiung's industrial zones and my complaints about pollution, both industrial and vehicular, Lu always exclaimed as we buzzed around on his motorcycle, "It's a hard job trying to keep clean in Taiwan."

Ron Boccieri and James Collignon on the way to Ilan with the Taiwan Foundation for Democracy, December 7, 2003. Lynn Miles and James Seymour behind them.

Rowland Van Es and Michael Fonte on the same trip. In recent years Michael Fonte has been the Washington D.C. representative for the Democratic Progressive Party, and he goes beyond the call of duty to protect Taiwan's security.

A person who befriended me greatly in Tainan was Robert Lin, head of the board of the YMCA there and a resident at the local seminary. The Presbyterian seminary in Tainan was said to be the center for the Formosan independence movement. It is the Taiwan Garrison Command (TGC), someone told me, who really controls the situation. Mr. Lin told me of a distant relative of his who used to be a Presbyterian minister at the seminary and made reports all the time to the TGC. When this informer heard one family was intending to move to Japan, he reported it and they were stopped.

Still others at the seminary were enthusiastic missionaries. One, an American born in Indonesia, denounced the Catholics as not indigenous to Taiwan and boasted how many native Taiwanese Presbyterian pastors there were. I met Dr. Siau (Hsiao Ching-fen), the unpretentious president of the seminary as he was riding a bicycle, moving files to his new office. We met the next day and he talked with me for two hours until his daughters' screaming ended my interview.

In Osaka I had spoken with Ben Wu, who had given me the names of four people to meet at the seminary, including Liz Brown. Liz handed me teaching materials for a two-week college preparatory English course that were enough for years of instruction. An Englishwoman, her heart was clearly in teaching and she had been in Tainan then for some fourteen years and was in charge of teaching centers in five other cities besides Tainan. [Editor's note: Elizabeth Brown 包佩玉 was later secretary to Rev. C.M. Kao.]

My notes reveal my frustration with other Americans I had met, who were concerned with mundane problems like people's materialism, traffic and industrial pollution, and petty crime. Me, I was concerned with more abstract issues like income distribution and political freedom. Ruefully, I wrote that I could not find a single person on the island who didn't want to sell me something or go into business with me once I was back in the States. I consoled myself with the thought that this was typical perhaps only for the people who wanted to learn English. I wrote in my journal on August 24, 1975 while still in Tainan, "The purpose of my project is not to liberate Taiwan or berate multinational corporations, but to liberate people in the U.S. and stimulate people in Japan." I thought then that "Korea and Taiwan may be the best places in the world to study unbridled and unchoked imperialism/capitalism." I got a letter from Mike Fidel, a student at Friends World College in Kyoto, chastising me as a bleeding heart liberal on issues of labor in the multinational corporations, because the MNC's were, in his view, the only way a country could develop, and he didn't trust multilateral aid institutions.

Writing in my diary as preparation for my trips to Kaohsiung's export processing zone, I asked myself: how many poor people are there? Was the land reform fair? Are state enterprises a good thing in some respects? Did U.S. "capital" control Taiwan's economy? Other questions on my mind then were more forward-looking: "Will China (the PRC) engulf or influence them? Or will they change the PRC? Will their people become free?" But I also complained more mundanely – like my friends – about the pollution and noise on the streets, noting that the roads were always bathed in a

To My Taiwanese Friends: I Am Most Honored to Be Your Adopted Son

by Michael J. Fonte

I have often told my Taiwanese friends that, since all my grandparents emigrated to the U.S. from Italy, I felt totally at home in Taiwan. Taiwanese and Italians both prize family and food, what more could one want in life!

When my Maryknoll superiors asked me where I wanted to work, I requested an urban mission -- either Tokyo/Japan, Caracas/Venezuela or Santiago/Chile. In their wisdom, they sent me to Taiwan to work with farmers. It was the best thing, after my wife and son, that has ever happened to me. I entered the world of Taiwan not knowing what to expect and found myself quite happy.

Several Taiwanese families "adopted" me and, to this day, my heart remains warmed by the Chen (Tan), Huang (Ng) and Wang (Ong) families of Taichung and the Cheng (Ten) family of Yuan-li, Miaoli County. They, and my wonderful teachers at the Maryknoll Taichung Language School, educated me about how rich and lively Taiwanese culture really was. They taught me how to not only speak Hoklo Taiwanese but also to get inside the words to the deeper dynamic of love and friendship at work.

I enjoyed sitting around the hot pot with the Cheng (Ten) family at New Year's, eating moon cakes with friends during the Mid Autumn festival, Chen family meals when I lived with them during language study, toasting the bride and groom during sumptuous rural wedding banquets, riding my motorcycle through Samgi and smelling the hinoki wood being carved, swimming with my young friends at Tunghsiao, and meeting with farmers in Yuanli to discuss credit union business.

However, during my three years in Taiwan (1967-70), there was always a cold wind blowing. I was schooled in an intense study of the Bible and the Roman Catholic theology of Vatican II. I believed my "mission" was to share my ideas of social justice and building community with my Taiwanese friends, to learn from them about their values and, together, try to make the world a little better place.

The repressive government of those years would have none of this. I had read *Formosa Betrayed* by George Kerr before I came to Taiwan but it took living on the island to sense the fear that still paralyzed everyone twenty years after the 2-28 massacre. The military, police and spies, who were everywhere, kept "order" with a vengeance, allowing no gatherings that were not approved, disrupting the right of people to share their hopes and to try to turn them into reality. The credit union movement, which gave poor farmers a chance to pool their funds and not be ripped off by loan sharks, was looked upon with suspicion and anything beyond that was considered subversive.

Privately, and with a few friends and like-minded colleagues, I railed at the repression but feared that any open activities would only get my Taiwanese friends in trouble. Unfortunately, the Catholic hierarchy was not willing to see its beloved institution

bluish gray mist of exhaust fumes, punctuated by potholes and blowing horns. To seek answers to these questions, I realized, I would need to move to Taipei. So I did, where thanks to a reference from Ben Wu of a lawyer I could look up in Taipei, I got what all my friends and I considered to be a plush, extremely well-paid assignment (NT$8,000 a month for three months) to write a handbook on foreign investment law in Taiwan for English readers. This allowed me to interview many government officials and businesspersons in Taipei.

When I moved to Taipei on October 8, 1975, my motorcyclist friend Lu and I searched for housing together on his motorcycle for several days, living at the start in a vacant room at a construction site until I ran into some of my former English students from Tainan who had an extra double bed in their apartment in Yung Ho that Lu and I shared for six weeks until we splurged and rented a single house near Shih Da (National Taiwan Normal University) together with Dirk Bennett, an American graduate student. Lu told me only mainlanders like the U.S. because they can flee there; Taiwan isn't their home. The government had banned 93 sad songs in Chinese, he said, and only allowed happy songs. Sad songs in English, on the other hand, he said, are permitted, because the people don't understand them. Lu had a way with pithy comments.

Other than Dr. Tso, it was not until I had moved to Taipei that I encountered specific expressions of disagreement with the Kuomintang (KMT). There, the Taiwanese college students I met — law students, political science students, and their friends and siblings — were unanimous in heaping scorn on the KMT, to which they nonetheless admitted they belonged because you had to in order to get a good job. But they reassured me that they never went to Party meetings. They felt disenfranchised but I didn't detect any desire on their part — or hope —- to change the status quo. When I asked questions in this regard, they ignored me and drank more beer, or asked me what Americans thought. And they were cautious in sharing such open talk with other fellow students, for example, a roommate who was a trade union representative in a factory.

But I found the same anti-KMT attitude elsewhere, too – in Bandou, the company where I taught English, and even in my mentor lawyer Mr. Lin Min-sheng, who had hired me to write the handbook on foreign investment. He was, I was told, one of the richest men in Taiwan and perhaps the richest lawyer. [Editor's note: This was Mr. M.S. Lin 林敏生 who founded Taiwan International Patent & Law Office in 1965 with a group of professional legal and technical associates specializing in intellectual property rights. TIPLO has been a staunch supporter of Taiwan independence organizations, and generally lends its facilities on Nanking E. Road for meetings.] Interestingly, of the two lawyers I worked closest with in preparing the handbook, one, Mr. Chen, was a former administrator at the Kaohsiung Export Processing Zone, and the other was John Kao, a former Catholic priest, a mainlander. Both Mr. Lin and Mr. Kao, to whom I showed my interview notes, were critical of MNCs on the grounds that they too often only came to Taiwan for cheap labor and neglected to file patents and trademarks (our office's specialty; I wasn't sure which of the abovementioned sins was the higher reproach in their eyes.). They hoped with my

"wrecked" by social justice actions, so I decided to return to the U.S., pursue a Masters degree at the University of Michigan and see what I could do States-side to change my own government's support for the Chiang family's repressive control of Taiwan.

Again, fortune smiled on me. At Michigan, 1971-76, I was to meet and become friends with both Professor Peng Ming-min, who had just escaped from Taiwan and was given a position at the University, and Dr. Lin Tsung-yi, whose father had been a Taiwanese leader during 2-28 and was murdered by Chiang's troops. Both of these Taiwanese patriots taught me to hope for Taiwan's future and to work to see changes on the island.

I vividly remember giving a talk about Taiwan to students and faculty and noting that many of the Hok-lo speaking Taiwanese would privately joke about a cheer they were supposed to use during national celebration days. Instead of "Long live the KMT (Kok-bin-tong, ban-soe)," they would use Hoklo words that sounded the same but translated into, "The country rice bucket, 10,000 taxes (Kok-png-thang, ban-soe)." After writing the characters on the board for those who didn't understand Hoklo Taiwanese, I almost got into a fight with some of the students from Taiwan who thought I was being disrespectful of their dear KMT. I believe they were raising their voices in protest to show whatever spies were there how "loyal" they were. Taiwanese students at that time had to fear for their own safety and the safety of their loved ones back home as well.

Another vivid memory was the trip I made to Taiwan in the early 1970s to smuggle in Dr. Peng's book, *A Taste of Freedom*, and deliver it to his mother. My nervousness about whether the customs officers would find and confiscate the book was more than offset by the joy of being able to actually meet Dr. Peng's mother and tell her of her son's new life in Michigan.

I began to meet Taiwanese students of a different cast as well, those who had chosen to organize and press for changes back home. At first, my meetings with these dedicated women and men were sketchy as I lived in Michigan and later the Los Angeles area.

Taiwan would just not let me go, however. When I moved to Washington, DC in 1985, I found that these activists had formed the Formosan Association for Public Affairs (FAPA) to educate U.S. policy makers and the American public about realities in Taiwan. Dr. Peng was the FAPA president at the time and I worked part-time with FAPA editing an English-language newsletter that we distributed to Members of Congress and the media. The newsletter highlighted concerns about political prisoners, human rights reports from Amnesty International and Asia Watch, and Congressional actions to press the U.S. Administration to exert stronger leverage on the KMT government to end martial law.

When the Democratic Progressive Party was formed in 1986, the U.S. National Democratic Institute (NDI), encouraged to do so by Taiwanese- American activists, invited the DPP founders, as well as KMT representatives, to Washington. Not surprisingly the KMT refused to show, but the DPP did accept this offer, a move by NDI to provide the newly formed, and still illegal, party with some umbrella of protection. A range of American politicians came to the NDI meetings to offer their support for democracy in Taiwan. Particularly enthusiastic about the changes taking place on the island was Walter Mondale, former Vice-President, the Democratic Party's Presidential nominee in 1984 and long-time Senator from Minnesota.

handbook to increase their foreign clientele.

In Taipei I found someone who arranged for me to interview workers at MNC factories located outside of export processing zones. This was Father Traugott, a Catholic Maryknoll priest working with a youth group called the Young Christian Workers [Editor's note: John F. Traugott 董加德, who came to Taiwan in 1965, was also, according to the grapevine, very dedicated to workers' issues and also affectionately known as "Harry the Rat."] John Kao used to work with this group and he had introduced me to Father Traugott and another foreign worker there, John Elliott. Father Traugott said that the average factory salary was (NT$2,000)/month for 192 hours, which worked out to US$ 0.25 an hour. While movies in Taipei cost NT$45 — half a day's wages — he still believed that as long as things kept improving, the workers would not grow discontented. He cautioned that if Taiwan were no longer run by mainlanders, things might be different.

Father Traugott invited me to a meeting of nine girls and three boys who were working at the General Instruments factory near Taipei. [Editor's note: This is the same early electronics manufacturer, founded 1965 in Hsintien to produce television components such as tuners and semi-conductors, where Linda Gail Arrigo began her research on women factory workers.] All of them came from the south of Taiwan. One girl acted as spokeswoman for the group in answering my general questions. They invited me to visit their factory.

While working on my handbook, I was also meeting regularly with Bill Armbruster, the journalist who had met me at the airport in July, as well as with my housemate Dirk, an American graduate student researching U.S. aid to Taiwan, and the three of us heatedly debated economic development issues such as whether the ten infrastructure projects touted by President Chiang Ching-kuo would only benefit the rich (Armbruster's view, not mine) and whether more money should be spent on agriculture. Dirk argued that the land reform in the 1950s and 1960s was a mechanism used by the Nationalists (KMT) for taking power from the Taiwanese and that the export industries were mostly unplanned, at most fostered by American aid, but not a prime objective at the time. Most early U.S. aid was military in nature; the export platform came later, in the mid-1960s and 1970s.

I knew that Taiwan's economic agenda called for moving up the chain of the division of labor from labor-intensive to capital-intensive work, but I was unclear what exactly Taiwan's economic planners had in mind other than the production of polluting plastics for the manufacturing industry and of electronic semiconductors for entertainment devices. (That this later amorphed into the information technology revolution was of course unknown to all at the time.)

Among my interview partners for the handbook were a Methodist missionary pair, the Knettlers, who graphically described the atrocities in mainland China they witnessed between 1949 and 1952 and had heard of since. Later, I met another Methodist missionary pair, Ruth and Carlisle Philips, who lived in Fukien province from 1947-1950, but were much less pro-KMT in their opinions.

Ken Kilimnik

I was able to get appointments for DPP representatives, including Chou Ching-yu and Hsu Rong-hsu whose husbands were political prisoners, with members of Congress sympathetic to their cause. Meetings were held with Senators Edward Kennedy and Claiborne Pell, as well as with Representatives Jim Leach and Stephen Solarz. The stories they heard deepened their dedication to pushing for democracy and human rights in Taiwan through their efforts in Congress.

Abroad when the Kaohsiung Incident took place, Hsu Hsin-liang was put on the KMT's wanted list and was threatened with arrest if he returned to Taiwan. He made his first attempt to return at the end of November 1986. A delegation formed to accompany Mr. Hsu included Ramsey Clark, former Attorney General of the United States. As a member of the delegation, I was to act as the translator/companion for a public relations person hired to get media coverage of the return. At our Tokyo stop, officials refused to let Mr. Hsu, Clark and others in the delegation board the plane for Taipei. About six of us were allowed to go forward, however, and we arrived at CCK Airport in Taoyuan to find the remnants of the great standoff between the riot police and DPP supporters. [Editor's note: Lynn Miles was also recruited by Hsu Hsin-liang to work in the U.S. public relations for this effort to "do an Acquino" for Taiwan. But it was known that Lynn Miles was *persona non grata* in Taiwan; he got only so far as the tarmac of the Chiang Kai-shek Airport, before he was physically carried back to the plane.]

After being briefly detained by customs officials, we were allowed to enter Taiwan. What we saw on our bus departure was like a movie set: helmeted riot police still standing guard with the smell of tear gas lingering in the air and barbed wire barricades everywhere. Once in Taipei we learned of the tumultuous events that had taken place: about 5,000 demonstrators peacefully waiting for Hsu's arrival had been blocked from access to the airport.

When KMT media control started to loosen, Mr. Kang Ning-hsiang 康寧祥 began publication of the first independent newspaper, *The Capital Morning Post* 首都早報, in 1989. I had met Mr. Kang during the NDI meetings of 1986 and he asked me to be the paper's Washington correspondent.

This was a dynamic time in Taiwan and there was much to cover concerning Washington developments. My most interesting memory was filing a story reporting that Senator Claiborne Pell had said Taiwan Independence "was a question of when not if." Antonio Chiang, then the editor in chief, had someone call me to check on the accuracy of the quote. "None of the other reporters have that in their stories," Antonio said. "I just want to check before we run this story." I assured him that I had the quote on tape. This was but one more lesson in how even good media personnel, and there were many good Taiwanese reporters in Washington, were so cowed by KMT censorship that they self-censored the news they filed.

Unfortunately, Mr. Kang was a bit ahead of his time and it was simply not financially possible to continue to publish the newspaper. By 1991, I was looking for another job.

After working for eight years on a variety of arms control and foreign policy issues, I came back to FAPA to work full-time in 1999. My three years at FAPA were filled with educating members of Congress and their aides about changes in Taiwan and hoped for changes

I also interviewed Father José Ellacuria, a contact of John Traugott's, who worked with the Taiwan Provincial Federation, a local labor union, and tried to run labor education courses. I met with a trio I called the "three stooges" at the Chinese Federation of Labor, since their organization was said to be controlled by the Ministry of the Interior and the KMT, and they came across to me as obedient servants of some higher power. Father José, a Basque Spaniard, echoed what Peter W. had told me in my first meeting, cautioning that everything I would hear or read in books were lies, that Chinese have two faces, etc., and whispering to me of an Amnesty International report claiming that there were 8,000 political prisoners in Taiwan. He was doubtful I would ever learn "the truth" from interviews.

[Editor's note: Father Jos'e Ellacuria stayed in Taiwan for many years, often under great governmental pressure. It is noted in Taiwan Communiqué, April 1989, that "At around the same time as Father Magill's expulsion (March 1989; Magill was also a labor activist), another Roman Catholic clergyman, Jesuit father José Ellacuria, originally from Spain, was given notice that his visa was not being renewed for 'violating his religious duty with his involvement in labor activities.' Father Ellacuria has lived in Taiwan for 31 years. He set up a center in Taipei City for educating workers on their legal rights." This was not the only shock for Father Ellacuria in 1989. His brother Ignacio Ellacuria, 59, rector of the Central American University and a widely respected leftist intellectual, was murdered by government military forces along with five other Jesuits on November 16, 1989, in El Salvador. It would seem that the two Basque brother priests sought out the most repressive regimes under which to serve humanity, on opposite sides of the globe.]

By January 1976, my contacts with José had paid off and I was able to visit Sanchung City, an industrial suburb of Taipei then with 300,000 inhabitants. Sanchung City was often the first stop for people moving from the south of Taiwan and was lined with small, family-scale enterprises in which children often worked daily after they finished school. The place was crammed with metalworking shops and sewing shops. I spoke with the deacon of a local church who explained that in the summer there were floods frequently that inundated all the streets and homes, and described families of ten living in one room. Like their wealthier counterparts, the deacon told me most parishioners only cared about making money, saving enough to move to Taipei, and neither cared nor thought about politics.

That same attitude I found reported by Ron Boccieri 郭佳信, a missionary running an orphanage consisting of thirteen kids in the countryside near Lao Tsu, Changhua County. Ron said reproachfully that the Taiwanese had sold their souls for their stomachs, and that he tried to give his orphan kids a sense of sharing and community rather than to compete with each other – no doubt his was a voice in the wilderness.

By the time I had finished the foreign investment handbook, I had met the American commercial attache', Dwight Cramer, and had grown to like him very much. The feeling was mutual, and he treated me like an adopted son. But I also felt welcomed by Mr. Lin Min-sheng both in his law firm and family, and of course in my first Chinese host family in Tainan, not to speak of the numerous friends I made, largely

in U.S. policy, writing press releases and opinion-pieces, speaking to groups across the country about Taiwan's new democracy, and training a growing number of Taiwanese Americans as they sought to become stronger advocates for their homeland.

During this time, the best memories are of returning to offices of people like Senator Ted Kennedy, who was there in the darkest hours for Taiwan, to introduce him to former political prisoners who were now members of the Legislative Yuan. The miracle that is Taiwan today is a constant source of inspiration to many here in Washington as they see an authoritarian regime be transformed by the struggle of its citizens into a true human rights respecting democracy.

Taiwan's story has not been told to enough of the world's audiences, so I introduced Maysing Yang 楊黃美辛 and Michael Tsai 蔡明憲 to the Project on Justice in Times of Transition at Harvard University. Taiwan is a wonderful case study that the Project wants to use to show others how countries of conflict can move toward open, inclusive societies without cycles of revenge undercutting democratic development.

You have miles to go before you sleep, my Taiwanese friends, and promises to keep. You have fought the good fight for your own country, now you have to let your light shine for others as well. I am most honored to be your adopted son.

Michael J. Fonte

but not entirely from my English students and their friends. I met many people on the streets when they began talking to me spontaneously (something that never happened in Japan.) I wrote in my notes that the most interesting people in my law firm – a place where I spent a lot of time towards the end of my stay in order to finish the handbook were the night cleaners — a pair of lively high school students in love with each other – as well as Mr. Lin himself, who seemed to govern the place by snoozing in his big armchair most of the time but still managed to know exactly who was doing what. Before I left Taiwan for Japan in February 1976 I returned to Tainan and visited my former student and roommate Raymond Chuang, my host family, Lu's parents' house, Robert Lin, and other friends, exchanging red envelopes stuffed with modest amounts of cash.

On balance, I don't think that I had any influence in any way on what my friends or contacts thought politically. I recall that Mr. Lin's brother, a naturalized American citizen, visited Mr. Lin's apartment when I was there and he praised the *Taiwan Political Review*, a pro-independence, pro-democracy publication that had started up in Taiwan. Outside of the presence of his brother, Mr. Lin bitterly criticized his brother for fleeing Taiwan, and then commented, "I would respect him," he told me in confidence, "if he had said the same things (while living) here." Lin himself thought the magazine great but the writers foolish to take a stand against the government. He told me he was a believer in Lao Tse – live in the present and ignore the future. Lin, like the majority of people, expected mainland China to eventually absorb Taiwan because it was bigger, and he saw no place for capitalism or democracy in China's future. But as to Taiwan, his prediction was wrong, at least seen some three decades later, and his judgment as to the mainland has been at least partially superseded.

My criticism of Taiwan's economic and political development then also seems fortunately in hindsight to have missed the extraordinary progress Taiwan has made since the 1970's both economically and politically even as I faithfully recorded the abiding insights of my English students. As to democratic developments, I don't believe one can hold anyone other than Taiwan's residents themselves responsible for its remarkable progress towards democracy.

We cannot predict how the balance of military power or the judgment of political leaders may shape Taiwan's future. One thing is sure: a Kosovo-style declaration of independence is not likely from Taiwan. Rather than causing subjugation, however, economic integration with the rest of the world contributed to the development of democracy. As for Taiwan's influence on me, my stay there left fond impressions not only of the tasty food but also of the many wonderful, friendly and kind people I met.

Ken Kilimnik is an American attorney now practicing U.S. and international law in Germany, and a member of the German-Taiwan (ROC) Lawyers Association. He authored several articles on Taiwan's economy after his 1970s stay, such as "Taiwan Behind the Economic Miracle," published in Free Trade Zones & Industrialization in Asia, AMPO, December 1976.

Chapter Five

We Are Willing to be Jailed for the Future of Taiwan

Many of the generation growing up in post-war Taiwan remained unaware of the draconian past. By the late 1970s a new native-Taiwanese middle class began flexing its economic muscle and seeking political voice. From 1975, rigged elections met increasing resistance. In 1977 a Chungli police station was burned down, with ICDHRT-linked Linda Gail Arrigo and foreign news on hand to report. Then impending US rapprochement with the Peoples Republic of China put Taiwan's future into immediate question. In early 1979 a democratic movement broke into the open and defied harsh martial-law reprisals. Overseas, Taiwanese settled in the U.S. and Japan rallied in support and took on the old China Lobby. The showdown was the Kaohsiung Incident, December 10, 1979, a pretext manufactured for wholesale arrests. But in their arrogance, the security agencies were slow to realize that they could no longer fully cow resistance, nor hoodwink the media with concoctions of communist conspiracies.

第五章 1977-79： 我們願爲台灣民主的前途坐牢

成長於第二次世界大戰後的台灣新世代，大部分都是幸福而不知慘酷的過去事。1970年代末期，有一群新興的本土台灣中產階級，開始展現其經濟實力並尋求政治發聲。國民黨因其惡質的選舉作票行徑，面臨民眾日增的抵抗，1977年中壢警察局因而被燒，ICDHRT 的成員艾琳達及外國記者就近報導。此外，因美國即將承認中華人民共和國，也使台灣的未來成爲直接且迫在眉睫的問題。公開的民主運動最後以勢如破竹之勢掙破了戒嚴令，無懼勇敢的參與者一再被捕入獄。在美國及日本定居的海外台灣人，整合力量對抗老中國集團的遊說。國民黨於1979年12月10日在高雄事件中攤牌，藉口進行全面性的大逮捕。但傲慢的情治單位似乎未意識到，反抗精神未滅，爾以往哄騙外國媒體說民主人士是共產黨的老套之詞，都已無法繼續奏效。

Three Years and a Lifetime: Swept Up in Taiwan's Democratic Movement, 1977-79

by Linda Gail Arrigo

Memory and Sources

It is now over thirty years since I embarked on several defining turns in my life; I would claim from my memory that they were intentional, and yet it is just as likely that when I hoped to turn back to relative safety, the route was blocked, and I continued with an impetus that came from the previous experiences, which is to say not entirely by free choice. In my distant memory, I was strongly motivated and self-directed to discover what it was that seemed to instill such fear and revulsion in the hearts of the Taiwanese people I knew. This was intellectual curiosity, and something more, perhaps a drive to witness the depths of human society and experience.

Since it was my role in the democratic movement period to interview, translate and brief reporters, and because I have frequently made presentations on this history in the years since – and have not had much of an important role since then that would crowd out my earlier memories – I think I have a clearer memory of these events than most people. And then there is the infamous pattern of aging, to remember what you did thirty years ago in the glory of youthful adventure, but not to remember what you did two weeks ago. Adding to this the effect that each of us remembers most vividly the challenges that we personally encounter, the following account naturally writes large my own perspective on these events, and it does not claim to fairly encompass the contributions of others. This is especially so given that most of the early crucial work in human rights reporting depended on secrecy, whereas as the democratic movement coalesced and broke through to public activity, my role was in the public eye, especially in the international media campaign following the Kaohsiung Incident. However, I do believe also that due to my academic training I have a sociological eye that tries to analyze beyond the level of personal experience.

The following account was written first from memory, aided somewhat by my review of historical materials and books written by others and of my own documents brought back from the United States (my mother Nellie G. Amondson must be appreciated for preservation of these materials that fell into her hands 1978-1980). They were carried back to Taiwan during my period of post-doctoral award at the Institute of Sociology, Academia Sinica, 2002-2004. Second, I have then tried to verify the dates and names and sequence of events, but it has not always been possible to check all the details, and this condensed narrative can only sketch the main themes.

However, a further source for verification of dates and much of the threatening atmosphere in the period of the opposition mobilization is to be found in the surviving records of the government and its security agencies (mainly the Taiwan

Linda Gail Arrigo at the picturesque old town of Tahsi, Taoyuan, on November 18, 1977, the day before the Chungli Incident. Note election poster on pillar.

Garrison Command 台灣警備總部, the National Security Bureau 國家安全局, the Ministry of Justice Investigation Bureau 法務部調查局, the Government Information Office 行政院新聞局, and the Ministry of Foreign Affairs外交部 and its overseas offices), all of which have been collected by the National Archives國家檔案局, established after the KMT's fall from ruling party in 2000. On March 1 -12, 2003, a collection of documents was displayed at the National Archives building on the Kaohsiung Incident trials (more sympathetically dubbed the "Meilitao" or "Formosa magazine" Incident in Chinese; the public assembly that precipitated a struggle with government forces was on International Human Rights Day, December 10, 1979). I made a brief report on this exhibition, from memory. Soon after, I was finally able to get access to some of the documents; the staff made a lengthy search for the items that I was legally allowed to access under the restrictive regulations and practice of the National Archives, and provided me with a 10-cm.-thick stack of copies of documents and reports that had my name somewhere in them, or that dealt with international human rights appeals.

It is also important to my account here that, over the 18 years since I was able to return to Taiwan in May 1990, I have met again, whether by arrangement or by chance, a huge number of people involved in these events, even some on the side of the government authorities, and gotten small pieces of the picture in my head filled in or confirmed or revised. No doubt there will still be some contentious interpretations, especially since it is my proclivity to emphasize rather than gloss over disagreements among the participants, in order to highlight the historical choices. And I will not mince words: that this is my own narrative shaded by my particular political persuasion that is infused with 1970's leftist revolutionary fervor.

From Catholic School and J.F. Kennedy to Taiwan: Vietnam War Spillover

When I came to Taiwan in June 1963, age 14, with my father, formerly an officer with the Military Assistance Advisory Group, it was a great adventure that I had prepared for for some time. I had begun to learn Chinese at age twelve in a summer program at San Francisco State College. I was fired with the spirit of Catholic missionaries, from St. Monica's School on 25th Avenue and Geary in the Richmond District of San Francisco; a Catholic Democrat, John Kennedy, had become president of the United States, and he directed the young people of America, particularly as embodied in the Peace Corps, to carry American ideals of freedom and democracy to the benighted and oppressed nations of the world. I read a child's version history of Sun Yat-sen's Chinese revolution as well as Tom Dooley's odyssey as a doctor in Laos to Catholic refugees fleeing communist persecution. Myself rather a lone iconoclast and dissenter at school (at age 13, following Confirmation, I embarked on quest for the foundations of my faith, and eventually concluded that Christianity was only one of many belief systems), I resolved to myself even before I went to Taiwan that I wanted to break through racism to experience another culture, and marry someone from a different culture as well.

We arrived at Sungshan airport through space-available military air transport,

Linda Gail with pet rabbit, age 2, in Silver Springs, Virginia.

Linda Gail Arrigo, Notre Dame High School, San Jose 1962

Major Joseph Arrigo, 1958, San Francisco

stopping at Manila on the way. The green mountains surrounded the city; the old Grand Hotel, like a golden temple, crouched on the hillside above. My father's girlfriend Miss Chu Chi-hua 褚啓華, a.k.a. "Orchid", and her brother Eddie met us at the airport and took us to the Omei Restaurant on Po-Ai Road downtown for lunch. Dazed, I thought the Szechwan food was delicious, but didn't know not to swallow the blackened peppers together with the chicken chunks and peanuts; they burned in my intestines for days. After a few days at a parquet-floored hotel, we settled into a boarding house near National Taiwan University, No. 55 Lane 269, Section 3, Roosevelt Road, where the lane intersected at an angle with Wenchou Street; now there is a small park on the triangle where pedicabs used to park. It was a relatively new building, with four rooms and a common bathroom on each of two floors. We rented two, later three, rooms and the rest were occupied by overseas Chinese students. Orchid's father, from Shanghai, was a professor of adult education at NTU and the Ministry of Education. He had been educated in the United States in the late 1930's and was sent to Taiwan in 1946. They lived in an old Japanese-style tiled-roof house within walking distance on Taishun Street, rather modest, with the usual broken glass embedded at the top of the walls around the small front courtyard, and the plaster crumbling and showing plaited bamboo beneath in some of the bedrooms.

My father's friends were military personnel and civil servants, all "mainlanders"; soon I realized that the language of the markets was different. But Mandarin was unchallenged in Taipei, and I absorbed it as quickly as possible, my mouth becoming sore from the unfamiliar vowels and singsong tones. Gradually, as I made out the large slogans painted on walls, I came to realize the ominous and paranoid sense of the place, with military at every corner and a megalomaniac president that signs on his route to office on Chungshan North Road proclaimed was "the savior of the Chinese nation." The MAAG Officers Club 美軍軍官俱樂部 there that my father and I frequented had, to my later perception, an ingratiating colonial air: a swimming pool, weekly Mongolian barbecue with American beef, and high-ranking Chinese officers and Mrs. Claire Chennault occasionally conspicuous among the casual Americans. Aside from the Grand Hotel 圓山大飯店 that was Madame Chiang Kai-shek's exclusive lair for visiting dignitaries, the Officer's Club was the realm of important people. Only government officials and American military had private cars. But I knew from casual conversations that the American military were dismissive of Chiang Kai-shek; they insinuated that he only ruled at their pleasure. Meanwhile Orchid's father and other mainlanders railed at General Marshall and his mission that had caused them to lose their homeland to the communists.

Along the long daily bus trip to Taipei American High School, I bought scallion-pancakes from old soldier street vendors or ate mutton dumplings at the Muslim tent area in front of the Taipei train station. At school I mostly took Latin, but exchanged Chinese/English language lessons with local teachers at night. The American military brats found it easy to ignore me; my bookish manner and my ill-fitting local-made clothes did not fit in. That bothered me little; I disliked popular teenage music and dance. My interest for friends were intellectual Chinese girls (Chinese boys did not attend American school due to military service) or cultural oddities like Shanghai-

Linda enrolled as a foreign student at National Taiwan University for 1966-67. Her student identification card and library card show Taipei American School 1966 graduation pictures with standardized neckline drape.

Linda Arrigo Chen with father-in-law Raymond Chain in Taipei, December 1974. Mr. Chain, educated in English in the Japanese period, in 1947 founded Formosan Magazine Press which distributed Readers' Digest and Time-Life books in Taiwan. He was a lifelong member of the English-speaking Rotary Club chapter in Taipei.

born Alex Moosa, son of the English journalist Spencer Moosa. Escaping from my father's oversight with my linguistic skills (except that I was pressed into service for his commercial ventures, including illegally changing money on the local economy and investigating local companies for Dun & Bradstreet, which also gave me wider exposure to Taiwan society), I wandered through temples and markets and red-light districts after school. I graduated as valedictorian from Taipei American High School in 1966, also taking the English prize and the Chinese prize and a US$500 scholarship from the U.S. Embassy.

Through the late 1960's the role of Taiwan as staging theatre for the Vietnam War became more pronounced. Suzie Wong joints took over Chungshan and Linshen North Roads. Although the Star and Stripes never explained the reasons for the war, I got what I could out of the "anti-insurgency" literature at the small library at the U.S. 13th Air Force Base near Kungkuan 公館. I could draw a parallel with U.S. support for the dictatorship in Taiwan, and felt disturbed by the young GI's on R&R who talked about killing "gooks." Overseas Chinese at National Taiwan University and a few bold native Taiwanese students, in hurried whispers, gave me a different view of "Free China."

My father's delusions of grandeur as an international businessman led him to join the English-speaking Rotary Club of Taipei, the first one; and thus I met the son of Raymond Chain 陳國政 (1903-1991), a native Taiwanese who farsightedly learned English in the Japanese period and became the major importer of English magazines in Taiwan, founding Formosan Magazine Press in 1946 after he was repatriated from the Japanese war effort in Indonesia. I felt intuitively that native Taiwanese were more genuine than the mainlanders and rooted in their own culture and land; I began to see Taiwan history and my first direct knowledge of 2-28 through their eyes. My future father-in-law was pleased to have a native speaker of English to potentially help the business. But his son and I wanted to study in the U.S. first, and we left Taiwan in June 1968, for me an elopement and escape from my racist father as well.

Discovering the Horrors of Taiwanese History with the Taiwanese-Americans

I took a double major in Anthropology and Chinese Studies at the University of California, San Diego, in 1973. The National Defense Education Act was revving up Chinese studies throughout the U.S. in preparation for rapprochement with China, and it was easy for me to get scholarships. I was interested in joining the State Department, and passed the written exam in 1972. But I found the explanations of State Department officials for the reversals in policy towards China quite disingenuous; they intended to drop Chiang Kai-shek, but had no concern for what happened to the people of Taiwan.

At the same time, through my husband, I was a member of Taiwanese student and Taiwanese-American community groups. From 1971, the Diaoyutai Movement 釣魚台 運動broke into a searing criticism of the Chiang regime, following on the anti-Vietnam War movement that shook California campuses, especially UCSD. I think that my five

Linda Gail Arrigo

Teh Hua Girls' Dormitory, Hsintien, 1977: Linda, Theresa Yuan, Liao Hsiu-mei a.k.a. "Bala".

Linda's house on Dafeng Road, Hsintien: Research assistant Chiang Ying-chu, Linda, "Stone", an indigenous girl from Puli working at General Instruments.

Girls working at a Japanese-owned asbestos fiber factory in the Kaohsiung Export Processing Zone, 1978.

formative adolescent years in Taiwan and my sense of identity with my Taiwanese family made me feel these issues much more deeply than other Americans would. Ironically, this (as well as the women's liberation movement, etc.) also led me later to leave my Taiwanese husband and son and return to Taiwan.

My original perspective was academic and intellectual; I was the highest-ranked applicant to the Department of Anthropology, Stanford University, in Fall 1973. I focused on practical issues of world population and birth control. The graduate program was demanding, and I neglected my family. My advisor, Professor Arthur Wolf, the first American in anthropological fieldwork in Taiwan following World War II, assigned me to study change in family roles with the rise of employment for young women, and I immediately (December 1974) found my field site at General Instruments in Hsintien, where a priest, Father Edward Wojniak, a friend of my father's, had founded a dormitory for factory girls in 1967. I went out for a pilot study in summer 1975. Fateful moment.

As part of the Taiwanese Alliance for Interculture, a Bay Area Taiwanese-American community organization with links to the World United Formosans for Independence, my husband and I had met Kang Ning-hsiang 康寧祥and Peng Ming-min 彭明敏and Lu Hsiu-lien 呂秀蓮, among others, in 1975. This reflected of course the growing activism of the Taiwanese abroad, and the open challenge to the status quo in Taiwan represented by *Taiwan Political Review* 台灣政論. I had only arrived in Taiwan about ten days to begin my fieldwork when I met Kang, visiting, in my father-in-law's parlor in the Manka District 萬華 not far from Lung Shan Temple 龍山寺. He immediately suggested sending his secretary, a young woman named Chen Chu 陳菊, to interview me about my fieldwork and write an article for *Taiwan Political Review*. Soon after, Chen Chu met up with me at the Teh Hua Dormitory 德華女子公寓, and we had some round-table discussions with groups of girls that explained a lot about their migration, work conditions, and hopes for future life. Chen Chu in short order introduced me to Professor Chen Ku-ying 陳鼓應 who lived just across the river in Chingmei 景美, 15 minutes walk from the dormitory; Professor Chen, though purged from the NTU Philosophy Department, had secret links to KMT sources that leaked information on arrests and repressions. Chen Chu also took me to meet other intellectuals and members of *Taiwan Political Review*. Given the general suppression of information on social issues, I felt these intellectuals were important sources for my understanding of Taiwan social development, and thus for my academic research.

About the end of the summer, two events that had great personal significance to me occurred: there was a strike at General Instruments that led the American personnel manager to explain to me how he indirectly used martial law to put down the strike; and Professor Chen Ku-ying directed me to attend a political trial at the Taiwan Garrison Command. Together, these revealed to me the neo-colonial nature of Taiwan under U.S. economic (as well as military) imperialism, and the connection of this with serious human rights violations. In my fieldwork I seemed to see young lives chewed up in the huge machine of industrial development, trampled callously for the accumulation of super-profits (Taiwan wages were less than a tenth of U.S. wages,

The Sky-blue Backpack: My Experience with Taiwan's Human Rights

by Rosemary Haddon

(Account combined from her submitted writing plus interview on December 9, 2003.)

My present home is in New Zealand. Here, the natural environment is clean and green and the political environment is close to ideal: New Zealand has one of the most representative, democratic governments in the world. Needless to say, all this is a far cry from Taiwan with its broken environment and the injustice, repression and purges that comprise the story of the past. During the seven years I lived in Taiwan, I encountered and struggled with repression and my experience of happy times was often shaded over with pain. Now, as I recall the past, the anguish that accompanied those times comes back to me and I ponder if it will ever be put to rest. The anguish is a reminder of fate and, more important, of how love and passion determined the course of my life. To this day, I live with the consequences of this and wonder if what I did was right.

I was born in the city of Victoria on the southern tip of Vancouver Island, British Columbia, Canada. As a child, I spent my formative years there and in the surrounding countryside of Saanich where my grandparents had their home. I had a childhood that was not very different from that of any child growing up in the North American context. This childhood, nonetheless, did little to prepare me for the extraordinary times that I experienced as a young adult. In my early twenties, I moved to Vancouver and completed a major in Chinese at the University of British Columbia (UBC). After I graduated (Class I) in 1973, I worked in the restaurant business for a year earning and saving money for a trip overseas. My intention was to travel to either China or Taiwan in order to further my Chinese studies. At the time, my interest lay in pre-Chin thought but I also hoped to acquire proficiency in spoken standard Mandarin.

In 1974, China was still in the throes of the Cultural Revolution. Thus, on the advice of teachers and friends I traveled to Taiwan and enrolled in what was then called the Mandarin Training Center, which was attached to Taiwan Normal University. After four months at the Center, I subsequently enrolled in a Master's program at Taiwan National University. Initially, I had intended to stay in Taiwan for only one year, but I revised my plans and sold off the return half of my ticket. What with one adventure following another, my sojourn in Taiwan lengthened and extended to a total of seven years. I didn't return to Canada until 1981.

During those seven years in Taiwan, I became involved in the struggle against the violation of human rights, got married to a Taiwanese national who was a former political prisoner, and undertook research into Taiwan history and culture. The latter has particular value to me because it has since become an important part of my professional career. My Taiwan experience was intriguing, heart-wrenching and profound and, needless to say, it changed my life in ways that continue to affect me today.

As a young Canadian, I came to Taiwan with a naive understanding about the political

and health and safety standards were ignored). Wage work did give daughters some opportunities for education and advancement; but the conditions of work were blatantly exploitative and unfair, prone to serious accident and spurring alienation from family and community. Somehow, living in the dormitory with the factory girls, fielding their questions and perhaps suspicions of my presence, presented me with a challenge as to the meaning of what and why I was doing this research. Was it only my selfish academic career pretensions? I reshaped my priorities; I stopped treating my subjects as if their heads were glass globes for me to plunge for information. I felt I owed my knowledge and my personal commitment to them. Martial law shaped their conditions of work. And as an American, Taiwan's martial law was my business, too.

The trial was the re-trial of Lee Ao 李敖, Hsieh Tsung-min 謝聰敏, and about nine others who were accused of bombing the Bank of America and USIS in 1969/1970. Under international pressure, the Taiwan Garrison Command announced that it would hold an open trial on September 15, 1975. But arriving at the Chingmei prison with about three or four foreign journalists, including Fox Butterfield, we found that we would not be allowed access. The military officers who received us at a reception building had masking tape covering their name plates. It was frightening just to go to the entrance of the Taiwan Garrison Command, given the chill of their reputation; but seeing them hide imparted a strange sense of power. But then they mostly left us there, and relatives of the accused, also refused entrance, appeared. I thought to interview them, take notes, and translate for the journalists. The military officers looked discomfited but could not stop us. Later in the afternoon at Chen Ku-ying's house I met Dr. James Seymour who had been dispatched from New York by Amnesty International but had been turned away at the gate of the Garrison, and I handed on to him the information on names and treatment.

This summer of fieldwork, after many years away from Taiwan, imbued me with a new sense of purpose. I thirsted to understand the crux of oppression in this society. The structure of social inequality and injustice in general. Now there was a stirring of questioning and challenge to the authorities by the lone dissidents I had met. Political prisoners were being released following the death of Chiang Kai-shek in April 1975. People were beginning to talk.

Seeking Sociology in the Real World: My Ejection from Stanford University

Returning to Stanford, I discarded the wordy, empty tomes of modernization theory as "the apologetics for the failures of imperialist development", and studied political economy from Economics Department Marxists instead. The United Nations personnel I met at conferences, spouting platitudes about economic development and women and child welfare, seemed like bald hypocrites consuming huge salaries; regimes of inequality, they admitted when pressed, stymied any reform. I dared to argue directly with Arthur Wolf, my economic determinism versus his cultural determinism. I thought academia meant intellectual freedom.

Meanwhile, due to renovations of the beautiful old carved sandstone buildings in the

circumstances of developing countries, particularly those in Asia. My political orientation was leftist, which stemmed from UBC's Chinese program and Canada's pro-China stance. Within a year or so after arriving in Taiwan, my political initiation began to unfold and my sheltered worldview cracked. In 1976, I was introduced by Dirk Bennett, who was an aspiring stringer/journalist, to Chen Ku-ying.

Chen Ku-ying was a professor in the Philosophy Department, NTU, but he had lost his job because of an allegation of political misconduct. What was called the "banchang"班長 – some people translate that as "professional student," people who aren't really students, but pose as students to serve as stooges for the government, and are posted in all the classes in order to monitor the behavior of the students and the teachers – had made a report on him. And if anybody does anything that they feel is problematical, or could be construed as being critical of the government, these banchang would write up a "xiao bao gao", a report, and present it to the government. So Chen Ku-ying was under a sort of house arrest.

My American flatmate Kathy Kearny and I and other friends used to go to his house in Chingmei on the south side of Taipei, where he would offer private tutorials in Chinese philosophy, for nothing, so we went along and got these lessons in Han-fei-dze, and Chuang-dze, and classical philosophers. He put an interesting political spin on his interpretation of these classical documents, for example how Han-fei-dze was a writer under a totalitarian regime in China, between 210 and 206 B.C. And you could draw parallels between that period and the KMT in Taiwan, or China under Mao, and he was perceived as being highly critical of the regime under the KMT.

While we were going to his house on a weekly basis, we were introduced to many of his friends, and his house was like a meeting place for a lot of different intellectuals. Some were native Taiwanese 本省人, some were Chinese mainlanders 外省人. But they were all politically aware and openly critical of the repressive aspects of the KMT regime. So it was really interesting for me to meet these people. Because everyone else was so quiet in Taiwan. They presented a sort of façade that life is fine, and nothing is wrong – and yet there was this circle of people that were speaking out about political abuses, the infringements on human rights. And prior to that time, I didn't know that Taiwan was under martial law. And they were saying that there were violations of constitutional rights, and freedom of assembly, and freedom of expression. So gradually I became educated as to what the real situation was all about in Taiwan.

I came to understand that what was presented to us foreigners by the government was nothing but a set of lies, this big myth. A lot of foreigners who were students like myself, or business people from the outside, were taken in by these lies that were presented to us. But once you scratched beneath the surface, you saw the real situation, one that was pretty horrific.

During our visits, Ku-ying introduced us to his close-knit circle of friends. These friends included critics, activists and writers, such as Wang Hsiao-po 王曉波, Hu Chiu-yuan 胡秋原, Chen Ying-chen 陳映真 and Wang Tuo. I was intrigued and felt fortunate in having the opportunity to become acquainted with people who were not afraid to articulate their concerns and, more important, their ideals and utopian visions. Chen Ying-chen, for instance, had served a six-year jail sentence for his part in Taiwan's first local-grown leftist

central quad of Stanford University, I was assigned an office in the Physiology Building, and got a terrible cold in November 1975 that dragged into chronic asthma, dizziness, and even fevers for over a year. Pressed by Professor G. William Skinner's usual inhumane threats to students, that qualifying exams must be completed in several weeks, etc., I did not know until over a year later, after allergy diagnosis, that there were experimental animals in a basement room that connected to my first-floor office by vents. I do not know if I would have been better able to deal with ideological clashes with Wolf and Skinner if fully fit; but at any rate they flunked me, and I determined to go and continue my fieldwork anyway since my award of US$7,000 from the Rockefeller-Ford Foundations Program on Economic Development and Population Policy did not depend on enrollment. Though they doubtlessly would not recognize the ancestry, my Ph.D. research finally completed in 1996 drew on the basic debates on inequality in Chinese peasant economy and demography that I encountered in study with them. But before I left, I traveled to New School for Social Research in New York by Greyhound bus together with my son Roger, and was much encouraged by assurance of future admission there by Stanley Diamond, Chair of the Anthropology Department; he said I woke up to international realities earlier than most graduate students.

In 1976 I received a letter from Chen Chu concerning the suppression of *Taiwan Political Review*, with arrests; she had lost her job at the library of the Chengchi University Economics School as well. Taking a human rights petition around the Stanford campus, I found that those who championed the Chinese revolution would not stand up publicly for democracy and human rights in general; they were, in my impression, opportunistically afraid that being identified with the Taiwan opposition would limit their access to China, just when research possibilities seemed to be opening up.

By April 1977 when I set off for fieldwork again I had made several nearly inexplicable decisions. In those days travel to the other side of the Pacific was extremely expensive, and had a sort of finality to it; years could pass. My husband was an upcoming young engineer at Lockheed, the center of the military-industrial complex, and I was filled with a nameless terror of ending up, after advanced education, as a dependent housewife in a beautiful suburban Menlo Park luxury house. He said he could not stand to live without me for a year, and if I insisted on going he would divorce me; but perhaps it was meant to be an empty threat. I said, okay. I remember my tough eight-year-old son breaking into tears when I told him I was leaving. I rewrote the divorce agreement to a very mild, non-contestant wording. The divorce lawyer asked if we knew what we were doing, because he saw that we were holding hands as we waited to sign the divorce papers. I felt as though I were stepping off a cliff, willingly, driven to know the unknown. Two months later I was packing frantically and two hours late to the airport, almost as if I wanted to miss it; but the China Airlines plane was two hours late as well.

Linked up with the Osaka Human Rights Network

Pausing in Japan for a week at the end of April 1977 on the way to my anthropology

Rosemary Haddon (left), Wu Yao-chung (also imprisoned in Chen Ying-chen's 1968 case), and roommate Kathy Cearney. Taipei, 1978

Rosemary Haddon (left), Linda Gail Arrigo, Chang Mei-chen, and Chen Chu. At home of Chang Chun-hong in Nantou, 1978; Mei-chen is his younger sister.

political case and had recently been released. Chen had headed a reading cell that had access to and studied contraband publications from China. He surmised that among the cell members there was a KMT operative whose report led to the arrest of the members and their subsequent charge of sedition — a word that at the time I only barely fully understood. When I first made Chen's acquaintance in the 1970s, he was writing stories that centered on the dependency theory reflecting his anti-American, pro-reunification stance. As I got to know Chen Ying-chen, Chen Ku-ying and Wang Tuo, I became drawn into a world of underground leftist politics in which the intent was passive resistance of the repressive structure of the KMT regime.

I will never forget the day in Chen Ku-ying's house when I met Lin Hua-chou 林華洲 — the Taiwan national to whom I was drawn because of his leftist thought and with whom I fell in love and later exchanged vows. Hua-chou had been a member of Chen Ying-chen's reading cell and, like Ying-chen, had recently obtained his release from serving a six-year jail sentence for sedition. He had not been in jail quite the ten years of his sentence, because Chiang Kai-shek had died in 1975, and there was a partial amnesty that had been granted to political prisoners, so they actually only served six years of their sentence. They had been in prison on Green Island, which was also called Burning Island火燒島, and places like Taiyuan, which was the location of another earlier political prison in Taiwan. So I met Lin Hua-chou about a year after he had been released. My association with Hua-chou became the key factor in my life that, at times, seemed to spiral into madness.

I was immediately drawn to these people, because I empathized with their socialist viewpoint and their concern for the lack of social welfare in Taiwan, the need for labor reform, and the suffering of the common people of Taiwan老百姓, what is called the "little people"小人物, or the lower classes, under Taiwan's rampant modernization: the farmers, the people in the countryside, the workers and women workers, especially in the new export industries: the proletariat, if you want to use Marxist terminology.

In 1978, Lin Hua-chou and I embarked on a honeymoon that was as unlike the usual honeymoon as one can possibly imagine. The honeymoon comprised a tour of Taiwan and visits to places that included sites such as Orchid Island. But besides this, the tour

fieldwork in Taiwan, I followed a series of leads to find those with similar interests in the political economy of dictatorships supported by U.S. imperialism. From David Satterwhite with American Friends Service Committee in Tokyo I was referred to Miyake Kiyoko, a petite woman of about 35, who came to meet me and put me in touch with a Lynn Miles in Osaka. I knew a Japanese family in Osaka that I would be staying with; I had helped Professor Ichioka when he was a visiting professor at UCSD in 1970 or so. So aside from visiting castles I had ample time to meet Lynn Miles and his network of activists, including Ron Fujiyoshi, an American from Hawaii who worked organizing Korean-Japanese workers in Japan. Ron's Maoist-Christian motivations and later correspondence had a great impact on me. Various disheveled Western backpacking students in Japan, under Lynn's networking, carried materials in and out of Taiwan and Korea on their travels and language-learning throughout Asia. By Lynn's memory of my visit, I was interested in hearing about his work, but said I could not get much involved because I was busy with my academic research. Famous last words.

Finally back in Taipei on May 7, 1977, I met immediately with Chen Chu; within a few days I met Wei Ting-chao 魏廷朝, just released from jail on September 23, 1976, and other political prisoners released early due to sentence reduction after Chiang Kai-shek's death, and for the first time I heard their experiences directly. I met also Rosemary Haddon and Cathy Kearny, associated with the anti-U.S. intellectuals at Tamkiang University in Tamsui, and with Chen Ku-ying, and also Dennis Engbarth 安德毅, aspiring to be a journalist and in close correspondence with Lynn Miles. It was not clear to me then what the role of the Osaka network was, but in Taipei there was a parallel mix of students learning Chinese and dabbling in political analysis, and journalists trying to report provocatively on "the Republic of China" while doing more than the obligatory tours of Kinmen with guns at the ready facing Red China. Melinda Liu of Newsweek was then known as the foremost irritant to the Government Information Office, which of course did not want any foreign airing of suppressed dissent within "Free China."

Officially, I was affiliated with the Population Studies Center, in the top floor of the new white four-story library at National Taiwan University. Fatefully, this was also later the building from which the body of Professor Chen Wen-cheng of Carnegie-Mellon University was thrown, almost certainly by the security agency thugs, on July 3, 1981 after his interrogation, some related to myself. I took one course in the Agricultural Extension Department as an auditor foreign student. National Legislator Kang Ning-hsiang was my guarantor for my one-year visa, next due to be renewed in late October 1978. For a while I was still exhausted and depressed from my expulsion from Stanford and separation from my son. I rented a modest one-story tile-roof house (No. 12, Lane 31, Dafeng Road, Hsintien) just five minutes walk from the Teh Hua Dormitory, for NT$3,000 a month, i.e. US$75. I had a bunk in the dormitory, but there were no electric outlets in the rooms and no space to work. The house had a large open front room, two bedrooms at the side, and small kitchen and bath; the usual terra cotta floors and moldy wooden doors and windows; and a small yard with a *lienwu* tree and a cement tank pond. I had to heat water separately in large

Rosemary Haddon and Dirk Bennett at Dangwai activity, 1978.

also included visits to a secret compound or "concentration camp" for the incarceration of political prisoners, Taiyuan, which was the location of a jail housing similar sorts of prisoners; and, finally, Green Island, the infamous penal colony that lay off the southeast coast. On Green Island, we went by taxi along a gravel road which led up a hill that offered a view of the compound lying below. From inside the taxi, I secretly took photographs of the place where my lover had spent several years of his life and that he and his jail-mates referred to facetiously as "the Ph.D. program." The experience was uncanny and augured a future for me that became more hair-raising and dangerous as the days went by.

In general, Taiwan in the 1970s was a paradise for foreigners. We enjoyed good treatment by the government and an easy lifestyle studying Chinese and teaching English in corporations and buhsiban (cram schools). The flip side of the coin, however, was the ubiquitous presence of the KMT, including rhetoric and anti-Communist sloganeering; banned Chinese publications; the military police; a curfew; and censorship, all of which were the reminders that we were living under Martial Law. Everywhere, walls, placards and buses displayed sloganistic rallying cries, such as "Recover the Mainland" and "Everyone is responsible for defending against Communist spies" 防衛匪諜,人人有責. Most foreigners ignored this aspect of Taiwan life and went about their daily life oblivious to the repression. There were those such as Dirk, however, who looked below the surface and perceived what lay beneath — a fragmented and distorted world that was constructed on the basis of lies; the whitewashing of the past; and the erasure of a separate Taiwan history that was the marker of identity and difference. The more I came into contact with this darker, hidden side of Taiwan life the more I felt that the easy-going lifestyle that the foreigners were living was similarly a lie.

The whitewashing of the past was brought home to me one day when Hua-chou took me to meet two young women — a pair of twin girls in their twenties who had the family name of Lin. The girls were pale and thin and shared a tiny, dark room in a concrete block in which they had little more than a bunk bed, a couple of desks and a stove where they cooked their food. One of them looked ill and her expression was very sad. After we left, Hua-chou told me that the twins had been orphaned when their father was arrested and executed during the February 28 Incident. I had never before heard of this incident but learned that it had occurred in 1947 at the outset of KMT rule. I learned more about this from two other sisters to whom I taught English. These women filled me in on some other details and told me about the sea of bodies that were seen floating in Keelung harbor at the time. They also told me about an execution ground in the middle of Taipei that they used to pass every day when they took the bus to school. The women were quite outspoken about the purge and I wondered at their insouciance and fearlessness at a time when everyone else seemed either ignorant or afraid. In my conversations with these two students, I similarly learned for the first time about Taiwan's Japanese colonial past,

pots for bathing. After a trip to the used furniture street, the front room was mostly taken up with three desks and a manual typewriter. A graduate student from the University of Hawaii, Ruth Sando, shared the house with me for a while, and other American graduate students, including Don Nonini from Anthropology at Stanford University on his way to fieldwork in Malaysia, occasionally crashed with me as well. The house made it possible for me to put up backpacker visitors from Lynn Miles, as well as to invite girls from the dormitory over for private chats or small parties. Gradually it also became a place for impromptu meetings till all hours of the night of young Taiwanese dissidents including Lin Cheng-chieh 林正杰 (Jackie), his friend Wu Hsueh-tao 吳學道 (nicknamed Shadow; Jackie and Shadow were young mainlanders who objected to the martial law regime and joined the Taiwanese dissidents), Chen Chu, Tien Chiu-chin 田秋堇, and Chiang Chun-nan 江春男 (Antonio Chiang, a liberal journalist and favorite interviewee for foreign reporters),.

My immediate concern in getting my research underway was finding a motivated research assistant. In 1975 I found that the elitist women studies graduate students at National Taiwan University could not tolerate the heat and dust of fieldwork. I sought an assistant recommended by Su Ching-li 蘇慶黎, the editor of the leftist, PRC-leaning *China Tide* magazine. Professor Wang Jing-ping 王津平 of the English Department at Tamkiang found for me Miss Chiang Ying-chu 蔣英珠, a thin, earnest, hard-working assistant with a social conscience, and her boyfriend Huang Chao-chou 黃潮州 came along to help me and volunteered to find and photograph all the American and foreign electronics factories in north Taiwan, so we would have a census of the total number of girl workers. That finished, in September he had to enter military service. Tien Chiu-chin 田秋堇, a very lively young woman with dark eyebrows and big round eyes who was the daughter of Dr. Tien Chao-ming 田朝明, a Taiwanese doctor with an office on Chungshan North Road who was the main contact for Japanese-speaking human rights visitors, volunteered to explore the General Instruments factory conditions by working on the assembly line for two months (her ID card did not list her NTU degree), and she also camped at my house a few nights a week, bringing more contacts with young dissidents.

I was also in frequent contact with Reverend Kao Chun-ming 高俊明, General Secretary of the Presbyterian Church, and his secretary Elizabeth Brown; the church headquarters was on Lane 269, Roosevelt Road, Section 3, near National Taiwan University and on the same lane where I lived in 1963. The Presbyterian Church was embattled in trying to fight off the proposed new laws on religious establishments, which would allow the government to confiscate the property of churches whose pastors made "seditious" statements violating government property. I was among those charged with smuggling out the Church's 1977 statement on human rights.

It was abundantly clear that nearly all foreigners were under close scrutiny, and those of us in contact with dissidents in particular. The government wanted to look like the ROC was the beacon, not the PRC, for all those who wished to study the great ancient Chinese civilization (so the importance of the Stanford Center and the Mandarin Center at National Normal University, heavily implanted with spies), a period that was similarly hidden and little talked about.

My friendship with Chen Ku-ying, his wife Shan-shan, and their circle of friends deepened. This was the period when the Dangwai (politicians in opposition to the ruling party) came into being; the nativist literature movement 鄉土文學 was in full swing; and *China Tide* began publishing critical articles about politics, history and culture. The journal similarly published re-prints of Japanese colonial fiction, bringing to light the fifty-year period of Taiwan's past that had been obliterated and shrouded in shame. In my daily life with friends I was surrounded by conversations about *Free China, Taiwan Political Review* and the political thought of Lee Ao. Often, I didn't understand the content of the talk; nonetheless, I felt I was in the midst of great change and that history was being made.

In 1977, elections were called for the Taiwan Provincial Assembly, and political tensions unfolded as the time approached for the people to go to the polls. The tensions were marked by increasing political and social disturbance. This was a year of the Chungli Riot. In August 1977 as the tensions peaked, the government convened a forum about the meaning of "native literature." The KMT maintained that this was a form of literature of workers, peasants and soldiers 工農兵文藝. Critics such as Yu Kuang-chung similarly maintained that it was inspired by Chinese communism. Needless to say, his charge added fuel to the debate and was followed by counter-charges that highlighted Taiwan's lack of freedom of expression and publication. In the midst of these tensions, news came about arrests taking place around the island and people began to disappear. My foreign friends and I were cautioned about our telephone conversations and we devised codenames that we used when we discussed our Chinese and Taiwanese friends.

Eventually as the confusion grew, the day came when Shan-shan approached me with an unusual request. I was planning to take a trip to Hong Kong in order to renew my visa. Shan-shan asked me if I could take some material with me that she said I would need to pass on to a contact in Hong Kong.

Rosemary and husband Lin Hua-chou.

Li Ching-tung, Chen Ku-ying, Dirk Bennett out hiking, 1977.

Rosemary Haddon with former political prisoner Mr. Huang, from Kuangtung, jailed 30 years.

but these unruly foreigners also had to be warned subtly or not-so-subtly to stay in line. Supposedly all policemen had to memorize at least 200 foreign faces, to report wherever they appeared. Within a few weeks of my return, my former father-in-law was warned, but he demurred that I had already divorced his son and he had no control over me.

Amateur Human Rights Spies: Busted

The precise time escapes me, but sometime in 1978 three other foreign women and I formed an underground cell together for a division of labor and hopefully less chance of detection: I would do the usual translation and guide service for foreign reporters and visitors wishing to meet directly with dissidents, while others would do pickups and dropoffs of donations and materials from abroad, and according to plan quietly pass the messages to me. Two of the other women involved were Helen Chauncey, a tall thin American studying Chinese at the Stanford Center and affiliated with the *Bulletin of Concerned Asian Scholars*, and Penny Simpson, a short round Trotskyite from the Quebec independence movement, who wanted to eventually expose the falsity of the PRC's minority programs. We would not talk at length in our apartments or on the telephone, assuming bugs and recording, so generally we had to walk around and eat at tiny sidewalk restaurants while we exchanged information and plans. On one gray day Penny came out to my house and we walked to the remote countryside- like areas at the end of Dafeng Road. True, this is the area of "Central Village" in Hsintien, the home turf of the feared Ministry of Justice Investigation Bureau; but the markets are all Taiwanese. We were talking heatedly in English in a tiny crowded open-air eatery, and did not notice a tall man in a gray trench coat, back to us, leaning closer and closer. As we paid the tab, he turned to us and spoke in perfect English, making it clear that he had been eavesdropping on us, and worked at the MJIB, and intended to politely intimidate us with this information. Not long after, Helen Chauncey went to visit China through Hong Kong, and found when she went to board the plane back to Taiwan that her long-term visa had been cancelled. After a week of hurried cables with the Stanford Center, she was finally readmitted; but no more activity for our cell. She did however make a long report to Lynn Miles in March 1978 concerning the March 18 security agency raid on the printing of *Elections Forever* 『選舉萬歲』. Penny stuck with me as much as she could till she went back to Canada.

Following up on addresses received from Lynn Miles, I saw Dennis Engbarth frequently in the first few weeks after my arrival; he kept up contact with Chen Chu, Su Ching-li, and Kang Ning-hsiang. After several months, however, we came to some disagreement as to modus operandi. In my view, we should inform as many people as possible, and in particular educate and recruit other foreigners to participate in human rights materials smuggling. There was no reason to conceal what the security agencies already knew, and of course they knew the crimes they had perpetrated in suppressing dissent. Dennis wanted to operate clandestinely on the basis of "need to know", and his proclivity was not to share information. I considered his approach to be "conspicuous secrecy." In particular I held it against him that he did not inform me that a letter of mine to Lynn had been confiscated from him on the way

I agreed, although I had little notion about what the request entailed. On the evening prior to my departure, Shan-shan came with a friend to the apartment that I rented with my American and Taiwanese flatmates. She then asked me to bring out my sky-blue Canadian backpack. She examined it closely and said that we would need to take it apart. I wondered why she said this, but helped her to dismantle one section of the hollow aluminum tubing that formed the framework of the backpack. Shan-shan then unrolled several letter-size sheets of paper and handed them to me to read. I took the pages and saw that at the very top of the first page was a row of tiny characters that ran across the full width of the page. Crammed beneath this was a second row, then a third, which was followed by more and more rows running down the full length of that page. The rows continued on to the next page and the next. As I looked more closely, I saw that each line commenced with a name that was followed by an age in years, a place and, finally, the time or circumstances in which that person had been arrested or had disappeared. My eyes scanned the pages and I realized with a shock that they recorded the names of hundreds of people, who were silently and without a trace disappearing off the face of the Taiwan map. I was stunned and my head reeled in shock. I had known, of course, that people were being arrested, but I had no idea that the situation had become so bad. Like other things that happened to me in Taiwan, this incident profoundly affected me and awakened within me a first-hand awareness of the impact of political repression. I understood that what was taking place in Taiwan was on a par with the political abuses that had taken place in countries such as Argentina.

Shan-shan had spent the preceding day and night writing up the sheets of paper in preparation to give to me prior to my departure. Silently, she tightly re-rolled the pages into sheathes the shape and size of pencils or straws. Together we pushed the sheaths into the hollow tubing of the backpack and reassembled the frame. The backpack was ready for my departure. As I went to bed, I thought of my departure the next day and, more important, my cargo that was more precious than gold.

The next day at the airport and on each occasion thereafter, I approached the emigration desk with trepidation. My heart was thumping and, unreasonably, I felt like a criminal. I convinced myself that the official behind the desk had X-ray vision and could see through the tubing to the precious material inside. Forcing myself forward, I smiled cheerily and engaged in meaningless banter as the man checked my passport and bags. A moment later, my departure was approved and I passed through the checkpoint. My spirits soaring, I walked to the gate, looking forward to the plane ride to Hong Kong and to meeting Li Yi, my Hong Kong contact, who was the editor of a Chinese-language magazine called *The Seventies* 七十年代. After I arrived in Hong Kong and phoned Li Yi, we arranged to meet in a nearby coffee shop. Over coffee, I surreptitiously handed to him the rolled up sheets of paper, and he received them nonchalantly and without a word. It was as though what we were doing was a normal, routine part of everyday human exchange.

During the period of martial law, the curtailment of civil rights extended to the banning of publications from China. Several times during the late 1970s, I traveled abroad to Japan and Hong Kong. Each time, I was requested by Chen Ku-ying or Chen Ying-chen to bring back into Taiwan contraband Chinese publications. In order to buy these publications, I went to bookstores where the owner understood the nature of my request and carefully disguised the books with a false cover. On the surface, it thus appeared as though I were

out of the airport, nor did he notify me of Ron Fujiyoshi's scheduled visit in early February 1978 because it was "too dangerous" to go to my house. I looked to Ron for ideological guidance and meaning in what I was doing, even if I didn't share his religiosity. Fortunately Ron Fujiyoshi called me directly when he came back through in late February. From Dennis' point of view, no doubt, I was too flamboyant to be able to operate without detection (and it will be seen below that I was soon out of the pan and into the fire), and would endanger our Taiwanese contacts. (As can be seen from Lynn's files, namely Wu San-lien archives 081-10-003, Helen Chauncey reported this dispute to Lynn in August 1978, when Dennis was suggesting Lynn cut communication with Linda because "she talked too much.") Lynn did not send all of his missions to Taiwan to see me. The matter of endangering Taiwanese associates was a difficult issue; as foreigners we were in general only in danger of deportation, not arrest and torture. Of course deportation could still be a high cost, in my case my friendships and my research project. My view that developed over time was that I would do at least whatever Taiwanese activists wanted me to do; those who were brave enough (or even not brave enough, the victims) needed the world to know their suffering.

We were obviously all amateurs with little experience or resources. At first I did not realize why Taiwanese people were generally so fearful, including the intellectuals with respected positions; gradually I understood that there were spies and infiltrators and secret government reporters everywhere. Even the intellectuals at Academia Sinica walked a thin line, trying to be convincingly relevant without incurring the wrath of the authorities. There were even some spies recruited from among the teenage factory girls I spent time with. There was no way human rights reporters could entirely thwart the heavy surveillance and interference. But the amateur nature of the foreign participants, plus persistence and diffuseness, made it impossible for the security agencies to totally stop us, either. Help in smuggling the human rights materials often came from unexpected quarters; for example, Adrienne Ropa, a robust blonde-haired young woman who came to Taiwan occasionally to help Father Wojniak at the dormitory, volunteered to carry letters when I mentioned what we were doing, and from her later note to me I knew that this act was very meaningful to her. The techniques we used were mostly low tech, except that Lynn Miles (whom then I hardly remembered as a face, only as a reliable outside contact) had access to special equipment in his job as an advertising typesetter, and could insert messages into what appeared to be printed contract forms or advertising. I resorted, among others, to sending printed contracts in which the carbon paper carried the real typed message, which could be read by reflection in a mirror. Handing over letters to be carried was not always safe, either; some untrustworthy carriers got cold feet and threw letters in the mail box. When the security agencies intercepted them, they sometimes mailed you back a photocopy, for intimidation effect.

One case that I investigated personally in 1977 was the case of a mainlander, surnamed Wang. I had received from others his home address, an old four-story walkup near Chungshan North Road, and I visited without prior arrangement. His wife would not tell me much, but his son happened to come home, and then the story

buying cookbooks or books on poetry or other things. Little did the Taiwan immigration officials know that, at the bottom of my sky-blue backpack, I was smuggling back into Taiwan Chinese publications on the thought of Karl Marx, Mao Zedong and Lu Hsun. I was proud to be able to do this for my friends and believed that, as the freedom of publication and reading was a normal part of Canadian life, it should be in Taiwan, too.

In Taipei, my life with my American and Taiwanese flatmates continued relatively undisturbed. One day in 1978, out of the blue, Chen Chu came flying up the stairs and pounded excitedly on our door. She pleaded with us to take her in. Chen Chu had worked for the opposition politician Kuo Yu-hsin and a warrant had been issued for her arrest. That night and the next day, we kept her hidden in our apartment and discussed what we should do with her. Finally, we contacted the local branch of the Presbyterian Church and explained the situation to one of the ministers who was active in the area of human rights. The second night we dressed Chen Chu up as a peasant with a shawl over her head and waited for the minister to arrive. Finally, a white van arrived at our apartment. We smuggled Chen Chu down the stairs and into the van and it disappeared into the dark.

The previous day while we had waited for nightfall, Chen Chu discussed many things with us, then added that she had left her home in such a hurry that she had taken no change of clothing or other things with her in her panic to escape the police. She explained that she needed to take some things if she were to spend some time in hiding. Cautiously, we liaised with the wife of Yao Chia-wen. Mrs. Yao told us that she would get the provisions and take them to her husband's office where one of us could pick them up. I volunteered to make the journey there and decided to ride my bicycle, which would make me appear less conspicuous than a trip there by taxi. I made my way to Yao Chia-wen's office where I picked up the provisions. A minute after I left his building, I realized that I was being followed by a spy who was similarly on a bicycle. In a panic, I ducked into a lane and weaved my way in and out among alleyways, shops and stalls in an attempt to throw him off my trial. I succeeded and, relieved, made my way cautiously back to Wenchou Street. If I had arrived back at Chen Chu's hiding place with an operative on my tail, the consequences would have been unthinkable.

Would you like me to talk more about Lin Hua-chou and my relationship with him? At that time I was living in Taipei, and about 1978 we moved to Taichung, and I started teaching English at Tunghai University. I lived in the home of Hua-chou's maternal uncle, who was similarly a former political prisoner. I actually lived out in an old traditional farming house in Dachia, and commuted to Taichung for my classes. Shortly after that time, Lin Hua-chou had an invitation to work for an opposition politician by the name of Huang Hsun-hsin 黃順興 who was in Changhua. Lin Hua-chou became very active in the campaign there in the runup to the elections for the Legislative Yuan in December 1978. In the countryside, I was the first in the household to learn of the intentions of the United States to break off diplomatic relations with Taiwan.

During the day, I taught English at Tunghai University and, on several occasions, visited Yang Kuei 楊逵, the writer who was active during the time of the Japanese occupation. Yang Kuei operated a flower garden opposite the university and, in the course of discussions, enlightened me about the period of the Japanese rule and presented me with a collection of his fiction. The collection contained the complete, unedited version of his story "Paperboy" 送報夫, which I translated into English and published in the Hong Kong

came out. Wang was a graduate of the famed Hwangpu Military Academy 黃埔軍校 in Shanghai, which should have given him many influential classmates among the KMT to plead his case. After coming to Taiwan in 1949 he left the military and went into business; in the 1960's he was fairly successful. However, he needed foreign currency for his business occasionally, and changed illegally on the local market (there were small currency exchange and foreign check cashing windows at the back of all the jewelry shops on Hengyang Road downtown; I did small exchanges for my father's business in the 1960's too). The Ministry of Justice Investigation Bureau (MJIB) arrested Wang for currency violations, which could be a serious charge, and blackmailed his family for a large sum of money. Wang's son was outraged, and reported the MJIB corruption to the Taiwan Garrison Command. The TGC arrested the MJIB officers involved – but then charges were trumped up that Wang was a communist spy, no doubt by confession through beating in which he lost many of his teeth, and he was sentenced to 15 years. Then his property was under threat of confiscation as well, but the agents said they wouldn't take the house if his wife kept her mouth shut. The son told me that the case had been reported overseas, and sometime later I saw an account about Wang in a human rights publication that was smuggled in. Interviewing in this case, especially going in alone cold and introducing myself, I think it was a definite advantage to be an American, because the general belief was that the security agencies could not coerce foreigners to serve as spies.

In September 1977 a tragedy occurred that however also provided occasion for venting of the opposition to the regime. Lee Shuang-dze 李雙澤, a leftist Filippino-Chinese who was part of the Tamkiang University activists, about thirty, tall and heavily rotund and a strong swimmer, drowned while trying to save two swimmers caught in a rip tide off a Tamsui beach. He saved one, but drowned with the second. A guitar player and prolific writer of poetry and political criticism, his funeral was a display of his writings and quotations written in huge black Chinese characters on lengths of white cloth – he could no longer be arrested for them. I had met him only once; but there had been schemes afoot by my friends to link us up, given the similarities of age, weight, and political bent. The scuttlebutt on this occasion, I don't know from where, was that Melinda Liu of *Newsweek* had received notice from the GIO to leave within a week, but now I was tops on the security agencies' list of foreign irritants.

Appealing to the Enemy: The United States Embassy

When I first arrived, before I was pegged as an ally for dangerous dissidents, some personnel in the U.S. Embassy were very much interested in my research on industrial workers, in particular an analyst by the surname of Laurey (precise spelling I no longer remember). Yang Ching-chu 楊青矗 and his short stories on workers were then in the news, and Mr. Laurey on one occasion invited both of us to his house on Yangmingshan for dinner. The guest of honor was a man surnamed Clark who had spent seven years as a prisoner of the Khmer Rouge in the hills between Vietnam and Cambodia. He told us many macabre stories of the captured GI's being fed elephant foot and monkey paw, as well as cannibalism between the Vietnamese and the Cambodians in the jungles, where protein was scarce. One GI was reported to have

Lin Hua-chou.

Lin Hua-chou, left of Linda, on an outing to Pinglin together with electronics factory workers.

journal *Renditions*. In Dachia, I began a translation project that entailed the translation of fiction from the Japanese period and the 1960s and 1970s. In 1996, Professor Helmut Martin agreed to publish the book in his Edition Cathay series. *Oxcart: Nativist Stories from Taiwan, 1934-1977* stands as a testament to the courage of Taiwan's writers who persisted in writing and publishing despite the curtailment of the freedom of expression.

I was still in Taichung in early 1979, but I knew what was going on. And Linda, you know Ai Linda 艾琳達, on one occasion she came to me, and she scolded me, "You're not sufficiently politically involved. I want you to get more involved. You've got to do this, do that." But I really quite hesitant, because I felt I was already quite involved, and I didn't want to jeopardize our situation.

One day, the banchang (classroom monitor) of my class at Tunghai University came up to me and asked if I could stay after class so we could have a chat. We went to an empty classroom and, after sitting down, she began to question me concerning my views about Taiwan's political situation and the views of Lin Hua-chou and his background. I quickly realized that she knew some things, but was unaware of others and, in my answers, was able to skirt around the real intent behind her questions and, after a while, she left. Through this encounter I realized that I, too, was being watched and that my freedoms were being curtailed. I felt indignant and reasoned that, as a foreigner, I should be immune from this violation of my rights. I recalled words spoken by China specialists who maintained that, although things were bad in China, the situation was actually worse in Taiwan. Anger and frustration surged within me and I began to feel a strong need to return home. Daily, I pressured Hua-chou to apply for a passport and an exit permit, so we could leave. At the time, I refused to entertain the possibility that, because of the political situation and his background as a former political prisoner, it was unlikely that he could leave.

In late 1979, Hua-chou and I returned to Taipei and rented an apartment in the suburb of Chungho, which was just around the corner from Chen Ying-chen. Almost every day, Hua-

been eaten as well, he said; to which a Chinese woman guest quipped shrilly, "So it must have been Western-style cuisine!"

The social significance of Yang Ching-chu's short stories about changing farm families and young factory workers was not lost on Tom Gold 高棣民, who was in 1977 still on sociological fieldwork in Taiwan. He translated one of Yang Ching-chu's books of short stories into English, and I corrected the galleys. Tom later published his Ph.D. as *State and Society in the Taiwan Miracle*, a favorable account of state-directed economic development that was the first for Taiwan, but still not acceptable within Taiwan because of some frank depiction of the authoritarian state.

Other interest in my research came from a Professor Allan Schwartzbaum, on a Fulbright and teaching in Taichung once a week, an orthodox Jew from New York who still managed not to eat pork and not to travel on Fridays. He had been charged by the Asia Foundation with planning a conference on industrial relations to be held at Tunghai University, Taichung, in April 1978. Over a lunch at an eatery near National Taiwan University, he asked me to help him with contacts, and soon I produced a list of social critics from the *China Tide* group, plus a Taiwanese personnel manager from RCA who would talk frankly about management of the women workers. More to be said about this conference later.

My study of girl factory workers was not entirely separate from intellectual interest in the social critiques by the more daring local academics (e.g. Yang Kuo-shu 楊國樞, Hsu Cheng-kuang 徐正光, and Hu Tai-li 胡台麗 at Academia Sinica, and Chang Hsiao-chun 張曉春 in industrial sociology at National Taiwan University) and opposition figures. Yet in public conferences they only talked in abstract statistics; when at the end of a conference downtown I took the microphone and merely asked where was the flesh and the human experience in these statistics, a newspaper report denounced me by name, to my surprise.

Despite frequent flurries of activities with dissidents, no doubt what the government thought was a small group that could be easily contained, most of my time in 1977 was taken up with doing life histories of women factory workers, and preparing and administering a detailed questionnaire that could define a socio-economic "life trajectory", and relate it to the girls' aspirations for marriage and reproduction. My assistant Chiang Ying-chu was a stoic and steady worker, but in late November and December 1977 it gradually became apparent to me that she was becoming irritable and then tearful. I pressed her several times for what was wrong, before she finally blurted that she had been threatened not to tell, but that her fiancé Huang Chao-chou had been arrested while in military service, one of three students said to be involved with the case of Tai Hua-kuang 戴華光, an assistant lecturer at Tamkiang University, who allegedly sent anonymous threatening anti-imperialist letters to the foreign electronics manufacturers; one foreign manager had told me about receiving such a letter.

The students at Tamkiang University had held discussion groups on "toothbrushism" 牙刷主義, the increasingly-apparent phenomenon of government officials holding U.S.

chou visited his former cell-mate, while I worked in a publishing company downtown and compiled material about Taiwan history and culture that I eventually used for my Ph.D. A few times during that period, we had visits from KMT operatives who arrived with little or no warning at our front door. Seated in our front room, these people questioned Hua-chou about his views, his activities and his associates. My mail was read and there were other signs of censorship that I deeply resented. I began to sense that I possessed few skills to deal with the violation of my freedoms that the local people were accustomed to through long periods of repression.

One day in October 1979, Chen Lina, the wife of Chen Ying-chen, made her way in a panic to our apartment, yelling that Ying-chen had been detained. Although he was released a few days later, the uncertainties generated by this incident deepened my awareness about the complexities of our lives and the dangers that seemed imminent. My nerves were frayed and I began to doubt the meaning and value of my life living abroad in a place that was far from my home. At one point I felt I was coming down with ulcers. Even my health was being jeopardized. What Ai Linda was doing, and what the other people were doing, that was their decision to get more actively involved. But I wasn't sure whether I wanted to go that far.

Life became bewildering, especially in the wake of the Kaohsiung Incident that erupted in December 1979. By 1980 we had moved back to Taipei, and we were back more in the mainstream. We heard all about the arrests and the response on the part of the foreign community to the arrests. What everyone was trying to do to get information out of Taiwan, to get the outside community aware of the peril. We assumed that habeas corpus was being violated, and we were not sure whether the defendants were going to have a fair and open trial. Because it was court martial, wasn't it?

There were attempts to organize the families of those who were arrested, and to take care of their interests and to raise money for them. I remember going to some of those meeting organized by Chou Ching-yu (Mrs. Yao Chia-wen), and listening to their concerns. There were people like Nicki (Monica Croghan). She went in another direction, and she got very involved. And maybe also Vallaurie (Vallaurie Crawford). But I had decided that I had done my bit, and it was time for me to pull back. Perhaps I could help in different ways. I felt I could contribute by translating stories from the "native literature" movement and collecting information on Taiwan history and culture. I did start writing up articles, and I tried to get them published abroad, but they were rejected, maybe because people didn't understand what was going on here.

The day came in 1981 when Hua-chou returned to the apartment and informed me that his exit permit had been denied. With the impulsiveness of youth, I mused that our life together was over, destroyed by an abusive system that had little feeling for the rights, lives and emotions of others, foreigners and Taiwanese alike. The announcement was accompanied with no apologies and few explanations. In the days that followed, I was forced to ponder whether I possessed the ability to live on in a situation that, by the day, denied me the freedom to pursue personal goals that could lead to happiness. Soon after, I left Taiwan and, as I did so, I bade farewell to the confusion and pain that had haunted me.

Once I got back to Canada, it was really difficult, because I tried to explain to the

green cards and taking off a few weeks each year to maintain their U.S. permanent residence, like rats ready to abandon the sinking ship of the ROC at any moment. Like an extension of the Diaoyutai movement 釣魚台運動, this revelation could be considered either ROC Chinese patriotism, or a debunking of the hypocrisy of the Chiang regime. The police hesitated to crack down directly. But the Tai Hua-kuang case, which I believe was a genuine case and not a police ploy, gave the security agencies occasion to dampen student activism and also electioneering, ten days before the Provincial Assembly elections scheduled for November 1977.

I didn't know whether Huang Chao-chou's arrest had anything to do with my assigning him to photograph the multinational factories in north Taiwan, though it could certainly seem like circumstantial evidence for the Tai Hua-kuang case. I knew that Huang Chao-chou had written an article on the civil rights movement of American blacks for the *China Tide* magazine , and that that movement had become a sensitive topic in Taiwan military propaganda, i.e. black civil rights (and by extension Taiwanese civil rights demands) accused of infiltration by communist sympathizers. But now was the era of human rights as proclaimed by Jimmy Carter; the U.S. Embassy was required to pass on to Washington any reports of human rights violations. Within two days I wrote up a report on Huang Chao-chou and marched to the Embassy with it, perhaps mid-December. The tall man in a three-piece suit who received me sat back in his high swivel chair and turned away from me while he read the report. Then he swiveled back to face me, and said, with a slight sneer, "So you like those *China Tide* anti-imperialist types?" I was later to realize from subsequent incidents that probably from that moment I was blackballed by the Embassy, and dropped from further consultation for the Asia Foundation conference on industrial relations.

By about April or May of 1978 I knew for sure that the American Embassy was actively cooperating with the security agencies in my persecution. On a Friday night I met with a young American named Larry Riddle who was studying Chinese and political science (later a teacher at San Jose State University), and whom I hoped would join our document-smuggling operation; on Monday morning he was called into the Embassy and warned of further contact with me. Obviously Taiwan security agents had protested to the Embassy over the weekend. I heard vaguer reports from other quarters. A few months after the November 1977 election in which she was successful in reaching the Provincial Assembly with her human rights platform penned by a mysterious Hsu Yi-wen 許一文, Su Hong Yueh-chiao 蘇洪月嬌 and her husband 蘇東啓, a former political prisoner, asked me to accompany her to the Embassy to report on the KMT harassing her with a spurious travel agency violations case. Once admitted past the door, I was separated from her in a demeaning way, and she was assigned a translator who was no doubt a KMT informant and didn't know the background. The next year, when, in some contact with the Embassy, an official told me they were legally forbidden from keeping records on American citizens, I almost laughed in his face. About the Asia Foundation-sponsored conference on industrial labor, though frozen out of further preparations, my earlier name list of invitees already had the desired effect, and the government officials who appeared

Canadian community what was going on in Taiwan, that there had been this terrible case of political oppression, and demonstrations, and something should be done about it. But my words were falling on deaf ears. I went to local Canadian politicians, the NDP party, in British Columbia, which is quite leftist, and I explained. I also went to people in Amnesty International, and explained what was going on in Taiwan. I felt I needed to do something, get word out, but I didn't know how to go about doing that, so I felt quite frustrated. And then being back in Canada was such an enormous culture shock. My family and friends couldn't understand what I was talking about. Canadians are pretty complacent and apolitical, and everybody believes that Taiwan is Free China. How could there be these terrible things that you are talking about? Maybe in China under the Cultural Revolution. There were terrible abuses, political abuses. But Taiwan, it's this wonderful place, it has a fairly democratic government. People had this kind of outlook, and they couldn't believe what I was saying.

I mused that, during those seven years, I had helped a soul or two and had made friendships that I knew would last a lifetime. At the same time, I felt that I had trespassed and had strayed into forbidden territory that belonged to others alone. In doing so, I had hurt both them and myself. As I write this report, it is a warm spring day in New Zealand. As I gaze out at the warmth, I realize that there is no answer to the question of whether what I did was right, just as there are few answers to any questions about the power of fate, love and the choices we make. Gradually, I have come to accept the inexplicable nature of those choices and consign to the past my time spent under a dark, repressive regime in a little country located off the coast of southern China.

Election posters for KMT candidate for Taoyuan County Executive, Ou Hsien-yu.

Election poster for Provincial Assemblyman candidate Huang Wan-shen, touting his expulsion from KMT party membership, together with Hsu Hsin-liang.

at the April Tunghai University meeting of about 30 people met excoriating criticism from *China Tide* social activists. However, although Professor Chen, chairman of the sociology department, promised the proceedings would be out in June, no further record of it was ever seen. It took this personal experience with Embassy personnel for me to totally reject any belief in the democratic intentions of the United States, even though I would acknowledge that we owed some appreciation to the Jimmy Carter human rights policy. I don't know if anything useful came from my visit to the Embassy on behalf of Huang Chao-chou; I heard from my assistant Chiang Ying-chu that he was released from detention in March 1978 or so, but since he was still in the military he was under continuing harassment.

Finally the Lid Blows: The Chungli Incident

I have skipped by my own witnessing of the Chungli Incident of November 19, 1977. And my own involvement soon after came to a new point of decision because of this. I had met Hsu Hsin-liang at Chang Chun-hung's house a few months earlier. He showed me his book on KMT corruption in the Provincial Assembly and explained some of his strategy in going up against the Party – predicting the popular reaction against the KMT when he was expelled from the Party and ran for Taoyuan County Executive. It just happened that one of the factory girls I knew well was getting engaged in her home village near Kuanyin, Taoyuan, two days before the election. Aside from hearing about Hsu's campaign there, I visited the rallies of Hsu and his KMT opponent, a scion of the security agencies, Ou Hsien-yu 歐憲瑜, the evening before the election. Ou's rally was populated thinly by mainlander soldiers; when I got closer to the podium I discovered the applause was being broadcast from the speakers, not rising from the audience. In contrast, Hsu Hsin-liang, though addressing his audience in Hakka with his usual hesitant stutter, was surrounded by a rapt, dense crowd of thousands, his bald pate shining in the far distance under the lights. Hsu warned his followers ominously that if they wanted him to win, they would have to watch the ballot boxes themselves.

The next afternoon while I was still in Taoyuan County I heard that a crowd had gathered at the Chungli police station to protest a school principal manipulating the ballots. It was near twilight when I got there. It was indeed a huge crowd, at least 10,000, but strangely silent, craning necks to watch the scene in front of the unlighted police station. As darkness fell, I could barely make out teams of men systematically rocking and rolling over the police cars around the station. Then after a while a fire could be seen in the windows of the police station. It grew higher, up to the second floor, the flames licked the electric lines over the station, and then suddenly they exploded. The crowd stampeded briefly, but no one seemed to be hurt. There was a red public phone a few blocks away, and I ran and made a report by collect phone to some international newsman I knew, as I remember two international calls, to whom and by what means I don't remember. A ways from the crowd there were policemen surrounding the area, but they were being conspicuously polite, even smiling, as if afraid of becoming the object of public anger. Later there were stories that Chiang Ching-kuo flew over the area in a helicopter, and decided to let Hsu Hsin-liang and all

The day after the Chungli Incident of November 19, 1977. A crowd overturned police cars and set the police station on fire after a school principal was discovered engaging in election fraud on behalf of the KMT, and police failed to charge him. Pictures taken by Linda Gail Arrigo.

the opposition candidates win election without further vote manipulation that might enflame the population.

The sequel to the Chungli Incident was a hearing in the Provincial Assembly. Chen Chu came to get me early in the morning to take the train to Taichung; as I remember, it was my birthday, January 16, 1978. I knew that this was a public appearance on my part; Chen Chu wanted me to go with her, openly. I thought of Huang Chao-chou, fate still unknown, and felt this was the time to take a public stance. Chen Chu said deliberately, with some show of arrogance as if to dismiss our fears of the authorities, "The security agencies will not be happy. We do not require them to be happy."

Chen Chu and I got to the Provincial Assembly at about 11 am and went first to Chang Chun-hung's office before taking seats in the wooden balcony of the hall. I do not remember any other audience of dissidents, except the few who were members of the Provincial Assembly. The guards did not seem to know what to make of me, a foreign visitor, and did not interfere. After the lunch break the interlocution began. Chang Chun-hung's voice resonated throughout the hall; with his rhetoric in precise Mandarin, he warned the Kuomintang that it must not discard the people, or the people would discard it. (Later I understood that this was his usual rhetorical stance, taking up the voice of a loyal opposition to warn the KMT for its own good, which of course saw him as an enemy rather than loyal opposition.) Tsai Huang Yu-chao 蔡黄玉嬌, the representative from Taoyuan, a fiery middle-aged woman in the mold of the traditional clan-based Dangwai, presented the sequence of events in which a young man was killed when hit in the head by the firing of a tear gas canister, the trigger for the ransacking and burning of the police station. This was much more specific than I had known before.

In the 1990's I met industrial workers who were Hsu Hsin-liang's supporters, and they said that they set off the Chungli disturbance in coordination with his strategy for achieving election. Six or seven persons were given jail sentences, but probably not the planners.

The Axe Falls: Expulsion from National Taiwan University

Earlier I had heard some rumor, I can't remember from where, that the security agencies had noted my presence at the Chungli Incident and had also confiscated some materials I had tried to smuggle, and would deal with me. I did not know what that meant until I went to register for the spring semester at NTU, in late January 1978, a complicated process following from desk to desk in the gymnasium, and was told that I would not be allowed to register. The supposed rationale was that I had failed to take the examination in Professor Huang Ta-chou's class – I was an auditor, so of course I didn't take the examination. Huang Ta-chou 黃大洲 declined to make any clarification on my behalf. (Known as an obedient Party functionary, Huang later was appointed mayor of Taipei; but he was never good enough at double talk to get farther.) While I knew very well (by word from the Agricultural Extension Department's chairman, Professor Liao, who was wringing his hands) that the order to expel me came to the university from the security agencies, I did not let this pass

Letter to Lynn Miles Concerning March 18, 1978 Confiscation of *Long Live the Elections*

(Source: Retyped from Wu San-lien archives lynn081.07-005)

I am writing to you on behalf of Ms. Chen Chu (陳菊) concerning events which have occurred recently in Taipei. Two days ago I notified Mr. Chen Ku-ying of my plans to return to the U.S. for a visit. He sent Ms. Chen to my house this morning. Ms. Chen asked that I write to you immediately and relay to you her account of an incident which took place on March 18 and the morning of March 19 in Taipei. She also asked me to relay some requests to you and your organization.

The events concern the seizure of a book by Taiwan plainclothes police and security agents at the factory where it was being bound for publication. The book is a detailed account (complete with an excellent set of photographs — the first I have seen in any publication appearing in Taiwan) of the riot which took place in Chung Li (中壢) in Tao Yuan district (桃園縣) last November during the elections. It is entitled Hsuan Ju Wan Shui (選舉萬歲, Elections Forever) and is co-authored by a student at Chengchi University (政治大學) named Lin Cheng-chieh (林正杰) and Chang Fu-chung (張富忠). The incident developed in the following way.

On the afternoon of March 18 Ms. Chen was at the factory where the book was being printed. The owner of the factory informed her that police had been to the plant to inquire about the contents of the material being printed there. Nothing was taken, although in Ms. Chen's opinion they knew about the book and probably had obtained the cooperation of the factory owner. Ms. Chen says that she assured the owner that there should be no trouble, since the book had not yet appeared on the market. Pre-publication seizure was unlikely, although the book might later be banned.

Ms. Chen then took several printed copies of the book to another factory for binding. She was joined there by several friends who assisted in the effort to put covers on the books and expedite publication. About 8 people took part. While they were doing this, at about 6 p.m. 2 men (one a policeman in plainclothes and another from the Security Division (National Security Bureau?)) suddenly entered the factory unannounced and asked what they were doing. Ms. Chen and the others refused to cooperate or to show them the material, surrounding it to protect it from their view. The two men produced identification but no warrant and departed empty-handed. Ms. Chen immediately called their lawyer Mr. Yao Chia-Wen (姚嘉文), as well as the assemblyman (立法委員) Mr. Kang Ning-hsiang 康寧祥. Mr. Kang advised her to notify him immediately if any further incidents occurred, but told her that he would not be at home after 8 p.m. Mr. Yao came over to the factory immediately, accompanied by his wife and child. At about this time one of the authors, Mr. Lin Cheng-chieh, also joined them. Together they helped bind the books.

Some time later (about 11 p.m., I believe) about 12 plainclothes police and security agents suddenly entered the premises, accompanied by a "student counselor" from Chengchi University. They demanded to see the books. The "counselor" told Mr. Lin that the head of the school had the authority to demand to see what a student had written. Mr. Lin replied that his book was not a school thesis but his own project,

gracefully. Step by step I went up the hierarchy, and then I barged into the office of the Dean of National Taiwan University, the venerable old Professor Wu Huo-yao 吳活耀, and made him acknowledge that the security agencies had interfered in the affairs of the university. He seemed nearly on the verge of tears, and I almost felt sorry for this weak old man, accompanied by his sinister fifty-some secretary Miss Sa 沙小姐 who was obviously a security agency plant right next to him. (Fifteen years later I met an obstreperous Malaysian woman, his student, who said he named her "Linda" after me; she said that Wu Huo-yao had admired my courage, but there might be more than one reason for the name.)

Since I had already suffered the repercussions from involvement with the dissidents and human rights smuggling, I perhaps threw myself into it with more of a vengeance, with both anger at the treatment suffered by myself and others, and a kind of gleefulness at having already gotten away with a great deal. There seems to be a psychological process of developing resistance to authority: along with punishment, you find that the punishment can be endured or dealt with (at least the relatively mild consequences that I experienced as a foreigner), and also you recognize that the capacity of the police state to control and stop what you are doing is actually limited, in the face of persistence by even a small group of people. Finally, for me a strong motivation was a kind of general but personal love for, and desire to protect, people like Chen Chu who were determined to stand up for their own rights.

In general however I was intellectually closer to the *China Tide* group, and frequently had long discussions with Su Ching-li, the editor. She and some of her group lived at Garden City 花園新城, a new housing development in the hills south of Hsintien and on the way to Wulai. From the north side of Hsintien where I lived it took about 40 minutes to take the bus to Garden City, and then it was a long walk up the hill. I depended on Su Ching-li for political analysis and judgments of character. She was quite correct, I understood fairly soon, in her analysis of Hsu Hsin-liang and his populist manipulations, strategically using social issues and socially-committed youth to propagate his candidacy, but then bartering away that position to moneyed interests. Most of the Dangwai politicians had no pretensions to concern for social issues; for them the pervasive control and repression under the martial law of the mainlander Chiang regime was the obvious impediment to democracy, freedom of speech, and the opportunity for the populace to represent its own interests. In response to my pressing for a stance on social issues, Chen Chu once retorted that the Dangwai was already too busy with elections.

Lu Hsiu-lien's position in this was intermediate. In 1971 after she came back from obtaining an M.A. in law at the University of Illinois, she obtained a good job in a government bureau and held Party membership. However, she had greater ambitions, to shake up the status of women in Taiwan society. She wrote a book and many articles and introduced the issue of equality for women in legal and employment status to Taiwan, and she braved the vociferous attacks of the KMT old guard who slanted her words to imply that that meant sexual license. She recruited volunteers and set up a hotline for women in emergency situations. Lu Hsiu-lien,

and refused to cooperate. Meanwhile Mr. Yao was strenuously and angrily challenging the authority of the police to act as they had with no legal warrants or authority. The atmosphere was tense and angry. Ms. Chen tells me that Mr. Yao had earlier instructed her not to over-react to police provocation, since they had no authority to seize books that were still in press. On this occasion he was present personally to challenge them, and shortly the police left empty-handed. (However, this visit had not gone unnoticed in the neighborhood and Ms. Chen said that many people, including plainclothes police, could be seen at the mouth of the alleyway observing the visit on the second occasion.)

Meanwhile Ms. Chen had called Kang Ning-hsiang, who was not at home, and Chen Ku-ying. At this time it was decided that the 3 women present should leave, while the men should remain at the factory to protect the books. At the same time it was decided that the books which were already bound should be taken to Mr. Kang's house for safe-keeping. Mr. Yao departed with the books in his car, and Ms. Chen and the other women left for their homes. All those leaving the factory were followed by police. Mr. Lin Cheng-chieh accompanied Ms. Chen to her home (Ms. Chen also took a set of finished copies with her). This was at about 1 a.m. of March 19.

Not long after, at about 1:30 a.m., someone began to ring Ms. Chen's doorbell insistently. It was Mr. Lin, who had returned to tell her that "something bad" had happened at the factory. He warned her to hide any anti-Kuomintang materials in her home in case of a raid. Ms. Chen told me (I think) that Mr. Lin was accompanied this time by at least one other person, the "counselor" from his school, but if this is true he apparently was able to warn her in spite of this man's presence.

According to Lin's account to Ms. Chen, not long after she left, the neighborhood surrounding the factory (on Shuang-yen St.; I don't know the characters) was sealed off by police and martial law was imposed. Residents and all outsiders were forbidden entry. This included Mr. Hsu Hsin-liang, the newly elected head of Taoyuan district whose candidacy resulted in the tensions that touched off the Chungli riot. Mr. Hsu, who had also been called by Ms. Chen, arrived about this time accompanied by another lawyer and both were forbidden to enter the area by police even after identifying themselves. However, Kang Ning-hsiang, who by this time had returned home, and Yao Chia-wen were able to enter the factory, since Mr. Kang's home was in the same area under martial law. They confronted several agents in plainclothes (I think perhaps the total number of police involved was about 100) who had rushed into the premises to seize the books. Mr. Kang identified himself and began to argue angrily with them, challenging their right to seize the material. Mr. Yao joined in, but both men scuffled with police and were physically restrained from interfering with the police. The arguing and seizure continued until about 3 a.m. Approximately 3 truckloads of police, brandishing guns and rifles, maintained a tight cordon, and those police who entered the factory were also armed and made every effort to intimidate the people inside.

After the seizure the cordon was lifted. Mr. Hsu and the second lawyer were able to join Mr. Kang, Mr. Yao, and the others, and together they left the factory in the early morning.

Meanwhile, Ms. Chen was prevented from leaving her apartment by the presence of 2 men stationed to watch her apartment. By morning they had left, and she took

English name Annette, had a sense of social issues and of the need to motivate and mobilize followers with activities that let them speak and actively participate. She went again to the States in September 1977 to study at Harvard Law School under Professor Jerome Cohen, but settled for a second M.A. and came back in late 1978 to run in the national elections as an opposition candidate. Later she established her Pioneer Publishing House, and then was working on a venture that combined social innovation and commercial profit, a dating club for educated young career men and women, when the security agencies determined to run her out of business.

Ron Fujiyoshi reminded me by letter that bourgeois democratic movements were superficial, and suggested I stick just with labor issues. But despite this shallowness of social philosophy among the Dangwai, I could on occasion observe that the power of the grassroots was behind them in their struggle against the KMT, while the leftist intellectuals had their following mostly among students, and largely armchair at that. So I judged that social issues would not advance unless democratic rights were established, and human rights advocacy was basic to achieving democratic rights, however small a role I could play in this. I assumed my academic career would resume sometime in the future.

These ideological issues were important to me; more invidious was the struggle with my own feelings of weakness and helplessness, e.g. whether any action mattered in the face of such overwhelming forces of repression. Some sense of efficacy and human dignity was achieved just by the effort in resistance. But in action what was most difficult to surmount was the sense of propriety and social convention, of things in their proper place under an existing social order – as if by refusing to go along obediently and quietly with the conventions of martial law, by making a stink in insisting on your rights as framed in regulation (but which wordlessly did not apply to or protect those disloyal to the authority), you were doing something repulsive like blowing your nose in a pot of soup. Troublemakers were despised, disorderly, dangerous – and we felt this in the body language of the people around us, as well as in our own inhibitions. I had to be careful not to give away my own state of agitation; it was hardly possible to write anything down at such a moment because my hands were shaking. But conversely, when on some rare occasion I was thrown together with security agency personnel in a private situation, as waiting in a bus line, it was revealed that they secretly admired those who dared to challenge the authorities, and might feel diffident or even have a deep inferiority complex about their employment. These brief glimpses threw the relations of power on their head.

Occasionally I was followed when I went out from my residence. It seemed that young inexperienced agents were generally assigned to me. I watched a tall young woman, whether actually five months pregnant or fake, puff and sweat as she tried to keep up with me getting on and off buses in the summer heat. I knew the small gaps between the houses in my dead-end lane, and once I circled back behind the young agent who had lost me near a field of tall grass, and watched him jump when I greeted him. Small psychological victories, perhaps something to grasp at. The old mainlander neighbor whom I hired to fix my bamboo fence after a typhoon, and then

advantage of this break to move any incriminating material, together with the books she had removed from the factory, to a safer place. She had one of the copies with her when she visited me, but we decided it would be best if I did not attempt to take it with me on this trip. Mr. Chen tells me that they hope to mail all of the approximately 200 copies in Mr. Kang's keeping overseas as soon as possible and she hopes that in the future some mans can be found to publish it abroad.

To the best of my recollection that is her account. No one has been arrested or questioned thus far as a result of the raid, but the people present, including Ms. Chen, are being closely watched. Ms. Chen does not know what may yet happen, but as of now her situation is quite bad, especially because this is not her first trouble with the authorities. Thus far Mr. Lin has not been bothered by the police or school officials; this is his first involvement in an incident of this kind. But all are being closely watched.

Ms. Chen asked me to relay several requests to you.

1. Please send someone to Taipei as soon as possible to see her.

2. The cost of printing the book was about $200,000.00 N.T. dollars (about US$5,000 in 1978). If you can find funds to help cover this cost it would be a great help.

3. I will be seeing Mr. James Seymour of Amnesty International in New York to relay the same news. Ms. Chen wishes him to maintain closer contact with your people in Tokyo, since you are better informed about events in Taiwan.

4. Please notify Mr. Guo Yu-hsin（郭雨新）of what has happened. Tell him that Ms. Chen's present situation is not good. She feels that it would probably be best if she leaves Taiwan, but she sees little chance that she can do this. She also mentioned someone named Morris (I believe that's the name) whom she wished to know this news.

If you have any messages in the near future that you wish to have taken to Taipei, I will be happy to carry them when I return sometime in early May. You can forward letters to my home address (1207 Beaver Road, Sewickle Pa. 15143). Or, if you wish, you can contact me through Mr. Seymour in New York. It is possible that I will pass through Tokyo on my return, in which case I will certainly call you.

I have not been following events in Taiwan closely in the past few months, but from conversations with Chen Ku-ying, Chen Chu and others I have the impression that the situation is very difficult for them and likely will get worse. I hope that you can be in touch with Ms. Chen directly in the very near future. Ms. Chen is particularly anxious that I get this news to you by the fastest means possible.

Sincerely yours,

(Name has been cut out in the photocopy in the file, evidently cut out much earlier when this report was to be copied further and circulated. However, Lynn's note on the topic of the file is that the letter was probably penned by Helen Chauncey, and this seems to be confirmed by the home address near Philadelphia.)

retained for odd yard jobs, was often found standing below the window listening to conversations; I had to let him go. My local foreign affairs policeman, a handsome young man with a clear face, visited more and more often, obviously on assignment; but every time he came I gave him a full run down on the cases of arrests (current or past), closing of newspapers, and other security agency actions that belied "Free China," and his face seemed to yellow with each reluctant visit.

In July 1978, Becky Cantwell, Don Luce, and the civil rights lawyer Leonard Weinglass came through Taiwan, of course sent to me by Lynn, and I took them to tour the dormitory and meet industrial workers and a former political prisoner, from which they wrote the booklet *Made in Taiwan: A Human Rights Investigation* (New York: Asian Center Publication, 1978). This was one of many trips to Taiwan for Leonard Weinglass, who became a long-term legal counsel for Taiwanese-Americans in Los Angeles and later in New York; if I remember correctly, he told me that on one trip his hotel room was ransacked by agents.

Marriage to a Former Political Prisoner: Nori the Instigator

At any rate, in February 1978, faced with the threat of expulsion, I dug in my heels and schemed how to resist. I was not yet finished with my research nor with my human rights reporting. The obvious choice was marriage to a local, and I could not marry anyone except a former political prisoner, else I would be harming the partner by giving him a political association that would blot his future prospects. I will reserve for another day and another account the details of how I found (through Helen Chauncey and Chen Chu) and married former political prisoner Shih Ming-teh 施明德 (then a.k.a. Hsu Yi-wen 許一文, but known personally as "Nori" which is Japanese for "teh", virtue, the last character of his real name). In the light of later events, and particularly his championing the "Red Shirt Army" of 2006 that tried to depose the Democratic Progressive Party President, a man who stepped forward to serve as Nori's lawyer when he was on trial for his life, it is a difficult memory. But for the history of the time and for my personal history, it is not a decision that I would choose to undo if I had a time machine.

When Nori moved to my house in May 1978, the whole pace of my human rights activities escalated, and the repressive actions of the authorities towards us as well. Nori brought with him a cast of characters, each with his own story of torture and imprisonment and continuing police harassment. Half or so were mainlanders. The former Taiwan Garrison Command colonel of erect military bearing, who insisted on Sun Yat-sen's principles and ended up serving 15 years; now he drove a taxi. Major Chiang Yuan 姜元, air force officer, totally disillusioned after serving as a guard at the Presidential Office in the 1950's; just wanted to go home to his wife in Anhwei, but was caught in planning escape and severely tortured and imprisoned 22 years. He was still trying to go back to his wife. Yang Pi-chuan 楊碧川, self-tutored native Taiwanese Trotskyite, jailed for seven years from age 18 and nearly died from tuberculosis. Wu from Malaysia, touted as an anti-communist fighter and given a civil service job; but he complained a little too much, and ended up confessing to being a communist spy when his fingernails were pulled out. After 15 years jail

Linda Gail Arrigo and Shih Ming-teh married by signed agreement at the U.S. consulate on June 15, 1978, when Shih was reported in danger of arrest. Chen Chu was a witness to the agreement.

Linda and Shih held a formal wedding party on October 15, 1978 -- in effect a political gathering preparing for the year-end elections. Lei Chen, formerly jailed 1960-70, was the marriage witness. Lei Chen urged Shih Ming-teh to form an opposition party.

time, he was free and happy to be free of all possessions. I felt I saw laid out before me an astounding, explosive side of Taiwan's historical landscape that had never been revealed to me before. Walking down the street, we were occasionally greeted, "Nori, I thought you were still on Green Island!" and I came to sense that there were secret legions of former political prisoners, bereaved relatives, and security agency personnel as well. This was much more than I ever saw in associating with the Dangwai politicians and intellectuals. Yang Pi-chuan lived with us for a few months in the house on Dafeng Road, and also a young Japanese woman sent by Lynn Miles whom we gave the Chinese name of Ko Hui-hwa 柯惠華. But nobody remembers her real name now.

Despite this traffic at my house on Dafeng Road, Nori and I were not known outside of the circles of opposition politicians and political prisoners, people who hardly ever appeared in the public media, except rarely in government propaganda attack. However, I did play an increasing role for international media, especially with the deepening understanding I gained from Nori and his associates. When the outspoken newspaper *Taiwan Daily* 台灣日報 was forcibly bought out by the *Youth Warrior* 青年戰士報 in mid-1978, the ousted chief editor Wu Dze-lang 吳哲朗 came to my house and I interviewed him at length. I wrote this up in a report in English and distributed it to Lynn and to foreign press when they asked; I was moving to a slightly more organized method of operation, preparing fact sheets and narratives in English for journalists, to save time in translation and in the hope this would help them get names and facts right.

By mid-1978 I had also already collected a large portion of the 1,000 questionnaires and two dozen life histories I intended to do with young women electronics workers, plus some comparison groups of lower and higher status workers. However, due to inflation since I wrote up my research budget, finances were running short. One of the housemothers at the Teh Hua Dormitory, Theresa Yen-yen Yuan 袁嬡嬡, a tough young mainlander woman, a teacher of arts and crafts but also a black belt holder in judo with a solid square build, had been very supportive of my research since the beginning in 1975, and welcomed Chen Chu and other social critics to the dormitory as well. She tried to start an English class at the dormitory for me to teach, but the prospective students were intimidated by shadowy forces. Then I answered an ad for working in the compilation of a colloquial English-Chinese dictionary, an office with about a dozen employees near the train station. I was hired to work two days a week or so, and was very careful not to telephone home from the office. Most surprising, I found one of Nori's former prison-mates, a wiry Cantonese of about 60 surnamed Lee, was also working there; highly-educated, he had been jailed 10 years as a communist sympathizer. We spent several lunches in whispered communication about his experience, but unfortunately my presence made it more likely his past would be found out. It was less than two months on the job for me when the boss, a former KMT general, got orders from the security agencies to fire me. I refused to resign quietly with extra severance, instead informing all the employees about my political persecution; unexpected, the boss admired my spirit and told me in parting how he had lost all his paratroopers in the battle of Hainan Island when they were

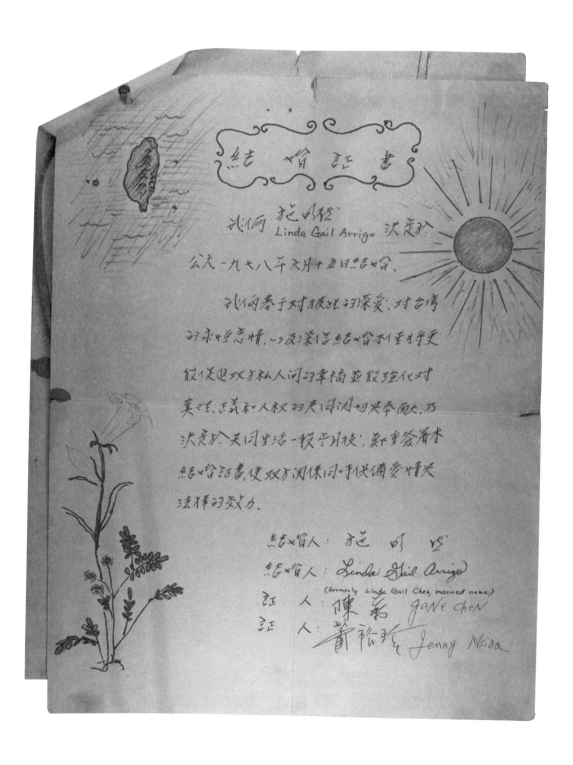

dropped into the ocean—the senselessness of the civil war with the communists. I didn't see Mr. Lee again.

Nori was actively attempting to mobilize students from Chengchi University (originally Chen Chu's recruits, such as Chiu Yi-ren 邱毅仁, a.k.a. Laba 外號喇叭, and from the Tainan Theological Seminary 台南神學院. He had also written and was beginning to distribute a small book with a bright green cover, "Suggestion for a Fourth National Assembly" that would in effect bypass the current geriatric bodies, a practical suggestion but including some jabs such as a reprint of a newspaper report about an 80-year-old National Assembly member who was unable to find his way home. Whatever the reason, about 8 am on the morning of June 15, 1978 as we were getting up, Nori received a telephone call that he would be arrested; that precipitated my decision to immediately carry through with registration of marriage at the American consulate, where the record could not be destroyed. Hsiao Yu-chen 蕭裕珍 and Chen Chu appeared there at 11 am to serve as marriage witnesses, and Nori immediately went into hiding after that. Chen Chu always laughs at the memory of two prospective brides showing up that morning. Whatever reservations I may have had personally, they were irrelevant to the immediate exigencies. I was sufficiently impressed with Shih Ming-teh's resolve to push forward for democratization and protection of human rights. And if I didn't marry him before he was (or was not) arrested, I would be deported in October when my visa expired.

Chen Chu is Arrested: But U.S. Intervention Foils the Garrison

That night Chen Chu's house was raided, and she herself was arrested late on the evening of June 23 when the security agencies traced her to the mission of Father Ron Boccieri in Lotsu, Changhua. That was the same evening that Nori returned to Dafeng Road, and I took apt revenge on him for the backup bride. All the same, we sprang into action as soon as we heard the news of Chen Chu's arrest the next morning. We could not make international telephone calls from my house; international calls required going to the main post office downtown, an hour's trip, and paying a deposit and using a telephone in a booth, of course recorded for surveillance. I slapped down my money and got a booth; fortunately Lynn Miles picked up his home phone right away, I delivered the information of Chen Chu's arrest within one minute, grabbed my change on the way out of the booth, and escaped from the post office. I was actually afraid that I would be apprehended on the spot. It was the first time I had made a direct report on an arrest, and Lynn Miles evidently made good use of it with immediate telex to Amnesty International and also mailings, also the first time such a quick reaction had reached AI.

Then I accompanied Nori to the apartment of my student, a young American military guy, in Tienmou close to the home of Chiang Wei-kuo. (I had been hired to teach Cultural Anthropology for spring 1978 in the University of Maryland program at the U.S. military base on Chungshan North Road. My student Kevin Burnor worked at the APO post office and also sent out packages for me, many for Chen Chu to Kuo Yu-shin.) What a place to hide; there were MP's all along the street. Nori lay low for a week, watching for signs of intent to arrest him.

When Chen Chu was finally released from custody and met with friends again, in a party in her honor on August 2, 1978, she suggested that Nori (Shih Ming-teh) and Linda Arrigo, married on June 15 by notary at the American consulate with Chen Chu as witness, hold a wedding party that would also kick off the election preparations.

The wedding party of Nori and Linda, on October 15, 1978, was the occasion for a gathering of about 400 opposition politicians and former political prisoners. Most celebrated among these was Lei Chen, the center of an effort to form an opposition party in 1969, for which he served ten years; Lei served as wedding certifier. Left, Dr. Tien Chao-ming, active in passing human rights information to Japanese visitors such as those sent by Miyake Kiyoko.

Nori instructed me to go buy a nightgown for Chen Chu and deliver it to the Taiwan Garrison Command, and then telephone all our friends to request concern for her. I found a beautiful turquoise-blue long gown, decorated with a red rose printed at the bosom, at the market for NT$200, and delivered it to the Chingmei Prison, within walking distance of Dafeng Road. It always required some steeling of nerves to walk into the Taiwan Garrison Command. We heard that Chang Chun-hung had delivered a basket of apples for her. But everyone who received my call sounded frightened and said as little as possible. Of course Nori knew the usual reaction to arrest, that all friends were chilled by fear and would deny close acquaintance with the arrestee, trying to put distance between themselves and the potential for arrest – the process of individualization that the security agencies counted on to squelch mobilization for the year-end elections. Hardly anyone telephoned or visited Nori and me for a long time; but still there had been some rudimentary effort at organization in the face of arrest. A group of the younger Dangwai in the next few days tried to get Kang Ning-hsiang to make a protest on her behalf, to no avail, although he acted at first as though he would lead in this effort. Kang Ning-hsiang had not taken well to my plan to marry Shih Ming-teh, in the first place; he joked that if he were the KMT, he would be smart enough to deport me right away.

The Chungli Incident had persuaded Chiang Ching-kuo to allow several important opposition figures into the Provincial Assembly (by not switching election results), as well as allow Hsu Hsin-liang's victory as Taoyuan County Executive. The Dangwai believed that the KMT would no longer dare to blatantly manipulate the balloting, and so their prospects for the December 1978 national elections were good. Chen Chu, nominally Kang Ning-hsiang's secretary since Kuo Yu-shin had gone to the United States, was the central coordinator of the Dangwai, and so her arrest struck at the impending mobilization, and filled us all with dread. We expected any day to hear that she had been sentenced to ten years for sedition; or that more arrests would follow.

In late June 1978 my mother Nellie Gephardt Amondson, a school teacher, came to Taiwan with my son Roger, and stayed with Nori and me for a few weeks. Despite the apparent strangeness of my activities, my mother, perhaps from her own family's roots in anti-slavery and civil rights campaigns, supported my human rights work and even my marrying a former political prisoner. My maternal grandfather Robert Gephardt was a vegetarian and a dedicated member of the Theosophical Society (a form of Buddhism/Hinduism that came to the U.S. from India in the early 1900's), and he believed Western/Asian marriage would produce a new enlightened generation; Harriet Beecher Stowe was a distant relative. Mother, Nori, Roger and I took a trip in late June through the neat Hakka countryside of Kuanhsi 關西 and Tahsi 大溪 that I was familiar with from many trips to the homes of girl factory workers. One morning when my mother went out walking early a quaint old Hakka woman came up, grasped hands with my mother, and was pleased to have her picture taken with my mother. In Tahsi my mother bought all the beautiful but worm-eaten carved wooden cornices that were being dismantled from an ancestor temple under refurbishment; it was quite a task to get them shipped.

August 1978

AN ACCOUNT OF CHEN CHÜ'S JUNE 23RD ARREST, DETENTION AND RELEASE

Chen Chü, 29 years old and a native of Ilan County (home address: No. 24, Yuen Mei Village, San Hsing Hsiang), was the secretary of Kuo Yu-hsin, the well-known legislator, since about the age of 19. Kuo left for the United States over a year ago, and especially since then Chen Chü has played an important role in the coordination of activities of non-Kuomintang (KMT) "party-less" candidates for election, and in publication of magazines and books critiquing the KMT's totalitarian and unconstitutional control of the government. She was instrumental in rallying college students to help in the November 19, 1977 elections, and later she helped in the publication of Hsuan-Chü Wan-Sui (Long Live the Election), a 446-page account of Hsü Hsin-liang's November 1977 race for Taoyuan county magistrate, how the campaign was organized and conducted, how Hsu ultimately overcame KMT dirty tricks and a wealth of well-funded tactics by the party machine to win by a landslide, and a close eyewitness of the culmination of the election day celebration -- the Chungli Riot -- penned by two of Hsü's campaign helpers, Lin Cheng-chieh and Chang Fu-chung. Hsüan Chü Wan-Sui fell victim to a midnight Taiwan Garrison Command raid in March, and the entire printing was confiscated at the binder's.

Two magazines that she had a hand in initiating and editing, Fu Pao chih Sheng (The Demo-Voice) and Hsin Sheng Tai (New Generation), were both banned after the appearance of only one issue each.

Chen Chü further helped arrange the printing of Hsü I-wen's Suggestions for a Fourth National Assembly, which came off the presses on June 9th. Hsü I-wen is the pen name for Shih Ming-teh, who served 15 years as a political prisoner from 1962 to 1977, but who went to work undaunted as campaign manager for Su Hung Yueh-chiao, now representative from Yunlin County in the Provincial Assembly and an outspoken defender of human rights in Taiwan.

On June 15, in the afternoon, Chen Chü accompanied Shih Ming-teh and American friends to the United States Consulate; on that day a warning had been received that Shih's book would be banned and the author arrested. After some other appointments, Chen Chu returned home to her 4th-floor apartment on Ching Tien Street, near the Moslem mosque in downtown Taipei, at about 11:00 p.m. She has one large room with attached bathroom, in an apartment shared with university students. The room is divided into two sections with large bookcases. Her younger brother was staying there on that day. Chen Chu had just finished washing some clothes and was going to sleep when there was a ring of the apartment door buzzer. A number of policemen requested a household registration check. After checking her ID card, they proceeded to ransack her room. She demanded that they show a search warrant, but they did not do so until several hours later. They shuffled through her voluminous files and shelves until about 5:30 a.m., then made a list of over fifty items and asked her to sign their confiscation receipt. Chen Chü and her brother rested until about 8:00 a.m.. Then she took a few items and told her brother not to worry about her if she didn't come back that evening; she was anticipating trouble, perhaps arrest, but she said she would do what she could to evade apprehension. Leaving the apartment, she found a car with four people in it waiting near her door. It followed her through several taxi trips to find friends and seek help. Finally the car was separated from her taxi at a stoplight. After a short visit with her lawyer friend, Yao Chia-wen, she left Taipei.

Ms. Chen spent several days resting at a Catholic mission at Lotsu, near Yuanlin, Changhua County. On June 23rd at 7:30 p.m., a Friday, the mission was surrounded by about thirty police. They demanded of the priest, an American of over eleven years' residence there, that Chen Chü be handed over to them. When she finally emerged from the room where she was staying, her arms were twisted behind her back by two burly policemen and flashlights were shined in her face. She was hustled off to a waiting van before she could say good-bye to the priest

Then in late July I caught a glimpse of Chen Chu on television, weakly recanting and asking forgiveness from the government. She appeared crushed and contrite, as no doubt the authorities wanted. The report said she would be released after a tour of the government's achievements. This was welcome news, but there was still unease over what information she may have divulged, or who had been implicated, during her interrogation. Later I interviewed her in depth, and sent a report on to Lynn. She had been interrogated, with sleep deprivation, for a week, and not allowed to wash or change clothes, despite personal needs. This would usually have been the prelude to a forced writing of confession and sentencing to a long term. At the time we heard rumors that she had been released under U.S. pressure, but it was not until the early 1990's that I received a detailed account from Harvey Feldman, formerly ambassador to Taiwan in the mid-1970's. During this time he had met and was well impressed by both Annette Lu and Chen Chu. In 1978 he was in charge of the Taiwan desk at the State Department. He said that he got news of Chen Chu's arrest from U.S. government channels, and on his own initiative just held up a Taiwan request for purchase of fighter jets on his desk until she was released.

I believe it was August 2 when Chen Chu returned to us. There is a happy picture of Chen Chu, Nori, and me at a restaurant near Taiwan National University. A few days later we had a gathering of about thirty people at a basement restaurant to celebrate. Chen Chu suggested that Nori and I have a wedding party, which would in effect be an occasion to kick off the upcoming election campaign. However, Kang Ning-hsiang poured cold water on her enthusiasm, and she failed to make the preparations. The simple logic for this was that Kang, up for re-election to the legislature, would be in danger of losing his seat if the Dangwai vote were split among more candidates. He no doubt saw his position of prominence challenged by the emergence of Hsu Hsin-liang, Chang Chun-hung, and Lin Yi-hsiung, all elected to the Taiwan Provincial Assembly in November 1977. From July 1978 or so Shih Ming-teh was in discussions with Hsu Hsin-liang to serve as campaign manager for a ticket of Chen Wan-chen (a young woman reporter at the Provincial Assembly, native Taiwanese from Changhua) and Chen Ku-ying (originally a Taiwan National University professor but purged from the Philosophy Department in 1971, a mainlander with a genteel manner and articulate Mandarin) in the Legislative Yuan/National Assembly elections in Taipei.

The Audacity of a Political Party in All But Name

By this time a secret coordinating group had been formed by the three new Provincial Assemblymen, plus Shih 施明德, and Yao Chia-wen 姚嘉文, a lawyer and friend of Lin Yi-hsiung 林義雄 who was also a candidate. Sometimes I was present at the furtive meetings, about twice a month, but I only partially understood Taiwanese. Since the three officials were very busy in their new roles, and Yao Chia-wen was still a practicing lawyer, only Shih (Nori) was fully devoted to political organization and coordination. Chen Chu seems to have been weakened psychologically and socially by her arrest; little was heard from her at this time. Nori received some small livelihood and expense subsidies from friends such as the usual photographer of the Dangwai, Chen Po-wen 陳博文. Nori worked like a man pursued by demons, racing

who sheltered her or even pick up her travel bag. She left with just the clothes on her back.

News of Ms. Chen's arrest was flashed in a New York Chinese-language newspaper, the Hsingtao Jihpao, on the same day [ed. note: in fact the Singtao Jihpao of 6/23 reported only that Ms. Chen had gone into hiding and that a Garrison Command arrest warrant was out; her arrest was first reported in that paper on the 24th]; and more detailed information about her appeared on June 24th and 26th. Newspapers in Taiwan denounced "subversive" American priests for the next day or two.

Chen Chü was whisked off to Taipei the same night, arriving there after 11:00. When she saw the massive gates of the Taiwan Garrison Command headquarters on Po Ai Road, she steeled herself to the resignation that she would not see the outside of prison walls for another ten years.

Upon arrival she was stripped naked and inspected. Interrogation began immediately. She was taken to a carpeted air-conditioned room; there was a bathroom adjoining and the walls were padded. She was told that she had been "invited" to talk, but she insisted on the fact that she had been forcibly arrested. Four persons, two men and two women, were assigned to be her "bodyguards." Two sat on each side of her during interrogation, and when she was allowed to go to the toilet the two women stood before the open door, and the two men stood just outside. Teams of four interrogated her at a time, some asking questions and some making notes. She saw over 30 people over the next few days, but five teams stayed with her over the period, in relays, through 24 hours. She was questioned and browbeaten with accusations without respite or rest. They tried to make her admit that she was a Taiwan independence advocate of violent overthrow of the government, and that she had connections with the communists.

Despite her physical condition and mental exhaustion, which deepened over four days without sleep or rest, she refused to accede to the Garrison's interrogators' accusations, and insisted that her participation in election activities is en-tirely legal and constitutional. She was confronted with the materials seized from her apartment, which included both Taiwan independence literature from the U.S. and leftist literature; and with a letter of hers concerning political prisoners, which was lifted from an American at the Taipei airport in January. Chen Chü admitted her concern for human rights in Taiwan.

Because the room was illuminated with artificial light, she soon lost track of time or even day and night, though she could count somewhat by the scheduling of the interrogators' meals. She was told she would be given what she wanted to eat, but had no appetite so merely drank some milk during the entire period. As she became more and more wrought up and exhausted, she sometimes sat with her eyes closed and refused to answer or respond to further questions. Then one of her interrogators would tap her on the knee and say, "Miss Chen, have a cigar-ette?" Sores appeared on her lower lip, and these were further irritated by the cigarettes, and became raw (Ms. Chen does not smoke). Her discomfort was heightened by the fact that she had begun to menstruate on the day before her arrest, and she had not been allowed to bathe since her forced stay at the "TGC hotel."

After four days of continuous interrogation, Ms. Chen sat on the floor and pro-tested that they had another ten years to question her anyway, so they could go ahead and kill her if they wanted, but she would not answer any more questions until she had been allowed to sleep. Then she was taken to a room with a bed and left there for one afternoon. But she was so exhausted that she was beyond the point of being able to sleep. Thereafter there followed days of the same routine, and the TGC ran her through a regular schedule of hours of interrogation, punctuated by meals and rest.

The TGC interrogators next demanded that she make a list of fellow activists in Taiwan independence activities, as well as assigning her the usual confessional self-biographical exposition, etc. They admonished her that Taiwan independence advocates were "being used by the Communists," and she responded that KMT abuses,

as though his time on this earth were brief, eating only plain noodles 陽春麵 outside of social engagements.

With the addition of the sponsorship of Huang Hsin-chieh 黃信介, elected life-long legislator in 1969, and the mechanism of the island-wide candidacy of the labor candidate Yang Ching-chu 楊青矗, an even wider project emerged in early October 1978. This was formally announced in Taichung on November 15: I gave this organization the translated name "the Non-KMT Candidates Campaign Coalition" 台灣黨外人士助選團, and it was in effect a nascent political party with a slate of about thirty candidates. (This was the earliest precursor of the Democratic Progressive Party, which was finally formally inaugurated in September 1986.) Shih Ming-teh was the general secretary. I was the unpaid English secretary. Deborah S. Davison, a friend of Nori's from her visit to the Lukang 鹿港 campaign of Su Hong Yueh-chiao 蘇洪月嬌 in November 1977, was also listed, as well as her friend David Gleit, but in November 1978 she was preparing to return to the States. (Bettine Birge, Helen Chauncey, and Debby met Nori when he served as Su's campaign manager under the alias Hsu Yi-wen, and all played some human rights role later.)

From this point on we were under the limelight with continual visits from foreign reporters, political scientists (Victor Li of the Stanford Law School, Richard Kagan of Hamline University in Minnesota), and visiting Taiwanese-Americans to the office in a grimy fourth-floor walkup on Mintsu West Road, a building provided by Huang Hsin-chieh a few blocks from his residence. Now my efforts were part of the political organization, not specifically human rights except as the organization met (frequently) underhand suppression, threats, and scattered arrests by the security agencies.

In late October 1978 former ambassador Harvey Feldman, then at the Taiwan Desk of the U.S. State Department, visited Taiwan and met with the major opposition figures, as Lynn learned from my letter of October 29 and many other sources.

The liaison headquarters for the coalition of candidates was just revving up when Nori was "invited" by the authorities to visit his old warden at the rehabilitation house where the political prisoners were sent for the last year before their release back to society, Ren Ai Chuang 仁愛莊, which can, shades of Orwell's *1984*, be translated as "Benevolent Love Villa." There was some reasonable doubt as to whether he would be free to leave after the "invitation." Nori mustered me, and I found two American reporters, Bill Kazer and Donna Liu, to accompany us on November 21 for this trip to the suburb of Tucheng 土城 on the southwest side of Taipei County. (This is reported in some detail in my November 26, 1978 letter to Lynn, Wu San-lien Archives no. lynn091.01-036.) This camp was a low-security prison in which the inmates lived in open military-style barracks, took political indoctrination and vocational classes, received frequent visits from their families, tended gardens (including a dense stand of small palms that facilitated conjugal visits), and improved their health and physical condition. The warden smoothly suggested that Nori go for studies abroad rather than bother with useless political activities. Despite the agitation of Nori's third elder brother, who had earlier also been visited by police with the same warning and who

Extract from Linda Letter to Lynn, 1978 / 11 / 26

Source: Wu San-lien Foundation archives, No. lynn091.01-036

November 26, 1978

Dear Vance,

Perhaps I have already told you in the last letter, but I don't remember, that Nori has been threatened. On November 5, the day of Chen Ku-Ing's very successful fund-raising dinner, at which Shih Ming-Teh and Wang Tuo were designated the joint masters of ceremonies, Nori's elder brother took the airplane up from Kaohsiung to talk to him. Third Brother had been visited by a plain clothes member of the Garrison in Kaohsiung, who warned that if Nori continued to be active in election activities, especially if he allied himself with the "leftist" Chen Ku-Ing, he was likely to be rearrested – whether or not he had a foreign wife. This has increased the emotional pressure on Nori, I can feel it, but it has not caused him to back down from his activities. He says he has a premonition that he will not live long.

On November 18 an administrator of the Panchiao "reformatory" called me up and asked very cordially if Nori would pay a visit to the head of the school. I asked if I could go along also, and that was approved. We went on November 21, and took along two American reporters, Bill Kazer and Donna Liu.

The reporters and I spent two hours on a guided tour of the premises (we have photographs too, and I may be able to get these from Donna and send them on to you with an article) while the head man very politely told Nori he was concerned about his future, and why, after all, did he have to go help those demagogues in their election. He insisted he had no orders from higher ups to warn Nori, but Nori felt from some phrases he let slip that the request to call Nori in came from official channels. We got another piece of news from Nori's brother in a letter, that the Garrison "welcomes him to go to study in the United States", i.e. "get out".

Huang Hsin-Chieh was also led to a meeting in Tainan – through a strange "non-availability" of airplane flights to Taichung – with the local police chief, who begged that Huang prevent any disturbances from occurring in his area. That was about November 15.

Political pressure on various people who are helping with the campaign has been felt – "reminders" through their schools or jobs.

All the same, there have been no election-related arrests, and no violent response yet to the literature which Chen Ku-Ing and also Nori have put out. Everything seems much more open than before. The dinner gatherings with political speeches are always well attended, and some incredible things have been said at them.

There seems to be more activity among high school students than among college students – in particular, rings of high school students whose political activities look rather like naughty pranks, distributing dangwai literature in government offices and putting up notices in the Sun Yat-Sen Memorial that it's about time the Three Peoples Principles were really put into action.

had gone to jail for five years in 1962 because of Nori, I saw no sign of Nori backing down.

The public organization of the Dangwai transformed our relationships and channels with overseas supporters and human rights organizations. For one, we were busy trying to disseminate public statements and get public recognition, rather than transmitting secret reports. For another, our contacts with overseas supporters became partially open as well. Eileen Chang (Yang Yi-yi 楊宜宜, wife of Morgan Chang張富雄) had just started a telephone call-up information service, *Voice of Taiwan*『台灣之音』, for her Taiwanese-American Presbyterian church community in Flushing and Jamaica, Queens suburbs of New York City, and she thought to telephone internationally directly to the number initially listed as the Campaign Coalition contact number, my house in Hsintien. I was surprised to get an international call, probably the first I had ever received in Taipei; as I remember, the service was only recently available, and having a telephone in the first place required a deposit of NT$16,000, over eight months income for a factory worker. Eileen recorded my account of the election preparation. Thereafter, she called regularly, or sometimes I called her collect, and the recordings were supplemented by news information and distributed to Taiwanese-American telephone services throughout North America. (Eventually by late 1979 there were over thirty lines in Hokkien, Hakka, and English, and a card with all the numbers had been widely distributed so anyone landing in North America or Japan from Taiwan could call locally. But then I did not understand the wide impact of it.) It was not until later, however, that others, at first Nori, were recorded on the phone: communication with overseas Taiwan independence organizations could be framed as sedition by the security agencies. (The recordings of the Voice of Taiwan have been fully transcribed into Chinese and published by the Wu San-lien Foundation, December 2006. See *Witnessing the Kaohsiung Incident –Selected Tape Recordings of Voice of Taiwan* 《見證關鍵時刻・高雄事件—[台灣之音]錄音記錄選輯》吳三連台灣史料基金會 2006年12月10日刊行.)

However, I had my own project in helping the labor candidate Yang Ching-chu; I made up a set of twelve cartoon posters illustrating labor issues. This project was undertaken together with an NTU Sociology student, Ke Chih-ming柯志明 (son of former leftist political prisoner Ko Chi-hua 柯旗化, more renowned as the author of a popular text for learning English), now head of the Institute of Sociology at Academia Sinica; and it was illustrated by the popular cartoonist Coco (whose real name is Chen Yung-nan 黃永楠).

The island-wide candidacy of Yang Ching-chu served as a device to allow the stars of the Dangwai, National Legislator Huang Hsin-chieh and the newly elected Provincial Assemblymen, to appear on the platforms of all 30-some candidates throughout the island. Otherwise, the KMT election regulations required registration of all campaign speakers, and forbade campaigns from sharing speakers – a means of preventing formation of party-like campaign slates. But this restriction was broken through with the momentous meeting at Chung Shan Tang中山堂 (the Sun Yat-sen Auditorium, venue of the National Assembly 國民大會) on December 5, 1978, that

The Campaign Coalition occupied a fourth-story walk-up on Mintsu West Road that was provided by permanent National Legislator Huang Hsin-chieh, whose brother Huang Tien-fu was also a candidate in the December 1978 elections.

The logo of the Non-KMT Candidates Campaign Coalition, a de facto political party founded in November 1978. "Human fist" in Chinese is a homonym for "human rights."

Yao Chia-wen, candidate for the December 1978 national elections, being interviewed by foreign media at the home of Linda Gail Arrigo. From late 1978 Yao and Shih Ming-teh carried out the main administrative activities of the united opposition forces, as executives for the undeclared leadership of five (also Hsu Hsin-liang, Lin Yi-hsiung, and Chang Chun-hung, all elected officials).

Yang Ching-chu, a worker at the state-owned oil refinery near Kaohsiung and an emerging author of native Taiwanese literature, ran for the island-wide office of labor representative, thus overcoming the restrictions on campaign speakers appearing in more than one district.

kicked off the ten days allowed for electioneering. As National Legislator, Huang was able to reserve it. Billed as a press conference for foreign reporters, the Dangwai in effect formed a *de facto* political party with an assembly of several hundred persons in the heart of the KMT's power structure, surrounded by hundreds of police and twice forcibly disrupted by a dozen "anti-communist heroes." The clenched fist with its incongruous olive branches, logo of the Campaign Coalition, loomed three-feet tall behind the center of the stage. The joint platform of the candidates of the Campaign Coalition (penned by Nori), calling for the end of martial law and political surveillance and the full popular election of the central government, was soon followed by an ultimatum that all offices of the Campaign Coalition would respond to attempts to suppress any one. The "anti-communist hero" surrogates for the KMT characterized this last statement as a threat by the Dangwai to Chungli-ize (referring to the burning of the police station) the whole west coast of Taiwan.

The election was abruptly cancelled on order from Chiang Ching-kuo on the morning of December 16 when Jimmy Carter announced agreement with the Peoples Republic of China for formal recognition to commence January 1, 1980. Many have suspected that the date of the announcement, just two days before an election in which the native opposition was poised to make great symbolic gains (the national bodies still were virtually frozen since 1949, 90% devoted to representation of mainland China), might have been the Carter administration's booby prize to Chiang Ching-kuo; but from scattered information I believe that the U.S. did not in the least consider the effect of that timing on Taiwan internally.

After the election cancellation, Nori spent a week traveling around Taiwan and then understood the tremendous impact of the traveling Dangwai stars and the Campaign Coalition in providing an advanced political ideology and a framework for island-wide coordination. While all the news organs were shouting hysterically about the betrayal of Free China by the United States and the treacherous fifth-columnists and communist sympathizers among the locals who criticized government policy in this moment of need when all citizens must unite against the communist threat (as school children donated their pennies for national defense armaments), the leadership of the Dangwai demanded control over the future of Taiwan be wielded by the people of Taiwan. There was a general sense of crisis that China could stage an attack on Taiwan at any moment, or that Chiang could announce a resolution for reunification with the PRC. Indeed, Lu Hsiu-lien's campaign had focused on the issue of the future of Taiwan, together with the distribution of her book that she had prepared while abroad, *Taiwan's Past, Present, and Future*. The imperative to challenge the KMT at this moment separated those demanding change from those who did not dare step much beyond a "safe" level of dissent. Kang Ning-hsiang made it clear he would not act together with the provocative Campaign Coalition, though he had participated in the Sun Yat-sen Hall 中山堂 inauguration. There were reports, later partly substantiated, that the security agencies were spreading rumors that the Americans had smuggled guns and police uniforms to Hsu Hsin-liang to prepare for an uprising – the kind of advance rumors of outrageous plots against the government that in the past were used to make subsequent announcement of large-scale political arrests more palatable

The public inauguration of the Non-KMT Candidates Campaign Coalition in a "press conference" of December 5, 1978, a few days in advance of the officially-approved ten days of electioneering. The slate encompassed about thirty candidates.

Yang Ching-chu, candidate for labor representative island-wide, allowed the opposition to overcome restrictions on campaigning across districts and form in effect a political party.

The candidate Hong Chih-liang from Changhua, signed on to the Campaign Coalition, was fated to play a reluctant role in a secret police scenario a year hence.

Professor Chen Ku-ying, a mainlander intellectual expelled from Taiwan National University in 1971 and long active in human rights work, ran for National Assembly.

Linda Gail Arrigo served as English secretary for the Campaign Coalition.

to the populace.

Nori planned the next event approved by the secret leadership core as carefully as guerilla warfare, beginning wider notification (when it was assumed the security agencies would catch wind of it) less than 48 hours in advance. He rented the top floor of the Ambassador Hotel for noon on December 25, 1978 for a meeting of the Dangwai, with the secret preparation of a "national affairs statement" demanding the end of martial law and the right to democratic determination. But on Christmas day the Ambassador Hotel was totally staked out by black vans and plainclothesmen by mid-morning, and the doorway to the hall was papered with a sign saying "closed for renovation." The fallback plan was to convene at the Campaign Coalition office, and by about 2 pm twenty or so persons had gathered quietly and signed the statement. First among them was Yu Teng-fa 余登發, the old founder of the Dangwai family clan in Kaohsiung, the "black faction 黑派", who had in earlier years been removed from office and jailed by the KMT. Yu's continuing role as local kingpin was shown in that his son-in-law was the head of Kaohsiung County, and he had fielded several candidates in the election. At the beginning of the campaign he thought these Taipei intellectuals couldn't do anything for him, and he ignored the Campaign Coalition; but suddenly in the middle he printed huge numbers of "human rights fist" logo decal stickers, about four inches across, for all his candidates. Now he had come to Taipei prepared to bankroll a new challenge to the KMT, and he was the first to sign the statement signature page, in clear large characters.

There was relative quiet for a week while the government braced for the visit of the Warren Christopher mission which was to "explain" U.S. policy. High school counselors (the usual KMT arm in the schools) organized a "spontaneous" mob of high school students to attack the Christopher cavalcade as it departed. At the same time, on December 31, 1978, Nori and I and probably other Dangwai leadership as well were totally staked out and followed by security personnel, apparently to prevent our attempting to make contact with the Christopher mission.

"Martial Law in No Longer a Virgin": The Chiaotou March

In the following three weeks Nori went down to Kaohsiung twice for planning with Yu Teng-fa. The plan was to hold Lunar New Years banquets starting from Kaohsiung and moving north, occasions for issuing thousands of copies of the National Statement. Late on the evening of January 20, 1979, there was an informal meeting of a dozen dissidents at Su Ching-li's apartment in the Garden City suburb, to listen to Professor Huang Yueh-chin's 黃越欽 take on labor issues, and continue with an all-night discussion. Nori, back from Kaohsiung, came straight from the train station some time after midnight. Not one to be totally deprived of sleep, I probably slept on the carpet for a few hours. At 6 am or so Su Ching-li got an electrifying telephone call: Yu Teng-fa and his half-witted son had been arrested, implicated in some communist association. The date was January 21. Hurried plans were made for a meeting at Lawyer Chang Teh-ming's office in mid-morning; Nori was to immediately inform others. Under these circumstances, we would scatter but preferably not return to our houses since they were probably staked out by agents. I took a taxi down the

Following the December 16 cancellation of the elections when the United States announced impending recognition of the Peoples Republic of China, Yu Teng-fa and the twenty-some most determined dissidents on December 25, 1978 signed a new demand for the end of martial law. Huang Hsun-hsing left sitting, Shih Ming-teh and Chen Chu standing. Photograph taken by Linda Arrigo.

The Chiaotou march of January 22, 1979, protesting the arrest of elder statesman Yu Teng-fa, in his hometown in Kaohsiung County: The first such protest since the massacres of 1947.

自稱「國際赦免組織工作者」的美籍艾琳達
與其夫施明德遊行煽動群眾。

In 1980 the Government Information Office produced a booklet with a picture of Linda and Nori (taken at the Chiaotou march) "inciting the masses."

Two women, Chen Wan-chen, left, and Chen Chu, right, headed the Chiaotou march.

Tseng Hsin-yi, feminist author and second-generation mainlander, shrilly drove off police harassment.

mountain together with Prof. Chen Ku-ying and two others. Halfway down, Prof. Chen began laughing inexplicably. I looked at him quizzically. "The KMT always says they are apprehending important communist spies, but all they catch are us little mice!" he quipped with incongruous glee.

It was close to 11 am but dull under a gray sky when a dozen or so of our usual dissident circle, both right and left, had glumly assembled at Chang Teh-ming's office. Hsu Hsin-liang made the first concrete statement: if we do not react to Yu Teng-fa's arrest together, we will be picked off one by one. Chen Ku-ying immediately seconded this view. No one disputed it. It seemed that the plan to visit Yu Teng-fa's home, in Chiaotou, Kaoshiung County, early the next morning for a concerted demonstration of concern was formulated quickly; few spoke. No doubt texts of political trials echoed in everyone's heads: trials that quoted the confessed evidence of the prisoner having urged seditious actions in secret meetings. Nori prepared to execute his part, visiting the Dangwai members of the Provincial Assembly. Notifications of others were to be made in person without the use of telephones. Su Ching-li would man a telephone for later coordination and communication in Taipei. It was dark when Nori and I took a long-distance "wild chicken" taxi (sharing with others) from the Taipei train station, without going home for clean clothes, and ended up in the Provincial Assembly outside Nantou when it was still dark on January 21/22; the Provincial Assemblymen had small suites for private quarters. There were hurried, hushed consultations for diffused travel to the site of the demonstration while I dozed on a sofa, and we slept briefly at the home of Nori's former political prisoner friend in Kaohsiung, Huang Chung-kuang 黃重光, before we set out again.

We arrived at Yu Teng-fa's home near the market center of Chiaotou: a narrow shop-front-like house facing on the street, parlor and several rooms deep to the back. Some of his supporters were there, and well-known Dangwai figures strolled in in twos and threes. By about 10 am the police realized that something was afoot, and the police chief barged in for a while to harangue those gathered and issue vague threats to Yu's daughter. As time for the secretly planned demonstration was being frittered away in indecision, the intrepid woman reporter Chen Wan-chen and I hatched a side-plot. I ducked out to the market to buy cheap cloth and ink, and within about forty minutes working in the loft above the back room, Chen Wan-chen and I produced rough red name sashes of those present and large white banners tied to bamboo poles protesting the arrests. We quietly brought these downstairs. A written statement had been prepared and copied earlier at the Provincial Assembly.

Somehow the will to act was galvanized and overcame the images of 2-28 that were no doubt playing in many heads: immediate arrest, maybe even machine guns. The column of forty persons or so, about half of the marchers Yu Teng-fa's local supporters, made a slow wide loop around the market area. Plainclothesmen clicked pictures from the roofs. Chen Po-wen recorded the Chiaotou demonstration for our posterity, and I took pictures as well, which were sent immediately to Lynn as undeveloped negatives. A picture of me taken by the agents, published in a 1980 Government Information Office-sponsored hate booklet, shows me marching by the

U.S. Air Force Mailman "Trying to Make a Difference on Behalf of the Taiwanese People"

by Kevin Burnor

I was in the American Air Force serving PACAF in the AeroPostal Division out of the Phillipines, but stationed in Taipei serving the Navy for the most part by working at the Sung Shan Air Base as a warehouse laborer basically, as well as being responsible for processing of registered mail and delivering loaded igloos to the departing aircraft en route to their respective destinations. Later I moved to the Chung Shan North Road American Military Compound where I worked as a public mail clerk. During my months at Sung Shan Air Base I was also responsible for weekly mail runs to Kaohsiung and Tainan as I remember.

I remember the first day I arrived in Taiwan. I stayed just outside the military compound in a hotel on about the 7th floor. There was no elevator. The city was a mixture of urban and rural as large buildings shared were attached to vacant lots where one could find a water buffalo, chickens, a pig, etc. One thing that comes to mind is the trash truck. They were playing what Americans consider ice cream truck music. Instead of everyone rushing to the truck for ice cream they were rushing to the truck with their trash. I also remember the great deals on tailor-made clothes. I designed a few outfits myself and had the local tailor, Lee I believe, make them for me.

I had many friends in the local community. As I remember, I lived on Tienmou 1st Road, No. 22. I had a great two bedroom apartment on the third floor. My friend Gail Parton was a Navy nurse who lived on the second floor. We shared an amah once per week who cleaned our places as well as our clothes for a song. Practically every day when I returned from work I would have brown eggs, tofu, and seaweed at the little restaurant on the first floor owned by my landlord.

My experiences eating food on the streets began with chicken feet and noodle soup. Whatever it was it was 25 cents in U.S. money. As I sat there trying to learn how to use chopsticks I witnessed mangy cats and rats prowling around where I was eating. The noodles and the feet were great. I never got sick from the food the entire time I lived there. Including the time I was eating with the Chinese soldiers at the Sung Shan Air Base and noticed that my mouthful of green beans had something crunchy. I realized it was the other half of the large cockroach staring me in the face. I moved it aside and finished my lunch. As regards dog meat, I never ate dog. I did drink snake blood mixed with rice wine at the night market. I also drank snake blood fresh out of the snake with the sex organs in the glass also. I tasted the blood for about three days as it was not diluted with rice wine and stuck to my mouth forever, it seemed.

As I first remember Linda Arrigo was my Anthropology professor in February-June 1978 at the University of Maryland, Extension Program, Taipei Campus on the military base on Chung Shan North Road, and I attended evening courses towards by bachelor's degree.

What is memorable for me about our time together is serving the human rights group exposing corruption of the Kuomintang under Chiang Ching-kuo, son of Chiang Kai-shek, who I now know to be a CIA puppet responsible for atrocities of 228, for example. I helped with this by sending information to Amnesty International Offices in Tokyo, Japan, and San Francisco and New York, USA.

side of Shih Ming-teh, incongruously gleeful. I remember trying to look solemn as everyone else was, and wondering whether I should avoid marching in the column because of my foreign nationality (not for safety, rather for lack of citizenship entitlement), but there was a strange and happy exhilaration in finally being able to openly express public outrage after all the acts of aggression that the KMT had perpetrated on us.

As the group stopped to offer prayers for Yu at the local temple, Tseng Hsin-yi 曾心儀, a delicate-looking second-generation mainlander young woman known for feminist novels, was confronted by a policeman and she shrieked at him like a harpy. (The police seemed inhibited in dealing with mainlander women, whereas they could easily take on roughing up dark-skinned Taiwanese men; Tseng Hsin-yi often proved her worth until she began to suffer nervous ulcers and dropped out of demonstrating.) Tseng Hsin-yi was later famously quoted: "Today the KMT's martial law order is no longer a virgin; we raped the thirty-year old virgin!" 「國民黨的戒嚴令已不是處女了，我們已強暴了這個三十歲的老處女！」 (Shih Ming-teh's account of the Chiaotou march, dated January 29, 1979, was published in *Formosa* magazine No. 4, November 25, 1979, pp. 82-88; Tseng Hsin-yi's quote is on page 88.)

Now that the protest, the first since 1947, had been openly performed and found the police unprepared, new plans were hatched. We would distribute a mimeographed statement at the railway station, and then charter a bus for the group to go back to Taipei. At the railway station I strayed a ways from the rest of the group and was encircled by shouting police and agents; but Nori led a phalanx of supporters to grab me back. Under Su Ching-li's telephone coordination, the bus and supporters in Taipei converged on Kang Ning-hsiang's home in Wanhua 萬華 (Manka, the most historic area of Taipei) at 6:30 pm. Kang, originally the leading Dangwai National Legislator though junior to Huang Hsin-chieh, and cultivating special relations with the KMT, was thought to have the power to be instrumental in requesting Yu Teng-fa's release; and Nori evidently wanted to heal the rift in the Dangwai. Kang, with a great deal of bluster and bravado, announced that he would negotiate tomorrow with the Taiwan Garrison Command and demand that Yu and his son be released, or else … tomorrow we would meet again at his house to decide on action. Those of us who had dealt with Kang before when Chen Chu was arrested in June 1978 felt a sense of deja vu, that he was actually defusing protest, and no doubt expecting brownie points from the KMT for his ambitions to be head of a ministry. Tseng Hsin-yi stood up and denounced Kang to his face. A few dozen people showed up at Kang's house again the next evening, but he came late and said he couldn't get a channel to the Garrison, or some such, and disbanded the meeting inconclusively.

However, the news of the Chiaotou march, though only reported in a few obscure sentences in the press, immediately rippled through the grapevine and drew a tremendous response. Theresa Yuan 袁嬿嬿, the housemother at the Teh Hua Dormitory, insisted on meeting with me as soon as she saw the newspaper, and instantly became one of the most militant and dependable activists of the Dangwai, particularly in regards to human rights reporting. She probably would have

I had a girl friend from Germany at the time who was also a tutor for the children for Chiang Ching-kuo's son. She gave me information about personal and private possessions and actions of Chiang Hsiao-wu which I passed on to Linda and got published in the underground newspaper Chao Liu. Later people involved with publishing Chao Liu got arrested.

Right after Linda and Nori got married by notary on June 15, 1978 when it looked like Nori would be arrested, I gave Nori shelter as there was fear for his well-being and possibly life as well. Linda and Nori stayed at my apartment, secretly, for about three days then, and again later. I lived in Tienmou and my house was right next to that of Chiang Wei-kuo, the brother of Chiang Ching-kuo. I took Linda and Nori up on the roof to look down at his compound, and we joked that we could easily dump a barrel of pig blood down on it. He was a military general responsible for a tank rolling up on some building on Roosevelt Road during some show of force by the Kuomintang against the opposition, as I remember vaguely.

I was one of six best men at Linda's wedding party on October 15, 1978. I went also in order to receive one large manila envelope containing similar documentation which I sent on to Amnesty International as well.

Once Linda and I took a hike through the countryside and a jungle where we found an old homestead with various wooden tools. I saw a chard of a clay bowl on the ground which ended up being a bowl which was intact but had been repaired with a piece of tar where there had been a crack. I had never eaten dog, which I still have not, and we joked about eating Linda's puppies. We also attended a couple of shui jiao (pork dumpling) parties on Yangmingshan (Grass Mountain).

Prior to the normalization with China the social climate was great. I knew of nothing negative between the American military and the local peoples. As you must remember, ships would come in regularly and many service men contributed to the local economy in many ways. To be more exact with regard to the issues surrounding Carter normalizing with China and recognizing the PRC rather than the ROC, here's my account.

I believe it was 19 Dec 1978 when it all went down. It was about 2:00 pm and I believe it was a Saturday afternoon, but I cannot be sure. I was working at the time at the Post Office in the U.S. military compound on Chung Shan North Road. A civil service person came into the lobby and was quite distressed as she reported that Carter had just normalized with China and all Americans were in jeopardy. None of us had been warned of what was to happen and we had no time to prepare. Within no time at all there was a crowd at the front gate; local nationals were storming the compound to express their negative feelings about what had happened. I believe a flag was burned out at the front gate but I cannot be sure. We were ordered to close up and go home.

I lived in Tienmou at the time. I don't remember how I got home without any trouble but I did have my 1965 mustang at the time, as you may remember, so I probably drove home. I didn't have any trouble with my neighbors as I was friends with all of them, but someone did spit on me as they passed me on their motorcycle. I remember saying, " Wo shi Deguoren. Wo ye bu shi Meiguoren." (" I'm German, and I'm not American.") Ha ha ha!!! It was more a joke than a betrayal.

My friend Joseph Keri was stabbed at the China Seas NCO Club along with some others who were trying to stop angry locals from rolling and burning the cars there. That is all I can tell you about Joseph except he and I studying martial arts together with a northern Shaolin master on a terrace downtown. Our master was famous for some of his feats. He could palm a 5-gallon glass water bottle. I remember being there each day at about 4 am. I also remember the children lining up for school or school bus. They were all in uniform and stood rather quietly and quite orderly which astounded me as they were anywhere from five years old and up. I believe we studied near the plaza where it was rumored a mass grave

gone to jail after the Kaohsiung Incident, except that her father had been a senior KMT general. The next demonstration was planned for the next weekend, at the Kaohsiung County Executive's official residence, and 200 or so people showed. The Executive, Huang You-ren 黃友仁, that is, Yu's son-in-law, and Chang Chun-hung were persuaded by liberal KMT figures to call off the march. The next Saturday, February 4, in the Lunar New Year vacation period, even more people gathered at the Taoyuan train station and marched to Hsu Hsin-liang's official residence with a large sign board (as usually bestowed for official awards and hung on a wall in commemoration) inscribed "Human Rights Forever." Huang Hsin-chieh announced that a human rights organization would be formed, and Lin Yi-hsiung supported this proposal strongly, but in practice nothing came of it at the time (see Linda's letter to Lynn, February 12, 1979, pp. 1-3, in Wu San-lien Archives). But from this point on, droves of people connected through diverse grapevines, but particularly working class people in self-employment, flocked to the activities of the democratic movement, to the point that the snowballing could hardly be controlled by the leadership. The mass activities broke down the sense of helplessness in isolation and the individual's fear of reprisal from the KMT. It was not so much a matter of the logic that the KMT couldn't identify everyone if so many people were involved; it was a transformation to a hope and belief that change must come.

In my opinion, the formation of the Campaign Coalition and the Chiaotou march, a development in the short period of October 1978 through January 1979, was the crucial breakthrough in the coalescence of organized resistance to martial law. Of course this built on the gradual accretion of grassroots opposition and student participation, especially from the election campaign of Kuo Yu-hsin in Ilan in 1975; from the native Taiwanese intellectuals Chang Chun-hung and Hsu Hsin-liang that were purged from the liberal KMT magazine *The Intellectual* 大學 and joined Kang Ning-hsiang's strategic challenge to the KMT, *Taiwan Political Review*; and the crowd action of the Chungli Incident in ransacking and burning down the police station, a riot which provided a counter to the KMT's previous monopoly on political violence.

Of course on this level the interaction moves far beyond liberal appeals to human rights and the conscience or international embarrassment exerted on the oppressor. As the activities, grassroots mobilization, and formal organization of the opposition continued to escalate through 1979, there was an internal critique (by Lu Hsiu-lien, among others; her 1997 book *Retry Meilitao* 『重審美麗島』 still maintains this position), that this provocation to the KMT would exceed its tolerance and lead to a costly crackdown; it would be more advisable to proceed more slowly to stretch the limits of tolerance, and appeal to the respectable liberal intellectuals and seek their influence on the KMT. In my view, the events of September 1979 at the formal inauguration of *Formosa* magazine that Lu Hsiu-lien tried to make a glittering event attended by influential literati, proved that the KMT's security agencies would allow no such dignified liberal opening for the opposition. The liberal-sounding faces of the KMT such as John Kuan 關中 had no real power to negotiate, no personal commitment to democratic opening, and were themselves cowed by the security agencies; they were only window-dressing meant to placate and perhaps buy off

exists from the 228 massacre.

I believe there was also a local national who doused himself with gasoline and set himself ablaze on Roosevelt Road. [Editor's note: at that time the U.S. 13th Air Force Base was located near Kung Kuan on Roosevelt Road. There is no confirmation of Kevin's report on this.]

The U.S. military compound was trashed and our cars were rolled and burned. I also witnessed the government stage university protests during this time as well. The U.S. military was ordered to leave Taiwan in compliance with an agreement with China. After a short time the US allayed the concerns of the Taiwanese and the Taiwan government by explaining they would remove the U.S. military and U.S. Embassy but would maintain a center for trade and would not allow China to take over Taiwan. Things seemed to settle down and an official agreement was in place soon afterwards. I was ordered to move into the Grand Hotel where I lived for two to three months before leaving in April 1979. I was the last military enlisted person to leave Taiwan followed only by the last military officer who was taking roll.

One night, when I lived at the Grand Hotel, I had gone out for a run. I bumped into a Prince from Saudi Arabia in the lobby and witnessed a pig being hit by a car during my run just a few minutes later. I never got any social diseases the entire time I was there even though some of my girl friends were prostitutes. However, my last days in Taiwan, I caught crabs from the sheets at the Grand Hotel. When I tried to treat them there was no treatment available and I had to use flea powder for dogs.

As regards telling my superiors about my interactions with human rights work: I was followed by the secret police when I left Linda's wedding party, and had to lose them by going through the night market and changing directions several times until I didn't sense them after me anymore. I was not afraid; however, I did believe I should tell my commander, MSgt. Tague, about what was going on and what I was doing. A local friend of mine told me of his uncle coming up missing after a black limousine pulled up and took him away right off the street, and he was concerned for my well-being. With this in mind, I told him what I was doing and he just warned me to be careful and never told me to stop. However, even though I had no idea I was doing anything wrong, later when I went through Officers Training School I learned that interfering in local politics and other social matters in a foreign country is prohibited. By the time I learned this it was about two years after leaving Taiwan.

Partly from my experiences in Taiwan, later I came to a different understanding of the U.S. military role. Today they have replaced "communism" as the buzz word for "enemy" with the label "terrorist". In the name of fighting terrorists the United States is violating every national and international human rights law with their electronic and psychological devices and powerful weapons.

A while after I left Taiwan, I received word from Linda that Nori had been put back in prison. He had already served 15 years in prison as a political dissident as I remember and had just been released when I met them.

I loved Taiwan and had arranged to stay there when I got out of the military but after Carter normalized we were all ordered to leave. I loved my time in Taiwan. I loved our adventures. I loved trying to make a difference on behalf of the Taiwanese people.

opposition figures with flattery or promises. Rather, it was only the mass mobilization and veiled threat of mass action, as well as a real concern for international reaction at a time when Taiwan's status with Washington was uncertain, that staved off a concerted crackdown by the security agencies. However, in cat-and-mouse fashion, they continually made arrests of peripheral figures through 1979, and those arrested were only released if mass protest were mobilized for them. The leaders of the opposition were riding the tiger as both government attempts at suppression and mass organization escalated over the course of 1979.

"The Revolutionary Circus": The Trial of Yu Teng-fa

However, some small level of advance was also made within the system. The Government Information Office and other international faces of the KMT, under more pressure since the leaking of the list of political prisoners at the Chingmei Prison in 1970, continued criticism issued by Amnesty International, and then Jimmy Carter's human rights policy of 1976, assured foreign observers that prisoners were allowed legal representation. When Yu Teng-fa and his son were brought to trial on March 9, 1979, Yao Chia-wen served as his lawyer and put up much more argument than usually seen in military trials, including the central challenge to the right of the military to try civilians. About thirty of us, Theresa Yuan and Chiu Ching-mei邱靜美 (younger sister of Chiu Yi-ping, the dentist who testified to KMT ballot-manipulation at Chungli) and others from Taoyuan among them, milled around in front of the trial site at the Chingmei Prison of the Taiwan Garrison Command in inchoate protest. Amnesty International sent a representative from Japan, Professor Nishikawa, who was only allowed as far as the reception room, where I took a picture of him to show that he had appeared for the trial.

Yu was all the same sentenced to seven years for "failing to report a communist spy", the self-proclaimed "spy" Wu Tai-An. Shades of the December rumors, the government displayed several faux police uniforms. Lynn Miles investigated in detail Wu Tai-an's activities in Japan in 1978 before he returned to Taiwan; there was reason to suspect Wu was an agent provocateur who had been directed by the security agencies to ferret out Taiwan Independence contacts in Japan. He subsequently visited a number of mutually-unrelated KMT critics and thus provided an excuse for arresting them, including six or so in Taitung who had challenged the KMT in elections. In Taiwan we translated Lynn's report into Chinese and printed 10,000 copies; I remember seeing them being put into the trunk of a car for distribution, but no sign of them after that. More will be said about the Wu Tai-an case later in my account (I visited the families of other defendants in a November 1979 trip to Taitung).

When Nori and I finally returned home to Hsintien after the Chiaotou march, we found that the gate of our Japanese-style house had inexplicably been painted with fresh red paint, perhaps to look as if we had moved. The landlady had said before that these last few Japanese-style one-story houses were to be sold for building the standard four-story concrete blocks; but soon afterwards she apparently was ordered by the police to expel us. We moved in March 1979 to a first-story apartment of a four-

Yuan Yen-Yen (Theresa) 袁嬿嬿, Tien Chiu-chin 田秋瑾, Chiu Ching-mei 邱靜美, women all involved in human rights defenses, Chiu because her brother the dentist Chiu Yi-ping 邱亦彬 was persecuted for supposedly making false witness against KMT ballot fraud in Chungli. Tien Chiu-chin is daughter of Dr. Tien Chao-ming.

Shih Ming-teh 施明德, Chen Chu 陳菊, Chen Ku-ying 陳鼓應, Linda Arrigo 艾琳達. Professor Chen lived only a 15-minute walk from the Chingmei Prison, and had long been quietly feeding out information on political cases from his sources within the KMT.

Shih Ming-teh, left; Provincial Assemblywoman from Taoyuan Huang Yu-chiao, center, who protested loudly over Chungli Incident police violence.

Chang Hua-ming 彰化民 and Hsieh Tsung-min 謝聰敏, former political prisoners. Given the severe torture Hsieh had suffered at the Chingmei Prison in 1971, his habitual cheer is especially amazing here.

Professor Nishikawa, Amnesty International representative sent to observe the supposedly-open trial of Yu Teng-fa on March 9, 1979. He was not allowed entry to the court.

Taiwan Garrison Command, Chingmei complex with courtrooms and large prison built 1968. Entrance to the courtyard. On the date of the trial of Yu Teng-fa, March 9, 1979, lawyer Yao Chia-wen represented him, and a few dozen supporters milled around in front, not quite a demonstration. Pictures taken by Linda Arrigo.

story building on a dead-end lane of Fuhsing Road (which runs along the south side of the Chingmei River), where it would be more convenient for relatives of prisoners to drop by to see us on their way to visit them at the Chingmei facility of the Taiwan Garrison Command.

We were also increasingly contacted there by international news services, no doubt channeled to us through Lynn Miles; European reporters spent the time to interview and film former political prisoners, while American TV reporters mostly wanted something fast in political statements and were disappointed if there was nothing immediately sensational ("no bleed, no read") after I had spent a great deal of time traveling with them and translating for them gratis. We met with a great deal of international reporting within two months or so after the U.S. established relations with the PRC. For example, I translated for Nori when he, among others, was interviewed by an American television team, NBC (National Broadcasting Corp.); he took out his full set of false teeth for dramatic flourish to explain that he knew what faced him, but he was prepared to go to jail again. The program was broadcast on Sunday, April 8, 1979, in the U.S., and a transcript was obtained later. But soon after the flurry in which several major American broadcast companies did segments on Taiwan, the major international news agencies decamped from Taiwan and centralized in Hong Kong.

A Place Among Nations: Reunificationists and Independence Advocates Part Ways

An occasion for an explicit split in the opposition camp between pro-Taiwan independence/generally liberal (the large majority of the candidates in the Campaign Coalition, plus the secret leadership of five) and vague pro-PRC/socialist ideals (the *China Tide* group, with former National Legislator Huang Shun-hsin 黃順興, the writer Wang Tuo 王拓, and Chen Ku-ying 陳鼓應 among the candidates) occurred in April 1979. The leadership of five hatched a plan to try to woo some liberal KMT figures into cooperation with the Dangwai through a campaign for the island to join the United Nations again under the name of Taiwan. A meeting was called, without explanation, for the morning of April 12, 1979. I translated the statement into English and typed it up the day before. It was presented as a *fait accompli* to be signed at the meeting, with Huang Hsin-chieh as chair. About 30 persons were present. Chen Ku-ying expressed disagreement in a hurt tone: "Brother Ming-teh, we met together yesterday noon, why didn't you mention this plan to me?" Only the pro-TI Dangwai figures signed. Obviously the *China Tide* group was far in the minority; it would perhaps provide an opening for the KMT to arrest them, for them to fragment off. But this incident marked a more explicit division in the opposition, and a frame of speech of "us" and "them." Although Su Ching-li continued in active participation, many of the *China Tide* intellectuals sunk back into armchair positions of critique. As for the campaign for Taiwan to enter the UN, no liberal KMT figures responded, and it was not heard of again for a long time.

The KMT did however respond to the threat of formation of a formal human rights organization by the opposition; its tactic was to form the Chinese Association for

Witnessing the Kaohsiung Incident –Selected Tape Recordings of Voice of Taiwan.

by Morgan Chang 張富雄

原文 「台灣之音」的回顧 張富雄 載於《見證關鍵時刻・高雄事件 – [台灣之音]錄音記錄選輯》吳三連台灣史料基金會 2006年12月10日刊行 p.43-47
Wu San-Lien Foundation For Taiwan Historical Materials.

The newly appointed president of the Taiwanese Association of New York in America, Mr. Stephen Lin 林俊提, held an officers meeting back in early 1977. During that meeting, I suggested that we could use an answering machine to form the Voice of Taiwan, as an avenue for distributing news for the Association. I had gotten this idea from the fact that, back then, in the United States, we could call a phone number at any time to get the day's weather. I used this service every morning and thought it was very convenient. During the meeting, it was decided that I would be responsible for carrying out my suggestion. Soon after, President Lin personally delivered a new answering machine and audio tapes over to my house. At the time, my wife Eileen Yi-Yi 楊宜宜 and I lived in a rented apartment in Woodside, Queens. I was working at the securities brokerage firm, E. F. Hutton, on Wall Street, and Eileen stayed at home to take care of our two-year-old daughter, Gloria.

The Voice of Taiwan 「台灣之音」 made its first test broadcast on April 1st, 1977, and formally started operating on May 1st, using the telephone number (212) 726-3023. The contents of the broadcast were first entered by me onto a keypunch card, then recorded after Eileen's edits. The first answering machine could only produce a three minute segment, and soon I discovered that this limitation was too short and hard to work with. President Lin went to search for better machines and finally found one in which the recording time could be as long or short as we wanted, and could even include interview segments. I remember our first interview being on site at a violin recital at which the two Wang daughters, Linda and Grace, performed. They were very cute and exceptional violin players, and the location was at the New York Queens Botanical Garden.

When the Voice of Taiwan first started broadcasting, the content changed once a week. On August 16, 1977, the Presbyterian Church in Taiwan published a "Human Rights Declaration 人權宣言" urging the Kuomintang government to establish Taiwan as a "new and independent" country. This Declaration was immediately censored by the government in Taiwan. Coincidentally, my third sister, Emma (Chang Hui-Jen), and her family were about to migrate from Taiwan to Los Angeles. A Presbyterian pastor, John Tin, quickly decided to use this opportunity to visit my sister at her home, and asked her to send an envelope to me via express mail as soon as she got off the plane. My sister, being the beautiful and innocent person she was, did so without hesitation or suspicion of motives. I did not tell her until twenty years later that what she sent was

Human Rights, registered in 1979, headed by the elderly National Legislator Han Lih-wu杭立武, and sharing offices with the World Anti-Communist League. Under the laws for formation and mandatory registration of civic organizations, any subsequent Taiwan-based association for human rights would be required to accept tutelage and oversight from the Chinese "national" organization. Therefore this move both provided government window-dressing for foreign consumption, and prevented legalization of a real human rights organization.

Surprises in the Philippines: The Asian Forum for Human Rights

In April we received vague information through the Presbyterian Church that an international forum on human rights was going to be held in the Philippines, and it was hoped that Taiwan would send a representative. Lin Hung-hsuan林弘宣, a graduate of the Tainan Theological Seminary who had recently returned from theological study in the States, was slated to go, but at the last minute was unable to get permission to leave the country. I was the substitute. Although I was afraid that I might not be allowed back into Taiwan, I wanted to escape the claustrophobia of Taiwan for a while; news was tightly controlled, and even *Far Eastern Economic Review* was not generally available. On the way out of Chiang Kai-shek Airport on the morning of May 3, I was thoroughly shaken down, and all my materials on Taiwan labor and human rights that I intended to present were confiscated. I arrived in Manila with a card on which I had written "Asian Forum for Human Rights" clipped to my lapel, expecting a welcome committee to pick up visitors. The immigration stopped me and copied it. They tried to confiscate the book I was reading, and I demanded and got it back. Despite the little booklets on Asian political economy that Ron Fujiyoshi had brought me, I did not realize that the Philippines was also under martial law! I took a taxi and finally found the address of a church compound. The meeting was hidden in the basement.

There were seventeen countries and areas represented at the meeting of the Asia Forum for Human Rights (AFHR), as I remember, Southeast and South Asian as well as the Pacific and Japan. Like Taiwan, Korea was too repressive for a native human rights representative to appear, so it was represented by Pharis Harvey from the Korean human rights office in Washington D.C. There were a few Maoris and others from developed countries who left after the two days in Manila, as well as some shrill radical chic Australians. A tall thin soft-spoken young man named Luingan Lithui represented Nagaland's aspirations for separation from India; in the mid-1990's I ran into him again as the head of the Asian Indigenous Peoples Pact. The Filipina who ran the meeting was adamantly anti-American, with good reason from the Philippine experience, as we learned from the relatives of those "salvaged" and disappeared, and in a trip to areas clandestinely governed by the Peoples Liberation Army. We heard talks by Sister Marianni who was organizing the families of the victims, and by "Father Ed" Edicio Gan de la Torre who had been imprisoned in 1974 and released recently, especially at the later venue, hidden in a convent in Baguio. Philippine activists were being continually targeted and murdered by the military, but the regime did not have a total registration of the population as in Taiwan, so escape was

the Human Rights Declaration. After receiving the document in New York, in addition to broadcasting it repeatedly on the Voice of Taiwan, a month later I also invited sixty-eight members from the Taiwanese Associations and Taiwanese churches all over America and American church friends to collectively purchase an advertisement in the New York Times. It appeared on page A14 in the September 21, 1977 issue with the English title "Listen!! Outcry Within Taiwan: 'A New and Independent Country'" and a separate Chinese title of "Taiwanese Want Independence" 台灣人民要獨立 drafted by Dr. Teng-Lung Hsu (許登龍), and written by Mr. Rei-Fung Hsu (許瑞峰) in calligraphy. This ad cost us around $10,000 (U.S. dollars), and at that time we depended entirely on voluntary contributions to pay for it.

On November 19, 1977 the Chungli Incident 中壢事件 took place, and from then on we greatly increased the number of news reports on Taiwan politics on the Voice of Taiwan. 1978 saw the formation of the Tangwai Island-Wide Candidates Campaign Coalition 黨外助選團 and the normalization of diplomatic relations between the United States and China. In 1979, Chen Wan-Jen protested with a fast, *Formosa, The Magazine of Taiwan's Democratic Movement* 美麗島雜誌, was formed, and the Kaohsiung Incident高雄事件, the Lin Yi-hsiung 林義雄 family murders, and the trial for the Kaohsiung Incident all followed in rapid succession. All these political events left us with barely any time to catch our breath. In crisis situations, we could be found changing our program five times in one day. Back then, we were often awoken in the middle of the night by long distance phone calls from Taiwan, and we started production of the broadcast as soon as we received the news, often working until 5 am. I had to leave the house for work at 7 am. Thinking back, I can't believe how we got through those days. Sometimes, Eileen and I closed our doors while we were busy taking phone calls and making recordings to reduce any extraneous noise, but on some tapes you can still hear our two daughters crying outside the door.

New and urgent events kept occurring in Taiwan, and many exiles here were eager to absorb the information. They called into our phone lines day and night; people in Taiwan were even calling in to hear the latest information. One of the tales I recall with excitement and pride occurred on the day of the large Kaohsiung Incident demonstration. We were on the phone with Ms. Chang Mei-Jen張美貞, sister of Provincial Assemblyman Chang Chun-hong張俊宏, who was at the scene in Kaohsiung, and suddenly we heard her shouting out: "Ah! The police released tear gas!" The explosion of the bombs following that statement was loud and clear, and made all of us listeners feel as if we were on location, experiencing it ourselves. This event remains unforgettable in the minds of many to this day.

In the beginning, all expenses incurred by the Voice of Taiwan were completely covered by the Taiwanese Association of New York. After 1978, the Association became overwhelmingly burdened by the staggering cost of the collect calls and suggested that the hotline start encouraging voluntary contributions from its listeners. Naturally, the Voice of Taiwan operations then became increasingly independent of the Association. Even so, Stephen Lin's successor, Mr. Martin Tsai 蔡明峰, still contributed $500 to the hotline. I remember clearly the day that we received our first $1,000 check, from a Kuo-Chung Liao 廖國仲. At the time we did not know who he was. This Mr. Liao, who passed

possible. Father Ed labeled middle-class democratic movement leader Ninoy Aquino as just another elite that was out of power. When we reached the final session and joint statement, however, I allied with a labor activist from Sri Lanka, George Caius, in arguing that the statement should keep to a narrow definition of human rights as freedom from government-sponsored terror (e.g. not define economic well being as a human right) and minimize anti-American rhetoric, so that we could publicly issue it in Taiwan and other very repressive anti-communist states like South Korea, and form local chapters of AFHR. But we were in the minority; and after I made plans to attend a United Nations conference (UNCTAD) then being held in Manila and told them I had a Rockefeller-Ford grant, some of the Filipinos spread aspersions that I was a CIA agent. Still, later a few of us from the AFHR gathering got a tour of urban slums and underground organization from clandestine members of the National Democratic Front. Despite the immediate negativity of the Filipino AFHR leadership towards me, I arranged to take this opportunity, out of Taiwan, to set up a visit to Sam Ho, the head of AFHR, a Malaysian Chinese, at his office in Hong Kong. During the activity in the Philippines, Sam Ho was very careful not to be photographed. I guessed that the security organs of Malaysia must also have a long reach, like in Taiwan.

The UN conference, a huge two-day affair held at the international conference center in Manila that seemed to express the megalomania of the Marcos regime, taught me a great deal. Imelda swept down in her butterfly gown with a royal retinue to talk about housing settlements for the poor; the Eastern European delegates snickered and were negatively impressed. I learned the pattern of empty rhetoric of democracy, actually oligarchy masquerading as populism. I approached the three delegates from the Peoples Republic of China who were sitting not far from me, and discovered that, although my information should be an intelligence bonanza for them, they were terrified to talk to anyone from Taiwan, leading to suspicions they were under paranoid political controls even worse than the KMT's.

I was very impressed by this conference, and in later years continued to find Filipinos such as Father Ed, Sonny San Juan (E. San Juan, Jr.) in Washington D.C., and Walden Bello impressive in incisive social analysis and unwincing political judgment; I noted their analysis of the opportunistic behavior of local opposition political clan machines, sometimes rallying resistance to exploitative authorities and sometimes making deals with them, and found it applied to Taiwan.

I had only been in Hong Kong briefly before, but Sam Ho of AFHR was very helpful when we met there; he visited us in Taiwan in October and then I could provide hospitality. Moreover, I was able to make or renew acquaintance with some of the China-watching foreign reporters who were stationed there, such as Ed Moritz of the *Christian Science Monitor*, and some social activist organizations such as Asia Monitor. Lastly, I met Lee Yi, editor of *The Seventies* 『七十年代』, an influential Chinese magazine that was critical of the KMT and later of the PRC as well.

away two years ago, was known within the Association as the man who "participated in a 'truckload' of charitable deeds, but barely uttered a word." He knew of our financial situation and quietly contributed so generously. Other listeners were like him, giving us financial support in large and small sums, without recognition, to keep us in operation for the next five years. Another gentleman who donated $1,000 when we first started the project was Mr. Pei-Long Hsu 許丕龍 of Los Angeles. My older daughter (now renamed Sister Mary Gloria) had Mr. Hsu's older brother, Dr. Teng-Lung Hsu, as her godfather at her baptism. Beginnings are always hard; the early aid of all our supporters is especially hard to forget.

To encourage donations to support our immense telephone bill, painter Tsin-Fang Chen 陳錦芳 supplied us with his limited edition paintings "Looking Towards the Homeland 望鄉" at low cost and donated one hundred cassette tape recordings of his "Taiwan Historical Poems." Dr. Teng-Lung Hsu's other younger brother also presented us with fifty "Let's Sing Together 大家唱" song books as gifts. We were showered regularly with letters from all over the world and they warmed our hearts and encouraged us immensely. An anonymous gift of a silk painting depicting lotus flowers and birds was small, but the love contained in it was heartfelt. Eileen framed and hung it on the wall, and throughout the last quarter century, even though the decorations in our house have changed many times, this silk painting has never been removed. Eileen believes it is the only thing we have left that commemorates the Voice of Taiwan, and it has always held a special place in our hearts.

In July of 1978, we moved from Woodside to Jamaica Estates, and thus the Voice of Taiwan found a new home. In addition to broadcasting in Taiwanese, we added a Mandarin line, and sometimes delivered news in Hakka, another dialect in Taiwan). The telephone number also changed to (212) 523-7855 (Taiwanese) and (212) 523-5672 (Mandarin). Eileen was always the main broadcaster; I and a couple of other Taiwanese individuals occasionally participated in the broadcasting too. Association President Lin continued to support our recording hardware needs, even after he stepped down from the post. To keep up with the increasing number of listeners, we had to keep updating our machine. The last two machines we used were a then-advanced model that had ten incoming lines and could service ten consecutive listeners at a time. However, because of limited funding, we could only support seven lines: five in Taiwanese and two in Mandarin/Hakka. The machines were not big in size and comparable to the size of a desktop PC today, only a little thicker. We also installed a counter on the machines so that we could tally the total number of incoming calls. And because we had around 30 to 40 affiliated stations, we also purchased an answering machine for their re-distribution and assigned to them the "internal" number of (212) 523-7856. In all, from the first day of our broadcast, the machines we employed were sturdy and top-of-the-line models available in the U.S.

Living in our Jamaica Estates neighborhood was an older couple, Mr. and Mrs. Chao-Yin Chang 張超英, who happened to be good friends with my oldest sister and her husband. We benefited from their generosity when Eileen and I first came to New York. Mr. Chang gave us a very old and large tape recorder and an outdated-format tape that contained folk songs from Taiwan. We used it to archive some of our work, and these became the

After about twelve days abroad I was very relieved to get through the Chiang Kai-shek airport immigration in mid-May without incident and see Nori and Theresa Yuan waiting for me. I brought back quite a stack of reports on other countries from the AFHR, but Nori and Yao Chia-wen and the usual Dangwai were not even interested in hearing about the meeting; I only met with Su Ching-li, Huang Hsun-hsin, and two others at her house to report on it. Su Ching-li got a thick manuscript on exploitation of farmers in Korea translated; this will appear again later in my account.

The Challenge to Martial Law Gains Momentum: *Formosa* Magazine

In March through May 1979 large activities of thousands were convened under a number of ruses, such as the birthday for Hsu Hsin-liang just as the KMT began to discuss disciplining him for leaving his Taoyuan Executive post for the Chiaotou march. Many of these activities I did not attend; my research still had much to be done in coding of questionnaires.

On May 28, magazines suddenly announced that Wu Tai-an吳泰安 (real name Wu Chun-fa吳春發) had been executed, apparently more as a threat to the snowballing opposition than punishment intended for the very cooperative "communist spy." The big man with his thick shock of black hair was shown in magazine pictures first shackled and grinning with a kind of gallows bravado, and then his twisted body lying on the ground, face turned to the side and the same white shirt splotched with dark blood. But this did not seem to deter the rising tide of public participation in opposition rallies.

By this time I had mostly gone through my research money, could not get the usual English-teaching employment, and still had to put out for the expenses of telephone, copying, photography, and mailing, etc., incurred in our communications, both open and surreptitious. Occasionally some small assistance came from overseas; once Huang You-ren 黃友仁 (real name Huang Chao-tang 黃昭堂), whom I only vaguely knew was a Taiwan independence figure in Japan, sent a package of some expensive Japanese shitake mushrooms, and I took them downtown to a consignment shop to sell them to pay the rent for the Fuhsing Street flat. Another time we received by registered mail a check for US$5,000 from a Taiwanese-American club; I cashed the check and it immediately went to cover Dangwai organization expenses. The money had been collected and sent by Professor Chen Wen-cheng 陳文成 of Carnegie-Mellon University, I learned much later. I also did not know until 1980 that Chen Wen-cheng was a member of *Taiwan Era*. How it happened I don't remember, but we began to get copies of Taiwanese-American newsletters through our hand-carried sources more regularly, from the Taiwan Association for Human Rights 台灣人權會 in New York, from Kuo Yu-shin's 郭雨新 Overseas Alliance for Democratic Rule in Taiwan 台灣民主運動海外同盟 in Washington, D.C., which also used our fist in an olive wreath logo, from Lin Hsiao-hsin's 林孝信 OSDMT (Organization for the Support of the Democratic Movement in Taiwan 台灣民主運動支援會; Newletter No. 16 is dated May 1980) in Chicago, and even copies of *Taiwan Era* 台灣時代, the ideological masthead of the leftist Taiwan independence organization with spokesman in Philadelphia.

three rolls of tape that were mentioned in this book.

Thanks to the Voice of Taiwan's timely and accurate broadcasts and our faithful service to our listeners, our program had a high tune-in rate and affirmation from our listeners. After the Kaohsiung Incident, overseas Taiwanese groups came together to form a "United Front for the Formation of the Country of Taiwan 台灣建國聯合陣線." Next came the bombing of the Coordination Council for North American Affairs Office 北美事務協調會in New York (the Taiwan government's representative organization in the U.S. at the time). Many Kuomintang Offices in the U.S. came under attack. Then, on February 28, 1980, the brutal Lin family murders occurred. As in the past, the Voice of Taiwan reported on these events immediately. But after this series of incidents, we started noticing several unfamiliar and questionable Chinese individuals loitering around our house. Eileen told me that she also saw young Chinese men with close-cropped hair surreptitiously monitoring her when she went to the post office box of the Jamaica Post Office for the mail of the Voice of Taiwan. Some of our Taiwanese friends feared for our safety, suggesting we apply for a gun license so we could carry one in self-defense; some of them even suggested that we flee to Brazil, where we could stay with Eileen's brother Simon Suh-wen Cheng 鄭士文 for a while. However, we did not follow through on any of these suggestions. I only made one change, and that was to move the Voice of Taiwan's answering machines from my house to a Forest Hills phone service company. The hotline number had to change once again, to (212) 261-5111 (Taiwanese), and (212) 261-5551 (Mandarin). We just rented a small space from this company to house our machines, and in the morning I would exchange the tape on my way to work after recording a new program at home. This phone service company was operational 24-hours a day, so we had access to our machines at all times. We made this move in fear of the Kuomintang's secret service cutting the telephone lines at our house, which seemed to us like something they could easily have done.

On August 7, 1979, Ms. Chen Wan-chen 陳婉眞, the founder and editor of the first Taiwan underground publication in decades, Chaoliu (潮流, "Tide"), was a guest at my house when she suddenly received news that two of her Chaoliu co-workers, Chen Po-wen 陳博文 and Yang Yu-rong 楊裕榮, had been incarcerated by the Kuomintang in Taiwan. She immediately decided to fast in protest and proceeded to write a letter which she brought to the Coordination Council for North American Affairs Office in New York on August 9. From that day on, Chen Wan-chen sat at the office entrance, sleeping in a sleeping bag at night. Except for going to the bathroom, she stayed at her post day and night and fasted. Eileen stayed on-site to take care of her, living in a nearby hotel with several other supporters and providing up-to-date information to me, without coming home for the next twelve days. I passed the Voice of Taiwan broadcasts, along with a recording of Chen Wan-chen's declaration, on to Mr. Shih Ming-teh 施明德 in Taiwan, who said he was going to distribute them within the island. I had also left my daughters, one-and-a-half year-old Karen Im-Im (音音) and four year-old Gloria Mi-Mi (敏敏) with our neighbor Mr. Chau-song Ou's 歐昭松wife Alvina for caretaking. Because of this non-stop, twelve-day fasting protest, I constantly had new material for the Voice of Taiwan, and it attracted people from numerous states near and far who showed up in person to support Chen Wan-chen, until her body gave in and she was rushed to the hospital on August 21.

From May 1979 Nori was beginning to put into effect a plan that he had been hatching for some time, and for which he had gotten a promise of sponsorship from Huang Hsin-chieh. Opposition figures had historically launched their efforts with a flagship magazine, often quickly closed down. Nori proposed that Huang Hsin-chieh apply for permission for a new magazine, and it was approved, about the same time as *The Eighties*『八十年代』 for Kang Ning-hsiang. Perhaps the KMT figured that these usual activities would keep the Dangwai busy without much harm. But Nori's scheme was to recreate the organization of the Campaign Coalition in the branch offices of *Formosa, The Magazine of Taiwan's Democratic Movement* (the Chinese name Meilitao 美麗島 means "beautiful island", the literal meaning of Formosa; the subtitle for the English name on the cover was my idea, to label it clearly for foreign media), and that was instantaneously clear from the picture and text on the back cover of the first issue, August 16, 1979: the listing of the nominal staff was virtually the same as the candidate slate for the Campaign Coalition. The editorial tone was the direct, strident prose of Chen Chung-hsin 陳忠信, close to the *China Tide* group; second editor was former political prisoner Wei Ting-chao 魏廷朝. The first issue sold 60,000 copies and later printings reached 110,000. Kang's magazine, on the other hand, while drawing a staff of young, active intellectuals, kept a safe distance from street action.

Taking a Blow Below the Belt: The Scandal Letter

In about August 1979 we were again forced out of our residence, then Fuhsing Street, after only half a year there. By then I felt ambivalent about staying there, anyway; it was dark and dank, although it had several large bedrooms and we could put up visitors from the south such as Rev. Lin Hung-hsuan林宏宣. We had found that the other side of the high wall at the end of the lane and the side of our house was a military camp. One night in June I heard my two dogs barking furiously, and I went around the side of the house and in the faint light saw a head above the high wall, not five feet from our bedroom window; then the man disappeared. The next day I climbed up and found that there was a ladder on the other side of the wall, apparently a listening post. Then about two weeks later my two dogs died at 2 am in terrible spasms seemingly from time-release nerve poison, evidently set by a middle-aged mainlander who knocked on the door about 8 pm and asked if we wanted to subscribe to the *Youth Warrior* newspaper『青年戰士報』 (military-owned). We buried them on the river bank around the other side of the Taiwan Garrison Command, hoping the dog spirits would haunt them. Nori said the poisoning was a warning to us.

On Sunday, July 15, Nori and I went on a rare outing, to hike and swim with some friends at Green Lake (Bitan碧潭) to the south of Hsintien. In those days before it was overbuilt it was beautiful and deep green and natural, and you took a small boat across the end of the lake for NT$5 and could walk on shady paths for an hour to temples that seemed dreamily beyond the world of the red dust. We came back at dusk; Nori seemed uneasy. After fifteen minutes home he suddenly got dressed again, saying he had seen plainclothes men with military-issue black shoes loitering in the lane when we came back. He sped off on a bicycle borrowed from Yang Pi-

Before the Kaohsiung Incident, twenty-nine affiliate stations of the Voice of Taiwan had already been established in various locations. Several locales attempted to produce their own programming, and others called our "internal line" to relay the news we recorded in New York. In the early 1980s, long distance telephone fees were very expensive, so having additional numbers across the country not only made it more affordable for the listeners, it also alleviated the problem of long wait times to get through to the New York lines. In Europe, France and Germany both had a Voice of Taiwan station. Since international calling was too expensive, we mailed tapes to those overseas stations every two weeks.

In December of 1981, my father-in-law, Dr. Yang Tien-Ho 楊天和, who had been the only doctor for ten years on the island of Okinoshima in Shikoku 四國, Japan, was suddenly diagnosed with pancreatic cancer and was admitted to the hospital in Kobe. Eileen immediately flew to Japan and took care of him for the last three months of his life. During this time, I recorded programs at night, exchanged the tapes in the morning, and then went to work. A relative remained available to help take care of my four- and seven-year-old daughters, but work on the Voice of Taiwan never ceased. Up until February of 1982, that is, when our machines stopped functioning. I also realized that I was extremely exhausted, so I reached out to the San Francisco Bay Area Voice of Taiwan host, Mr. Chieh Huang, to take over for me, and announced that, effective immediately, his station would be responsible for production.

Several months after the New York Voice of Taiwan went off the air, we received a letter from New York telephone company. We were told that our private home telephone line had been on a request list to the U.S. Federal Court for wire tapping for the past 33 months. The first request was approved for three months, and the request was renewed 10 times thereafter, for a total of 33 months. The telephone company was informing me that they would no longer be wire tapping our line.

In the summer of 1980, after the Kaohsiung Incident, we discovered an FBI agent's card in our house mailbox, telling us to call him. He wanted me to meet him at the FBI headquarters in Manhattan. I met him for over half an hour, and he wanted to know the sponsoring organization and money sources for the Voice of Taiwan. I told him the truth, that the Voice of Taiwan was not affiliated with any groups, and the only people responsible for it were my wife Eileen and I. I also told him that our funding came completely from voluntary donations of our listeners.

After 1979, we tried hard to further develop the Voice of Taiwan by recruiting professionals to run and manage the project as an enterprise. Sadly, we did not succeed in doing so. After 1980, publications like the *Formosa Weekly* 美麗島周報, *Asian Business News*, *Taiwan Tribune* 台灣公論報, etc. all made their debut, so it was no longer as difficult to obtain news on Taiwan as it was in the 70's. Thus, the New York Voice of Taiwan's mission for this period was declared completed in early 1982.

The Democratic Movement Riding the Tiger:

The security agencies pick off the dissidents one-by-one, while the December 1978 elections are postponed indefinitely. The opposition mobilizes the populace in order to spur release of arrested comrades, and the escalation spirals to a final confrontation.

chuan, who lived nearby. Perhaps another fifteen minutes, and three policemen rang the bell and barged into the house. They saw Shih Ming-teh was not there and left. Later in the evening more police came and left. But the house was staked out for a week. I sent telegrams to Jimmy Carter and telephoned out a human rights alert. Fearing a police raid, I smuggled the "seditious" materials, including the copies of *Taiwan Era*, out of the house under a tight girdle; I gave them to Professor Wang Shao-po 王曉波 of the *China Tide* group, who later destroyed these precious materials, but no blame. Later the young gangsters watching the house were withdrawn. On July 25, I penned a long sarcastic letter directly to the Taiwan Garrison Command, asking if they wanted to arrest my husband, and on what grounds. Nori came back safely – perhaps having weathered arrest attempt number three.

But that was not the only tactic the security agencies could unleash. On July 26, Yen Wen-suan 嚴文閂, a well-known reporter of the *United Daily News* 『聯合報』, and a young woman reporter with him showed up at our doorstep about 7 pm and insisted they would interview us, separately. They had copies of my personal mail – a long bitter handwritten letter dated September 29, 1978, very unhappy with Shih Ming-teh even while facing public marriage to him on October 15 (we had been married by notarized written agreement on June 15, but in local custom you are not really recognized as married until you have the party), a letter that I had sent to a former paramour at Stanford University. The letter had been carried out, I had thought, by a Western reporter, and the other party had received it and sent back a note; but it had obviously been intercepted and saved for future dirty tricks. The letter had been distributed to churches and media throughout Taiwan by a "patriotic youth group" that claimed to be scandalized by this foreign hussy. The letter labeled Nori a "fanatic Taiwanese nationalist" and myself a correspondent for Amnesty International. The next day, July 27, 1979, the *United Daily News* devoted a quarter page to the exposé, together with a facsimile of the letter section saying "sex and politics are intertwined" and a picture I provided of Nori and me standing sweetly in front of a Japanese wedding kimono I bought used in Kyoto in 1977 – provided with the hope it would slightly counterbalance their poison pen. Nori's mug shot on the wanted poster of December 1979 was later taken from this photo. This scandal was a crisis and paralyzing embarrassment for personal life, the kind of below-the-belt tactics often perpetrated on the KMT's political opponents. [This letter is translated in summary in an August 1, 1979, report by the Ministry of Justice Investigation Bureau, No. 情字第 054556, to the National Security Bureau, held by the National Archives; the document leaves an impression that the reporter was put up to this smear.] A foreign Catholic Maryknoller who supported the Dangwai asked me with tears in his eyes if the letter were true, and I could only nod yes. But incongruously the letter incident catapulted the previously publicly unknown Shih Ming-teh into the known ranks of Dangwai figures, and the information that a foreign woman human rights worker had linked up with a former political prisoner was read as hopeful news by sympathizers. For example, a desperately isolated youth who hated government propaganda located our house from the information in the newspaper and immediately joined the Dangwai activities.

This cartoon, drawn by Linda Arrigo, originally appeared in the underground newspaper Chao Liu ("Tide" 潮流) and was reproduced in the July 18, 1979 newsletter of the International Committee for the Defense of Human Rights in Taiwan, from which this English version has been redrawn. The cartoon shows a general of the Taiwan Garrison Command throwing darts at posters of opposition figures, plotting arrests.

Yu Teng-fa, the old opposition standard-bearer in Kaohsiung, was arrested January 21, 1979, after planning island-wide statements against martial law together with Shih Ming-deh on January 18. He was arrested on the pretext of meeting with self-proclaimed "spy" Wu Tai-an months earlier, and for distributing copies of an article in the Japanese newspaper Asahi Shimbun, and sentenced to eight years. Hsu Hsin-liang, elected County Executive of Taoyuan in November 1977, marched in the January 22 protest against Yu's arrest, and was removed from office on July 1, 1979, for taking leave without permission. Shih Ming-deh, General Secretary of the 1978 opposition coalition, was sentenced to life imprisonment for sedition in 1962 but released in 1977 on amnesty. Minor accusation by "anti-communist hero" could return him to life imprisonment. There was an apparent attempt to arrest Shih on July 15, 1979.

At any rate, by the time we had to move our residence yet again, Nori was so busy at the *Formosa* magazine headquarters in the Bailing Building 百靈大廈 on Renai Road near the Shinsheng South Road intersection that it was better to move into town. As general secretary, after huge sales of the first issue, he drew a salary (NT$12,000) in August, and the next month I was also provided a reasonable salary (NT$10,000) to serve as English secretary. We heard that a large apartment was available on the second floor above Lin Yi-hsiung's first floor apartment on a lane of Hsinyi Road, not far from the *Formosa* headquarters. By that time the headquarters was so overrun with volunteers and visitors that the editorial department could not find quiet space to work; so we divided the apartment up between the editorial department and our personal residence, plus a guest room for Chen Chu. Moving in, I personally scrubbed the toilets and found the furniture for the office from the Hsiamen Street used furniture shops. The arrangement gave me the opportunity to get to know the editors and layout artists better.

Among the staff for the magazine, Chang Fu-chung 張富忠, just returned from the States in September, was full of radical sentiments and information but insufferably arrogant. Chen Chu later took off for a trip to the States as well. Lin Yi-hsiung was invited to visit Washington about this time, and it seemed a time of wondrous possibilities, that those who were thorns in the side of the government were shown respect by the Americans, and the magazine provided an income stream while exhorting the populace to rise up for democracy. In activities our public sometimes treated us with admiration close to reverence, and the sympathizers seemed to feel that the Dangwai and not the KMT were the rightful authorities. Local offices of the magazine were opened one by one by the local Dangwai candidates; at each opening a big rally would be held with the leadership coming down as speakers, and banned books would be sold openly. Police who tried to stop the activities would be overrun by the masses of participants. Each crisis successfully surmounted lent an increasing sense of invincibility, even while the Dangwai leadership penned a statement entitled "We are willing to go to jail for Taiwan's future." This was not an empty promise.

Beginning from April 27, 1979, Chen Wan-chen 陳婉眞 had put out twenty-four issues of a biweekly handwritten two-sided newspaper centering on the Provincial Assembly with the new Dangwai members, titled *Tide* (*Chao Liu*『潮流』), one sheet in B3 size. She printed 1,000 copies of each issue, and the new availability of copier machines did the rest in reaching circulation of probably 10,000 or more. On August 7 the security agencies arrested two of those involved, our old friend Chen Po-wen (pen name Chen Yun-chung 陳允中) the photographer and the printer Yang Rung-rong 楊裕榮, while Chen Wan-chen was on a trip to the U.S. They were released however on August 23 after she held a 24-hour hunger strike and vigil on the street below the ROC office in New York for twelve days, before collapsing.

Those for whom there was no public mobilization, however, were not released. On August 30 Hong Chih-liang 洪誌良, a candidate in the December 1978 Campaign Coalition from Changhua, was arrested, but little was known specifically (more about this case below). On September 4, Chang Hua-min 張化民, associated with Kang's

Investigation of the Wu Tai-an Case:

Research by Hsu Chen-shu (Mrs. Chang Kuo-lung) and Linda Arrigo in November 1979 led to their article "The Tragedy of the Revolutionary Circus" in the final issue of *Formosa*, No. 4, November 25, 1979.

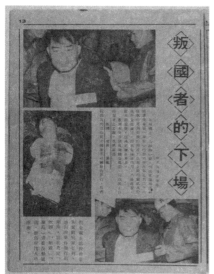

Photographer: "We scripted them together into the picture; now you can take them out and hang them."

Pictures of Wu Tai-an before and after execution, published in magazines about May 20, 1979. The timing seemed calculate to terrorize the opposition, and in fact pictures of his execution were later shown to prisoner Lu Hsiu-lien under interrogation in early 1980.

China Post 中國郵報

THURSDAY, JANUARY 25, 1979   中華郵政台字第五九二號執照登記證為第二類新聞紙類   局版台郵字第壹零壹玖號

: urges 'new ation' for U.S.

. 24 (UPI) saying the n is sound, can people in building n'' for the ing inflation ice through s limitation

to us is to firmer foun- ture. for a a more ef- nt, political le peace," second state ess.

hat contain- cific legisla- told a joint s and a na- udience that every sign our union is

it unemploy.

not one American had died in combat.

"Towerinver all this volatile changing world, like a thunder- cloud in a summer way, looms the awesome power of nuclear weapons," Carter said.

"We have no desire to be the world's policeman. Amer- ica does want to be the world's peacemaker."

Carter said that the SALT II agreement—now in its final stages with the Soviet Union— was based "not on sentiment (but self-interest of the United States and the Soviet Union."

"I will sign no agreement which cannot be verified," Carter said. "I will sign no agreement unless our deter- rent forces will remain over- whelming."

Woman nabbed

The five defendants in the trial yesterday; (from left) Wu Chun-fa, alias Wu Tai-an; his co-inhabitant Yu Su-cheng; Lin Jung-hsiao, restaurant owner in Japan;   Chang Sen-yuan, businessman; and Huang Che-tsung, also a businessman.   (CHINA POST photo)

Five admit role in Peiping plot

Evidence unfavorable to former Kaohsiung County Magistrate Yu Teng-fa emerged yester- day in a military tribunal in Taipei, as Com-   munist agent suspect Wu Chun-fa, alias Wu Tai-an, pleaded guilty to charges of plotting to overthrow the government by force last year.

Wu's testiminy was also unfavorable to present Hsinchu County Magistrate Hsu Hsin- liang and Kaohsiung County   Wang Yun-tao.

Two witnesses identified Wu in the court as the man who ordered two dozen green uni-   certificate' in advance but did not give it to him," Wu re- plied.

Plans   their organization to lead the authorities to launch a crack- down.

Maj. Fang defended Wu's mistress, Yu Su-cheng on the

magazine *The Eighties*, a debonair older mainlander and former political prisoner still championing the spirit of the Chinese May 4th movement of 1919, was arrested. Chang came to my house often in 1977, and when he heard I was looking to marry a former political prisoner, he fancied I would marry him; but he was much too traditional for my taste. He also told me about his investigation of security agency connections of the Cathay Insurance group, perhaps the real reason he was again hustled off to jail. Chou Yu 周渝, a young mainlander writer who had long joined with the Dangwai, wrote up a protest poster, and I tacked it to the front of the *Formosa* office hallway. It did not ignite further reaction, though a statement of concern appeared in the No. 2 issue (*Formosa* September 25, p. 81).

In June we had seen newspaper reports that the government had purchased riot equipment from South Africa. We first saw these close up in Taichung on July 28, 1979, when the Candidates Friendship Association planned a group trip to Taichung to support Wu Tze-lang 吳哲朗 in the spurious case that had been brought against him. The Candidates Friendship Association had been formed by Lu Hsiu-lien and Chang Chun-nan 張春南 (a former pig farmer, National Assemblyman, and candidate from Changhua; a tall man with thick, combed-over hair and a steady, booming voice, he took the bullhorn at the Chiaotou march), somewhat in reaction to the autocratic and unexplained directions of the leadership of five. Nori was somewhat scornful of it, feeling Lu Hsiu-lien had no sense of tactics, and that it was impossible for the Association to pull off an activity before the security agencies countered it, because the local loudmouth candidates would be spouting off to reporters. Yao Chia-wen and I went on the trip and I took along my 10-year-old son Roger, but Nori didn't; the program conveniently arranged to use a chartered bus on the newly-completed north/south freeway. As soon as the bus turned into the city, it was apparent that the KMT had totally mobilized to meet this affront to authority, in fact illogically creating much more disruption to the city than 30 people on a tour bus could ever have created. I estimated they must have mobilized 5,000 police to cover every intersection and separate off other traffic, every way that the bus turned. We got out in the park to rally our small group, and were met by a hundred or so plainclothesmen in jogging suits, a phalanx of uncertain riot police with the batteries falling out of their cattle prods (we walked between their ranks chanting "Return to the mainland!" giving them no excuse to attack), and finally two fire engines that turned their water hoses on us. Back on the bus, we were then followed by a dozen gangsters on motorcycles who closed in and shattered the Plexiglas windows with their bare fists when the bus stopped. At least no one was injured. It is hard to see what the KMT accomplished with this comical total overkill, other than field practice for their riot equipment – which we saw again several times.

The opening of the Nantou office I remember quite vividly. Nantou then was a small city on a low plateau surrounded by mountains near the center of the island, a 40-minute drive inland from Taichung. We drove there in the morning, and on the single route into the city I counted over a hundred military vehicles, e.g. jeeps and personnel carriers, parked by the side of the road. About thirty persons gathered at noon in a large office downtown. No sooner had we begun the meeting than a

The back of the first cover featured a picture of the editorial staff and a long list of names, in effect proclaiming that Formosa was a de facto political party that continued the organization of the Non-KMT Candidates Campaign Coalition. Most of the candidates were represented.

Formosa: The Magazine of Taiwan's Democratic Movement| made clear its claim to represent the masses of people in Taiwan with its cover showing a crowd of supporters at a rally. The first three covers were brick red (August 16), grass green (September 25), and golden yellow (October 25), inspired by Taiwan's lush countryside. These became the colors that represented the democratic movement in the sashes marking the leadership at the Human Rights Day march in Kaohsiung, December 10, 1979. The last cover, November 25, was originally designed black with red highlights, but was changed at the last moment to blue.

The Formosa office décor was designed by Lu Hsiu-lien to be unmistakable in pictures. The banner reads "Democracy, Solidarity, Love Taiwan."

horrendous rumble began; the military was driving tanks around the block, and the whole building was shaking so loudly discussion was almost impossible. The public speeches were scheduled for about 5:30 pm at a movie theater. The police had cordoned the whole area off, but as a crowd gathered a process of pushing began, in which whiplines of people with their arms closely intertwined bounced off the police lines until they broke through. Nori's hopeful view was that not only would the populace grow used to resisting the police, the police would get used to seeing the people exercising their right to assembly and free speech, and no real violence would ensue. Later the movie theater was full; I estimated a thousand people. But it was unusual that we had an indoor venue with seats, allowing a clear estimate.

These are only a few of the large public events in this period, which cannot be fully covered here. Only one more must be mentioned in passing. The opening tea party of Formosa magazine, designed by Lu Hsiu-lien and held at a fancy new hotel, the Mandarin Crown Hotel 中泰賓館, on September 8, was the important point at which Formosa tried to achieve acceptance by liberal intellectuals. But the tactic of the security agencies was to turn the street in front of the hotel into a brawl with "anti-communist" demonstrators and deny *Formosa* the dignity of a formal event.

Human Rights from Politicians to Political Prisoners: The Psychology of Denial

As *Formosa* became organized as a vehicle for the candidates in the aborted election (with no stated date for resumption), it became clearer that there was a distinction between the organization seeking democracy, specifically election, and human rights work per se, although *Formosa* introduced international human rights organizations to the public as well. Most clearly, the immediate reaction to an arrest was still for politicians to deny association with the arrestee, and for friends to scatter, rather than to demand explanation for the arrest from the security agencies. If concern were shown, it was only for high-profile people who shared the same political position.

On two or three occasions Nori wistfully suggested that I help him emigrate out of Taiwan before he was arrested, the last time in early November when we visited Green Island; he had no expectation that the established Dangwai politicians would stand up for him. Everyone knew that association with former political prisoners -- persons already proven seditious -- could be trumped up as an excuse for arresting current Dangwai politicians, and so the former prisoners were often avoided. Perhaps Nori was excepted from this pattern because his marriage to me gave him some immunity. However, it was perhaps callous of me that I never seriously considered Nori's suggestion, and in fact in June 1978 I had demanded a marriage agreement from him stipulating that I would not arrange U.S. immigration for him or his family, and that either party could request an end to the marriage after a year.

About September, with the magazine providing more resources and an apparently stable mouthpiece that interested foreign reporters and political scientists, I planned recruiting foreign friends to translate part of the magazine and also to do more active human rights research and translate it, to produce an English newsletter. This would

我們願為台灣民主的前途坐牢

全世界矚目的余登發案件，經過政府三個月的考慮與猶疑，判處有期徒刑八年。對這個七七高齡的人這樣判決，無異是宣告死刑，關心台灣民主前途的人們，不但感到震驚，而且感到萬分的悲痛。

余登發案件，從抓人到判決，暴露了許多懸疑與破綻。案件的內容實在令人難以置信。政府指責日本數一數二有代表性的大報「朝日新聞」為共匪宣傳文件，但是日本與我國同為自由民主國家，閱讀外國報紙竟然是犯罪，縱然走訪過余登發，但飯館自古為殺頭罪，誰敢初見面即大談叛亂之事，即使有，余登發怎會相信與是叛諜，為了這種事情，余登發竟然被判重刑，是何等殘酷的事呀！

余登發日治時代參加抗日運動，光復後歷任水利會長、國大代表、縣長，一生主張經由自由民主的選舉方式為地方服務，日據時代，日本人在「六三法案」的鎮壓下，對反抗異族的台胞，也不會受到如此的重罰，一個熱心競選的老人，竟在同族相煎之下，遭受無情的處罰！

三百年來連抗議的自由都沒有的台灣人，除了再度噤息以外，還能為自己的命運做什麼呢？

我們不願意看到台灣民主潮流落暴戾之氣與暴行之風所摧毀。

我們也不願意看到余登發老死監獄中，也為台灣民主和平的前途坐牢。我們寧願捨身支持余登發老先生坐牢——有的一天，有的一星期，有的一個月，有的一年，來挽救千千萬萬糊起的「良心罪犯」的不幸，來挽救台灣進一步走向軍事統治的不幸。

希望藉著眾人自動的服刑來免除一位垂危老人在冷酷的鐵窗中抑鬱悲憤而死的命運，希望藉著眾人對「良心罪犯」關懷的熱烈情感感動著早日終止古老的同類相殘凌弱暴寡的慣行，迎接安祥道德而寧靜的未來！

我們請您共同寫信或打電話給余登發的家屬（〇七一六一三八二六），表示大家的關懷！

我們決心關起窗門，停止嬉樂，放下工作，共同分擔余老先生的刑期。

替余登發坐牢。

為台灣民主和平的前途坐牢。

我們似乎隱約約的看到一種悲劇命運正在萌芽，我們幾十年來辛辛苦苦建立的微小民主政治的成就，已經搖搖欲墜，我們擔心這一代人政治錯誤所遺留的仇恨與不滿，會為下一代人創造無可挽回的悲劇。這是我們萬萬所不願意看到的。

但是我們能做什麼呢？

一切抗議示威的和平途徑，都已被絕望；老百姓公開和不公開的企求，都不受重視；我們呼天無門，喚地不應，除了默默禱告，除了同聲一哭外，還能做什麼呢？

台灣人的命運真是這樣悲慘嗎？

臺灣人權委員會

On May 21, 1979, in response to the sentencing of Yu Teng-fa, the leaders of the democratic movement penned a statement, "We are Willing to be Imprisoned for the Future of Taiwan's Democracy," signed in the name of the "Taiwan Human Rights Committee." It stated exasperation that peaceful demonstrations and demands for democracy had been met with government violence through arrests and bannings, and ended with a plea for sympathizers to telephone Yu's family to express concern.

The tea party for the official inauguration of the Formosa magazine was held on September 8, 1979 at the ritzy Mandarin Crown Hotel, and was intended by the program designer, Lu Hsiu-lien, to be an elegant affair that would entertain liberal intellectuals and gain respectability for the democratic movement, generally lampooned by the authorities as motley betel nut-chewing rabble.

The security agencies spoiled the polish of this event by unleashing a protest by "anti-communist heroes", encircled by assisting police lines that in effect sealed off the site and trapped those inside. Finally *Formosa* mobilized a phalanx of volunteers to break out of the blockade, only to be accused of fomenting violence.

also feed material to overseas human rights organizations more systematically and help us brief reporters. In September and October, I think, Sam Ho of Asian Forum for Human Rights and Kazuyoshi Nishikura 西倉一喜, a young Japanese reporter who had learned Chinese in the PRC and was in close coordination with Lynn Miles in actively covering Taiwan issues, came to study Formosa magazine and the political opening in depth. By contrast, for mainstream media visiting Taiwan at ROC largess, the Government Information Office would take them for an obligatory 30-minute visit to the offices of the opposition after feeding them silly at lunch, and then whisk them away at 3:30 pm for an "important" subsequent activity – shopping at the government-run Chinese Handicraft Center. Of the few remaining locally posted foreign reporters, Bill Kazer kept in close contact with us, while Dirk Bennett, a stringer for *Newsweek*, seemed to have been intimidated.

Nori was the main local collaborator in the plan for human rights reporting, and as manager of *Formosa*, together with Yao Chia-wen, could provide the minor funds needed for the English newsletter. Theresa Yuan, who spoke fair English, also promised wholehearted participation. I met over several weeks with Herbert Thomas, James Decker, and Monica (Nicki) Croghan, all studying Chinese at a fairly advanced level and planning to stay in Taiwan for a while. During the breakthrough period of the democratic movement, I was generally the only foreign participant around to help in or witness the activities; Rosemary Haddon and her partner had moved from Tamsui in Taipei County to Taichung, and Dennis Engbarth had gone to Hong Kong. Now the atmosphere of fear was ebbing, it seemed to be a new era, and foreigners were emboldened as well. By Dr. Mark Thelin's memory, in November I showed up at his place at Tunghai University to request writing contributions from his students. But new crises were boding.

On October 3, 1979, the leftist intellectuals Chen Yung-shan 陳永善 (pen name, Chen Ying-chen 陳映眞, previously served ten years, 1968-1975, for running a Maoist study group; mouthpiece for Beijing since the mid-90's, and now hospitalized unconscious in Beijing following a stroke) and Lee Ching-rong 李慶榮 (briefly editor of *Tocsin* 『富堡之聲』) were suddenly arrested. It seemed as if the authorities wanted to see if less vocal parts of the opposition could be picked off piecemeal. I participated in a meeting at *China Tide*; Wang Tuo said something like, if we don't stand up for ourselves the Taiwan independence opposition won't respect us. At about 4 pm about fifteen persons, myself included, marched into the front office of the Taiwan Garrison Command 台灣警備總部 headquarters on Po Ai Road 博愛路 (Universal Love Road, such an Orwellian address), demanded to know why Chen and Lee had been arrested, and occupied the reception area until 5:30 when the office closed. As for the *Formosa* office, there was no apparent reaction to the arrests of the leftists. However disappointed, Nori did not leave it at that. We called up what I believe were the *China Tide* sympathizers, a group of artists (Nieh Hua-ling 聶華伶), in New York. Sitting at his big swivel chair in his office, Nori intoned, "Now, don't you people in the U.S. do anything rash about these arrests…," with a tone of sarcasm that made it clear he was inciting something incendiary. The next day or so the wives of the two men came over to my house in the early evening, and with their information I immediately made

Tensions mounted in October 1979 with rumors that the security agencies had met and decided to close down the magazine. *Formosa* magazine rallied mass support to ward off suppression, at the same time proceeding to quickly open new branch offices in defiance of police forces and render its popular organization a fait accompli. It did not back down from escalating government threats as plans for Human Rights Day activities in Kaohsiung, December 10, 1979, were set in place. The night before, two volunteer workers were apprehended and severely beaten by police.

Huang Hsin-chieh on sound truck under the visage of Sun Yat-sen; Yang Ching-chu and Shih Ming-teh donning three-colored sashes and name banners.

The sign proclaims "Oppose exploitation of labor!" The signs and songs for the evening were designed by young ministers from the Tainan Presbyterian Seminary, steeped in liberation theology. The songs included "We Shall Overcome" in Taiwanese, and the repeated cry was "The beautiful island (Formosa) is ours!"

Several hundred marchers were surrounded by riot police lines in the traffic circle in front of the First Precinct Police Station. Thousands more were blocked outside the lines. When huge riot trucks faintly spewing tear gas could be seen approaching, the march leaders directed the crowd to break out of encirclement in the other direction.

several long international telephone calls to Taiwanese-American and human rights organizations in the States. Within an hour my phone went dead. However, I believe it was the next day, October 6, in the afternoon, that Chen and Lee were released from the Garrison, and came straight over to my house. Chen Yung-shan gave me a bear hug and ran out again. I have no idea how the overseas supporters reacted, or what the process within the Taiwan Garrison Command was.

Right after their release, the wife of a candidate in Changhua, Hong Chih-liang 洪誌良, who had published a banned magazine together with Lee Ching-rong, came to me with news that Hong had been arrested August 30 together with his assistant surnamed Wu, and he was being held at the Chingmei Prison. In September I accompanied her on a visit there, but she was not allowed to see him. Few were inclined to protest his arrest because he was just a peripheral figure of the pro-Chinese group, and was rumored to be an agent of the MJIB. However, after listening to the details provided by Mrs. Hong, which acknowledged some regular contacts with the MJIB and Wu apparently placed as a watcher, I suspected that Hong was being coerced to serve as another "communist spy" in the Wu Tai-an mold, to frame someone else in the future. I made a detailed report to Lynn. And I was, unfortunately, right.

The opening of the offices changed the relationship of the Dangwai with the populace in many ways, providing broader contacts. Interesting enough, in some cases even mainlander former soldiers looked to the opposition forces for relief from oppression. Once when I went down to the Taichung office, the office manager Lin Hui-chen (the same Lin Hui-chen who has been the long-time partner of Chang Chun-hung 張俊宏, till recently) told me about a retired mainlander soldier, named Ho Chi-hsing 賀吉星, unemployed since losing his hand in an industrial accident, who had written some political tracts and left them at the office. I took copies back with me. Two weeks or so later she called me and told me the old soldier had been arrested; I got more information from Chen Po-wen and made a human rights report which is now to be found in Lynn Miles' files at the Wu San-lien Foundation (lynn084.18-005). The pamphlet, printed in green with a silver star in a circle as a logo, is dated October 15, 1979; Ho was arrested November 28.

Deepening Pressure on *Formosa* Magazine: Weathering the Crisis

The second issue of *Formosa*, dated September 25, 1979, carried the first half of the article on exploitation of Korean farmers that I brought back from the Philippines and Su Ching-li had gotten translated into Chinese (now titled "Expose the Myth of Korea's Economic Miracle", *Formosa* No. 2, p. 52-60); the second half was to be published in the next issue. The Foreign Ministry objected that this article had offended the South Korean embassy; more to the point, the security agencies believed that the article was criticism of Taiwan's farm policy but disguised as purporting to be about Korea, and demanded to see the original. Our editorial department always shredded the original handwritten draft, and the English was not found. The magazine was threatened with closure. Nori issued a statement in the name of all the offices that Korea was meddling in the internal affairs of the country, and

The lead truck, with march directors Yao Chia-wen and Shih Ming-teh at the fore, turned in the direction of the breakout, pushed from behind as well by a mass of the marchers.

，兩人互相握手，常司令並親以座車將介送到美麗島雜誌社的服務處，且陪同

偏激的言論

七時正，宣傳車上開始發表演說、唱歌，

美麗島雜誌社於民國六十八年十二月十日晚間在高雄非法集會，四百餘名暴力份子，用火把、木棍、鋼條、鐵鈎、石頭、磚塊、破酒瓶、斧頭等凶器，擊傷了一百八十多名維護治安

This breakout was subsequently alleged by the government prosecutors to be an attack on the police and an attempt at inciting armed uprising. The widely-used tilted picture in the above government propaganda is labeled: "*Formosa* magazine on the evening of December 10, 1979, held an illegal assembly in Kaohsiung. Four hundred and some violent elements utilized torches, wooden staves, metal bars, iron hooks, stones, bricks, broken glass bottles, axes, and other weapons to attack and injure over 180 military police personnel who were forbidden to strike back – and one citizen who went to the aid of the police was also injured."

After several clashes in which there were perhaps a dozen police injuries, the column returned to the front of the Formosa office, and speeches continued peacefully for over an hour with an audience of perhaps 50,000. At about 10 pm over a dozen riot trucks massed and bore down on the assembly, and with tear gas clouds billowing and bamboo torches flailing, the *Formosa* leadership was forced to abandon the speech truck. This was the fateful Kaohsiung Incident, the beginning of both a tragedy and a turning point in Taiwan's thirty years of martial law.

Formosa would demonstrate in front of the Korean embassy. Forbidden from printing the second half of the article, *Formosa* printed a protest (*Formosa* No. 3, October 25, Table of Contents) plus a full page of black (p. 8). The president of South Korea, Park Chung-Hee, was shot by his own chief of security a few days later.

Our crisis in Taiwan continued to escalate. It was conveyed from shadowy sources that on October 16 – this date is only from my vague memory – there had been a high-level meeting of Taiwan's security agencies, and they had decided to shut *Formosa* down. The leadership of five sprang into action. I only know the part I participated in: Nori and I paid a visit on Mark Pratt, ranking official at the American Institute in Taiwan, at his home in the Hsinyi area of Taipei. Mark Pratt was soothing, saying that Chiang Ching-kuo had taken a turn for liberalization, and the fact that Wu San-lien, the venerable old native politician and newspaper founder, had also staked his reputation on it, meant that there would be no crackdown. I believe that Chang Chun-hung and others visited liberal figures in the Kuomintang. There was no further immediate move from the authorities.

Investigation of the Wu Tai-An Case: Threatening the Security Agencies

In this brief lull in the first days of November, I took a trip to Taitung, the most remote city at the south of the east coast, together with Hsu Chen-shu 徐慎恕, long an acquaintance from the women's movement, sprightly wife of Chang Kuo-lung 張國龍, the professor of nuclear physics at National Taiwan University (later one of the leaders of the anti-nuclear movement, and head of the Environmental Protection Agency 環保署, 2005-2007). She had some personal leads to the families of the eight from Taitung arrested in the Wu Tai-an case. We spent about a day and a half visiting four families and the temple where Wu had resided for a while, and were soon being pursued within 40 minutes of our arriving anywhere by ominous visitors and phone calls to the families. At about 5 pm I decided we may as well confront the cockroaches. I got the number of the local Investigation Bureau, called, and introduced myself. There was a commotion in the background of their office, some kind of worried uproar with my name in it. Now it seemed *Formosa* magazine wielded a powerful public voice that was feared by the secret police.

It was clear that three of those arrested in the Wu Tai-an 吳泰安 case had tried to breathe life into the Taitung branch of the China Youth Party 青年黨, one of the small parties that had come from China in 1949 and served as a fig leaf for the regime, and they had actually challenged the local KMT machine in elections in 1977 and 1978. Wu's appearance there was a ploy to snare them in September 1978 while preparing for the December national-level election, and they were sentenced to 10-12 years. The abbot of the large temple who had known Wu and helped the Youth Party candidates was sentenced to life. Within a week Hsu wrote up the article, under her pen name Hsu Hsin許心; my contribution was just the title, "The Tragedy of the 'Revolutionary Circus'", and the photographs. The editorial department got a cartoon from Coco that was a stroke of genius, Wu the self-proclaimed spy waving to the camera in a group picture of the defendants. Somehow the typed text got lost on the way to the printer, and it had to be reset before printing in the final issue of *Formosa*, No. 4, November 25,

The Asian Forum for Human Rights

Immediately following the Kaohsiung Incident, AFHR sent an investigator to Taiwan and with the assistance of Denis Wong produced the following booklet, dated January 4, 1980. This booklet was distributed widely among its members in Southeast Asia, providing rare first-hand news and resulting in newspaper reports in faraway places.

Preface

This booklet is a collection of essays relating to the recent Kaohsiung (or Formosa magazine) incident that occurred on December 10, 1979 -- Universal Human Rights' Day. Much confusion has arisen over the Democratic *tangwai* Movement in Taiwan due to stringent control of the press in Taiwan by the Kuomintang government authorities and their highly selective choice of facts in their press releases. This booklet hopes to provide a more balanced account of the background and events that led to the incident.

Section A focuses on the incident itself and contains a report from a fact-finding mission that visited the island soon after the event.

Section B includes an analysis of the historical and socio-economic context under which the Democratic Movement in Taiwan has developed, firstly as an opposition movement to an aging KMT bureaucracy and finally as a force reflecting and voicing the needs of the people.

Section C contains three translations taken from *Formosa* and *Spring Breeze*, magazines lying at the centre of the controversy.

The AFHR hopes that this collection is able to bring attention to this much-neglected "orphan of Asia" -- Taiwan.

Published by:

Asia Forum on Human Rights

568, 12/F, Nathan Road,
Kowloon, HONG KONG

Land Area: 35,981 square kilometres

Population: (1978) 17.01 million

Gross National
Product: (1977) US$19,490 million

CONTENTS

1979.

Nori met up with me in Taitung, and on November 3 or so we took a small airplane to the prison island offshore from Taitung, Green Island, that had recently been opened to tourist travel. A year previous we had been unable to go because of high winds. I had made matching shirt and shirtdress for us for this occasion, yellow and green weave in light cotton, a feeble protection. Nori seemed to have some compulsion to look at the place from the outside, the fortress-like building where he had been imprisoned from about 1971-76, mostly in solitaire (which he claimed he liked, though he almost lost the ability to speak), and where he almost died from appendicitis. It was low tide, and we found a group of prisoners collecting seaweed, under guard; Nori walked over to them, people he knew, and they shouted exchanges until the guards intervened. As we walked around the island we were trailed by a man on a bicycle. A little way past the main prison for political offenders, we found that a new larger prison compound was under construction, not far from the graveyard, and I photographed it surreptitiously, changed the film, and hid the canister on my body. Two weeks later I gave a set of the pictures to Laurie Wiseberg of Human Right Internet, during her visit to Taiwan, and that is the only set of the pictures that survived the subsequent confiscations.

Laurie Wiseberg, founder of Human Rights Internet, came to Taiwan November 15-20, and within that time we just happened to have scheduled a meeting of the Dangwai wives, the as-yet-unorganized organization that had been promoted by Lu Hsiu-lien in August/September. Lu Hsiu-lien did not attend, however. Myself and Su Ching-li and others who wanted the organization to focus on human rights and assisting the families of political prisoners had arranged for the wives of Chen Yung-shan (wife, Chen Li-na 陳麗娜) and Lee Ching-rong (Lee Feng 李豐, herself a doctor, who in recent years has written a book on her survival over cancer) to tell about the experience of their husbands' arrest and release the previous month. Very importantly, the venue was provided by Huang Hsin-chieh's wife; the second floor of their house was a very large parlor, quite enough for the dozen or so participants. Probably Nicki Croghan was there, too. After the account by the wives, we discussed whether we could formalize an organization concerned with the families of political prisoners; Chou Ching-yu, the beautiful and scholarly wife of lawyer Yao Chia-wen, was interested, but said with her usual diffidence that it would be a provocation to the authorities. No concrete plans were made, but when Laurie arrived later in the meeting, I translated for her explaining her activities, and further sketched the overseas organizations and channels that our human rights work in Taiwan was linked to. It was perhaps not an auspicious occasion, but it was a fortuitous preparation.

Formosa Magazine: Riding the Tiger

The magazine continued to open new offices, one after another. Many more were planned, even for the east coast. Nori sometimes staged ruses to make me show up even when I wanted to devote my time to finishing my research; he indicated that the presence of the foreign witness emboldened the participants. Then Wu Tze-lang, the

The December 10 Kaohsiung Incident

THE CRISIS OF THE DEMOCRATIC MOVEMENT

Report of a fact-finding mission in the days
following the clash of forces in a rally to
celebrate Universal Human Rights Day.

"The Democratic Movement in Taiwan has suffered its
greatest tragedy since the February 28 Incident." That
was the way in which one Taiwanese described the events
associated with the December 10 Human Rights Day rally
and the following suppression campaign on *Formosa*
monthly publication and its supporters. *Formosa* was a
legal publication, begun in August 1979 by a coalition
of *tangwai* (non-party, i.e. non-*Kuomintang*) legislators, dissidents, writers, lawyers, activists and young
supporters. It has produced 4 issues and established
some 15 service-centers across the island before being
shut down by the ruling KMT authorities following the
incident at Kaohsiung.

Background to the Incident

Towards the end of November, two *Formosa* service-
centers were simultaneously attacked in Taipei and Taichung. Using similar tactics, the intruders described
as *hooligans* attacked the offices and disrupted publication activities. A third incident occurred in Pin-
tung on December 6 which, according to one witness, may
have involved the same people. As a result, all *Formosa* service centers around the island were urged by
the editors to be on their guard. These and other acts
of harassment over the past months were seen by the
leaders of the Democratic Movement to be deliberate
acts of government intimidation.

On December 8, leaders of the magazine drove to Pin-
tung to prepare for the rally in Kaohsiung to celebrate
Universal Human Rights Day. All of them were followed
by the familiar *"special police cars."* On the way, one
car was almost forced off the road by the police car,

10

which had been following so very closely and danger-
ously. This resulted in an exchange of insults and
a minor scuffle with the police.

In another meeting scheduled in Kaohsiung on December 9, a group of police went to *Formosa* office and
drew a crowd of onlookers outside. The police came to
inform that the rally had not been approved, but they
did not show any statement to that effect. The police
also asked that the sound trucks announcing the rally
be not sent out. However, such announcements were
within the limits of the law, the two trucks went out
as planned.

In the early evening, workers preparing the rally
heard that two volunteers in the sound truck had been
detained. Representatives of *Formosa* immediately went
to the police station to demand an explanation. They
were told that there had been no arrests and that the
two had merely been called in for questioning. So they
suggested the police escort the two back to the *Formosa*
office. The negotiators, however, then asked for the
immediate release. After signing the release, the two
were brought out.

Both had been severely beaten. One of them, Chiou
Ah-su, a young Taiwanese worker, had suffered a con-
cussion. The other, Yao Kuo-chien, a sturdy mainlander
whose parents had been loyal KMT functionaries, had
received a gash down his neck. When his shirt, completely soaked in blood, was removed at the hospital,
the doctors said that he had been repeatedly kicked
with boot heels.

The same evening, two *Formosa* editors went to a
judge to seek a court order for the arrest of people
who were responsible for Chiou and Yao. Although the
application was made in the early morning, no action
was taken.

December 10 and its Aftermath

On December 10 morning, police barricades were set
up around the *Formosa* office in Kaohsiung. A large
number of police and security forces were practicing

11

MAP -- Kaohsiung Incident
December 10 Night

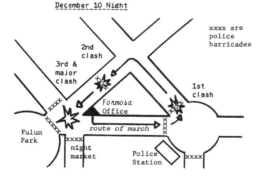

xxxx are
police
barricades

in the park where the rally was to be held. In view
of the increasingly tense situation, it was decided
not to hold the rally in Fulun Park, but to shift the
route of the march to a traffic circle in the other
direction.

The march was to be led by one person carrying a
large human rights torch, followed by 24 persons
carrying smaller torches made out of bamboo poles,
and then several cars carrying the *Formosa* leaders,
after whom would follow other marchers and volunteers.
Only bamboo poles, wicks and alcohol for the torches
were prepared in advance.

At 6.00 p.m., the procession set out for the traffic circle. The people who eventually gathered around
the circle numbered between 10,000 and 20,000. Security forces were grouped around three sides of the
crowd, but kept their distance.

12

Speeches were made without incident. The speakers
continually urged the people to remain peaceful and
orderly especially on the occasion of Human Rights
Day. However, as with many crowd control situations,
some minor scuffles began to occur around the fringes
of the audience, especially as the crowd increased
and the distance between the people and police became
reduced.

*(What follows is somewhat contradictory and unclear,
and is based upon three eyewitness accounts and comparison with newspaper reports. Hopefully, greater accuracy and more details will emerge as more and more
people write up their own accounts of what had happened that night.)*

Sometime 8.30 p.m., Yao Chia-wen spoke as the crowd
was getting increasingly restless. He said that he
and another representative would go to the police station at the traffic circle to make two requests. First,
to ask that the crowd be allowed to proceed peacefully
to Fulun Park, where it was reported that some 30,000
people were waiting for them. Second, to reiterate
Formosa request from the night before that the three
officials responsible for the beatings of Yao Guo-jian
and Chiou Ah-su be disciplined and removed. He told
the people if he did not come out within 30 minutes,
then it would mean that he too had been arrested.

After which Yao Chia-wen left and went in. The
crowd paid little attention to the speeches that followed. Instead, they began a countdown based on his
final remark. Finally Yao came out of the police station in time, but without any concrete results. As a
consequence *(and there are conflicting reports here)*,
several people   began moving in a direction out
of the traffic circle. The masses from behind pushed
forward. This was the first clash with the police at
which some 10 to 20 policemen were injured.

The leaders continued to urge restraint as the
crowd and police moved around the block back to *Formosa* office. Another clash occurred here as the people

13

former editor of *Taiwan Daily News*『台灣日報』, was arrested on November 20 on a trumped-up charge of physical attack, after several months of hiding out. The rally for the office opening in Taichung County, held in the schoolyard of an elementary school at night, turned militant. About 200 riot police in full gear lolled in the back corridors of the school. There were almost no lights in the schoolyard, with a crowd of a few thousand; but when car lights flickered from the street beyond, a faint outline could be seen of what seemed to be machine guns on the top of the nearby two-story wing of classrooms. Nori wanted a show of defiance, I believe; it had been planned in advance, but whether and how it would be executed was the question. A few dozen bamboo torches were lit, handed to those who dared, carried one-by-one a hundred feet or so to the exit to the schoolyard, and extinguished.

It would be too much to give a detailed account here, but from early November the security agencies let loose their lackey gangsters to physically attack the facilities of the magazine, first the office in Kaohsiung. Nori put out statements that Formosa would organize its own self-defense and apply for guns. At the same time, the security agents began to trail the Dangwai leadership closely, e.g. surrounding the cars carrying *Formosa* leaders with their own black sedans, precipitating incidents like that at the opening of the Pingtung office when a tour bus full of supporters ran a black sedan off the road into a dry rice paddy and chased the agents. On December 4 or so Lu Hsiu-lien put out an appeal for help, reporting that her "new women's movement" publishing house office was totally staked out by agents. The event planned for human rights day, December 10, 1979, in Kaohsiung (it was clear that the political sentiment was different in the south, very anti-KMT) was originally just one among many activities. We had achieved direct communication with the International League for Human Rights in New York and planned to announce the establishment of a Taiwan branch at the event. (I learned later that Professor Chen Lung-chu 陳隆志 had helped arrange this. I knew his book, with Harold D. Lasswell, entitled *Formosa, China, and the United Nations: Formosa in the World Community*. New York: St. Martin's, 1967.) But planning for December 10 rose to a pitch as it shaped up to be a confrontation to determine whether the authorities would prevail in controlling assembly and speech, or whether *Formosa* would continue to flout martial law.

A few weeks earlier I had purchased the fabric and planned three-color campaign sashes in the colors of the first three *Formosa* issues (grass green for spring rice fields; brick red for farm houses; golden yellow for afternoon sun reflecting on the rice paddies, also hope). I couldn't write articles, but I had some kind of artistic empathy with the *Formosa* layout artist. I had planned the colors to distinguish us wordlessly from the KMT red-white-blue long before the magazine was begun, and he used them without mentioning any coordination. The 27 finished sashes and 20 armbands only arrived on the evening of December 10, and I personally ran around draping the sashes and armbands on the leading marchers.

The vicious police arrest and beating in custody of two *Formosa* volunteers who were manning the announcement truck the evening before (the Ku Shan Incident; I interviewed Yao Kuo-chien 姚國建, a young mainlander, and Chiu A-she 邱勝雄, a

went around the block. After which the crowd stayed in one place and listened to more speeches, sang songs and chanted slogans.

Shih Ming-teh urged the people to stay calm; for restraint was better than action. He also said that Taiwanese people could now only rely on themselves in settling their legal problems but then this would have to be done orderly and in accordance to the law. By this time, the crowd was estimated to be from 15,000 to 70,000 to include the many people who came over from Kaohsiung's night market.

(What happened next is most unclear.)

At one point, Huang Hsin-chieh surrendered the microphone and a number of unauthorised persons took it over. People began throwing stones and torches at the police. The police in return threw them back into the crowd.

At another point, a small group of security forces became detached from the rest, and this led to what was described by one person as the most violent clash. The arrival of a fleet of riot trucks, the marching of police towards the crowd when the people had no room to move, and the firing of tear gas into the people who were literally trapped — all of these further exacerbated the violence.

It is true that the police did not strike back at the demonstrators when they were in the front line. But the throwing of rocks and beatings of the people who eventually moved behind the police were acts of violence. Further, all witnesses *(whom I spoke with)* confirmed the presence of one to two dozen "hooligans", dressed in identical leather jackets, and who indiscriminately struck at both the police and the people. One witness believed these "hooligans" to have come from a prison for reform, for he had seen a newspaper advertisement recalling these people to Kaohsiung several days before the rally.

Reports are that somewhere between 40 and 180 police were injured before the melee ended at 2.00 a.m. (A news report said that only 62 were treated

14

in the hospital). But there were no reports in Taiwan newspapers of the hundreds of demonstrators who were also injured.

In the next day, newspapers described the events as an *"unfortunate incident"*. On December 12, news report of deliberate violence appeared. By December 13, there was *"evidence"* of a conspiracy to foment violence, led by *Formosa* staff, 19 of whom had been arrested the day before.

On December 12, the editors of *Formosa* Monthly held a press conference in Taipei expressing their regrets for what had happened and also charged the KMT with provocation. To date, there has been no report of this press conference.

The names of 26 persons who have been arrested or detained have appeared in the newspapers. There have been at least 17 others arrested or detained while at least another 20 are in hiding. The government has not yet managed to capture *Formosa* general manager, Shih Ming-teh.

In addition to *Formosa*, two other magazines of the opposition, *The Eighties* and *Spring Breeze*, have also been shut down *"for distorting facts and treating the government with malice."* Also, newspaper reports have made sweeping accusations at the political and intellectual opposition, as well as at *"a small group of people within the Presbyterian Church."*

In short, the KMT has attempted to silence in one swipe the most prominent voices of dissent around the island. This has, in effect, decimated the Democratic Movement in Taiwan.

The KMT's Role in the Creation of Violence

All was not right with the demonstration in Kaohsiung. But there is no way in which the violence which erupted can be seen as the demonstrators' premeditated action to create trouble. Instead, it must be viewed as what happens when a crowd gets out of control after years of pent up feelings against a regime which has imposed its will on the people of Taiwan. People

15

should be punished for acts of violence, and the leaders should be criticised for not maintaining order. But the one charge which has not been adequately dealt with is the government's direct role in creating violence.

What needs to be more clearly understood is not the Kaohsiung incident in isolation, but rather the suppression of the Democratic Movement.

The widely held view in Taiwan is that the KMT took advantage of an unfortunate incident to play its final card in a trap which they had been waiting to spring on for a long time. Thus, the arrests may be seen as a major victory for the KMT *"hawks"*, led by Wang Sheng.

The following four points need to be pursued to get a better understanding of the KMT's role in creating violence in Kaohsiung:

1) An investigation of the facts of the case in comparison with government charges and reports in the tightly controlled press. There are too many questions which have not yet been answered.

2) An investigation of incidents of provocation prior to the incident, especially the use of "hooligans" to incite and intimidate *Formosa* editors.

3) Concern for the wide-ranging questioning of the who may not even have been present on the December 10 evening.

4) The future of the Democratic Movement.

It is difficult at this time to say much about the future of the Democratic Movement in Taiwan. Although that was one of the purposes of the mission, little information could be obtained. Many are the varying and contradictory reports that it is best to remain alert. But one can say that this has been a severe blow against democracy.

I went to Taiwan, expecting to come away feeling

16

quite depressed about the situation. And yet, that was not the case. I was continually inspired and strengthened by the witness of people at many levels. Towards the end of my stay, I was asked, "Was Kaohsiung a victory or a defeat? Now is the time for testing the Taiwanese people." A great tragedy has been suffered in Taiwan. We must however be with the Taiwanese people as they seek to transform an end into a new beginning. ¤

January 4, 1980.

17

middle-aged taxi driver, in hospital on the morning of December 10; they had lost some teeth and were covered with bruises in knuckle patterns) was perhaps part of a security agency master plan to incite a conflict, but that cannot be proven from the interviews of lower-level riot police and activists compiled by the New Taiwan Foundation 新台灣研究文教基金會 (Shih Ming-teh's foundation) in the mid-1990s and published by *China Times*. But from my own observations on the evening of December 10, 1979, as well as later revelations about gangsters hired by the mayor Wang Yu-yun 王玉雲, I conclude that the authorities did intentionally precipitate physical conflict (military camps in the Kaohsiung area were put on alert two weeks in advance), not once but twice, but then were hard-put to strategically place their own formidable forces, in the face of active mass resistance by the Kaohsiung populace, up to 150,000 present. The first time, the cavalcade of 300 Formosa marchers standing in formation in the traffic circle in front of the First Precinct Police Office was sealed off by police lines on all four sides; then huge riot trucks faintly spewing tear gas were brought up on one side, leading Shih Ming-teh and Yao Chia-wen standing on the back of the small lead truck to rally a charge through the police lines on the other side, an exodus to escape tear gassing. The picture of this, slanted to make it look like the marchers were bearing down on the police, was used as evidence of an attack on the police with bamboo torches intended as the first volley in an armed uprising – certainly enough to warrant a martial law Article 2, Paragraph 1, sentence of sedition, for which the death sentence was mandatory. But after some period of disorder, the Formosa cavalcade returned to the intersection in front of the *Formosa* office, was joined by a spirited mass of supporters, and continued with speeches (notably Lu Hsiu-lien's impassioned and articulate address on the right of the people of Taiwan to determine their own future), songs such as "We Shall Overcome" in Taiwanese led by the Presbyterian seminary youths who had designed the program including social protest posters, and electrifying chants such as "Formosa is ours!" At about 10 pm, the riot trucks began sweeping the populace out of the area around the *Formosa* sound truck, but they kept returning; Shih Ming-teh said quietly, "If I go to jail for the rest of my life for this night, I am willing." His ultimate goal, I surmise, was to light the fire of resistance in the hearts of the people of Taiwan. We telephoned reports to the overseas from public telephones, I think, right in front of the scene. We left as clouds of tear gas engulfed the area. Hundreds were gassed, and the crowd tore up the railings on the traffic islands of make blockades, skirmishing with the riot police till 2 am.

About 10:30 pm we met up with the sedan of Chang Chun-hung, I believe, and raced to the Tainan Hotel. Nori was frozen and silent, steeling himself for arrest and torture, I knew. In that moment of silence, I narrated to Nori the end of the Japanese novel *Running Horses* that Nicki had lent me and I had just finished reading: the young nationalistic hero, his deed as assassin done, commits hari-kari as the sun rises. He gave no sign of listening, but a muffled sob escaped from Nori's throat.

We met up with about twenty Dangwai there in all-night discussion in a horrified, mystified tone; no one knew what the regime intended, nor had a realistic strategy; Lu Hsiu-lien's draft of a statement failed to face the facts. But by the time we saw the afternoon papers on December 11, we knew the regime intended a crushing blow

Nicki, December 1979: The Human Rights Link for the Formosa Magazine Defendants' Wives at a Crucial Moment

by Nicki Croghan

(Text combined from her October 20, 2003 draft and December 9, 2003 interview.)

I was raised in Alexandria, Virginia in the American South and as a child I soon learned about how racism persisted in all aspects of society. In the fall of 1964 my high school became integrated when the Black high school was closed and the city embraced integration, ten years after the Supreme Count decision of Brown v. the Board of Education. In fact, my high school was "turned" into the Black high school, which to me seemed like they were just reestablishing segregation in another school.

I attended a small women's college in New York City and became involved in a variety of issues including: human rights, Asian Studies, feminism, prison rights and international affairs. After graduation, I attended University of Pennsylvania for graduate study in Asian Studies. Learning a foreign language in the United States seemed impractical and time consuming, so I decided to study Chinese in Taiwan in January 1972.

Prior to my departure, I was well aware of the Kuomintang (KMT) political oppression in Taiwan and the various attempts to resist it. After arriving in Taipei, I began to study Chinese and to teach English to support myself.

Shortly thereafter, I attended the initial meeting of a new feminist group in a Taipei coffee shop on March 8, 1972. At that time it was illegal to have a political meeting or group without formal governmental recognition. A small group of women gathered that day, and I believe that I was the only non-Taiwanese at the meeting. The obvious leader, Lu Hsiu-lien, announced that the KMT had failed to recognize the group so we were not allowed to meet. There were plainclothes secret police from the KMT in the coffee shop watching us. I had some coffee, talked to some of the women and left. I believe that this group was never recognized officially. This was a good example of the political oppression at this time.

In 1973 I met Peng Shu-yuan in one of the English classes at The Language Center in Taipei. She invited me to her house for dinner and I soon discovered that she was the older sister of the well-known political activist and law professor Peng Ming-min. I had read about him when I was a college student in the U.S. As soon as she said there was political trouble in her family, I realized who her brother was. I began to teach her English privately and noticed that there was always someone stationed outside her house and whenever we went out to eat together someone followed us either by foot or on a motorcycle. At times we were even asked where we were going. The secret police were always brazen, looking for ways to intimidate even relatives of dissidents.

I tried to keep abreast of political activities. I read a well-worn copy of George Kerr's *Formosa Betrayed*, which was passed around by teachers at The Language Center. I

to the opposition, and was grinding out an ominous atmosphere of indignation with exaggerated reports of hundreds of injured policemen (probably actually six significant injuries). But it was generally thought that those targeted for arrest would be those directly involved with planning the demonstration: certainly Shih Ming-teh, and then Chen Chu and Lin Hong-hsuan who were the responsible officers in Kaohsiung. Minimally, Nori would be returned to life imprisonment. We got on a freeway bus back to Taipei; the security agencies were still in disarray and it seemed we were not followed. Midway, getting off at a rest stop in the dark, I urged Nori to make a break for it now (logically he could head for the smuggling port of Tungkang south of Kaohsiung); but he seemed resigned to being the scapegoat and said nothing. Going first to Huang Hsin-chieh's residence not far from the bus depot, Nori was treated to a reprimand from Huang about letting those "communist" youth from the Presbyterian seminary take over. Next, about fifteen people were gathered at Yao Chia-wen's house at 11 pm, and the discussion went around in circles like a broken record, a mesmerized recounting of the events and then a break off. Nori was silent. I had seen this psychological phenomenon before in interviewing former political prisoners: the possibilities are too horrific to be dealt with. After a while, I suggested twice that Formosa make a show of solidarity, returning en masse to the Kaohsiung office and speaking directly from there to the populace, even if they faced arrest. Then Chang Mei-chen (Chang Chun-hung's sister, Nori's secretary) blurted out hysterically, "Say arrest, and you will be arrested!" The lawyers Yao and Lu begged off that they had cases to attend to the next day: an escape to normality. The concrete conclusion was that *Formosa* would hold a press conference at its office at 7 pm, December 12, and that Kang Ning-hsiang would be asked to beg for the good graces of liberal KMT figures; a high-level KMT Party Congress was in session.

The Other Shoe Falls: The Arrests

December 12 was quiet, a day to purge the apartment of incriminating political papers; Nori was out. But I was not thorough enough, and all the name cards of my personal, non-political friends that I failed to destroy were visited by the police later. Then the press conference, a huge crowd of reporters/agents with strobes flashing. Lin Yi-hsiung and the other Formosa leaders who spoke must have felt like pieces of meat thrown to vultures. We retreated to a usual restaurant haunt near National Taiwan University, and then back to our house, with Chen Chu and Lu Hsiu-lien sleeping in the back bedroom. I made whatever international telephone calls I could. Nori went out, came back at midnight, and informed me the arrests were pending, and I should go back to the States with the news. He lay down stiff at my side, as usual sleeping only in shorts, or maybe not sleeping this time although his eyes were tight shut, his skin cold to touch. All night I heard the slamming of car doors and muffled shouts from the lane in front of the house, a kind of psychological warfare notifying us that only a few hours remained.

With the first light of dawn loud pounding on the door below began. From the balcony I glanced at the knot of black cars below, called Nori, and we dressed quickly; he said nothing. I put my purse and address books in the corner by the bed and tossed

studied a little Taiwanese language, read the Taiwan Political Review and tried to learn about the activities of the Dangwai. There were often rumors of crackdowns and some of us would try to purchase books or magazines before they were confiscated by the police.

In early 1978 I returned to Taiwan after spending approximately a year and a half in Japan. I began attending various meeting with former political prisoners and wives of current prisoners. I met ardent activists who knew they would be imprisoned again and men who had suffered greatly in prison. Some of those in attendance were clearly spies, but you never knew who the spy was. I also met Linda Arrigo and Rosemary Haddon at this time. After attending the first meeting, a KMT secret police agent visited me in my apartment and told me that I should stop all political activities immediately. I believe that I did reduce my activities, but I certainly did not stop them. I was convinced that this was the right thing to do.

The political atmosphere grew tenser when the United States announced that it would establish an embassy in China and break off relations with Taiwan, and the subsequent announcement by the KMT that they would cancel the scheduled elections indefinitely.

I was excited with the publication of *Formosa* magazine and read them cover to cover. Linda asked me to translate some of the articles into English. *Formosa* magazine established local offices all over Taiwan and the Dangwai became a de facto political party. Linda and Shih Min-teh had married to try to forestall his arrest. Around September or October 1979 Linda gave me a list of human rights organizations and activists outside of Taiwan and asked me to contact them if there were massive arrests.

The events leading up to and on the December 10, 1979 rally to commemorate the anniversary of the Universal Declaration of Human Rights certainly were confrontational. The police and secret police agents beat up activists announcing the rally and the police attacked the crowds during the rally. I did not attend the rally, but I did meet with Linda and other activists the following day to discuss the possibility of arrests and next steps. I believe it was that night or the next night that I went to Yao Chia-wen's house. I remember clearly that he was flipping through a book of the law of Taiwan, and saying, "Well, we didn't break any law in this book." But of course breaking the law does not necessarily mean anything — even if you had not broken the law doesn't mean that you weren't going to be arrested.

On December 13 Linda called me about 6:00 AM and said that the secret police were coming into her apartment as she spoke and that several prominent Dangwai leaders had already been arrested. The telephone line was cut in the middle of our conversation. She asked me to immediately contact Amnesty International and other human rights organizations in Japan and in the United States and also Hong Kong, as we had arranged previously. So I called Amnesty International and a few other people on the list.

Later that day I met with the wives and families of the Dangwai leaders that had been arrested that morning. Hsu Rong-shu, Chang Chun-hong's 張俊宏wife was extremely important because she had been through this before since her husband had been arrested before. She knew the kinds of thing that needed to be done: they needed to find some quilts, covers, to take in. Some tooth brushes. She was particularly worried about the various people who had been arrested — their health problems — whether they would be

a blanket over them. Without any prior planning, I jammed a small sofa against the front door, and it just fit in the niche so the door could not be opened. Agents were pounding on the door, and Nori shouted to them coolly, "My wife has put a bomb next to the door." Chen Chu tossed me an envelope with US$1,000 and a jade Goddess of Mercy pendant on a thick gold chain, her gifts from Kuo Yu-hsin on her recent trip to the States (other than that I only had US$20). Soon after I saw her rush down the back stairs in back of the kitchen; our apartment was unusual in that it had a narrow flight of stairs connecting the floors in the back, aside from the usual front stairway. But although we did not think that Lin Yi-hsiung downstairs would be arrested, about the same time I heard the large glass doors at the front of Lin's house being shattered. I was standing in the kitchen wondering if I could go to the apartment next door through the back balcony door and ask to use the phone; our phone was dead that morning. Suddenly Nori flew past me over the balcony, silently. A few moments later several agents, some women, burst through the back balcony door and grabbed me. Not to take this quietly, I let out a piercing shriek, and they picked me up physically, broke my glasses, and stuffed my mouth with cloth. Years later, Nori told me he heard that shriek as he was clambering over the tiled roofs of the one-story buildings in the middle of the block, not a minute after leaping off the second-floor balcony.

The agents threw me down in the front room and fanned out to all the rooms. Then they started knocking their knuckles on the walls to find hidden compartments. Within fifteen minutes I dared to suspect that Nori had really gotten away. "No point in asking her, she won't tell," they grumbled. I saw the agents drag out Lu Hsiu-lien, still partly in pajamas, and shouted after her. Then they left me alone. In an instant I found that the telephone was working again, and in a few words instructed Nicki Croghan to report on the arrests as previously arranged. A fat agent charged into the house and yanked the phone out of the wall. Then they ransacked the house, carried off boxes of my research papers as I shouted abuse after them, and left. It was about 7:30 am. I found that they had not discovered my purse and had not taken my diary and the photographs of Dangwai activities that we always threw in a bedroom drawer. I quickly packed these in a satchel, and however it happened I don't know, but a woman I didn't know who was an employee in a Canadian bank in Taiwan immediately picked them up for safekeeping and delivered them to a friend. (Until just five years ago when Chen Po-wen, also arrested at the same time in December 1979, found the negatives of his 1978-79 photography hidden in a pile of X-ray plates -- medical X-ray was his business -- these photographs the agents overlooked were the main cache extant from the raids. Unfortunately they are now in the custody of Shih Ming-teh's New Taiwan Foundation, and could be treated as exclusive property.

I knew the pattern, that the secret police wanted to be able to snatch people quietly and hold them incommunicado and without social reaction while they were broken to confess and submit. Then the prisoner would be trotted out, contrite, for a mock trial, and safely put away for many years, with no heroics and no manifesto. With two telephone calls I knew that the same scene of arrest, no doubt with torture in store, had been played out at Yao Chia-wen's house and elsewhere. At 8 am I walked

able to get medication for hypertension or other diseases that they might suffer from. I remember that Annette Lu's sister was very worried about her health since she had had cancer before and her health was precarious. So, from that time on, I met with family members daily. Any day we had an ongoing meeting to talk about the different issues in their lives. The other major issue was financial. Many of these people were dependent on their husbands or whatever relative for financial support. They were the breadwinners. So how were all of these people now to support their own families without help? So this was another major worry about how to proceed.

I met with them daily to help them organize. I arranged to have photographs of the rally and of the police beating up the rally participants to be taken to Hong Kong and them mailed to Amnesty International and other human right groups. I found various people who were not Taiwanese to take those out of the country and to mail them to various human rights organizations so that they could have that material. Since Linda was detained, I went to her apartment and packed some of belongings. Linda was deported on December 15. I continued to make phone calls to international human rights groups either from my home telephone or from the international telephone office. My telephone was tapped and I was followed. My two American roommates were especially upset when our apartment was broken into and they came home to find a uniformed police officer sitting in the living room! In fact, the police officer stayed for hours until I finally successfully got him to leave.

Leonard Weinglass, a prominent human rights attorney in the United States, visited Taiwan in late December since he had promised Yao Chia-wen to provide legal assistance if and when Yao was arrested. I served as his interpreter.

On about January 3, 1980 I was called to a special secret police office that dealt with foreigners living in Taiwan. I was told that since they "...could no longer guarantee my safety" that they were going to revoke my visa and expel me on January 10, 1980. The level of intimidation was intense for me, a woman alone in a room with several frightening plain-clothes men. It took me a couple of days to realize I had done nothing wrong; in fact, what we were doing was necessary. From that meeting I was followed by three secret agents at all time. When I left the meeting where I was told that I would be deported, I had one KMT agent on my right and one on my left. Then there was a small yellow car that followed me wherever I went. Everywhere I went those people were there. There was no way to avoid having them around. I would try sometimes and maybe I was successful once or twice when I would jump on a bus, ride a couple stops and get off. For example, when I went to get my typewriter fixed, they entered the shop with me and told the proprietor that since I was being expelled on the 10th that they needed to fix the machine fixed immediately. I remember going back to the local dry cleaners where I lived. It was a very small store. There was only room for one or two people in it, and of course since two men followed on either side of me, everybody had to go into the dry cleaners. I gave the clerk the clothes that I wanted to have cleaned, and the KMT agent yelled at the store clerk, "She's being deported on the 10th, you had better have these clothes ready before then!"

I continued to meet with the wives and family members of the arrested leaders and provide assistance and moral support. I was very much impressed with their ability to come together, to support the political actions of their family members, and to stand firm

to the American Institute on Taiwan, ten minutes away on Hsinyi Road, barged into Mark Pratt's office, and demanded that, under the terms of the Taiwan Relations Act which stated the goal of enhancing human rights in Taiwan, AIT stop issuing visas immediately to ROC officials until the prisoners were released. Mark Pratt laughed in my face and recited a remarkable piece of doubletalk: that "enhance" meant to do the same as before, so business as usual. He further divulged that thirteen leaders of *Formosa* had been arrested that morning up and down Taiwan. Had he given prior or *post facto* or tacit approval, I wondered? Distraught and furious, I determined not to go quietly, to shout the news of the arrests throughout foreign institutions in Taipei, and further feed the grapevine. Like a madwoman, I sped through the Stanford Center and other language centers and shouted the news in the lobbies and classrooms. Late in the afternoon I discovered that there were fourteen agents in cars or on motorcycles trailing after me, and I led them on a chase down alleys and through department stores and shook them off for a while. In later years I still occasionally recapitulate frantic Road Runner-type dreams where I leave the KMT agents in the dust.

The wives of those arrested had made a plan to meet at 5 pm at the home of Mrs. Chang Chun-hung (i.e. Hsu Rong-shu 許榮淑, a pragmatic school teacher who supported the family of four children with her salary and business on the side while Chang Chun-hung played out his political pipedreams; she was easily recognizable because her left eye looked outward). At this extreme moment, Hsu Rong-shu held together because she was used to taking care of herself and taking charge; Mrs. Yao Chia-wen (Chou Ching-yu 周清玉) who had always depended on her husband oozed tears continually, and even over a year after the arrests when I saw her in the States she still had a pathetic, almost whining, tone of voice.

When I got to Hsu Rong-shu's house about twenty relatives had gathered, and Nicki Croghan was very competently taking information from the wives as well. My younger sister Sue Ann Arrigo in San Diego, California had been frantically contacting U.S. media ever since the night of the Kaohsiung Incident, and Taiwanese-Americans had contributed the international telephone charges for Bob Aldrich of KPFK, the Pacifica station in Los Angeles, to interview me by telephone. The call went through from Hsu Rong-shu's house, and in one hour I gave a detailed pre-recorded account of the growth of the democratic movement, the issues, and the arrests. I feared that I would be cut off from international communications, or even be myself detained and neutralized; I had to give the most complete historical record, because I was the last witness who could impart understanding of the tremendous sacrifice of my friends. When the call ended, I was told that someone was waiting for me outside: an agent delivered the message that I was to be deported on orders of the Government Information Office, and I was requested to report the next day to the Foreign Affairs Police at 2 pm.

That night I did not dare to go back to my house. I went and stayed at Nicki's house overnight. I had been resolute and purposeful all day; but near midnight I asked her to come over and put her arms around me, and I sobbed uncontrollably for half

with their beliefs. The leadership qualities that Hsu Rong-shu, for example, exhibited in this stressful time still impress me today. The KMT was using these methods to intimidate not only me but Taiwanese too. Those car accidents that happened to Hsu Rong-shu obviously were very suspicious. There is no question about that. She was very important to the support of the family members of the other people who got arrested. So to try threaten her or hurt her, or to kill her, would have a major impact on any response to the KMT and on the treatment of the other family members who were in jail.

Several news articles in the Taiwan press inaccurately stated that I was being expelled since I had helped Shih Min-teh escape. Shih had gone out the back door of his apartment as the police came in the front. He remained at large for 22 days, which obviously was very embarrassing to the authorities. While I had no hand in his escape, I had tremendous admiration for his political organizing skills.

I went to the American Institute in Taiwan (AIT), the de facto American embassy, and asked for some assistance and was told that I had got what I deserved. I was angry that the American government's representative not only would not help me, but also was helping to maintain a dictatorship in Taiwan. They finally agreed to accompany me to the airport on January 10. A young, inexperienced staff person was assigned to go with me to the airport. I was separated from my luggage, which the officials wanted to search with a fine tooth comb. The AIT staffer had no idea that it was important for him to accompany me closely and I had to explain to him what kind of support I needed.

After I was expelled from Taiwan on January 10th, I went to Japan and started to work with Lynn Miles and the International Committee for the Defense of Human Rights in Taiwan (ICHRT) in Osaka. Lynn Miles worked tirelessly to investigate and publicize political oppression in Taiwan under the auspices of ICDHRT. So it was at that time that I worked outside of Taiwan on information about the trials and Lin Yi-hsiung's 林義雄 family's murder. We worked putting out a newsletter several times a year. I helped to send people into Taiwan to get information about what was going on. Of course the whole Lin Yi-hsiung story was very important in that. Then in July of 1980, I made a trip to the United States. After visiting my family, I went to several other cities to talk to Taiwanese groups about Taiwan. I went to Philadelphia, Boston and Los Angeles. And in each of these sites, I talked about the situation with the Kaohsiung Incident and the implications of that. So, I guess I must have worked with Lynn Miles for more like seven years in Osaka.

In December 1986 I joined with a group of activists accompanying Hsu Hsin-liang back to Taiwan. I was among a large number of people who were not allowed to enter Taiwan. Since then I have tried several times to obtain a visa to enter Taiwan and each time I have been denied.

My hope now on my return to Taiwan in December 2003 is to reconnect with the many courageous Taiwanese friends who so generously welcomed a foreigner in their midst.

PNicki Croghan, left, and Rosemary Haddon, right, December 9, 2003, at the conference "A Journey of Remembrance and Appreciation: International Friends and Taiwan's Democracy and Human Rights" sponsored by the Taiwan Foundation for Democracy.

Nicki Croghan

an hour. That night I dreamed scenes of terror, and I woke up in a cold sweat, as described in novels for dramatic flourish, but it was real and my skin was chill and wet and I shivered violently despite warm quilts.

On the morning of December 14, I kept an appointment with an impatient British reporter briefly outside the Taiwan Garrison Command, and then joined with the wives and relatives, many of whom had made a special trip from the south, to send gifts to the prisoners as a group. Theresa Yuan took the picture of us in front of the prison wall. We had lunch together, and then I met with Phil Kurata, the new Japanese-American correspondent for the *Far Eastern Economic Review*, at the Hilton near the Taipei train station. He was new to the cast of characters, and I insisted on giving him a blow-by-blow recital of the Kaohsiung Incident. I was just describing the first phase, with Shih Ming-teh charging through the police lines, when, close to 2 pm, a circle of agents began to close in, and Phil got cold feet and left suddenly. No wonder his report sounded much like the GIO's, and in fact was later copied and distributed by the Government Information Office to foreign inquirers.

Deported, Still Defiant

I was taken to the Foreign Affairs Police and then to an office in the Police Administration. A General Peter Lee of Foreign Affairs demanded my passport, and his face turned livid with anger when I refused. I told him I had given my passport to Phil Kurata, and they believed me and shook down Phil's house that night, whereas when I went to the bathroom I slipped it in between the layers of the cardboard liner of my purse. At one point I slipped past the keepers and ran down the corridor screaming to embarrass them (a kind of strategic hysteria) and prove I was being held under duress, even if I couldn't get away. They requested a deposition from me, and showed me a huge binder of color pictures of myself at the Kaohsiung Incident, proving I was "guilty." I looked like the Statue of Liberty, full-figured in the flowing white embroidered dress I bought in the Philippines. I was pleased to give an account that showed that the government had set off the violence; but the recorder did not write what I said. I insisted on writing it out myself, but as it got closer to 5:30 pm the recorder leaned over and hissed to me, "It doesn't matter what you write anyway, so don't bother so much." I had not known that they intended to deport me on the spot; but my ruse forced them to contact AIT to get papers for me, and an official from AIT came at about 6 pm to take note of my condition. I think the authorities were dismissive of me, as they usually were of women, and they assumed I was just a pawn of Shih Ming-teh, so deporting me would solve the problem of this noisy woman.

I made a fuss about my personal belongings and research materials, actually to distract them from my intentions to press the human rights campaign, and in the time that I was at the Police Administration somehow Theresa Yuan and other friends packed my personal belongings at my house in a big suitcase and my remaining research materials in several cardboard boxes. The police said I could not go home and pack myself because my house was surrounded by reporters. I was taken to the women's barracks of the police at the Chiang Kai-shek Airport for the night, very thankfully with James Decker who had come to the Police Administration

Linda Gail Arrigo was taken into police custody on the afternoon of December 14 after visiting the Chingmei Prison together with other wives of those arrested. She was deported the morning of December 15, 1979.

accompanying me in the police van, and when I looked in the suitcase (the young women police did not understand anything about the political context) I found that Theresa and I had a wordless understanding, and she had packed the three-color sashes and clothes that Nori and I had worn on the night of the Kaohsiung Incident. I secretly stashed one of the sashes in the sleeve of my bulky winter jacket.

The next morning James Decker brought the satchel of pictures, diary, and address book that had been taken for safekeeping, along with other school papers of mine, to where I was being held in the airport. It was hard to make him understand that I could not take the address books and diary while I was under police custody, or they would be confiscated and compromise other people, but finally he took them back. When the police came to question him that night he finally understood, and destroyed the hidden address books. I heard rumors that my diary was given to Cathy Kearney to hold, but it was never seen again. When finally it came time for me to get on the plane, after all the other passengers had boarded, there was a gauntlet of reporters waiting for me in a line on the way. The same AIT official had come again also. I took off my jacket and in one motion arrayed the three-color sash across my chest, a statement of "keep the faith" for the movement. A murmur went up from the reporters. Some agent made a grab at the sash, but I held on to it, and it was too embarrassing for them to struggle with me in public. The first newspaper pictures just showed the jacket swirling, but then the full picture appeared, even on television (Nori, in hiding, saw me being deported), and in that moment of painful defeat the symbolic gesture of defiance, however futile, gave me some scrap of comfort. In later years I learned that it had resonated far.

Over the last two years, as the movement went public, the foreign publicity I had helped to generate was useful, but increasingly peripheral, to the accelerating internal social dynamic. However, I was a functioning part of the operation. Now separated from my circle of friends in the democratic movement, I was alone and exposed as the most obvious bearer of their cause, and feverishly anxious as I pictured the suffering and despondency they must be enduring. Later I realized that going through this experience of seeing my husband and friends physically apprehended and my house ransacked had a long-term psychological effect on me, though I knew it was only a small portion of the experience of those arrested and totally at the mercy of a vicious system,. The sense of personal violation and expropriation of personal papers and property hung with me for a year; I could not bring myself to psychologically invest in organizing my own materials, and I began to understand why Nori continually crammed his personally valuable papers, such as the linguistic study of Taiwanese that he did while he was in prison before, in musty corners where they would probably be lost.

The Rioters Are On Trial, Not the Government

American officials on Taiwan appeared to tacitly endorse the December 1979 arrests, despite the human rights clause in the Taiwan Relations Act. However, the ROC Government Information Office claim that the Kaohsiung Incident was an attempted armed uprising was immediately challenged by the deported American wife of one of the arrested opposition figures, a former political prisoner. Under scrutiny of international media, the authorities finally yielded to long-standing Amnesty International requests for open trials, promising that the martial law proceedings would be conducted under international observation. Thus began the unraveling of the carefully-laid plans of the Taiwan Garrison Command to trot out repentant "conspirators." Domestic media likewise demanded full court access, and for the first time barely-censored transcripts of the trial of the March 1980, ten-day trial were printed in full in the local press, a watershed of political consciousness in Taiwan.

第六章 1980： 國際媒體似乎在公審中華民國

美國在台官員完全無視於台灣關係法的人權條款，首先對於1979年的大逮捕保持緘默。不過，中華民國新聞局的宣傳—高雄事件是一樁企圖武裝暴動—隨即受到被驅逐出境的前政治犯施明德美籍妻子艾琳達的挑戰。在國際特赦組織的堅持要求下，國民黨最後被迫同意公開大審，以往作爲保衛其政權的戒嚴令，就在國際媒體的注目下首當其衝被審視—台灣警備總部所精心設計「叛亂共謀者」的圈套於是被逐一拆穿。國內媒體也要求同樣的權利，且相當令人驚訝地是，1980年3月18日大審中的文字記錄，居然可不受檢查的全文照登，持續十天全部刊登在每天的報紙上—這是台灣的政治意識上一個分水嶺。

In Mortal Combat with the Government Information Office
"Is Linda the Liar, or James Soong?"

by Linda Gail Arrigo

Debunking the KMT Propaganda: Hong Kong to San Francisco

As I was being deported, I was given a free ticket on Northwest, through Tokyo to Los Angeles. They never asked me where I wanted to go; their consideration was probably that my home address in the United States was San Diego. But I knew the center of international reporting for Asia was in Hong Kong, and when I discovered the stopover on the ticket and reasoned it through in the quiet of the plane, the landscape of Taiwan quickly disappearing behind the clouds – if I would ever see it again – I determined that I must go to Hong Kong quickly. At the transit lounge in Tokyo, I begged an immigration official to let me disembark in Tokyo, which did not require a visa for a three-day stay. The official told me to pull myself together and stop blubbering if I wanted in.

That done, I had to call my mother collect in San Diego to get the contact numbers for Lynn and others in Japan, because I had shoved my address book back at Jim Decker rather than have it confiscated by my keepers. The number of James Seymour in New York, the Society for the Protection of East Asians' Human Rights (SPEAHR), was no problem, because it was easy to memorize, then 212-222-9012. That night I joined Shih Ming 史明 (Su Beng in Taiwanese), the elderly Taiwanese independence revolutionary trained by the Chinese communists who had schemed to assassinate Chiang Kai-shek in 1951, at his modest restaurant and residence in the Ikebukuro area of Tokyo. However, as I learned later, this was not just a small noodle shop with tatamis on the next floor up for the workers; it was a five-storey center of communications for an underground national liberation movement organization, and the waiters who served big bowls of udon were Taiwanese with a mission. Shih Ming was just completing the Chinese version of his *400 Years of Taiwan History*, and I added to it my map of Green Island and the penal facilities there, hand-drawn from the recent memories of our trip in November 1979.

There were demonstrations (very small because Taiwanese could not get secure immigration status in Japan, and in the past the KMT had kidnapped dissident Taiwanese from Japan) and meetings with reporters in Japan. Japanese newspapers ran only the most minimal of reports; the Japanese had an amoral attitude towards the rest of the world. Lynn Miles sent me to visit Nishikura Kazuyoshi 西倉一喜for a day, and Nishikawa wrote a long article that was the major report on the Kaohsiung Incident in Japan, published in Japanese Playboy, which shows less flesh and has more serious articles than the U.S. original. Also in Osaka with Lynn, I met a slight young Japanese man with the last name Watarida 度田, a member of the Taiwan

Immediately following the arrests of the Formosa magazine leadership, the urgent mission was to counter the government's depiction of the Kaohsiung Incident as an attempt at armed uprising. Linda, left, in protest with Shih Ming's group in Japan a few days after her deportation on December 15, 1979. Below James Soong, head of the Government Information Office,

Political Prisoner Rescue Association in Japan, who had volunteered to go to Taiwan to visit the families of those arrested; I sketched a map for him to explain how to get to the homes of foreign helpers and the prisoners' families.

Then I flew to Hong Kong using Chen Chu's money, and my central media effort began. The contacts I had made in April 1979 bore fruit. Sam Ho of Asian Forum for Human Rights immediately sent press releases on the Kaohsiung Incident and the arrests throughout Southeast Asia, and subsequently made up an English booklet with a light green cover that laid out the details of the Kaohsing Incident, based on a fact finding trip there in late December, and explained the issues of Taiwan political economy and KMT oppression. *The Baltimore Sun* and the *Christian Science Monitor* published sympathetic reports. Most importantly, I knew, from the point of influencing those in Taiwan, Lee Yi 李怡 of the Chinese magazine *The Seventies* 《七十年代》 interviewed me at length on December 18. I drew diagrams of the Kaohsiung Incident location and narrated a very detailed account in Chinese, hoping this would influence the trial. This was the major topic of the 1 January 1980 issue, and as soon as it was published, the tide of media coverage, which had reproduced the KMT's reports and photographs, substantially changed direction, although the largest newspapers in Hong Kong, the "yellow" (sex sensationalist) press, were KMT patsies and at least once deliberately quoted me the opposite of what I said in a recorded interview, by deleting a "not". However, I had little time in Hong Kong, because the strong Taiwanese- American organizations in San Francisco wanted me to arrive immediately, and I knew the Taiwanese-Americans in fact were opposed to my going to Hong Kong at all.

I landed in San Francisco in the afternoon a few days before Christmas, on December 22, and although I knew there would be some publicity to meet me and on the way I had prepared a handwritten timeline of the last year of Dangwai activities, I did not realize until I got off the plane the scale of the activity. There were about 150 Taiwanese-Americans led by Kuo Ching-chiang 郭清江 waiting for me in the airport with large signs, plus Chinese-language reporters, and local English news reporters, radio and NBC TV, set up for immediate interviews at 4 pm. They had brought my mother, Nellie Amondson, up from San Diego, as well, and with her quaint and patient school teacher ways she was an engaging figure to serve in press relations. The next afternoon the same game plan was repeated in San Diego with about 40 Taiwanese- American supporters, and even more thoroughly covered by the media. This airport welcome, moreover, provided the model for making national news in about twelve major cities in the next two weeks; in major cities it was even covered by local and national television networks.

Whatever my personal relations with Shih Ming-teh had been, they were far overshadowed by the urgency of the larger situation, that dozens of people had been arrested following the Kaohsiung Incident (my overall guess now is that several hundred people were picked up and interrogated, and the security agencies might well have originally intended to sentence 200), were likely being terrorized or tortured at that moment, and the issue of democratization for the whole society

A Japanese Reporter Witnesses Struggles for Democracy in Taiwan, Korea, and the Philippines

by Nishikura Kazuyoshi 西倉一喜

Interviewed by Linda Gail Arrigo on December 9, 2007.

My first involvement with Taiwan was as a result of a book entitled "Sainara, Zhai-Jen", i.e. "goodbye", written by Huang Chun-ming 黃春明. It is a kind of very humorous exposé, a novel, about a group of Japanese tourists who come to Taiwan, for, you know, prostitution. And this book was so interesting, then I realized that although Taiwan and Japan have had such a close relationship historically, even after the end of the Second World War, there really was no attention paid to Taiwan, for several reasons. I read that book in 1976. I introduced it to Japanese newspapers. That was the first that modern Taiwanese fiction that reached Japan. So people were very surprised, but not pleased about me.

I was born August 1947, and I studied Chinese in the university in Japan. How did I become involved with China? I studied for one year in the U.S., in Lynchburg, Virginia, where I happened to go to the library of Randolph-Macon Woman's College that used to be the college of the famous American female novelist, Pearl Buck. There I started reading Pearl Buck. And then I got really interested in China while I was in the States. So many things happened while I was in the States. I went through a kind of identity crisis, being in an overwhelmingly powerful civilization like the United States. How can I understand my Japanese-ness. But I thought, maybe study China.

I met the very famous scholar of Japanese literature. His name was Donald Keene. He was teaching literature. And I was the only Japanese at the school. And we talked a lot. And I asked him what kind of field he thought I should study for the future. He said China. So I got decided to take up study of Chinese. Or course my English got better in the United States too. I came back to Japan and studied Chinese.

I came back to Japan and I joined Kyodo News Service and after several years of local reporting I was transferred to the foreign news department. While I was doing that, there were some issues of China. But there was the problem of access. Taiwan was accessible, but nobody was paying attention to it. So I visited Taiwan in 1979. I went to the *Formosa* office. At that time I met Linda in Taiwan, and I met Dennis. I found the contacts through some human rights organization and through Chen Yu-hsi, the former student at the University of Hawaii who was arrested and jailed in Taiwan for a while. He was pro-unification, and with some pro-unificationists in Japan. They gave me some information. After I came back I was involved then in using the materials provided

stood in the balance. I was the witness to the events, and, as the American wife of the arrested leader, I was the figure to make the appeal to the American audience. Also, in those early days of Taiwan immigrants coming only for graduate school study, there were very few Taiwanese who could express themselves well in English and deal directly with the press.

Quite fortuitously, at that time the work of the Formosan Association for Human Rights (FAHR台灣人權協會) had mainly moved from New York to San Diego, specifically to Leucadia and other northern suburbs of the city where many Taiwanese-Americans worked in electronics and aeronautics industry and an easy drive from my mother's home on the north side of San Diego. This facilitated our coordination in the first crucial days. Dr. and Mrs. Fan Ching-liang 范清亮, the Chengs (wife Lai Shu-ching), Chen Chiu-shan 陳秋山 (whose thesis I had typed when he was a Ph.D. student at UCSD in the late 1960s) and others sprang into action to coordinate a campaign among Taiwanese-Americans throughout the United States, designing a rapid speaking tour for me, while my mother sent a day or an afternoon in advance to firm up press relations. FAHR was founded originally in New York in 1976 by Tina Chang 張丁蘭, wife of George Chang 張燦鍙, long the chairman of the self-proclaimed revolutionary World United Formosans for Independence 台灣獨立聯盟(WUFI).

With just two days to pause at my mother's house in San Diego, we were strained by some strange phenomena. Our phone clicked and blanked out and a few times a Chinese voice could be heard in the background. An American woman named Johnni Smith, formerly with CAT airlines in Taiwan, called to interview me for her newsletter *Taiwan My China,* and then when her voice turned nasty I realized she was a front for KMT propaganda. She later sent me several issues of the newsletter with its bright Republic of China flag; perhaps at some point she was sincere; because the newsletter ended in a few issues. I received numerous surrealistic, bullying, telephone calls from an American man who claimed to be a special operations Marine who could fly in with a helicopter and snatch Nori, still on the run, to safety. There was a Mr. Liu I met in Japan who claimed some connection to Ku Kuan-min, and who had dangled some huge sum of money to help get Nori out of Taiwan; he pursued me to the United States as well. I concluded that there was some kind of KMT effort to dig information from me about where Nori was, but truthfully I had no idea.

When the airport reception was repeated in San Francisco on December 28 with 40 forty supporters and a very large banner, KMT agents were in attendance taking pictures as well (to identify the demonstrators), and a skirmish broke out that gave the KMT the later opportunity to harass the Taiwanese-American community leaders with exaggerated lawsuits. My mother was flown up the day before to facilitate contacts with American press.

From being part of the Taiwanese Alliance for Interculture a few years earlier, I knew the more militant Bay Area Taiwanese-Americans, such as Chen Tu 陳都 and his wife Nancy (Chen Tu was a covert member of World United Formosans for Independence, which secretly coordinated my trip around the U.S.), rather well and we all pitched into the human rights appeal operation to meet the crisis. I look very grim in most

by Lynn Miles to write a news story in Japan about Taiwan. I started writing about Taiwan, and what the Taiwanese were thinking about themselves. Ms. Chen Chu also came to stay at my house for one day in late 1979.

So that year later after I came back to Japan, there were the arrests. But no Japanese newspaper was talking about it or interested in Taiwan. There are a couple of reasons. Only one newspaper picked it up, but that newspaper was pro-Kuomintang. That newspaper was printing a story based on the version of the Kuomintang. I heard there was a big crackdown in Kaohsiung. Then I found I might be the only one who could write the real story. The other newspapers were only interested in mainland China.

I wanted to write about the Kaohsiung Incident, but without Linda's account, I would have had no materials to do it. So I interviewed her. I remember I saw her within a few days after the Incident. Linda came with her mother the second time a few months later, February 1980. I wrote this article on the Kaohsiung Incident in early 1980, January, and got it published in the Japanese *Playboy*, which has one serious article each issue, and that is a very good place for non-fiction writers to get published. And it has very wide circulation. When I wrote it, the Japanese audience was surprised; they only knew about Chiang Kai-shek. There was no news about Taiwan.

And there was an immediate reaction, from the mainland and from the Kuomintang. I thought, what about my China career? The Kuomintang's office in Tokyo called me up, and they said you are now *persona non grata*. Then there was the reaction from the China side, saying more indirectly, too much involvement in Taiwan affairs would not beneficial for my future career as a China-watcher. Anyway, I had already published it, so what could I do.

And then I got the assignment to go to Korea. I was a young active writer, and they decided to send me down to Seoul. And in Seoul I got to see more demonstrations again, against the dictator Chun Do-hwan, who had taken over by coup d'état. I wrote many stories about the Kwangju Uprising while I was in Korea. Then I was kicked out, and our office in Seoul was closed up. So I came back.

They couldn't figure out what to do with me. So they decided to send me to China for one year, till things would cool down. While I was in China I was traveling, in fact riding by bicycle over a large territory, and I decided to write a book, *The China Grassroots*, which won a prize. Then China kept me away for the next ten years.

Then I spent several years in the Philippines, just in time for the overthrow of Marcos.

And now I am a professor of political science in the Faculty of Law at Ryukoku University.

of the pictures. Our emergency telephone calls from Taiwan and the long account of the democratic movement development and the Kaohsiung Incident I gave to KPFK radio and other from Taiwan on December 13 was already transcribed by my elder sister Jean Arrigo, and distributed in advance of my arrival by Gerritt van der Weiss and his wife Mei-Chin in Seattle. They had in late 1979 gradually taken over the English newsletter function from Lynn Miles in Osaka, since most of the copies were mailed to Taiwanese-Americans.

After the San Francisco airport press conference, which demonstrated we were mobilized to deal with the American media, the Government Information Office under James C.C. Soong seems to have been goaded into reaction. On January 8, 1980 the GIO issued materials for rebuttal by the overseas offices, a report two-pages each in Chinese and English entitled "Background Report on Linda Gail Arrigo" (in Chinese, 艾琳達其人其事), attaching two pictures from the Kaohsiung Incident. This was reported in a classified document to the National Security Bureau with copy to the office of the head of the Executive Yuan [See copies in National Archives, bar code National Security Bureau 069300Z00059, GIO no. 00569]. The report utilized excerpts on my marriage and relationship with Shih Ming-teh from the scandal letter reported on by United Daily News on July 27, 1979, apparently in the belief that my violation of traditional Chinese values, e.g. against remarriage by women, would sway Western press against my witness of the events.

My Black Propaganda Gambit: United Daily News Takes the Bait

In the last few days of 1979 I planned my own intelligence counter-strike against the KMT. In late 1978 or early 1979 (when I still lived at Da Feng Road, I remember) one of my friends obtained a small booklet, about 4 cm x 4 cm with a bright grass green cover, evidently circulated by the some forces in the government, which depicted the Dangwai as a scheme of the Americans and claimed that Lu Hsiu-lien and Ai Lin-da (myself) were agents of the U.S. CIA. Of course the KMT always needed some scapegoat to explain its reverses, either communists or liberal Americans. If some elements in the government believed that, it could perhaps somewhat explain why the authorities were rather tardy in moving against me. Moreover, I thought now that if I could reinforce that impression it might gain some breathing space for my friends in the hands of the security agencies, and give encouragement to the supporters of the *Dangwai*. I penned a detailed alternative biography for myself, including that my real name was Catherine Borgio (an alias I had once used in a report to Lynn that had been confiscated; my grandfather was from Burgio, Sicily), and that I had been trained in Chinese from a young age at the Monterey military language school, et cetera. After several tries, I managed to recruit someone plausible, ostensibly my classmate at Monterey, to anonymously telephone this information to the *United Daily News*聯合報 and the Taiwan Garrison Command. My "classmate," whose identity I will not reveal here, said both even accepted the reversed international telephone charges, but the Taiwan Garrison Command sounded incredulous. At any rate, on December 27, 1979, the *United Daily News* printed a large report on my alleged CIA connection, even embroidering the details to make me out to be an electronics communications

United Daily News, December 29, 1979. "An American friend calls international at own expense to expose that Ai Linda belongs to the Central Intelligence Agency! Real name Catherine Borgia, recruited 1972. Came to Taiwan four years ago, complex relations with the political opposition."

expert as well. That stacks of incomprehensible computer printouts, just numbers, had been found at my house, could be whipped into such a story; but actually they were just a computer simulation of demographic processes that I had been working on for years. Then as part of the *Washington Post's* reporting on the events in Taiwan, they cited the rumor that Linda was a CIA agent, and quoted the denial of the CIA headquarters. This planted information of mine did seem to have some repercussions as I had hoped in the diplomatic relations between Taipei and Washington D.C. According to a brief newspaper report, an old mainlander soldier attacked AIT. Later in 1980 the story grew thicker, when the colorful weekly magazine of *China Times* in June did a full feature on the three supposed attempts of the U.S. to overthrow the Chiang regime, Linda and the Kaohsiung Incident being the most recent, and Senator Edward Kennedy lodged an objection. In later years I heard that the PRC believed the allegation as well, no doubt confirming their mindset that Taiwan independence must be a creation of the CIA, else why would Taiwanese not embrace the motherland?

In fact it would be accurate to say that I functioned as a mouthpiece for the Taiwanese-American activists who championed the Taiwan independence movement (TIM for short), even at the displeasure of the United States. The added element was that I was also a direct participant in the events – and my difference with the Taiwanese nationalists was that I insisted on recognizing the human rights contributions of figures like Professor Chen Ku-ying, part of the *China Tide* group, that the TIM people did not want to mention.

As can be seen from the documents saved from that period, FAHR issued emergency reports on the arrests in both Chinese and English mostly to overseas Taiwanese, and ICDHRT, which had shifted from Osaka to Seattle (with Gerritt van der Wees, his wife Mei-Chin, and also Chen Fang-min) over the course of 1979, issued materials in English to a broader audience. The FAHR organization paid for the travel of myself, my mother to accompany me and help with press work, and for my tremendous telephone bills to Japan, Hong Kong, and sometimes even direct to Taiwan; they also collected the donations when I went to speak, and did not inform me about either bills or receipts, though in the rush of things it would have been nearly irrelevant to me. (Late in 1980 FAHR in New York produced an English booklet just on the Kaohsiung Incident, with a full translation of the transcript of the recordings taken on the sound truck that night; Herbert Thomas, who had been with me and Nicki in Taipei in late 1979, did the translation and editing for this.) Taiwanese-Americans all over the U.S. began writing and calling their senators and congressmen to exert pressure in concern for those imprisoned; a year later this lobbying effort was formalized in the structure of the Formosan Association for Public Affairs (FAPA, "fa-pa" in Taiwanese roughly means "strike a blow" or "make an effort") through the efforts of Trong Chai (Tsai Tong-rong, a Taiwanese-American professor of political science in New York who had served in past years as chairman of WUFI).

In San Diego a Taiwanese who ran a photo shop, Ken Wang, immediately made a set of slides for me from the dozens of photographs that I had been able to stash in my luggage, and these proved invaluable. I made a slide-show narrative from them, plus

United Daily News, December 29, 1979. "The Kaohsiung riot is distorted by foreign sources. The head of the Government Information Agency condemns ill-intended rumors."

some historical pictures I got from Lynn Miles and my November 1979 photographs of Green Island that I got back from Laurie Wiseberg: the history of martial law in Taiwan, the rise of the young Dangwai intellectuals from the generation that as children witnessed the tragedy of February 28, 1947 but were still able to achieve entrance into national universities, and then the details of the democratic movement breakthrough from the Chungli Incident through to the Kaohsiung Incident, garnished with personal vignettes of those pictured who were at that moment in the clutches of torturers (some of these early rumors of torture were later confirmed). The slides added immeasurably to what I could impart in a two-hour presentation, especially when I was exhausted from day after day of meeting with supporters and reporters, this physical exhaustion superimposed on my own emotionally wrought state of mind.

I remember finishing my presentation in Chicago to a large Taiwanese-American group including many influential doctors, on Saturday, December 29, and seeing many faces streaked with tears as the lights turned up. Those arrested were their classmates or friends or distant relatives; or they had felt a surge of identification with the voice of the democratic movement and its condemnation of KMT injustice. I have probably shown the final set of 80 slides a hundred times, and was very pleased when I found a blue plastic crayon box that they just fit into neatly, where they still reside. (Within a year the North American Taiwanese Professors Association was initiated by doctors from Chicago; this organization expressed great concern for democratization in Taiwan, and is still functioning.)

World United Formosans for Independence: Keeping Tabs on the Taiwanese-American Community

In Washington D.C. my mother and I stayed in the apartment of N.H. Wang (Wang Neng-hsiang 王能祥), who had been very systematically cultivating relations with the U.S. Congress from the mid-1960's. We were trailed a few times by a fake telephone company panel truck manned by Americans (the same later seen taking zoom pictures of us and demonstrators at the Taiwan government office in Washington D.C.), and at some point we saw "telephone company" men opening up the telephone connection panel in the hallway. But we could not afford the time and effort to expose them.

The efforts of the overseas spy system to track our activities can be seen particularly in an early combined report to the Ministry of Foreign Affairs, which lists our itinerary more clearly than I could do myself. Not long after the Kaohsiung Incident, the overseas Taiwanese attacked and/or ransacked the overseas offices, formerly the consulates, of the ROC in Washington D.C., Los Angeles, and even in Germany. Not surprisingly, the now-declassified spy reports obtained from the National Archives often report in great detail on the internal meetings of overseas Taiwanese, and especially note plans for demonstrations and whether I advocated militant tactics.

I met George Chang, chairman of the underground World United Formosans for Independence, and some of his lieutenants at his home in New Jersey just across

Inside!
INTERVIEW WITH TAIWAN DISSIDENT'S WIFE

██████, Reporter
Newsroom, OAKLAND TRIBUNE
P. O. Box 24304
Oakland, CA 94623

NEWS FROM THE PEOPLE OF

TAIWAN MY CHINA

Editor/Publisher Johni Smith | JANUARY 1980 | VOL. III No. 1

WHO IS LINDA SHIH?
TMC Editor Interviews American Woman Deported from Taiwan

This article, compiled from facts revealed during a two-hour telephone interview with former San Diegan, Linda Arrigo Shih, serves as a timely follow-up to the last two articles in this series, "The Closing of the Sixties" (Sep/Oct issue '79) and "No Phoenix in the Ashes" (Nov/Dec '79). It is published in keeping with a promise to the man on the street in Taiwan, out of whose pockets this publication is funded, to write only the truth about his country.

In 1977, Linda Arrigo Chen filed for divorce, left her 8 yr. old son with his father in California and took off to "make a statement" in Taiwan. She'd been there only twice since 1968 when she and Chen, the son of a prominent Taiwan-born businessman, returned to the states to live. Linda, who speaks fluent Mandarin, learned the language during the five years she lived in Taiwan as a teenager with her father, Joseph Arrigo (whom this writer knew), a free-lance entrepreneur who retired there from MAAG (U.S. Military Assistance Advisory Group). She was 18 and had just graduated from Taipei American School when she married Chen.

Child of the sixties had no interest in politics 'til 1968

Until 1968 Linda says she wasn't interested in politics. Her decision to rescue the native Taiwanese from the clutches of the Kuomintang she claims was prompted by a summer stay in 1975 to "research a doctorate on girl factory workers" and, by a course she took in anthropology at Stanford. A child of the sixties, Linda now 31, claims attendance in no less than five institutions of higher learning: Taiwan University and Maryland U. Extension Program in Taipei, La Mesa College in San Diego, Univ. of Calif. at La Jolla, and Stanford. She makes no claims however, of ever having been gainfully employed.

Upon her return to Taiwan in 1977 Linda immediately embarked on a campaign to recruit supporters for her fight against the "Nationalists" (her name for mainlanders in general, the ruling KMT in particular). She found them almost exclusively among former political prisoners. For the first fifteen minutes on the telephone Christmas Night I was inundated by a breathless torrent of horror tales told to her by one ex-convict after another, which prompted me to ask, "Good grief Linda, don't you know anyone in Taiwan who hasn't been in jail?!" She paused briefly to express indignation, then continued with her broken-record list of brutalities. "Of course you saw all this with your own eyes?" I asked. "No, but I know it's true because they told me so."

"Waiting at the prison gates" for perfect helpmate Shih Ming-teh

In June 1977, the ink barely dry on her divorce decree, Linda found the perfect helpmate for her campaign, Shih Ming-teh. You could say she was waiting at the gate when he got out of prison after serving 15 years of a life sentence for inciting armed rebellion while in the ROC army. They were married that same month. Of her first marriage, Linda speaks of "love at first sight". Of her second, she speaks of love not at all. Despite the fact that Shih 38, now has a price on his head as a ringleader—along with Linda—in the Kaohsiung riot last month, and was told his life sentence would be reinstated if he ever ran afoul of the law again, Mrs. Shih doesn't seem to be the least bit emotional over the fate of her husband. At no time during our two hour conversation did she express any wifely distress over her separation from him or fear for his safety. It appears her marriage to Shih was as her American friends in Taipei said "a match of political convenience".

As the wife of a Chinese national, Linda could now take advantage of dual citizenship—use her ROC citizenship to justify her right to oppose the government, her U.S. passport to open doors to outside support. Moreover, Shih could open doors to the underworld in Taiwan where his prestige would be enhanced considerably as the spouse of an American schooled in all the techniques of civil protest in which no Taiwanese had been schooled heretofore.

In the aftermath of what is now known as the "Kaohsiung Incident", the ROC authorities arrested some 50-60 persons responsible for the brick, bottle and axe attack on the unarmed police that night (Dec. 10, 1979). Only Shih is still at large. Among those in custody are oppositionists who also participated in a similar incident in Chungli in the fall of 1977. Evidence now links Shih Ming-teh, "General Manager" of FORMOSA magazine, and Linda, "Foreign Public Relations Secretary", to the Chungli election riots of two years ago which, until last month, was the first anti-government violence on the island in more than a decade.

Dual citizenship open doors to outside and Taiwan underworld

In any event, in early 1978 when CBS Reports came to town to film a documentary on Taiwan, the Shihs were readily available. His American wife at his side, Shih demonstrated the tortures he'd endured under the "Nationalists" by removing his dentures on camera. When I asked Linda about this toothless dissident and his wife, she interrupted proudly, "That was me! That was me!"

continued on page 4

from the Washington Bridge, New York City. After traveling from city to city, I was aware that WUFI was a powerfully motivated organization that represented the aspirations of the Taiwanese-Americans, and could coordinate hundreds of people quickly. So I took this discussion seriously. I presented as detailed an analysis as I could of the democratic movement. But George Chang seemed to me to have only a rather casual interest in my intelligence from Taiwan; or perhaps he did not think that I could tell him anything he didn't already know. From this and later interactions I surmised that WUFI was largely preoccupied with keeping control of Taiwanese-American organizations and their donations for political causes, and although to the community WUFI espoused violent revolution against the KMT, it was actually engaged in lobbying the U.S. public and government. It seemed that WUFI resented any competitors, including the exiled Professor Peng Ming-min, lobbyist N.H. Wang in Washington D.C., or even the Voice of Taiwan.

WUFI had played a crucial role in setting up networks of coordination between Taiwanese-American community organizations in the United States, Canada, Japan, and Brazil, and kept the fires of Taiwan independence sentiment burning. But to my view they were hopelessly conservative and amateur as political revolutionaries, since they did not recognize the global pattern of U.S. support for anti-communist dictators.

To George, I outlined my plan that I must return to Hong Kong during the trials, then scheduled for February, to influence international reporting (news generated within the United States reached local populations on local news pages, but was not respected as the expert word on Asian affairs) and also the Chinese-language reporting that could get back to Taiwan. More than enough money for such a trip had been raised during my speaking tour; FAHR controlled the funds. George said nothing in response. FAHR declined to provide my air ticket to Hong Kong. I later heard WUFI opposed my going to Hong Kong; no doubt they also wished to prevent me from approaching contacts with the PRC.

This was parallel to my experience arriving in Chicago. In Taiwan we had received several newsletters of the Organization for the Support of the Democratic Movement in Taiwan, based in Chicago and headed by Lin Hsiao-hsin 林孝信, a native Taiwanese, originally a graduate student in chemical engineering in Chicago. Leaving for Chicago, I called up Lin, whom I had never met before, and told him what time my plane would arrive. He came to the airport, but was blocked from seeing me by the WUFI members assigned to meet me. Lin is a man of shy demeanor and slight build, and it took him something of a shoving match to reach me. With great reluctance, my WUFI sponsors allowed me to set aside an afternoon to meet with the members of OSDMT. Then I understood that the OSDMT group was mostly younger students who had mixed opinions on Chinese and Taiwanese nationalism, in fact probably leaning towards the former; but their concern for human rights and also social movements seemed genuine. The following year OSDMT put out a thick booklet entitled KMT Spies on Campus compiling newspaper reports on "professional students" and Taiwan government surveillance in the United States, from 1975 to the

TAIWAN MY CHINA

4075 Mississippi St., San Diego, CA 92014

Editor/Publisher **JOHNI SMITH**
Art Director **ANNETTE CUMMINGS**

Circulation: 2500. Distributed subscription-free to: the President of the United States, members of the Cabinet and White House staff, all members of Congress, State Governors, Presidents of leading U.S. universities, Chief Executives of Fortune 500 companies, major U.S. media and individual contributors to the TAIWAN MY CHINA publication fund.

History

TAIWAN MY CHINA, edited and published single-handedly by Johni Smith of San Diego, California, began in February 1978 after acceptance of a personal donation from Taiwan businessman H.C. Tony Lin in response to his plea, "I want to do something to help my country." Additional funds were obtained between May and July 1978 after Miss Smith's "Open Letter to Free Chinese Everywhere" was published in the ROC's leading daily, the UNITED DAILY NEWS, on May 12, 1978. The appeal for support, copied by other Chinese language papers in Taiwan (and overseas), evoked an unprecedented nationwide campaign to raise money for TAIWAN MY CHINA. Over $100,000.00 was donated to Miss Smith in less than seven weeks, mostly out of the pockets of school children. The $70,000.00 donated by the readers of the UNITED DAILY NEWS alone was reported as the largest amount of foreign exchange ever approved by the ROC for remittance to a private individual.

JOHNI SMITH, writer, author and former PR/Advertising executive, whose TAIWAN MY CHINA speaks for the *people* of Taiwan lived and worked among them 11½ years. Originally brought to Taiwan in January 1965 by the now-defunct former flag carrier CAT, Miss Smith resigned from that organization in 1966 and opened her own PR/Ad Agency in Taipei — becoming the first foreign woman to register a corporation in the Republic of China on Taiwan, the first American female member of the ROC American Chamber of Commerce. In February 1971 Miss Smith sold her company, Smith & Associates Co. Ltd., and went to S.E. Asia for 18 months in airline PR and advertising. Upon her return to Taiwan in the fall of 1972 she was subsequently employed as English Advisor to the Taipei City Government Department of Information and concurrently English copywriter for China Airlines' international advertising agency, which positions she held until June 1976 when she returned to the United States.

Editorial content of TAIWAN MY CHINA, format and distribution remain the sole responsibility of Editor/Publisher Johni Smith, independent of any political, governmental, or private group affiliation.

AMERICAN MATERIAL WITNESS IN SLAYING OF RIOT LEADER'S FAMILY
continued from page 1

Road, only blocks away from the Lins ground-floor apartment in the same building where Shih Ming-teh and his American wife Linda Arrigo had lived.

Though Jacobs has been unable to verify his whereabouts at the time of the murders, and there have been some conflicting reports as to whether he visited the Lin apartment that day and exactly how many times he telephoned them, the American political scientist is not a suspect in the case. The surviving daughter's description of the suspected killer as well as other evidence so far uncovered has ruled him out. Nor is Jacobs under arrest. At his request, he is under police protection, and has been advised he will not be permitted to leave the country until the Lin murder case is resolved. Officially, Dr. Bruce Jacobs is a "material witness" detained by the Taiwan authorities primarily in the hope that he may be able to shed some light on the motive for the slayings.

Latest report is that the investigation has shifted overseas in pursuit of the suspicion of an international conspiracy in the case involving expatriate Taiwan independance advocates and their foreign friends, notably Shih Ming-teh and his deported American wife Linda Arrigo.

As additional facts become available, we'll report them.

LINDA ARRIGO, deported American wife of riot leader Shih Ming-teh, preparing to strike a blow for democracy in Kaohsiung last December.

In Reply To A Letter From Hong Kong

DEAR LINDA. . .

Doubtless, your "disappointment" with WHO IS LINDA SHIH? (TMC January), as well as your inability to refute any of it, will be welcomed news to the people of Taiwan. Moreover, I'm obliged to thank you for your recent letter from Hong Kong in which you refer to me as "part of the propaganda network of the Kuomingtang" in as much as it affords me a long-awaited opportunity to publicly thank the government of the Republic of China. I am grateful to them, not only for keeping hands off TAIWAN MY CHINA, but for approving the foreign exchange for the money their citizens donated to finance this publication without ever questioning what I would write or even if I would indeed use over $100,000 of their citizens' pocket money for the purpose for which I solicited it. My "moral responsibility", as you so aptly put it, is to keep faith with the Majority of the people of the Republic of China by continuing to tell the truth about their country. I join them in admonishing you to "seek deeper knowledge" of that truth.

JOHNI SMITH

murder of Professor Chen Wen-cheng of Carnegie-Mellon University in Taiwan in July 1981.

The "Anti-Communist" Writer Chen Ruo-hsi Dresses Down Chiang Ching-kuo

Parallel to the efforts of the Taiwanese-Americans that were closely associated with the Taiwan independence movement, many organizations of people from Taiwan (both native Taiwanese and mainlanders) that had rallied in the 1971 Diaoyutai Movement 釣嶼台運動 and were generally pro-PRC, like OSDMT, took a stand against the arrests. On December 31, 1979, the *People's Daily* in Beijing published pictures of the Kaohsiung Incident and said this was the result of the KMT's "long dictatorship." On January 28, pro-PRC groups in the U.S. urged China to make a statement in support of the democratic movement in Taiwan; but this apparently did not happen. One influential leftist Chinese-language publication in New York, *Taiwan and the World* 台灣與世界, devoted its whole January issue to the *Formosa* magazine defendants; I provided rare pictures of Nori taken in prison in Taiyuan in the 1960s.

More importantly, and related to *Taiwan and the World*, a group of Chinese intellectuals and artists centered in Manhattan quickly penned a letter to President Chiang Ching-kuo politely but persistently expressing concern for the case. This group, including the artist Nieh Hua-ling, had mobilized the first time in October 1979 over the arrest of Chen Yung-shan. This simple letter, written up hurriedly with modern pen on white paper rather than traditional Chinese brush, as would be expected for a formal presentation, and signed by sixteen recognized Chinese intellectuals abroad, was taken to Taiwan on January 7, 1980 and presented personally to Chiang Ching-kuo by Chen Ruo-hsi 陳若曦 (English name Lucy) on January 10. Chen Ruo-hsi, a native Taiwanese writer, had gone to China from the U.S. with her husband, a mainlander, in the late 1960's to contribute to the socialist reconstruction of the motherland. However, they became disillusioned with totalitarian control of personal life during the Cultural Revolution, and left in 1973. Chen Ruo-hsi's collection of short stories entitled The *Execution of Mayor Yin* was considered a masterpiece of anti-communist writing by the Chiang regime, which had long been seeking her visit to Taiwan. Her words could not be ignored, and she met twice with Chiang Ching-kuo during her 10-day visit, her first since leaving Taiwan 18 years before. (Dates for her visit and background are given in the New York Chinese-language newspaper *North American Daily* 北美日報.) Chen Ruo-hsi was quoted in press headlines as saying the incident resulted from "first repression and then violence, not first violence and then repression" 先鎮後暴，不是先暴後鎮. I would like to think that quick and detailed accounts of the Kaohsiung Incident had made the difference.

The Manhunt Creates a Legend: Nori the Man on a Thousand Posters

It was the late afternoon of January 7 and I was just preparing to return from New York to Washington D.C. when someone whispered to me that Nori had been apprehended by the authorities, Taipei time January 8, 3 am. (We had had reports that there was a huge manhunt for Shih Ming-teh throughout Taiwan, with his picture

pasted on all street corners and continually on television, all fishing ports under surveillance, and buses continually stopped en route to check the passengers. In later years I met an indigenous man in a remote mountain area who had been nabbed just because he had a superficial resemblance.) I placed a phone call to Shih Ming in Japan, and Shih Ming, who seemed to have some shadowy sources within the security agencies, told me that Nori would likely be done away with before he could come to trial. A few hours later I went into kind of a trance in which I felt Nori's state of mind, actually peaceful and triumphant in a martyr's death. In fact, I had long known by watching him that Nori had a kind of death wish or a resignation to death that permeated his motivation and his actions; he would die with the same steeliness of will that he had faced the KMT. He would have no regrets for what he left behind. I narrated my trance to Voice of Taiwan as if speaking to myself. But I knew thousands of Taiwanese felt that moment deeply.

In retrospect, we can surmise that Nori's eluding the authorities for 26 days did change the course of the put-down planned by the security agencies. There was a reward of US$62,000 offered for information leading to his arrest, and the threat that those harboring him would be subject to the same punishment – even the death penalty. The huge manhunt for Nori was a tactical error on the part of the authorities, I believe; it magnified his value and the spirit of resistance. It also delayed the trial somewhat until international pressure could kick in and those arrested were allowed friendly lawyers. Finally, from reports then and later, Nori's heroic appearance in the Kaohsiung Incident trial, grinning in the face of death, and his brief whispered encounters with other defendants in the halls helped raise their spirits and turn the trial transcript into a manifesto for the democratic movement.

The details soon came out in the Taiwan newspapers about Nori's arrest on January 8, just following the arrests of the two youthful Presbyterian ministers who had been Nori's lieutenants. These were Lin Hung-hsuan and Tsai You-chuan, deputy managers of the Formosa offices in Kaohsiung and Taipei, respectively (Lin and Tsai before their arrests met clandestinely with Philip Wickeri who made a trip into Taiwan on behalf of the Presbyterian church; later in Hong Kong he gave me a letter from them, and was helpful in our efforts there). The newspaper accounts of the arrests made it appear that Nori had been sold out by Hsu Chun-tai 徐春泰, nickname "Thailand" 泰國, a former political prisoner who was a habitual visitor and helper at our house. Thailand, a plump, jovial-looking man of Chinese ancestry, had told me this story of his background: he had infiltrated the KMT embassy in Bangkok and was working there, as part of an assassination plot of Thai communists to kill the Crown Prince, when the plot was foiled and he was kidnapped to Taiwan and sentenced to 15 years. He claimed to have been with Nori when the 1970 Taiyuan prison break attempt failed, but he did not rat on Nori's role even though he was tied in a cold pond in February for two days to try to make him talk. Nori warned me twice not to trust Thailand, but he did not object to the man frequently helping us with moving and other tasks.

On the night of the Kaohsiung Incident Thailand had been on the command truck

Background Report on Linda Gail Arrigo

Linda Gail Arrigo was deported by the Republic of China for participation in the riots at Kaohsiung December 10, 1979. Her husband, Shih Ming-teh, believed to have been the mastermind behind the riots, escaped temporarily but was apprehended January 8, 1980.

There is conclusive evidence that Linda Gail Arrigo engaged in subversive activities against the government of the Republic of China and is a member of the "Taiwan independence movement" supported by groups of international conspirators.

The Kaohsiung incident was planned and carried out by the Formosa magazine. Ringleaders assembled more than 200 lawless and radical elements from various parts of the island and armed them with steel bars, iron hooks, wooden clubs, brickbats, chemicals and torches. This force was instructed to undertake civil violence under the pretense of celebrating World Human Rights Day. The authorities withheld a parade permit because of the threat to social order but sanctioned a rally in front of the magazine's offices. Instead of holding a peaceful rally, the participants took to the streets in defiance of military and civilian police who were standing by unarmed. Under strict orders to avoid bloodshed, the police resisted only passively and 180 of them were injured. None of the rioters was hurt. People at home and abroad have denounced the violence and those who instigated it. Arrest of such ringleaders as Huang Hsin-chieh, Chang Chung-hung and Yao Chia-wen won wide public support, as reported in the press and television interviews.

Linda Gail Arrigo took advantage of the government's leniency to continue her attacks on the Republic of China and its authorities. She distorted the facts and defamed the government. She joined in harassing activities organized by elements of the "Taiwan independence movement" abroad.

After her deportation on December 15, Miss Arrigo went to Tokyo for a few days, then flew to Hongkong to bear false witness against the government. At a press conference in Hongkong December 20, she misrepresented arrests of the rioters as "political persecution" and an "abuse of human rights." She returned to Tokyo December 20. The next day she assembled about 20 Taiwan independence movement elements and members of Amnesty International and persuaded them to harass the Tokyo office of the Association of East Asian Relations of the Republic of China. These activities were ignored by the Japanese press.

Returning to the United States December 22, she was interviewed by the Los Angeles Times. She claimed that the government of the Republic of China had tortured her husband, Shih Ming-teh, in an attempt to wring a confession from him. Her motive was to place the law enforcement authorities of the Republic of China in a bad light. On December 28, she told the San Francisco Chronicle that the Kaohsiung riot was part of a "democratic movement" intended to win a larger voice in government for the "Taiwanese." She did not say how a violent at-with Nori, and then when the conflict broke out he followed me as I ran around trying to figure out what was happening, either to protect or watch me. On the early evening of December 12 it was his heavily-pregnant common-law wife, a seamstress from Sanchung City, who came to gather the incriminating papers I cleaned out of my house, from so far away. Was he a plant of the security agencies? I think it is possible. But in San Diego I received two letters from him, mailed from Thailand, insisting that he did not sell out Nori but had to leave Taiwan under threat of death from TIM supporters. In the rush of events, I did not answer the letters. Later I heard reliable accounts that he had raped a young woman, a *Formosa* magazine supporter, when he took her to a hotel after she was overcome by teargas on the evening of December 10, and she was so traditional in mentality that she could not face her fiancé (who among those arrested following the Kaohsiung Incident) and followed Thailand back to his country. Who betrayed the location of Shih Ming-teh's hideout is one of the many mysteries that we may never know the full truth of. I don't believe the conjecture that the security agencies let him go just to enmesh the Presbyterian Church; and those who sheltered him successfully shielded some who participated.

Looking back in retrospect from the replay of his role at the head of a rabble in 2006, however, I sometimes wonder if it would not have been better for Nori's own historical legacy and for the future of Taiwan if he had been executed then in 1980 as a hero and a martyr. Now he is likely to be spat upon if he shows his face at a gathering of former political prisoners. I recently heard that he was stung to be excluded from the December 10, 2007 dedication of the Chingmei (now Jingmei) prison as a national memorial, the same venue where he was photographed in 1980 striding into court with the bravado of a romantic revolutionary. But no wonder President Chen, formerly one of his lawyers at the trial of the Kaohsiung Incident, did not welcome him, considering Shih Ming-teh led the September 2006 "Red Shirts" campaign in the name of deposing the president for corruption. We learn a great deal about human nature by facing such painful memories and unanticipated historical reversals.

Linda's Mother Nellie Amondson Captures Congress

Back in Washington D.C. again with N.H. Wang, my mother, N.H., other Taiwanese-Americans in D.C., and Darlene Meyer, a delicate older American woman who had long been concerned with Taiwan issues but largely behind-the-scenes, laid out a campaign to bring the issue of human rights in Taiwan to the attention of Senators and Congressmen. My mother, with her decades as a patient school teacher, was much more effective in this than I was. My mother made up a handwritten sheet with a beautiful picture of me and Nori on it, plus the glaring query below it, "Has my son-in-law been executed?" She took it personally to every office in Congress, blue eyes smiling in her sweet grandmotherly way. She got lists from the Department of Agriculture and elsewhere, and wrote to 500 companies doing business with Taiwan, reportedly leading to endless headaches for David Dean, head of the American Institute on Taiwan.

Myself, I viewed the United States as the Great Satan (and it was interesting that the interns in Jimmy Carter's office of human rights at the State Department seemed to

- 2 -

tack on unarmed police was to be equated with democracy.

Linda Gail Arrigo was born in San Diego, California, January 16, 1947. From 1969 to 1873, she was enrolled at the University of California at San Diego. After her graduation, she pursued advanced studies at Stanford University on a U.S. Defense Department scholarship. In May of 1875 she came to Taiwan as a social researcher subsidized by the Rockefeller and Ford Foundations. At that time, she had frequent contacts with elements of the "Taiwan independence movement." She returned to the United States after September, 1975, and since then has shuttled back and forth between her own country and the Republic of China. In Taiwan, she first was married to a man named Chen. She expressed regret that he was a middle class member with no interest in politics. She said: "What I need is a sweetheart, a father for my children and a political comrade."

She was remarried on October 15, 1978, to Shih Ming-teh, who was to be involved in the Kaohsiung incident. According to a United Daily News report of July 27, 1979, Linda wrote to a friend in the United States on September 29, 1978: "I'm getting married October 15, but I don't really want to. How have I gotten to this position? When will I get out of it! It is a long story, but I don't suppose I can tell you all the intrigues in a hundred words or less. It all the more compels because love and sex are entangled with politics."

The political union of Linda Gail Arrigo and Shih Ming-teh came about hastily, because Shih had just been released after serving a 15-year prison term for sedition and again was in danger of arrest for publishing articles to instigate Taiwan independence. The marriage gave her opportunity to cover up her husband's illegal activities with her U.S. citizenship. At the same time, she hoped that by marrying another Chinese she could obtain Chinese citizenship and stay in Taiwan to engage in activities against the government of the Republic of China.

Linda Gail Arrigo was active in Taiwan in the guise of a worker for Amnesty International. She reportedly said that the Kuomintang would be dealt a heavy blow when a political prisoner married an Amnesty International worker. She claimed to be the spokeswoman for the "Taiwan Democratic Alliance" organized by her husband and others. She made false accusations against the Republic of China's government and joined in anti-government activities. When foreign journalists came to Taiwan, she sought them out and fed them false information. She was a primary source of some of the misleading articles about the Republic of China in the world press. With the inauguration of Formosa magazine in August of 1979, 14 anti-government political activities were undertaken in quick succession. Linda Gail Arrigo participated in all of them.

feel the same way about U.S. actions in South America), and I would not beg for U.S. mercies, even when National Public Radio tried to maneuver me into it. I visited the Embassy of Iran, where the Shah had been recently overthrown, suggesting they welcome me to Tehran to make a statement against U.S. support for vicious police regimes; this was planned but later called off. I even visited the Embassy of the Peoples Republic of China, and naively urged them a make a statement or action in sympathy with the people of Taiwan suffering under their perennial enemy, the Chiang regime.

James Soong, Government Information Office Head, Blames Linda for Bad Press

By the beginning of January the security agencies in Taiwan were no doubt kicking themselves that they had deported me rather than detaining me. The Government Information Office under the smooth-faced James Soong 宋楚瑜 launched a clumsy counter-attack by sending a letter on January 19 under the banner of a public relations agency, "registered agent of a foreign government" Hugh Newton, to newspapers throughout the U.S. denouncing my account of the Kaohsiung Incident, and attaching a literal translation of the propagandistic version of the Government Information Office, which asserted guilt of sedition in advance of the trial. Three days later they followed up with another letter introducing Alice Kao, a conservative reporter and since then a New Party legislator, as a speaker to be invited to unmask the lies of Linda Arrigo. According to one report, when asked if Linda were a CIA agent, Alice Kao said she doubted it. Overall, it seems this GIO effort elevated attention to Taiwan and provided me more newspaper interviews.

In fact by reading the National Archives materials I recently learned that the security agencies had by December 28 prepared and distributed on January 8 the first volley of their attack on me, a quick biography with several errors of fact, in English and Chinese both. This was provided for the use of the CCNAA offices abroad. A discerning reader would note that the Government Information Office clearly considered advocating the independence of Taiwan, an act of speech, sufficient for imprisonment for sedition.

The KMT's past harassment of foreign reporters in Taiwan came to its just deserts when *Newsweek* reported on the Kaohsiung Incident and Nori's arrest. I was just visiting Melinda Liu at the New York office when they were putting it together in early January, and gave her my detailed account; it was the first I had seen her since September 1977 before she was expelled, but she knew my deep involvement then. She discarded Dirk Bennett's GIO-flavored report, and started all over for the January 21 Asian edition of Newsweek. James Soong made a public protest over the Newsweek report, again blaming the lies of Linda Arrigo. Newsweek did not retract.

On January 22, 1980, the anniversary of the Chiaotou march protesting political arrest, a bomb went off at 3:20 am in the baggage handling facility of China Airlines in Los Angeles, causing damage of US$25,000. China Airlines had added a considerable sum to the price on Nori's head (according to a report on January 17, the total reward

Jingmei Prison dedicated as a National Human Rights Park, December 9, 2007. International human rights activists gather together with former political prisoners.

Kazuyoshi Nishikura of Ryukoku University on left, Masahira Watarida of Globalization Watch Hiroshima on right.

TAIWAN（台湾の政治犯を救う会ニュース）速報 No.6（その2）　　80年1月12日

台湾警備総司令部
渡田さんの逮捕を正式発表（1月4日）

日籍旅客渡田正弘涉嫌爲暴徒充交通警總說明已予羈押偵查

The Taiwan Political Prisoners Rescue Committee in Japan on January 12, 1980 reports on the December 21, 1979 arrest of Masahira Watarida while on a mission to Taiwan. Watarida was tortured and held for 84 days, until mid-March.

was NT$2.5 million, equal to US$62,500, which then would have bought perhaps five apartment flats in Taipei). I made a lot of telephone calls to try to explain the significance of the date to the U.S. media, which later was added to my FBI file of suspected connections with terrorists. This was not the only violence. A bomb set at the Los Angeles home of the son of Wang Sheng, the penultimate head of the security agencies, killed the son's father-in-law. Other bombs went off in California without injury. Some years later I heard through Taiwan independence organization sources that one of the group of police who had been charged with apprehending Nori had been murdered in the mountains of Brazil together with his girlfriend. The ROC security agencies at that time had close links with anti-communist forces in Brazil and Paraguay, with considerable travel among them.

The American government's tardy response to the wave of repression unleashed by the ROC's security agencies was probably jarred by the protests of the Taiwanese-Americans, and was at the same time concerned for backlash in the Taiwan government and among allies of "Free China." Under Carter, the State Department's Office of Human Rights (then headed by Ms. Pat Derian) would be charged with reporting on Taiwan's repression. Early on, American officials counseled the Taiwan government against exercising the death penalty (recently confirmed to me also by a former Taiwan Ministry of Foreign Affairs official). In mid-January, David Dean, head of the American Institute on Taiwan in Washington (the quasi-diplomatic front for the State Department's relations with Taiwan), traveled to Taiwan and on January 17 met with relatives of the Kaohsiung Incident defendants in the AIT offices there, a relatively strong display of concern.

Senator Edward Kennedy made early strong statements condemning repression in Taiwan, and later in May 1980 entered a protest concerning the heavy sentences.

On February 5-6 the U.S. Congress held a hearing on human rights in the Philippines, South Korea, and Taiwan, sponsored by Congressmen Richard Lugar, Tony Hall, and others. Ed Morrell spoke for the Philippines, Pharis Harvey for South Korea, and Richard Kagan for Taiwan. My testimony on the Kaohsiung Incident was entered into the record.

Professor Richard Kagan of Hamline University, long concerned with Taiwan issues and also a member of the Committee of Concerned Asian Scholars (CCAS) that opposed the Vietnam War, nevertheless put effort at this time into lobbying the U.S. to seek clemency for the Kaohsiung defendants. Professor James Seymour of Columbia University, also a CCAS member and closely associated with Amnesty International as well, was an expert witness for issues in Taiwan, and his publication SPEAHRhead reported closely on the developments following the Kaohsiung Incident.

The Congress passed a resolution in early March expressing concern for democracy in Taiwan. Though continually countered by the huge resources of the officials of the Coordinating Council for North American Affairs (CCNAA, the Taiwan government's quasi-diplomatic representative), the Taiwanese-Americans had quickly put together a successful lobbying effort, one later formalized in the organization of the

"I Thank the Kuomintang for Making Me Strong" The Arrest and Torture of Human Rights Investigator Masahiro Watarida 渡田正弘

by Yoshihisa Amae and Linda Gail Arrigo

Yoshihisa Amae and Linda Gail Arrigo interviewed Masahiro Watarida and others during the commemoration events for the establishment of the Chingmei (now Jingmei) Prison as a national park, December 7-10, 2007. Watarida is now the Secretary General of Globalization Watch Hiroshima. His mother is a hibakusha, survivor of the atom bombing. The following is written from personal discussion and written sources.

Soon after the Kaohsiung Incident arrests, the Taiwan Political Prisoner Rescue Association (台灣の政治犯を救う會) made plans to send a member of the group, Masahiro Watarida 渡田正弘, into Taiwan to visit the families of those arrested. Watarida, a slight young man of modest demeanor, was born November 7, 1951, in Hiroshima City, Japan. Lynn Miles brought Linda to meet with Watarida on December 16 or 17 in Osaka, to brief him for the trip, and translated for them. Linda drew rough maps of the addresses of the relatives and other contacts, and also wrote out a note of instructions for recovery of her personal papers and research materials. Before embarking on December 18, Watarida carefully copied the information to his own notes, retaining the name pronounced "Linda" in Japanese script.

Watarida first visited Dr. and Mrs. Tien Chao-ming 田朝明, in the 1970s and 80s a main contact for Japanese human rights visitors, and they took Watarida to meet Hsu Jung-shu, wife of Chang Chun-hung, a defendant of the Kaohsiung Incident. With Hsu, he also met other families. Mrs. Tien recalls that when Watarida visited their house, she and her husband circled Linda's address in red (this was also the same apartment building as Lin Yi-hsiung's home, on the first floor). After the Tiens sent Watarida to Hsu's house, officers of the Investigation Bureau visited them at their residence and questioned the couple about the Japanese visitor. A couple of days later, they received a call from Japan, only to find out that Watarida had not returned to Japan as scheduled. They checked with the hotel where he was staying but were informed that he had checked out already. That was when they realized that he was arrested. (Testimony given December 9, 2007, by Tien Meng-shu 田孟淑, "田媽媽", at the Gi-kong Presbyterian Church, Taipei, formerly the home of Lin Yi-hsiung.)

To Watarida's impression, he was apprehended as a result of random checks. When departing from Taiwan on December 21, 1979, he was found by the airport security to be carrying newspapers and magazines covering the Kaohsiung Incident in his bags. Then his name was checked again against a list, and he was detained. He was driven blindfolded to an unknown prison. He was arrested, tortured, and imprisoned for 84 days. The authority arrested Watarida on suspicion that he was on a mission to help Shih Ming-teh escape abroad. Shih, who lived on the second floor over Lin Yi-hsiung's home, had eluded arrest on the morning of December 13.

Formosan Association for Public Affairs.

By the end of January I was in a rush to get back to Asia since the KMT had put out statements that the trial was to be held in February, and I had made speaking engagements for mid-February at the University of Hawaii. After passing through Texas, where David Tsay, to my relief, agreed to provide money for my airfare, my mother and I had only two nights in San Diego before we were off again, my mother a day later while she got together funds for her own ticket. She sold part of her collection of antique clocks and took leave from her teaching job to accompany me. We bought tickets on PanAm that were billed as "Around the World in Eighty Days", 12 stops within that time limit, which was the cheapest way we could also cover Europe. I had tried to get Edward Tanng 陳黃義敏 of Loyola University, Department of Communications, who was very helpful in Chicago, one of the few Taiwanese-Americans I met with very good linguistic and political skills and motivation, to go on this international press campaign, but he could not take leave from his university on such short notice.

Around the World in Eighty Days: Countdown to a Trial

Landing in Japan, we heard that the government had postponed the trial. Lynn's hospitality was not strained by all of us sleeping in one tatami-floored room in his tiny apartment in Osaka. The bathtub was covered over with a board to provide a space for a large copy machine; we bathed in the public baths two blocks away. The prosecutor's indictment was published on February 20, charging the Kaohsiung Incident defendants with seditious intent and actions to try to overthrow the government, under Article 2, Section 1, which carried a mandatory death sentence. From the indictment I could see that my suspicions that Hong Chih-liang 洪誌良 would be used to implicate others had come true, and I spent some time briefing my mother in detail on his case from my previous report to Lynn and from memory (long notes in her handwriting are preserved). I was hoping she could go to Taipei, and attend Nori's trial as a relative. My mother bought an Osaka-to-Taipei ticket for February 26, but the day before, this sweet little old lady with big blue eyes was named a terrorist by the Taiwan government, and the ticket was refunded. Finally, since our PanAm airplane tickets had a fixed end date and we figured the government could not put off the trial much longer, we planned to move on, by March 1.

My mother and I were in Tokyo on February 28, 1980. That morning, a bomb shook a China Airlines flight about to take off in Manila, it was reported. Later I came back to an office to meet with Miyake Kiyoko at about 5 pm, just as she received a telephone call and began to shriek inconsolably. It was a few minutes before she could coherently explain that she had received the news of the murder of Lin Yi-hsiung's mother and two five-year-old twin daughters; the older daughter had survived. For me, I had a strange flashback to the last time I had seen the little girls, playing on the doorstep of their home just below my house in November 1979, and then for no apparent reason had had a sudden overpowering sense of foreboding. Was it a real memory or a recreation of one? As a materialist, I would prefer not to answer the question I posed to myself.

According to a United Daily News article of January 4, 1980, the airport security found a notebook which contained contact information of Hsieh Hsin-chieh, Linda Arrigo, Hsu Hsin-liang, Yao Kuo-chien, and government high officials. Also found in his bag was a Taipei tourist map, on which "important sites" were circled in red. Watarida's arrest was reported in Japanese in *Taiwan no Seijihan wo Sukuu Kai* (in Japanese), No.6, January 12, 1980: 2. The Taiwan Political Prisoner Rescue Association made appeals to the Japanese authorities to demand his release, but reaction was slow.

Watarida returned to Taiwan for the first time since his arrest to attend the opening ceremony of the Taiwan Human Rights Memorial Park in Jingmei. He gave a testimony about his detention at the Gi-kong Presbyterian Church on the evening of December 9, 2007. Gi-kong Presbyterian Church was the former residence of Provincial Assemblyman Lin Yi-hsiung, a leader of the *Formosa* magazine group. (On February 28, 1980, probably an hour after Lin's mother had told an international caller from Japan that Lin had been tortured in prison, an assassin broke into the residence and stabbed to death his mother and the twin daughters. Many Taiwanese believe the murder date echoing the February 28, 1947 massacres was intentional.) Below is the summary of Masahiro Watarida's testimony:

> While I was imprisoned, the interrogator told me about the murder of Lin Yi-hsiung's mother and twin daughters. He asked me if I knew Lin or not. I told him that I've heard of him but have never met him in person. They thought I was lying. The interrogator then told me that if that is the case, he will let me meet Lin. He took me to another room not so far away from where I was staying to see Lin. Lin might not remember it, but we met at the time. I felt frightened and also felt deeply sad for Lin...
>
> Since I was a Japanese citizen, I believe the torture which I received was not as bad as that a Taiwanese would have suffered. On the day of arrest, they would not let me sleep for 24 hours. They forced me to stand and each time I fell asleep they would slap me in the face. They asked me whether I came to Taiwan to help the escape of Shih Ming-teh. I told them I knew nothing about him, but they would not believe me. They also made me kneel on the bed and hit my knees with a rubber stick. They also whipped the back of my feet when I was tied down on the bed. I believe they chose these parts to prevent the evidence of torture from being too noticeable. The torture seems to have stopped after Shih was arrested. Moreover, they seem to have been aware of the rescue campaign initiated by my friends in Japan. As I look back, the torture made me strong. So, perhaps I should thank the KMT for the experience.

He himself does not know what prison he was is in, but it was almost certainly the Chingmei Prison of the Taiwan Garrison Command. Another Taiwanese political prisoner who was there says that the hoses on the shower heads were changed, reportedly so that a Japanese prisoner would not be able to attempt suicide. According to Lynn Miles, upon his return to Japan, Watarida looked traumatized and remained silent, although at that time Japanese newspapers wanted to interview him. Lynn believes that Watarida was threatened with further punishment if he talked, and given the KMT ability to kidnap Taiwanese from Japan, it might have been a credible threat.

The next day, March 1, we were to take a 3 pm flight from Narita to Hong Kong, and we were driven to the airport by a Mr. He 賀 who donated US$500 cash to my efforts as he dropped us off. (I remember that on the way to the airport Mr. He told me the story of how he had gone back to Taiwan in about 1968 for a break during study in Japan, where he had been labeled a student leader; and while driving from his family home in the countryside he was hit intentionally by a military truck from a camp nearby, and came very close to dying, spending months in the hospital. The child with him was not seriously hurt.) But having spent over two hours in traffic jams, we missed the plane boarding time by 10 minutes, and could only stay at the airport and wait for the next day's plane.

My watchword has been to do whatever you can immediately with the resources at hand. Walking around the airport late in the evening, I saw that there was a telex office open till midnight, manned by a lone young man. I asked to borrow and got a book of telex numbers for Taiwan. I composed a message in 30 words (US$1 charge) in English to summarize that Lin's family was murdered right after his mother divulged his torture in the morning telephone call with Japan. I picked out 500 telex address that I judged to be small and medium-size businesses throughout Taiwan, but more in the peripheral and southern areas. The puzzled young telex operator complied. I do not know what impact this may have had, but it was probably amplified by Taiwan's grapevine effect. (Nellie Amondson's letter of May 5, 1980 from Hong Kong to Lynn in Osaka confirms the date and action.)

The next day, discussing with my mother what our next move would be while on the plane to Hong Kong, I suggested she might be able to get into Taiwan on her valid visa with a quick flight from Hong Kong. She quipped, rather cheerily, "You would sacrifice your own mother, wouldn't you?" I had to answer, "Yes." We knew only vaguely that Watarida, the young man that the Taiwan Political Prisoners Rescue Association had sent to Taipei, had been detained. Since my mother was an American who had recently been visible in Washington D.C., I did not expect anything serious to happen to her; but there was still a risk. However, I knew it would be an invaluable encouragement to the families of the prisoners and to Nori if my mother could appear to witness the trial, which the government had claimed would be open to international observation.

There are lengthy documents in the National Archives concerning my mother's intent to come to Taiwan, starting with a late January letter from the government's New York office asking the Ministry of Foreign Affairs for advice, noting that Nellie E. Amondson held a valid visa and was rumored to be planning a trip to attend the trial. As it happened, my mother was pulled aside as soon as she stepped off the Cathay Pacific flight Hong Kong to Taipei on March 9; the agents had a picture of her in Washington D.C. with the same leopard-print coat. A "reporter" jumped out and took a picture of her, which in fact appeared in the newspapers with a line that she sought to attend her son-in-law's trial: a valuable snippet of news about international concern for those reading the martial law-controlled press. The agents tried to grab her passport, but my mother wouldn't let go; after a frightening tussle a Cathay

Masahira Watarida relating his 1980 experience in the clutches of the Taiwan Garrison Command on the evening of December 9, 2007, at the Gi-kong Presbyterian Church in Taipei, formerly the residence of Lin Yi-hsiung. Lin's mother and two small twin daughters were stabbed to death there on the morning of February 28, 1980.

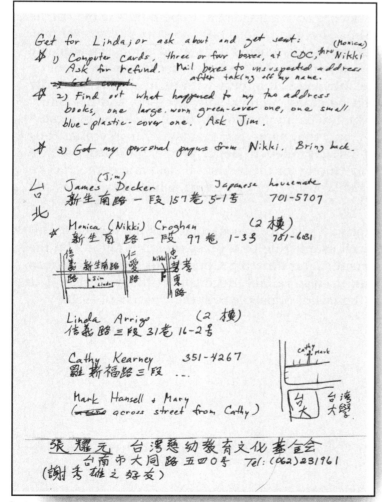

Instructions and addresses Linda wrote out for Watarida.

Watarida at the prison, December 2007: "I was not tortured as badly as a Taiwanese would be. ... Maybe I could thank the Kuomintang for making me strong."

Pacific officer intervened and shepherded her back to the airplane for a return flight.

The Chinese-language Hong Kong press reported at great length on the Taiwan situation, but it was a yellow press among which at least the largest papers had strong ties to the KMT. The remaining press and non-governmental organizations were aligned with the PRC to varying degrees, and virulently against Taiwan independence as well on nationalistic grounds. The overall ethic was, make money and don't rile any authorities. The *Far East Newspaper*, the one with the largest circulation, was eager to interview me and twist what I said to please their KMT backers – to the point of falsifying what I said in interviews with a tape recorder running (for example, deleting one "no" in a sentence with double negatives, completely reversing the statement). Later I learned that the owner of the *Far East* had fled to Taiwan following a drug case, and was given sanctuary there. For television cameras, I had to say what I intended in 30 seconds and stop, or they would edit out the significant content. I had visited Asia Monitor and other social activist organizations in Hong Kong before; but after the indictment in Taiwan named it a case of sedition by Taiwan independence advocates (albeit supposedly as a ploy of the Chinese communists), these left-liberal organizations became skittish. For example, my mother and I had reserved Caritas House, where I had stayed before, a reasonable religious-run hostel, but after two days they asked us to leave, citing harassment by newspaper reporters. We had no Taiwanese to appear with us in public, or hardly even to help. Shih Ming-teh's second eldest brother, Shih Ming-ho, and his family lived in Hong Kong, but didn't want to be implicated. Finally I met some dedicated Hong Kong Trotskyite students, and they were our mainstay for miscellaneous tasks; they were not in favor of Taiwan indepen- dence per se, but their political line was that they wanted the opportunity for the industrial class and democracy to become mature in Taiwan as a model for the future of China, which they saw as still predominantly a feudal dictatorship.

Before proceeding with this narrative, I wish to present a table of my itinerary. This provides dates and details, as well as a listing of sources (notably reports by the overseas offices of the government's Coordinating Council for North American Affairs, CCNAA) that have been used to reliably reconstruct this program. The activities involved or influenced thousands of people over the first half of 1980.

Introduction to National Archives Documents

by Linda Gail Arrigo

Not long after taking office in May 2000, President Chen Shui-bian called for the establishment of a national archives. This ultimately required passage of nineteen pieces of legislation to effect the release of stipulated documents from military, bureaucratic, and administrative organs of the government. A 1970s building originally held by the military was refurbished to provide an initial home for the National Archives Administration檔案管理局, http://www.archives.gov.tw, but it has now moved to specially-built quarters in Shihlin on the north side of Taipei (11160台北市士林區文林路731號1樓, Tel: (02) 2838-8166, Fax: (02) 2838-1988.)

The first imperative for the organization was to collect materials on political history that had been largely suppressed under the long rule of the Kuomintang: the 2-28 1947 civil unrest and massacres, the White Terror, the 1978/79 democratic movement and subsequent agitation leading to the emergence of the now-ruling Democratic Progressive Party. Special visits were made to the National Security Council, Department of National Defense, Ministry of Justice, local courts and Appellate Court, Presidential Office, etc. Some 50,000 documents concerning 2-28 were collected (exhibit was held beginning March 15, 2003 at the Sun Yat-Sen Memorial Hall), and nearly 5,000 concerning the Formosa Incident, of which 20% are still classified.

Under the confidentiality regulations of the National Archives, the copies of the documents I was able to obtain in 2004 through a request under my own name, about 400 pages, had the names of personnel in government agencies and the names of most other than public persons or applications blacked out. However, for the foreign language correspondence about half of the foreign names were missed in this filtering, and so we can know many of the Amnesty International chapters who wrote on behalf of the Kaohsiung Incident, and many of those who applied to attend the trial.

It is also clear from these documents that the dissidents, myself included, were under very heavy surveillance both in Taiwan and abroad; there are reports, obviously made by informants, covering my movements and public presentations following deportation on December 15, 1979. These are now convenient reference materials, often much more detailed and organized than my own records. Reviewing these documents now, it seems that the Republic of China government was much more worried about its international image and even letters from foreign private citizens (which were roughly translated and passed through with cover letters up the chain of command) than I ever imagined at the time, even with my fresh experience of the terrifying and encompassing power of the authoritarian regime. They tried to come up with a strategy to deal with the international news and international human rights groups, but in the initial stages could not adjust their own overbearing mentality quickly enough, and the English translations of their Chinese materials made for very bad PR. In particular, the efforts of the Government Information Office focused on attacking what they saw as the libelous testimony of Linda Gail Arrigo, dubbed "the international conspirator Ai Linda" in internal Garrison documents, as the explanation for the bad press received by the ROC. Although at least hundreds of

The Itinerary of Linda Gail Arrigo's Campaign for the Formosa Magazine Defendants,

December 1979-May 1980

This itinerary of travel and activities has been reconstructed from memory supplemented by various documents such as notebooks kept by Nellie Amondson (Linda Arrigo's mother, who accompanied her for most of this travel and arranged much of the press contacts) announcements in Taiwanese-American community newsletters, airplane tickets, current newspaper reports, and now-declassified reports by the overseas representatives of the Republic of China government, the offices of the Coordinating Committee for North American Affairs. Travel document was Linda Gail Arrigo passport Z3186836 issued Taipei Sept. 5, 1978. Items in square brackets are related events at which Linda was not present.

Date	Place	Linda Gail Arrigo Itinerary, Page 1	Comments
1979 Dec 14	Taipei, Hsu Rong-su's house	Telephone narration of Kaohsiung Incident and political situation to Bob Aldrich of KPFK, Pacific stations, Los Angeles, arranged by Sue Ann Arrigo, Linda's sister.	Made into English transcript for detailed narrative of night of Dec 10 1979.
Dec 15 11 am	Taipei CKS airport	Deported from Taiwan by GIO order. Gauntlet of local reporters at airport. Stayed at Shih Ming's 史明 place in Ikebukuro, Tokyo, first night in Japan.	ROC provided ticket Northwest airlines, Taipei- Tokyo-LAX
[Dec. 15 am]	[Seattle]	50-60 Taiwan independence protesters, most from California and Vancouver, led by seven (names blacked out), attack ROC office and official residence, latter protected by police.	See Jan 15 1980 spy report 0094
Dec 16-18	Tokyo	Activities with Shih Ming. News interviews arranged by Lynn Miles. Interview with Nishikura Kazuyoshi西倉一喜 for *Playboy* article; Nishikura was in Taipei late 1979.	Shih Ming, in Japan since 1950's, leftist Taiwan independence revolutionary.
Dec 18-20	Hong Kong	Met with international media, e.g. *Baltimore Sun* and *Christian Science Monitor, South China Morning Post*. Long narrative to Li Yi李怡, editor of *The Seventies* 七十年代 monthly magazine in Chinese, published January 1, 1980 issue.	Began to turn tide on KMT propa- ganda Kaohsiung Incident was armed uprising attempt.
Dec 20	Hong Kong	Press conference.	
Dec 21	Tokyo, Osaka	Demonstration at ROC office in Tokyo with 20 Taiwanese and Japanese Amnesty International members.	Tokyo ROC office report MOFA rec'd No. 22266.
[Dec 22]	[New York]	Demonstration at ROC office in New York.	Chinese news.
Dec 22 pm	Los Angeles	Met at LAX by Kuo Ching-chiang郭清江 and 150 Taiwanese-Americans. 4 pm press conference at airport with NBC TV news, KPFK, etc., assisted by Nellie Amondson, also contacts of Richard Kagan. Linda prepared handwritten chronology on plane. Press conference transcribed for later use.	See LA CCNAA report Dec 23, NA068300Z00086.

Linda Gail Arrigo

Taiwanese-Americans and a few dozen foreign friends were engaged in intense efforts for rescuing the imprisoned leaders of the democratic movement, I was the wife of the "ringleader" of the Kaohsiung Incident and the figure on hand that Western press could frame a human interest story around. It is not surprising then that its overseas propaganda initiative the GIO was preoccupied with attacking me, while in defensive mode it insisted that the ROC followed the legal processes of a democratic country. Within two weeks of the international outcry, the Government Information Office promised, as a sop, I believe, an open trial. Then step-by-step under accumulating international pressure, the security agencies, which believed in their accustomed ability to completely cow the defendants, along with their kangaroo court proceedings, were laid open to observation by local and international media. And this brought about a watershed in the consciousness of Taiwan's populace and its subsequent political development. Overall, the history reflected in these internal documents should be a considerable encouragement to Amnesty International and to human rights workers who often wonder what their efforts are worth in the face of the stony silence of repressive regimes.

The documents at the National Archives concerning the Kaohsiung Incident begin near the output end of the black box of political surveillance and control, i.e. when the "suspects" are already in custody, presumed guilty of sedition under the definitions of a martial law state that outlaws questioning of the "national goals" of the Republic of China. There do not seem to be any documents from the most feared of the security agencies, the Ministry of Justice Bureau of Investigation, which conducted much of the surveillance and generally dealt with political prisoners until they were handed over to the Taiwan Garrison Command for trial. So motivation and strategy on the part of the government agencies remain hidden. However, in these documents there is still much to be useful, in dates and events that have slipped from clear memory of the participants.

The documents now partially available at the National Archives provide only a few hints of the internal thinking at the high levels of the regime. The first draft of the directive to design the case of sedition against the opposition is dated the day after the incident. Finalized December 20, 1979, it designates three categories of dissidents in the case:

A.   Communists 共產黨: Huang Hsin-chieh 黃信介, Ms. Su Ching-li 蘇慶黎, Wang Tuo 王拓, Chen Chung-hsin 陳忠信.

B.   Taiwan Independence 台獨分子: Yao Chia-wen 姚嘉文, Chang Chun-hung 張俊宏, Lin Yi-hsiung 林義雄, Ms. Lu Hsiu-lien 呂秀蓮, et al.

C.   Shih Ming-deh 施明德and others.

Given this lacuna in internal official documents about what preceded December 10, much of the interpretation of the actions of the regime and its security agencies can only come from seasoned conjecture of those who have experienced its wrath over a period of time and even garnered tidbits of inside information from their captors.

In this chapter, these documents have been used to assist in preparation of 1) a recreation of my itinerary from December 15, 1979, through June 1980, 2) an analysis of the internal discussion of the Taiwan Garrison Command on sentencing of the Kaohsiung Incident defendants, with translation of two key documents, March 19 and April 19, 1980, and 3) a listing of letters of human rights concern and requests to attend the trials.

Date	Place	Linda Gail Arrigo Itinerary, Page 2	Comments
Dec 23 pm	San Diego	Met at airport by 40 Formosan Association for Human Rights (FAHR) members. Press conference led to *San Diego Union*, *Sentinel*, Los Angeles Times articles. KOGO, KFMB radio. KGTV, CBS national TV.	San Diego *Sentinel* article by Linda Matt.
	San Diego	Telephone interview by Johnni Smith, *Taiwan My China*, English KMT-affiliated newsletter, producing derogatory report in January issue. Travel schedule for Linda and Nellie coordinated by Fan Ching-liang 范清亮 of FAHR	Thomas Metzger of UC San Diego publishes pro-KMT article in *San Diego Union*.
Dec 26?	LosAngeles	Activities w Taiwanese-American community.	
Dec 28 pm	San Francisco	Met at airport by Chen Chang Fu-mei of Stanford and about 40 supporters. Press conference, CBS, NBC TV, *SF Examiner*, *San Francisco Chronicle*, *SF Journal* (Chinese language, contact with Maurice Chuck through Rita Yeh).KMT agent taking pictures pushed off by 5 persons, 2 identified, case later used for harassment lawsuit by KMT.	See FAHR and Nellie planning notes. Also Jan 15 1980 spy report 0094, Jan 8 GIO report NA069300Z00059.
Dec 28 pm	San Francisco	Evening meeting with members of Bay Area Taiwan Alliance for Interculture in church hall, 200-300 participants. Contact was Tu Chen 陳都, others cited in spy report.	See Jan 15 1980 spy report 0094.
Dec. 29 am Sat	San Francisco	Linda and over 100 Taiwanese-Americans, 50 from Los Angeles, protest at San Francisco office of CCNAA. CCNAA says office protected by 20+ volunteer students.	See Jan 15 1980 spy report 0094, Dec 29 CCNAA NA068300Z00084.
[Dec 29 am]	[Honolulu]	Leftist activists, over 30, led by two (names blacked out), protest at ROC office, faces obscured with white cloth. Police presence.	See Jan 15 1980 spy report 0094.
	[Taipei]	Taiwan government continues huge manhunt for Shih Ming-teh, announces US$62,000 reward for his arrest, states that those who harbor him will get same sentence, even death sentence.	Shih Ming-teh's mug shot is from *United Daily News* scandal letter report, July 1979.
Dec 29 pm Sat	Chicago	Met at O'Hare airport by Maurice Lin and Thomas Lin, WUFI supporters, also Lin Hsiao-hsin 林孝信, Organization for Support of the Democratic Movement in Taiwan (OSDMT). Press release by Chicago Committee for Rescuing Political Prisoners in Taiwan, for Linda's talk to Annual Meeting of Taiwanese Assn. of Greater Chicago at Hinsdale Community House. Participants 800 or so for New Years dinner. Many doctors present, later formed North American Taiwanese Professors Assn. Long *Chicago Tribune* article by Rogers Worthington. *Christian Science Monitor* report 12/30.	News efforts later assisted by Edward Tanng 陳黃義敏, Communication Dept., Loyola U. of Chicago. See Jan 15 1980 spy report 00942: 7 ROC govt reps ejected, allegedly student from Singapore beaten.

President Chen Shui-bian shaking hands with Nellie G.. Amondson and daughter Linda Gail Arrigo at commemoration of Green Island prison memorial, December 10, 2002.

Wang Neng-hsiang at a conference on Kuo Yu-hsin, 2006. Wang assisted elder statesman Kuo after he settled in Washington D.C. in 1975, putting out a human rights newsletter. Wang was of invaluable assistance to the 1980 campaign for the Formosa defendants, both housing and instructing Linda and Nellie how to lobby Congress.

Date	Place	Linda Gail Arrigo Itinerary, Page 3	Comments
Dec 30 pm Sun	Urbana, Ill.	University of Illinois, Champagne. Large attendance, tense accidental disruption.	See Jan 15 1980 spy report 00942
Jan 1 pm	Washington DC	Met 2:30 pm at National Airport by 40+ Taiwanese, press conference attended by UPI and Channel 5 TV. See UPI Stewart Kellerman story. Talk at United Methodist Church 4:00 pm attended by 156 (only members of Taiwan association allowed to enter). 100 vote to demonstrate at CCNAA Saturday Jan 5.	See Jan 15 1980 spy report 00942, MOFA rec'd No. 00114. No. 00115 quotes Linda "1/3 of Taiwanese support TI", "peaceful means no use."
Jan 2-3	Washington DC	Linda and Nellie visit Congressional offices as directed by N.H. Wang王能祥, also State Department.	
Jan 4 pm Friday	Washington DC	Twenty persons accompany Linda to visit American Institute in Taiwan; AIT head David Dean agrees to meet with her and representatives for two hours. Formosan Assn for Human Rights petitions AIT.	See Jan 15 1980 spy report 00942, Wash. CCNAA Jan 4 NA069330Z00263.
Jan 5 am	Washington DC	Demonstration at CCNA postponed due to snow storm.	See Jan 15 1980 spy report 00942
Jan 5 pm Sat	New York City	Speech at Robert Wagner High School Auditorium, 220 E 76th St, Manhattan, audience 500, 2 – 5 pm. Taiwanese-Americans nation-wide requested to lobby their congressmen for resolution on Taiwan human rights.	Announcements. Also Jan 15 1980 spy report 0094: organizers warn that disrupters will be dealt with.
Jan 6 pm Sunday	New Jersey	Talk to Formosa Association in New Jersey at Kendall Park Community Center. Interview with local reporter, feature story.	Jan 15 1980 spy report 0094. 8-page CCNAA report, Jan 7 307.
Jan 7 Mon	New York 5 pm EST	News received that Shih Ming-teh has been arrested, Taipei time Jan 8 4 am.	
Jan 8 am	New York	Linda, Nellie Amondson, Eileen Chang (Yang Yi-yi, Voice of Taiwan) and Chen Wan-chen hold press conference at New York Internat'l Correspondents Club, attended by over 40: UPI, AP, WPIX radio, WPA radio, Washington Post, and North America (Chinese) newspaper. Linda reports on previous visits to the U.S. by four of those arrested, Shih's arrest that day and effects of Shih's earlier torture.	New York CCNAA report Jan 9 2 pm, MOFA rec'd No. 0519.
Jan 8 pm	New York	Speech at International League for Human Rights, 236 E. 46th St., New York City	
Jan 9-10		Voice of Taiwan broadcasts Linda's emotional vision of Shih Ming-teh facing execution with peace of mind. Hong Kong BBC broadcasts as well.	

"Has My Son-in-Law Been Executed?"

by Nellie G. Amondson

The following information is summarized from the December 2003 Conference "International Friends and Taiwan's Democracy and Human Rights:"

Nellie Gephardt Amondson was born on August 11, 1921 in Kiowa, Colorado, 50 miles south of Denver. The descendant of German pioneers, she grew up on a chicken farm, the eldest of six brothers and sisters. Later her father took up a post at a weather station in Arkansas, and she even trained to fly weather planes. She graduated in math and physics from University of Colorado in 1954, setting a standard of intellectual achievement for her daughters and grandson. She worked over a period of 10 years towards a degree at the Scripps Institute of Oceanography, but is best known for her 39 years as a math teacher at Mesa College in San Diego; she just retired in 2002.

Nellie visited Taipei in 1975, and again in 1978 to meet her daughter Linda Gail's new husband, former political prisoner Shih Ming-teh. The Gephardt family had a tradition of involvement in black civil rights issues, going back to ancestor Harriet Beecher Stowe; and Nellie gave moral support to Linda's involvement in Taiwan. When she received an international telephone from Linda on December 9, 1979, Nellie and her youngest daughter Sue Ann Arrigo sprang into full-time action, in cooperation with the Formosan Association for Human Rights, then also headquartered near San Diego.

Nellie continued in the next phase of the campaign with Linda, internationally, February-June 1980. She took a leave of six months from her teaching job, and sold some of her collection of antique clocks to cover household expenses during her absence. In Hong Kong, the task was to brief international reporters going into Taiwan to cover the Kaohsiung Incident trials, slated to begin March 18.

Nellie especially took notes on Edith Lederer's (Associated Press) talks with Bruce Jacobs, in detention at the Grand Hotel as a material witness following the Lin family murders. In fact now, over 20 years later, Nellie's voluminous letters and notes and the three boxes of archives she kept safe for so long are an important resource for studying the overseas human rights campaign for the Kaohsiung Incident defendants.

The participants were interviewed individually on December 9, 2003, in Taipei:

I am Nellie Amondson, the mother of Ai Linda.

Linda was learning Chinese when she was eleven years old. I was teaching in San Francisco, and once I went to San Francisco State College, where there were fifty teachers of Chinese language from all over the United States and from Canada, in training. They were lamenting that they had fifty teachers and no students to practice on for the summer. So I told Linda, and she brought one of her friends, and all summer long they had the best teaching equipment, fifty teachers, and eleven students. So that was a great advantage for her.

So after that she would ask anybody who came to visit if they would take her to

Date	Place	Linda Gail Arrigo Itinerary, Page 4	Comments
[Jan 10]	[Washington DC]	State Dept Taiwan Desk rep meets informally for lunch with Washington DC CCNAA, hopes rumors of torture of defendants can be dispelled. Senator Edward Kennedy and his assistant eat dinner with CCNAA officials, expresses concern re. Linda's report that Shih will be executed, says he might make statement.	Washington CCNAA report Jan 10 3 pm, MOFA rec'd No. 0662, 7 pm No. 00635.
Jan 11?		Shih reported as actually executed on Jan 11 at 7 am by Chinese news in New York. Taiwan government denies Shih has been executed.	World News 世界日報 (Chinese) Jan 14 editorial.
Jan 10-11	Boston	Linda talks to Taiwanese Assn of Greater Boston and in English at MIT.	
[Jan 9-13]	[Taipei]	News received that over ten persons have been arrested for harboring Shih as fugitive, including Presbyterian ministers and Ms. Shih Rui-yun, secretary to General Secretary Rev Kao Chun-min.	
Jan 12 am Sat	Washington DC	50 demonstrators at ROC government office in Washington D.C., signs "End Martial Law", "Free Political Prisoners", 3-color banners. Linda receives NBC TV interviews. Demonstrators photographed by white agents with zoom lenses.	Washington DC CCNAA report Jan 12 7 pm, MOFA rec'd No. 00783.
Jan 15	New York	Linda goes to New York office of CCNAA with sign, "Taiwan KMT Murderers: If you haven't executed my husband, let family or lawyers see him." Refused entrance, vigil outside in cold.	Picture and story, Overseas Chinese News Jan 17 p. 5.
Jan 17 on	Washington DC	Linda and Nellie canvass Congressional Offices, submit report for hearing, visit offices of Korean and Filipino human rights organizations. Linda records National Public Radio interview.	
Feb 5-6	Washington DC	Congressional Hearings on Human Rights covering Philippines, Taiwan, South Korea. Richard Kagan testifies for Taiwan, Linda submits written statement.	
Feb 9-10	Houston	Talk to Houston Taiwanese Assn. David Tsay, President, promises $800 contribution for Linda's trip to Hong Kong for the trial, funds sent Feb 20.	
Feb 11-12	San Diego	Rest and pack. Nellie sells some of her antique clocks to raise funds.	
Feb 13&14	Los Angeles	Linda departs on PanAm "Round the World in 80 Days" ticket for $1119; Nellie delayed till next day for lack of funds.	
Feb 14-16	Honolulu	Several talks at East-West Center, U. of Hawaii, arranged by Larry Meacham, concerned with KMT spies on campus. Confrontation with CCNA officials and KMT professional students at presentation on Thursday, Feb 14, with about 100 audience. Nellie's letter: "She handled the situation quite well, giving soft answers with informational clout."	Larry Meacham challenged KMT spies on campus in 1979; local news articles. Linda's visit generated more local news.

Chinatown. Then at age 14 she came to Taiwan with her father, with whom I was recently divorced, and she stayed with her father during that time (1963-68) and went to Taipei American School. She ran his import business while he was flitting and flirting, and she was sometimes lonely, so she would go on buses and she would always talk to Taiwanese people, because, she said, they were her family. She was also in a Hei Song Cola ad that was played in the movie theaters between movies, for eight years. Well, Taiwanese people got quite used to her.

I visited Taiwan in 1975 on a family trip to the Orient, and in 1978 I came to meet Shih Ming-teh, whom Linda had just married. On April of 1979 I got a letter from Linda that had been censored, and it had a hole in it, like this (Nellie shows the letter pasted in a photo album, with red paper backing highlighting the sections cut out). It made me quite frightened about what she was doing, that they would be censoring her mail. But I realized that she was a very determined person, and she had to do what she wanted to do.

Then on December 9, 1979, I got an emergency telephone call from Linda. And on December 13 my doctor daughter Sue Arrigo got in touch with KPFK, a liberal Los Angeles radio station, to call Linda long distance. Linda gave a long, intense, interview, and it was the first detailed account of the Kaohsiung Incident, and what had happened in Taiwan. The KPFK interview was while Linda was talking with the wives of the arrested men, urging them to be brave. Nicki Croghan was there also

Linda was notified by the police to report to the Foreign Affairs office the next day, just while she was talking to the wives. She was deported (on December 15). She went to Japan, and gave a ten-page interview that was printed in Japan. Then, she shouldn't have done this, but as she came back through Taiwan on the way to Hong Kong she got off the plane and called a lot of her friends in Taiwan from the transit area at the airport). Then she suddenly realized that they were about to arrest her, and she got on the plane again.

Before she got back to the United States, some Taiwanese friends called me and urged me to go to the Taiwan government office in Los Angeles with them. And I didn't quite know what it was about, but they seemed friendly, so I went with them to the office. As I went into the inner office to talk to the officials about helping Linda in Taiwan, I heard the biggest commotion, a big smashing, and these Taiwanese people were smashing the Taiwan office while I was in the inner room. In other words, they were using me for a decoy. That was quite frightening. I still remember the picture of Chiang Kai-shek hanging on the wall, all smashed up but still hanging by its corner on the wall.

So then I got home, and I got quite a few threatening telephone calls. I still don't know who they were from.

On the 24th of December, back in San Diego, we saw an editor of the San Diego Tribune, and we had hoped to get some sympathy from him for the Taiwan cause. But he said, "There's no problem in Taiwan." And he had mementos from Taiwan all over his walls. "There's no problem in Taiwan. I just went there about six months ago. We went on a beautiful trip, everything paid for, expensive hotels, expensive food, they even furnished me a girlfriend while I was there. And if I don't print anything bad about Taiwan, I'll get another trip next year." So that's how the government kept

Date	Place	Linda Gail Arrigo Itinerary, Page 5	Comments
Feb 17	Osaka	Meet up with Lynn Miles in Osaka, make contacts with Japanese and foreign press, wait for announcement of trial dates.	
	Tokyo	Press conference held in Tokyo, but little news appears in Japanese.	
Feb 25 pm	Osaka	Plan for Nellie Amondson to fly to Taipei to on Feb 26 to attend Kaohsiung Incident trial cancelled after Singapore Airlines instructed not to let her on plane, supposed terrorist.	
Feb 26	Osaka	Linda prepares detailed write-up on background and arrest of Hong Chih-liang 洪誌良, and calls Huang Hsin-chieh's daughter in Taipei to explain this material and states it has been distributed abroad to try to prevent TGC from concocting a communist connection to Huang.	"Rainbow" 彩虹資料intelligence report No. 1203, Feb. 27, full translation of telephone call.
Feb 28 5 pm Thurs	Tokyo	News of murders of Lin Yi-hsiung's mother and little twin daughters that morning reaches Miyake Kiyoko三宅清子 and Linda. Japanese friend of Miyake telephoned Lin's mother in the morning, last words.	
Feb 29 Friday	Tokyo, Narita airport	Leap year. Linda and Nellie miss 3 pm airplane. At airport telex office Linda sends 500 random telexes to Taiwan reporting Lin family murders.	
March 1	Hong Kong	Mail contact through Rev. Philip Wickeri in Hong Kong. Stay at Holy Carpenter Guest House.	
March 1-8		Visit foreign correspondents in Hong Kong: *Baltimore Sun*, *Christian Science Monitor*, *Newsweek*, *Time*, etc., particularly with background on Lin Yi-hsiung. Press conference at Foreign Correspondents Club.	See Nellie Amondson letter to Lynn Miles March 5.
March 9 am	Hong Kong/ Taipei	Nellie attempts to enter Taiwan with valid visa, flight on Cathay Pacific; detained briefly by agents who try to grab her passport; sent back to Hong Kong. Brief notice with picture in Taipei news: Shih's mother-in-law attempts to attend trial. See MOFA correspondence Jan 9 80 (National Security Bureau NA No. 069300Z00005) through Feb 25 (MOFA 03648) concerning Nellie's intended entry; denied.	Intelligence report 檢情要報 Mar 13 02051 fully translates March 10 international wire reports on Nellie's attempt to enter Taiwan.
March 13-21	Hong Kong	Ramsey Clark has visited Taiwan. Linda telephones Shih's lawyer You Ching in Taipei several times to clarify Kaohsiung Incident sequence and 3-color sashes.	Content recorded by intelligence reports 3030, 3103.
March 13 pm evening	Hong Kong	Chris Vertucci of Asia Monitor returns from courier trip to Taiwan; she has obtained typed materials on Kaohsiung Incident from wife of Yao Chia-wen.	
March 14 am Fri	Hong Kong	Linda holds press conference at Foreign Correspondents Club, presents recently-obtained materials from Taiwan, Hong background. Huge attendance.	See handwritten press release with newspaper picture.

a lid on bad news from Taiwan.

On the 27th of December, we left San Diego for a trip across the United States, Linda and I. We went to San Francisco, Chicago, Washington D.C. -- about one week I lobbied in Congress. We went to New York, we went to Boston, and the Taiwanese constantly were calling everybody about what was happening. The Taiwanese were wonderful about financing our trip, taking care of us, and so on. Whenever we went to these new cities, I would go three hours or more on a plane ahead of Linda, and I would talk to the airport officials, and say, these people are just friends of Linda's, and they're just having a welcoming committee. There won't be any violence, everything's fine. I think it was a good idea I did that, or otherwise they might have gotten upset about the banners and the songs and everything.

During this time I was helped by Mark Chen（Chen Tang-shan 陳唐山）and N.H. Wang （Wang Neng-hsiang 王能祥）. In Washington D.C. we went with a Taiwanese Christian group and we held a candlelight vigil in front of CCNAA (Coordinating Council for North American Affairs). In Washington D.C. and New York both we were followed constantly by an 18-foot panel truck, spying on us. They had a tripod with a camera mounted on the back of the truck. That was a little bit nerve-racking. We didn't know exactly what they were doing. We went to Congress and talked to Jack Anderson on the 13th of January.

In New York City Linda talked to five hundred people at a school. My sister Maesel Nagy came from New Jersey, to come to the talk. And when we first came from California, with our sandals with little tiny straps, it was very hard on our feet, so I bought some old army boots for us at a surplus store. And when my sister saw Linda talking to a big crowd wearing army boots, she said, "So your mother wears army boots?" with the implication as in Germany that your mother is going with a military person. So my sister bought us beautiful Hungarian suede boots; her husband is a Hungarian. And we wore these on our trip around the world.

We heard about six o'clock a few days later that Shih Ming-teh would be executed. But then someone called from the Taiwan government, and said he would not be executed, they would give him a trial. I don't know where that message came from, but at least we felt a little bit easier about the seriousness of what might happen.

So then I stayed at N.H. Wang's house, and visited every Senator and Congressman. One night, Linda was off giving speeches, and N.H. Wang was out, and I stayed up all night writing a letter, starting out like this, "Has my son-in-law been executed?" And it had a story of Linda Gail and Shih Ming-teh, and a little bit about the Kaohsiung Incident, and then I also had this big picture of them. It made quite a splash. I was trying to bring some personal interest into the story.

David Dean was head of AIT (American Institute on Taiwan) in Washington D.C., and so many hundreds of people called him about this letter, that he was very annoyed. He said something like, "You can send Linda after me, but don't ever send her mother. She's too much trouble."

We went to Houston, Texas, and there Linda got huge donations. Whenever she got money she tabulated it very carefully. She wouldn't use it for any of our own expenses; she was very careful about just using it for Taiwan expenses. So I was very proud of her for that. A man named Dr. David Tsay in Houston paid for our

Date	Place	Linda Gail Arrigo Itinerary, Page 6	Comments
March 18, Tues	Hong Kong	Kaohsiung Incident trial begins in Taipei. Major Chinese newspapers in Hong Kong print daily courtroom transcript, same as in Taiwan.	
[March 20-30]	[Taipei]	Intelligence reports 雲霓資料 (classified secret, burn after handling) translate in detail the content of reports by foreign observers at the Kaohsiung Incident trials.	Intelligence reports 3159, 3166, 3167, 3178, 3196, 3198, 3202
March 22	Hong Kong	Nellie's letter: "As to the effort of a 'white face', Linda and I are now seeing the results of our 16-hr-a-day work. Taiwan military courts have never had an open trial like this one. Linda personally spent hours briefing people from UPI, AP, *Time*, *Newsweek*, etc., before they went. Edith Lederer, who is writing the AP articles, has now been barred from the courtroom for her stories. Luckily she has the names of about 20 former political prisoners which Linda gave her. We stayed up until 3:30 am again last night clipping news articles. Nori is doing an amazing job."	March 22 Nellie Amondson letter.
March 24-27	Hong Kong	Lynn Miles comes to Hong Kong to assist. Talk at Amnesty International office, HK. Learning of Lin murders, Shih Ming-teh requests death sentence, Linda statements.	See Nagorski, *Newsweek* article, AP releases.
March 26	Hong Kong	One full day at Iranian Embassy with Consul General Roshanger, planning trip to Teheran for April 2-7 to express solidarity with revolution against US-sponsored dictator; cancelled due to new upheavals in Iran.	
April 1	Bangkok	Discussion with activists met through Asian Forum for Human Rights (AFHR).	
April 7	Bangkok	Receipts for $1794 mailed to Formosan Assn for Human Rights, including copying, mailing, telephone, and lodgings for Linda and Nellie in Hong Kong, plus air ticket for a courier's mission RT HK to Taipei and $150 contribution to Asian Forum for Human Rights office in Hong Kong.	
April 8	Bombay	Tourism; unable to get onward flight for a week.	
April 15?	Vienna	Received by Chen Chao-nan 陳昭男 and Taiwanese-born judge in Austria.	
April 17?	Frankfurt	Program set by local Taiwanese Assn. Nellie's letter lists: Frankfurt, Heidelberg, Mannheim, Berlin (meet with Amnesty International), Hamburg, Bielefeld, Wuppertal, Bochum. Interview in Chinese for shortwave broadcast of Germany public radio.	
April 26	Paris	Meet with Chang Wei-chia 張維嘉, network of Shih Ming, and Taiwanese Assn.	

trip around the world; it was US$1,200 each, on Pan American Airlines' Around-the-World-in-Eighty-Days. That was the type of ticket we got. Because we wanted to be in Hong Kong while the trial was in progress. So we went to Hawaii first and Linda gave some speeches there at the University of Hawaii. In Japan we stayed at the home of Lynn Miles, who was working with Amnesty International. We got a call about the Lin family murders. So that was quite frightening. From Osaka where Lynn Miles lived I tried to go to Taiwan, and the travel agent said he got a message back saying, no, Nellie Amondson is a terrorist, and she cannot come. It kind of hurt my feelings, but that is what they said. I tried to get into Taiwan again from Hong Kong. When I got off the plane they took me to a separate room, and somebody with a camera came up suddenly and took a picture of me. A man with a nasty expression demanded my passport, and I took it out to show my visa, but he tried to grab it. I held on with two hands and wouldn't give it to him. He struggled with me and my passport pages got crumpled. Then a Cathay Pacific attendant came over to protect me, and he took me back to the plane. But at least from the newspaper people knew that Shih Ming-teh's mother-in-law had tried to attend the trial.

Then Linda and I went together to Hong Kong. The KMT people harassed us a great deal. They said we wouldn't leave there alive. We stayed in a church guest house, on the fifth floor. And whenever we came home in the evening or in the afternoon, we'd look under every bed, we'd look in the closets to see if somebody was there, we'd look out the window to see if we could still get out if we had to get out in a hurry.

I need to go back to our activities in Hong Kong. Linda had a press conference, and after the press conference a reporter came up to her named Edith Lederer, who had just come back from Taiwan. She said that Bruce Jacobs, an American who was teaching in Australia, told her that his situation was very serious. He was totally frightened, because he was a suspect in the Lin murder case. The government of Taiwan was trying to pin the murder of Lin's mother and two twin daughters on somebody, and someone had noticed that there was someone with a beard coming out of the Lin house about the time of the murders. He had already been held about a month, I think. He hadn't been tortured, but they were definitely holding him and trying to pin something on him. So I found out all I could about Bruce Jacobs, and I wrote up a long paper that I sent to every newspaper in Australia, to every college in Australia, and I said, please write to the American ambassador, please write to everybody you can about Bruce Jacobs' situation. Also, when we went around the world we went to every American embassy and told them about what was happening to him. He had other people working for him, too, but what we did may have helped.

So after we left India, we went to Frankfurt, Germany. And there Linda gave a talk in Chinese, and it was translated into German. The talk was at the University of Heidelberg, and the place in which it was given was a house that Hitler had given to Max Schmeling, the boxer, just as a gift. So it was kind of a strange place. After the talk, they had some appetizers, and one was a plate with ground up meat with a lot of fat in it. But it was hard, like butter. We were supposed to spread it on bread, like our dessert. That was kind of unusual to me.

Then we went to Paris, and we had a tremendous amount of work to do there. We stayed in a very old building that was about to be demolished, but it was owned by Taiwanese person. When you walked across the floors they would kind of bounce.

Date	Place	Linda Gail Arrigo Itinerary, Page 7	Comments
April 27	Paris	Two discussions with Taiwanese in France, one hosted by Chen of WUFI (identified by spy report as lacking one thumb). Detailed account of Linda's political analysis by spy.	Handwritten spy reports of May 4, 6 for "Overseas Intelligence".
	London	BBC radio interview.	
May 1-18	Washington DC	Nellie Amondson continues lobbying Congress with the assistance of N.H. Wang. She highlights the plight of Prof. Bruce Jacobs, detained in Taipei.	
[May 22]	[Taipei]	Bruce Jacobs released.	
May 1980	Seattle, Vancouver	Linda talks to Taiwanese associations in Seattle and Vancouver.	
June 1980	San Diego	Linda goes back to mother Nellie's home in San Diego. Nellie takes Greyhound from Washington DC for lack of plane ticket.	
July 1980	Los Angeles	*Formosa Weekly* founded by Hsu Hsin-liang and Chen Wan-chen in Los Angeles, after split with World United Formosans for Independence. Linda joins in, then makes first of two extended trips by Greyhound bus through Taiwanese-American communities in college towns in Midwest and South, ending in Orlando and Miami.	
Late July – August 8	Managua, Nicaragua	Flying from Miami, Linda visits Nicaragua to understand revolution there, visits FMLN international office and Ministry of Foreign Affairs, interviewed by *La Prensa*.	

The ceilings had beautiful, beautiful paintings on them, but all of this was going to be destroyed soon. We had only a few minutes to go to the Louvre, and they were on strike that day. We didn't get to do any sightseeing; we just took care of our business.

Then we went to London, and Linda talked on BBC (British Broadcasting Corporation), quite a long talk. We went to the headquarters of Amnesty International, and Shih Ming-teh's picture was right in the middle of all the pictures of people that Amnesty International was working for. I kind of suspect that they put the picture of the visiting person's relative right in the middle whenever a family member came. They were very nice to us. It turned out that some people in Norway had been doing a lot of work on behalf of Shih Ming-teh. So we were quite proud of that.

Then Linda was going to fly to Seattle, Washington. I had to go to Washington D.C. and do more lobbying. I stayed again at the home of N.H. Wang. I went to the offices of every Senator, every Congressman. Nobody was rude to me except one person who had a six foot by six foot human rights poster behind the desk. Sometimes it took quite a bit of waiting to see some people. But my usual process was that I would go to the Library of Congress before going to the offices, and I would give them a list of the books I would like to see at noon and after work. And these would be books about Taiwan history, about things that were happening in Asia, because I needed to improve my knowledge. So I would go all morning to the offices, and at noon I would sit and look at these books, and all afternoon go to the offices again, and then come and read again. So I had lunch and evening meal while I was doing that.

Finally when it was time to go home to San Diego, I had run out of money, and my ticket for Around-the-World-in- Eighty-Days had expired. I think I had a hundred dollars left, and the air ticket across the United States would have been about US$650. So I took the Greyhound Bus. It was quite an interesting experience, because Canada had saved some of our prisoners who were in Iran, and the Greyhound had given free trips to any Canadians who wanted to go across the country. So the bus was full of mostly Canadians. I stopped in Denver to see one of Linda's Taiwanese friends, and they gave me quite a few things, in addition to all the things I had brought from around the world.

I was very thankful to the Taiwan people for helping us go on this trip. And everywhere we went they were very gracious to us, they arranged housing for us, and they invited us for meals. In Germany, especially, there was a Taiwanese man married to a German lady [Ursula Chao], and she had started schools for Turkish children who weren't allowed by the Germans to go to school. And she did many other brave things like that. So I think the whole trip was very rewarding from a human standpoint, and in getting acquainted with some wonderful people.

Nellie Amondson

First Task in Hong Kong: Countering Prejudiced Reporting on the Lin Family Murders

The immediate issue when we landed in Hong Kong was the press depiction of the murder of Lin Yi-hsiung's family. The KMT was casting ridiculous aspersions on the Presbyterian Church and on unknown overseas TIM assassins, supposedly their revenge for Lin's cooperation with the authorities (Lin's later testimony, however, tells how he was savagely beaten for his pithy and penetrating comments on the KMT). The further wrinkle was the supposed involvement of a foreigner nicknamed "Big Beard" 大鬍子 in the news, later more precisely called Chia-bo 家博, Professor Bruce Jacobs in political science from Australia.

Since I had lived on the second floor and knew Lin's role in the democratic movement and also the usual operating practices of the agencies towards us – for example, that the house was watched by four different security organizations plus informants – I had a great deal of relevant information. But *Asiaweek*, which sent a very young Linda Jaivin into Taiwan, printed the GIO version of foreign Taiwan independence-related assassins, garished with sleuthy details. *Time* in Hong Kong told my mother that their founder Henry Luce was a very good friend of Chiang Kai-shek. Even after I had spent a great deal of time providing material, the PRC-leaning *Ta Kung Pao* 大公報 printed virtually a KMT version in brief. Only the new Chinese-language *Centre News* 中報 (invested in by Fu Chao-su after he was forcibly bought out of his outspoken Taiwan newspaper *Taiwan Daily* by the military in mid-1978, as mentioned in the previous chapter) with its editor Lu Kang 陸鏗, tall and strident but graying even then after years of imprisonment under both Chiang Kai-shek and Mao Tse-dong, printed a detailed report on the Lin murders, utilizing largely my sources.

Still we made some headway in Hong Kong, especially since my January interview in *The Seventies* had reached currency since then. The KMT version that the Kaohsiung Incident was an unprovoked attack on the police intended to incite insurrection against the government was no longer cited. I was invited to give a talk at Hong Kong University that was attended by perhaps 500 students; the auditorium was full. Five minutes before start time, I was sitting outside the projection room of the auditorium, and had almost finished loading my slides into the projector carousel. A man came up and made some small conversation. Then suddenly he deliberately knocked the carousel out of my hands, scattering the slides all around. The lecture started ten minutes late as I scrambled to reorganize them, fortunately mostly numbered in subject topics. Afterwards I felt that the majority of students were receptive to the human rights issues, if not to Taiwan's right to self-determination.

The murder of Lin Yi-hsiung's mother and two small twin daughters on February 28, 1980, while he was under detention following the Kaohsiung Incident, is one of the inexplicable atrocities of the Chiang Ching-kuo era. An older daughter survived. Internal security agency documents of March 19, 1980, recently declassified, reveal police relief that the start of the trial had distracted public focus on the murders.

The Mysterious Tragedy of the Lin Family Murders: Some Memories of a "Foreign Big Beard"

by J. Bruce Jacobs 家博

When I arrived in Taiwan during mid-January 1980, I went to the Government Information Office, which had previously helped me on several occasions, expressed the concern of many people overseas about the arrested persons, and requested permission to visit them in prison. This request was ignored, though I did receive some assistance in my research. This period in early 1980 was the most xenophobic I had ever seen Taiwan from 1965 to the present.

Many people both in the *dangwai* and among Taiwan's more liberal elements were concerned about the possible fates of the arrested *dangwai* leaders. Death sentences seemed possible and long prison terms a certainty. In addition to conducting research into Taiwan's political system, I spent time with the families of prisoners. Thus, I got to know the families of Yao Chia-wen 姚嘉文 and Lin Yi-hsiung 林義雄, near where I was staying at International House on Hsin-yi Road.

Sometime during January 1980, I received a message from a visiting Amnesty International team saying they wished to meet with me. We had a discussion about the Kaohsiung Incident and the Amnesty team said they wanted to pair me with a lawyer to observe the trial of the Kaohsiung Incident defendants. They requested that I contact them if anything in particular happened.

In the afternoon of February 28, 1980, I had two key interviews scheduled with Tao Pai-chuan 陶百川, one of the key older liberals in Taiwan, and Lien Chen-tung 連震東, one of the important *banshan* 半山Taiwanese who had been involved with the Kuomintang. I spent the morning preparing and ate a box lunch in my room. I had heard that Fang Su-min 方素敏, Mrs. Lin Yi-hsiung, had gone to the prison to visit with her husband, so around noon I rang to hear if there was any news about Lin. Fang Su-min was not home, but her youngest daughter answered the phone and we chatted for a while. I was going to hang up, but she said her twin sister wanted to chat. So we chatted some more before hanging up.

Both of my afternoon interviews went on for some time and I returned home late in the afternoon. I asked Prof. Parks Coble, another young scholar staying at International House, to join me for a drink of Johnnie Walker Black Label — then a really precious drink in Taiwan. During our conversation, I remembered that I had not gotten through to Fang Su-min at noon, so I rang the house. The man who answered the phone said that Fang was not home. I asked when she would return and he answered, "I don't know. Something has happened at home." At the time, this did not seem anything special. When we arrived at the Lin house about 6 pm, it was already dark. There were many reporters and policemen there, but no one would tell me what was going on. I rang the doorbell and several people took photos that later appeared in the press saying I had been to the house at noon, but the reflections of the flash clearly indicated these photos were taken at night. Finally, someone said that Fang Su-min was at the Jen-ai Hospital 仁愛醫院. I rushed there and saw Kang Ning-hsiang 康寧祥, who told me that someone had killed Lin's mother and twin daughters and left their nine-year old daughter severely injured. She was then undergoing an operation in the hospital. Fang was in the hospital under sedation. Several friends said that the secret police had done the murders. At the time, I responded that that was impossible. I said the security agencies could not be so stupid. I told police at the hospital that I had talked on the phone to the twins at noon, and, if I could help with the timing of the crime, I would.

Many of us were afraid. That night, several of us stayed in the hotel near the hospital. The next night, I joined several friends and we stayed at the Lin residence giving some comfort to Lin Yi-hsiung's sister. This was helpful as a neighbor came by to give the money that Auntie Lin had earned washing clothes while her son was in prison. Auntie Lin basically was illiterate, though she did "read" Buddhist texts, and washing clothes helped take her mind off her son in jail.

The next morning, the *United Daily News* 聯合報 said that possibly a foreigner with a beard was involved in the case. My friends were worried, but I tried to crack a joke and told the many police guarding the house that I was here if they wanted me. They said, "Of course, we don't want you."

In the meantime, I had been to visit Lin Huan-chün 林煥均 in the hospital. She was under 24-hour guard as she could identify the murderer. The police let me in and Huan-chün greeted me as her "foreign uncle" 外國叔叔. There were rumors that Huan-chün had said that the murderer was an uncle that had come to the house, but the doctors and nurses made clear to me that Huan-chün had never said anything like that.

The third night I went back to International House to sleep. The next morning, a Sunday, I read the *United Daily News* which said that the foreigner with a beard might have a PhD from Columbia University. Since Taiwan did not have many foreigners with beards in those days, I thought this pointed to me. I rang two friends, who held the equivalent of vice-ministerial positions in the Kuomintang, at home and asked what I should do. Both Kuan Chung 關中 and Chao Shou-po 趙守博 said I should contact the Detective Bureau of the Police Department 刑事警察侷.

The Detective Bureau did not seem particularly interested, but said I could come if I wanted. I had felt it strange that the police had not contacted me about the timing of my telephone talk with the twins at noon on the day they were murdered, so I went to the Detective Bureau to give this type of information. To use a Chinese expression, "I walked into the tiger's lair" 深入虎穴. The Detective Bureau was pleasant. They did not really ask me any questions, though they videotaped a bit. They said this was for "good memories," though I later found out these videos were used when the police talked to so-called witnesses. They asked me if I had contacted anyone internationally after the murders. I said that I had cabled Amnesty International. They asked what I had said and I showed them my copy of the cable. Clearly, from my perspective, nothing was secret.

It was getting late, so I prepared to leave. The police said there were reporters outside. Later reporters told me that the police had called them. As I was hoping to keep a low profile so that I could represent Amnesty at the trial and because any newspaper coverage would tell the murderer where I was, I did not want to make a big public splash. The police offered me "protection" and I signed a paper for twenty-four hours of protection. They asked where I wanted to go and I said I had never been to the Grand Hotel before. So, about 3 am we went to the Grand Hotel. As it became clearer that the press was saying that I had gone to the Lin house at noon and had seen the murderer, I was happy to have police protection. Things at the hotel were rather quiet, though my room was shifted when my college classmate, journalist Don Shapiro, was close to tracking me down. My main difficulty was an inability to sleep after the murders and I was becoming exhausted.

After several days the police said we were going out and I assumed that we were going to hold a joint press conference indicating that I was not guilty of anything. Instead we went to a "safe house" near the old stadium on Nanking East Road. I was happy to answer questions as I wanted to provide any information that I had to help solve the murder case, but we did not seem to be making any progress on the case and, even from my inexpert perspective, it seemed that the police had left many potential leads unexamined. I realized that all was not right when I went to the toilet and was closely guarded. About 2 am, totally exhausted, I said was going home. The police said I was not going anywhere.

About this time they started interrogating me in one-hour cycles, changing the questioners each time. They kept saying someone else had to talk to me. I was exhausted and told them to bring anyone who needed to speak to me there now. Finally, about 4 am they promised that they would not have another cycle and that I could sleep. Then they started again. In my anger and my fatigue, I swore in Hokkien quite foully at the interrogating policeman. When I realized what I had said, I apologized, but feared that I would really get beaten. The policeman thought he had an advantage. My fatigued brain thought quickly. I said, "I never thought..." He answered, "You never thought what?" I said, "I never thought..." He again asked, "You never thought what?" I said, "I never thought that the Republic of China used methods of torture." He asked, "What torture?" I replied, "Deprivation of sleep is a famous type of torture." After that they let me sleep a while. In line with Taiwan's procedures at that time, they asked me to sign a statement of what we had discussed. We agreed on the text and I signed the document in Hokkien as "Bruce Jacobs wants to sleep" 家博愛睏.

I did not know it then, but the law gave the police twenty-four hours with a suspect after which the police had to deal with a case more openly. The time was over and I was met by several representatives of the American Institute in Taiwan, the then *de facto* American embassy. The Americans had spent the night looking for me. Fortunately, in dealing with a foreigner, the police had to respect the law. The newspapers were proclaiming that I had seen the murderer, and there was some concern that the murderer might believe that and come and kill me to prevent any identification. After discussion with AIT, I agreed to continue with protection, with several explicit provisions. I had to re-sign for protection every twenty-four hours. And I had to call the Americans at least once every twenty-four hours. I was to have access to a telephone, a television and newspapers. And, I was to be protected by the Foreign Affairs Police, not the Murder Case Task Force 專案小組.

We went back to the Grand Hotel. This time I was in a basement room with no windows. At least two or three policemen were in my room all of the time. I was desperate for some exercise, so each night I went out around midnight with three police, one of whom had a gun and another of whom had a special expandable metal billy club. They told me that I had a larger group of police guarding me than a visiting premier, though not quite so many as a visiting president. For one month, I never saw the sun.

Virtually, everyday the press had news of the "foreign big beard" in its social news pages. The term "big beard" 大鬍子 means a full beard as opposed to a "small beard" 小鬍子 or a mustache. Clearly, giving such attention to the foreign big beard was an attempt to make it seem that foreigners were involved in the Lin family murders.

Because I was pressuring to be released, the police decided to issue me with a subpoena to go to the Procurator. The reason provided on the subpoena was "Murder" 殺人. Working closely with my lawyer, Henry Hau-min Rai 賴浩敏, I called a press conference for a couple of hours before the time I was subpoenaed to go. In preparation, I photocopied seventy-five copies of all of the key documents including the subpoena. It turned out that in fact I needed 125 copies because so many reporters came to the press conference. At the press conference, I noted that I had nothing to do with the murder case and that I was quite healthy. I said that I did not know if I would be able to come out after seeing the Procurator, but if I came out saying something different, they would understand what had happened. This sensitive statement went to air that night on one of the TV stations.

When I got to the Procurator's, I began to feel more optimistic as members of the press and cameramen filled the area outside. Clearly, they wanted to know if I would come back out from the Procurator's court. I felt much more confident that I would not be jailed in front of such a large press corps, and, in fact, I was released to go back to the Grand Hotel. The next day, the morning press wrote in some detail and reasonably accurately. Many newspapers printed copies of the documents I had distributed.

I had several sessions with such senior security and police personnel as Wang Ching-hsu 汪敬煦, the Commander of the Taiwan Garrison Command, and Tsao Chi 曹極, the chief of the Detective Bureau. Wang told me that they knew I had not committed the murders, but thought I knew something that I was afraid to tell. I told him that if I knew anything more, I would have told them long before. Tsao asked what I was doing in Taiwan. When I said "research," he started to attack Professor John Fairbank of Harvard. I told him I was from Columbia, a different faction, as he was pleased to hear.

Eventually, after a month, I could no longer stand not seeing the sun. I was moved to a room with a nice balcony and view. Clearly, it was much better being in the Grand Hotel than in a prison. But, I had lost my freedom and could not see my daughter. Though the police paid for my room and food, I had to pay for my lawyer, my laundry and my international phone calls back home. These cost me several thousand dollars.

The Americans and the Taiwan government had long planned a US-ROC economics conference to be held in May at the Grand Hotel. Some 48 of the 50 American lieutenant governors were to participate. AIT had long told the Taiwan government that they could not control me at the Grand Hotel and privately told me that they thought I would be released before the conference. On the day before the conference began, the Procurator again subpoenaed me.

All along, the Procurators had said two unnamed people had seen me at the scene of the crime at noon. Finally, at this late date, the Procurator brought out an older Hakka woman who was a neighbor of Lin Yi-hsiung's. She said she had seen me go to the house at noon on February 28. The Procurator then gave me a chance to cross-examine her. I had had no training in cross-examination, but my freedom depended upon my skill. I asked the witness, "How many foreigners have you seen with a beard?" She replied, "One." I asked, "If you have seen only one foreigner with a beard, how do you know it was me?" She replied, "Because I have seen only one foreigner with a beard, therefore I know it is you."

The Procurator clearly saw that this case would not hold up in an open courtroom. I was told that I could leave that evening. I booked flights to Hong Kong and Melbourne, and arranged to overnight in Hong Kong with a close friend there. When I got to Hong Kong, I was pleased to be free after three months of "police protection." It was only later that night after some celebrations, when I opened my suitcase and discovered that it had been gone through thoroughly, that I finally broke down.

Many people over the years have asked me, "Who murdered Lin Yi-hsiung's mother and twin daughters?" I do not know, but the death of Chen Wen-cheng 陳文成 in 1981 and the murder of Henry Liu Yi-liang 劉宜良 (pen name Chiang Nan 江南) in 1984 in the United States clearly raise questions. In the latter case, the FBI obtained material proving that the Taiwan security forces were involved. Possibly in the Lin case a superior told some subordinates, "We have to teach these bastards a lesson" and a subordinate took such an instruction too literally. While many opponents of the KMT regime had been killed, the murder of the Lin family was the first time that family members had been attacked. Despite the efforts of Chen Shui-bian, when mayor of Taipei, and of the Control Yuan to investigate the murders of Auntie Lin and the twins, the case remains unsolved after twenty-eight years.

Professor Bruce Jacobs knew Lin Yi-hsiung and his family well. On the morning of the murders, he telephoned and talked to the little girls, but did not visit. All the same, the police detained him as "a material witness" nearly three months, housed at the Grand Hotel, and the press hinted darkly that the "Big Beard" and Presbyterian Church forces somehow played a role in the murders. This may have been a desperate effort on the part of the police to create a distraction from the plain fact that the homes of those arrested were totally staked out by the security agencies. According to rumor at the time, Jacobs was offered US$250,000 to "tell the truth" about his witness of the murderer. He did not return to Taipei till 1992.

Hong Kong Press Conference on the Eve of the Kaohsiung Incident Trial

As the revised trial date of March 18 approached, our preparations in Hong Kong came to more effect. The KMT had no doubt again postponed the date to avoid the presence of Ramsey Clark, who had prepared to come to Taiwan for three days in early March, trip funded by the Formosan Association for Human Rights. We had time to prep the foreign press corps in Hong Kong on the Taiwan issues and the arrested figures of *Formosa* magazine. In particular I gave out background on the contact that the February 20 indictment used to link Huang Hsin-chieh to a communist conspiracy, Hong Chih-liang, who had been arrested August 30, 1979. Less than a week in advance, I finally got Chris Vertucci of Asia Monitor to go into Taiwan unannounced and visit the relatives of those arrested. Nicki Croghan had been ushered out of Taiwan when her visa expired January 12, 1980, but she had helped the prisoners' wives a great deal in those few weeks. It was extremely fortunate that Chou Ching-yu, wife of the imprisoned lawyer Yao Chia-wen, had just then prepared typed materials in Chinese, about ten pages, such as a transcript of the accounts of the two men beaten up at the Ku Shan Incident, as well as descriptions of violation of legal practice in the access of the prisoners to their lawyers.

I only received these important materials on Thursday night, in preparation for our scheduled press conference at the Foreign Correspondents Club on Friday morning, March 14, with the trial to begin on Tuesday. I thought it was hopeless to try, but my mother went out at 7 am and was able to find a copy shop that would open early, by pounding on the doors and flashing a bonus of US$5. That was before the days of automatic collators, however, and when we arrived at the venue my mother was unable to get all the pages in Chinese sorted correctly and collated before the mob of reporters descended on her and made off with whatever pages they could grab. But I felt that in the thick of this information war we had captured much of the initiative from the KMT.

When the trial finally commenced on March 18, the defendants had been through choreographed pre-trial depositions previously, and had not been able to see each other. But from later information, we know that their lawyers had been subtly communicating with them to raise their spirits and the possibility of violating the Garrison's script of confessions. There were observers both from the local press and the foreign press, as well as officials such as the American Institute on Taiwan and Professor John Kaplan of the Stanford University Law School (Victor Li had gotten Kaplan to stand in when he couldn't come because of the time shift; Kaplan quickly wrote a thin but important book on the trial). One of the Western TV crews sent into Taiwan kindly gave me the short film provided them by the Government Information Office of the arrival of the defendants from their prison cells to the court room, and the government display of evidence: three-color sashes, broken military police helmets, and wooden sticks with nails that had fastened placards.

In Hong Kong my mother and I, joined for a while by Lynn Miles who came to help with media relations, were amazed to read daily transcripts of the trial that covered a whole page or more in the Chinese-language newspapers, especially in the KMT-

The announcement for Linda's press conference on Friday, March 14, 1980, just a few days before the first Kaohsiung Incident trial, shows Nellie's neat school teacher handwriting, as do the background briefing sheets on Hong Chih-liang 洪誌良, slated to play the communist connection in the prosecutor's scenario.

Press
Conference

Foreign
Press
Club

Announcing Press Conference
10:00 a.m., Fri. March 14 by
Linda Gail Arrigo Shih
(added information below)
Main Topic: Trial and indictment
of Democratic Movement Leaders
in Taiwan slated for March 18. Shih
Ming-Teh, Linda's husband, is one of
the 8 leaders being tried on
sedition charges in the military
courts.

Associated topics:
1) Pre-arrest activities of "communist-connection"
against Huang Hsin-Chieh from human rights investigation by
Mrs. Arrigo Shih Sept-Nov. 1979.
2) Relationships of the democratic movement in Taiwan with
supporters in the United States over the last year, and international conspiracy charges.
3) Background on Dr. Bruce Jacobs, American in "protective
custody" in Taipei as witness to the Lin murder.

linked newspapers. The same was being printed in Taiwan. By a recent account to me from Yu's daughter Anne, Yu Chi-chung 余紀忠 of *China Times*, himself of significant standing in the KMT, notified President Chiang Ching-kuo that if foreign newspapers were allowed into the trial and would write about it, his newspaper would insist on national pride and would also; and all others, not to be outdone, followed his lead.

The eight defendants in the sedition trial were the National Legislator Huang Hsin-chieh, the Provincial Assemblymen Lin Yi-hsiung and Chang Chun-hung, the candidates for the December 1978 election women rights advocate Lu Hsiu-lien (Annette) and lawyer Yao Chia-wen, the central election campaign coordinators Shih Ming-teh (Nori) and Chen Chu, and finally the young minister from the Presbyterian seminary in Tainan Lin Hung-hsuan, who was no doubt included in the sedition trial because captured letters tied him to George Chang and WUFI. Of the core leadership of five up to the *Formosa* magazine phase, only Hsu Hsin-liang had escaped arrest; after being stripped of his seat as Taoyuan County Executive July 1, 1979, he went abroad "for study."

As I had feared, Hong Chih-liang, the candidate in the Campaign Coalition who was arrested in August 1979 (recognizable by a round head and a few strands of comb-over in the December 1978 photo), was used to "bite" Huang Hsin-chieh. The scenario concocted by the military prosecutor was that Huang Hsin-chieh had lent money to Hong to do illegal business with China, and Hong had secretly visited China and connived with the Chinese authorities to fund the Dangwai by buying eel fry in China that were then to be raised in Taiwan and sold to Japan at a good profit. In sum, the scenario painted the Taiwan independence movement as a dupe or a front for the Chinese communists. (Remember the categorization of Huang with the pro-PRC group in the "A-B-C groups" planning by the prosecutors right after the Kaohsiung Incident, December 11-20, 1979 -- documents previously displayed at the National Archives Administration exhibition on the *Formosa* trials, March 2003. Exhibition booklet with ISBN 957-01-3621-9 describes the collection but not the specific documents. 『美麗島事件檔案導引』，行政院研究發展考核員會，發行人林嘉誠 February 2003.)

According to Yao Chia-wen's account *Court Martial Taipei* 景美大審判－美麗島軍法審判寫真 (self-printing, April 2000), he was completely demoralized after exhaustion induced by interrogation and over two months of being held incommunicado in bare chilly cells. His interrogators nearly convinced him that he and the other conspirators would be convicted of intent to overthrow the government by violent means with action towards that goal, sedition as defined under Article 2, Paragraph 1, carrying a mandatory death sentence. Particularly inflammatory was the *Formosa* magazine policy of pushing activities to "the brink of violence" 暴力邊緣, a phrase ascribed to Yao Chia-wen. Their advice was that his only hope was to admit his errors and throw himself on the mercy of the authorities. But the brief audiences beginning in the last few days of February with his wife and his lawyers, long his good friends, began to restore his spirit. He reasoned a defense that was both legal and political, a persistent demand for democratic rights. Yao was himself a professor of law, and his outbursts

In this picture of the courtroom from the April issue of *Taiwan My China,* the foreign press attending are shown. Edith Lederer, writing on the desk at the right, was soon expelled for reporting on Annette Lu Hsiu-lien's tearful outburst that she had been threatened by being shown a picture of the executed Wu Tai-an. Edith Lederer brought Nellie a detailed account of her interview with Bruce Jacobs, and in early May, back in Washington D.C., Nellie made this a main topic of her congressional appeals.

TWENTY MEMBERS OF THE FOREIGN PRESS were among the sixty reporters attending the Koahsiung riot leaders' sedition trial last month and yet, little news of the trial has been published in the U.S.

Kaohsiung Incident sedition trial defendants, in martial law court at the Taiwan Garrison Command, Chingmei Prison, March 18, 1980. Left to right, Chang Chun-hong, Huang Hsin-chieh, Chen Chu, Yao Chia-wen (white shirt), Shih Ming-teh (in back of Yao), Annette Lu Hsiu-lien, Lin Hong-hsuan. Lin Yi-hsiung was allowed leave to attend to the funerals of his mother and twin daughters.

in court concerning violation of proper procedure seemed to have been heard through rather than stifled; the usual political detainee would have been throttled. The judges ranked lower than himself in judicial learning and experience. He noted the presence of domestic and international media.

As the trial proceeded for ten days with much more than the half-day process usually accorded political offenders, the eight defendants in the sedition trial, and especially Nori who had watched television reports before he was apprehended and knew the old half-day routine of military trials, realized that even though it was a show trial the proceedings would be broadcast to the world. The defendants began to rise to the occasion, though nearly broken in spirit through interrogation and intimidation.

Shih Ming-teh's defense, delivered with machine-gun speed as he feared being cut off and silenced, more specifically drew on international political analysis. He reasoned that the ROC government had sought to maintain international diplomatic relations after expulsion from the United Nations and U.S. recognition of the Peoples Republic; it implicitly operated on the premise that Taiwan and the outlying islands under ROC control are an independent political entity. Therefore, "Taiwan has already been independent for thirty years." Although rebuked by the judge on this point, Shih's testament was printed in the press and reverberated widely. Moreover, if *Formosa* magazine were to be judged guilty of intent to overthrow the government, it could only be intent to demand democratic process, the same way democratic governments are "overthrown" when the ruling party is voted out.

My mother and I talked at length with Edith Lederer of the Associated Press before the trial, and again when she was disbarred from the trial and ejected a few days later after writing a press dispatch on Lu Hsiu-lien breaking down in tears and describing how she had been taunted with pictures of the executed Wu Tai-an while under interrogation. My mother Nellie Amondson took detailed notes on Edith Lederer's narration of her interview with Bruce Jacobs, "Big Beard" as he was labeled in the Taiwan press, the American professor at Australian National University who was under police detention at the Grand Hotel after he was alleged to have been at the front door of the Lin residence on the morning of the murders. Aside from the threat that he would be held as a material witness or worse, we heard a rumor from Edith that he had been offered US$300,000 by the police to make false witness as to the identity of the attacker. (In her second stint in Washington D.C. in May 1-18, 1980, my mother made Bruce Jacobs' detention a major issue of her lobbying, and I hope that was a contributing factor in his being released on May 22.)

Learning the shocking atrocity of the Lin family murders during the court proceedings, Shih Ming-teh broke down sobbing and asked to be executed if it would dissipate the hatred against the political challengers. Lin Yi-hsiung had been released temporarily in early March for the funerals of his mother and little daughters, but he returned voluntarily to take his place in the trials.

The sentences announced on April 5, 1980 were: return to life imprisonment for Shih Ming-teh, 14 years for Huang Hsin-chieh as the senior figure, and 12 years for

Hong Chih-liang 洪誌良 being led into court. Hong was only sentenced to five years in a later trial, although supposedly he was part of a communist conspiracy. After release he wrote a book explaining that he was coerced into testifying against Huang Hsin-chieh.

3.

Hung was arrested on August 30, 1979 while on the way to Taipei. His home and office were searched for 6 hours, 4 to 10 p.m, and letters, address books, name cards, etc., carted away. Later his friends and even distant business associates were grilled. The newspapers charged him with going to the mainland in March-April 1979, and "failing to make a clear account" after his return. Because of his uneasy relationships to the opposition members they were not willing to make much protest over his arrest.

According to information attributed to Hsia, Yuanlin, Bureau of Investigation, Ministry of Justice, (BIMJ) head, Hung made a report to the Taipei BIMJ immediately after return to Taiwan, on his trip to PRC. Hung was to be given NT $100,000 reward, but then BIMJ decided to arrest him after they checked with agents in Japan and "discovered he had withheld information."

In early September I went to visit Hung's wife, Liu Ming-Yueh (劉明月) about her husband's arrest. A local BIMJ official "happened" to visit her at the same time. On another occasion Hung's wife talked frankly about her debts when I witnessed a group of visitors dunning her for payment, and said Hung owed NT $300,000 to the printer of the magazine and NT $200,000 to Li Ching-Rung. She never mentioned Huang Hsin-Chieh or possible eel business. By Feb. 1979, Hung had no business but the magazine, having lost his fertilizer franchise

the other six in the sedition trial. In the document of the sentencing, the contacts of the defendants with overseas Taiwanese organizations figured heavily in the determination of seditious Taiwan independence intent: these included not just George Chang 張燦鍙 of World United Formosans for Independence which had a declared goal of overthrowing the KMT, but also the community information service Voice of Taiwan and its operators Eileen 張楊宜宜 and Morgan Chang 張富雄. Ironically, Chen Tu 陳都 of Saratoga, California, mentioned repeatedly as a seditious contact in the United States, safely returned briefly to visit his home in Taiwan in January 1980 while the prosecution was preparing its indictment, Chen Tu not knowing he figured prominently in it.

The sentencing further attempted to link Huang Hsin-chieh to the Peoples Republic of China through Hong Chih-liang 洪誌良 and eel business profits, but only devoted two sentences to this, and did not claim others than Huang Hsin-chieh were implicated. Hong himself was later separately sentenced to only five years. However, it is to his credit that soon after his release in 1985, while still under martial law, he wrote and distributed a little-known book that narrated how he was coerced into making false testimony.

A list of those arrested in December 1979-January 1980 was originally issued by the government on January 17, and it included 151 names to be charged with sedition. We had expected all of them to be slapped with heavy sentences; but as time passed and international pressure accrued, the government's published lists grew shorter, and most names were shifted to trial for physical attack on the police, plus "problems with thinking" and three-years sentence for wearing the three-color sash, now declared an emblem of Taiwan independence advocacy. I had had the sashes custom made, picking out the colors myself, and had them brought down to Kaohsiung; I remember how cheered the main figures in the columns were to don a colorful sash or armband, and for some I had adjusted the sashes on their shoulders personally. Was the affiliation now to be seen as a curse or a badge of courage?

The trial was held the following month, April, in the same military court. The 33 finally tried were mostly the candidates of the Campaign Coalition, including national labor candidate Yang Ching-chu, and also the founders of the branch offices of Formosa magazine, and the activists and volunteers of the organization. Charges that they physically attacked the police were ridiculous, but some had been severely beaten after arrest (one presented his bloody underpants in court in seeking, unsuccessfully, to have the court recognize retraction of his confession made under torture) and were sentenced to four or five years each in civilian prison. A few unknown ruffians caught on the spot were thrown in to bolster the charges, and given light sentences.

Ten persons charged with aiding and hiding Shih Ming-teh as a fugitive from the law were arrested at or soon after his apprehension on January 8. Among these were Lin Wen-chen, a woman minister who held high rank in the Presbyterian Church, and Shih Rui-yun, the sweet, demure secretary to General Secretary Reverend Kao

Internal Documents of the Taiwan Garrison Command Concerning the Sentencing of the Kaohsiung Incident Defendants, 1980

Analysis and translation by Linda Gail Arrigo, February 20, 2008

Among the copies of documents Linda was able to obtain from the National Archives in 2004 are a number of reports in a series prepared by the "Taiwan Garrison Command Special Investigation Office" (台灣警備總伺令部特種調查室情報報告).

These reports are uniform in format. They have a printed cover sheet with four large characters at the top, which may be roughly translated as "Intelligence Summary Report," and a logo of a white dove perched on a globe, wings extended and one foot clutching a scroll, perhaps figuratively a carrier pigeon. The right side of the page has a printed box for filling in the classification level and the serial number, i.e. this was seemingly a report reproduced in very limited numbers and each copy would be accounted for. The classification level "secret," the serial number (either 1 or 6 on the copies held), and the dates at the bottom of the page are filled in with rubber stamp imprints. The next page is a standard form with the distribution instructions and the summarized content, and apparently most of the reports had further attachments.

However it happened, there is no National Archives bar code tab with number on these reports (which may have been interspersed with other materials in a file), but the top page has penciled on it "(2) 275, 319, partially provided," i.e. full access was not allowed for these materials although they were over twenty years old. It appears that the National Archives numbered all the pages of the consecutive reports in pencil, and the items on hand are in the page range 031-208.

The interest in these reports is, first, that they show how closely the top security agencies were following the foreign reports on the Meilidao trial; and, second, two of these reports are internal memos discussing the authorities' perception of public reaction to the trial and the sentencing, and suggesting how the defendants should be sentenced and treated. The latter two reports provide a very rare glimpse into the internal deliberations of the security agencies, in fact the only such discussion in the materials on hand from the National Archives, and so warrant reproduction and full translation into English, though the implications of the language and tone as used within these security agencies cannot be entirely clear to the translator. To further provide more of the context, the issues of these reports on hand, certainly only a few of the total, are listed in the following table.

The two most interesting of these internal documents are the March 19 and April 19 discussions on recommended sentencing. These two internal memos, as far as they have been made available, are rather chilling in that they evidence that the security agencies could very likely have imposed death sentences, if only domestic reactions were their consideration.

Chun-ming. Others were fellow political prisoners or old friends of Shih Ming-teh and his family. Then Rev. Kao himself was taken into custody, and on April 24 the trial for aiding and abetting the fugitive commenced. Reverend Kao was given a sentence of seven years, the same as others who had directly aided Nori in flight and concealment. This was no doubt an opportunity for attack on the Presbyterian Church that the security agencies relished.

How Do We Tally the Price for Democracy?

Looking back from the present time, we still do not know the full tally for those who paid a heavy price for their role in the democratic movement of 1978-79. I believe that hundreds suffered serious consequences. For one, Chiu Yi-pin 邱亦彬, the dentist who testified to KMT ballot manipulation in the November 1977 election in Chungli, was also arrested in December 1979, and some years later medically analyzed his experience for me. After seven days under interrogation without sleep, he became delusional. He was told, or imagined, that his sister had been violently raped and his family was in mortal danger. (Threats to the prisoner's family are a recurring theme in accounts of interrogation.) Distraught, he attempted suicide by biting his tongue. Finally psychotic, he was not brought to trial and was released, but it was a year before he returned to full sanity.

For another, Su Ching-li, the editor of *China Tide*, told me how she was arrested and her offices ransacked. Her office documents and also all the negatives of my women factory workers study, then on loan to the magazine, were lost. Her interrogators arrogantly told her that she was in for at least ten years; but then she was released in two months.

I believe this was because of a strategic decision by the KMT to decrease resistance to the trials by first dealing with the main challenge, the Taiwan independence dissidents, while leaving the dissidents adhering to Chinese nationalism for later. Lee Ching-rong 李慶榮, for example, was re-arrested at a later date. Some other significant figures in the Campaign Coalition, such as candidates Chang Chun-nan 張春男 and Liu Feng-sung 流峰松, eluded capture in December 1979 (Chang Chun-nan hid in a pigsty in the mountains for six months, with elaborate ruses for his family to deliver food), but still ended up serving three and a half years for defaming the government following his unsuccessful bid in the December 1980 elections.

Many of those who paid a price are not known publicly. For example, Huang Chin-yeh 黃金也, a judo instructor who owned the second floor apartment above Lin Yi-hsiung's place and rented it to us in August 1979 over police objections, dodged three arrest attempts and left the country on an alternative passport; he was suspected of providing military training to Formosa magazine volunteers. Ironically, a few unrecorded persons I have met who were taken in for grilling seemed to have identified more with the democratic movement after their ordeal than before; I think the heroic stature of those on trial seized the imagination of those who had been even remotely involved with Formosa, as well as those far beyond.

In retrospect, the daily news reporting on the trial most certainly had more impact

Intelligence Summary Reports (Selected)		
Prepared by Taiwan Garrison Command Special Investigation Office, 1980		
Date / (69)You-Ching Report No./ National Archives page numbers	Translation of Subject of Report	Summary of Contents
1980.02.23 0223 pp. 031-032	Situation of lawyers defending Huang Hsin-Chieh et al. case	Lawyers have obtained full tape recording of Kaohsiung Incident, can document the words of the defendants there. Also obtained original receipt for $NT200,000 Huang loan to Hong Chih-Liang. Chen Chu and Lin Hong-Hsuan can be linked to overseas seditious organizations by letters. "Because Chen Chu has a thick streak of individualistic heroism, and her personality is rash, under a mistaken consciousness she might in court openly acknowledge that she is an advocate of Taiwan independence, and if so it will be difficult to reprieve her." 又陳菊個人英雄主義色彩濃厚，個性衝動，在錯覺意念下，可能在法廷上公開承認是〈台獨〉份子，果如此則難求平反。 Be careful with intelligence reports obtained through undercover contacts.
1980.02.27 0248 pp. 051-052	American Linda Arrigo's mother holds a visa and is coming to Taiwan.	Nellie G. Amondson, mother of Linda Gail Arrigo, is planning on coming to Taiwan; this will create news troublesome to the government.
No cover sheets; pp. 108-118	Wide Arrests	Typed account in Chinese of arrests of main defendants. [Prepared by wife of Yao Chia-wen before trial; distributed by Linda at Hong Kong press conference March 14.]
1980.03.19 0351 pp. 130-133	Reaction of cultural, news media to trial of Meilitao sedition.	Internal memo after second day of trial, recommending heavy sentences to prevent recurrence, with later lenience. [See full translation below]
1980.03.20 (no summary page) pp. 151,155-159	Translation of Lederer API dispatches on trial.	Copies of English dispatches by Edith Lederer: March 17-2 (extract) "The government claims eight dissidents conspired with Communist China and Taiwanese independence groups in the United States and Japan to seize power …" March 17-3 (extract) "Another editorial in the semi-official *China News* Monday accused the foreign press of trying the government and not the defendants in the press…"

on political consciousness in Taiwan than the whole previous year-and-a-half of the mobilization of the democratic movement; the whole period is recognized as a watershed in modern Taiwan history. The trial and the reporting was an incredible precedent under martial law, though at the time I felt an overwhelming despair that the democratic movement had been destroyed. Daily, our Trotskyite student helper clipped and pasted up the newspaper transcripts for us in B3 format so that my mother and I had a package that we could copy and distribute by mail just before we left Hong Kong when our entry visas expired on April 1, fortuitously just after the end of the main trial.

A remaining matter concerning Hong Kong. If I remember correctly, Asia Forum for Human Rights in Hong Kong and its head, Sam Ho, were themselves under difficulties in 1980. However, later in 1980 after the trial, when Shih Ming-teh's third eldest brother Shih Ming-hsiung 施明雄 (who was himself a former political prisoner, jailed for five years in the same case) could not continue in his Chinese medicine practice in Kaohsiung because of political pressure and fled to Hong Kong, Sam Ho helped him get asylum in Canada, and he immigrated to Toronto with his family. However, a while later Sam Ho himself was forced out of Hong Kong, and Shih Ming-hsiung helped Sam relocate to Canada as well.

Taiwanese-Austrians, Taiwanese-Germans, Taiwanese-Frenchmen Maoists

My mother and I visited Thai contacts of the Asian Forum for Human Rights in Bangkok and then were stuck in Bombay for a week on our around-the-world PamAm air tickets, before we landed in Frankfurt. Taiwanese in Austria, Germany, France, and the United Kingdom arranged for me to speak at several universities, notably the University of Heidelberg, and on public radio stations in Germany and England, as well as to Taiwanese community groups. In Germany, I met Reverend Roger Chao (Chao You-Yuan) 趙有源 and his German wife Ursula, Helmut Martin 馬漢茂, and others who had responded vigorously to the human rights crisis in Taiwan. However, in Europe the Taiwanese were limited in their capacities, because they were few and widely dispersed, and mostly made their living through Chinese restaurants, even if they came to Europe to study music; only a few had professorships, though one strong supporter of Taiwanese democratization was a judge in Vienna.

My most vivid memory of this trip is my visit to German public radio, recording for a shortwave broadcast in Chinese. The host was a middle-aged German Orientalist with a full brown beard; his office was decorated with classical Chinese brush paintings and gilded awards from the Kuomintang. As I continued with my graphic litany of injustice and torture under the Chiang regime, my host made every effort to speak and smile politely, but could not help grimacing with outrage. I do not know how much of the recording was broadcast, or how he reconciled his personal views. Traditionally, the KMT, denouncing the godless and anti-elitist communists, was able to capture the allegiance of those who were enthralled by ancient Chinese high culture.

Intelligence Summary Reports (Selected, continued)		
Prepared by Taiwan Garrison Command Special Investigation Office, 1980		
1980.03.25 0381 pp. 163-165	American Institute on Taiwan in Washington DC on March 20 provided contents of New York Post article to its Taipei office.	Information obtained from undercover contact. Summary translation of New York Post, March 18, relating indictment of communist connection, i.e. Hong Chih-Liang going to PRC from Japan, seeking profits through purchase of eel fry to raise in Taiwan; Shih's arrest; forced confessions.
1980.04.11 0445 pp. 181-186	Translation of American reporter's report on trial.	Translation of Phil Kurata, "Democracy goes on trial with the dissidents", Far Eastern Economic Review, April 9, 1980.
1980.04.19 0484 pp. 122-124	Response from all sectors on sentencing in Huang Hsin-Chieh et al. trial.	Internal memo discussing outcome of sentencing and negative impact of the light sentences on public opinion – will give appearance of gov' t bowing to overseas threats of violence and pressure from the US, and encourage further histrionics. [See full translation below]
1980.04.29 0527 pp. 204-208	Newsweek story critical of sentencing in Huang Hsin-Chieh et al. sedition trial.	Translation of "Taiwan's Dissidents: Guilty", Newsweek, April 28, 1980, by Bob Levin with Dirk Bennett in Taipei and Andrew Nagorski in Hong Kong.

They seem to be oblivious to obvious hypocrisies and issues, e.g. whether the defendants had actually been coerced or abused, and totally secure in the defendants' guilt. It cannot be known here whether the drafters were making a frank internal assessment as seen from the perspective of the security agencies' intelligence, or whether, as is also likely, they were couching their findings in terms that would be less displeasing to the superiors to whom the reports were addressed. The quick and accurate translations of international news undoubtedly had their own impact.

Most of the writing on the last page of the April 19, 1980 report was covered when copying, i.e. not provided by the National Archives Administration. Considering that the report starts out with "I" and "A" sections that have no continuing sections here, it is likely that most of this report, and the even more revelatory sections, have been excised. Hopefully these will in some not-too-distant future be available to historians; these documents are nearly 30 years old already. At any rate, we do also know, due to a leaked internal report that was picked up and translated by James Seymour, that in 1984 the ranking security agencies, including the Government Information Office and the Culture Bureau of the Kuomintang, then headed by James Soong, crafted a new policy to charge and jail bothersome opposition figures through libel suits (e.g. the *Peng-lai-dao* magazine case that sent Huang Tien-fu and future-president Chen Shui-bian to jail for eight months each), thus avoiding sedition trials that would draw international attention. This report plus Seymour's commentary is to be found in *Index on Censorship*, March 1985. With this additional information, it is possible to deduce that the Kaohsiung Incident trials and international and domestic reactions were pivotal in modifying and decreasing the repressiveness of the martial law authorities. This permitted resurgence of the opposition organization within a few years.

According to the report of the Taiwan government office in France, I arrived in Paris on April 26, and gave a talk at a Taiwanese community gathering of about 50 people the next day.

By late April my mother and I were close to the expiration of our Around-the-World-in-Eighty-Days tickets and the end of our funds, and had to use the last leg quickly to get back to the States. My mother flew to Washington D.C. and spent two more weeks in lobbying, going from office to office, now also concerned about the fate of Professor Bruce Jacobs in Taipei, and methodically searching the Library of Congress for documents on Taiwan's history. Then she took the Greyhound bus back to San Diego.

I flew straight to Seattle, Washington, where I finally met those who were dedicated to putting out the newsletter transferred from Osaka, now renamed *Taiwan Communiqué*, and then to meet the Taiwanese community in Vancouver, including Professor Harry Hsiao (Hsiao Hsin-yi), influential in English communications for the Taiwanese community.

Nationalism Right and Left: Who Shall Lead?

There were tumultuous ideological and organizational struggles in the Taiwanese communities in North America following the mobilization of the democratic movement and the shock of the repression. I had a period for rest and reflection in San Diego. I felt Taiwanese, especially those in the United States who had comfortable professional jobs, often in defense-related research, were naive or in denial about the callous attitude of the United States during Taiwan's suffering under the Chiangs, a regime that the United States propped up with economic and military aid and recognized as the legitimate ruler of China, no doubt mainly to keep the Peoples Republic of China and its veto power out of the United Nations. At least the organization of left-Taiwan Independence students known as Taiwan Era had the same internationalist view I did, and I coordinated with them as much as I could. In mid-1980 Taiwan Era, assisted by Chang Chin-tse 張金策, began to attack the World United Formosans for Independence on its conceptualization of Taiwan nationalism, and promote the standard of nationalism as defined by national liberation movements worldwide in the 1970s and 1980s, that is, a civic citizenship definition rather than an ethnic definition.

Not long after returning from the round-the-world trip, I set out again on a very low budget to continue the mission. I took mostly Greyhound buses, visiting small college towns where there were Taiwan Student Associations or Taiwanese community clubs, and presenting my slides and analysis to groups of 15-30 Taiwanese, or sometimes to their academic or church American friends. After making my way through the Midwest, e.g. Ann Arbor, I went to Toronto, Canada, where I paired up with Chang Chin-tse and his young adherent Jimmy Tan 陳慶榮 at the June 1980 annual Taiwanese gathering there. This was the first volley of challenge to WUFI. Then I went through several more college towns in the southern states, and ended up in Orlando, Florida, and Miami, from whence I took a cheap flight from Miami to Nicaragua.

I wanted to understand the Sandinistas and the revolution there, just as they were celebrating their one-year anniversary and beginning to suffer sanctions from the United States. The new foreign ministry there, with the Asia section run by young college students, knew about the recent repression in Taiwan only from church bulletins concerning the arrest of Reverend Kao. I was interviewed by *La Prensa*. Then I returned to Los Angeles in early August and joined the staff of the Chinese-language newsprint-format *Formosa Weekly*, formed by Hsu Hsin-liang and Chen Wan-chen, with an office hidden in a Latino district of East Los Angeles.

The American presidential campaign heating up in the fall of 1980 provided the Taiwanese-Americans with another opportunity to try to put the issue of Taiwan's repressiveness on the front burner, especially since new U.S. diplomatic relations with China were in the news. They held a lavish event in Los Angeles with Edward Kennedy in September 1980, and I was pleased to be on the stage with him.

President Jimmy Carter, who in his 1976 campaign had put forth a policy of considering human rights in international relations, was challenged by Ronald Reagan, a conservative Republican in the anti-communist Goldwater tradition. Reagan's staff had put out a booklet entitled "A Friendship Based on High Ideals" – friendship with the Chiang regime – after Reagan visited Taiwan. Steve Chung 鍾 金江, a restaurateur living in Fountain Valley, south Orange County, put together a plan for me to go on hunger strike near the offices of Reagan's lawyers Deaver and Hannaford, close to Los Angeles Airport. Deaver and Hannaford were on a US$5,000 a month retainer from the Taiwan regime, as well as similarly contracted with the Guatemalan generals; this had been reported in reliable news sources.

Our hunger strike activity involved rallying the Taiwanese community for two weekends of demonstrations, and there was considerable logistics in contacting press, setting up signs, having a team to protect me from KMT harassers (including apparently KMT-hired American provocateurs as before), and taking me back to rest safely each evening, of course much less wearing on my physiology than sleeping on the sidewalk as Chen Wan-chen had done earlier in New York. (Although I drank a little juice and broth, after three days I fell into a stupor that made it difficult to focus in talking with the press, and twelve days was pushing my capacities. From my later experience in 1985 I would say hunger strikes should not be casually declared; neurological damage can occur even with fat on the body.) Aside from a sizeable article in the *Los Angeles Times*, we drew solidarity from Philippine and South Korean activists, leading to further joint activities. I suggested to a Taiwanese student that he write up this hunger strike as if he were outraged by these Taiwan independence seditionists camped out at the Los Angeles Airport vilifying the ROC, and the *Central Daily News* in Taipei printed it as a letter to the editor. Another notch for creative propaganda techniques.

With the immediate campaign for human rights directed to English speakers and the international community behind me, I took on a new role in the internal debates within the Taiwanese-American community. The formation of *Formosa Weekly* in Los Angeles was in effect a challenge to WUFI's grip on the Taiwanese-American

台灣警備總司令部特種調查至情報告（通報）

民國六九年三月十九日
(69)友情字第○三五一號

受文者	軍法處　保安處	來源	原報者 ▓	地點 ▓	日期	69.	3.	19.	分發單位	國家安全局總司令汪上將 副參謀總長鄭中將 副參謀長史少將 三處
			轉報者 ▓	地點 ▓	日期	69.	3.	19.		
事由摘要	文化、新聞界對審判美麗島叛亂犯之反應。	來源	蒐集方法 ▓						定鑑	甲二
			傳遞方法 ▓							

內容：

一、本室本三月十九(69)友情字第○三四九號情報諒達。

二、經透過關係訪談文化、新聞界人士，對軍法審判美麗島叛亂犯一案，綜合反應如下：

（一）本案審判官均甚年輕，審判經驗似有不足，當被告律師競相發言時，肆應略欠週全。本案被告在法庭上全部翻供，否定叛亂罪行，其所聘辯護律師亦似已互相串通，今後對本案之審判勢必非常棘手。

（二）從被告辯護律師之「程序」之辯，便可看出彼等經過詳細的分工，並對軍事法庭之組織程序法研究得十分透徹，今後數日，法庭似宜加強準備彼等藉機挑剔，以「程序」、「管轄權」、「權益」、「證據」等細節問題，干擾審理，尤應注意自白書之運用，並防被告藉「非出於自由意志」而抵賴。

（三）昨天庭上出示之證據有實物、文字、照片等，今後若審及現場情形細節，似有蒐集各電視台及其他公司機構現場錄影播放，對被告及中外記者等，將有說服力。

（四）許多外籍記者及外籍旁聽人士，對我國法律並非深入了解，尤以平民以軍法審判一節，彼等均弄不明原因。因此有關當局，似宜利用一適當時機，單獨對外籍記者與旁聽人士，舉行每日記者招待會，解釋被告等不明瞭之問題，以免彼等一知半解閙發消息。

（五）對於法律之外，尤其沿途必要之交通指標外，似不必以武裝憲兵佈崗哨，若有需要，也宜由便衣人員擔任，以免給人「如臨大敵」之過份緊張之印象。

（六）對於八名被告，政府應依法嚴懲，勿再姑息養奸。全國民心均支持政府嚴懲不法，民心不可違，而且時機適宜，設若此時不辦，今後更難辦了。即使政府要表示寬厚，也應重判，死刑或無期徒刑，然後由總統大赦，如此即可以服眾又可以示寬大胸懷，顯示政府德意，可謂一舉兩得，不失為兩全之策。

（七）八人之公審，吸引了新聞的注意力，使林宅兇案的「新聞性」及民間的注意力轉移了方向，減輕了治安單位的精神壓力，對承辦林宅兇案的警方是一件意外的收穫。

三、請參考。

（依原件重新打字，一○○八年四月十三日）

community, in terms of ideology, direction of action, and control of donations. Hsu Hsin-liang and Chen Wan-chen had direct contacts with those who were slowly becoming active again in Taiwan after the Kaohsiung Incident crackdown. WUFI founded its own competing newspaper, *Taiwan Tribune* 台灣公論報, and the competition was on as to who could marshal the most community support. Within *Formosa Weekly* also the editorial staff was rift with left/right and Taiwanese/Chinese nationalism divisions. Shih Ming came to the rescue from Japan after one split and collapse. And at the same time there was fear that the KMT would penetrate our associations, find our location, and maybe even carry out a hit. Later, when Henry Liu was assassinated in 1984, it was rumored that Hsu Hsin-liang and others overseas were also on the hit list. This is to me an interesting period of ideological debate, but it is the stuff of a different book.

In September 1980 I again took off on an extended Greyhound trip through small Taiwanese campus communities, still personally carrying the story of the democratic movement and its imprisoned leaders in my blue crayon box with the slides of the Meilitao days. In early November I was on the way back, in Lawrence, Kansas, when I was so congested and dizzy that I was unable to speak to the thirty or so Taiwanese-Americans who had driven far from Manhattan, Kansas, and elsewhere. My condition had been gradually getting worse over the months back in California with the grass pollens, but I had no medical insurance or idea of how to deal with it. Dr. Shin-fu Hsu 許信夫, a nose, ears, and throat specialist, came up from the audience and took an expert glance up my nose. He announced that my sinusitis was too serious for me to talk any further. Dr. Hsu immediately took me to his house, and a few days later he and a Taiwanese anesthesiologist did a long, delicate operation cutting out some huge amount of swollen membranes. I remember how safe I felt in their hands, and grateful that they and the Taiwanese-American community covered all my medical costs; I had no savings. Then I slept for two weeks, only briefly waking twice daily to be fed nutritious and healthy Taiwanese food by Mrs. Hsu. When I was well enough to build snowmen with Dr. Hsu's little girls Jenny and Annie, I went out and bought a huge turkey and made a huge Thanksgiving dinner with fixings for the people who missed my talk before. They said they would bring a few side dishes – but of course that was a feast in itself, and my turkey went uneaten. At least I had a lot of turkey sandwiches before they put me on a plane back to San Diego. I felt, perhaps I knocked out my academic career by participating in the Taiwan democratic movement, but I had made a mark on so many hearts, and these Taiwanese friends were there for me. What could be worth more in a lifetime?

A Light at the End of the Tunnel

Not too much later, it also became apparent that the democratic movement of the *Meilitao* movement, despite the repression, had not been totally cowed as I had thought, and in fact had left a substantial legacy.

With most of the candidates and cadres of the Campaign Coalition safely in jail, the Taiwan government finally announced the resumption of the aborted December 1978 election, for December 6, 1980. Despite the recent and continuing heavy hand of the

----

SECRET

Taiwan Garrison Command Special Investigation Office Report (Notification)
台灣警備總伺令部特種調查室情報報告（通報）

Republic of China 69th Year [1980], 3rd Month, 19th Day
(69) You-Ching (Friendly Intelligence) No. 0351

Recipients:

Military Law Office 軍法處
Preserve the Peace Office 保安處

Rationale:

Reactions of cultural and news media worlds to trial of the Meilidao sedition criminals.
Source of Report: (all names and locations blacked out).

Distribution:

National Security Bureau 國家安全局
TGC Commander Major General Wang 總司令汪上將
TGC Vice-Commander General Yu 副總司令于中將
Chief of Staff General Chung 參謀長鐘中將
Vice-Chief of Staff Lt. General Shih 副參謀長史少將
Political Section 2 政二處

Classification: A-2

Content:

A.   This office on this month (3) 19th has delivered the intelligence report (69) You-Ching No. 0349.

B.   After interviewing cultural and news media personages through various channels, the reactions to the military court trial of the Meilidao sedition case are summarized as follows:

1.   The judges assigned to this case are all very young, and their experience seems to be insufficient. When the lawyers of the defendants compete to speak, (the judges') reaction lacks circumspection. The defendants in this case have all overturned their previous testimony, and they deny their seditious criminal actions. The lawyers they have engaged also seem to have coordinated their strategy. For the further developments, it seems the situation in this case must be extremely thorny.

2.   From the procedural objections raised by the defendants' lawyers, it can further be seen that they have devised a detailed division of labor, and that they have become completely familiar with the organizational procedures of the military court. In the next few days the military court must make appropriate reinforcement of its preparation to meet their challenges on "procedure", "jurisdiction", "rights", "evidence", etc., these details which are interfering with the trial. In particular care must be paid

security agencies, the KMT could not totally control the agenda or the candidates. The wives of Chang Chun-hung and Yao Chia-wen won landslide victories in the races for National Legislator. Even though these elections affected only 10% or so of that body, the moral victory was tremendous, demonstrating an upwelling of support for the imprisoned leaders of the democratic movement. Chou Ching-yu 周清玉 (Mrs. Yao Chia-wen) and Hsu Rong-su 許榮淑 (Mrs. Chang Chun-hung) started an organization called "Care" 關懷 that linked relatives of the arrested, and delivered blankets, items of comfort, and cards to all political prisoners of every political stripe. Gradually the intellectuals and the local people who had come together in the democratic movement began to regroup under various organizational names, including magazine staffs.

For the foreigners in the human rights efforts, we could be pleased that Taiwanese and Taiwanese-Americans were taking over the role of collecting, writing up, and smuggling information in and out of Taiwan. *Formosa Weekly* funded Vallaurie Crawford (sent to Taiwan by Professor Richard Kagan as a student in 1978, when I first met her and helped with her study of abortion in Taiwan) to go into Taiwan for the December 1980 election. She was openly aided by Robert (a.k.a. Eric) Lu Hsiao-chih 呂孝治, a Taiwanese businessman who had been surreptitiously carrying human rights materials in 1980, and finally it was Robert (over a decade later an aide to County Executive Lu Hsiu-lien) who got most of the material through to *Formosa Weekly*. Back in the States after this adventure, Vallaurie wrote articles about the election as a cub reporter. This example was I believe being repeated on many fronts, in communications with Taiwan, aided by increasing business traffic and telecommunications, and in Taiwanese-American lobbying of Congress.

Therefore it is appropriate to take the end of 1980 as a point of transition that can end this book and begin another. Perhaps the murder of Professor Chen Wen-cheng of Carnegie-Mellon University on July 3, 1981 during his visit home to Taiwan was an attempt by the security agencies to turn back the rising tide of activism and openness among Taiwanese abroad; but it incited anger more than fear. The tide was not turned.

Short Sequel, in Case You Want to Ask "What Happened After That?"

For the reader who has not been following the news of the last two decades in Taiwan, I may sketch in a little of the aftermath, for the democratic movement and for myself. All of the Kaohsiung Incident defendants were released by 1985-86, except for Shih Ming-teh. Nori embarked on a determined hunger strike in April 1985 demanding government forbearance of the founding of an opposition party; his weight eventually fell to a skeletal 47 kg. In the United States, Hsu Hsin-liang 許信良 and Hsieh Tsung-min 謝聰敏 (1964 declaration, 1970 smuggling of political prisoners' list) and Lin Shui-chuan 林水泉 (former political prisoner) mobilized Taiwanese-Americans around public action to "take the Taiwan Democratic Party back to Taiwan" in late 1986. The Democratic Progressive Party was finally established in Taiwan with the same basic personnel as the 1978 Campaign Coalition, in September 1986. There were no immediate arrests.

to the utilization of the confessions, and the defendants must be prevented from using the refutation that the confessions "did not come from free will".

3.   Yesterday, concerning the evidence displayed by the court, including objects, writings, and pictures, etc., if in the continuation of the trial there is a detailed accounting of the incident events, it might be advisable to collect on-the-scene reports from the television stations and from public and private institutions in order to broadcast these, to be persuasive to the defendants and to the Chinese and foreign reporters.

4.   Many of the foreign reporters and foreign auditors do not have a deep understanding of our country's law, particularly on the matter of why civilians are tried in military court. They cannot figure out the reason. Because of this, the relevant institutions might appropriately utilize a suitable time, and separately hold daily press conferences for the foreign journalists and auditors, to explain the problems that they don't understand, else they may make careless reports with their half-knowledge.

5.   Outside the court, especially on the major traffic routes along the way, it is perhaps not necessary to make an excessive show of military might. If it is necessary, duties can be appropriately taken over by plainclothes personnel, to avoid giving an extreme impression of "confronting a great enemy".

6.   Concerning the eight defendants, the government should punish them severely according to the law, and not allow a recurrence and nurturing of such evils. The will of the whole people of the nation supports the government's strict punishment of illegality, and the will of the people cannot be violated. If there is concern whether the time is appropriate, then it should be seen that if this is not done on this occasion, in the future it will be even harder to do. Even if the government wants to display tolerance, it should (first) sentence heavily with death sentences or life imprisonment, and then later exercise presidential pardon; in this way the masses can be served, while the government can also show its "broad chest" and manifest its benevolence. This could be said to be a solution that meets both purposes.

7.   The public trial of the eight persons has absorbed the interest of the media, causing the newsworthiness of the Lin family murders (to decrease) and attention among the public to change direction. This has decreased the psychological pressure on the security personnel, and provided an unexpected benefit for the police forces dealing with the Lin case.

C.   Attached materials (not attached to materials made available).

Huang Hua was jailed three times, total twenty-some years. He returned to see his old cell at the Taiwan Garrison Command Chingmei Prison on December 9, 2007.

A native Taiwanese technocrat, Lee Teng-hui, had been appointed Vice President to President Chiang Ching-kuo, who died in January 1988 soon after declaring the end of martial law. However, there were many more struggles to come and a few martyrs to die before actual civil rights and democratic process were established, after 1992. Lee Teng-hui freed the remaining political prisoners (some had been imprisoned over 30 years), in May 1990, and I was allowed to return to Taiwan.

Although Nori and I maintained a political marriage, I divorced him in 1995 when he was National Legislator and DPP party chairman on an issue, among others, of international human rights. As when I decided to marry him, my main consideration was the political principles involved. The Republic of China's two dozen remaining diplomatic ties were mostly with countries that had been fellow members of the World Anti-Communist League, such as Paraguay, and had had their own White Terror. The DPP itself took on increasingly conservative international relations, totally oblivious to this history. The matter on which I parted ways with Shih Ming-teh was related to South Africa, occasioned by a trip by the DPP to South Africa in July 1994, apparently when the KMT government wanted to show the new Mandela government that they were liberalizing and had an opposition, too. Subsequently Shih Ming-teh appointed to the post of DPP representative in Washington D.C. a professor of political science who advocated ties with Chief Mangosuthu Buthelezi and had a background with the Rand Corporation as well as with KMT institutions. The Taiwan press totally misreported the reason I divorced him even when I explained it to them; they couched the explanation in sexist stereotypes, i.e. Shih Ming-teh's extramarital affairs.

The Democratic Progressive Party took the presidency by thin margins in 2000 and 2004, bringing basic civil rights and greater welfare and wide changes in Taiwan's society, but also compromises in its stated goals of national independence and egalitarian democracy for Taiwan. In eight years in power, it was not able to gain a majority in the legislature, establish any diplomatic relations in the name of Taiwan, or wrest back the properties that the KMT had appropriated from the state during its decades of monopoly. At the same time, the KMT in the role of an opposition party was compelled to take on some of the trappings of Taiwanese culture and populism, and occasionally promise that the determination of sovereignty should be a democratic right.

						中華民國六九年四月十九日
台灣警備總司令部特種調查室情報報告(通報)						(69)友情字第○四八四號

受文者	國家安全局	來源	原報者	■	地點	■	日期 69. 4. 19	分發單位	副總司令王上將 總司令王上將 副參謀長鍾中將 參謀長史少將
			轉報者	■	地點	■	日期 69. 4. 19		保安處處長 軍法處處長
摘由	黃信介等叛亂案宣判後各界反應。		蒐集方法	■				定鑑	甲 二
			傳遞方法	■					

內容：

一、綜合各工作關係提供黃信介等叛亂案宣判後反應如後：

(一)文化新聞界：

1 新聞界原預測該案應在決議良判決後宣判，而今突然提前，出人意料。為何提前宣判？當局想必另有考量。

2 一般經濟犯(票據)尚有判刑三十餘年之案例，而美麗島二十人，以暴力顛覆之叛亂罪行，僅分別判刑十四年、十三年，最高僅無期徒刑(施明德)，似嫌太輕。

3 原先同業們談起此案，也會預料到會從輕發落，但總以為會從重依法判決，事後再予減刑。如此既可以收攬部分民心，又兼顧到法律尊嚴，此際一概從輕發落，至少有以下影響：

(1)不能服人心，愛國同胞憤憤不平。

(2)今後類似案件也將輕科重刑，否則易遭人批評「雙重標準」。

(3)易使人誤認政府受了海外叛國份子威脅，不敢重判嚴懲(怕渠等報復)，也因此助長了叛國份子及國內少數政治野心份子的氣焰。

(4)別有用心之人及國際陰謀份子，易藉此曲解「寬大」為「心虛」，認為政府從輕發落乃是羅織人罪，起訴之犯行(叛亂)，乃是「欲加之罪」。國內偏激刊物及中央民意代表將來選舉時，也可能借此題發揮，大作文章。

(5)留下這些人等於留下無數麻煩：今後海外叛國份子及國際陰謀份子，必將在彼等服刑期間，以他們為「題目」，大作「文章」，惹是生非，如要求「放人」，指稱他們為「政治犯」，說他們「遭受虐待」，這些傢伙也可能會配合海外作表演。

4 也有少部分人士(必多為台籍年輕記者或同情陰謀份子者)認為：國家需要團結，如此判決也可以了，每人刑期均在十年以上，十年冷藏，他們的政治生命等於死亡，有何必去判他們死刑呢！

5 此人在叛國份子陰謀集團及反政府份子心目中，已成為「民主鬥士」、「革命英雄」，今後若逢大赦或減刑，提前出獄，必成為他們的「偶像」，更具號召與影響力，所以務必不可假釋或大赦，使其提前出來，否則，如放虎歸山，不可不慎。

(以下文字檔案局未提供影印)

(依原件重新打字，二○○八年四月十三日)

Witnessing Taiwan's 1980 Elections: What the Dangwai Taught Me at 22

By Vallaurie Crawford

what gets lost in translation
reappears in disbelief...

things lost in translation
band together symbiotically
and haunt the world

-- Andrei Codescru

Because Americans' access to China in 1978 was limited to tour groups, most aspiring China hands studied in Taiwan, sharing an oral lore of great restaurants and the evils of the Nationalist dictatorship. So when a college consortium paid my airfare to Taiwan for research in 1978, I prepared for nine months by watching kung-fu movies, baying Mandarin tone drills and waitressing at the Village Wok (where I was called Whale, as Val is unpronounceable in Chinese).

Most English sources on Taiwan at my university were propaganda: statistical yearbooks and magazines touting an isolated Cold War regime. How isolated? The *Far Eastern Economic Review* referred to Taiwan's ties to Israel and South Africa with the headline "The Skunks of the World Unite." In 1978 Taiwan was still a leading recipient of U.S. foreign aid, and it hosted American military facilities and the remnants of a Vietnam War-era R&R (rest and recreation) industry.

My fascination with Taiwan's politics began as our Minnesota student group followed Richard Kagan, a Hamline University history professor, and his two children around the island. Over evening-long meals in private dining rooms we met Taiwanese activists and foreign human rights volunteers. I was researching a thesis on working women's changing roles, but my first-year Chinese improved on talk of censorship and prison sentences.

I went with some of our group to an opposition rally where the speeches were in Taiwanese (therefore gibberish to us); we were ready to run photo film away from the site if anything happened. I thought it was low-tech cute that someone was holding a fluorescent strip lamp aloft until someone told me the light was to help police agents photograph and intimidate the audience.

A few days later I met Linda Gail Arrigo, a Stanford anthropology graduate student

----

Secret

Taiwan Garrison Command Special Investigation Office Report (Notification)

Republic of China 69th Year [1980], 4th Month, 19th Day
(69) You-Ching (友情 Friendly Intelligence) No. 0484

Recipients:
National Security Bureau 國家安全局

Rationale:
Reaction from all sectors following the sentencing in the sedition case of Huang Hsin-Chieh and others.
Source of Report: (all names and locations blacked out).

Distribution:
TGC Commander Major General Wang 總司令汪上將
TGC Vice-Commander General Yu 副總司令于中將
Chief of Staff General Chung 參謀長鐘中將
Vice-Chief of Staff Lt. General Shih 副參謀長史少將
Political Section 2 政二處
Military Law Office 軍法處
Preserve the Peace Office 保安處

Classification: A-2

Content:

I. The summary of all work connections providing information and materials in the case of sedition of Huang Hsin-Chieh and others, following sentencing, is as follows:

A. Culture and news media worlds:

1.   The news media originally expected that sentencing in this case would be announced after the case of Hong Chih-Liang was judged and his sentence announced, but now suddenly the sentencing of Huang et al. has been moved forward, which is out of people's expectations. Why has it been moved up? The government must have had other considerations.

2.   In general economic criminals (like in notes-of-receipt) have set the precedent of sentencing to 12 years or more. But the Meilidao bunch, who committed the crime of sedition by attempting to overthrow the government by violence, have only each been sentenced to 12 or 14 years, and the highest sentence is just life imprisonment (for Shih Ming-Deh), which all seems too light.

3.   Originally, those in the same field discussing this case also had expected that the sentencing outcome would be light, but still they thought there would be heavy sentences and then later the defendants would be given reductions. This outcome perhaps can encompass part of the people's will, and at the same time maintain respect for the law. But this general light punishment at least has the following effects:

i. It cannot serve the people's will, and patriotic countrymen are angry and uneasy.

who talked fast in both Chinese and English. She had married a former political prisoner, Shih Ming-teh, with the hope that her American leverage would keep him out of jail, as he continued to organize fearlessly against the KMT. The day I met him, the plainclothes agents outside their apartment (thugs in sweatsuits) had killed the couple's puppy out of casual malice, so Linda buzzed like a hornet while her wiry husband was silent.

I thought I'd walked into a movie: Here was Evil, standing right across the street! Here were coded names for tapped phone lines! As a post-Watergate journalism student, I fell in love with Taiwan as a story, an unfolding melodrama of oppression and passionate activists.

When we visited the factory dormitory where Linda was researching women workers, she talked about the Dangwai, literally "party outside": the nascent opposition to the Nationalist Party (Kuomintang or KMT). With her help I finished my interviews, met more of the activist network, and later helped with PR for Taiwan-related events in Minnesota. I typed the furtive democratic movement's press releases about political prisoners and visiting speakers, wearied my journalist friends with anti-KMT editorials, and spent Chinese New Years at secret feasts with paranoid scholars. (They were wise to worry. They were spied on by the same KMT agents whose reports sent University of Minnesota student Rita Yeh 葉島蕾 to prison after she went home: Rita was sentenced to 14 years in January 1981.)

Then came the crackdown. After a Human Rights Day rally became the Kaohsiung Incident of December 1979, Linda was expelled from Taiwan; over a hundred others were jailed. The KMT dictatorship was murderous, and monied enough to cover up its crimes. For example, detainee Lin Yi-hsiung told his wife how he had been tortured, and the wife told human rights groups. Within days, Lin's mother and daughters were stabbed to death by "mysterious intruders."

I heard of this from a Taiwanese in Minnesota, but when I wrote about it my college newspaper was picketed by a group that included the same student; he said he risked losing his government scholarship if he didn't picket.

Linda toured America telling her story, so I met her again in Chicago in mid 1980. She had just cut her arm to bleed on the carpet of a China Air Lines office [Editor's note: By Linda's memory, she probably used lipstick], denouncing the regime's flag carrier in loud Mandarin for providing a reward for Shih Ming-teh's capture, and garnering newspaper photos. Maybe because I was gung-ho and could get by on a backpacker budget, Linda later invited me to help document the 1980 elections for the exiled opposition. What an exciting opportunity! I'm still grateful for it, because this experience changed my life in many ways. For two weeks I toured West Coast Taiwanese communities as Linda Arrigo arranged, never asking for money directly, but appearing at various gatherings as the exiles' hope of getting information out of Taiwan, and the funds for the trip were raised. I assured them I wouldn't turn out to be a leftist or Taiwan independence sympathizer, nor would I implicate anyone if questioned. I was eager, but my limitations were obvious: I lacked enough Mandarin

ii.In the future similar cases can hardly be punished severely, or else it will be easy for people to make the accusation of "double standard".

iii.This outcome easily gives the mistaken impression that the government capitulated to the threats of overseas seditionists, such that it did not dare to impose heavy punishment (for fear of their revenge). So also for this reason it tends to raise the blazes of seditionists and a few ambitious and opportunistic domestic politicians.

iv.People with untoward motives as well as international conspirators will easily interpret the government's "breadth of tolerance" as "emptiness of heart" [i.e. fear and uncertainty, e.g. following perpetration of a deception], and consider that the government's light sentencing outcome is because of (the defendants') entrapment into a crime; and the crime for which they are indicted, sedition, is merely "a crime inflated as wanted" (by the authorities). Domestic extremist magazines during the upcoming elections for national representatives may also take this as grist for their mill and write exaggerated articles.

v.Leaving these people [alive?] is equivalent to retaining endless troubles: from now on the overseas seditionists and international conspirators will, while they are in jail, take them as "subjects", write a lot of articles, and whether or not they are alive, do things like demanding their release, point to them as "political prisoners", say they have "met with abuse", etc. These scoundrels may even coordinate with the overseas to create a show.

4. There are also a small portion of people (most are young native Taiwanese reporters or sympathizers of the conspirators) who feel that: the country needs to be united, and this sentencing is okay, because each person has been sentenced to over ten years, ten years in cold storage, and their political lives are the same as dead, so why is it necessary to sentence them to death!

5. In the hearts of the conspiratorial group of seditionists and those who oppose the government, these eight people have already become "fighters for democracy" and "revolutionary heroes". If in the future there is a general pardon or reduction in sentences, such that they would be released from jail early, these eight would certainly become their "idols", and will have even greater attraction and influence. So by no means can they be released or given amnesty that can let them out of jail earlier, or else the consideration cannot be avoided that that would be like "returning a tiger to the mountain".

Lin Shui-chuan returns to the Chingmei Prison on December 9, 2007. Exercise courtyard looking up at the cell blocks.

fluency (never mind the Taiwanese dialect) to comprehend and record what I was to witness, and I lacked the reporting experience to do much with it. I'd parrot what I could, but would parroting be enough?

For a girl from pallid Minnesota, this multicultural milieu was thrilling. A decade before David Rieff called Los Angeles "the capital of the Third World," I caromed between cultures there, staying in a Taiwanese house in Hispanic Boyle Heights, buying chiles rellenos from a drive-in while walking to the Little Tokyo office where a big Chinese typewriter produced *Formosa Weekly* 美麗島週報, the voice of the exiled opposition. The cultural collision nearly became literal when tense ex-political prisoner Roger Hsieh 謝聰敏 first drove U.S. freeways; I rode shotgun a few times when he had his learner's permit. (He and his wife also joined me to see Muddy Waters play at the Roxy; Muddy and Roger were the only guys in suits.)

In Seattle I met Gerrit van der Wees, a soft-spoken Dutchman working with the International Committee on Human Rights in Taiwan. In a few days we assembled a slick, detailed Taiwan issues packet for reporters covering candidate Ronald Reagan. We arrived at the "Reagan Posse" rally in a suburban hotel, at first pacing in the parking lot with a few Taiwanese and Koreans carrying confusing signs. Then I strode into the lobby, found the press room and passed out our packets. I asked the reporters hiding out from the speeches what they knew about Reagan's links to the KMT: they knew nothing, and didn't care. When the rest of the reporters rushed in I had nowhere to loiter unobtrusively, so I stepped outside the press room. I was suddenly pinned against the wall and frisked -- just before Ronald Reagan shook my hand, his face freezing on the "Reagan for Shah" button on my proper gray suit coat! Then he moved on; such rude surprises are common enough in politics.

And then in November 1980 it was time to go to Taiwan. I sublet my apartment and told my parents about a vague job offer, and at age 22 I returned as a spy. Even if I had been caught, I faced no risk beyond deportation -- but the Taiwanese who helped me risked their lives. Thus we were serious about protecting their identities with amateur spycraft, right down to a coded address book and a false-bottomed suitcase (to hide documents). I went off to Asia, stopping in Japan for about a week with Lynn Miles and company. He was a charismatic leader in Osaka, and I was really impressed by these young people with him.

After arriving in Taiwan and finding a room with the enemy at a China Youth Corps hostel, I beat my head against the phone, garbling Chinese names and passwords, waiting for callers to bring help and take me to interviews.

I also sought editing work for money, a cover story and a routine, and was lucky to find a temp job at the China Economic News Service. (This otherwise prudish export-promotion agency had selected a penis-enlarger called Handsome Up! as one issue's featured product, so I enforced grammar and vagueness on its ad copy, eliminating all references to "happiness.") I liked office life, as my rewriting desk wasn't far from the Frankenstein-sized tea boiler where gossip and small talk sharpened my Chinese. The office ladies told me I was daring for traveling while unmarried, and they fed me

Vallaurie Crawford, left, and William Armbruster, right, both of whom first came to Taiwan as young aspiring journalists

Foreign human rights activists were invited to attend the dedication of the Jingmei Prison Human Rights Park on December 9, 2007. Here those from Europe and Japan are photographed together with Hsieh Chih-wei (white tie, center), head of the Government Information Office under the Democratic Progressive Party administration. (Photograph courtesy of Ronald Tsao.)

soymilk and "Mexican buns" after I'd slip in late, having interviewed some Dangwai figure the night before (when my visits were less likely to be noted by lurking KMT agents).

These interviews were usually dominated by complaints about the repressive new election law and examples of KMT dirty tricks. One woman visited me regularly to translate to me the newspapers' campaign-related stories, and give me phone numbers and names. A young intellectual code-named Brian took me to visit rallies, meet candidates, take photos and gather documents to send to the Formosa exiles. During the campaign, Brian and two other activists took me on a memorable road trip to see the democratic opposition across Taiwan. We went to Peikang, Tainan, Yuanlin's "democracy wall," Chungli, Changhua and Taichung, visiting campaign headquarters, rallies, and candidates' homes.

These guys weren't the best translators -- their English and my Mandarin made for ludicrous quotes -- but they tolerated my toddler-level queries like kind uncles. I remember eating strange specialties in open markets where people stared and commented (I'm left-handed and big-nosed, as was noted with good cheer). I was most visible in small towns, and when plainclothes agents questioned Brian and followed our cab after a rally in Nantou I panicked about names and stories, as I expected to be questioned too. I wrote that day in my journal: "I scolded Brian for I knew the danger he put himself in, and I wanted to physically hit back when KMT agents photographed me ... I'm sitting in the car near a small-town gathering, bored and cramped by fear of stares. We're running out of money and it's my fault, I forgot film and batteries and haven't paid much ... KMT sound trucks scream like monsters."

One night I had had enough of such worries, and was also fed up with the prevailing double standard of booze for men and orange soda for women. So I poured potent kaoliang into my teacup at my hosts' table. It was a rude and inappropriate thing to do -- particularly when it turned out that this was the night Su Ching-li 蘇慶黎 was available for an interview. I'd interviewed Su in 1978, when her *China Tide* 夏潮 magazine focused on social issues: she had been my favorite interview subject and I admired her analysis. Two years later she seemed changed: her political imprisonment as part of the 1979 crackdown left her careful and vague in her speech, and far less hopeful about changing the conditions she had once crusaded against.

So went November and early December of 1980, gathering interviews, photos and documents. The Meilitao folks wanted a timely packet of campaign information for a special issue, so I flew to Hong Kong to send the best of my collected campaign notes and materials via an international courier service. But I had misdeciphered the coded address, and the parcel never got to Los Angeles. Worse, I had sent it under a code name and purposely dumped the receipt to protect my hosts. Since I couldn't prove that identity, I had no authority to trace my precious envelope, much less to do so from Taiwan ("...and why did you use a false name?").

I returned to Taipei with a raw cough and fever to monitor coverage of the December

Human Rights Letter Campaigns for the Kaohsiung Incident Defendants: Letters from the Files of Taiwan Garrison Command, February-June, 1980

by Linda Gail Arrigo

The following report on overseas concern for the Kaohsiung Incident arrests has been prepared from materials requested by Linda Arrigo from the National Archives of Taiwan in 2004. A stack of about 200 pages was received. In principle, the person making the request is only allowed to access materials in which the person is cited; but here whole files seem to have been copied. The source of these materials seems to be mostly the Taiwan Garrison Command (TGC), but includes letters forwarded from other organizations. Only a few of the pages have numbers and bar codes of the National Archives that can be used to precisely locate the document; probably these are the first page of a file folder. But after sorting the pages by date and topic, the relationship with the file number has generally been lost.

Only a few days after the Kaohsiung Incident, on December 14 at 10 am, an urgent secret transmission, typed and accompanied by a typed table, was directed from the National Security Bureau 國安局 to all the security agencies (literally, Commander, Vice-Commander, and Chiefs of Staff of the Taiwan Garrison Command 總司令汪上將, 副總司令于中將, 參謀長鍾中將, 副參謀長史中將; the Security Bureau 安全局; the Peace Preservation Office 保安處; and the Intelligence Research Section 情研組) to report on 17 telegrams to or from overseas organizations. This was included in a distributed report, Intelligence Summary, No. 10474 for 1979, dated Dec 14, National Archives No. 068300Z00007. The 17 communications included 14 from overseas to Taipei: three from the International League for Human Rights and from James Seymour of SPEAHR to President Chiang Ching-kuo; two from the League to Linda Arrigo and a person feared arrested; five directed to the American Institute in Taiwan from the Indiana Chinese Students Friendship Association, the Taiwan Association for Human Rights branches in Detroit and Greensboro, North Carolina, and others in the U.S.; and Kuo Yu-hsin in Washington D.C. to the Formosa magazine. The three telegrams out of Taipei were news reports on the Kaohsiung Incident and arrests by Reuters, AP, and UP. It is perhaps surprising that the security agencies, apparently so impervious to external criticism, immediately gave such attention to these minor foreign communications.

The materials from the TGC cite 34 letters from abroad stating concern for the Kaohsiung Incident (KI) defendants written in the period February-March 1980, most forwarded from the Ministry of Justice (MJ) to the Taiwan Garrison Command, with TGC receipt number stamped on the cover sheets; most of the letters are attached. Most of the names and addresses were blacked out on the copied documents in the course of provision by the Archives, but not all. It can be surmised that the letter-writing campaign of Amnesty International was noted by the government authorities and probably had immediate effect.

6 vote; luckily I had smuggled back some traditional cold medicines for my host's family (all products from China were illegal, even soothing lohanguo and Po Sum On herbal oil). The returns from Saturday's vote came in slowly; only Monday night we heard of election irregularities in Taoyuan.

Then the elections were over. It was time to write my eyewitness report and try to sell it. I remember looking at my typewriter and piles of typed notes: my stomach would tighten. I knew how little I understood; with different dialects, romanization systems and pronunciations, I couldn't even be sure I'd gotten the names right! Isn't that journalism's first rule, Get the names right?

So I'll end this story with that clumsy story, my attempt to understand the 1980 elections' heroism and unfairness. I learned then that it takes confidence to cook assembled facts into useful knowledge, and that failures teach more than successes. (Or as Grace Paley wrote, "You come to doing what you do by not being able to do something.")

Taiwan's ruling Nationalists claimed an overwhelming victory in the December 6 elections, a claim accepted as fact by pro-regime TV networks and newspapers. Democratic activists also spoke of victory, though few reporters sought their statements: A dozen major opposition candidates won seats in two national parliamentary bodies. Chou Ching-yu, wife of imprisoned lawyer Yao Chia-wen, pulled 150,000 votes, the island's highest vote total. Days earlier, she had been called a threat to the nation at a KMT Central Committee meeting because she and another political prisoner's wife were forcing a public vote of confidence on last year's crackdown.

The opposition won 27 percent of the vote despite an unpopular new election law and its unequal enforcement, a comparative lack of funds, and documented bribery and ballot-fixing by the ruling party. The election law enforced that:

- The opposition is forbidden to form a party, and the mutual endorsements and cooperation that had strengthened the opposition in 1977 and 1978 campaigns are illegal under the new law. Enough opposition candidates braved the unfavorable conditions to split the anti-KMT vote, but KMT sympathizers who ran as independents received more publicity...

- With up to 30 candidates, districts are large enough that funding problems are insurmountable for all but the rich or those with KMT assistance, as contributions are restricted. Students, formerly a source of opposition strength, were banned from helping in campaigns under the new law, and assistants to opposition candidates were called in for questioning and threatened by police...

- Bribery accusations surfaced as candidates accused each other with evidence of free feasts and entertainment, gifts of wallets and other products, and lottery parties in KMT offices. Despite solid evidence, few were disqualified; yet Dangwai candidates remain in jeopardy of losing the seats they won for

Document No.	Letter to:	Letter from:	Letter Date:	Concern:
MJ forwarded to TGC No. 1771 Feb 20 1980	Ministry of Justice	Lynne Reade USA.	Feb 5 1980	Only cover sheet in file.
	Dear Sir	AI British Section Durham University Group Dunelin House	Handwritten Jan 30	8 defendants Kaohsiung Incident
	Minister of Justice Li Yuan-Tsu	AI USA Group 80 Marianne Smith 207 Corbett Avenue San Francisco, CA 94114	Feb 8	8 defendants hiding Shih Ming-deh. Oppose death penalty for all.
	Minister of Justice Li Yuan-Tsu	Name blacked out. Member of AI USA	Typed letter. Feb 6	Release those non-violent. Oppose death penalty for all.
No. 1774 Feb 20	Minister of Justice Li Yuan-Tsu	Cecile Dorgeval AI Saint Germain en Laye	Telegram Feb 11	Physical safety of KI defendants
No. 1775 Feb 21	Minister of Justice Li Yuan-Tsu	Name blacked out. NW Roden Holland	Telegram Feb 11	Yao Chia-wen, Lin Yi-hsiung, Chen Chung-hsin, Lu Hsiu-lien
	Minister of Justice Li Yuan-Tsu	Name blacked out. Venlo Holland	Telegram Feb 11	Wei Ting-chao, Chen Chu, Chi Wan-sheng, Chang Fu-chung, Hsu Chiu-chen
No. 1908 Feb 23	Minister of Justice	AI member USA Jane Mayers "I am writing again…"	Handwritten Feb 9	KI defendants and those hiding Shih. Oppose death penalty.
	Minister of Justice Li Yuan-Tsu	AI Belgium, Section FrancophoneGroupe 33 Av. Penelope 39 1190 Bruxelles Signed by Claude-Gisele Verheyen, seven others	Feb 11	Protest suppression of non-violent demon-stration in Dec 1979 to celebrate human rights day. Guarantee physical well being.
	Minister of Justice Li Yuan-Tsu	AI Danish Section Kaj Baago, Kirsten Baago Teglvaerksvej 80 3460 Birkerod, Denmark	Feb 13	Nine KI defendants and those hiding Shih. Oppose death penalty for all.
	Minister of Justice Li Yuan-Tsu	Margaret C. Monsarrat AI member Lambert Road Sharon, Connecticut	Feb 8	Publish names and whereabouts of those detained. Oppose death penalty for all.
No. 1909 Feb 23	Dear Sir	Name blacked out. USA	Handwritten Feb 5	Heard 65 detained, 8 may face death. Request defense, no death penalty.
No. 1910 Feb 23	Your Excellency	Two names blacked out. Japan	Hand printed Feb 14	Unconditional release.

such minor offenses as allowing an assistant to speak first at a rally...

• Candidate-organized rallies were allowed only during the first half of the two-week campaign period. Dangwai candidates were hurt by the new requirement for a letter of permission from rally site landlords, as secondary harassment of the landlords made sites difficult to find and sometimes forced rallies to be cancelled. The new requirement that a printer's name must appear on campaign literature achieved similar results, making it difficult to publish even uncensored material...

• Speeches could not legally be transcribed, and candidates could not speak from their campaign trucks, which had to broadcast tapes by assistants...

• Dangwai election-related books were banned, further limiting fund-raising. Officials sat onstage at all rallies to halt "improper" speeches, and Dangwai crowds were openly taped and photographed, officially for security reasons. One candidate told me, "I know I'm in danger. I know there are a hundred cameras here."

Yet official censorship was frequently violated, as was the blanket ban on any mention of *Formosa* magazine, the Kaohsiung Incident, and the names of those convicted of sedition, including the husband of eventual top winner Chou Ching-yu. Opposition rallies drew crowds of up to 30,000 people, but KMT rallies drew far fewer; one candidate resorted to bringing his audience with him on buses.

The ending of my Taiwan adventure was surreal: I flew home sandwiched between a Hong Kong pragmatist (who said Taiwan democracy activists were right, but would never succeed) and a Tokyo-based American psychologist who called himself "one of Ronald Reagan's Asian advisors" -- and knew nothing about Taiwan. Flanked by seatmates who said my efforts were useless, I turned up the squalling Peking opera channel on my China Airlines headset and slept until it was morning in America, at least for me.

Document No.	Letter to:	Letter from:	Letter Date:	Concern:
	Minister of Justice Li Yuan-Tsu	Name blacked out. Tranas, Sweden	Feb 1	Arrest for non-violent exercise.
	Minister of Justice Li Yuan-Tsu	Three names blacked out. USA	No date	8 defendants.
	Minister of Justice	Name blacked out. Newnham College Cambridge, UK	Telegram Feb 13	Urgently release.
No. 1913 Feb 23		Cover letter to TGC mentions 5 letters from AI members in UK, Brussels, Denmark, and US, but letters not attached.		
No. 2006 Feb 26	Minister of Justice Li Yuan-Tsu	AI Sezione Italiana Gruppo 18, Gve Bossi Bariosto 25, Varese, Italy	Handwritten in English Feb 10	Disturbed by news of arrests. Universal Declaration of HR.
No. 2119 Feb 27	President Chiang Ching-kuo	Jacques Cottier, Vice-Batonnier, Ordre des Avocats de Geneve 1204 Geneve, Palais de Justice, Switzerland	Feb 15	Special concern for three lawyers, Yao Chia-wen, Lu Hsiu-lien, Lin Yi-hsiung.
	Minister of Justice Li Yuan-Tsu	Dr. Jean-Flavien Lalive Lalive & Budin Attorneys-at-Law Ch 1211 Geneva 12 Switzerland	Registered letter Feb 14	"That demonstration was merely exercise of the rights duly recognized by Article 18 of the Universal Declaration..."
	Minister of Justice Li Yuan-Tsu	Andreas M. Suit AI German Section Group 217	Jan	8 KI defendants
No. 2120 Feb 27	Minister of Justice Li Yuan-Tsu	AI Danish Section Mette Dossing Frimestervej 81 Copenhagen, Denmark	Feb	73 persons in detention. 8 accused of harboring Shih.
	Minister of Justice Li Yuan-Tsu	George E. Beilby AI USA Central Cape Group 95 c/o Box 309 South Orleans MA 02662 USA	Handwritten Feb 11	"It would be in the best interest of your gov't to conduct fair trials rather than lock up and persecute those who happen to disagree with the party in power."
No. 2373 March 4	Minister of Justice Li Yuan-Tsu	Jerome N. Frank Legal Services Org. Yale Law School New Haven, Conn. 06520	Feb 18	"I am writing to you as an attorney to express my serious concern..."
No. 3176 March 26		Cover letter mentions March 10 letter from AI Switzerland Ruedi Joct, but letter not attached.		

The Story of Taiwan Communiqué

By Gerrit van der Wees

Interviewed by Stefan Fleischauer at the Conference "International Friends and Taiwan's Democracy and Human Rights" held in Taipei, December 8-9, 2003

Stefan: I am very honored to have Dr. Gerritt Van der Wees here with me today; he was active in the human rights struggles in Taiwan, publishing the *Taiwan Communiqué* from 1979, now 105 issues over a period of 24 years. Mr. Van der Wees, you could perhaps first tell us how you got involved in human rights issues in Taiwan.

Gerritt: That happened in the 1970s. I was a graduate student at the University of Washington in Seattle, and it was quite an international university. There were students from many countries, including Taiwan, China, India, Pakistan, Iran and so on, and we had quite an active international student organization, which I was the chairman of for one year. I got to know many of the students from those countries, and got to know some of the Taiwanese students who lived in Bedford. One day one of them came up to me and said, I want to talk to you about Taiwan. I said, sure, fine, talk to me about Taiwan, no problem. He said, no, no, not here, I have to do that in a little room so nobody can see me talking to you. So we went into a little room, and he began to tell me about the human rights violations and lack of democracy in Taiwan, and the yearning of the Taiwan people for Taiwan independence.

So I got rather fascinated by that, and I started to read books, e.g. George Kerr's *Formosa Betrayed*, and Peng Ming-min's *A Taste of Freedom*, and other books that I could find in the library. And gradually I got so fascinated by it that I decided that I would try to do something. I was also the founding member of Amnesty International in the northwest of the United States, in Seattle, in the 1970s. And through that we tried to apply our Amnesty International training, so to speak, and our experience on Taiwan by focusing attention on the plight of political prisoners in Taiwan.

At one point I also thought it would be very interesting to invite Professor Peng Ming-min to the University of Washington at Seattle, and through some contacts that was possible. And in December 1975 he came to Seattle to give a speech at the university. I organized that. We made posters beforehand that we put up around campus to advertise the event for the students of the university, but I found the next day and the day after that, that a lot of posters had been damaged and torn off the walls. Then I realized that this was the Kuomintang campus spies, the professional students, who were doing that. And we were prepared for that, so we had made a whole big pile of posters, so we put more and more posters back up on the walls of the campus. So it was a major event on campus.

And also I saw at the entrance on that evening that there were some student spies

Document No.	Letter to:	Letter from:	Letter Date:	Concern:
No. 3178 March 26	Minister of Justice Li Yuan-Tsu	Name blacked out Hong Kong	Telegram March 17	"We American friends of Chinese people deeply concerned … court March 18."
No. 3469 April 7	Minister of Justice	Names blacked out West Germany	March 16	KI defendants
No. 4032 June 21	Minister of Justice Li Yuan-Tsu	AI Norway Group 19 Torunn Kvaal Pedersen Alsteinsgate lo 4000 Stavanger Norway	March 20	Publish names and whereabouts of all detained.
TGC form May 29	Taiwan Garrison Commander Wang Ching- hsi	Germany (several names)	March 20	"Reports have reached us that up to 200 people have been arrested in the Kaohsiung area."
TGC form June 14	Taiwan Garrison Commander Wang Ching- hsi	AI Austria Gruppe 78 Mitterbergerweg 2 4040 Linz Ereu Bohm Glenda Haupert Josef Vuhboch	March 13	"22 prominent people who engage in activities for freedom of thought were arrested on 13th Dec. 1979."

On May 15, 1980, the President of the Chinese Association for Human Rights, Han Lih-wu, transmitted one set of letters asking for mercy for the defendants to the Taiwan Garrison Command. The original letter to CAHR was dated May 1, from a Howard Brody (spelling of last name not certain because it was blacked out but also translated into Chinese 布魯第 in the CAHR correspondence) from San Francisco, noting "…I'm a TV

newsman in America, who covers most of the important criminal trials. I have also covered executions. As a human being, I am very much opposed to executions, whether occurring in my own country or in others." In attached copies of similar letters written within the United States, Mr. Brody noted that he had witnessed executions in California and Florida, as well as at executions in wartime (WWII, Korea, and Vietnam), and was convinced that these created additional damage to society.

Requests to Attend the Trial

Another aspect of international concern for the Kaohsiung Incident is found in requests to attend the trial. These are also found in correspondence of the Taiwan Garrison Command, as early as January 17, 1980, from the Chinese Association for Human Rights (CAHR; government sponsored). The Garrison claimed that the seats available in the courtroom were limited; moreover, a large number of seats were relegated to applicants from the CAHR, the Police University, the Central Committee of the Kuomintang, and other institutions not sympathetic to the defendants.

One of the most interesting of these letters is directed to the Government Information Office, dated January 21, 1980, from a group of American and Canadian foreign students studying Chinese in Taiwan. In laboriously hand-written characters and formal Chinese, they write (translation):

> "Respected Sirs: Our group of foreign students who are studying in China very sincerely request your permission to attend and audit the court during the opportunity of the trial of the violent elements of the Meilitao Incident. We have

who were trying to threaten the Taiwanese students, in particular, telling them not to come into the meeting. Even in the meeting itself we had several of these professional students that tried to cause problems for Professor Peng. But still it was a major success, and it gave large exposure to Professor Peng at the university.

And that event happened to be in the same week that I married my wife, Chen Mei-chin, who was from Taiwan, and we got to know each other and we have been active in Taiwan politics since that time.

Stefan: During this early period, in the 1970s, was it easy to get accurate information about Taiwan?

Gerritt: No, it was very difficult. A little bit later, I am talking about 1977 and 78 now, we got quite a lot of information through the Taiwanese community itself, through people who were active. When they went for family visits to Taiwan, they brought out information from Taiwan. So that was one source. Another source was Lynn Miles and Linda Arrigo, with whom I came into contact in the 1978, 79 period. And they had their links with Taiwan, and of course we tried to publicize the information they provided us, in the United States.

We started to set up a small newsletter, and now I'm talking in the summer of 1979, and in that summer there was a major conference of Taiwanese in Seattle, I'm talking about the "Shih Tai Hui", the World Federation of Taiwanese Associations. And after that weekend, which Peng Ming-min attended, and Lynn Miles attended, as well as two or three hundred people from around the world, we started to publish a newsletter on a regular basis. This first one was one sheet, and then the next one was two sheets, three sheets, and so on. And after about half a year, the Kaohsiung Incident happened, and of course then the thickness of the publication went higher yet, and the circulation also became much larger.

Stefan: How much was the circulation?

Gerritt: The very beginning circulation was only about 40; we basically collected the few names of people who were either interested in Taiwan, or active in human rights, or some key people in the United States Congress received it in the beginning. But of course after the Kaohsiung Incident we added other names, and it grew to two, three, four, five hundred. That was the very initial period. So that was basically the period before the Kaohsiung Incident where all this happened, and as I said through those newsletters we tried to publicize the cases of the political prisoners, people like Yang Ching-hai, who is here today, and people like Chen Chu who had been arrested in 1978. So that was the very beginning of our newsletter.

Stefan: Before we go to the Kaohsiung Incident, one more question: How could you fund your activities?

Gerritt: Basically we were very poor students at that time, and we only had teaching assistant or research assistant income, so we had to get funding from the Taiwanese community, but usually the Taiwanese community was very helpful and provided us

all come to Taiwan to learn the national language, and live at the International Youth Activity Center (Hsin Hai Road, Section 3, No. 30). This gives us the opportunity to meet Chinese friends, and visit museums, temples, parks, night markets, schools, and the ten great economic projects, etc. But we have not yet had the chance to learn about the situation of legal cases and decisions. Perhaps we could take this chance understand these. So we earnestly hope you will allow us to do so. Thanking you, (four names blacked out)."

They seem to have been put off with a letter from the TGC that the period for application to attend has not yet begun.

On February 5 Han Lih-wu (杭立武) of CAHR relayed the request from Laurie Wiseberg of Human Rights Internet for Linda Arrigo to attend the trial (request denied), along with a request from Dick Oosting of Amnesty International (document received at TGC with No. 07949).

Other requests mention David Hulme, February 21; Mark Pratt of the American Institute on Taiwan requesting two seats, February 25 (given high priority); and Harris Wofford of the International League for Human Rights in New York; Victor Li of the Stanford University Law School; and Michael Posner of the Lawyers Committee for Human Rights.

In response to the February 27 request of World Pen, China Branch, to attend the trial, the Garrison drafted a letter (no date) with instructions to provide background material to them, and allow the head of the organization a seat in the courtroom so that: "He will represent our country in the annual meeting of the international organization in May, and then can make a correct explanation of the Kaohsiung Incident."

In response to an urgent telegram from the ROC governmental office in the U.S.(the Coordinating Council for North American Affairs), the Government Information Office in a document numbered Year 69 (1980) Yu-ji No. 3 stamp 02697 (date March 1), advises CCNAA to tell three friendly organizations, the Free China Forum Monthly (自由中國評論月刊), the Austria Free China News Materials Service (自由中國評論月刊) (自由中國新聞資料供應社), and the East Asia Relations Association Tokyo News Office (亞東關係協會東京辦事處新聞組), that outside interference in the trial is not welcomed by the government, and an international trip might not be worthwhile because the courtroom seating is limited.

President of the Tri-Forces Military University General Chiang Wei-kuo on March 3 provides the credentials for a representative of the school to attend the trial.

On February 26, the General Assembly of the Presbyterian Church in Taiwan, on stationery from the office of General Secretary C. M. Kao (Kao Chun-ming, who was himself to be arrested on April 24 and on trial on May 16), requested three to five seats, since Rev. Lin Hong-hsuan was among the eight main defendants charged with sedition, in addition to several ministers among the remaining defendants to be tried on lesser charges; and on March 17 they urgently requested a seat for Edwin Luidens of the World Alliance of Reformed Churches.

Finally in these Taiwan Garrison Command documents there are listings and seat number charts for observers at the trial, with English names including John Kaplan of Stanford University Law School, and Angus Taylor Simmons, aside from Edwin Luidens, AIT, and World Pen.

with sufficient funds to make possible the printing and mailing of the newsletter.

Stefan: How did you find out about the Kaohsiung Incident?

Gerritt: We actually found out about it during the time it was happening, because when it was still going on, Linda, who was in Kaohsiung, called us from the Meilitao office in Kaohsiung, and she gave us a whole report of what had happened that evening, and so, although in those days it was of course so difficult to get information from Taiwan, we always recorded our phone calls and I had a tape recorder connected to my phone, so her whole story I had on tape, and that was very helpful. Two or three days later we published the next issue of our newsletter, and in this newsletter you could get a very accurate account of what had happened on that evening, based on Linda's eye-witness review. And of course added to that, information we had gotten from other sources in the Taiwanese community.

Stefan: Were these telephone conversations later edited and published?

Gerritt: The conversations themselves, no, but we did edit and publish the so-called Kaohsiung Incident tapes, which were tapes of the trucks at the Kaohsiung Incident. The trucks had a loudspeaker system, and attached to the loudspeaker system they also had tapes. And those tapes were smuggled out of Taiwan, first to England. There they were translated by good friends in the Presbyterian Church, and then we received the translation, and together with Professor Seymour, who was also at this meeting, we published those. And those were the literal words that were said at the Kaohsiung Incident, and you can read those now on our website at www.taiwandc. org, if you go to the history page, and on the history page click on the Kaohsiung Incident, and you find this document. And that document gave every word of what the speakers said on that evening. And if you read that, you find that the speakers were primarily interested in human rights and democracy in Taiwan, and the international status of Taiwan.

Annette Lu, Lu Hsiu-lien, now the Vice President, actually gave the longest speech, and she argued for Taiwan's acceptance in the international community as a full member. There were no words about sedition, or overthrowing the government in any fashion. But those were precisely the charges, the accusations of the Kuomintang authorities against the defendants later on. You can see from that that those were outrageous charges, and they were not based on any facts. They just were political charges to get those people out of the way and to silence them, preferably for good, from the perspective of the Kuomintang.

Stefan: And the Kaohsiung Incident itself, did that come as a big shock to you? I heard that some kind of crackdown had been expected for a while.

Gerritt: On the one hand it was a shock, on the other hand there was a gradual buildup to the incident itself, in the weeks and even months before that. It was quite an increase of the activities of the Kuomintang against the Dangwai. At that time there were at least two magazines, *Formosa* and *The Eighties*, and those two were the only two magazines in Taiwan that tried to advocate democracy and self-determination.

Gerrit van der Wees

Thirty-three defendants who had originally been among those accused of sedition were charged on March 31, 1980 with "inciting a group of people to commit or threaten violence" or "being accomplices in acts of violence" (AI report of August 5, 1981, p. 15). The subsequent trial was carried out April 17-19 (from the pictures, it seems to be in the same courtroom of the Taiwan Garrison Command, although this was stated to be a civilian trial), and seemed devised to put a large number of the Formosa magazine staff and the candidates still awaiting the national elections out of the way for several years. Including the main trial, the count of opposition politicians put behind bars included three elected officials, six candidates, and a dozen leading officers of the island-wide Formosa magazine organization. Many in court reported severe beatings, but this did not alter the use of their "confessions". This trial received less international attention, but the pictures of the accused being led into the courtroom still appeared in the press, and it was considerable encouragement to see them proud and unbowed.

The trial of Reverend Kao Chun-ming, twice elected General Secretary of the Presbyterian Church of Taiwan (and once again while imprisoned), and nine others, on charges of harboring Shih Ming-teh, named a fugitive from justice, commenced on May 16, 1980. Of course the ROC government had long been seeking a pretext to punish the Presbyterian Church for its public statements. Aside from Kao's indirect involvement, a thin, frail woman minister, Rev. Lin Wen-chen, had allowed Shih to stay at her house for several days, and Rev. Wu Wen, a Lutheran who had never met Shih, served as a messenger. Reverend Kao was sentenced to seven years, and the others who had directly sheltered Shih to seven or less. (Most tragically, Rev. Lin's son, 20, later died of a sudden asthma attack while she was imprisoned.) The trial was attended by, among others, Rev. James M. Phillips, and his detailed report of May 19 explained that he had served as a Presbyterian missionary in Korea (1949-52) and Japan (1959-75), during which latter time he had met Rev. Kao; and he had come for the trial while serving as a professor of Church History at Tokyo Union Theological Seminary, Japan. Rev. Phillips clearly felt he was attending "one of the most significant trials in Taiwan's recent history". News of this trial spread worldwide through religious channels. Years later, Rev. Kao, with his usual studied dignity, said that his five years in prison, though difficult, were personally and socially "meaningful", and in fact gave him an opportunity to understand and minister to common criminals that he would usually not be able to meet.

So when this increase of political pressure happened, everybody said, okay, that will pass, but then when the Kaohsiung Incident, indeed, happened, and the response by the Kuomintang authorities, that really galvanized the Taiwanese community overseas into action.

And that was also the theme of my presentation this morning, that it was a very significant incident. Before Kaohsiung, there had been many groups throughout the world, mainly students, who were in some way active for Taiwan: we had Formosans for a Free Formosa, which was established in 1956 in Philadelphia by five young students, and that grew into the U.S. branch of the United Formosans for Independence, and then together with the Japan branch, "Taiwan Ching Nien", called *Taiwan Youth* magazine in the 1960s, those two merged together into the World United Formosans for Independence in the early 1970s. And there were still small groups of people here and there. But the importance of the Kaohsiung Incident was that after that these small groups suddenly became big groups, and it really mesmerized the Taiwanese community, and prompted them into political action. They became really important centers of influence in the United States, and to a lesser extent in Europe.

Stefan: To my understanding, after the incident you also invested a lot of time and energy in the campaigning for the people who were arrested in the incident.

Gerritt: Yes, of course, that was the main purpose after the incident. There was a lot of international attention for what was happening in Taiwan: that the people not be executed was the first concern, because the Kuomintang was known to execute people pretty frequently. And secondly, once they received a trial, it should be a relatively open trial. We knew it would never be a fair trial. The conclusion was a foregone one, that the government had concluded already that these people were not innocent, and that they were guilty of trying to overthrow the government. So that belief prompted us all overseas to write as much as possible.

I think the important thing at that time was also that there was fairly little attention to Taiwan in the international press. The *New York Times* had five lines of reporting about the Kaohsiung trials, the first and second and third day. Only by the end was there a little bit longer report on that. That was the extent of coverage by the *New York Times. Newsweek* had a better article by Melinda Liu. *Time* had a so-so article that was pretty biased. So overall there was not so much attention. And we hoped that by our activities at least the English language world could find out more about what was happening in Taiwan.

Stefan: You were just talking about your activities in the United States after the Meilitao Incident. Were your energies mostly directed towards the media, or towards politicians?

Gerritt: All of that. I think it's important to emphasize that both media and the Congress were very little aware of the situation in Taiwan. As I said, I was a student at the University of Washington, and all of this involved a lot of phone calls. And during the month after the Meilitao Incident, I had a telephone bill each month that was about US$800, and I had an income of only US$512. I still remember that. But

Letters Send Directly
to the Taiwan Garrison Command Following the Trial

Following the main trial, there seems to have been another Amnesty International campaign of letter-writing directly to the head of the Taiwan Garrison Command, General Wang Ching-hsi 警總司令汪敬熙, which is perhaps related to the fear that death sentences would be imposed. The Liaison and Translation Office of the TGC dealt with these letters by devising a check-off form, which is of itself of interest. In the following it is recreated in English.

Main points of letters from Amnesty International or related persons:

1.   Source of letter

     ( ) Amnesty International _____ National Section

     ( ) Person from _____ country, Name _____

2.   Language of letter

3.   Date of letter

4.   Content of letter is concerned with persons:

     (E.g., defendants in Kaohsiung Incident case, or listed names)

5.   Requests in letter: (several may be checked)

     ( ) fair and open trial.

     ( ) make public the criminal condition and list of names.

     ( ) no torture.

     ( ) immediately release.

     ( ) tell where the person is being held.

     ( ) provide information on the situation of trial.

     ( ) allow the person contact with family and lawyers.

     ( ) maintain the health of the person.

     ( ) other.

Taiwan Garrison Command

Central Office Liaison and Translation Office

  (OVAL RUBBER STAMP)

Date: Year   Month   Date

---

fortunately the Taiwanese community was very helpful, and they paid our phone bills. Otherwise we could never have done that. We made a lot of telephone calls to Taiwan, and we made a lot of calls to Congress in Washington.

In Washington there was not really organized Taiwanese activity yet. We had Mark Chen, Chen Tang-shan, who is presently in the Legislative Yuan, who was working in Washington, so he did a lot of his work after hours in Washington, but he was basically just a single person. And it wasn't until 1982 that FAPA, the Formosan Association for Public Affairs, was established. And their main purpose was to lobby Congress about human rights and democracy in Taiwan. So they got a little office; it was at the most two, or three, or four people who worked there at one time. And they really made a tremendous difference in the attention that Congress had for Taiwan.

I mentioned already this morning that at that time we had our own "gang of four" in the Congress: those were, in the Congress, Stephen Solarz and Jim Leach, and then on the Senate side, Senator Edward Kennedy and Senator Claiborne Pell. So those four people really helped a lot. And they helped focus attention on the plight of the prisoners, but also started to hold hearings about human rights and democracy in Taiwan, about martial law which still existed at that time. And that pressure, I think, really helped a lot to get rid of martial law.

Just right as we are speaking, there is a forum discussion going on about the role of Chiang Ching-kuo in the ending of martial law and democratization of Taiwan. I think that we should emphasize that he did not move until he was really pushed very hard. He was pushed by the people in Taiwan themselves, by the Dangwai, by the magazines in Taiwan, and he was also pushed by the U.S. Congress in particular to go towards a more democratic system – to end martial law, to respect the human rights of the people in Taiwan. So he did eventually move in that direction, but not until he was put under great pressure. It was not his own benevolence.

Stefan: In this early phase, before the establishment of FAPA, who were the people who devoted a full-time effort? How many people were involved?

Gerritt: Well, it was never a full-time effort for people. People had their regular jobs; they were students, or professors at the university. So they devoted their spare time on this, and once in a while people like myself went to Washington to talk to people in Congress. It was very much of a part-time effort. But for this network, you have to mention the Formosan Association for Human Rights with headquarters in California. Mrs. Fan was heading it. They really did a tremendous job in focusing attention on human rights in Taiwan. And they had a network of people all throughout the United States, which would write letters, and so on. That was really the beginning of the coalescence of these little clusters of activity that I talked about previously, into a massive movement of Taiwanese organizations. After that we have FAPA, we have North American Taiwanese Professors Association, North American Taiwanese Women's Association, so those organizations all really helped build overseas support for democratization in Taiwan.

Stefan: In 1981, you left the United States, and continued to work in the Hague?

There are fourteen such forms dated May 29 through June 14, 1980 (through two refer to letters written in March, as above) in the files received from the National Archives, most accompanied by the letters to which they refer. There are also several letters with other cover sheets, and internal messages mentioning many letters from Germany, and thus reason to think that the letters obtained from the National Archives are only a portion of the letters sent. Since the letters from individuals have the names and addresses rather thoroughly blacked out, it is not very useful to list them individually; the AI addresses were not blacked out. Most of these messages are concerned with Lin Yi-hsiung's hunger strike after he was taken back into custody on May 1, and are aggrieved at the murders of his daughters.

- There is a petition with a page of signatures from Porthcawl (name not clear in copy), UK, May 20.

- There is an aerogram from Australia that the TGC lists as AI-related.

- There is a telegram from San Francisco, May 23.

- There are individual letters from Austria, Switzerland, and Washington DC, USA.

- There are three letters from the UK, including one from Durham, and one from "a doctor and head of a research institution".

- There are formal Amnesty International letters, some on stationery, from Sweden Group 20 (Agneta Gorfelt, Uppsala), Sweden Group 63 (G. Ahnberg, Malmo), Sweden Group 268 (E-L Neth Johansson, Goteborg), and Germany Group 1-226 (Michael Spring, Steinenfeld).

Amnesty International's February 1980 official visit to Taiwan

The direct efforts of Amnesty International are not mentioned in the files obtained, but from AI report "Memorandum Submitted to the Government of the Republic of China by Amnesty International" that was made public on August 5, 1981, Amnesty International evidently made a considerable effort in early 1980 that was not publicly announced. From February 16-26, 1980, Professor C. F. Rüter, in Criminal Law at the University of Amsterdam, and Françoise Vandale, of the Asia Research Department of AI, visited Taiwan and interviewed both relatives of prisoners and government officials. They were allowed to visit Green Island and talk to three long-term prisoners, though not those that they had requested to interview, and heard that one of those they met was later punished for his temerity.

According to the abovementioned AI report of August 5, 1981, "Memorandum Submitted to the Government of the Republic of China by Amnesty International", AI was represented at the March 18-28, 1980, trial of the Meilidao magazine eight by Dr. Michael Sandor, lecturer in law at Hong Kong University. However, AI was also concerned with and commented at length on the trials of the 33 defendants charged with involvement in violence at the Kaohsiung Incident, and with those charged with harboring fugitives, including the Presbyterians. Within its 21-page report is the following:

Gerritt: Yes. We moved back to the Netherlands. I had completed my Ph.D. at the University of Washington, so we moved back to the Netherlands and continued to live there, and we continued to publish *Taiwan Communiqué*. In the early years we focused on human rights, but also on press freedom.

You may remember that in those days they had the Dangwai magazines, from about 1982 to about 1986-7. And many people in the Dangwai movement would publish a little magazine, but usually the government authorities would confiscate and ban those magazines. And one of our tasks was to record all of those bannings and confiscations, so in the early issues of *Taiwan Communiqué* you will find all the statistics that I drew, e.g. how many issues a month banned, etc., to document the lack of press freedom in Taiwan.

So that was the early phase, until about 1986, and then of course the Democratic Progressive Party, the DPP, was founded, and then our work was focused more on support for democratization, to end martial law, which was ended in 1987. But then there were still severe restrictions on freedom of expression, Article 100 and the National Security Law, which still prevented people from openly speaking about full membership of Taiwan in the international community as an independent country. And that's a basic freedom for a people. So we continued to fight for that.

Stefan: After 1987?

Gerritt: Actually until 1986 we were still able to go to Taiwan, because the Kuomintang authorities never knew about our activities. We were very low-key, and we didn't publicize our activities, so they really didn't know about them. But in 1986 we came to Taiwan to attend the election campaign in November and December of that year. It was really the first time there was nearly open, I won't say fully open, elections for the Legislative Yuan and the National Assembly.

And so we came to Taiwan, and we went to various campaign rallies. We went to one in Panchiao, and there was a large crowd in the evening, 15,000 people. And on the stage there was You Ching, who had studied in Germany, in Heidelberg. We had known him in Heidelberg; we had visited him there. So You Ching was there on stage talking to all these people, and telling them about Taiwan's international status, a very legal analysis of Taiwan's political situation. So I wanted to get a picture of that; I like to take pictures. So I got behind him on the stage to take his picture like that, and the crowds saw that a foreigner "high nose" was taking the picture, and the audience started to applaud. And the whole crowd was applauding, and You Ching was wondering why they were applauding, because he was in the middle of a very serious discussion of Taiwan's legal status, and he turned around and saw me, and he said, "Oh, my friend from the Netherlands," and he introduced me to the crowd. And the crowd applauded more, and then he went on with his speech.

But the next day, I actually had an appointment at the Government Information Office with Chiang Ching-yu. I think he is presently the ambassador to the Vatican. And he was deputy GIO head then. And he began to scold me, "You are interfering in the internal affairs of the Republic of China, and it is terrible..." But I could only

"The Amnesty International delegates who went to Taiwan in 1980 met a number of people who had been interrogated either by the local police or by the military authorities about their participation in the Kaohsiung Incident, and had subsequently been released. Some of those interviewed said they had been interrogated continuously throughout their detention – in some cases, for less than 10 hours; in others, for as long as seven days and nights. They had all been released after signing a statement.

"The delegates were also told about the following types of ill-treatment meted out during incommunicado interrogation to some of the 33 people who were later tried for ttheir participation in the Kaohsiung Incident. They were told that (4 names given) had been tortured; and that Chen Fu-lai ... had been beaten with a leather belt and given electric shocks. The delegates were told too that most of the suspects who were interrogated by the Southern District of the Taiwan Garrison Command were made to wear fetters and iron balls, some at night, others all the time. ..." (page 6)

In response to the AI report, James C.Y. Soong, Director General of the Government Information Office, in a letter of May 13, 1981, addressed to Mr. Thomas Hammarberg, AI Secretary General, provided a seven-page rebuttal, which claimed "Human rights enjoyed by the people of the Republic of China in the economic field have approached the level enjoyed in the advanced western countries", that the "witnesses and evidence showed the ringleaders (eight in military court) planned the riot in advance", that allegations of mistreatment were "groundless", and that the defendants had been convicted of sedition as defined under ROC law. Mr. Hammarberg restarted AI's position in a three-page letter of July 1. All of this exchange was finally made public on August 5, 1981.

Conclusion

It is clearer in the statements of the Government Information Office that over a period of months they shifted their public utterances from unmitigated castigation of the "violent rioters" with assurances that they would be duly punished, to more measured statements that guilt was not presumed before trial, and that the proceedings would demonstrate the justice of the government's action. This seems to have created a promise of open trials and a momentum towards international observation of the trials. For the Taiwan Garrison Command it is harder to say whether the voice of international human rights concern really weighed on those military men; but we now know they watched the international reporting keenly. Some of those imprisoned, such as Lu Hsiu-lien, have since said that treatment in prison improved considerably after letter-writing campaigns. Overall, the evidence of the treatment of these letters and requests, as they made their way along a bureaucratic track, as well as the fact that the government formally received the Amnesty International delegation, should be a great encouragement to organizations such as Amnesty International and their members, who must often wonder whether their pleas fall on deaf ears. Finally, the opening of the trials to observers and media resulted in a pervasive impact both internationally and domestically, far beyond the individual fates of the defendants.

say, "I don't know what I did..." He said, "You are associating with members of the Dangwai in the United States, you cannot do that, you are interfering in our internal affairs." Well, that was apparently very serious. I didn't realize that taking a picture was such serious business.

So after we left we were told we had better not apply for a visa to come back to Taiwan anymore. Yes, we tried, we tried several times, until 1991 or 1992 we tried seven or eight times, and even with the help of people in the Dutch parliament who wrote letters for us, but the Kuomintang was very insistent that we were trying to destabilize their system, I guess.

And finally, in 1992, there were elections again, and these were elections for all the seats in the Legislative Yuan – the election in 1986 had been for only a very small part of the Legislature, the part representing Taiwan in all of China represented by the whole Legislative Yuan. So in 1992 we wanted to go to those elections, too, and then the office of the Kuomintang in the Hague, the Taiwan representative office, said, "It is not convenient for you to go to Taiwan." I told them, "I can determine what is convenient for me, right? How can you determine that?" And then our visa was approved. So we went back for the first time in 1993, after our blacklist period. Of course it was a happy occasion to see many old friends again, in a much freer atmosphere. You could really see the change between 1992 and 1993, in terms of how people behaved in the streets, talking to each other. You could have a conversation with any of the political activists in 1993 in a restaurant. before 1993 it was never possible.

So that was the exciting moment of the story, in the transition to democracy. Of course we came back again in 1996, and then in 2000 to attend the inauguration of the president. And that was really the culmination of so many years of hard work for the Taiwanese people, and for our own involvement, of course.

It has been a long but rewarding journey of 24 years, because we were able to witness the transformation of Taiwan from an authoritarian state into a full and blossoming democracy. We are happy and proud to be part of the human rights and democratic movement that brought about this transformation.

Gerrit van der Wees

Index